CONWAY'S

ALL THE WORLD'S
FIGHTING
SHIPS
1947-1982

Post World War II Soviet warship
development exemplified by the classic big
gun cruiser *Sverdlov* at the June 1953
Coronation Review and the 'Krivak I'
missile frigate *Strorozhevoy* proceeding
down the English Channel 14 April 1976.

CPL/UPI

CONWAY'S
ALL THE WORLD'S
FIGHTING SHIPS
1947-1982

PART II:
THE WARSAW PACT
AND NON-ALIGNED NATIONS

NAVAL INSTITUTE PRESS

Editorial Director
ROBERT GARDINER

Editor
RANDAL GRAY

Assistant Editor
CAROLINE MORDAUNT

Contributors
PRZEMYSŁAW BUDZBON (Albania, Burma, Indonesia, Korea, Philippines, Thailand, Warsaw Pact, except Soviet Union, Vietnam, Yugoslavia)
NORMAN FRIEDMAN (Soviet Union)
ANDRZEJ M JASKULA (Middle East, Malta)
HUGH LYON (Asia, except countries above and below, Eire)
ANTONY PRESTON (India, Malaysia, Pakistan, Sri Lanka)
ROBERT L SCHEINA (Latin America)
ADAM ŚMIGIELSKI (Middle East)
IAN STURTON (Africa)
KARL-ERIK WESTERLUND (Finland, Sweden)

Line drawings
By Przemysław Budzbon (with the assistance of Marek Twardowski)

Book design
By Dave Mills

Index
By Patricia Moore

First published in 1983 by Conway Maritime Press Ltd,
24 Bride Lane, Fleet Street, London EC4Y 8DR

Published and distributed in the United States of America
and Canada by the Naval Institute Press,
Annapolis, Maryland 21402

Library of Congress Catalog Card No. 82-42936
ISBN 0-87021-418-9 (Volume 1)
ISBN 0-87021-919-7 (Volume 2)
ISBN 0-87021-923-5 (2 volume set)

Manufactured in the United Kingdom

Contents

Foreword

This is the second part of *Conway's All the World's Fighting Ships 1947–82* and covers the navies of the Warsaw Pact and all outside NATO, Japan and Australasia, a grand total of 125 countries. They are arranged in alphabetical order within their groupings which are themselves in alphabetical order from Africa to the Warsaw Pact.

The organisation within each country is exactly as in Part I except that the six type division headings have been dispensed with for small navies and in the case of very small forces ships are detailed in the introduction itself. Unlike in Part I the data on sensors does include ECM gear, where known, more as a reflection of its growing importance than as a completely accurate record. A few abbreviations additional to Part I are listed below, notably FAC for fast attack craft, a ubiquitous type in this part.

It should be noted that although the period in the title ends in 1982, information is included as far into 1983 as time permitted. This is especially true of the addenda, after the index, which also covers Part I as well as Part II, with photographs relevant to both. Accents are omitted from capital letters as a matter of style.

ILLUSTRATIONS

Classes of frigate-size and upward are usually represented by both a photograph and a line drawing; wherever possible these are complementary, representing either sister ships, or the same vessel before and after alteration. The emphasis on appearance changes is carried into the captions for both types of illustration, which are dated wherever and as accurately as possible.

The line drawings, which were specially commissioned for this book, are mostly reproduced to 1/1250 scale. A few very large ships are reproduced to 1/1750 scale to allow them to fit horizontally onto a page, and quite a few small ships are reproduced at 1/750 scale, so that a reasonable degree of detail could be included. All exceptions to the standard 1/1250 scale are clearly marked.

ACKNOWLEDGEMENTS

For help with photographs we are indebted to the following individuals and organisations: T A Adams, Giorgio Arra, Argentine Navy, Brooke Marine, Przemyslaw Budzbon, Chilean Navy, Fairey Marine, Norman Friedman, Ross Gillett, L & L van Ginderen, Israel Aircraft Industries, MG Photographic, Micinski Collection, MoD, John Mortimer, Jacques Navarett, Salamander Books, Robert L Scheina, South African Navy, Royal Swedish Navy, C & S Taylor, Marek Twardowski, US Coast Guard, US Navy, Verolme-Cork, Vosper Thornycroft, Xinhua News Agency, Yarrow, Karl-Erik Westerlund.

NOTE

As always we welcome 'alterations and addtions' to information in this book. All correspondence on this subject should be directed to Conway Maritime Press Ltd, 24 Bride Lane, Fleet Street, London EC4Y 8DR, Great Britain.

Robert Gardiner

ABBREVIATIONS

Not listed in Part I. See introduction to Soviet Union for her warship terms, weapons and sensors.

CBR Chemical, Biological, Radiation protective systems
CEP Circular Error Probability or the radius of a circle round a target in which there is 50 per chance of a weapon landing
EW Electronic Warfare
FAC Fast Attack Craft

L/F low frequency
MIRV multiple independently targetable re-entry vehicle(s)
MRV multiple re-entry vehicle(s)
ONI Office of Naval Intelligence (US)
RL rocket launcher
RR recoilless rifle (Army anti-tank weapon)

Algeria

The Algerian armed forces (including a fourth service, the National Gendarmerie) are formidable and well-equipped, much military effort having been devoted to the 150,000-man army, the fourth strongest in Africa, with a reputation and traditions based on winning the prolonged guerrilla war leading to independence in 1962. Algeria's merchant marine, boosted like much else by the country's recent oil wealth, expanded from 75 ships (239,815grt) in 1974 to 130 vessels (1,218,621grt) in 1980.

The Navy, which began with a pair of Egyptian (ex-US) coastal minesweepers, has been gradually expanded and modernised in the past 15 years, personnel being increased from 3000 to 6000, with about 9000 reservists, and it is now probably stronger and certainly more efficient than the Libyan Navy. Previously a force of large patrol and fast attack craft, it was reinforced in 1980 by the first of two Soviet missile corvettes and a 'Koni' class frigate, giving some cruising capability. From January 1982 a Soviet 'Romeo' class submarine was giving training to Algerian crews at Mers-el-Kebir, so it is thought Algeria will, like Libya, buy new 'Foxtrot' submarines.

But Soviet requests for Mediterranean Fleet harbour facilities have not been approved despite heavy routine visits since 1966 and the Russian arms monopoly has recently been offset by an order placed in Italy for coast guard patrol craft. Italian weapons have been specified for the first indigenous Algerian warships, four Brooke Marine-designed missile-armed fast attack craft under construction at Mers-el-Kebir. The other main bases along the 800-mile coast are Algiers, Arzew, Philippeville, La Senia and Annaba (Bône). The naval personnel, commanded by a lieutenant-colonel, and regarded as reasonably well trained (many officers in the USSR) and educated (a special recruitment drive was launched in 1980 for 17-23 year old technical specialists), loyal to the regime and likely to perform well in combat.

Soviet 'KONI' class *frigates*

No	Name	Builder	Launched	Comp	Fate
901	MURAT REIS	Zelenodolsk SY	c1979	1980	Extant 1982
902	RAIS KELLICEN	Zelenodolsk SY			Extant 1982

901 was delivered from Black Sea 20.12.80 and 902 was transferred 4.3.82.

Soviet 'NANUCHKA II' class *corvettes*

No	Name	Builder	Launched	Fate
801	RAS HAMIDOU	Petrovskiy SY, Leningrad	c1979	Extant 1982
802	SALAH REIS	Petrovskiy SY, Leningrad	c1979	Extant 1982

801 delivered 4.7.80, 802 received 9.2.81. Reported that more (perhaps three) are to follow.

KEBIR class *fast attack craft (missile)*

Particulars:	See Omani *Al Bushra* class

Brooke Marine 37.5m design. The first pair ordered Oct 1981 were delivered, without missiles, early in 1983. Four more are being built with Brooke Marine assistance by ONCN/CNB, Mers-el-Kebir for delivery in 1984. They are the first locally-built Algerian warships. Armament is not yet clear but includes 1–76mm/62 OTO Melara Compact, and 2 Otomat SSMs and/or 1–30mm may be added.

Ex-Soviet 'OSA I' and 'OSA II' *fast attack craft (missile)*

Three 'Osa I' class boats transferred in 1967 and numbered *641* to *643*; nine 'Osa II' boats transferred (4 in 1976–77, 2 in 1978, 2 in 1979, 1 in 1981) have been numbered *644* to *651*. Two damaged by a missile explosion in 1981. All 12 are to be re-engined with MTU diesels and receive modernised electronics.

Ex-Soviet 'KOMAR' class *fast attack craft (missile)*

Six transferred in 1966 and numbered *671* to *676*, will be re-engined with MTU diesels.

Ex-Soviet 'P 6' class *fast attack craft (torpedo)*

Twelve transferred 1963–68. Four, numbered *631–634*, remained in service in 1982, two discarded in 1975, two transferred to the Coast Guard, two used for training and two are hulks.

Ex-Soviet 'SO 1' class *large patrol craft*

Six boats transferred Oct 1965–Oct 1967 and numbered *P 651* to *P 656*. All in ¬vice 1982. Three have two 533mm TT taken from the 'P 6' FAC.

Ex-US BYMS type *coastal minesweepers*

Class (former name):
Djebel Aures (ex-*Tor*), *Sidi Fradj* (ex-*Darfur*)
    Acquired from Egypt in July 1962. *Djebel Aures* wrecked off Algiers in April 1963, and *Sidi Fradj* discarded c1971.

Ex-Soviet 'T 43' class *ocean minesweepers*

Class:
M 521, M 522
    Launched c1950–56. Both transferred 1968 and in service 1982.

MISCELLANEOUS
Ex-Soviet 'Polnochny' class landing ship, transferred in August 1976 and numbered 555.
    Ex-Soviet 'Zhuk' class coastal patrol boat received from the Black Sea 22.5.81.
    Ex-Soviet 'Poluchat' class coastal patrol craft, used for torpedo recovery.
    Sixteen coastal patrol craft built in Italy (1976–78) for the Algerian Coast Guard.
    Two logistic landing ships of the 93m design were ordered from Brooke Marine England, in Oct 1981. The first was launched 20.12.82. See under Oman for particulars.

Angola

Angola's internal problems since her civil war-wracked independence from Portugal in November 1975 make excursions by her armed forces unlikely. Support has been given to the Ovambo guerrillas in Namibia (South-West Africa), but the ruling MPLA alone have neither the strength nor the ability to resist South African reprisals in the frontier area, or wipe out UNITA's increasing inland territory, and the 17,000–20,000 Cuban troops are stationed well to the north. In the short period since 1976, when a 20-year Treaty of Friendship and

One of the 37.5m Brooke Marine fast attack craft for Algeria

Co-operation was signed with the USSR, Angola's capital city and port, Luanda, has become the Soviet Navy's third most visited Atlantic port for all the years since 1953, behind only Guinea and Cuba.

The very young Angolan Navy, commanded by the Deputy Minister of Defence, is and will almost certainly remain a small ship patrol force for a 1000-mile coastline. Most of its boats were transferred by Portugal at independence, and there are also ex-Soviet craft delivered since February 1977. Maintenance, which must present considerable problems for the former, depends on Soviet and Cuban technicians, and training for the 1000 sailors is by advisers from these countries, with a Nigerian team; some officers go to the USSR. The Eastern bloc has given relatively little economic assistance, and sometimes even harmed the economy – Soviet trawlers and factory ships have fished the local waters bare. Future plans for the Navy are not available, although the defences of its HQ on the Ila de Luanda are being strengthened. The other bases are to the south at Lobito and Moçâmedes.

Ex-Soviet 'SHERSHEN' class *fast attack craft (torpedo)*

Four transferred, one on 16.12.77, two on 16.12.78 and one in Feb 1979.

Ex-Portuguese ARGOS class *patrol vessels*

Seven units transferred, four in 1975 (*Lira, Orion, Escorpiño, Pegaso*) and three in 1976 (*Argos, Centauro, Dragao*); names/numbers after transfer not available. Ex-*Argos* and ex-*Dragao* believed to be non-operational, having been transferred for spares.

MISCELLANEOUS
The following minor fighting and amphibious force vessels have been acquired since 1975: from Portugal the former coastal patrol boats *Venus* (*Jupiter* class), *Espiga, Formalhaut, Pollux, Altair* and *Rigel* (all *Bellatrix* class), and the LCT *Alfance*.
From the USSR two 'Poluchat' class and at least one 'Zhuk' class coastal patrol craft (in Feb 1977), and three 'Polnochny' class landing ships (delivered 16.12.77, 16.12.78 and 1.2.79).

There are also up to nine ex-Portuguese LDM 400s and five ex-Soviet 'T 4' LCMs. The latter distributed Soviet arms to the MPLA along the coast during the critical fighting with UNITA and South Africa in 1975–76. It was reported that three, perhaps Soviet-crewed, shelled the port of Moçâmedes for two days (10–11.2.76) before several hundred Cubans landed in or near the port.

Benin (ex-Dahomey)

In early 1978 the People's Republic of Benin (Dahomey until 1975) began forming a naval force at Cotonou; its Army personnel now totals about 200. The Soviet Union delivered two 'Osa I' class fast attack craft (with missiles removed), two much smaller P 4 class torpedo boats and three 'Zhuk' class coastal patrol craft in January 1979 with another in September 1980. These craft would seem more than sufficient to patrol the country's 75-mile coastline and limited EEZ.

Cameroun

The United Republic of Cameroun is the result of a successful 1961 merger of the former French Cameroun and the southern part of the British Cameroons, two territories with different colonial pasts.

The French trained and equipped armed forces are small, and intended mainly for internal security among the nine million inhabitants. France guarantees external security by 1974 treaty. The 600-man Navy, under French command until 1973, operates a coastal patrol force of fast attack craft and patrol craft from its HQ in Douala, where an American company built a new $9 million naval base that became operational in 1982. Other ports along the 250-mile coastline are Victoria, Man O'War Bay (base for the 100 Cameroun Marines), Kribi, Tiko Idabato, Garoua and Lobé. The republic's merchant marine

expanded from 18 ships in 1974 to 44 by 1980 which was the year the French firm of Cofras Marine delivered a study on how Cameroun is to protect her 200-mile economic zone.

No indication of future naval plans or proposed new construction is available, but, in view of the closeness of expansionist Libya and the occasional border skirmishes with Nigeria, any available money will probably go to the Army and Air Force.

Ex-Chinese 'SHANGHAI II' class *fast attack craft (gun)*

Class (no):
Cap Cameroun (101), *Man O'War Bay* (102)
Transferred in July 1976. 70 Cameroun sailors trained in China before their delivery. Repaired in the Douala floating dock during 1980. Both extant 1982.

L'AUDACIEUX *large patrol craft*

Particulars: As Ivory Coast *Le Valeureux*

P 48 type boat ordered from SFCN in Sept 1974, laid down 10.2.75, launched 31.10.75 and commissioned 11.5.76. An enlarged P 48 boat was ordered 14.12.80 and laid down in Dec 1981. 8 Exocet MM40 ordered for her in 1982.

MISCELLANEOUS
The French seaward patrol craft *VC 6* (P 756) and *VC 8* (P 758) acquired in 1964 and ?1969 respectively, and named *Vigilant* and *Audacieux*; both discarded in 1975. The smaller French seaward patrol craft *VP 747* (ex-British *HDML 1423*) transferred in 1961 and named *Patrie du Cameroun*. Replaced in 1963 by *VP 768* (ex-British *HDML 1228*) which was assigned the same name and discarded c1972.

There are 3 French-built small coastal patrol craft and 6 landing craft, built in the Ivory Coast and Gabon, as well as 9 smaller assault boats.

Cape Verdes

This republic of nine major islands, some 250 miles off the coast of Senegal, became independent by referendum from former Portuguese Guinea-Bissau in 1975. Since January 1979 the Soviet Union has supplied its left-wing government with three 'Shershen' class fast attack craft (configured as gunboats, the usual torpedo tubes not being fitted) and one 'Zhuk' class coastal patrol craft.

Comoros

This four island group NW of Madagascar declared unilateral independence from France in 1975; France later recognised the transfer of power, but allowed one of the islands, Mayotte, to remain French. The French LCT 9061 (ex-HMS *Buttress*, LCT(8) 4099) was transferred in 1976, probably as an inter-island transport.

Congo

The history of Congo (formerly Middle Congo, of French Equatorial Africa) since independence in 1960 has been turbulent and confused. Another coup in 1979 returned the People's Republic to its version of Marxism-Leninism. There are about 100 Soviet advisers and a similar number of East Germans in the country; several hundred Cubans, many of them military advisers, occupy strategic sites in the country.

Congo (population 1.6 million), like Guinea and Angola, is not, however, a Soviet satellite in the Eastern European sense. She retains freedom of action in foreign and economic affairs and has improved relations with China. The main trade and development partner is France (Congo remains a member of the franc zone) with assistance also from the USA, West Germany and the Netherlands for specific projects.

The Congolese armed forces have expanded rapidly in the past decade, the Army increasing from 1500 to 8000. The French and Chinese military aid formerly received have mostly been replaced by the technical and other assistance from Cuba already mentioned. The 180-volunteer Navy (formed 1963) operates four fast attack craft from its base at Pointe-Noire, and has also some smaller Brazzaville-based patrol craft for the very long Congo and Ubargi river frontier with Zaire. The 1982 five-year plan envisaged five new river bases equipped with hovercraft.

Ex-Soviet 'SHERSHEN' class *fast attack craft (gun)*

Three transferred in Dec 1979 without TT.

Ex-Chinese 'SHANGHAI' class *fast attack craft (gun)*

Three transferred in March 1975 and numbered P 401 to P 403. Renumbered P 201 to P 203.

Spanish PIRANA class *large patrol craft*

Displacement:	125t standard; 134t full load
Dimensions:	118.7ft × 19ft × 6.2ft
	36.2m × 5.8m × 1.9m
Machinery:	2 shafts, 2 Bazán/MAN V8V 16/8 TLS diesels, 3200bhp = 25kts. Range 1100nm at 17kts.
Armament:	1–40mm Breda-Bofors (144rds), 2–20mm Oerlikon (1000rds), 2–12.7mm Browning M2 MG
Sensors:	Radar Raytheon RN-1220
Complement:	19

Class (no):

Marien Ngouabi (ex-*L'Intrepide*, P 601) launched 7.7.82 and completed Nov 1982, *Les Trois Glorieuses* (ex-*Le Vaillant*, P 602), *Les Maloango* (ex-*Le Terrible*, P 603)

Very similar to Spanish *Barcelo* class FAC. Ordered from Bazán, Cadiz, in Aug 1980. All arrived Pointe-Noire 3.4.83.

MISCELLANEOUS

The French seaward patrol craft *VC 4* (P 754) purchased in 1962 and renamed *Reine N'Galifourou*. Returned to France in 1965, and subsequently transferred to Senegal.

There are 3 ex-Soviet 'Zhuk' class coastal patrol craft (V 301 to V 303), 4 ex-Chinese *Yulin* class patrol boats (transferred 1966) and about 12 other small craft for river patrol duties.

Djibouti

This tiny state (formerly French Somaliland) independent since 1977 and outlet for half Ethiopia's trade, relies on French land, sea and air forces for its protection. A French Navy minesweeping flotilla has been based there since November 1980. There is a 30-ton glass fibre Tecimar patrol craft (ex-French P 771) as the nucleus of a 20-man naval force; at least nine harbour craft are also reported.

Egypt

The Royal Egyptian Navy was negligible in 1947, its most important unit being the weakly-armed sloop *El Amir Farouk*. Plans to acquire 3 sloops, 2 'Castle' class frigates, 4 *Algerine* class minesweepers and smaller craft were interrupted by the 1948–49 Arab-Israeli War, in which the Egyptian Navy succeeded only in losing *El Amir Farouk*, and when implemented in 1949–50 were modified, the actual ships acquired being detailed below.

Further warship purchases were made by Nasser's new republic in 1955–56. Two old British destroyers were delivered in July 1956 as tension over the Suez Canal was increasing, while from the Soviet Union came 2 new destroyers, 4 minesweepers and 12 MTBs. In spite of these reinforcements, the Navy was badly mauled in the Suez Operations (29 October–7 November), losing 3 frigates, 1 LST and about 6 MTBs in the face of overwhelming Anglo-French strength. Egyptian claims that two officers sank the French battleship *Jean Bart*

by unspecified means were unfounded, and duly ignored by the non-Arab world. On the other hand the Navy's blocking of the Suez Canal was efficiently done.

The naval losses were soon made good by the Soviet Union, which also transferred submarines for the first time. During the 1967 Six Day War, despite it being precipitated by Egypt's blockade of the Gulf of Aqaba at Sharm el Sheikh, the larger Egyptian units were kept in port, and the fighting was left to motor torpedo-boats. No successes were reported, and four Egyptian boats are believed to have been sunk, two by Israeli boats and two by the destroyer *Eilat*.

Between 1962 and 1967 the Soviet Union transferred 12 'Osa I' and 8 'Komar' class fast attack craft, armed with SSN-2 'Styx' surface-to-surface missiles (SSM). In a celebrated encounter on the night of 21 October 1967, one or more of these boats, moored at Port Said, launched 'Styx' missiles at *Eilat*, patrolling some 13 miles offshore. *Eilat* took evasive action and opened fire on the incoming missiles, but was totally disabled by two hits in her machinery spaces, and sank an hour later after a third hit. This incident attracted widespread attention in Western navies, which then had no operational SSM, and no modern shipborne defence against them.

Eilat was avenged physically when Israeli jets sank the Egyptian destroyer *El Qaher* in May 1970; the Israelis also rapidly developed counter-measures to deal with the missile threat. The results were seen in the October 1973 War (War of Ramadan), in which for the first time opposing sides fought with SSMs, and engagements were almost entirely between fast attack craft; of these, there were 19 Egyptian and 6 Syrian, armed with 'Styx', to 14 Israeli, armed with the new Gabriel I, which had half the range of the 'Styx' and a much smaller warhead. The Egyptians operated their boats piecemeal, and did not make the best use of their missile superiority, often electing to fire their 'Styx' at distances beyond the Gabriel's range and then withdrawing to harbour. Out of an estimated 50 'Styx' fired, none hit, because of Israeli ECM, high-speed manoeuvring and gun attacks on incoming missiles, while Gabriels are believed to have sunk between three and five Egyptian boats.

The USSR did not replace these losses (coming after the 1972 expulsion of 20,000 Soviet advisers and followed by the ending of Red Fleet Egyptian port facilities in April 1976), so Egypt was compelled to rely more on Western shipbuilders and repairers. The re-opening of the Suez Canal in 1975 was a moment of glory for the Navy and a commercial blessing, but the canal had been cleared by British and American mine warfare ships. Her situation at the end of 1982 with regard to large units is unsatisfactory, as no ships are known to be on order, under construction or due for transfer to replace the eight vintage ex-British and ex-Soviet destroyers and frigates, and to counter new construction in other Arab states. The proposed construction of two *Agosta* class submarines in France and two *Lupo* class frigates in Italy has been postponed or abandoned. An order for the latter was reportedly placed in September 1981. In 1978 the frigates *Lincoln* and *Salisbury* were purchased from Britain, with the guided missile destroyer *Devonshire* and the submarine *Cachalot* to follow, but Cairo had second thoughts and cancelled the transaction (although not before *Salisbury* reached Gibraltar), probably because the ships were too old. Two elderly US *Gearing* FRAM I destroyers were subsequently also offered and rejected.

The main strength of the Egyptian Navy lies in its 12 submarines and 24 missile-armed fast attack craft. Six of the latter have been modernised in Britain, where six more are fitting out, while a number of the ex-Soviet boats have been re-engined. The naval personnel (6000 in 1960, 14,000 in 1970 and 20,000 in 1982, of which 15,000 are 3-year conscripts) are considered to be well-trained, adequately educated, and possessing reasonable initiative and fighting spirit; small-scale joint exercises with the US Navy ensure that they are kept up-to-date. There are also about 15,000 reservists.

The Egyptian Navy's Mediterranean bases are Alexandria, Port Said, Sollum and Mersa Matruh while Port Tewfik, Hurghada, Safaqa and Ras Banas (106 million dollar modernisation being funded by the US) cover the Red Sea. Since 1980 a unique Otomat missile coastal defence system has been installed; 30 truck-mounted batteries with mobile radar to replace the 1960s Soviet 'Samlet' system.

FLEET STRENGTH 1947

The sloop *El Amir Farouk* built by Hawthorn Leslie (Newcastle-on-Tyne) was sunk by Israeli action off Gaza 22.10.48, possibly by limpet mines or an explosive motor boat.

There were also the transport *El Amira Fawzia* (1929, 2640t, 2–3pdr, renamed *El Quseir* c1953, discarded 1967); the veteran royal yacht *Mahroussa* (built 1865 by Samuda, London, 3417t, renamed *El Horria* c1953), still active in 1982 as a training ship and occasional presidential yacht after by far the longest career of any sea-going ship in a modern navy); and the small motor boats *Darfeel*, *Noor el Bahr*, *El Sarea* and *Raqib* (used by the RN as harbour defence boats during World War II and discarded 1948–*c*1953).

MAJOR SURFACE SHIPS

Ex-Soviet 'SKORY' class *destroyers*

No	Name	Builder	Acquired	Fate
	EL NASSER (i)	USSR	11.6.56	Returned USSR 1967
822	EL ZAFFER	USSR	11.6.56	Extant 1982
	DAMIET (i)	USSR	Jan 1962	Returned USSR 1967
888	SUEZ	USSR	Jan 1962	Extant 1982
666	6 OCTOBER (ex-*Al Nasser*)	USSR	Apr 1967	Extant 1982
844	DAMIET (ii)	USSR	Apr 1967	Extant 1982

El Nasser (i) and *El Zaffer* (one possibly ex-*Stoikii*) transferred at Alexandria in June 1956; one reported damaged by British aircraft 1.11.56 and the other set on fire and damaged by French aircraft on 2.11.56. *Damiet* and *Suez* (one possibly ex-*Bessmennyi*) transferred in 1962. In 1967 *El Nasser* and *Damiet* returned to the Soviet Union and were replaced by modified *Skory* class ships, given the same names. *El Nasser* (ii) renamed after the day Egypt crossed the Suez Canal in 1973 Arab-Israeli War. *El Zaffer* modernised as a guided missile destroyer; 2–85mm (3.4in) and 2–37mm AA guns have been replaced by two SSN-2 SSMs, probably taken from a 'Komar' class FAC (1978). *Damiet* (also given as *Domiat*) commemorates the frigate sunk in the 1956 Suez operations.

Ex-British 'Z' class *destroyers*

No	Name	Builder	Acquired Fate
833	EL FATEH (ex-*Zenith*, ex-*Wessex*)	Denny	July 1956 Extant 1982
	EL QAHER (ex-*Myngs*)	Vickers-Armstrong, Tyne	July 1956 Sunk 16.5.70

Purchased from the RN in 1955 and refitted before delivery. Modernised in the UK between 1963 and 1964, (TT removed and short mainmast replaced by a tall thin lattice mast with Type 960 search radar). *El Qaher* was sunk in the Red Sea by Israeli aircraft at Ras Banas (Berenice).

Ex-British BLACK SWAN class *frigate*

No	Name	Builder	Acquired	Fate
555 ex-42	EL TARIK (ex-*El Malek Farouk*, ex-*Whimbrel*)	Yarrow	1949	Extant 1982

Modified *Black Swan* class sloop, purchased from the RN in late 1949. Now completely obsolete and may be converted into a submarine depot ship.

Ex-British 'FLOWER' class *frigate*

No	Name	Builder	Acquired Fate
	EL SUDAN (ex-*Mallow*, ex-*Partizanka*, ex-*Nada*, ex-*Mallow*)	Harland and Wolff	28.10.49 Discarded *c*1975

This ex-'Flower' class corvette, launched in 1940 and loaned to Yugoslavia 1943–49, was transferred to Egypt. Used for training from *c*1970.

The frigate *Misr* (ex-mercantile *Malrouk*), sunk by collision S of Suez during the night of 16–17.5.73, is listed as a sister ship of *El Sudan*. However, her original 'Flower' name has not been located, and she may have been of another class (numerous 'Castle' class corvettes and *Bangor* class minesweepers were also sold to commercial interests after the war).

Ex-British 'HUNT' class (Type 1) *frigates*

No	Name	Builder	Acquired	Fate
525, ex-11	PORT SAID (ex-*Mohamed Ali*, ex-*Ibrahim el Awal*, ex-*Cottesmore*)	Yarrow	July 1950	Extant 1982

No	Name	Builder	Acquired	Fate
	IBRAHIM EL AWAL (ex-*Mohamed Ali*, (ex-*Mendip*, ex-*Lin Fu*, ex-*Mendip*)	Swan Hunter	Nov 1949	To Israel 1956

Former escort destroyers, launched in 1940, transferred from the RN. They exchanged names about 1951–52. *Ibrahim el Awal* surrendered off Haifa on 31.10.56 after coming under fire from the French destroyer *Kersaint*, and subsequently became the Israeli *Haifa* (see under Israel). *Port Said* lost her 5–2pdr guns in the 1960s, and her remaining light AA guns were replaced by 2–37mm and 2–25mm Russian-made weapons *c*1972. She has only one navigation radar and no ASW equipment.

Ex-British 'RIVER' class *frigates*

No	Name	Builder	Acquired	Fate
	ABIKIR (ex-*Usk*)	Smith Dock	Apr 1950	Scuttled 1.11.56
	DOMIAT (ex-*Nith*)	Robb	May 1950	Sunk 1.11.56
511 (ex-43)	RASHID (ex-*Spey*)	Smith Dock	Dec 1949	Extant 1982

These ships, launched 1941–43, were purchased from the RN in 1949 and refitted before delivery. *Abikir*, scuttled as a blockship in the Suez Canal, was refloated on 8.4.57, beached and abandoned. *Domiat* was sunk by gunfire from the cruiser HMS *Newfoundland* 8 miles S of Suez; there were 69 survivors. *Rashid* has been used as a submarine support ship since *c*1975, and has a large deckhouse aft.

EX-US TACOMA CLASS
In addition to the above, the ex-US *Tacoma* class (British 'Colony' class) frigates *Papua* (ex-*Howett*) and *Tobago* (ex-*Hong Kong*, ex-*Holmes*) were acquired by Egypt in 1950 as mercantile passenger vessels. They were taken over by the Egyptian Navy on 17.5.53 for refitting as warships, but so far as is known no work had been done when they were scuttled as blockships in the Suez Canal on 1.11.56. They were later refloated, beached and abandoned.

SUBMARINES

Ex-Soviet 'WHISKEY' class *submarines*

Class:
415, 418, 421, 432, 455, 477
Eight transferred (4 in June 1957, 3 on 24.1.58 and 1 in January 1962), but two returned to the Soviet Union in 1966 and were replaced by 'Romeo' class boats. Two more exchanged in 1971–72 at Leningrad. *455* is in reserve, and may be used for spares; the rest remain in service.

Ex-Soviet 'MV' class *submarine*

One (number unknown) transferred in 1957 and deleted 1971.

Ex-Soviet 'ROMEO' class *submarines*

Class:
711, 722, 733, 744, 755, 766
Five transferred in 1966 (two replacing two 'Whiskey' class boats returned to the USSR) and one in 1969. Two (*733* and *744*) may have been cannibalised for spares, but the rest are still in service. Two ex-Chinese-built 'Romeo' boats were delivered under tow in March 1982.

AMPHIBIOUS WARFARE VESSELS

LST *Aka* (ex-US *LST 178*, acquired 1950) was sunk as a blockship near Lake Timsah in the Suez Canal on 1.11.56. Refloated in Feb 1957, beached and abandoned. Three ex-Soviet 'Polnochny I' class LCTs (acquired 1974) were in service 1982. Numbered *910, 912* and *915*.
Ten ex-Soviet 'Vydra' class LCUs (acquired 1968–69) were in service in 1982; numbered *640, 643, 645, 648, 649, 682, 684, 685* and *688*. Some temporarily refitted as gunboats after the 1973 war, with 122mm 8-barrelled rocket launchers and 37mm or 40mm guns. Four Soviet 'SMB-1' class LCUs (acquired 1965) were in service in 1982.
Twenty very small LCTs of the LCM type were acquired in 1948 and numbered 1 to 20. Nos 15 and 20 were sunk in the 1956 Suez operations, eight have been discarded and ten remained in service as harbour craft in 1982.

SMALL SURFACE COMBATANTS

Ex-Soviet 'KOMAR' class *fast attack craft (missile)*

Eight transferred to Egypt in 1962–7. Four believed to have been sunk (one by Israeli aircraft on 16.5.70 and two in the October 1973 War) and four, numbered *393*, *395*, *397* and *399*, remain in service in 1982. Refitted with Italian CRM-12 D/S-2 diesels.

Ex-Soviet 'OSA I' class *fast attack craft (missile)*

Twelve transferred to Egypt in 1966. Four believed to have been sunk (some in the October 1973 War) and eight, numbered *301*, *310*, *323*, *341*, *356*, *378*, *389* and *390*, remain in service in 1982. At least four of these, numbers not known, have been refitted with 3 MTU diesels and had 2 MG added. All carry SA-N-5 'Grail' shoulder-launched missiles, new Kelvin Hughes 1006 surveillance and Decca 916 navigation radars.

Ex-Soviet 'SHERSHEN' class *fast attack craft*

Class:
310, *321*, *332*, *343*, *354* and *365*
Transferred 1967–68 and all extant 1982. Two were configured as torpedo boats, with 4–21in TT, and four as gunboats, with tubes replaced by 122mm BM21 multiple rocket launchers and one SA-N-5 'Grail' SAM.

'OCTOBER' class *fast attack craft (missile)*

Displacement:	71t standard, 82t full load
Dimensions:	84ft oa × 20ft × 5ft
	25.5m × 6.1m × 1.3m
Machinery:	4 shafts, 4CRM-18 DS/2 diesels, 5400bhp =40kts. Range 400nm at 30kts
Armament:	2 Otomat Mk 1 SSM, 4–30mm A32 (2×2)
Sensors:	Radar Decca AC 1226, Marconi S810; ECM Decca Cutlass RDL-1, 2 Protean decoy launchers
Complement:	20

Class:
207–212
Launched 1975–76 at Alexandria, with Soviet 'Komar' class wooden hulls and Italian machinery. Weapons and electronics installed in 1979–81 by Vosper Thornycroft, Portchester. Last pair (*207*, *212*) reached Alexandria 25.4.81. The Marconi-Sperry Sapphire radar/tv fire control system is fitted. They are very cramped, access to the engine room hatches being by a removable GRP operations room. Three more may be building.

RAMADAN class *fast attack craft (missile)*

Displacement:	258t light; 307t normal; 350t full load
Dimensions:	170ft 7in oa × 25ft × 6ft 7in mean
	52.0m × 7.6m × 2.0m
Machinery:	4 shafts, 4 MTU 20cyl 20V-538 TB 91 diesels, 18,000bhp = 37kts. Range 2000nm at 15kts. Oil 43.3t
Armament:	4 Otomat Mk 1 SSM (2×2), 1–76mm 62 OTO Melara Compact, 2–40mm Breda Bofors (1×2)
Sensors:	Radar Marconi S820, S810, 2 ST802, Decca AC 1226; ECM Decca-Racal Cutlass, 2 Protean MEL decoy launchers
Complement:	40

No	Name	Builder	Launched	Fate
561	RAMADAN	Vosper	6.9.79	Extant 1982
562	KHYBER	Vosper	12.6.80	Extant 1982
563	EL KADESSEYA	Vosper	19.2.80	Extant 1982
564	EL YARMOUK	Vosper	12.6.80	Extant 1982
565	HETTEIN	Vosper	17.6.81	Extant 1982
566	BADR	Vosper	25.11.80	Extant 1982

Laid down and completion dates: *Ramadan* (23.11.78, 20.7.81), *Khyber* (26.2.79, 15.9.81), *El Kadesseya* (23.4.79, Jan 1982), *El Yarmouk* (16.5.79, March 1982), *Hettein* (29.9.79, June 1982), *Badr* (March 1980, June 1982). Ordered from Vosper Thornycroft, Portchester 4.9.77 for £153 million to a design derived from the RN *Tenacity* class FPBs. Numbered 670, 672, 674, 676, 678 and 680 until 1982. *Ramadan* and *Khyber* arrived at Alexandria 9.11.81. They have the very advanced Marconi-Sperry Sapphire fire control system, 2 + 1 OFD trackers and Ferranti CAAIS action information system. A Ferranti operation room simulator due for 1983 delivery.

Ex-Soviet 'SO 1' class *large patrol craft*

Class:
211, *217*, *222*, *228*, *230*, *233*, *239*, *244*, *251*, *255*, *262*, *266*
Eight transferred in 1962–67, and four after 1970. Armament varies: six have BM21 rocket launchers, others 2–21in TT or SA-N-5 'Grail' SAMs. All in service 1982. Decca 916 radar is fitted.

MINE WARFARE VESSELS

Ex-British BANGOR class *minesweepers (corvettes)*

No	Name	Builder	Launched	Fate
	MATROUH (ex-*Stornoway*)	Robb	1949	?Sunk 1968–69
	NASR (ex-*Bude*)	Lobnitz	1949	Expended *c*1972
	SOLLUM (ex-*Wedgeport*)	Dufferin	1949	Lost 7.4.53

Former minesweepers, launched 1940–41. Details of *Matrouh's* loss are not available. Transferred from the RN and rated as corvettes. *Nasr* sunk as a target for 'Styx' SSMs, and *Sollum* foundered off Alexandria in heavy weather.

'October' class no *210* on trials   *Vosper Thornycroft*

Ramadan on trials   *Vosper Thornycroft*

Ex-US YMS type *coastal minesweepers*

Class (former BYMS no):
Arish (2028), *Darfur* (2041), *Gaza* (2013), *Kaisaria* (2075), *Kordofan* (2212), *Malek Fuad* 2035), *Naharia* (2069), *Rafah* (2149), *Tor* (2175)
Wooden-hulled boats launched 1942–43 and acquired 1949–50; all single-funnelled except *Arish*, which had two stacks. *Gaza* blew up off Mersa Matrouh in a fuel tank explosion on 26.7.50, *Darfur* and *Tor* transferred to Algeria in 1962, rest hulked or discarded *c*1967–70.

Ex-Soviet 'T 43' class *ocean minesweepers*

Class (no, former no):
Assiut (675, ex-*303*), *Bahaira* (659, ex-*301*), *Charkieh* (650, ex-*304*), *Dakhla* (672, ex-*305*), *Gharbia* (656, ex-*306*), *Miniya* (302), *Sinai* (679)
Four transferred from the USSR in 1956–59; *Assiut* and *Sinai* after 1970. *Miniya* sunk in the Gulf of Suez by Israeli aircraft on 6.2.70; the other six remain in service in 1982.

Ex-Soviet 'T 301' class *inshore minesweepers*

Class (no):
El Fayoum (708), *El Manufieh* (619)
 Transferred 1962 and in harbour service 1982.

Ex-Soviet 'YURKA' class *ocean minesweepers*

Class (no):
Aswan (695), *Giza* (690), *Qena* (696), *Sohag* (699)
 Transferred from the USSR in 1970–71 and slightly modified for Egyptian service (with hull scuttles and no 'Drum Tilt' radar), and all remain in service in 1982.

MISCELLANEOUS

The following light craft and amphibious force units have seen service with the Egyptian Navy:
 Five Fairmile 'B' type motor launches acquired from Britain (1948–50). Two (names not known) sunk *c* 1949–50; *Hamza* (ex-*ML 134*), *Sab el Bahr* and *Saker el Bahar*, hulked in the late 1960s.
 Two Fairmile 'D' type motor launches acquired from Britain in 1950 and named *El Naser* and *El Zafer*. Both discarded *c* 1965.
 Six Yugoslav '108' type MTBs (similar to US Higgins boats) bought in 1956. Four discarded in 1975 and two relegated to targets.
 Thirty-six Soviet 'P 6' type MTBs were acquired 1956–70 (a few may have been built at Alexandria). At least 10 have been sunk, 2 in the 1956 Suez operations, 4 in the Six Days War and 4 by Israeli aircraft in 1969–70, and 4 discarded (in 1975); 20, numbered from *201*, are believed to be in service in 1982. Armament varies; two boats have 4–21in TT, some have had the aft 25mm mounting and all TT replaced by a 122mm 8-barrelled 40 tube RL and 2–12.7mm MG.
 Four ex-Soviet 'P 4' type MTBs, transferred from Syria in 1970, were in service in 1982.
 Two ex-Soviet 'K 8' class minesweeper boats, named *Safaga* and *Abou El Ghoussoum*, were delivered 1968 and deleted 1980.
 Three British SRN-6 hovercraft, delivered 1976–79, may be minelayers.
 The large patrol craft *Nisr*, *Nimr* and *Thar* were built at Port Said in 1963 for the Coast Guard (110t, 1–20mm). The Coast Guard also operates six GRP MV 70 class coastal patrol craft (70ft, 33t, 2–30mm, 1–20mm, 2 MG) and has six more on order from Italy. It received three *Timsah* class Egyptian-built patrol craft in 1981 (99t, 25kts, 1–30mm, 13 men) with another 12 of the 42 ordered building.

Equatorial Guinea

Equatorial Guinea, sandwiched between Gabon and Cameroun, became independent from Spain in 1968. West Africa's smallest state (est pop 260,000) received a Soviet 'P 6' class torpedo boat and a 'Poluchat' class patrol boat in 1974. The 100 officers and men are based at Malabo (Fernando Po), Guinea's island dependency, and the capital Bata (Rio Muni). They receive some training from China and Spain.

Ethiopia

The history of Ethiopia between 1947 and 1982 shows a sharp discontinuity in September 1974, when the so-called 'creeping revolution' finally deposed the venerable Emperor, Haile Selassie, the effective ruler of the country since 1916 (except for the years of Italian occupation), and replaced his paternal feudalism by the Marxist military rule of the Dergue. The immediate cause of the revolution was the disastrous drought and famine of 1973, which cost up to 400,000 lives, but the Imperial Government had long been unable and perhaps unwilling to face the task of unifying and modernising their gigantic, primitive and ramshackle country. Eritrea, an ex-Italian territory forcibly amalgamated with Ethiopia in 1962 and providing its outlet to the Red Sea, was a battleground for vigorous independence movements, while to the south and east Somali irredentism in the Ogaden Desert also threatened national unity.

In international affairs the changes between 1974 and 1977 ended the pro-Western stance of Imperial days and left the Ethiopian government as the most pro-Soviet in Africa (and the most dependent on Soviet and Cuban military support). Arms shipments from the USA ceased in 1977, shortly before deliveries from the USSR began. The swift Ethiopian defeat of Somalia in the Ogaden during early 1978 could not have happened without assistance from Soviet and Cuban advisers and Cuban troops; these 'volunteers' helped shortly afterwards to roll back to the Sudan frontier the Eritrean liberation movements which, by 1977, had come to control nearly all the province, almost isolating Addis Ababa from the sea. In November 1978 Ethiopia and the USSR formalised their new alliance into a 20-year Treaty of Friendship and Co-operation.

The Ethiopian armed forces have been greatly expanded in recent years, the Army totalling 244,500 in 1982. Military efficiency and political reliability are alike low, the regime looking ultimately to the 13,000 Cubans and 1000–2000 Soviet and East German advisers for protection against internal and external opponents. The Imperial Ethiopian Navy was founded in 1955, and a naval base and college were established at Massawa in 1956. The first ship was received there in 1957. Personnel increased from 129 in 1958 to 1200 in 1970 and is now about 1500. Training, initially by 25 Norwegian officers, was later shared among other NATO countries, India, Israel and Yugoslavia. The modest naval force supplied by the USA, the Netherlands, France and Yugoslavia has been supplemented since 1977 by ex-Soviet fast attack craft; only the latter can now be considered fully operational. By contrast Ethiopia's tiny coastal merchant marine has shrunk from 23 to 17 ships (1974–80).

The naval base at Assab, scene of the 1977–78 Soviet arms sealift and close to the strategic Bab el Mandeb Strait, is being expanded to include repair facilities, while a small Soviet-constructed forward base in the Dahlak Islands is used as an anchorage for Russian warships. It has the 8500-ton 'Kherson' type floating dock removed from Berbera in 1977. Both harbours are protected by Soviet Sepal coast defence missiles. No details of future Ethiopian plans have been published, but more transfers to replace ageing ex-Western units may be expected.

Ex-Soviet 'PETYA I' class *frigate*

Transferred Sept 1981.

Ex-Soviet OSA II' class *fast attack craft (missile)*

Three transferred 1978, Sept 1980 and 13.1.81. Based in the Dahlak Is with Soviet advisers presumed to be aboard. More transfers expected.

Ex-Soviet 'MOL' class *torpedo-boats*

Three transferred 1978, may not have TT.

Ex-US PC type *large patrol craft*

Class (former no):
Belay Deress (ex-*PC 1616*)
 Built for W Germany at Brest, France, during 1953–55 under MDAP, but not delivered, being transferred to Ethiopia in 1957 under the MAP as her first warship. Found to be too advanced for the then state of Ethiopian naval training, and returned to the US in 1958, subsequently becoming the Italian *Vedetta* (discarded 1977).

Ex-US 'CAPE' and 'PGM 53' class *large patrol craft*

Class (former no):
PC 11 (ex-USCG *WVP 95304*), PC 12 (ex-*WVP 95310*), PC 13 (ex-USN *PGM 53*), PC 14 (ex-*PGM 54*), PC 15 (ex-*PGM 18*)
 The two ex-US Coast Guard cutters transferred in 1958, the three ex-USN patrol gunboats in 1961–62. *PC 12* sunk by Ethiopian aircraft in April 1977 while her crew were defecting; the other four were in service 1982.

Ex-Netherlands WILDERWANK class *large patrol craft*

Class (former name and no):
MS 41 (ex-*Eist*, M 829)
 Acquired from the Netherlands in 1971. Used for patrol duties, but minesweeping fittings remain. May have been fitted with SS 12 missiles. In service 1982.

Ex-Yugoslav 'KRALJEVICA' class *large patrol craft*

PBR 509 was transferred in 1975; her Ethiopian number is 51. In service 1982.

US 'SWIFT' type *large patrol craft*

Displacement:	118t full load
Dimensions:	105ft oa × 23ft 7in × 6ft 6in
	32.0m × 7.2m × 2.0m
Machinery:	2 shafts, 2 MTU MD 16V538 TB90 diesels, 7000bhp = 30kts.
	Range 1200nm at 18kts
Armament:	4–30mm Emerlec (2×2)
Sensors:	Radar Decca RM 916
Complement:	21

Class:
P 201, P 202, P 203, P 204

Six ordered from Swiftships, Louisiana in 1976; four delivered in April 1977 before US arms deliveries to Ethiopia ceased. In service 1982. *P 203* and *P 204* have 4–23mm (2×2) and 2–12.7mm MG (2×1) Soviet armament.

AMPHIBIOUS WARFARE SHIPS
Four ex-US landing craft (two LCM type, purchased 1962, and two LCVP type, purchased 1971).
Two French 'EDIC' LCU class (L 1035 and L 1036, launched May 1977).
Ex-Soviet 'T 4' class LCVP (transferred May 1979) and ex-Soviet 'Polnocny' class landing ship (L 1037, transferred 9.11.81).

Gabon

The Republic of Gabon, formerly part of French Equatorial Africa, became independent in 1960, and has since been politically stable, with a right-of-centre autocracy firmly in control and black Africa's highest per capita income; a one-party state was formally instituted in 1968. French military intervention quickly ended the one coup so far, in February 1964.

Gabon, like Ivory Coast, follows a 'moderate' foreign policy, usually taking the French line; a flirtation with Libya in 1973–74 has now cooled off. She consistently broke trade sanctions against Rhodesia, and was accused of complicity in the guerrilla attack on Cotonou in Benin (Dahomey) in January 1977. The continued French interest is mainly the consequence of Gabon's mineral wealth (iron, manganese and uranium); under 1974 bilateral defence arrangements, France keeps four Jaguar aircraft and 900 marines at Libreville, and has another 1500 men near at hand in the landlocked Central African Republic.

These forces protect Gabon from external threats, and give France effective control over her 660,000 inhabitants, as the Gabonese Army is only of reinforced battalion strength. The 170-volunteer Navy, based at Port Gentil, south of Libreville and just below the Equator, has a French commanding officer and operates a few fast attack craft and patrol craft along the 500-mile coastline. Port Gentil (opened March 1968) was enlarged in 1981.

PRESIDENT EL HADJ OMAR BONGO
fast attack craft (missile)

Displacement:	150t full load
Dimensions:	138ft oa × 25ft 4in × 6ft 6in
	42.0m × 7.7m × 1.9m
Machinery:	3 shafts, 3 MTU 20V 672 TY90 diesels, 9450bhp = 38.5kts.
	Oil 28.4t, range 1500nm at 15kts
Armament:	4–SS12M SSM (2×2), 1–40mm Bofors, 1–20mm
Sensors:	Radar Decca RM 1226
Complement:	20

Class (no):
President El Hadj Omar Bongo (GC 05, ex-P 10)
Triple-skinned mahogany-hulled boat launched by CNE, Cannes, on 21.11.77 and commissioned 7.8.78, and in service 1982. Reached 40kts (10,500bhp) on trials. Wire-guided optically fired missiles.

N'GOLO class *fast attack craft (gun)*

Displacement:	65t standard; 88t full load
Dimensions:	88.5ft oa × 22.3ft × 6.9ft
	27.3m × 6.8m × 2.1m
Machinery:	2 shafts, 2 MTU 16V538 diesels, 7000bhp = 40kts. Range
	600nm/1200nm at 40kts/35kts
Armament:	1–40mm Bofors, 2–20mm Rheinmetall RM 202
Sensors:	Radar Decca RM 916
Complement:	16

N'golo (GC 04) ordered from Intermarine, Sarzana, Italy, laid down in June and launched Dec 1976. She was completed in March 1977 but burnt out on 13.3.80. Replaced in 1981 by craft of same name and number, three more reported on order. Largest high-speed GRP hull in service. *N'golo* reached 43.8kts (7960bhp) on measured distance trials off Italy. Galileo fire control systems.

N'GUENE *large patrol craft*

Displacement:	90t standard; 118t full load
Dimensions:	95ft 9in pp, 105ft 7in oa × 22ft 4in × 7ft 7in
	29.2m, 32.2m × 6.8m × 2.3m
Machinery:	3 shafts, GM 16V 149TE diesels, 4800bhp = 27kts. Range
	825nm/1400nm at 25kts/15kts
Armament:	1–40mm Bofors, 1–20mm, 2–12.7mm MG (1×2)
Sensors:	Radar Decca RM 916
Complement:	21

N'guéné (GC 03) is an aluminium-hulled boat built by Swiftships, Morgan City, USA (1974–75) and in service since Feb 1976. Armament 2–40mm when delivered. A report that five more are on order has not been confirmed.

MISCELLANEOUS
The French seaward patrol craft *VP 775* (ex-*VP 25*, ex-British *HDML 1021*) was acquired as Gabon's first warship in 1961 and named *Bouet-Willaumez*. She was hulked in Feb 1968 and deleted in 1975. In service are the patrol craft *Colonel Djoue Dabany* (ex-*President Albert Bongo*, (GC 02, 1972, CNE, Cannes, commissioned March 1972, 80t, 2–20mm, 30kts, 17 men) and the Gabon-built *President Léon M'ba* (GC 01, launched 16.1.68, 85t, 2–12.7mm MG, 12.5kts, 16 men), a Senegalese-built LCM *Manga* (two more were ordered from Bazan, Cadiz, in Aug 1981) and a coast guard of about ten small coast patrol craft and launches.

President Albert Bongo as completed
Navarret Collection

Ghana

Ghana under Kwame Nkrumah became in March 1957 the first British black African territory to achieve independence, largely because of her relatively advanced electorate and strong cocoa-based economy. The initial promise was not, however, maintained; within a few years, strains appeared in the carefully imported pseudo-Westminster constitutional arrangements, and, as a result of extravagance, mismanagement and a catastrophic fall in the world cocoa price, the economy almost collapsed.

This first democratic experiment ended with Nkrumah's overthrow by the Army in February 1966, since when Ghana has had military rule rather than not and an economy that has not recovered. Internationally, the fledgeling state became the centre of pan-African nationalism and a vigorous denouncer of 'neo-colonialism', but by 1966, as Nkrumah's outlook moved left, the official policy had become an ill-defined amalgam of Pan-Africanism and 'African Socialism', entitled 'Nkrumahism'. Since 1966 domestic matters have swept these 'isms' out ot sight.

The volunteer armed forces, initially derived from the modest colonial army, have gradually expanded in the years of independence. At present, more than 12 per cent of the gross national product is spent on the armed forces, a very high figure for a country under no threat from her neighbours, and emphasising the privileged role of the military in tropical Africa. Despite this huge sum, the training of the armed forces has deteriorated and their development stagnated, affecting the soldiers' professionalism and dedication to duty.

The Ghanaian Navy, very much a junior partner, has been built up into a modest coast defence force split into Western and Eastern Commands, mainly useful for coast guard purposes and fishery protection. By the end of 1981 fish piracy was so rife that Eastern Command issued a shoot to sink warning. The volunteer personnel, planned in 1960 for 500, reached 800 in 1970 and 1360 in 1982. The first ships, two ex-RN inshore minesweepers, reached Sekondi-Takoradi (Tema, east of Accra, is the other main base) in November 1959, and subsequent construction and purchases have been very moderate, except during the last years of Nkrumah, when there were grandiose plans for a sizeable fleet. Two corvettes of a novel type completed in 1964 and 1965 were to have been followed by two more, and by two frigates and a support ship but of the latter five, only one frigate materialised, and then not in Ghanaian service.

BLACK STAR *frigate*

Particulars:	See British *Mermaid*

Modified RN Type 41 frigate, to serve also as presidential yacht, ordered in 1965 as *Black Star*, but cancelled after President Nkrumah's deposition in 1966. The British Government accepting responsibility for the hull, the ship was completed by the builders. Acquired by the RN in 1972 after six years lying idle in the Clyde and commissioned in 1973 as *Mermaid*. See under United Kingdom (Part I) and Malaysia (Part II). Another such frigate was projected, but never begun.

Kromantse as completed
NB 1/750 scale

KROMANTSE class *corvettes*

Displacement:	380t light; 440t standard; 500t full load
Dimensions:	177ft oa × 28ft 6in × 13ft
	54.0m × 8.7m × 4.0m
Machinery:	2 shafts, 2 Bristol Siddeley Maybach 16cyl diesels, 7100bhp = 20kts. Fuel 60t. Range 1100nm/2900nm at 14kts/18kts
Armament:	1–4in/40 Mk 23, 1–40mm/60 Mk 9, 1 Squid Mk 4, 2–2in RFLs
Sensors:	Radar Plessey AWS-1, Type 978 navigation set; Sonar Type 164
Complement:	54

No	Name	Builder	Launched	Fate
F 17	KROMANTSE	Vosper, Portsmouth	5.9.63	Extant 1982
F 18	KETA	Vickers, Tyne	18.1.65	Extant 1982

Kromantse running trials   *Vosper Thornycroft*

Vosper Mk 1 corvettes, designed in conjunction with Vickers, and the first in the series of Vosper (now Vosper Thornycroft) corvette and frigate designs. Laid down 10.12.62 and 25.10.63. Completed 27.7.64 and 18.5.65. Novel, compact and relatively cheap ASW patrol vessels. Both refitted 1974–75. Two more units were projected, but never begun.

Yogaga as completed
NB 1/750 scale

ACHIMOTA class *fast attack craft (gun)*

Displacement:	380t standard; 410t full load
Dimensions:	190ft 7in oa × 25ft × 9ft 2in
	58.1m × 7.6m × 2.8m
Machinery:	3 shafts, 3 MTU 16V 538 TB91 diesels, 11,400bhp = 33kts. Range 3300nm/5200nm at 16kts/12kts
Armament:	1–76mm/62 OTO Melara Compact (250rnds), 1–40mm/70 Bofors (750rnds)
Sensors:	Radar Navigational, Thomson-CSF Canopus A
Complement:	40

Class (no):
Achimota (P 28), *Yogaga* (P 29)
PB 57 type, launched 14.3.79 and delivered 27.3.81 by Lürssen, Vegesack. Larger and faster than *Dzata* class. In service 1982.

Sahene 1976
NB 1/750 scale

DELA class *large patrol craft*

Displacement:	160t full load
Dimensions:	115ft 6in × 21ft 4in × 5ft 11in
	35.2m × 6.5m × 1.8m
Machinery:	2 shafts, 2 MTU MD 16V 538 TB90 diesels, 3000bhp = 30kts. Range 1000nm at 30kts
Armament:	1–40mm Bofors (RFLs attached)
Complement:	32

Class (no):
Dela (P 24), *Sahene* (P 25)
Built 1973–76 for fishery protection by Ruthoff Werft, Mainz, West Germany, and in service 1982. The builders' 1975 bankruptcy prevented construction of four further units. Refitted by Lürssen 1981.

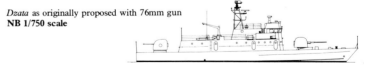

Dzata as originally proposed with 76mm gun
NB 1/750 scale

DZATA class *large patrol craft*

Displacement:	212t standard, 255t full load
Dimensions:	147ft 4in oa × 23ft × 7ft 6in
	44.9m × 7.0m × 2.3m
Machinery:	2 shafts, 2 MTU diesels, 7200bhp = 27kts. Range 1100nm/2000nm at 25kts/15kts
Armament:	2–40mm/70 Bofors, 2–7.62mm MG
Sensors:	Radar Navigational, Thomson-CSF Canopus A
Complement:	35

Class (no, in service):
Dzata (P 26, 4.12.79), *Sebo* (P 27, 2.5.80)
TNC 45 type, laid down Jan 1978 and launched 19.9.79 by Lürssen, Vegesack, in W Germany, and in service 1982.

British 'FORD' class *seaward defence boats*

Class (no):
Elmina (P 13, 18.10.62), *Komenda* (P 14, 17.5.62)
  As RN ships, but built for Ghana and commissioned in Nov 1962. Still in service 1982.

Ex-British 'HAM' class *inshore minesweepers*

Class (no):
Afadzato (M 12), *Yogaga* (M 11)
  Formerly *Ottringham* and *Malham* respectively, transferred from the RN in 1959. Fitted with funnels. The Foden diesel and centre shaft were removed in 1967. Discarded 1977.

Ex-British 'TON' class *coastal minesweeper*

Ejura (M 16) formerly HMS *Aldington* (M 1171) loaned by the RN in 1964 and transferred permanently in 1974. Discarded 1979.

MISCELLANEOUS
The British maintenance repair craft *MRC 1122*, a converted LCT (4) type, was purchased in 1965 and named *Asuantsi*. Used as a base workshop and for sea training, she was discarded in 1970
  Four 'Poluchat I' class coastal patrol boats, numbered *P 20*, *P 21*, *P 22* and *P 23*, were transferred from the USSR in 1967. *P 22* discarded 1970, the others 1973. There are also four coastal patrol craft of the 'Spear 2' class, built by Fairey Marine in 1978, and two Rotork service craft.

Guinea

Guinea became independent in 1958, when her people voted against continued association with France in the referendum held in French colonies and territories. For thus spurning de Gaulle's offer of participation in the great Francophone community, the new republic was cut off without a sou; the estrangement lasted 20 years until reconciliation in December 1978. Traditional agriculture accounts for about half the gross domestic product, but the most important and dynamic area is mining, Guinea having about 30 per cent of the world's crude bauxite, and iron ore deposits of an estimated eight billion tons.

Internationally, Guinea, although a one-party state and leftward-leaning under Sékou Touré, is not a Soviet satellite despite arms deliveries going back to 1960. Since 1975 there has been a generally steady improvement and normalisation of relations with the West and Guinea's neighbours; in 1980, refuelling facilities formerly granted for Soviet naval long-range reconnaissance aircraft at Conakry airport were withdrawn, another straw in the wind. Guinea strengthened her 1971 defence agreement with neighbouring Sierre Leone into a Mutual Defence Pact in August 1981.

The armed forces are small, but well supplied, with some 500 Cuban advisers; the Army of about 8500 is Russia-, Czech- and Chinese-equipped. The 600-man conscript Navy operates an ex-Soviet minesweeper and about 20 attack and patrol craft, delivered from 1971 and almost all from Russia and China, a large force when one considers that Guinea's merchant marine numbers 14 ships. On past performance, both the efficiency and loyalty of the Guinean military must be considered questionable. On 11 November 1970 a four-ship attack on Conakry by 350–400 Portuguese-led armed dissidents from the then Portuguese Guinea (now Guinea-Bissau) achieved complete surprise and reached its objective before being defeated in three days fighting. Soon after the first Soviet warships arrived at Conakry which became the Red Navy's most visited Atlantic port over the next decade, surpassing all of Cuba's combined. Its peak importance came during the 1975–76 Angolan Civil War. As of 1981 West Germany is to invest 7.3 million dollars in Conakry's development.

Ex-Soviet 'T58' class ocean minesweeper transferred May 1979 with all sweeping gear removed and renamed *Lamine Sadji Kaba*.
  Three ex-Soviet 'Shershen' class FAC (T) two transferred 1978, one in Dec 1979 minus TT.
  Six ex-Chinese 'Shanghai II' class FAC(G) transferred in pairs, 1973, 1974 and 1976. Pennant numbers 733–738.
  Four ex-Soviet 'P 6' class FAC(T) transferred 1971–72 and deleted 1981. French-built coastal patrol craft delivered by CNE in 1979.
  Three ex-Soviet 'Poluchat I' class coastal patrol craft.
  Two ex-Soviet 'MO VI' class coastal patrol craft transferred 1972–73.
  Two ex-Soviet LCUs.

Guinea-Bissau

The independence of this republic was recognised in 1974, ending a guerrilla war (since 1959) against the Portuguese Army. Her Navy, based at Bissau, has 250 volunteers who operate 2 ex-Soviet fast attack craft (one 'Shershen' minus TT, one 'P 6', transferred in 1978), 5 French and Spanish-built coastal patrol boats, 2 ex-Soviet 'T 4' landing craft and smaller units. A Dutch-built patrol craft was delivered in May 1981 and named *Naga*. No expansion is likely, although there is a dispute with neighbouring Guinea (almost seven times richer and more populous) about oil prospecting in coastal waters.

Ivory Coast

The Ivory Coast under Houphouët-Boigny, a political veteran, obtained independence from France in 1960, and has since been a model of stability and prosperity for tropical Africa. Her gross domestic product in 1980 almost matched neighbouring Ghana's and this from only two-thirds the population.

The conservative and anti-Communist policies followed externally have made her sometimes into France's mouthpiece in Africa, and have kept the country out of the most important black African councils and groupings. Similarly, Ivory Coast was one of the few countries to recognise breakaway Biafra, and granted asylum to her defeated leader in 1970.

The selective service defence forces are small, with an Army of about 4500 (including a marine battalion) and a Ministry of Marine-controlled Navy of 500–550 men (150 in 1974) manning a coastal and river patrol force. Two Exocet missile-armed 'Patra' or *Trident* class patrol boats have been delivered, and more will follow, allowing two coastal patrol squadrons to be formed. The ports of Abidjan (shipyard), Sassandra, Tabou and San Pedro are all used for the Navy's work which includes fire fighting and anti-pollution patrols. The Ivorian forces are, and are likely to remain, almost entirely trained, supplied and maintained by France; a 450-strong French marine infantry battalion is stationed near Abidjan as the ultimate guarantor of Houphouët-Boigny's rule.

Ex-US SC type *large patrol craft*

Wooden-hulled submarine chaser, formerly US *SC 1337*, transferred to France in 1943 (as *CH 71*, re-rated as patrol vessel *P 699* in 1951), and from France to Ivory Coast as *Patience* in 1961. Discarded *c*1972.

Vigilant as completed
NB 1/750 scale

LE VIGILANT class *large patrol craft (missile)*

Displacement:	235t full load (*Le Valeureux* 250t)
Dimensions:	155ft 10in oa (*Le Valeureux* 157ft 6in) × 23ft 7in × 7ft 6in 47.5m (48.0) × 7.0m × 2.3m
Machinery:	2 shafts, 2 MGO diesels, 2400bhp = 18.5kts (*Le Valeureux* 4200bhp = 23.0kts). Range 2000nm at 16kts
Armament:	4 MM40 Exocet SSM, 2–40mm/60 (1×2)
Sensors:	Radar DRBN-32, Decca (*Le Valeureux*)
Complement:	34

Name	Builder	Launched	Fate
LE VIGILANT	SFCN	23.5.67	Extant 1982
LE VALEUREUX	SFCN	8.3.76	Extant 1982

Franco-Belge type P 48 boats ordered in 1966 and 1974. Laid down 20.1.67 and 28.10.75, completed 29.2.68 and 25.9.79 respectively. *Vigilant* refitted at Brest, France 1981 when both vessels received Exocet.

L'ARDENT class *large patrol craft (missile)*

Class:
L'Ardent, L'Intrépide
   Ordered from Auroux, Arcachon in 1977, launched 21.7.78, and in service since 6.10.78. Differ from the French *Trident* class in having a 20mm gun instead of a 12.7mm, and an increased crew of 19. An Exocet quadruple launcher replaced the original 6 SS12 in 1981.

MISCELLANEOUS
The French 70t seaward patrol craft *La Persevèrance* VC 9 (P 759) was acquired 26.4.63 and named *Sine Saloum*. The 450t training ship *Locodjo*, built in W Germany in 1953 and seized in 1970 when gun-running to Biafra. Both were stricken in 1979.
   There are also four coastal and river patrol craft, the 750t 'Batral' type *Elephant* landing ship launched 1975 and commissioned 2.2.77 and refitted at Brest 1981, similar to the French *Champlain*), one LCVP (built in Abidjan, 1970) and one LCPS.

Kenya

This East African colony became independent in December 1963 and a republic within the Commonwealth one year later. The new state was led from 1963 to 1978 by Jomo Kenyatta, who, while setting up a one-party state, preached moderation and conciliation; the legacy of Mau Mau was forgotten, white farmers and some Asian traders allowed to remain, and in general the regime came to be accepted as one of the most stable and pro-Western in tropical Africa. Although tribal politics have occasionally led to uncertainty and unrest, the transition to Daniel Moi's leadership after Kenyatta's death was peaceful.

The volunteer armed forces have traditionally been small in numbers and lightly equipped. Kenya receives military assistance from Britain, and is re-equipping her air force with US credits; she could almost certainly rely on overt military support from these powers if threatened by a neighbour. US naval forces have in the past made routine visits to Mombasa, making use of the usual supply facilities that are available to other countries, including the Soviet Union since 1968. More recently, Kenya has responded to the crises in the Gulf and the Horn of Africa with a 1980 mutual defence and assistance agreement allowing US forces access to Kenyan airfields, and making Mombasa, where an 18,000-ton dry dock was opened in 1978, a possible storage and revictualling depot for the US Navy.

Plans for the Kenyan Navy were announced in March 1964, and it was inaugurated on 12 December 1964, the first anniversary of independence; training, supply and maintenance have been almost entirely British (initial equipment worth 3,640,000 dollars). The present strength of about 350 men and seven large patrol craft, four of which are being retrofitted with Israeli Gabriel missiles, is adequate for patrolling Kenya's 350-mile coastline, but construction of larger vessels for offshore duties seems likely.

SIMBA class *large patrol craft (gun)*

Displacement:	96t standard; 109t full load
Dimensions:	95ft wl, 103ft oa × 19ft 10in × 5ft 10in
	31.4m × 6m × 1.8m
Machinery:	2 shafts, 2 Paxman Ventura 12YJCM diesels, 2800bhp = 24kts. Oil 14t. Range 1500nm at 16kts
Armament:	2–40mm/60 Mk 7 (2×1), 2–2in RFL Mk 5
Complement:	23

Class (no, launched, in service):
Simba (P 3110, 9.9.65, 23.5.66), *Chui* (P 3112, 25.11.65, 7.7.66), *Ndovu* (P 3117, 22.12.65, 27.7.66)

Vosper type ordered 28.10.64 from Vosper, Portsmouth. All sailed 22.8.66 and arrived Mombasa 4.10.66. Extant 1982. Similar to Malaysian *Sri* class.

MAMBA *large patrol craft (missile)*

Displacement:	125t standard; 160t full load
Dimensions:	123ft oa × 22ft 6in × 5ft 2in
	37.5m × 6.9m × 1.6m
Machinery:	2 shafts, 2 Paxman Ventura 16YJCM diesels, 4000bhp = 25kts. Range 3000nm at 12kts
Armament:	4 Gabriel Mk 2 SSM (4×1), 4–30mm (2×2)
Sensors:	Radar Decca RM-916
Complement:	25

Class (no, builder, launched):
Mamba (P 3100, Brooke Marine, Lowestoft, 6.11.73).
   In service since 7.2.74. Original 2–40mm/60 Mk 7 replaced in 1981 by Israeli guns and missiles plus EW gear.

Harambee 1976
NB 1/750 scale

MADARAKA class *large patrol craft (missile)*

Displacement:	120t standard; 145t full load
Dimensions:	107ft oa × 20ft × 5ft 7in
	32.6m × 6.1m × 1.7m
Machinery:	2 shafts, 2 Paxman Valenta 16RP 200M diesels, 5400bhp = 25kts. Range 2300nm at 12kts
Armament:	4 Gabriel Mk 2 SSM (1×4), 2–40mm/60 Mk 7
Sensors:	Radar Decca RM-916
Complement:	21

Class (no, launched):
Madaraka (P 3121, 28.1.75), *Jamhuri* (P 3122, 14.3.75), *Harambee* (P 3123, 2.5.75)
   Brooke Marine type ordered 10.5.73 from Brooke Marine, Lowestoft. First two in service since 16.6.75, *Harambee* since 28.6.75. Israeli missiles fitted 1981–82.

Ex-British 'FORD' class *seaward defence boat*

Nyati (P 3102) Formerly HMS *Aberford*, RN loaned in 1964 and transferred permanently in 1967. Sold 1971.

ROYAL EAST AFRICAN NAVY 1950–64
Mention must be made of the Royal East African Navy, the colonial forerunner of the navies of independent Kenya and Tanzania.
   At the end of World War II, the Kenyan RNVR operated the *Rosalind*, a 'Shakespearian' class minesweeping trawler loaned by the RN as a training ship at Mombasa, while the Zanzibari RNVR, which combined for certain purposes with the Kenyan, used the *Ndovu* and *Alhathari*, two tugs fitted for minesweeping (380t, 1–3in, 2 Lewis guns, 1 DCT, 10kts, built Paisley 1928). *Ndovu* was discarded in 1948 and *Alhathari* in 1951.
   The East African Naval Force was formed in 1950 as successor to the Kenyan RNVR, with additional financial contributions from Tanganyika and (in later years) Uganda and Zanzibar. In 1953 the new force was designated the Royal East African Navy. Ships in service were *Rosalind* at Mombasa and the *MFV 206* at Kilindini (the *Mvita*, the base ship at Kilindini, seems to have been the MFV 204). In addition to training, the REAN performed usefully in famine relief operations. The inshore minesweeper *Bassingham* was acquired on loan in June 1958 to replace *Rosalind*, by then nearing the end of her useful life, but proved unsuitable and was returned to the RN in October 1961. No replacement had been transferred when the decision to disband the REAN was announced in December 1961. The government of newly independent Tanganyika considered the REAN unsuitable in its existing form and the other three governments were unable to meet the extra costs of modernising the force. *Rosalind* was discarded in 1963 and *Bassingham* was on the sales list in 1964. The fate of the MFV 204 *Mvita* has not been traced.

Simba as completed
Vosper Thornycroft

Liberia

Although Liberia has been independent since her foundation in 1847, there is no long-standing naval tradition, her naval forces having generally been negligible or non-existent. In 1982 the 445-man volunteer Coast Guard (set up c1956) operates from Monrovia and three other bases, three CG 27 class Swedish-built 87ft patrol boats (50t, in service 27.9.80, 3 MGs, 25kts), two US-built Swiftship 65ft boats (38t, in service 22.7.76, 81mm mortar and 3 MGs, 24kts) and a US-built 42ft craft. The large patrol boat *Alert* (ex-US *PGM 102*, transferred 1967) was deleted in 1981. Two ex-USCG motor launches (*ML 4001* and *ML 4002*, sold in 1957) were discarded in 1976. The 1980 coup by Army NCOs ended 133 years of civilian rule and completely upset the power structure in the country, but will probably not affect the Coast Guard adversely.

Libya

After World War II, the provinces of Libya were placed provisionally under British and French administration until the country became independent in December 1951, the first independent state created by the UN. The conservative, pro-Western rule of King Idris was bolstered by an American and British military presence, but this did not prevent its overthrow by a military coup in September 1969. The new Arab Republic reversed previous policies – Western bases and troops were evacuated by 1970 – and has subsequently steered a somewhat maverick course internationally, a course apparently often dependent on the whims of her erratic yet mercurial leader – Colonel Muammar el Gaddafi.

In the world arena, oil-rich Libya has developed love-hate relationships with both Western and Eastern blocs. Nearer home, the main enemies are Israel and Zionism, but realistic appreciations of Libya's current military capabilities and her oil installations' vulnerability have prevented direct armed conflict. As a fervent exponent of pan-Arab Socialism, she has proposed (and occasionally effected) unions with other Arab states, but these have always proved transitory. No money or effort have been spared in attempts to destabilise less revolutionary Arab leaders, or even revolutionary leaders following different roads to socialism. Libya has replaced Algeria as the main arms supplier to the Polisario Front in the Western Sahara, and has also begun economic and military penetration southwards, alarming the fragile and vulnerable state of the Sahel and tropical Africa; attempts in 1979 to shore up Idi Amin in Uganda and Bokassa in the Central African Empire brought only ignominy and ridicule, but the Libyan intervention in Chad in 1980 successfully ended traditional French influence.

Libya's armed forces are numerically weak, as expected for a population of only 3,250,000, but make up for this by being lavishly equipped with the most modern weapons, which look good on paper but cause formidable problems of training and maintenance; in major July 1977 border clashes with Egypt, Libyan forces performed badly. Some 1800 Soviet advisers were reported in the country in 1982, but the USSR has never secured bases in avowedly anti-Communist Libya.

The Navy was set up in November 1962 by a British Naval Mission, with technical assistance and training that began in Malta. Since 1974 it has been expanded rapidly with defence spending rising 250 per cent; the volunteer personnel increased from 2000 to 3000 between 1974 and 1980. Libya's merchant marine quadrupled over the same period. The Fleet, which is obtaining up-to-date ships from both West and East, now includes submarines, missile-armed corvettes and fast attack craft, an amphibious force in theory able to land 2000 troops plus units with a minelaying capability. Italy received an order for 240 A244 ASW torpedoes in 1979. The bases are Tripoli (5000-ton floating dock), Benghazi, Derna, Tobruk and Bandiyah.

However, inadequately trained and inexperienced sailors have mishandled delicate equipment; thus the frigate *Dat Assawari* probably sustained engineering damage on her delivery voyage in 1973, and the landing ship *Ibn al Qis* was destroyed at sea by a fire in 1979. The existence of other avoidable hazards is indicated by the Malta liberation movement's sabotaging of *Dat Assawari* while refitting in Italy in October 1980.

MAJOR SURFACE SHIPS

Dat Assawari 1973

DAT ASSAWARI *frigate (missile)*

Displacement:	1325t standard; 1625t full load
Dimensions:	310ft pp, 330ft oa × 36ft × 11ft 2in *94.5m, 100.6m × 11.0m × 3.4m*
Machinery:	2-shaft CODOG: 2 Rolls-Royce Olympus gas turbines, 46,400shp = 37.5kts, plus 2 Paxman Ventura 16Y JCM diesels, 3500bhp = 17kts. Range 5700nm at 17kts
Armament:	1–4.5in/55 Mk 8, 2–40mm/70 (2×1), 2–35mm/90 Oerlikon (1×2), 2 Seacat SAM (2×3), 1 Limbo Mk 10 ASW mortar. See notes
Sensors:	Radar Plessey AWS-1, RDL-1; sonar Types 185, 170, 174
Complement:	132

No	Name	Builder	Launched	Fate
F 01	DAT ASSAWARI	Vosper Thornycroft	13.10.69	Extant 1982

Vosper Thornycroft Mk 7 frigate, ordered in Feb 1968, laid down 27 Sept and completed 1.2.73, slightly larger than the two Iranian Mk 5s and has a different armament. Vibrates strongly at speeds over 27kts. *Dat Assawari* was refitted (1979–81) by CNR, Riva Trigosa (Genoa) despite bomb damage on 29.10.80 with the following changes: 4 Otomat Mk 1 SSM (4×1) added aft, 4 Albatros SAM (1×4) in place of Seacat forward, 6–12.75in ASW TT (2×3), Decca TM 1229 radar, Diodon sonar and Selenia RAN-12/X combat data system added. Italian RAN-10S search radar gives a reported 50 per cent range improvement on the old British set. Now numbered 211 (ex-101).

SUBMARINES

Soviet 'FOXTROT' class *submarines*

Class (no):
Al Badr (311), *Al Fatah* (312), *Al Ahad* (313), *Al Matrega* (314), 315, 316

Constructed on a re-activated Sudomekh SY building line in Leningrad; *Al Badr* reached Tripoli 27.12.76. Rest delivered late 1977, early 1978, 17.3.81 and Feb 1982. One more on order and building. Libyan crews receive training in USSR and up to 12 Soviet advisers serve in each boat.

Yugoslav MALA class *midget submarines*

Two ordered 1979. First delivered Jan 1982.

Dat Assawari as completed   *Vosper Thornycroft*

AMPHIBIOUS WARFARE VESSELS

IBN OUF class *landing ships*

Displacement:	2200t standard; 2800t full load
Dimensions:	326ft 5in × 51ft 2in × 7ft 10in
	99.5m × 15.6m × 2.4m
Machinery:	2 shafts, 2 SEMT-Pielstick diesels, 5340bhp = 15.4kts. Range 4000nm at 14kts, 30-day endurance
Armament:	6–40mm/70 Breda AA (3×2), 1–81mm mortar
Sensors:	Radar Decca 1226, Thomson-CSF Triton
Complement:	35 (+ 240 troops)

No	Name	Builder	Launched	Fate
130	IBN OUF	CNIM, La Seyne	22.10.76	Extant 1982
131	IBN HARITHA	CNIM, La Seyne	18.10.77	Extant 1982

Can carry 570t cargo inc 11 tanks. Stern helicopter platform. 130 laid down 1.4.76 and completed 11.3.77; 131 laid down 18.4.77 and completed 10.3.78. Renumbered 132 and 134.

Soviet 'POLNOCNY-C' class *landing ships*

Class (no):
Ibn al Hadrani (112), *Ibn al Qis* (113), *Ibn Omaya* (116) and *Ibn el Farat* (118)
Number 112 transferred Dec 1977, 116 and 118 in June 1979. 113 lost by fire at sea 14/15.9.78 during landing exercise. Like Iraq's export versions with helicopter deck fwd of superstructure.

Turkish 'C 107' class *large landing craft*

Class (no):
Ras el Hilel (ex-Turk *C 132*), and *El Kobayat* (ex-Turk *C 133*)
Transferred 7.12.79. Another 14 ordered direct and delivered by April 1981, perhaps up to 50 may be bought by Libya. Built Taskizak N Yd, Istanbul and Gölçuk N Yd. Cargo: 5 tanks, up to 100 troops, up to 350t. Slow and short-ranged (600nm at 10kts, unloaded).

Ibn Haritha 1979   *L & L van Ginderen*

Susa on trials   *Vosper Thornycroft*

SMALL SURFACE COMBATANTS

TOBRUK *corvette*

Displacement:	440t standard; 500t full load
Dimensions:	177ft oa × 28ft 6in × 13ft
	54.0m × 8.7m × 4.0m
Machinery:	2 shafts, 2 Paxman Ventura 16 YJCM diesels, 3800bhp = 18kts. Oil 60t. Range 2900nm at 14kts
Armament:	1–4in/40 Mk 23 LA, 4–40mm/60 Mk 9 (4×1), 2–2in RFL, 2–12.7mm MG
Sensors:	Radar surface warning
Complement:	63

No	Name	Builder	Launched	Fate
C 411	TOBRUK	Vosper, Portsmouth	29.7.65	Extant 1982

Type 1 corvette, laid down 22.2.65 and completed 30.3.66; arrived Tripoli 15.6.66. Generally similar to *Keta* and *Kromantse* built for Ghana but with less powerful machinery, and AA armament. Two 40mm guns removed *c*1970. Apartments for use as state yacht. Vosper anti-roll fins and air conditioning.

Wadi M'Ragh as completed

WADI M'RAGH class *missile corvettes*

Displacement:	545t light; 670t full load
Dimensions:	189ft 7in pp, 202ft 5in oa × 30ft 6in × 8ft 10in
	57.8m, 61.7m × 9.3m × 2.7m
Machinery:	4 shafts, 4 MTU type MA 16V 956 TB91 diesels, 14,000bhp = 31.5kts. Oil 126t. Range 1400nm/4150nm at 33kts/18kts, 15 days endurance
Armament:	4 Otomat Mk 1 SSM (4×1), 1–76mm/62 OTO Melara Compact, 2–35mm/90 Oerlikon (1×2), 6–12.75in ASW TT (2×3), 16 mines on 2 rails (as minelayer)
Sensors:	Radar Selenia RAN-11L/X, Decca TM-1226, RTN-10X Orion; Sonar Thomson-CSF Diodon; ECM Selenia ISN-1 intercept
Complement:	58

No	Name	Builder	Launched	Fate
C 412	ASSAD AL TADJIER (ex-*Wadi M'Ragh*)	Muggiano, La Spezia	29.9.77	Extant 1982
C 413	ASSAD AL TOUGOUR (ex-*Wadi Majer*)	Muggiano, La Spezia	20.4.78	Extant 1982
C 414	ASSAD AL KALIJ (ex-*Wadi Marseat*)	Muggiano, La Spezia	14.12.79	Extant 1982
C 415	ASSAD AL HUDUD (ex-*Wadi Magrawa*)	Muggiano, La Spezia	21.6.79	Extant 1982

Missile corvettes ordered in 1974: 412 and 413 laid down 25.5.76; 414 on 26.10.77; 415 on 25.5.78. 412 entered service on 14.9.79, 413 on 12.2.80, 414 and 415 on 28.3.81. All renamed 1981. Four more ordered May 1980. Slower than comparably armed FAC, but have much greater range and sea-keeping qualities. NBC protection. Six similar ships are building for Ecuador.

Soviet 'NANUCHKA II' class *missile corvettes*

Ain Mara (C 416) reached Libya Oct 1981. Three more expected 1982–83; one, *Ain Algazala* (C 417) delivered Feb 1983.

SUSA class *fast attack craft (missile)*

Displacement:	95t standard; 114t full load
Dimensions:	100ft oa × 25ft 6in × 7ft
	30.5m × 7.8m × 2.1m
Machinery:	3-shaft CODOG: Bristol Siddeley Proteus gas turbines; 12,750shp = 54kts; 2 GM 6–71 cruising diesels, 190hp
Armament:	8 SS12 SSM (2×4), 2–40mm/60 Mk 9 (2×1), 2 RFL
Complement:	20

Class (no, launched):
Susa (P 512, 31.8.67), *Sirte* (P 513, 10.1.68), *Sebha* (ex-*Sokna*) (P 514, 29.2.68)
Wooden, nylon sheathed boat ordered from Vospers 12.10.66 and modelled on Vosper's Danish *Sölöven* class. All commissioned Jan 1969 as the West's first missile-armed FAC after Vosper and Nord Aviation had designed a sighting turret for the wire-guided SS12. All completely refitted 1977 in Italy and in service 1982.

Ex-Soviet 'OSA II' class *fast attack craft (missile)*

Class (no):
Al Katum (205), *Al O'Work* (206), *Al Rwae* (207), *Al Baida* (208), *Al Nabhaa* (209), *Al Fikar* (210), *Al Safhaa* (952), *Al Zakab* (954), *Al Zuara* (956), 953 and 513 plus one other.

Libya has 12; the first transferred in Oct 1976, 4 in 1977, 1 in 1978, 3 in Oct 1979 to Tobruk and 3 in 1980.

BEIR GRASSA class *fast attack craft (missile)*

Displacement:	258t standard; 311t full load
Dimensions:	160ft 8in oa × 24ft 11in × 7ft 11in
	49.0m × 7.6m × 2.4m
Machinery:	4 shafts, 4 MTU 20V538 TB91 diesels, 18,000bhp = 40kts. Range 1600nm at 15kts.
Armament:	4 Otomat Mk 1 SSM (4×1), 1–76mm/62 OTO Melara Compact, 2–40mm/70 Breda Bofors (1×2)
Sensors:	Radar Thomson-CSF: Triton search, Castor track, Vega II fire-control; ECM Thomson-CSF
Complement:	27

No	Name	New name:	Launched	Fate
518	BEIR GRASSA	*Sharara*	28.6.79	Extant 1982
519	BEIR GZIR	*Shehab*	22.1.80	Extant 1982
520	BEIR GTIFA	*Wahg*	20.5.80	Extant 1982
521	BEIR GLULUD	*Waheeg*	30.9.80	Extant 1982
522	BEIR ALGANDULA	*Shouaae*	14.1.81	Extant 1982
523	BEIR KTITAT	*Shouala*	22.4.81	Extant 1982
524	BEIR ALKARIM	*Shafak*	23.6.81	Extant 1982
525	BEIR ALKARDMEN	*Bark*	23.6.81	Extant 1982
526	BEIR ALKUR	*Raad*	30.11.81	Extant 1982
527	BEIR ALKUESAT	*Laahibe*	28.1.82	Extant 1982

'Combattante IIG' type boats ordered from CMN, Cherbourg in May 1977 at an estimated cost of about £300 million. Laying down dates: 518 (13.3.78), 519 (10.6.78), 520 (30.1.79), 521 (20.10.79), 522 (12.9.79), 523 (17.12.79), 524 (11.3.80), 525 (9.6.80), 526 (20.10.80) and 527 (20.1.81). *Beir Grassa* was to have been delivered in Feb 1981 but the French embargo on arms sales to Libya, imposed because of Libyan intervention in Chad, delayed her handover till 5.2.82, that of *Beir Gzir* until 3.4.82. 520 and 521 were delivered in July 1982 and 522 in Sept, 525 on 11.3.83. Renamed, and probably renumbered, 1983.

GARIAN class *large patrol craft*

Displacement:	120t standard; 159t full load
Dimensions:	106ft oa × 21ft 2in × 5ft 6in
	32.3m × 6.5m × 1.7m
Machinery:	2 shafts, 2 Paxman 12cyl Ventura 10 YJCM diesels, 3600bhp = 24kts. Range 1800nm/2300nm at 13kts/11kts
Armament:	1–40mm/60 Mk 9, 1–20mm (690rds for both), 2–2in RFL
Complement:	15–22

Class (no, launched):
Garian (PC 1, 21.4.69), *Khawlan* (PC 2, 29.5.69), *Merawa* (PC 3, 30.9.69), *Sabratha* (PC 4, 25.10.69)

Ordered from Brooke Marine, Lowestoft, England, in Dec 1967. First two commissioned 30.8.69, second two early 1970. At least one has Soviet BM21 122mm 20-barrel MRL instead of the 20mm gun. All extant 1982.

FARWA class *large patrol craft*

Displacement:	100t full load
Dimensions:	100ft oa × 21ft × 5ft 6in
	30.5m × 6.4m × 1.7m
Machinery:	3 shafts, 3 Rolls-Royce DV8TLM diesels, 1740bhp = 18kts. Range 1800nm at 14kts
Armament:	1–20mm Oerlikon Mk 7
Complement:	18

Class (commissioned):
Ar Rakib (4.5.67), *Farwa* (4.5.67), *Benina* (29.8.69), *Misurata* (29.8.69), *Akrama* early 1969), *Homs* (early 1969)

Vosper Thornycroft type, for customs and fishery protection, launched 1967–68, *Ar Rakib*, *Akrama* and *Farwa* transferred to Malta in 1978; rest extant 1982.

MINE WARFARE VESSELS

Ex-British 'HAM' class *inshore minesweepers*

Class (former name):
Brak (ex-*Harpham*), *Zuara* (ex-*Greetham*)

Loaned by the RN in 1963 as the new Libyan Navy's first ships. Transferred permanently and renamed in Sept 1966. Both discarded 1973.

Soviet 'NATYA' class *ocean minesweepers*

Class (no):
Ras el Gelais (111), *Ras Hadad* (113)

Delivered 17.3.81. Names also reported as *Ishsaar* and *Tayyar*. As with India's six they lack the stern ramp of Soviet Navy units. Two minefields laid 8 miles from Tripoli in June 1973, several since using Italian-built ro-ro ship *El Timsah* (acquired 1979). Two further ships, numbered 115 (*Ras al Hamman*) and *Ras al Falluga* 117 were reported in transit Jan 1983.

MISCELLANEOUS

One 78ft Thornycroft coastal patrol craft (built Singapore 1962), the maintenance repair craft *Zleiten* (ex-British *MRC 1013*), bought 5.9.66 and now a hulk, the 2200t logistic support ship *Zeltin* (Vosper, launched 29.2.68, 15kts) can dock FAC of up to 120ft, 14 SAR 33 class customs patrol boats (150t, 40kts, 1–40mm and 2–12.7mm MG) of W German design ordered early 1980 from Taskizak N Yd, Istanbul, 2 customs patrol boats *Jihad* and *Salam* (120t, 27kts, 4–20mm Hispano-Suiza A32) bought from Müller of W Germany in Jan 1978 when Lebanon unable to pay.

The logistic support ship *Zeltin* as completed   *Vosper Thornycroft*

Madagascar

Madagascar regained independence as the Malagasy Republic in 1960, after 64 years of French rule. The new state, under a right-wing autocratic regime, maintained strong economic and cultural links with France and joined the usual Francophone African organisation. Military rulers (since 1972) renegotiated the cooperation agreement with France, French air and naval bases were evacuated by 4000 troops in 1973. A policy of 'active neutralism', *ie* non-alignment, denies the use of the important naval base of Diego Suarez to foreign powers, and includes routine denunciations of Western imperialism and neo-colonialism. Financial assistance from France remains vital, and trading with South Africa continues very quietly. The country is too remote and insignificant to influence African affairs appreciably; traditionally, the Malagasys (8,900,000 in 1982) have kept aloof from the mainland, perhaps because of indifference or a feeling of superiority.

The Malagasy armed forces, including the Gendarmerie, total nearly 30,000 18-month conscripts, and have been incorporated into the People's Armed Forces. Formed on 15 February 1961, the 600-man Navy (including a company of 150 marines) has doubled since 1974 and operates a coast patrol force of light craft from Diego Suarez (shipyard transferred from French ownership 1975), Tamatave and Majunga. Lesser bases in the south of the island are Tulear, Nossi-Be, Fort Dauphin and Manakara. Madagascar's warships have been supplied by France, W Germany and N Korea. No details are available of future plans for the Navy, or proposed new construction.

MALAIKA *large patrol craft*

Particulars: As Ivory Coast *Le Vigilant*

P 48 type boat ordered from SFCN in 1966. Laid down 5.12.66 and launched 22.3.67. In service since 11.4.68 still with original armament of 2–40mm.

Ex-US YMS type *coastal minesweepers*

Class (former name, no):
Tanamasoandro (ex-*Marjolaine*, ex-*D 337*, ex-*YMS 69*), *Jasmine* (ex-*Jasmin*, ex-*D 385*, ex-*YMS 29*)
    Wooden-hulled 1942 US-built ships and transferred to France in 1954. *Tanamasoandro*, bought 18.2.61 by Madagascar as her first warship and used as a patrol vessel, was discarded in 1968; *Jasmine*, acquired in 1965 and rated as a tender, was deleted in 1976.

MISCELLANEOUS
The French seaward patrol craft VC 8 (P 758) was acquired in 1963 and named *Malaika*. Returned to France in 1967. In 1982 the following were also in service:
    Five Maritime Police small coastal W German-built patrol craft (commissioned 1962, 46t, 22kts, 1–40mm).
    'Batram' class LCT *Toky* (in service Oct 1974, intermediate in size between the French 'Batral' and EDIC types and paid for by France although built at Diego Suarez: she is reportedly armed with 8 SS12 SSM as well as guns).
    Two ex-N Korean 'Nampo' class LCAs (acquired Feb and June 1979) rampless and used only as patrol craft) and two ex-US LCMs.
    The Coast Guard and training ship *Fanantenana* (1040t, 12kts, 1040t) is the ex-trawler *Richelieu*, Bremen-built in 1959 and refitted Diego Suarez Dec 1966–July 1967.

Malawi

Malawi (independent 1964) has no sea coast, but four small patrol craft (100 men) are in service at Chipoka on Lake Malawi (formerly Lake Nyasa) which is a quarter of the country. A Fairey Marine 'Spear' class boat joined the other three British-built vessels (acquired since 1968) in 1976.

Mali

This landlocked desert republic (independent 1960) has three small river patrol craft (50 men) on her long stretch of the upper Niger, operating from Timbuktu, Barnako (capital), Segou and Mopti.

Mauritania

Mauritania, an independent Islamic republic since 1960, is larger in area than Nigeria but mainly desert, with a population of only 1.5 million, uneasily divided between the 80 per cent Arabs and 20 per cent black Africans. There are few natural resources, and the country has been exhausted by her 1975–79 support for Morocco against the Polisario Front guerrillas of the Western Sahara. Several palace revolutions since 1978 have caused a change of sides, and the French and Moroccan troops that formerly assisted her weak army have left. The Islamic Navy was formed on 25 January 1966. The country's fishing fleet of French and locally built trawlers is aiming to catch 250,000 tons a year. South Korea is to help build a naval shipyard.
    The 320 volunteer naval personnel in 1982 manned a growing force of patrol craft based at Port Etienne, Nouadhibou, on Cape Blanc adjoining Western Sahara. In the south are the Senegal river ports of Rosso, Boghé and Kaedi.

Spanish BARCELO class *fast attack craft (gun)*

Class (no, in service):
El Vaiz (P 362, Dec 1979), *El Beg* (P 363, May 1979), *El Kenz* (P 364, Jan 1981).
    Ordered 21.7.76 from Bazán, Cadiz. First two delivered late due to trials collision in Dec 1978. Three more may be ordered.

Le 10 Juillet as completed   *Auroux*

French TRIDENT class *patrol boats*

Class (no, in service):
Le 10 Juillet (P 411, ex-French *Rapière*, 1.11.81)
    Laid down 15.2.81 and launched 3.6.81. May carry 6 SS 12M SSM. Second on order, also funded by Libya.

TICHITT class *coastal patrol craft*

Class (in service):
Tichitt (April 1969), *Dar el Barba* (Sept 1969).
    Built by CNE. First refitted at Dakar 1980, second in the Canaries 1982. Same as Tunisian *Istiklal* and Moroccan *El Sabiq* patrol craft.

French 18-metre *coastal patrol craft*

Class (in service):
Imrag'ni (Nov 1965), *Sloughi* (May 1968)
    CNE built 20t units (21kts, 2 diesels, 1–12.7mm MG, 8 men) given to Mauritania.

MISCELLANEOUS
Ex-Spanish patrol vessels *Centinela* and *Serviola* (1953, 270t, 2–37mm, 12kts) served as *Tekane* and *Keur Macenf* from 5.3.77, two ex-Soviet whalers, the *Boulanouar* and *Idini* (1956, 847t, 2–30mm, 1 MG), converted as patrol vessels and support ships. They were all sold to a Las Palmas (Canaries) ship-broker 12.1.81.

Morocco

The Sherifian Empire (now Kingdom) of Morocco obtained independence in 1956 from France and Spain, which had ruled it as a protectorate since 1912. Internally, initial and unsuccessful attempts at parliamentary goverment gave way to direct rule by King Hassan II. To obtain a national consensus for intervention in the Western Sahara since 1975, a four-party democratic system and parliament has been reintroduced, but ultimate power remains firmly in royal hands.
    Moroccan foreign policy in the Middle East and Africa has been pro-Western since independence. French interventions in the Shaba province of Zaire in 1977 and 1978 were supported, Moroccan soldiers being airlifted to put down the rebel forces. Morocco also publicly approved the Camp David agreements between the United States, Egypt and Israel, but modified her attitude to retain essential subsidies from the Saudis and the Gulf States. Her main external problem in recent years, however, has been the West Sahara War. Morocco and Mauritania jointly occupied the former Spanish Sahara when Spain withdrew in 1975 to secure the world's richest nitrate deposits, but faced growing resistance from the Polisario Front, sponsored by Algeria and more recently Libya. In spite of French and Moroccan military support, Mauritania gave up the struggle in July 1979 and transferred her portion of the territory to Morocco; a military stalemate resulted, with Morocco controlling the main towns and the phosphate mines, and the Polisario Front making sporadic guerrilla raids from its bases near the Algerian border. The Western Sahara extends Morocco's 2100-mile coastline by half as much again.
    Militarily, Morocco has concentrated her efforts on her Army and Air Force, with France as the main arms supplier. The United States has also supplied arms and in May 1982 concluded an agreement allowing the Rapid Deployment Force to use Moroccan bases. The self-esteem and prestige of the armed forces is high, as often happens when a right wing regime lacks a strong political base, but their loyalty to the throne has sometimes been justly suspect.

The Royal Moroccan Navy only dates from 1960 and is small (per sonnel 6000 in 1982 including a battalion of 500–600 marines), but expanding, with most warships and naval equipment from France, although important recent orders have gone to Spain. An analysis of the 18-month conscript sailors suggests that they are reliable politically and adequately trained, but operationally inexperienced.

The main Atlantic bases are Casablanca, Safi, Agadir, Kenitra and Tangier; none near the Western Sahara. The age-old Spanish colonial ports of Ceuta and Melilla continue to dominate Morocco's Mediterranean coastline. A fishing dispute in 1973 caused a brief Moroccan-Spanish naval action. A rapid increase in strength to counter the growing Algerian and Libyan Navies is considered probable; Morocco is reported to be interested in ordering a further four *Descubierta* class frigates which, properly manned and maintained, could put her well ahead of her rivals. Recently pennant numbers have had a 0 added between the original two figures, *eg* 51 became 501.

Ex-British 'RIVER' class *frigate*

No	Name	Builder	Acquired	Fate
31	EL MAOUNA (ex-*La Surprise*, ex-*Torridge*)	Blyth	1964	Discarded 1975

Ex-RN frigate bought by France in 1944 and by Morocco in June 1964. Transferred in 1965 after conversion as flagship and royal yacht, extra accommodation and a helicopter landing deck having been added aft.

Modified Spanish DESCUBIERTA class *frigate*

No	Name	Builder	Launched	Fate
51	COLONEL ERRHAMAN (ex-*El Maouna*)	Bazán, Ferrol	26.2.82	Extant 1983

Ordered 14.6.77 and laid down 20.3.79. Strikes delayed delivery till 10.3.83. Full details of modifications are not available, but Exocet MM38 or MM40 SSM will probably be carried instead of Harpoon in the Spanish ships. Further particulars are as for the Spanish *Descubierta* class. See Part I. Four more may be ordered.

French CHAMPLAIN class *landing ships*

No	Name	Builder	Comp	Fate
42	DAOUD BEN AICHA	Dubigeon, Normandy	28.5.77	Extant 1982
43	AHMED ES SAKALI	Dubigeon, Normandy	June 1977	Extant 1982
44	ABOU ABDALLAH EL AYACHI	Dubigeon, Normandy	Dec 1978	Extant 1982

Ordered 12.3.65 (first two) and 19.8.75.

French EDIC type *landing craft*

Lieutenant Malghagh (41, ex-21) ordered 1963 from CN Franco-Belges. Laid down 17.9.63, launched 10.1.64 and commissioned 1965.

Ex-French CHAMOIS class *corvette (minesweeping sloop)*

No	Name	Builder	Acquired	Fate
33	EL LAHIQ (ex-*Annamite*)	Arsenal de Lorient	1961	Returned France 1967

CORMORAN class *fast attack craft (missile)*

Displacement:	363t standard; 355t full load
Dimensions:	194ft 6in oa × 24ft 7in × 6ft 3in 59.3m × 7.5m × 1.9m
Machinery:	2 shafts, 3 MTU-Bazán 16V956 TB 91 diesels, 13,500bhp = 36kts. Range 700nm/2500nm at 27kts/15kts
Armament:	4 Exocet MM38 SSM, 1-76mm/62 OTO Melara Compact (300rds), 1–40mm/70 Breda Bofors (1472rds), 2–20mm/90 Oerlikon GK204 (2×1, 3000rds)
Sensors:	Radar Raytheon 1620, HSA WM-25 fire control, Decca TM-1229C
Complement:	41

Class (no, completion):
El Khattabi (P 35, 30.6.81), *Boutouba* (P 36, 11.12.81), *El Harty* (P 37, 25.2.82), *Azouggarh* (P 38, 2.8.82)
Ordered 14.6.77 from Bazán, Cadiz, as modified Spanish *Lazaga* class (derived from Lürssen Type 143 design). *El Khattabi* launched 1.7.80.

Okba as completed
NB 1/750 scale

OKBA class *fast attack craft*

Displacement:	375t standard; 445t full load
Dimensions:	177ft 1in pp, 188ft 9in oa × 25ft × 7ft 1in 54.0m, 57.5m × 7.6m × 2.1m
Machinery:	4 shafts, 4 AGO V16 diesels, 11,040bhp = 28kts. Range 2500nm at 16kts, 20 days endurance
Armament:	1–76mm/62 OTO Melara Compact, 1–40mm/70 Breda
Sensors:	Radar Vega system
Complement:	53

Class (no, launched):
Okba (33, 10.10.75), *Triki* (34, 1.12.76)
PR 72 type boats ordered from SFCN June 1973. Laid down 28.4.75 and 22.11.74, completed 16.12.76 and 12.7.77. Both extant 1982. Two more projected. Exocet SSMs may be fitted as Vega fire control is already on board.

Ex-US PC type *patrol vessel*

Name	Builder	Acquired	Fate
AGADIR (ex-*Goumier*, (ex-USS *PC 545*)	Defoe	1960	Returned France 1964

Transferred from the USN to France in 1944 and from France to Morocco in 1960, as the first ship in the new Moroccan Navy. Returned to France in 1964 and sold in 1965.

Modified French LE FOUGUEUX class *large patrol craft*

Lieutenant Riffi (32)
Built by CMN, Cherbourg, laid down May 1963, launched 1.3.64 and in service May 1964. Armament differed from French units, comprising 1–76mm, 2–40mm and two ASW mortars. In service 1982 with just 2–40mm.

AL BACHIR *large patrol craft*

Displacement:	125t light; 154t full load
Dimensions:	124ft 8in pp, 133ft 2in oa × 20ft 10in × 4ft 8in 38.0m, 40.6m × 6.4m × 1.4m
Machinery:	2 shafts, 2 SEMT-Pielstick diesels, 3600bhp = 25kts. Oil 21t. Range 3000nm at 12kts
Armament:	2–40mm Bofors, 2–12.7mm MG
Complement:	23

Numbered 22 (ex-12), ordered in 1964 from CMN, Cherbourg, laid down June 1965 and launched 25.2.67. In service since April 1967.

Ex-French SIRIUS class *coastal minesweeper*

Tawfic (ex-*Aries*). Transferred on 4-year loan 28.11.74 (renewed 1978). In service 1982 for patrol duties as P 659.

MISCELLANEOUS
There are 10 coastal patrol craft: one ex-French seaward defence motor launch (ex-P 762, VC 12), transferred free 15.11.60 and named *El Sabiq*; 6 Albatros CMN P 32 type (built 1975–76) numbered 23–28 – with 6 more planned – and 3 Arcor 31 type).

Mozambique

This Portuguese territory became independent in June 1975, when Samora Machel's Frelimo guerrilla movement, which had risen against the colonial government in 1964, took power. Compared with less populous but richer Angola, the period of transition was peaceful; nevertheless, the departure of some 80,000 Portuguese settlers, about 80 per cent of the total, coupled with the immediate and almost complete socialisation of the economy, left the country in ruins.

The Mozambican armed forces total about 21,600, but standards are low; raids by Rhodesian, and more recently, South African columns have penetrated deep into the country without encountering appreciable opposition. There are believed to be two Tanzanian battalions, and military advisers from the USSR, E Germany, Romania, Cuba and China. A Treaty of Friendship and Co-operation was signed with the Soviet Union in March 1977.

The 700-man Navy (volunteer whereas the Army and Air Force are 2-year conscripts) operates a force of small coast and lake patrol craft; the personnel have been trained by Tanzania and the USSR. Their four main bases, Maputo (HQ, formerly Lourenço Marques, a 4500-ton capacity Soviet 'Klaipeda' floating dock was installed there in October 1981), Beira, Nacala and Pemba (Porto Amelia), cover the long coastline while Metangula serves Lake Nyasa. The country is bisected by the mighty Zambezi. Future plans are not known, but a force of missile and torpedo armed fast attack craft to command the Mozambique Channel would seem desirable as soon as funds and training permit.

In 1982 the Mozambican Navy consisted of the following coastal patrol and other units:

Six ex-Soviet 'Zhuk' class transferred 1979 (2), Oct 1980 (2) and Oct 1981 (2).

One ex-Soviet 'Poluchat' class transferred 1977.

Ex-Portuguese *Sirius* and *Vega* of the *Bellatrix* class

Three ex-Portuguese *Jupiter* class (which operate on Lake Nyasa) and the smaller ex-Portuguese *Antares*.

Ex-Portuguese survey ship *Almirante Lacerda* (ex-RCN *Bangor* class minesweeper *Caraquet*), transferred in 1975 and reported as a training and support hulk in Maputo.

Ex-Portuguese *Bombarda* class LDG (LCT) *Cimitarra* and 2 ex-Portuguese LDM 100 type landing craft. A report that the last-named has been wrecked is not confirmed. The new names and/or numbers for the above are not available.

Nigeria

The Federal Republic of Nigeria, with her population of around 80 million and vast oil revenues, is by far the most populous African country and much the wealthiest and most powerful country in black Africa; her gross domestic product exceeds South Africa's and is four times that of Egypt. The merchant marine has expanded by 50 ships since 1974.

Nigeria's political history since independence in 1960 has often been troubled and turbulent. The original parliamentary government evolved into quasi-dictatorial rule by a corrupt elite, which manipulated elections and censuses. Increasing polarisation along tribal lines, followed by mounting chaos, led to the January 1966 Army coup. This temporarily eased tensions, but seemed after a short time to be leading to Ibo (Easterner) domination; it was followed after six months by a second coup, led by Northern elements in the Army, which put 31-year-old Lt-Colonel Yakubu Gowon into power. Massacres of Ibos in the north ensued. Attempts to keep the East in the Federation failed, and the proclamation of the 'Republic of Biafra' in May 1967 was followed by civil war.

The Navy (a frigate and five small combatants) remained loyal and, even though its former minister (later Biafra's foreign minister) joked 'What navy?', a naval blockade of the 200-mile Biafran Coast at the outset effectively isolated the rebel republic from outside recognition or help (except by air). Amphibious landings at Bonny (to capture its ocean oil terminal) and Calabar in the end proved major springboards to Federal victory.

Biafra collapsed in January 1970, and General Gowon started a successful programme of national reconciliation. He was, however, unable to cope with the rise in world oil prices in 1973 and 1974. There was general relief when Gowon was ousted in July 1975; a new dynamic military ruler corrected the worst abuses of his regime, and set Nigeria firmly back on the road to civilian rule. A new constitution, loosely based on the American was carefully drawn up and took effect on 1 October 1979.

The Navy has grown slowly from its 200-man pre-independence beginnings in 1956, volunteer personnel having increased from 555 in 1960 to 1720 in 1970 and about 4000 in 1980. Until 1964 British officers were in command. The build-up of ships since 1970 has been steady, the ex-British warships originally transferred having been discarded as they wore out, and replaced by new construction from the UK, Netherlands, W Germany and France. The Navy is now far ahead materially of other tropical African forces; it operates two frigates and four corvettes, and has the only surface-to-surface missiles and ship-borne helicopters, as well as the only admiral, between the Mediterranean and South Africa. Its expansion is likely to continue, although it will probably not grow beyond a frigate and SSM force for which Nigeria began seeking a replenishment ship from Franco-German builders in 1981. Two *Lerici* class minehunters were ordered on 9 April 1983.

The training of its personnel is considered less satisfactory than its material state although India, USA, Australia, France and W Germany all help. A shortage of skilled and experienced technicians has caused mishandling of delicate equipment and a corresponding reduction in operational efficiency. The leadership, although young, is of uncertain quality, lacking initiative and a sense of devotion to duty; promotion in the past has often depended on tribal factors and nepotism.

The Fleet is split between Flotilla Command at Lekki (for the Niger and its delta), Western Naval Command (based on Apapa-Lagos where a second dockyard is building) and Eastern Naval Command at Calabar and Port Harcourt (home of Nigerian Shipbuilders Ltd). These and the main naval staff sections are normally headed by a commodore. A Fleet Air Arm was set up in 1981 for which Westland delivered the first of three Lynx helicopters. From 1976 Decca installed a chain of four coastal radars that covers the country's 400 nautical mile coastline.

To conclude, Nigeria's Navy is impressive on paper, but it has so far failed to tackle the revival of piracy off West Africa and Lagos in particular. Its future will depend on national stability, unity and prosperity. It is not, at present, equal to a properly led, trained and maintained force of similar paper strength. Rhetoric aside, to match Nigeria, or a Nigerian-led coalition of tropical African states, against South Africa, an occasional dream of African nationalists, would have tragic consequences; at sea, the result would be massacre worse than Tsushima.

Nigeria as completed

Navarret Collection

MAJOR SURFACE SHIPS

Aradu during trials period, May 1981

Ordered 3.11.77 from Blohm & Voss, Hamburg, to the MEKO 360H design (see Argentina), the first frigate in the world using extensive modular pre-fabrication and 'containerised' weapons (46 modules) and sensors (76) to speed construction. One and then two Lynx helicopters will be carried. Renamed (1.11.80) after launch. *Aradu* means 'Thunder' and she arrived at Lagos 21.12.81 to become the Nigerian Navy flagship at a cost of $84.5 million or 10 per cent of the 1981 defence budget.

ARADU *frigate*

Displacement:	3600t standard; 4200t full load
Dimensions:	390ft 5in wl, 413ft oa × 49ft 3in × 14ft 2in
	119.0m, 125.9m × 15.0m × 4.3m
Machinery:	2-shaft CODOG (2 CP propellers): 2 Rolls-Royce Olympus TM3B gas turbines, 50,000shp = 30.5kts plus 2 MTU Type 20 V 956 TB92 diesels 10,00bhp = 18kts. Fuel 440t. Range 6500nm at 18kts. Endurance 90 days
Armament:	1–127mm/54 OTO Melara (460rds), 8–40mm/70 Breda Bofors (4×2, 10,752rds), 8 Otomat Mk 2 SSM (8×1), 1 Aspide Mk 2 Mod 9 SAM (1×8, 24 missiles) system, 6–12.75in STWS-13 TT (2×3; 18 torpedoes), 2 helicopters
Sensors:	Radar AWS-5A, WM-25, Decca 1226 navigation; sonar PHS 32; ECM Elsag/Breda 105mm chaff RL (2×20; 120rds) Decca RCM-2
Complement:	200–237

No	Name	Builder	Laid down	Launched	Comp	Fate
F 89	ARADU (ex-*Republic*)	Blohm & Voss	2.5.79	25.1.80	4.9.81	Extant 1982

Nigeria 1975

Ordered at original price of £3.5 million from the Netherlands Shipbuilding Bureau (NEVESBU) as combined escort, training ship and flagship; armed with RN-pattern armament. Fitted with a helicopter pad aft. Refitted Birkenhead (UK) 1973 and Schiedam (Holland) 1977. Renamed *Obuma* in 1981. Her 4in will probably be replaced by a 76mm OTO Melara.

NIGERIA *frigate*

Displacement:	1724t standard; 2000t full load
Dimensions:	341ft 3in pp, 360ft 3in oa × 37ft × 11ft 6in
	104.0m, 109.8m × 11.3m × 3.5m
Machinery:	2 shafts, 4 MAN 16 V8B cyl diesels, 16,000bhp = 26kts. Range 3500nm at 15kts
Armament:	2–4in/45 Mk 19 (1×2), 4–40mm/60 Mk 7 (4×1), 1 Squid ASW mortar
Sensors:	Radar Types 293, 275, Plessey AWS-4; Sonar Types 170, 174 (removed 1977)
Complement:	216

No	Name	Builder	Laid down	Launched	Comp	Fate
F 87	NIGERIA	Wilton Fijenoord	9.4.64	12.4.65	16.9.65	Extant 1982

AMPHIBIOUS WARFARE VESSELS

West German type RO-RO 1300 *landing ships*

Displacement:	1470t standard; 1750t full load
Dimensions:	285ft 5in oa, 242ft 1½in pp × 45ft 11in × 7ft 6in
	97.0m, 74.5m × 14.0m × 2.3m
Machinery:	4 shafts, 2 MTU 16V 956 TB92 diesels, 6694bhp (4920kW) = 17kts. Range 5560nm at 14kts
Armament:	1–40mm Bofors (300rds), 2–20mm Oerlikon (2×1; 3000rds), 81mm mortar (optional)
Sensors:	Radar Decca 1226
Complement:	56 (plus 220–1000 troops)

No	Name	Builder	Launched	Fate
L 1312	AMBE	Howaldtswerke, Hamburg	7.7.78	Extant 1982
L 1313	OFIOM	Howaldtswerke, Hamburg	7.12.78	Extant 1982

Built as Type 502 landing ships, a design not bought by the *Bundesmarine*. Laid down 3.3.78 and 15.9.78, completed 11.5.79 and July 1979. Bow and stern ramps, former can unload 52t tanks. Typical loading could be 400t of vehicles plus troops. Names mean 'crocodile'. Cost $30.8 million each. Extant 1982.

Ambe 1979

L & L van Ginderen

AFRICA

SMALL SURFACE COMBATANTS

Dorina 1972

DORINA class *corvettes*

Displacement:	500t standard; 650t full load
Dimensions:	185ft pp, 202ft oa × 31ft × 11ft 4in *56.4m, 61.6m × 9.5m × 3.3m*
Machinery:	2 shafts, 2 MAN type V8V 24 30B diesels, 8000bhp = 22kts. Oil 68t. Range 3500nm at 14kts
Armament:	2–4in/45 Mk 19 (1×2), 2–40mm/60 (2×1), 2–20mm Mk 7a (2×1)
Sensors:	Radar Plessey AWS-1, M-22, Decca TM-626; sonar Plessey MS-22; ECM Decca
Complement:	67

No	Name	Builder	Launched	Fate
F 81	DORINA	Vosper Thornycroft	16.9.70	Extant 1982
F 82	OTOBO	Vosper Thornycroft	25.5.71	Extant 1982

Vosper Thornycroft Mk 3 corvettes, ordered 28.3.68, larger and faster than the
Mk 1 versions built for Ghana and Libya. Laid down 26.1.70 and 28.9.70,
completed 21.7.72 and 10.11.72. Both were refitted by Vosper 1975–76. The
4in guns are hand-loaded and there is no ASW armament to exploit the sonar
carried. Air-conditioned living spaces include quarters for flag officer and staff;
12 watertight compartments.

Otobo April 1976　　　　　　　　　　　　　　　　　　　　*C & S Taylor*

Erin'mi 1980

ERIN'MI class *corvettes*

Displacement:	700t standard; 850t full load
Dimensions:	210ft pp, 226ft oa × 31ft 6in × 9ft 10in *64.0m, 69.0m × 9.6m × 3.0m*
Machinery:	2 shafts, 4 MTU type 20V956 TB92 diesels (2 CP propellers), 17,600bhp = 28kts. Range 2200nm at 14kts
Armament:	1–76mm/62 OTO Melara Compact (750rds), 1–40mm/70 Bofors, 2–20mm Oerlikon GAM 204 GK (2×1), Seacat SAM (1×3; 15 missiles), 2–375mm Bofors ASW RL (1×2; 24 rockets)
Sensors:	Radar Plessey AWS-2, WM-24, TM-1226; sonar PMS-26; ECM Decca Cutlass system
Complement:	90

No	Name	Builder	Launched	Fate
F 83	ERIN'MI	Vosper Thornycroft	20.1.77	Extant 1982
F 84	ENYIMIRI	Vosper Thornycroft	9.2.78	Extant 1982

Vosper Thornycroft Mk 9 corvettes ordered 22.4.75 for $40 million. Laid down
14.10.75 and 11.2.77, completed 25.2.80 and 14.7.80. Funnels were heightened
during trials so that smoke would not blind the Bofors fire-control system at the
stern. Names, like those of the *Dorina* class, mean 'hippopotamus' in different
Nigerian languages. F 83 sailed for Nigeria May 1980. Can maintain 20kts on 2
diesels. *Erin'mi* renamed *Erin Omi* 14.8.81 during a Vosper refit for both ships
after much damage from faulty navigation.

Erin'mi on trials 1979　　　　　　　　　　　　　　*Vosper Thornycroft*

Damisia as completed
NB 1/750 scale

EKPE class *fast attack craft (missile)*

Displacement:	295t standard; 378t full load
Dimensions:	187ft wl, 200ft oa × 25ft 7in × 7ft 11in *57.0m, 61.0m × 7.8m × 2.4m*
Machinery:	4 shafts, 4 MTU 16cyl 956 TB92 diesels, 20,840bhp (15,298kW) = 38kts. Range 1300/3300nm at 30/16kts
Armament:	4 Otomat Mk 1 SSM (4×1), 1–76mm/62 OTO Melara Com- pact, 2–40mm/70 Breda Compact (1×2), 4–30mm Emerlec (2×2), 2–533mm TT
Sensors:	Radar Decca TM-1226C, HSA WM-28; ECM Decca RDL-1 intercept
Complement:	40

Class (no, launched):
Ekpe (P 178, 17.12.79), *Damisia* (P 179, 25.5.80), *Agu* (P 180, 7.11.80)
　S 143 type W German boats ordered with different armament from Lürssen,
Vegesack, 14.11.77. Laid down 17.2.79 and arrived Lagos together 29.9.81.
They are fitted with Dutch WM-28 fire control. TT are aft, firing Seal wire-
guided torpedoes.

SIRI class *fast attack craft (missile)*

Displacement:	385t standard; 430t full load
Dimensions:	184ft 5in oa × 26ft 3in × 6ft 11in *56.2m × 8.0m × 2.1m*
Machinery:	4 shafts, 4 MTU 16V956 TB92 diesels, 20,840bhp (15,298kW) = 37kts. Range 2000/800nm at 15/30kts
Armament:	4 Exocet MM38 SSM (2×2), 1–76mm/62 OTO Melara Com- pact (250rds), 2–40mm/70 Breda Compact (1×2, 1600rds), 4–30mm Emerlec (2×2; 1970rds)
Sensors:	Radar Decca 1226, Thomson-CSF Triton and Castor ESM Decca RDL-1
Complement:	42

Class (no, launched, completed):
Siri (P 181, 3.6.80, 19.2.81), *Ayam* (P 182, 10.11.80, 11.6.81), *Ekun* (P 183,
11.2.81, 18.9.81)
　'Combattante IIIB' type boats ordered from CMN, Cherbourg, 14.11.77.
Laid down 15.5.79, 7.9.79 and 14.11.79. Fitted with 2 CSEE Panda fire control
directors. Names mean 'tiger' in the three main Nigerian languages. Did not
leave France until 9.5.82 when Nigeria completed payment. Commissioned
6.2.82. Nigeria ordered 18 Exocet MM38 missiles from Aérospatiale in 1980.

Ex-US PC type *patrol vessel*

Name	Builder	Acquired	Fate
OGOJA (ex-*Queen Wilhelmina*, ex-*PC 468*)	Lawley & Sons	1965	Lost Oct 1969

Old patrol vessel, presented to the Netherlands in 1942 and laid up from 1953,
was lent to Nigeria while the frigate *Nigeria* was building. Transferred permanently *c* 1966 and wrecked off Brass (Niger Delta) in Oct 1969 during the Civil
War.

Hadejia after refit 1982
Brooke Marine

ARGUNGU class *large patrol craft*

Displacement:	90t full load
Dimensions:	95ft 1in oa × 18ft × 5ft 2in
	32.0m, 29.0m × 5.5m × 1.6m
Machinery:	2 shafts, 2 Paxman 8cyl Ventura YJCM diesels, 2200bhp = 20kts
Armament:	1–40mm/60 Mk 9, 1–20mm, 2–2in R(F)L (see notes)
Complement:	25

Class (no, launched):
Argungu (P 165, 4.7.73), *Yola* (P 166, 12.6.73), *Bras* (P 169, 12.1.76), *Epe* (P 170, 9.2.76)

Ordered from Abeking and Rasmussen, Lemwerder (FRG) in pairs (1971 and 1975). *Argungu* laid down 4.7.73 and units completed in pairs (Oct 1974 and March 1976). Rearmed with 4–30mm Emerlec (2×2) in 1978. All extant 1982.

MAKURDI class *large patrol craft*

Displacement:	115t standard; 143t full load
Dimensions:	107ft oa × 20ft × 11ft 6in
	32.6m × 6.1m × 3.5m
Machinery:	2 shafts, 2 Paxman Ventura 12cyl diesels, 3000bhp = 20.5kts. Oil 18t. Range 2300nm at 12kts
Armament:	2–40mm/60 Mk 9 (960rds). See notes
Complement:	21

Class (no, launched):
Makurdi (P 167, 21.3.74), *Hadejia* (P 168, 25.5.74), *Jebba* (P 171, 1.12.76), *Oguta* (P 172, 17.1.77)

First pair ordered June 1972 and second Oct 1974 from Brooke Marine, Lowestoft (GB). P 167 and P 168 commissioned 14.8.74. P 171 and P 172 29.4.77. First pair refitted with 4–30mm Emerlec (2×2) by Brooke Marine 1981, second pair likewise in Nigeria.

Ex-British 'FORD' class *seaward defence boats*

Class (former name):
Benin (ex-*Hinksford*), *Bonny* (ex-*Gifford*), *Enugu* (–), *Ibadan* (i) (ex-*Montford*), *Ibadan* (ii) (ex-*Bryansford*), *Kaduna* (ex-*Axford*), *Sapele* (ex-*Dubford*)

Enugu was the first warship built for Nigeria 1960–61. *Benin*, *Ibadan* (i) and *Kaduna* bought from the RN in 1966, *Bonny* and *Sapele* (1967–68) and *Ibadan* (ii) in 1968–69. *Ibadan* (i) served as the Biafran *Vigilance* May–Sept 1967; sunk by the Nigerian Navy at Port Harcourt on 10.9.67, she was salved and later broken up. *Kaduna* and *Ibadan* (ii) were deleted in 1965; *Benin* (P 03), *Bonny* (P 04), *Enugu* (P 05) and *Sapele* (P 09) were in service 1982.

Ex-British ALGERINE class *minesweeper*

Name	Builder	Acquired Fate
NIGERIA (ex-*Hare*)	Harland & Wolff	July 1959 BU 1962

A war-built minesweeper, transferred from the RN; returned to UK in 1962 with boiler and other defects, and scrapped as beyond economic repair.

MISCELLANEOUS

Besides the above, the following minor fighting vessels were acquired from the RN in 1959: the seaward defence motor launch *Kaduna* (ex-*SDML 3515*) deleted 1965, the Fairmile 'B' type minesweeping motor launches *Calabar* (ex-*MSML 2223*) deleted 1969, and *Sapele* (ex-*MSML 2217*), discarded 1967, and the landing craft *Lokoja* (ex-*LCT(4) 1213*), refitted in 1966–67 and deleted in 1978.

Three ex-Soviet 'P 6' class MTBs, acquired in 1967 and assigned the names *Ekpen*, *Ekun* and *Elole*, were discarded in 1975.

The Nigerian Coast Guard operates 15 GRP coastal patrol boats (21t, 33kts, 1–20mm, 2 MG) ordered from Intermarine, Italy, in Oct 1978, delivered July 1981–May 1982 for the anti-smuggling role. It also has a Fairey 'Tracker' and 2 Fairey 'Spear' boats for fishery protection (since 1978). The Marine Police operate a large force of fast launches (including 6 small hovercraft, delivered 1982) in the Niger Delta and on Lake Chad.

Senegal

This West African republic, 80 per cent Muslim, gained independence from France in 1960, and has since maintained a fair degree of political freedom and stability under Léopold Sédar Senghor, one of Africa's best known and most distinguished leaders. Senghor retired at the end of 1980, the first recorded voluntary withdrawal from office of a civilian black African President. Senegal has tried various parliamentary arrangements, and is at present successfully operating a multi-party system. On 1 February 1982 she united with her tiny riverine neighbour The Gambia to form the Confederation of Senegambia.

In foreign affairs, demonstrations of solidarity with liberation movements in Africa and the Middle East have increased; thus Senegal, like most African countries, broke diplomatic ties with Israel in October 1973, during the Yom Kippur War. Relations with the former colonial power have generally been good, with numerous cooperation agreements in operation. The March 1974 defence agreement allows France to keep a reinforced marine infantry battalion near Dakar and a French Navy Breguet Atlantic maritime patrol aircraft there, emphasising its strategic location on the South Atlantic and South American sea routes.

Senegal's French trained and equipped armed forces total about 9700. The small Navy (formed in 1961) of 350 two-year conscripts operates a coast patrol force craft from the capital, Dakar. The other Atlantic base is St Louis at the mouth of the Senegal river which is patrolled from Rosso, Podor and Kaedi. Kaolack is another river base. Banjul (ex-Bathurst), capital of The Gambia, covers the 50 miles coastline added by the two countries' union. Greater expansion, including proper offshore patrol vessels, is probably held up by Senegal's parlous financial state.

NJAMBUUR *fast attack craft*

Particulars:	As Moroccan *Okba* class

PR 72M type ordered from SFCN in 1978, launched 23.12.80 and delivered Sept 1981. She entered service in July 1982 as P 773. Fire control by two CSEE Naja optical directors. Armament also differs from Moroccan boats being 2–76mm/62 OTO Melara Compact and 2–20mm F2. Could be fitted with Exocet.

ST LOUIS class *large patrol craft*

Particulars:	As Ivory Coast *Le Vigilant*

Class (launched):
St Louis (5.8.70), *Popenguine* (22.3.74), *Podor* (20.7.76)

P 48 type. *St Louis* was ordered from Ch Franco-Belges, other two from SFCN. Laid down 20.4.70, 20.11.73, 5.2.76, completed 5.8.70, 22.3.74, 20.7.76. Decca navigation radar. All extant 1982.

MISCELLANEOUS

Wooden-hulled submarine chaser, formerly the US SC 1344, transferred to France in 1943 (as *CH 24*, re-rated as patrol vessel P 700 in 1951) and from France and Senegal in 1961 as the first Senegalese warship – *Sénégal*. Discarded 1974.

The French seaward patrol craft *VC 5* (P 755) and *VC 4* (P 754) (ex-Congolese *Reine N'Galifourou*) were acquired in 1963 and 1965, and renamed *Casamance* and *Siné-Saloum* respectively. Both discarded 1979.

There are also 3 coastal patrol craft of the 62ft Canadian-built 'Interceptor' class named *Senegal II*, *Casamance II* and *Siné-Saloum II* (in service since 1979) used for fishery protection, an ex-French LCT of the EDIC type *Falémè* (transferred 7.1.74) and two ex-US LCM(6) boats, transferred July 1968 and named *Djomboss* and *Douloulou*.

The Gambia adds 3 British-built coastal patrol boats (20mm guns, delivered 1974–78) and 50 men to Senegal's Navy which received 2 16-metre 20kt Spanish-built patrol craft on 10.2.82.

Sierra Leone

Sierra Leone, which became independent in 1961, acquired her first naval units in June 1973, when two 'Shanghai II' class fast attack craft were acquired from China. Both were transferred to the Freetown Port Authority in 1979, making their present status uncertain (according to other reports, three boats, numbered *001*, *002* and *003*, were acquired in 1973, two being transferred in 1979 and one deleted). A Fairey 'Tracker' Mk II class coastal patrol craft, *Siaka Stevens*, (in service August 1981) is also operated by 150 volunteers in the harbour and coastal patrol unit of the Republic of Sierra Leone Military Force. Freetown (anchorage for over 200 ships of unlimited draft), Pepel, Bonthe and Sulima give well-spaced coverage of the 250-mile coastline. Particulars of three LSTs, *Pompoli*, *Gulama* and *Kallondo*, launched for Sierra Leone in Japanese shipyards during February–March 1980, are not yet available.

Somalia

The Somali Republic was formed in 1960 by the union of the former UN Trust Territory (and ex-Italian colony) of Somalia and the former British Somaliland. The country is wretchedly poor and under-developed; since time immemorial a sparse, predominantly nomadic population has scratched a subsistence living from arid savannah and barren uplands. Many clans straddled the old colonial boundaries, so that Somali communities inhabit the Ogaden Desert region of Ethiopia, northern Kenya and much of French Somaliland (Djibouti). The young republic fervently claims these areas as 'Greater Somalia'.

Politically, the corrupt and divided civilian government since independence was overthrown in 1969 by an authoritarian military regime. China provided aid for major civilian projects, while the Army came to rely on Soviet equipment and training; in return, the Soviet Navy developed a small base at Berbera, in the north adding a floating pier and drydock, barracks, missile store as well as expanding oil storage and the airfield. The Russian Indian Ocean Squadron used this port more than any other in the period 1962–80. In 1974 the creeping transformation of the Ethiopian Government to military socialism was accompanied by spreading internal chaos and led to increasing demands by the Ogaden Somalis for self-determination. Soviet and Cuban support for Ethiopia caused Somalia to break her Communist ties and expel all Russians in November 1977, realigning herself with the West.

Open fighting flared in the Ogaden in 1977 and 1978; initial Somali advances were halted around Harar and Diredawa, and an Ethiopian counter-attack, spearheaded by Cubans, drove the invaders from the country. Guerrilla warfare in the Ogaden continues, and an estimated 1.3 million Somali refugees have fled from the fighting to a number of camps.

The Somali Army has doubled in size since 1977 and now totals about 60,000 men. The 1974 treaty with the USSR was abrogated in 1977, and Soviet military aid has ceased. In August 1980 the USA signed an agreement to provide Somalia with $17.4 millions' worth of defensive weapons and equipment in return for port facilities in Berbera and Mogadishu (Kismayu is the other main naval base), but has held back on more military aid because of continued Somali involvement in the Ogaden. The 350-man volunteer Navy under an army general operates a force of about 20 ex-Soviet craft; its operational efficiency will deteriorate unless spares and refits can be arranged outside the Eastern bloc, perhaps through Egypt which helps with training. Despite efforts to resettle nomads as fishermen, Somalia lacks a seafaring tradition. In the country's present plight, there is unlikely to be any money for new construction or for expanding existing facilties.

Two ex-Soviet 'Osa II' class fast attack craft (missile) transferred in Dec 1975.

Four Soviet 'MOL' class fast attack craft, new units transferred in 1976; two without TT.

Four ex-Soviet 'P 6' class fast attack craft (torpedo) transferred 1968.

Five ex-Soviet 'Poluchat I' class large patrol craft transferred 1965 (2) and 1966 (3).

Ex-Soviet 'Polnocny A' class landing ship transferred Dec 1976

Four ex-Soviet 'T 4' class landing craft transferred 1968–69.

South Africa

The South African Naval Service was founded in 1922, and between the wars operated two minesweeping trawlers and a survey ship; most of the seamen were South Africans while the Royal Navy provided the officers. From this very modest beginning, in a period when the RN's South Atlantic Squadron, based at Simonstown, still shielded South Africa, the SANS expanded enormously during World War II, providing personnel for RN ships and manning armed trawlers and whalers for coastal patrol work. In 1944–45 the RN transferred three 'Loch' class frigates, in addition to the two 'River' class frigates and some 80 smaller craft in service. Personnel totalled over 8000 by July 1945, and 3000 more were serving in the RN.

The South African Navy was officially proclaimed in 1946, but with rapid demobilisation the new Navy kept only the three 'Loch' class frigates, a minelayer, 11 harbour defence motor launches and two boom defence vessels. The RN protection remained, but the Nationalist Party government elected in 1948 found itself increasingly at odds with Britain, and took steps to increase its independence in defence matters; to its Navy, already strengthened by the acquisition of two fleet minesweepers in 1947, were added two destroyers in 1950–52 and two coastal minesweepers in 1954.

Under the 1955 Simonstown Agreement, Britain handed over her base to South Africa (1 April 1957) and the SAN was expanded to take responsibility for the Cape sea route. Six fast anti-submarine frigates (three conversions, later reduced to one, and three new construction), eight coastal minesweepers and four seaward defence boats would be purchased from Britain, as well as Buccaneer strike aircraft and Shackleton maritime patrol aircraft. Britain and her allies would in return be able to use the extensive fuelling, storage, repair and communications facilities at Simonstown even in a war which did not involve South Africa. Joint training and exercises with the RN and attendance of naval personnel at courses in the UK kept the SAN up to date, while Britain provided the arms and technical know-how when SAN warships were modernised.

As the Navy thus progressed, changes in world affairs began to work to South Africa's disadvantage. Her policy of apartheid, applied with steadily more rigour and rigidity in the 1950s and early 1960s, became increasingly unpopular in the Western world, and attracted much adverse publicity, while its whole concept was of course complete anathema to the states of black Africa, which became independent from 1957.

The trend of events were clearly shown in 1960, when the visiting British Prime Minister Macmillan's celebrated 'winds of change' speech was shortly followed by the Sharpeville shootings. On becoming a republic in the following year, South Africa was compelled to leave the Commonwealth, the first stage towards her present status of pariah among nations. Militarily, she increasingly began 'looking to her moat', but arms procurement became steadily harder; Britain first refused to provide submarines as offensive weapons, and then started making difficulties about defensive weapons, although supplying a survey ship in 1969. France, always alert to a profitable arms deal, was more accommodating, and three *Daphne* class boats were ordered from Dubigeon-Normandie. A new submarine base was built at Simonstown, with an enclosed repair yard and a Synchrolift marine elevator, for lifting any South African warship except the replenishment ship *Tafelberg*.

The year 1974 saw the British Labour Government abrogate the Simonstown Agreement, giving up her base facilities and ending all naval co-operation. Increasingly isolated, South Africa tried to replace obsolete tonnage and augment her naval strike capability by ordering two *Agosta* class submarines and two type A 69 corvettes in France in 1975–76, but the 1977 mandatory UN arms embargo prevented their delivery, and they were sold to Pakistan and Argentina. An important order for six missile-armed fast attack craft placed with Israel in 1974 was not affected by the embargo, which is not observed by Israel. Naval personnel reached 6758 (including 1574 two-year conscripts) by 1981 (plus 10,000 reservists), a notable increase on the figures of 2370 in 1960 and 3440 in 1970. A Marine Corps was formed for harbour defence in July 1979 and is now 900 strong. The Advokaat radar system scans the republic's 2100 nautical mile coasts and monitors 600,000 tons of shipping passing the Cape everyday. Principal naval bases are Simonstown, Cape Town, East London, Port Elizabeth, Durban and Walvis Bay, a highly strategic deepwater port on the otherwise inhospitable coast of SW Africa (Namibia).

The SAN can still boast of a high degree of competence, although its

10th Frigate Squadron was down to one ship by early 1982. It is going to become a navy of submarines and small surface ships, the latter missile-firing fast attack craft and corvettes, as local shipyards can build up to about 1000 tons. In September 1981 the C-in-C Vice-Admiral R A Edwards announced that home-built corvettes would be operational within ten years. They will probably be modelled on the Israeli helicopter-carrying *Aliya* class. The problems of obtaining modern armaments and electronic equipment may be overcome by co-operation with Israel and Taiwan (not now a UN member), but the replacement of the ancient Shackletons by modern maritime patrol aircraft will be more difficult, unless commercial planes can be modified. Another possible Achilles' heel is the country's lack of oil, only traces having been found near the coast, but large stocks are stored in disused mines, and a crash coal-to-oil programme that should produce 80 per cent of national requirements by the late 1980s is under way.

reception platform aft. *Transvaal* modernised along similar lines in 1962, but with the forecastle extended aft for extra accommodation. Both ships sunk as breakwaters in 1976; *Natal* sunk as a target in Sept 1972.

MISCELLANEOUS

There were also the following minor fighting vessels: the harbour (later seaward) defence motor launches *1197–1207*, built in South Africa during World War II and discarded between 1953–75; the controlled minelayer *Spindrift* (later *Skilpad*); an ex-German trawler, sold 1958; and the 'Bar' class boom defence vessels *Barcross* (later *Somerset*) and *Barbrake* (later *Fleur*), respectively in service 1982 and sunk as a target in Oct 1965.

President Pretorius refuelling from the Tafelberg 1981   SAN

FLEET STRENGTH 1947

FRIGATES

No	Name	Launched	Disp (std)	Fate
F 432	GOOD HOPE (ex-*Loch Boisdale*)	5.7.44	1435t	Scuttled 1976
F 10	NATAL (ex-*Loch Cree*)	19.6.44	1435t	Survey ship 1957
F 602	TRANSVAAL (ex-*Loch Ard*)	2.8.44	1435t	Scuttled 1976

Presented by RN in 1944–45. In 1955 *Good Hope* was modified as a despatch vessel/training ship, with 2–4in/45 Mk 16 (1×2) forward, a raised funnel and a

MAJOR SURFACE SHIPS

These destroyers, transferred from the RN, underwent modified Type 16 frigate conversions in 1962–66, their particulars being altered as follows: displacement 2105t standard, 2750t full load; draught (max) 17ft (*5.2m*); armament 4–4in/45 Mk 16 (2×2, in 'B' and 'Y' positions), 4–40mm/60 (4×1), 4–3pdr saluting, 4–21in TT (1×4), 2 DCT, 2 DC racks, 2 Wasp ASW helicopters; complement 192. The 21in TT were removed *c*1972, and 6–12.75in Mk 32 ASW TT (2×3) added. *Jan van Riebeeck*, sunk as a

Ex-British 'W' class *destroyers*

No	Name	Builder	Acquired	Fate
D 278	JAN VAN RIEBEECK (ex-*Wessex*, ex-*Zenith*)	Fairfield	29.3.50	Sunk as target May 1980
D 237	SIMON VAN DER STEL (ex-*Whelp*)	Hawthorn Leslie	1952	BU 1976

target in May 1980, was hit by a Skorpioen (Gabriel II) SSM from FAC *Jim Fouche* and subsequently torpedoed by submarine *Maria van Riebeeck*.

Type 15 conversion by Harland & Wolff of former 'W' class destroyer, purchased from the RN. Arrived Cape Town 19.2.57. Two further Type 15 purchases (one was to have been HMS *Roebuck*) were cancelled in 1956. *Vrystaat* was torpedoed in a submarine training exercise.

Ex-British RAPID class *frigate*

No	Name	Builder	Acquired	Fate
F 157	VRYSTAAT (ex-*Wrangler*)	Vickers-Armstrong, Barrow	29.11.56	Sunk as target April 1976

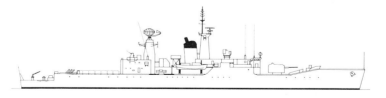

President Kruger 1979

As built, almost identical with the RN *Rothesay* class, although having a twin 40mm Mk 5 at main deck level in place of the STAAG Mk 2. All three refitted at Simonstown (F 147, 1968–70, F 150, 1969–71, F 145, 1971–77) with a plated foremast, French Jupiter surveillance radar on a new plated mainmast, and Italian Elsag NA9C fire control in place of the Mk 6M director (the latter not in *Kruger* until 1979). A small hangar for a Wasp helicopter added abaft the mainmast, with 2–40mm/60 singles on top, and the forward Limbo well was plated over to form a flight deck.

PRESIDENT class *frigates*

Particulars: As British *Rothesay* class

No	Name	Builder	Laid down	Launched	Comp	Fate
F 145	PRESIDENT KRUGER	Yarrow	6.4.60	21.10.60	1.10.62	Sunk 18.2.82
F 147	PRESIDENT PRETORIUS	Yarrow	21.11.60	28.9.62	4.3.64	Extant 1982
F 150	PRESIDENT STEYN	Stephen	20.5.60	23.11.61	26.4.63	Stricken 1981

Six 12.75in Mk 32 ASW TT (2×3) were added *c*1972. *Kruger* was given a modified funnel cap to carry smoke clear of the foremost radar arrays

*c*1975. *Steyn* was decommissioned in Aug 1980 to be cannibalised for her sisters. *Pretorius* was altered to give a resemblance to a *Leander* class frigate.

Kruger was lost 80 miles SW of the Cape on 18.2.82 with 13 of her crew in a night collision with the replenishment ship *Tafelberg* (A 243).

AFRICA

Replacements for the old 'Loch' class frigates with the same names ordered from France in 1976, two A69 units building for the French Navy being made available. Differed slightly from standard French design, having USN-pattern Mk 32 triple ASW TT on the quarterdeck. In September 1978, when both ships were almost ready, France cancelled the contract, because of the UN arms embargo on South Africa. Sold to Argentina 25.9.78 and renamed *Drummond* and *Guerrico* respectively.

GOOD HOPE class *corvettes*

Particulars: As French *D'Estienne d'Orves* class

No	Name	Builder	Laid down	Launched	Comp	Fate
F 432	GOOD HOPE (ex-*Lieutenant de Vaisseau Le Henaff*)	Arsenal de Lorient	12.3.76	16.3.78	Mar 1978	See notes
F 102	TRANSVAAL (ex-*Commandant l'Herminier*)	Arsenal de Lorient	1.10.76	Sept 1977	Nov 1978	See notes

SUBMARINES

Similar to those built in France for the French, Pakistani and Portuguese Navies, and in Spain for the Spanish Navy.

French DAPHNE class *submarines*

No	Name	Builder	Laid down	Launched	Comp	Fate
S 97	MARIA VAN RIEBEECK	A C Dubigeon	14.3.68	18.3.69	22.6.70	Extant 1982
S 98	EMILY HOBHOUSE	A C Dubigeon	18.11.68	24.10.69	25.1.71	Extant 1982
S 99	JOHANNA VAN DER MERWE	A C Dubigeon	24.4.69	21.7.70	21.7.71	Extant 1982

Ordered in June 1975, but in 1978 France cancelled the contract because UN arms embargo on South Africa. Became the Pakistani *Hashmat* and *Hurmat* respectively.

French AGOSTA class *submarines*

Name	Builder	Laid Down	Launched	Comp	Fate
ASTRANT	A C Dubigeon	15.9.76	14.12.77	17.2.79	See notes
ADVENTUROUS	A C Dubigeon	?	1.12.78	17.2.80	See notes

SMALL SURFACE COMBATANTS

'MOD' class *fast attack craft (missile)*

Particulars: As Israeli *Reshef* class

Class (no, launched/completed):
Jan Smuts (P 1561, Feb–Sept 1977); *P W Botha* (P 1562, Sept–Dec 1977), *Frederick Creswell* (P 1563, Jan–June 1978), *Jim Fouche* (P 1564, Sept–Dec 1978), *Franz Erasmus* (P 1565, Mar–July 1979), *Oswald Pirow* (P 1566, Sept 1979–4.3.80), *Frank Chappel* (P 1567, March–Sept 1980), *Hendrik Mentz* (P 1568, April 1982), *Kobje Coetzee* (P 1569, 25.11.82)

First three boats ordered from Haifa Shipyard, Israel, in late 1974. Material was supplied for three more to be built by Sandock Austral Navy Yard, Durban, and a further six are being built by Sandock at 50 million rands ($56 million) each under a contract signed on 15.11.77. All named after S African Ministers of Defence. Identical with the Israeli *Reshef*s, apart from using a S Africa-produced version of the Gabriel II SSM called Skorpioen (Scorpion). Fitted with ABCD sprinklers. Based at Salisbury Island, Durban.

'MoD' class boat on trials   *SAN*

British 'FORD' class *seaward defence boats*

Class (no, former name, transfer/launch/in service):
Gelderland (P 3105, ex-*Brayford*, 30.8.54), *Nautilus* (P 3120, ex-*Glassford*, 23.8.55), *Rijger* (P 3125, 5.2.58, Dec 1958), *Haerlem* (P 3126, Aug 1959), *Oosterland* (P 3127, 27.1.59, 6.12.59)

Two transferred from the RN in 1954–55, three built in Britain for the SAN in 1957–59. All in service 1982, *Haerlem* as an inshore survey craft (from 1963).

MINE WARFARE VESSELS

Ex-British ALGERINE class *minesweepers*

No	Name	Builder	Acquired	Fate
M 439	BLOEMFONTEIN (ex-*Rosamund*)	Port Arthur	1947	Sunk as target June 1967
M 291	PIETERMARITZBURG (ex-*Pelorus*)	Lobnitz	1947	Hulked 1976

Purchased from the RN in 1947. *Pietermaritzburg* converted to a midshipmen's TS in 1961–62, with new armament of 2–4in/45 Mk 16 (1×2), 2–40mm/60 Bofors, and accommodation added aft.

Ex-British 'TON' class *coastal minesweepers*

Class (no, former name, transferred):
Johannesburg (M 1207, ex-*Castleton*, 1959), *Kimberley* (M 1210, ex-*Stratton*, 1959), *Port Elizabeth* (M 1212, ex-*Dumbleton*, 27.10.58), *Mosselbaai* (M 1213, ex-*Oakington*, 1959), *Walvisbaai* (M 1214, ex-*Packington*, Dec 1959), *East London* (M 1215, ex-*Chilton*, 27.10.58), *Windhoek* (M 1498, launched 28.6.57), *Durban* (M 1499, launched 12.6.57), *Pretoria* (P 1556, ex-*Dunkerton*, Sept 1955), *Kaapstad* (P 1557, ex-*Hazelton*, Sept 1955)

Eight transferred from the RN in 1955–59, two built in Britain for the SAN in 1957–59. *Kimberley* (1977–78) and *Port Elizabeth* (1979–80) converted to minehunters – with Type 193M sonar, Type 1006 radar and 2 PAP-104 remote control devices. All in service 1982. *Pretoria* and *Kaapstad* as patrol vessels, *Walvisbaai* (P 1559) and *Durban* (P 1560) also being redesignated 1977–78. All 4 manned by Citizen Force reservists, retain sweep gear and carry a Gemini dinghy.

Sudan

The Sudan, by area the largest African state, became independent in 1956, when the Anglo-Egyptian condominium imposed after the fall of the Mahdist rule was terminated. Her subsequent history has been strongly influenced by her geography and demography, as she straddles the major natural link between the Arab world and tropical Africa, and has a population of 19 million divided between Arab Muslims (about 70 per cent) and various black minorities. Resentment of Arab rule by the partly Christian negroes of the south led to open revolt before independence, and trouble flared again repeatedly before the southern separatists were mollified in 1970 by the promise of autonomy. The 14-year Civil War ended in 1972 after 500,000 deaths and 250,000 refugees.

Two periods of civilian, parliamentary government were conspicuously unsuccessful, and the Army has been almost continuously in power. Foreign aid has come from the Eastern bloc (including the first major Soviets arms exported south of the Sahara) and, after the reversal of policy following the abortive Communist coup in 1971, from the West and the oil-rich Arab states. Even so the economy shrank by three per cent in 1980. Sudan's foreign policy attempts to conciliate all her seven neighbours, but Gaddafi's Libya is suspected of plotting to topple the Sudanese leader, and the problem of arms supplies through the Sudan to the anti-Ethiopian Eritrean guerrillas has not been solved.

Militarily, almost all expenditure has been on the 65,000-strong army; assistance has come from Egypt, with which there is a 1977 defence agreement. The Navy (600 volunteers since 1980) was set up in 1962 to protect the Red Sea coast (Port Sudan), and also operates on the Nile (Khartoum). The original Yugoslav training mission left in 1972; most Sudanese warships are ex-Yugoslav, dating from the 1950s and early 1960s, and have almost certainly deteriorated from lack of maintenance and spare parts. New units of the large patrol type are urgently needed, but no construction programme has been reported.

EL GIHAD class *large patrol craft*

Displacement:	86t standard; 100t full load
Dimensions:	103ft pp, 115ft oa × 16ft 1in × 5ft 2in
	31.4m, 35.0m × 4.9m × 1.7m
Machinery:	2 shafts, 2 MTU 12V 493 diesels, 1820bhp = 20kts. Range 1400nm at 12kts
Armament:	1–40mm, 1–20mm, 2–7.62mm MG
Complement:	20

Class (no):
El Gihad (PB 1, 1961), *El Horriya* (PB 2, 1961), *El Istiqlal* (PB 3, 1962), *El Shaab* (PB 4, 1962)

Built by Mosor, Yugoslavia, as the Sudanese Navy's first ships. All in service 1982.

Ex-Yugoslav 'KRALJEVICA' class *large patrol craft*

Class (no):
El Fasher (522), *El Khartoum* (523)

Transferred in 1969. Hulked in 1981.

MISCELLANEOUS

Ex-Iranian Coast Guard patrol craft *Sheikan* (128), *Kadir* (129), *Karari* (130), acquired 1975.

Six ex-Yugoslav Type 101 MTBs (gun version with 2–40mm, 2–20mm) acquired 1970 and discarded 1981.

Two ex-Yugoslav 'DTM 221' class LCTs *Sobat* and *Dinder* transferred 1969.

Tanzania (inc Zanzibar)

Tanzania was created in March 1964 by the union of mainland Tanganyika, which had gained independence in 1961, and the small island state of Zanzibar, where a left-wing African uprising had unseated the Arab Sultan soon after independence in December 1963. The ruler of Tanzania since her formation has been Julius Nyerere, a strong and uncompromising proponent of African socialism, to which he has given the name 'Ujamaa'.

Internationally, Tanzania has followed an erratic but generally left-wing course, quarrelling frequently with western countries, and less often with African and Communist states, for a variety of reasons. Chinese influence increased considerably after 1969, while the Tanzam railway from Dar es Salaam to the Zambian copperbelt was being built, but Nyerere has resolutely refused to be the puppet of any nation or faction. Zanzibar had complete internal autonomy and retains a small degree of freedom in international relations, but its Marxist government has mellowed greatly in the past ten years.

The armed forces are mainly for internal security duties, although the Chinese-trained Army performed well in its 1979 conquest of Uganda. The Navy is small, with volunteer personnel of about 700 in 1982, and operates from a main base built in 1971 at Dar es Salaam under Chinese supervision. Other coastal ports are Mtwara, Lindi and Tanga. Lake Victoria is patrolled from Mwanza, Bukota and Musoma while Lake Tanganyika is watched from Kigoma. Tanzanian warships, of the fast attack craft and patrol boat types, are from the Soviet Union, China and East Germany (1966–75), with two small craft from West Germany which with Indonesia and the Netherlands has also given training; no substantial changes are probable in the near future.

Six ex-Chinese 'Shanghai II' class fast attack craft (gun) transferred 1970–71. Numbered JW 9861–JW 9867. All in service 1982.

Four ex-Chinese 'Huchwan' class FAC (torpedo) transferred 1975 without hydrofoils (JW 9841–9844).

Three ex-Soviet 'P 6' class FAC (gun) transferred from E Germany 1974–75 with TT removed.

Four ex-Soviet 'P 4' class FAC (torpedo) transferred from USSR and E Germany 1970–73. Some minus TT.

Ex-Soviet 'Poluchat' class large patrol craft.

Two ex-E German *Schwalbe* class inshore minesweepers transferred Jan 1966 and Jan 1967 minus minesweeping gear and radar. Named *Araka* and *Salaam*.

Two ex-W German coastal patrol craft bought 1967 via Portugal. Named *Rafiki* and *Uhuru*.

Four ex-Chinese 'Yulin' class coastal patrol craft transferred Nov 1966 and operated on Lake Victoria.

Two ex-Chinese LCMs.

Japanese LST *Maendelo* launched 13.2.80.

Four coastal patrol boats loaned by West Germany in 1963 were discarded in 1967.

Zanzibar has four Vosper Thornycroft 75ft type GRP coastal patrol craft (*Unguja* and *Pemba* delivered 6.7.73, *Mnemba* in March 1974 and *Miwi* in April). One of the first orders for this Keith Nelson design, they displace 70t, can manage 24.5kts and have 2–20mm (2×1).

Togo

The West African republic of Togo, independent from France in 1960 and under a moderate military regime since 1967, has a short coastline of only 35 miles. The 200 volunteer naval personnel under a French Navy lieutenant operate two wooden coastal patrol craft, *Mono* and *Kara* (105ft, 30kts, 1–40mm, 1–20mm), built in France and delivered to Lomé on 5 October 1976 being named after the country's rivers.

Tunisia

Tunisia became independent from French protection in 1956, and has managed to keep her reputation of being the most peaceful and civilised of North African countries. Economic development has been generally successful, but tension caused by the widening disparity between rich and poor led to serious riots in 1979, and further strains have resulted from the growth in Islamic fundamentalism. A major future problem may be the succession question: Bourguiba, president since independence, is elderly and in poor health.

External policies have been generally neutralist but pro-Western, although relations with France in the early years of independence were sometimes very bad. In 1961 French paratroops caused 1000 casualties among Tunisian demonstrators protesting at France's retention of the Bizerta naval base, and matters again came to a head in 1964 on Tunisian nationalisation of foreign landholdings. More recently, it is relations with Libya that have caused concern, particularly after the 1980 Gafsa incident, and Tunisia now relies on France for military protection against her ambitious neighbour.

AFRICA

The military budget, expressed both absolutely and as a percentage of GNP, is much smaller than those of Tunisia's neighbours, so her armed forces are correspondingly weaker and more poorly equipped. The Navy, subordinate to the Tunisian National Army, comprises a number of patrol craft headed by an obsolete ex-US destroyer escort, and is no more than a coast defence force. This does not matter while France is prepared to send warships into Tunisian territorial waters whenever needed.

Tunisia has nine naval bases and 22 secondary ports along her 700-mile shore. The Soviet Mediterranean Fleet has made heavy use of Menzel-Bourguiba for repair work since 1977 and the expulsion from Egypt but has gained no permanent facilities. There seems little chance of significant Tunisian naval expansion in the near future, although some modernisation may be possible, perhaps with US assistance. The first of three 'La Combattante III' Exocet missile fast attack craft was laid down in August 1981 (ordered from CMN, Cherbourg, 27 June) with France bearing their 600 million franc cost. The personnel, totalling 2600 one-year conscripts since 1982 (2000 in 1974) with 3000 reservists, is considered fairly well trained and educated, and loyal to the regime, but likely to be unaggressive in action.

Ex-US SAVAGE class *radar-picket (frigate)*

No	Name	Builder	Acquired	Fate
E 7	PRESIDENT BOURGUIBA (ex-*Thomas J Gary*)	Consolidated, Orange	27.10.73	Extant 1982

Ex-US *Edsall* class DE (launched 21.8.43) converted to a *Savage* class radar-picket (SPS-10 and SPS-29 radars) in 1958 (DE 326, becoming DER 326). Transferred to Tunisia as the Navy's flagship in 1973. Hedgehog was replaced by 6–12.75in Mk 32 ASW TT (2×3). Replacement being sought.

Ex-French CHAMOIS class *corvette*

No	Name	Builder	Acquired	Fate
E 71	DESTOUR (ex-*Chevreuil*)	Arsenal de Lorient	13.10.59	Hulked 1972

Menzel Bourguiba on trials   *Vosper Thornycroft*

Ex-Chinese 'SHANGHAI II' class *fast attack craft (gun)*

Class (no):
Gafsa (P 305), *Amilcar* (P 306)
 Transferred late 1977. In service 1982.

French P 48 class *large patrol craft (missile)*

No	Name	Builder	Launched	Fate
P 301	BIZERTA	Ch Franco-Belges	20.11.69	Extant 1982
P 302	EL HORRIA (ex-*Liberté*)	SFCN	12.2.70	Extant 1982
P 304	MONASTIR	SFCN	25.6.74	Extant 1982

Laid down 5.6.69, 20.11.69 and 1.2.74; completed 10.7.70, Oct 1970 and 25.3.75. Exocet might replace the original wire-guided SS12 SSMs as with Ivory Coast's two units.

French LE FOUGEUX *submarine chaser*

Built as *P 9* by A C Dubigeon, Nantes, under US offshore order. Served as the West German ASW trials vessel *UW 12* 12.3.67 to 15.9.67. Bought by Tunisia 16.6.70 after transfer in Dec 1969. Hedgehog and all 4 DCT removed mid-1970s. In service 1982.

TAZARKA class *large patrol craft*

Displacement:	100t standard; 120t full load
Dimensions:	103ft oa × 19ft 6in × 5ft 6in 31.4m × 5.9m × 1.7m
Machinery:	2 shafts, 2MTU diesels, 4000bhp = 27kts. Range 1500nm at 14kts
Armament:	2–20mm
Sensor:	Radar Decca 916
Complement:	24

Class (no):
Tazarka (P 205), *Menzel Bourguiba* (P 206)
 Ordered from Vosper Thornycroft 9.9.75 and launched 19.7.76 and in service since 27.10.77. Original armament planned was 1–40mm.

US ADJUTANT class *coastal minesweepers*

Class (former name and no):
Hannibal (ex-*Coquelicot*, M 673), *Sousse* (ex-*Marjolaine*, M 640), ex-*Aconit*).
 Built for France in US shipyards under MDAP; *Hannibal* transferred in 1973, *Sousse* in July 1977. Both in service 1982 as patrol craft and for fishery protection, minesweeping gear having been removed.

MISCELLANEOUS
Four French 32-metre coastal patrol craft (60t, 28kts, 2–20mm, 17 men): *Istikal* (P 201, ex-French *VC 11* transferred March 1959); *Joumbouria* (P 202, ex-French *P 761* transferred Jan 1961); *Al Jala* (P 203, in service Nov 1963) and *Remada* (P 204, in service July 1967).

Eight French 25-metre coastal patrol craft (38t, 23kts, 1–20mm, 10 men): *V 101* to *V 106* in service 1961–63, *V 107* and *V 108* disarmed and transferred to Fisheries Administration in 1971.

Zaire

Zaire, formerly Congo-Kinshasa (independent in 1960) and black Africa's largest state, has a short coastline at the mouth of the River Zaire (Congo). Her 1500-volunteer Navy (600 marines) operates three flotillas, one coastal (based at Boma and Matadi in the Congo estuary), one river and one lake (mainly Kalemi for Lake Tanganyika). There are 70 river ports on the country's 9320 miles of navigable waterways. Since 1978 Chinese instructors have helped with training (begun by Norway in 1964) which is also obtained from Egypt and France. However, efficiency and maintenance are likely to be very low.

Four ex-Chinese 'Shanghai II' class FAC (gun): numbered P 101 to P 104, transferred in pairs Sept 1976 and Sept 1978.
Three ex-N Korean 'P 4' FAC (torpedo) transferred 1974.
Four ex-Chinese 'Huchwan' class hydrofoil FAC (torpedo) transferred in pairs Sept 1976 and Sept 1978.
The 70t *Zaire* (ex-*President Mobutu*, ex-*Congo*, ex-*General Olsen*) doubles as a yacht.
Six US Sewart type 65ft coastal patrol craft (33t, 25kts, 6–12.7mm MG, 12 men) bought 1972 and 1974.
Thirty Arcoa type patrol boats (1.7–7.5t craft, delivered from France since 1975 for river and lake operations).

Zambia

In September 1966 the Zambian Government purchased a tank landing craft of the LCT (8) type, the former HMS *Bastion* (L 4040). She was discarded in February 1969.

Bangladesh

The People's Republic of Bangladesh was proclaimed in what had been East Pakistan in April 1971. This was followed first by civil war and then in December by the Third Indo-Pakistan War, which resulted in the complete independence of Bangladesh. Although four Soviet 'Vanya' class minesweepers operated during 1972–74 in Bangladesh coastal waters to clear Chittagong of mines and wrecks these were not incorporated in the Bangladesh Navy, but returned to the USSR. The Navy came into being with its own river craft in 1972, and is formed around four old British frigates and a number of transferred gunboats. There is also a force of river gunboats. Volunteer personnel numbered 5300 in 1982. Their bases are Chittagong (HQ), Dacca, Kulna, Juldia and Kaptai. Bangladesh lacks the money to acquire new ships except for river gunboats.

Ex-British SALISBURY class *frigates*

No	Name	Builder	Acquired	Fate
F 16	UMAR FAROOQ (ex-*Llandaff*)	Hawthorn Leslie	10.12.76	Extant 1982
?	? (ex-*Lincoln*)	Fairfield	Feb 1982	Extant 1982

Karnaphuli 1976   *L & L van Ginderen*

Ex-British LEOPARD class *frigates*

No	Name	Builder	Acquired	Fate
F 17	ALI HAIDER (ex-*Jaguar*)	Denny	16.7.78	Extant 1982
F 15	ABU BAKR (ex-*Lynx*)	John Brown	12.3.82	Extant 1982

The RN AA Type 41 frigate HMS *Jaguar* was transferred to Bangladesh for £2m. Refitted by Vosper Thornycroft Aug–Oct 1978. The ASW weapons and equipment were removed while she was still in the RN.

Ex-Yugoslav KRALJEVICA class *large patrol craft*

Class (no, former name):
Karnaphuli (P 301, ex-*PBR 502*), *Tista* (P 302, ex-*PBR 505*)
Type 510 units sold to Bangladesh on 6.6.75.

Ex-Indian AKSHAY class *large patrol craft*

Class (no, former name):
Padma (P 201, ex-*Akshay*), *Surma* (P 202, ex-*Ajay*)
Transferred 12.4.73 and 26.7.74 respectively.

Ex-Pakistani *large patrol craft*

PNS *Jessore* was salvaged after the 1971 War of Independence and repaired at Khulna SY, recommissioned 23.11.78.

SHAMJALA class *large patrol craft*

Shamjala, first of a class of six built by Sumidagawa of Japan, was launched 2.7.81 and commissioned in 1982. She displaces 160t and measures 98ft 4in (30m).

Ex-Chinese 'SHANGHAI II' class *large patrol craft*

Class:
Shaheed Daulat, Shaheed Farid, Shaheed Mohibullah, Shaheed Akhtaruddin and 2 others.
Numbered P 101–106. Two transferred 1974, four more June–July 1980. All extant 1982.

PABNA class *river patrol boats*

Class (no, commissioned):
Pabna (P 101, 12.6.72), *Noakhali* (P 102, 8.7.72), *Patuakhali* (P 103, 7.11.74), *Bogra* (P 104, 15.7.77), *Rangamati* (P 105, 11.2.77)
Five were the first warships to be built in Bangladesh (by DEW Narayangon of Dacca) between 1972–77 and are based on river steamers. They are 75ft (22.9m) long, have 2 Cummins diesels giving 10.8kts (700nm at 8kts), displace 69.5t, a crew of 33 and are armed with 1–40mm. *Noakhali, Pabna* and *Patuakhali* have the gun aft but *Bogra* and *Rangamati* have it mounted forward. No more units are planned.

Brunei

Brunei became a British protectorate in 1888. In 1957 she became part of the Federation of Malaya and in 1963 joined the Federation of Malaysia. This oil and gas-rich Sultanate, a little larger than Washington DC, is self-governing internally but relies on Britain to assist with her defence. Independence for the estimated 230,000 inhabitants is due on 1 January 1984. The Navy is run by the volunteer Royal Brunei Malay Regiment and Britain provides its commander and many of the officers. It is divided into the 337-man First Flotilla for offshore patrols and the 120–strong Special Boat Squadron for policing the rivers. A powerful force of missile and gun armed patrol boats is based at Muara, and unlike many small navies is not confined to fishery protection and anti-smuggling work.

PAHLAWAN *fast attack craft (missile)*

Particulars: As Danish 'Söloven' class

The gas turbine powered *Pahlawan* was built by Vosper at Portsmouth between 1965–67 (launched 5.12.66, commissioned 19.10.67) to the same design as the Danish *Söloven* class. She had a wooden hull and aluminium alloy superstructure, and was originally armed with 1–40mm and 2–20mm (1×2). *Pahlawan* was refitted by Vosper Thornycroft, Singapore in May 1972 with 8 SS-12 SSM (4×2). She had Decca TM 616 radar. *Pahlawan* was discarded in 1977.

Waspada 1979
NB 1/750 scale

WASPADA class *fast attack craft (missile)*

Displacement:	150t full load
Dimensions:	110ft, 121ft oa × 23ft 6in × 6ft *33.5m, 36.9m × 7.2m × 1.8m*
Machinery:	2 shafts, 2 MTU 20V538 TB91 diesels, 9000bhp = 32kts. Fuel 16t. Range 1200nm at 14kts
Armament:	2 MM38 Exocet SSM (2×1), 2–30mm Oerlikon GCM-Bol (1×2), 2–7.62mm MG, 2–2in MoD(N) R(F)L
Sensors:	Radar Decca TM 1229
Complement:	24

Class (no, launched):
Waspada (P 02, 3.8.77), *Pejuang* (P 03, March 1978), *Seteria* (P 04, 22.6.78)
These boats were built for Brunei by Vosper, Singapore between 1976–79. They have identical welded steel hulls and aluminium superstructure to the Venezualan *Constitucion* class but have more powerful MTU diesels and a different armament controlled by Sperry 1412A digital computer and the Sea Archer missile system. *Waspada* (in service July 1978) differs from *Pejuang* and *Seteria* (both in service 1979) by having an enclosed bridge and training facilities. All are extant 1982.

'RAJA ISTERI' class *coastal patrol craft*

Class (no, launched):
Masna (P 12, 19.9.70), *Norain* (P 13, Nov 1971), *Saleha* (P 11, 18.9.70).

Built by Vosper at Singapore as 62ft wooden hull 25t units with aluminium superstructure, named after Brunei princesses. Their twin GM 71 16-cylinder diesels gave 1250bhp or 26kts (600nm at 23kts). The 8-man crews had 2–20mm Hispano Suiza (2×1) and 2-7.62mm MG. All were commissioned in 1972 and deleted 1978, *Norain* in 1979.

PERWIRA class *coastal patrol craft*

Class (no, launched):
Perwira (P 14, 9.5.74), *Pemburu* (P 15, 30.1.75), *Penyarang* (P 16, 20.3.75)

All-wood 30t standard/38.5t full load units (71ft × 20ft × 5ft, *21.7m × 6.1m × 1.2m*). Same armament as 'Raja Isteri' class. Twin MTU MB 12V 331 TC81 diesels give 2700bhp or 32kts (Range 600nm/1000nm at 20kts/16kts). *Perwira* was commissioned 9.9.74 with Decca 916A radar, the other in June 1975 with Decca 1216A radar. All extant 1982.

'LOADMASTER' class *landing craft*

Class (no, in service):
Damuan (L 31, May 1976), *Puni* (L 32, Feb 1977)

Built by Cheverton, IoW, England. These 64.3t units measure 65ft × 20ft × 3ft 7in (*19.8m × 6.1m × 1.1m*), have twin GM V71 6-cyl diesels giving 348hp = 9kts (300nm/1000nm at 8.5kts/6kts) and can carry 30t of cargo. Decca RM-1216 radar. Both extant 1982.

MISCELLANEOUS

Three *Bendahara* class river patrol craft (10t, 20kts, 2–7.62mm MG, 8 men, built 1974–75, deleted 1980).

The Marine Police operate two 14t GRP diesel/waterjet coastal patrol craft (Vosper, Singapore, built 1978–80, 28kts, MGs, 5 men) *Tenang* and *Abadi* extant 1982 with two more ordered early 1979.

The Special Boat Squadron has 24 Rigid Raider type fast assault boats and 3 Rotork 8.8t patrol boats (S 24 delivered Nov 1980 and S 25 and S 26 May 1981).

Burma

The Socialist Republic of the Union of Burma, as an exceptionally insular, almost 'forgotten' country, one quarter bigger than France, follows a policy of non-alignment and neutrality. Bordered to the north by China, and to the east by Thailand and west by Bangladesh, the 35 million Burmese are in a truly isolated position. Maintaining an isolated policy in the face of turbulence to east, north and south is a particularly difficult task. Up to the present this small Navy established on 4 January 1948 has relied upon ex-British and American vessels of principally Second World War vintage supported by some Yugoslav-built craft.

With the policy of neutrality the Burmese Navy does not require a vast force, just sufficient craft to police the 1900 mile coastline together with a number of small craft for patrolling the numerous rivers and waterways. These forces are maintained mainly for a counter-insurgency role, a necessary task as there have been a number of insurrections in the country and, as much of the countryside is a dense jungle, the main means of communications is by water. Lately the Navy embarked on a modest modernisation programme to police the 200-mile EEZ, receiving from Australia six *Carpentaria* patrol craft, and from Denmark three offshore patrol vessels of the so called British-designed *Osprey* class/Danish *Havørnen*. It is unlikely that Burma will consider any larger expansion programme and any new construction will be centred on light craft and the above mentioned OPV type vessels to replace overaged ex-British 'River', *Algerine* and US PCE ships.

There are three naval regions with seven major bases: Rangoon, Bassein (Irrawaddy Delta), Sittwe (Akyab), Moulmein in the Salween estuary, Mergui in the far south Tenasserim State, Sinmalaik and Seikyi. A 1958 strength of 3000 sailors with 42 ships had become 10,000 (including 800 marines) by 1982 with 106 ships. Service is by voluntary enlistment for two years and a rear-admiral (Vice Chief of Staff, Defence Forces, Navy) commands.

Ex-British 'RIVER' class *frigate*

No	Name	Builder	Acquired	Fate
	MAYU (ex-*Fal*)	Smith's Dock	1947	Deleted 1979

Ex-RN frigate (F 266) bought in 1947 and re-named March 1948. Had RN Type 974 radar.

Ex-British LCG (M) type *landing craft*

Class:
Indaw, Inlay, Inma, Inya

Former British LCG(M) type landing craft, gun medium. Employed as gunboats. Three deleted: *Indaw* in 1976 and *Inma* and *Inya* in 1980–82, and gave their names to OPVs built in Denmark.

Ex-US LCU 1610 type *utility landing craft*

Ex-US *LCU 1626*, transferred on completion at Rangoon under MDAP in June 1967 (launched 1963). Used as transport. Recently renamed *Aiyar Lulin* (603).

AIYAR MAUNG class *landing craft*

Displacement:	250t full load
Dimensions:	125ft 6in × 30ft × 4ft 6in
	38.2m × 9.1m × 1.4m
Machinery:	2 shafts, 2 Kubota diesels, 560hp = 10kts
Complement:	10

Class:
Aiyar Maung, Aiyar Min Thar, Aiyar Mai, Aiyar Min Tha Mee

Four landing craft launched March 1969 by Yokohama Yacht. Can carry 100t of cargo. Used as transports. All extant 1982

SINDE class *landing craft*

Displacement:	220t full load
Dimensions:	96ft 8in × 22ft × 4ft 6in
	29.5m × 6.7m × 1.4m
Machinery:	2 shafts, 2 Kubota diesels, 300hp = 20kts
Complement:	? + 30 passengers

Class:
Sinde, Htonbo

Two small landing craft built by Yokohama Yacht in 1978. Can carry 50t of cargo. Used as transports.

Ex-US LCM 3 type *landing craft*

Class:
LCM 701–708

Eight US-built 52t units (2 Gray Marine diesels, 4500bhp = 9kts, 2–20mm) used as transports able to carry 30t of stores. Extant 1982.

'OSPREY' class *offshore patrol vessels (corvettes)*

Displacement:	325t light; 480t full load
Dimensions:	164ft × 34ft 6in × 9ft
	50m × 10.5m × 2.8m
Machinery:	2 shafts (2 CP propellers), 2 Burmeister & Wain Alpha 16V23L-VO diesels, 4640bhp = 20kts. Range 4500nm at 16kts
Armament:	2–40mm (1×2), 1–20mm
Complement:	20

Class (no, completed):
Indaw (FV 388, 30.5.80), *Inma* (FV ?, Dec 1981), *Inya* (FV ?, 1982)

Ordered in Denmark at Frederikshavn Vaerft in 1978. Identical with Danish *Havørnen*. Built in 1979–82. Mercantile design of helicopter-carrying small fishery protection vessel. Sometimes known as FV 710 type. Carry a David Still 25kt boarding boat in an inclined ramp at the stern. Sailed by the Navy for the People's Pearl and Fishery Dept. *Indaw* operated effectively in her first six months against pirates, smugglers and illegal fishermen.

Ex-US PCE 827 class *patrol vessel*

Yan Taing Aung (41, ex-*Farmington* PCE 894) transferred 18.6.65. Built 1942–43 by Williamette Iron & Steel. Fitted with SPS-5 radar and QCU-2 sonar. Extant 1982.

Ex-US ADMIRABLE class *ocean minesweeper (corvette)*

Yan Gyi Aung (42, ex-*Creddock*, *MSF 356*) transferred at San Diego 31.3.67 with minesweeping gear removed. Built by Williamette Iron & Steel 1943–44, extant 1982.

US 'SWIFT' type *large patrol craft*

Class:
PGM 421–423
See under Ethiopia for data. Armament differs being 2–40mm (2×1), 2–20mm. MTU diesels are 12V331 TC81, crew 25. Built by Swiftships, Morgan City, USA. Launched 1976, completed 1977–78, extant 1982.

US 83ft type *motor gunboats*

Class:
MGB 101–110
Former USCG 83ft type patrol boat engines with new hulls built at Rangoon DYd, Burma. Completed in 1960. Three (*MGB 103*, *107*, *109*) are reported to have been sunk. Originally launched in 1938–42 and transferred by USCG under MDAP in 1951. Seven extant 1982.

Ex-British *motor launches*

Class:
ML 391, 414, 415, 418, 437 (Fairmile type, launched in 1946), *ML 1102, 1103, 1104* (smaller Thornycroft type loaned in 1946)
All 8 stricken *c* 1957–58.

Ex-British HDML type *motor launches*

Class:
MGB 1272, 1299, 1304, 1306, 1369, 1456, 1462, 1467, 1477, 1478, 1486
Eleven former RN HDMLs of same numbers transferred 1948–50. *MGB 1299, 1369, 1467, 1477* and *1486* deleted in 1957; others followed.

US PGM type *patrol gunboats*

Class:
PGM 401–406 (ex-US *PGM 43–46, 51, 52*)
Built by Marinette Marine, USA, 1959–61, austere export version, USCG 95ft type. Raytheon 1500 radar in *405* and *406*, EDO-320 in rest. Extant 1982.

Australian CARPENTARIA class *coastal patrol craft*

Displacement:	27t full load
Dimensions:	51ft 6in × 15ft 8in × 4ft 4in
	15.7m × 4.8m × 1.3m
Machinery:	2 shafts, 2 GM 12V 71TI diesels 1400hp = 30kts. Range 700nm/950nm at 22kts/18kts
Armament:	2–20mm
Sensors:	Radar Decca 110
Complement:	10

Six built by de Havilland, Sydney. Ordered Dec 1978 for fishery protection, launched 1979–80, completed 1980–81. First two delivered 1979.

British DARK class *fast attack craft*

Class:
PTS 101–105 (renamed during construction *T 201–205*)
Five interchangeable MTBs/MGBs built by Saunders-Roe and completed in 1956–57. Of aluminium construction, with riveted skin and aluminium alloy framework. The Saunders Roe slow-speed electric drive was fitted to facilitate manoeuvring in the confined inland waters where the craft were required to operate. Total cost of this order was £1.8 million. All stricken 1975.

Y 301 class *river gunboats*

Displacement:	120t
Dimensions:	104ft 9in × 24ft × 3ft
	31.7m × 7.3m × 0.8m
Machinery:	2 shafts, 2 MTU diesels, 1000hp = 13kts
Armament:	2–40mm (2×1), 1–2pdr
Complement:	29

Class:
Y 301–310
All ten launched in 1957 and completed in 1958 by Yugoslav yard Uljanik in Pula. Built to specific Burmese order. Extant 1982.

Nawarat as completed
NB 1/750 scale

NAWARAT class *river gunboats*

Displacement:	400t standard, 450t full load
Dimensions:	163ft × 26ft × 4ft 7in
	50.0m × 8.1m × 1.7m
Machinery:	2 shafts, 2 Paxman-Ricardo turbo-charged diesels, 1160hp = 12kts
Armament:	2–25pdr (Army), 2–40mm
Complement:	43

Class (in service):
Nawarat (25.4.60), *Nagakyay* (3.12.60)
Built at the Government Dockyard Dawbon, Rangoon, Burma. Launched 1959 and completed 1960. Extant 1982.

Y 311 class *river gunboats*

Displacement:	250t
Dimensions:	121ft 4in × 24ft × 3ft 6in
	37.0m × 7.3m × 1.1m
Machinery:	2 shafts, 2 MTU diesels, 1000hp = 14kts
Armament:	2–40mm, 2–20mm (both 1×2)
Complement:	?

Class:
Y 311, Y 312
Built in Burma by Simalak Dockyard in 1967–69. Extant 1982.
There are also six PBR 211–216 river patrol craft of American PBR type acquired in 1978; 8t, 25kts, 3 MG (1×2, 1×1).

Ex-British ALGERINE class *ocean minesweeper*

Name	Builder	Acquired	Fate
YAN MYO AUNG (ex-*Mariner*, ex-*Kincardine*)	Port Arthur	18.4.58	Extant 1982

Used also as an escort vessel (corvette). Canadian-built in 1943–45. Handed over to Burmese Navy in London. Fitted for minelaying and can carry 16 mines, eight on each side.

Ex-British MMS type *motor minesweepers*

Class (stricken):
MMS 197 (1957), *MMS 201* (1956)
Wooden units transferred from RN at Rangoon in Oct 1946. Both scrapped.

MISCELLANEOUS
Eight armed river transports (98t, 160hp = 12kts, 1–40mm, 3–20mm. Earlier just 6–20mm): *Hintha, Saban, Sagu, Seinda, Setkaya, Setyahat, Shwepazun, Shwethida* and *Sinmin*. All extant 1982.
Boom defence vessel *Barstoke* served on loan from RN 1946–59.

Cambodia (Kampuchea)

Cambodia (now known as Kampuchea) became a French protectorate in 1867 and a French colony in 1887. She became an independent Kingdom within the French Union in 1949 and became truly independent in 1954. The Marine Royal Khmer was set up on 20 April 1954 with French assistance. The Vietcong made use of Eastern Cambodia and Prince Norodom Sihanouk tried to steer a neutral course. This meant that the Navy received very few ships from abroad and the country lacked the money or inclination to purchase any.

There were border incidents in the late 1960s with Thailand and South Vietnam and in May 1970 the Americans and South Vietnamese invaded East Cambodia to eradicate the Vietcong. Sihanouk was overthrown and a pro-Western military government took over, renaming the Navy, Marine National Khmer. American aid was lavished on the armed forces, including the Navy, but the indigenous Khmer Rouge pushed them back and besieged the capital, Phnom Penh, from 1973 until, the river lifeline cut, it surrendered in April 1975. At that juncture the Navy totalled 11,000 men including 4000 marines, all 18-month conscripts.

Most of the major warships fled to Thailand or the Philippines, two MTBs were sunk during the American operations to recapture the freighter *Mayaguez*, and most of the remaining ships were sunk or discarded during the Khmer Rouge dictatorship or the subsequent Vietnamese invasion. Very few are likely to be in service in 1982. Cambodia's merchant marine totalled three ships (3558grt) in 1980 so the principal ports of Phnomh Penh (River Mekong), Kompong Som and Ream (Gulf of Thailand) see little traffic except that of Comecon states. The first Soviet warship visit was made in 1980.

Ex-French EDIC type *landing craft*

The French LST 606, built by Franco-Belge in 1968–69, was transferred to Cambodia on completion in Aug 1969, and renumbered *T 916*. She was discarded in 1979.

Ex-US *landing craft*

Two ex-USN LCT 6, transferred to France in 1951 for service in Indo-China, were transferred by the French to Cambodia in 1956–57. They were deleted in *c*1973–75. Two ex-USN LCU 501 Type were transferred first to France then to Cambodia at about the same time. Two more were transferred on 31.5.62, and two more in Nov 1972. Four were deleted in 1979. An ex-USN LCU 1466 Type was also transferred in Oct 1969. *T 919* (ex-USN LCU 1577) was sunk by a mine on 5.5.70. The remainder were either repossessed by the USN or deleted between 1973–75. In the early 1970s 20 ex-USN LCM 6 and 23 ex-USN ATC (converted LCM 6 or 8) were also transferred and suffered the same fate.

Ex-US PC class *large patrol craft*

Two ex-USN PCs, transferred to the French Navy in 1951 for use in Indo-China, were transferred to the Cambodian Navy in 1955–56. They were *E 311* (ex-*Flamberge*, ex-USS PC 1086), and *E 312* (ex-*L'Inconstant*, ex-USS PC 1171). *E 311* fled to Thailand on 16.5.75 and has been scrapped. *E 312* fled to the Philippines on 2.5.75, and was incorporated into the Philippines Navy in Dec 1976 as *Negros Oriental*.

Ex-Yugoslav Type 108 *fast attack craft (torpedo)*

Two were presented to Cambodia in 1965, and renumbered *VR 1* and *VR 2*. Both sunk by US aircraft on 13.5.75 during the *Mayaguez* incident.

Ex-US LSIL class *landing craft (support gunboats)*

P 111 (ex-USS *LSIL 9039*, ex-*LSIL 875*) and P 112 (ex-*Medecin Capitaine Le Gall*, ex-USS LSIL ?) had been USN rearmed large infantry landing craft transferred to the French Navy in 1951 for service in Indo-China. The French transferred them to Cambodia in 1957. Both escaped to the Philippines on 17.4.75, and P 111 was incorporated in the Philippines Navy on 17.11.77 as *Marinduque*.

Ex-US *patrol gunboat*

USS *PGM 70* was transferred to Cambodia under MDAP in 1964. She was deleted between 1973–75.

Ex-British *harbour defence motor launches*

Three RN HDMLs, among 26 transferred to the Free French Navy in 1943, were transferred by the French to Cambodia. *VP 762* (ex-*VP 42*, ex-*HDML 1457*) was transferred in 1956; *VP 748* (ex-*HDML 1223*) and *VP 749* (ex-*HDML 1229*) followed a year later. *VP 212* (ex-*748*) was the only one to survive the Khmer Rouge takeover. She may be in service in 1982.

Three ex-Chinese 'Yulin' type coastal patrol boats were transferred to Cambodia in Jan 1968 and renumbered *VP 1–3*. They may still be in service in 1982.

Two ex-USN AVR type, 17 ex-USN 'Swift' class PCF and 65 ex-USN PBR Mk 1 and Mk 2 river patrol craft were transferred to Cambodia in 1972–74. Several were sunk in 1973–75 and others reclaimed by the USN, but about 9 'Swift' class PCF and 25 PBR may be in service in 1982.

China
1947–1949

At the end of World War II no one group ruled all of China. The official government, the Kuomintang (Nationalists) controlled by Generalissimo Chiang Kai-Shek were based at Chungking on the Yangtze. They ruled over about half the land area, but this was mainly in the southwest of the country and did not include any of the major ports, which along with most of the rest of the coastline and the entire north-east were still in Japanese hands. The rest was dominated by the Communists under Mao Tse Tung. They were based in Yunnan but had troops and sympathisers scattered throughout the country.

The Japanese pulled out of Inner Mongolia, Manchuria, Taiwan (Formosa) and Hainan in September 1945, and with the help of the Americans the Kuomintang forces regained most of the major towns. However, the countryside was mainly Communist, and although the Kuomintang had several successes (the fragile truce between the Kuomintang and the Communists, dating back to 1936, had broken down well before the end of World War II), culminating in the taking of the Communist capital in Yunnan in March 1947, the Communists gradually gained the upper hand. China and the United States had signed a treaty of friendship on 4 November 1946, but American aid and military forces were gradually disengaged.

The Communists gained so much ground that on 1 September 1948 they proclaimed the North China People's Republic, and after a series of major battles they crossed the Yangtze into the Kuomintang's heartland in April 1949. On 16 July 1949 the Kuomintang commanders decided to withdraw to Taiwan and the other islands under their control. This massive evacuation was completed on 8 December. Meanwhile the People's Republic of China had been proclaimed at Peking on 1 October 1949.

All of the Chinese Navy's major warships had either been sunk or captured by the Japanese in 1937; the only ships to remain under the control of the Government were six gunboats and an MTB. Most of the latter remained at the Kuomintang capital of Chungking throughout World War II, and their numbers were swollen by one American and three British river gunboats that were also trapped at Chungking and which were transferred to the Chinese Navy in February 1942. The major prewar ships that had been taken over by the Japanese were all sunk by 1945, and the only vessels that were returned were two more gunboats.

Despite the political confusion in China, she was still thought of as a major power, especially by the Americans. It was therefore decided to build up her navy with British and American help. Britain supplied two frigates and several smaller craft, and a cruiser was purchased to act as the flagship. The United States provided rather more, including six destroyer-escorts, and large numbers of patrol boats, minesweepers and landing vessels. American aid to the Kuomintang forces temporarily ceased on 5 August 1949 though US vessels assisted with the evacuation.

China also claimed a number of Japanese warships as reparations. Because of the US desire to rebuild her navy and the justifiable claim that Japan had destroyed it, China obtained the lion's share of the surviving Japanese warships. Three destroyers, together with large numbers of destroyer-escorts and smaller craft, were transferred in 1946–47 after they had completed the repatriation of POWs and Japanese troops. In addition, a number of gunboats and other small warships were captured by Chinese forces in 1945, and these were also incorporated.

When the Chinese Navy was expanded after World War II it suffered badly from a lack of trained sailors among the 40,000 officers and men. In addition, although the Allied ships were operational when they were handed over, most of the Japanese vessels, including all the larger ones, were disarmed at the end of the War (almost all in Fleet Strength table). The country was in such disorder that none of them was rearmed prior to the collapse of the Kuomintang Government. The surviving dockyards had neither the trained men nor the equipment to put things right. On top of all of this, some of the officers and many of the men were sympathetic to the Communists, and a number of the Chinese Navy's ships, including the only cruiser, defected to the Communists during the last stages of the Civil War. Many more were captured either because they could not be moved or because they were cut off by the crossing of the Yangtze in April 1949. Finally, several ships were lost by accident, and several more were sunk in action with Communist land forces.

FLEET STRENGTH 1947

Ex-Japanese DESTROYERS

Name	Disp (std)	Acquired	Fate
Minekaze class launched 1922			
SHEN YANG '	1345t	3.10.47	To Taiwan 1949,
(ex-*Namikaze*)			BU 1960s
Kagero class launched 1939			
TAN YANG	2050t	1947	To Taiwan 1949,
			BU 1971
Akizuki class launched 1944			
FEN YANG	3485t	29.8.47	To Taiwan 1949,
(ex-*Yoitsuki*)			BU 1963
Ex-Japanese escort destroyers			
Matsu class launched 1944			
HENG YANG	1262t	6.7.47	To Taiwan 1949,
(ex-*Kaede*)			BU c1960
HUI YANG	1262t	31.7.47	To Taiwan 1949,
(ex-*Sugi*)			BU c1960
Tachibana class launched 1944–45			
HSIN YANG	1289t	6.7.47	To Taiwan 1949,
(ex-*Hatsume*)			BU 1964
HUA YANG	1289t	31.7.47	To Taiwan 1949,
(ex-*Tsuta*)			BU c1950

Tai Ping 4.2.54   *USN, courtesy Salamander Books*

Ex-US DESTROYER ESCORTS

Name	Disp (std)	Acquired	Fate
'GMT' class launched 1942			
TAI KANG	1150t	Aug 1945	To Taiwan 1949,
(ex-*Wyffels*)			deleted 1972
TAI PING	1150t	Aug 1945	To Taiwan 1949,
(ex-*Decker*)			sunk 14.11.54

Ex-British FRIGATE

Name	Disp (std)	Acquired	Fate
'Flower class'			
FU PO	1020t	Jan 1946	Sunk 19.3.47
(ex-*Petunia*)			

Fu Po sank in collision with the merchant ship *Hai Ming* in the Formosa Straits. *Matsu* class re-armed after 1950 with ex-Japanese weapons by Taiwan. *Tai Ping* torpedoed and sunk by Communist torpedo boats off the Tachen Islands. *Hsin*

Yang re-armed with 2–120mm (2×1), 8–25mm (4×2), 4–13mm, 36 DC after 1949. *Hua Yang* sailed to the Pescadores, was never re-armed and acted as a hulk. *Tai Kang* took Chiang Kai-Shek on his second exploratory visit to Taiwan, in July 1949. See under Taiwan for *Tan Yang*.

Ex-Japanese ESCORTS

Name	Disp (std)	Acquired	Fate
Etorofu Type A class launched 1942–43			
KU AN (ex-*Oki*)	870t	29.8.47	To PRC 1949
LIN AN	870t	31.7.47	To Taiwan 1949,
(ex-*Tsushima*)			deleted 1963
Ukuru Type B class launched 1944			
HUI AN	940t	6.7.47	To PRC 1949
(ex-*Shisaka*)			
Mikura (Type B) class launched 1944			
WEI TAI	940t	29.8.47	To Taiwan 1949
(ex-*Yashiro*)			
Kaibokan (Type C) class launched 1944–45			
MUKDEN	745t	1947	To PRC 1949,
(ex-*No 81*)			renamed
			Shen Yang
			and again,
			deleted c1980
CHI AN	745t	1947	To PRC 1949,
(ex-*No 85*)			renamed 1960s,
			deleted c1980
HSIN AN	745t	31.7.47	To Taiwan 1949,
(ex-*No 205*)			hulked c1960
CHAO AN	745t	21.8.47	To Taiwan 1949,
(ex-*No 107*)			deleted 1963
JUI AN	745t	June 1947	To Taiwan 1949,
(ex-*No 67*)			deleted 1963
LIAO HAI	745t	1945	To Taiwan 1949,
(ex-*No 215*)			hulked c1960
Kaibokan Type D class launched 1944–45			
CHENG AN	740t	29.8.47	To Taiwan 1949,
(ex-*No 40*)			deleted 1963
CHIEH 5	740t	6.6.47	To PRC 1949,
(ex-*No 14*)			renamed
			Wu Jang
CHIEH 6	740t	6.7.47	Renamed *Wei Hai*
(ex-*No 194*)			1948,
			to PRC 1949
CHIEH 12	740t	31.7.47	To PRC 1949,
(ex-*No 118*)			renamed *Jangsha*
CHIEH 14	740t	1947	To PRC 1949,
(ex-*No 198*)			renamed *Shian*
TAI AN	740t	29.8.47	To Taiwan 1949,
(ex-*No 104*)			deleted 1960
TUNG AN	740t	31.7.47	To Taiwan 1949,
(ex-*No 192*)			deleted 1960

Etorofu Type A class
Lin An rearmed after 1953 with 1–120mm, 1–76mm/50 and 8–25mm and fitted for minelaying. Reclassified as a frigate, deleted 1963. *Ku An* renamed by Communists – *Chang Pai* (230) and rearmed with 3–100mm (3×1) and 3–37mm (3×1) Soviet guns in 1950s, also fitted as minelayer. Extant with S Sea Fleet 1982.

Ukuru Type B class
Hui An not renamed by Communists. Rearmed in late 1960s or early 1970s with 2–120mm (2×1) and 6–12.7mm MG. Extant 1982 with 3–100mm (3×1) and 4–37mm (4×1) in E Sea Fleet.

Mikura Type B class
Wei Tai came to Taiwan in 1949, and was renamed *Hsueh Feng*. Rearmed in 1954 with 2–120mm (2×1) and 2–40mm (2×1) ex-Japanese guns – having been disarmed since Aug 1945. Renamed *Cheng An* in the late 1950s and deleted in 1963.

Kaibokan Type C class
Hsin An was rearmed with 2–76mm (2×1) and 6–25mm (6×1) but was wrecked on 26.9.54 in the Pescadores Islands. Laid up non-operational and renamed *Chang An*, and hulked c1960. *Chao An* was rearmed with 2–76mm (2×1) and 2–40mm (2×1) and deleted in 1963 as was *Jui An* which had been rearmed with 2–120mm (2×1), 1–76mm and 8-MG. *Liao Hai* was rearmed as in data and assigned to the Army. She was hulked and renamed *Tsing Hai* c1960 or possibly earlier.

Kaibokan Type D class
Cheng An and *Tai An* rearmed with 2–120mm (2×1), 11–20mm and 2-MG. Served as gunboats till deletion in 1963. *Tung An* never rearmed. The 4 Communist units armed with 2–76mm US Mk 26 (2×1), 8–37mm (8×1), 4/8–25mm (4×1 or 4×2) in 1955, all extant 1982, 2 each with N and E Sea Fleets.

ASIA

GUNBOATS

Name	Launched	Disp (std)	Fate
YI HSIEN (ex-*Yat Sen*, ex-*Atada*)	12.11.30	1520t	To Taiwan 1949, deleted 1960s
Chiang Chen class CHIANG YUAN	1905	550t	To PRC 1949, deleted 1963
Chu class CHU KUAN	1907	740t	To Taiwan 1949, deleted 1960s
CHU TUNG	1906	740t	To PRC 1949, deleted 1960s
Ming Cheun class MING CHEUN	1929	420t	To PRC 1949, extant 1982
Yung Chien class YUNG CHI (ex-*Hsai Hsing*, ex-*Asuga*, ex-*Yung Chi*)	1915	860t	To PRC 1949, deleted *c*1970
Yung Feng class YUNG HSIANG	1912	830t	To Taiwan 1949, deleted 1950s
Yung Sui class YUNG SUI	1929	650t	To PRC 1949, deleted 1970s

These were the only large ships left of the pre-1937 Navy. The sloop size *Yi Hsien* was the prewar *Yat Sen* retaken from the Japanese at Shanghai 25.8.46. In the early 1950s her Japanese poop deck was removed and she was refitted as a TS which she remained until deletion. Her post-1946 armament was 1–120mm, 1–76mm, 4–40mm (2×2), 5–25mm and 6–77mm MG. Radar and sonar were fitted. *Ming Cheun* was first renamed *Hsien Ning* then *Chang Chiang* by the Communist Navy. *Yung Chi* and *Yung Sui* were sunk by Communist forces in the Yangtze in April 1949 and salved by them.

RIVER GUNBOATS

Name	Launched	Disp (std)	Fate
Ex-British Peterel class YING SHAN (ex-*Gannet*)	10.11.27	310t	To PRC 1949, deleted 1960s
Falcon class YING TEH (ex-*Lung Huan*, ex-*Falcon*)	18.5.31	354t	To PRC 1949 deleted 1960s
Sandpiper class YING HAO (ex-*Sandpiper*)	9.6.33	185t	To PRC 1949 deleted 1960s
Ex-US Wake class TAI YUAN (ex-*Tatara*, ex-*Wake*, ex-*Guam*)	28.5.27	370t	To PRC 1949, deleted 1960s
MEI YUAN (ex-*Tutuila*)	14.6.27	370t	To PRC 1949 deleted 1960s

All except *Tai Yuan* were transferred to the Chinese Navy by the RN and USN at Chungking in February 1942. *Tai Yuan* had been captured by the Japanese at Shanghai on 8.12.41 and renamed *Tatara*; she was handed back in 1946. *Lung Huan* was renamed *Ying Teh* in 1948.

There were also *Wei Ning*, a 400t customs vessel launched in 1934, captured by the Japanese in 1937 and renamed *Bunsei*; she was recaptured by the Chinese in 1945, given back her original name, and used as a patrol boat. She was sunk in 1949 and salved by the Communists, being deleted in the 1950s. *Ku Ai 102* was a German-built 60t MTB, launched in 1937, taken over by the Communists in 1949 and deleted in the 1960s.

Ex-Japanese SUBMARINE CHASERS

Name	Acquired	Disp (std)	Fate
Ch 28 class launched 1943 YAI LUNG (ex-*Ch 49*)	3.10.47	420t	To Taiwan 1949, renamed *Hai Hung* then *Chu Chiang* deleted 1964
Cha 1 class KAO MING (ex-*Cha 220*)	Aug 1945	130t	To PRC 1949,
KUANG KUO (ex-*Cha 223*)	1947	130t	To PRC 1949

Ch 7 class launched 1938 FU LING (ex-*Ch 9*)	3.10.47	291t	*Hai Ta* 1948, to Taiwan renamed *Min Chiang*, deleted 1960s

Ex-Japanese COASTAL MINESWEEPERS

Name	Acquired	Fate	
Natsushima class launched 1914 CHIEH 29 (ex-*Kuroshima*)	14.11.47	450t	To Taiwan 1949, BU *c*1960
Wa 1 class launched 1942–43 No 200 (ex-*Wa 4*)	3.10.47	215t	To PRC 1949, deleted 1976
No 201 (ex-*Wa 14*)	3.10.47	215t	To PRC 1949, deleted 1976
No 202 (ex-*Wa 19*)	3.10.47	215t	To Taiwan 1949, renamed *Chiang Yung*, deleted *c*1970,
No 203 (ex-*Wa 22*)	3.10.47	215t	To Taiwan 1949, renamed *Chiang*, deleted *c*1970

Ex-Italian MINELAYER

Name	Acquired	Disp (std)	Fate
Ostia class launched 1927 HSIEN NING (ex-*Okitsu*, (ex-*Lepanto*)	1945	615t	To Taiwan 1949, deleted 1956

Ex-Axis RIVER GUNBOATS

Name	Acquired	Disp (std)	Fate
Italian launched 1918 KIANG KUN (ex-*Narumi*, ex-*Ermanno Carlotto*)	1946	180t	To PRC 1949, deleted 1960s
Japanese launched 1911 YANG CH'I (ex-*Toba*)	1945	250t	To PRC 1949, deleted 1960s
Japanese launched 1922 AN TUNG (ex-*Ataka*)	1945	725t	To PRC 1949, deleted 1970s
CHANG TEH (ex-*Seta*)	1945	305t	To PRC 1949, deleted 1960s
Atami class launched 1929 YUNG PING (ex-*Atami*)	1945	206t	To PRC 1949, deleted 1960s
YUNG AN (ex-*Futami*)	1945	206t	To PRC 1949, deleted 1960s
Fushima class launched 1939 KIANG SHIH (ex-*Fushima*)	1946	320t	To PRC 1949, renamed *Chiang Feng*, deleted 1960s then *Fu Chiang*
NAN CHANG (ex-*Sumida*)	1946	320t	To PRC 1949, deleted 1960s
Ex-Portuguese Macau class launched 1909 WU FENG (ex-*Maiko*, ex-*Macau*)	1946	95t	To PRC 1949, deleted 1960s
Hashidate class launched 1939 CHANG CHI (ex-*Uji*)	1945	999t	To PRC 1949

Hashidate class
Chang Chi renamed *Nan Chang* (53/224) and rearmed in 1950s with 2–130mm (2×1) *Gordyy* class destroyer guns and 6–37mm (6×1). Extant 1982 with E Sea Fleet.

Ex-Japanese LANDING SHIP

Name	Acquired	Disp (std)	Fate
T 103 class launched 1944 LU SHAN (ex-*T-172*)	3.10.47	887t	To Taiwan 1949, wrecked and BU *c*1954-55

Ex-Japanese MINELAYER

Name	Acquired	Disp (std)	Fate
Hirashima class launched 1941			
YUNG CHING (ex-*Saishu*)	3.10.47	720t	To Taiwan 1949, BU 1964

Hirashima class
Yung Ching was soon rearmed with 1–105mm, 1–40mm, 7–25mm, 1–20mm and 120 mines. At first classified as light minelayer, as before, but by 1953 reclassified as a frigate. This indicated the shortage of suitable frigates in the early 1950s.

MAJOR SURFACE SHIPS

Ex-British ARETHUSA class *cruiser*

Name	Builder	Launched	Acquired	Fate
CHUNG KING (ex-*Aurora*)	Portsmouth DY	20.8.36	19.5.48	To PRC 1949

The ex-RN cruiser *Aurora* was sold to China, fetched by a crew of 682, and defected to the Communists in Shanghai on 2.3.49 when she was renamed *Huang Ho*. The Nationalists claimed to have sunk her at Taku with bombers but she was salved and recommissioned by late 1951 undergoing another name change (allegedly) *Pei Ching*. China's largest warship was laid up *c*1954. BU in 1960s.

Ex-British 'HUNT' class (Type 1) *frigate*

Name	Builder	Launched	Acquired	Fate
LIN FU (ex-*Mendip*)	Swan Hunter, Wallsend	9.4.40	19.5.48	Returned to RN 27.5.49

Former RN wartime escort destroyer, with Type 285 and 290 radar, rerated AA frigate (F 160) in 1947, transferred to China for eight years but returned to RN at Hong Kong due to the Nationalist collapse on the mainland. Then transferred to Egypt as *Mohamed Ali El Kebir*. See under Egypt.

Ex-US 'DET' class *destroyer escorts*

Class (no, former name/no):
Tai Chao (ex-*Carter*, DE 112), *Tai Ho* (ex-*Thomas*, DE 102), *Tai Hu* (ex-*Breeman*, DE 104), *Tai Tsang* (25, ex-*Bostwick*, DE 103)
   Four ex-USN 'long hull' destroyer escorts, all handed over on 31.12.48. All sailed to Taiwan in 1949. *Tai Chao* and *Tai Tsang* deleted in 1973, *Tai Ho* in 1972 and *Tai Hu* in 1975.

AMPHIBIOUS WARFARE VESSELS

Ex-US LST class *tank landing ships*

At least 30 were transferred from the USN to China during 1946–48; 11 went to Taiwan including *Chung Shu* (ex-LST 520), and 16 to the Communists. In 1982 the latter were deployed as follows: *341–343* and *901–903* (Luda, N Sea), *921–926* (Shanghai, E Sea), *351* and *355* Canton, S Sea). In addition, the repair ship *Hsing An* (ex-USS *Achilles*, APL 41, ex-*LST 455*) was transferred in Sept 1947. She became the Communist *Taku Shan*, after salvage following grounding and fire in 1949. Taiwan units rebuilt late 1960s and all extant 1982, See under Taiwan. Two mainland LSTs transferred to N Vietnam as tankers, others used as merchantmen or fitted with RL.

Ex-US LSM class *medium landing ships*

About 30 were transferred from the USN to China during 1946–48; 15 went to the Communists and 11 to Taiwan. *Mei Lo* (ex-*LSM 157*) damaged by Communist gunfire and beached on Quemoy Island, 8.9.58. All 15 mainland (some merchantmen and most minelayers) and two of the Taiwan LSMs were extant in 1982. Mainland deployments in 1982: *394–396* (N Sea), *511* and *931–936* (E Sea), *352–354* and *393* (S Sea).

Ex-US LCT (5) and LCT (6) *tank landing craft*

More than 15 of these two classes were transferred from the USN during 1946–48. Built between 1942–43. The LCT(6) were modified versions of the LCT(5) with the bridge offset to starboard and bow and stern loading. Ten or eleven went to the Communists and 6 to Taiwan. At least 6–8 LCT(6) mainland units and 6 Taiwan craft (reclassified as LCU) were still extant in 1982.

Ex-US LCI class *landing craft*

About 25 USN LCI of various types, including at least seven LCI(G) and an LCI(M) were transferred to China during 1946–48. All built 1943–45. Fourteen, including at least three LCI(G), went to the People's Republic (some fitted with RL or minesweeping gear) and five to Taiwan, including an LCI(M) and four LCI(G). Four mainland ships are still extant in 1982.

SMALL SURFACE COMBATANTS

Ex-US PC (173ft) class *submarine chasers*

Class (former no):
Chien Fang (ex-*PC 1549*), *Huang Pu* (ex-*PC 492*), *Hung Tse* (ex-*PGM 26*, ex-*PC 1557*), *Kung Kiang* (ex-*PC 1233*), *Kan Tang* (ex-*PGM 15*, ex-*PC 1091*), *Chialing* (ex-*PC 1247*), *Pao Ying* (ex-*PGM 20*, ex-*PC 1551*), *Tung Ting* (ex-*PGM 13*, ex-*PC 1089*), *Wu Sung* (ex-*PC 490*), ? (ex-*PC 593*), ? (ex-*PC 595*), ? (ex-*PC 598*), ? (ex-*PGM 12*, ex-*PC 1088*), ? (ex-*PGM 14*, ex-*PC 1090*)
   Fourteen transferred to the Chinese Navy between 1946 and 1949, six of which had been rebuilt 1944–45 as PGM type gunboats. The PGMs had 1–60mm mortar and RLs in addition to guns, and the PCs had differing numbers of light AA guns. The first 11 except *Kan Tang* went to Taiwan in 1949, and the other four were taken over by the Communists. Three were deleted in the 1970s but one is still in service in 1982 as a S Sea Fleet training ship rearmed with 2–76mm (2×1) and 3–37mm (3×1). Taiwan fates and numbers were as follows: *Chien Fang* and *Wu Sung* deleted 1951–52, ex-*PC 598* deleted 1954, *Tung Ting* sunk by Communist torpedo boats 10.1.55, *Pao Ying* renamed *Ying Chiang* so badly torpedoed 20.1.55 that BU, ex-*PC 593* deleted 1955, *Hung Tse* and *Chialing* (renamed *To Kiang*, 104) deleted 1964, *Kung Kiang* (113) and *Huang Pu* (105, renamed *Fu Kiang*) deleted *c*1970.

Ex-US SC (110ft) class *submarine chasers*

Ten transferred 1946–49, ex-*SC 518*, ex-*SC 637*, ex-*SC 648*, ex-*SC 698* (renamed *Chu Chien 103*), ex-*SC 703*, ex-*SC 708* (*Chu Chien*, 102), ex-*SC 722*, ex-*SC 722*, ex-*SC 723*, ex-*SC 735*. All sailed to Taiwan and all deleted *c*1970 except *101 Chu Chien c*1955.

Ex-British *harbour defence motor launches*

Eight ex-RN HDMLs were transferred to China after World War II. They were named *Fang 1–8* (ex-*ML 1033*, *1047*, *1058*, *1059*, *1068*, *1390*, *1405* and *1406* respectively). They went to Taiwan in 1949. *Fang 3* and *Fang 8* were sunk in 1950 and the remainder were deleted *c*1970.

MINE WARFARE VESSELS

Ex-US ADMIRABLE class *minesweepers*

Class (former name/no, transferred):
Yung Ning (ex-*Magnet*/AM 260, Aug 1945), *Yung Sheng* (ex-*Lance*/AM 257, Aug 1945), *Yung Shun* (ex-*Logic*/AM 258, Aug 1945), *Yung Ting* (ex-*Lucid*/AM 259, Aug 1945), *Yung Chun* (ex-*Gavia*/AM 363, May 1946), *Yung Feng* (ex-*Prime*/AM 279, May 1946), *Yung Ho* (ex-*Delegate*/AM 217, May 1946), *Yung Hsing* (ex-*Embattle*/AM 226, May 1946), *Yung Kang* (ex-*Elusive*/AM 225), *Yung Chang* (ex-*Refresh*/AM 287, June 1948), *Yung Chia* (ex-*Implicit*/AM 246, June 1948), *Yung Hsiu* (ex-*Pinnacle*/AM 274, June 1948), ? (ex-*Nimble*/AM 266, June 1948), ? (ex-*Reform*/AM 286, June 1948), ? (ex-*Phantom*/AM 273, June 1948), *Yung Shou* (ex-*Pivot*/AM 276, Aug 1948)
   Last two PCE type gunboats. All 16 sailed to Taiwan 1949. Three, ? ex-USS *Nimble* (AM 266), ? ex-USS *Reform* (AM 286) and ? ex-USS *Phantom* (AM 273) were deleted almost immediately. Eight remained as minesweepers. Of these, one, *Yung Ting*, ex-USS *Lucid* (AM 259) was renamed *Yung Ming* in 1964 and later converted into a survey ship. She was deleted in 1976. Two more, *Yung Hsing* (ex-USS *Embattle*/AM 226) and *Yung Chia* (ex-USS *Implicit*/AM 246) were converted into coastguard vessels (early 1970s) and are still in service in 1982. The former was renamed *Hung Hsing*. Of the five other minesweepers, *Yung Ning* (ex-USS *Magnet*/AM 260) was deleted in 1963 and *Yung Hsiu* (ex-USS *Pinnacle*/AM 274), *Yung Sheng* (ex-USS *Lance*/AM 257), *Yung Shou* (ex-USS *Pivot*/AM 276) and *Yung Shun* (ex-USS *Logic*/AM 258) were deleted in the early 1970s. One, *Yung Feng* (ex-USS *Prime*/AM 279) was converted into a coastal minelayer. She was deleted *c*1970. The other four were converted into gunboats with 6–40mm (3×2) and 1–76mm. *Yung Chang* (ex-USS *Refresh*/AM 287) was sunk by a Communist escort off the South China coast on 14.11.65. *Yung Ho* (ex-USS *Delegate*/AM 217) and *Yung Kang* (ex-USS *Elusive*/AM 225) were scrapped in 1964 and *Yung Chun* (ex-USS *Gavia*/AM 363) was deleted *c*1970. The two ex-USN PCE class gunboats (which differ from the *Admirable* class mainly by not having minesweeping gear aft) were fitted with a second 76mm gun aft in 1955. *Yung Tai* (ex-USS

PCE 867) was damaged in action with Communist escorts off the South China coast on 14.11.65 and was deleted soon after. *Yung Hsiang* (ex-USS *PCE 869*) was renamed *Wei Yuan*, and was deleted *c*1970.

Ex-US YMS type *motor minesweepers*

Five ex-USN units transferred to the Chinese in 1948. Ex-*YMS 339, 346, 367* and *393* were built in 1942–43 for the USN, but ex-*YMS 2017* (ex-*YMS 17*) had served with the RN 1943–45. All were taken over by the People's Republic in 1949; ex-*YMS 339* was deleted in 1963 and the remainder in 1976.

China

PEOPLE'S REPUBLIC

The People's Republic of China was proclaimed at Peking on 1 October 1949; a 30-year mutual assistance pact was signed with the Soviet Union in February 1950, and in the same year the Chinese Red Army intervened in Korea and Indo-China and occupied Tibet and Hainan Island. Also in 1950 an attempt was made to invade Taiwan's island outpost of Quemoy, but this was foiled by the intervention of the US Navy. The United States introduced a 'no trade' policy with China, blocked the Republic's admission to the UN and ensured that no Western power recognised her. The Korean War ended in 1953, and by 1958 China had recovered sufficiently to try to take Quemoy, only to be stopped once again by the US Navy presence. Since then the only major actions fought by the People's Republic have been frontier disputes with India (1962), the Soviet Union (1966 onwards) and Vietnam (1977 onwards and especially 1979) and a continuing struggle for the islands in the South China Sea. The Navy has only been involved in the latter two, notably in the capture of the South Vietnamese Paracel Islands (January 1974). In addition, there have been clashes with the Taiwan Navy at odd intervals throughout the past three decades.

Between 1948 and 1950 the People's Republic acquired approximately half the combat vessels of the old Chinese Navy, either by their crews defecting or by capturing them in port or on the Yangtze. In January 1950 the Fleet comprised a cruiser, 7 frigates, 21 escorts, 5 minesweepers, 13 river gunboats, 6 patrol boats and about 60 landing vessels. Most of these ships were in bad condition and the larger ex-Japanese vessels were disarmed. In addition, the Kuomintang forces did their best to sink as many Communist ships as possible: their air force had a number of successes, including the sinking of the only cruiser almost immediately after she had defected. None of the larger ex-USN vessels defected, though large numbers of ex-USN small craft and landing vessels were acquired. Ships were patched up or salved and returned to service and a number of ex-British and Canadian vessels which had been demilitarised after World War II and sold to Chinese owners were rearmed and returned to service, but it was not until the mid-1950s that a serious effort could be made to get the ships fit for operational service.

SOVIET AID 1950–60

Although China has the largest population (and second largest land area) of any state in the world, in 1950 she was seriously underdeveloped industrially, quite apart from the after-effects of almost four decades of political confusion and civil war. What was urgently needed was foreign assistance. Despite the mutual assistance pact signed in 1950, the Soviet Union was herself so weakened by World War II and its aftermath that it was not until three years later that she could provide the Chinese with the kind of help they needed. As well as over 2500 trained staff, the Soviets provided machinery and equipment to rebuild China's shattered shipyards, and destroyers, submarines and small craft to build up the Navy. At first these were obsolescent vessels dating from the early years of World War II, but by the end of the decade new ships had been transferred and more were being built in Chinese yards. The first examples were assembled from parts made in the USSR, but gradually the Chinese yards built entire warships by themselves. Mid-1950s Soviet transfers totalled 4 destroyers, 13 submarines, 12 large patrol craft, 2 minesweepers and about 50 MTBs.

Ideological differences combined with Chinese distrust of the Soviet Union, which they felt was trying to take over China, led to a split that started in the late 1950s and culminated in the withdrawal of Soviet technicians in 1960. Militarily, this was a disaster for the Chinese. Although some aid did continue for a time, this eventually dried up,

Destroyer *Anshan* on training cruise 14.7.80   *Xinhua News Agency*

and the Navy was still in no condition to stand on its own feet. The problem was made worse by the failure of the 'Great Leap Forward' in 1958 and the first drive for industrialisation in 1961–62. The Navy went on building its existing Soviet warship designs, but these were already becoming outdated.

THE CULTURAL REVOLUTION

The ultimate disaster for the Chinese Navy was the Cultural Revolution that started in 1966. This cut off the People's Republic almost completely from other countries and dissipated her trained manpower. Development became almost impossible, and industrial production slumped. A number of new warships derived from Soviet designs were built from 1965, but much of their equipment was seriously out of date. This applied particularly to electronics, and, despite the acquisition of modern Soviet and US equipment as a result of the Vietnam War, little progress was made, partly because the trained development engineers were not allowed to do their jobs without serious interference.

THE FOUR MODERNISATIONS

An unexpected by-product of the Vietnam War was the rapprochement with the United States. The latter wished to find some end to her problems in South-East Asia, and a friendly China which was also hostile to the Soviet Union was the best solution. Talks started between the two countries in 1971 and in October of that year the People's Republic took her seat in the UN. Benefits to China from this friendship have included the US recognition of the People's Republic rather than the Republic of China in Taiwan as the Government of China in 1978 and access to US technology, including since 1980 military technology.

The four modernisations, announced in 1975, included that of industry and of the armed forces. As in the first drive for modernisation a decade and a half earlier, too much was attempted too soon, and much less has been achieved than was hoped. The only major new warship type in service is the nuclear-powered attack submarine, which is still experimental, and much of the Navy remains out of date by Western standards. Sufficient funds have not been available to buy new ship types and equipment from abroad. However, some improvements have been made: communications equipment is beginning to be refined and some of the rest of the electronics are being updated.

ORGANISATION AND ROLE

The Navy of the People's Republic of China is part of the People's Liberation Army (PLA), and comes under the PLA's high command, although in practice it is normally left to take its own decisions. It is divided into three fleets: the North Sea Fleet (*c*500 ships), HQ at Tsingtao with eight other Yellow Sea bases; the East Sea Fleet (*c*750 ships), based at Shanghai with a quarter of China's shipyards and seven other bases including four opposite Taiwan; and the South Sea Fleet (*c*600 ships), based at Chan Chiang with four other bases including two on Hainan. Most of the major surface ships and two submarine squadrons are in the Northern Fleet, whilst the South Sea Fleet is mainly composed of small craft with one submarine squadron of 25 boats. Most ships stay in the same fleet all the time, though there are occasional movements for special purposes. The sailors, almost all Party members, serve the longest PLA conscription term, five years, and pay is 10 per cent higher than the Army. Naval manpower totalled 284,000 in 1982 excluding 38,000 each for coast defence and the naval air arm which is the third largest naval air force in the world, with about 872 land-based aircraft. This suffers from the same defects as the Navy itself, with obsolete aircraft that compare very badly with those of surrounding countries.

The Chinese Navy has always been primarily a coast defence force. For the first two decades after the creation of the People's Republic, the major threat came from the power of the US Seventh Fleet, which twice prevented the PLA and the Navy from seizing the islands of Quemoy and Matsu, and which was able to cruise virtually with impunity off the Chinese coast. Since the early 1960s the Soviet Pacific Fleet has also become a possible threat and there has always been a danger of invasion from Taiwan if Chinese internal problems were to give the Nationalists enough hope of being able to take advantage of them. Therefore the Chinese Navy is composed principally of light craft and submarines, with a large force of fixed-wing aircraft and a powerful coast defence component of the PLA armed with guns and missiles backing them up. Until recently large surface warships have been much less important, but the discovery of offshore oil and the need to control the Paracels and other islands in the South China Sea have meant a reappraisal of their role.

The spectacular growth of the Chinese merchant fleet (300 ships bought and 100 built worth 4 million grt in the 1970s) and the use of warships for showing the flag in the last decade have also had their effect in changing the emphasis of the Navy. The last five years have seen a much wider deployment of major ships and the start of refuelling at sea with a small fleet train. Perhaps the most surprising gap, given China's claim to rule Taiwan, is the absence of a major amphibious capability. This is because the People's Republic has never seriously considered mounting an opposed landing on Taiwan, being content to wait for political rather than military developments. Moreover, the omnipresent US Seventh Fleet has made a successful operation impossible, so there was little point in wasting very scarce resources preparing for it.

THE FUTURE

The new access to advanced Western technology (Britain signed a £100 million Sea Dart missile, radar and electronics contract in November 1982, but the Central Committee then cancelled it) is likely to bring considerable changes to the Navy, but the weakness of the country's economy means that any change will be gradual. The Navy has been very good at keeping old ships operational, so existing vessels are likely to remain in service for many more years. Modern ASW sensors and AA missiles are urgent necessities, and are likely to be obtained in the very near future. A new type of missile fast attack craft is very probable, and new submarines are already being built. In another decade, the Navy of the Chinese People's Republic may really be as powerful as its numerical strength might mislead one to believe that it is now.

MAJOR SURFACE SHIPS

Ex-Soviet Type 7 destroyers

Other particulars: See 1922–46 volume
Armament: 4–130mm (4×1), 4 SS-N-2 SSM (2×2), 8–37mm (4×2), 60 mines. See notes
Sensors: Radar Cross Bird, Square Tie, Mina, Neptune; Sonar hull mounted
Complement: c200

No	Name	Builder	Acquired	Fate
101	ANSHAN (ex-*Razyaschy*)	Dalzavod, Nikolayev	1954–55	Extant 1982
102	CHANG CHUN (ex-*Reshitelny*)	Dalzavod, Nikolayev	1954–55	Extant 1982
103	CHI LIN (ex-*Retivy*)	Komsomolsk, Nikolayev	1954–55	Extant 1982
104	FU CHUN (ex-*Rezky*)	Komsomolsk Nikolayev	1954–55	Extant 1982

Two transferred in Dec 1954 and two in July 1955. Until 1971 armed with 4–130mm (4×1), 2–76mm (1×2), 4–37mm (4×1), 1–20mm and 6–533mm TT (2×3). Then during 1971–74 all had their TT replaced by twin SSM launchers and the single 37mm by twin mountings. This made them more effective, but their weapons and sensors are still obsolescent and their hulls, despite being very well maintained, are old even by Chinese standards. As they were lightly built, it is a tribute to the Navy that they have kept them in operation for so long, but they must soon be taken out of service. Current maximum speed is about 30kts, originally 37kts.

'Luta' 106 in 1980   *Courtesy Ross Gillett*

'Luta' class

'LUTA' class destroyers

Displacement:	3250t standard; 3750t full load
Dimensions:	430ft oa × 45ft × 15ft 131m × 13.7m × 4.6m
Machinery:	2-shaft geared steam turbines, 4 boilers, 60,000shp = c32kts. Oil ? t. Range 3200nm/4000nm at 18kts/15kts
Armament:	6 SS-N-2 SSM (2×3), 4–130mm (2×2), 8–57mm (4×2), 4–25mm (2×2), 2-FQF 2500 ASW RL, 2/4 DCT, 2 DC racks, mines
Sensors:	Radar Cross Slot, Wasp Head, Post Lamp, Square Tie, Neptune; sonar ?; ECM 2 Watch Dog
Complement:	c300

No	Builder	Laid down	Comp	Fate
105 (ex-240)	Lushun	c1966	1971	Extant 1982
106	Lushun	1968	1972	Extant 1982
107	Lushun	1968	1972	Extant 1982
108	Lushun	1969	1973	Extant 1982
109	Lushun		1974	Extant 1982
131	Lushun	1970	1974	Extant 1982
132	Lushun	1970	1975	Extant 1982
161		1971	1975	Extant 1982
162		1977	1980	Extant 1982
163			1980	Extant 1982
164			1980	Extant 1982
165			1981	Extant 1982

Similar to but slightly larger than the earlier Soviet 'Kotlin' class destroyers, armed with SSMs in place of the Kotlins' anti-ship torpedoes. Production (launch dates not known) appears to have been cut back in 1971 for political reasons, but in any case hull design, weapons and sensors compare very badly with contemporary destroyers, or even with Taiwan's refitted US World War II ships. The largest warships built in China since 1945, the 'Lutas' are her only truly ocean-going surface warships. They have recently been observed engaging in underway replenishment exercises. They are almost equally divided between the N and S Sea fleets. Some have 37mm in place of 57mm guns. ASW RL

12-barrel derivatives of Soviet RBU-1200. One unit lost by explosion near Zanjiang Aug 1978. 'Lutas' *105–107, 131, 132, 160* and *162* deployed to the C Pacific (Gilberts and Ellices) in May 1980. Eight were to have been modernised in China with operations room and Sea Dart SAM by British Aerospace and Vosper Thornycroft.

'Kiang Tung' class

'KIANG TUNG' ('JIANGDONG') class *frigates*

Displacement:	1800t standard; 2200t full load
Dimensions:	337ft 9in oa × 39ft 4in × 13ft 2in *103m × 12.8m × 4.3m*
Machinery:	2 shafts, 2 Pielstick diesels; 24,000hp = 28kts. Range 4000nm at 15kts
Armament:	4 SAM (2×2), 4–100mm (2×2), 8–37mm (4×2), 2-MBU 1800 ASW RL, 2 DCT, 2 DC rails
Sensors:	Radar ?
Complement:	195

No	Name	Builder	Launched	Fate
531	CHUNG TUNG (*Zhongdong*)	Hutong, Shanghai	1973	Extant 1982
532	?	Hutong, Shanghai	1974	Extant 1982

This class, also spelt 'Jiangdong', utilises an enlarged 'Riga'-type hull, with two large diesels (one per shaft) instead of four small ones. Laid down in 1971 and 1972, they were an attempt to provide an AA escort, something the Chinese Fleet badly needs. However, the SAM system caused many problems and is not yet operational, although *Chung Tung* was completed in 1977 and her sister in 1979. It will probably be abandoned in favour of a Western system if China can obtain one. Subsequent vessels using the same hull have been completed as *Kiang Hu* class SSM armed frigates, and the two *Kiang Tung* class have been delayed by the extended trials with the SAM system.

'Kiang Hu' class

'KIANG HU' ('JIANGHU') class *frigates*

Other particulars:	As 'Kiang Tung' class
Armament:	4 SS-N-2 SSM (2×2), 4–100mm (2×2), 8–37mm (4×2) 2-MBU 1800 ASW RL
Sensors:	Radar Slim Net, Square Tie, Neptune

No	Builder	Launched	Comp	Fate
510	Jiangnan, Shanghai	1975	1976	Extant 1982
511	Jiangnan, Shanghai	1975	1975	Extant 1982
512	Jiangnan, Shanghai	1976	1977	Extant 1982
513	Jiangnan, Shanghai	1977	1978	Extant 1982
514	Jiangnan, Shanghai	1977	1978	Extant 1982
515	Jiangnan, Shanghai	1977	1978	Extant 1982
516	Jiangnan, Shanghai	1978	1979	Extant 1982
517	Jiangnan, Shanghai	1979	1980	Extant 1982
518	Jiangnan, Shanghai	1980	1981	Extant 1982

These use the same hull as the earlier 'Kiang Tung' class, the major difference being the mounting of SSM rather than SAM. First two laid down 1974, *512* in 1975, next three 1976 and one each for next 3 years. Useful general purpose escorts but their armament and sensors (no ECM) are obsolescent (only optical rangefinder for 100mm fire control), and AA armament is very weak by modern standards. Pennant numbers changed from *520–525* in 1979. At least two more being built.

Ch'eng Tu after 1970s reconstruction

Soviet 'RIGA' class *frigates*

No	Name	Builder	Launched	Fate
507	CH'ENG TU (*Chengdu*)	Hutung, Shanghai	28.4.56	Extant 1982
505	KUEI YANG (*Guiyang*)	Hutung, Shanghai	26.9.56	Extant 1982
508	KUEI LIN (*Gulin*)	Kuang Chu, Canton	1957	Extant 1982
506	K'UN MING (*Kunming*)	Kuang Chu, Canton	1957	Extant 1982

These ships were assembled from Soviet components in Chinese shipyards and were of the Soviet 'Riga' class design. First 3 laid down 1955, completed in pairs 1958 and 1959. Two were completed with modified superstructures. All later rebuilt with a larger bridge and lattice mast. As originally built, they had 3–37mm (3×1) with 3–533mm TT (1×3) abaft the funnel. From 1971 onward the TT were replaced by a twin SSM launcher and the AA armament was modified to 4–37mm (2×2). Although this eliminated some of the worst weaknesses from the armament, it is still very poor for a modern escort. The ASW armament of 4 DCT is particularly weak. All serve with the S Sea Fleet.

'Kiangnan' class

'KIANGNAN' ('JIANGNAN') class *frigates*

Displacement:	1350t standard; 1600t full load
Armament:	3–100mm (3×1), 8–37mm (4×2), 4–14.5mm (2×2), 2-MBU 1800 ASW RL, 4 DCT, 2 DC rails, fitted for minelaying
Sensors:	Radar Ball Gun, Wok Won, Neptune; Sonar ?
Other particulars:	As Soviet 'Riga' class

No	Builder	Laid down	Comp	Fate
209	Kiangnan, Shanghai	1965	1967	Extant 1982
214	Kiangnan, Shanghai	1965	1967	Extant 1982
231	Kiangnan, Shanghai	1966	1968	Extant 1982
232	Kuang Chu, Canton	1966	1968	Extant 1982
233	Kuang Chu, Canton	1967	1969	Extant 1982

The first major warships, also spelt as 'Jiangnan' and named after their Shanghai builders, to be designed and built in China since 1945, even though they are an adaptation of the Soviet 'Riga' class design. Only the first ship's launch date (Jan 1966) is known. They use the same machinery and basic hull form, but the forecastle has been raised and extends three-quarters the length of the ship. This gives more room for living space and equipment. The armament has been rearranged, with one 100mm gun forward and two aft. They are efficient ships, but their sensors are obsolescent and their AA surface and ASW armament are all weak. Unlike the 'Rigas', they were not built with TT so it would be more difficult to find room for SSMs to improve the surface armament. However, their armament is so weak compared with probable opponents that it is surprising that something has not been tried, particularly as one of the class engaged S Vietnamese warships in 1974. It may be that there is inadequate stability due to the enlarged forecastle to make such an alteration to the armament. Four are in S Sea Fleet, one with E Sea Fleet.

Ex-British 'CASTLE' class *frigates*

Several that had served in the Canadian Navy were sold as merchant ships to China in 1947. After the Communist takeover of the mainland two were rearmed, at much the same time as the Nationalists also rearmed two. The ex-mercantile SS *Shih Lin*, ex-mercantile SS *Hsi Ling*, ex-mercantile *Ta Tung* (all 1947), ex-HMCS *Coppercliff* (1944), ex-British *Hever Castle*; and the ex-mercantile SS *Yuan Pei*, ex-mercantile SS *Ta Shun* (both 1947) ex-HMCS *Bowmanville* (1944) ex-HMS *Nunnery Castle* were both rearmed with 2–130mm (2×1), 1–45mm and 5–37mm (5×1). One was renamed *Kuang Chou*, but the name of the other is not known. There is some doubt about which one was renamed *Kuang Chou*. The other ship was discarded in the 1960s but *Kuang Chou* (602) is still in service in 1982.

Ex-British 'FLOWER' class *frigates*

Name	Builder	Acquired	Fate
KAI FENG (ex-*Cloverlock*, ex-*Clover*)	Fleming & Ferguson, Paisley	1949	Extant 1982
LIN I (ex-*Ziang Teh*, ex-*Heliolock*, ex-*Surprise*, ex-*Heliotrope*)	Crown	1949	Deleted 1979
? (ex-*Maw Hwa*, ex-*Tenacity*, ex-*Candytuft*)	Grangemouth		

Several were sold as merchant ships to China by the RN after World War II. During the last stages of the 1949 struggle for mainland China two, or possibly three, of these were rearmed by the People's Republic. By the early 1950s *Kai Feng* (formerly the mercantile SS *Cloverlock* ex-HMS *Clover*) and *Lin I* (ex-mercantile SS *Ziang Teh*, ex-mercantile *Heliolock*, ex-USS *Surprise*, ex-British HMS *Heliotrope*) were armed with Soviet weapons. In 1974–75 *Kai Feng* 2–100mm (2×1), 1–45mm, 4–37mm (2×2), was disarmed and refitted as a survey ship in which form she is still in service in 1982. *Lin I*, 2–100mm (2×1), 2–37mm (2×1), was deleted in 1979. The mercantile SS *Maw Hwa*, ex-USS *Tenacity*, ex-British *Candytuft* may also have been rearmed, but if so she was no longer in service by the mid-1950s.

SUBMARINES

Ex-Soviet Series VI 'M IV' class *coastal submarine*

One (built 1933–34) was transferred from the Soviet Pacific Fleet *c* 1955. She was used for training (only 2–533mm TT and 18 crew) and deleted in 1963.

Ex-Soviet Series VI bis 'M II' class *coastal submarine*

Ex-*M 39* (ex-*M 53*), launched 1935, was transferred from the Soviet Pacific Fleet in 1955. Used for training and deleted 1963.

Ex-Soviet Series XV 'MV' class *coastal submarines*

Four of this late 1930s design (built 1946–47) transferred *c* 1955. They were numbered *M 200*, *M 201*, *M 202* and *M 203*. They were used mainly for training. *M 200* was deleted in 1963 but the other three survived until the late 1970s. None remain in service.

Ex-Soviet SHCH class *submarines*

Four of these late 1930s units transferred in 1954–55. Their design was out of date when they were first built, and by the mid-1950s they were totally obsolete. All deleted in 1963.

Ex-Soviet Series IX bis STALINETZ class *submarines*

Class (former name):
S 400 (ex-*S 51*), *S 401* (ex-*S 52*), *S 402* (ex-*S 53*), and *S 403* (ex-*S 57*). Four transferred 1955. Launched 1939–40 by Dalzavod Yd, Vladivostok. Obsolete when transferred, but all remained in service until the 1970s. One is still in existence as a stationary harbour training boat.

Soviet 'WHISKEY' class *submarines*

Class:
119, 120, 122, 123, 127, 129, 131, 201–207, 221, 241, 243, 244, 265–267
Several transferred in the mid-1950s. The USSR supplied components for 5 more to be assembled in Chinese shipyards until eventually the Chinese built the entire submarine. A total of 21 entered service during 1956–64, most being built at Kiang Chou, Canton or Kiangnan, Shanghai. They are now obsolete. One was deleted in 1979 and several more are no longer operational and are used as harbour instruction boats. The rest of the class will probably be taken out of service in the near future.

Soviet 'ROMEO' class *submarines*

Class:
126, 140, 142, 143, 153, 172, 176, 208–212, 227–229, 245, 248, 249, 254, 267–270, 281–283 (plus 52 others)
Four supplied by the USSR prior to the Sino-Soviet split and between the early 1960s and late 1970s a further 67 have been built at the rate of 9 a year in the

Chinese 'Romeo' class 24.8.71   *Xinhua News Agency*

Kiang Chou, Canton and Kiangnan, Shanghai shipyards. Six of these Chinese-built 'Romeos' were transferred to N Korea, (1973–75) which is now building more of them. Another 2 went to Egypt (1982). When it first entered service the 'Romeo' class was a competent – if noisy – attack submarine, but it is now obsolete and very vulnerable to modern ASW vessels. Later Chinese-built 'Romeos' were built to a slightly modified design, but this is not much better. 'Romeos' form the bulk of China's submarine force. Now succeeded in production by the slightly enlarged 'Ming' class.

Soviet 'GOLF' class *strategic submarine*

The design for this Soviet submarine were supplied to China prior to the expulsion of the Soviet advisers in 1960, but although *200* was completed at Luda in 1964 with the three vertical tubes for SLBMs at the aft end of the conning tower the SLBMs themselves were not provided. China has not developed its own SLBM, so this submarine has always operated as an attack submarine, with an armament consisting entirely of torpedoes. Had the Sino-Soviet split occurred a few years later than it did, it is likely that SLBMs would have been supplied and that more of this type would have been built. An unnamed 'Golf' submarine was reported lost off China in Aug 1981 after a missile explosion during an 'underwater test firing'. The original 'Golf' SLBM was a surface only weapon.

'HAN' class *nuclear attack submarines*

Class (completed):
1701 (1974), *1702* (1977)
Experimental SSNs. They are the first nuclear powered vessels built (by Luta, Huludao SY) in China (*1701* was laid down in 1971–72), and are also the first submarines to be designed in China. They have an *Albacore*-type teardrop hull. Neither is operational, but they may presage future SSN developments. Considerable help was received from W Germany in the design of the nuclear reactor. Both boats extant 1982 with N Sea Fleet. A SSBN was reportedly launched by the same yard in April 1981.

'MING' class *attack submarines*

Displacement:	1500t surface; 1900t submerged
Dimensions:	*c* 250ft oa
	76m
Machinery:	2 shafts, 2 diesel-electric motors = 17kts; 15kts
Armament:	6–533mm TT
Sensors:	Sonar

Class (launched):
232 (1975), *233*

Slightly enlarged and improved versions of the Chinese-built 'Romeos'. The first unit was laid down in 1971–82. They share many of the faults of their predecessors, and are an obsolescent design. Since an improved hull form was used in the nuclear powered 'Han' class, it is surprising that it was not also used for these boats. Probably the improved 'Romeo' design was adopted for ease of production. It is also possible that the 'Han' class took up so much design effort that a relatively simple 'Romeo'-development was all that could be managed. Both extant 1982 with N Sea Fleet. More may well be built.

AMPHIBIOUS WARFARE VESSELS

YU LING class *medium landing ships*

About 10 of this 1500t, 250ft design have been built since 1971. Enlarged versions of US World War II LSMs.

YUKAN class *tank landing ships*

Class:
927, 928, 929, 934
New 1000t, 213ft (*65m*) class with 8–25mm (4×2) and Neptune radar. First unit completed at Shanghai in 1980.

YUNNAN class *utility landing craft*

Displacement:	133.2t full load
Dimensions:	90ft 2in oa × 78ft 9in × 17ft 8in × 4ft 6in
	27.5m, 24m × 5.4m × 1.4m
Machinery:	2 shafts, 2 diesels = 10kts
Armament:	2/4–14.5mm MG (1 or 2×2)
Complement:	6

Class:
3313, 3321, 3344, 5526, 7566, 7588 and many more.

Hangzhou Yd built 300 during 1968–72 and all are extant 1982. The 49ft × 13ft (*15m × 4m*) cargo deck can hold 46t or a tank. A stubbier 100t LCU *7568* was seen at Canton in April 1980.

SMALL SURFACE COMBATANTS

Ex-Australian BATHURST class *ocean minesweeper (escort)*

No	Name	Builder	Acquired	Fate
53/ 220	LOYANG (ex-*Cheung Hing*, ex-*Bendigo*)	Cockatoo D Yd	1949	Extant 1982

This ex-RAN minesweeper (launched 1.3.41) was sold on 5.5.47 and became the Chinese mercantile *Cheung Hing*. The Communist forces took her over and reconverted her from a merchant ship. She was originally rearmed with 2–130mm (2×1) and 2–37mm (2×1) but has since been fitted with 2–100mm (2×1) and 4–37mm (2×2). She is classed as an escort and serves with E Sea Fleet.

Chinese 'Osa' class 15.12.79   *Xinhua News Agency*

Ex-British 'ISLES' class *patrol trawlers*

Two which had been disarmed and sold to Chinese owners in 1946 for mercantile work were taken over by Communist forces and rearmed with 1–76mm and 3–20mm in 1949–51. Ex-HMS *Hoxa* (launched 15.1.41) became the mercantile SS *Sung Hwei* in 1946. The other may have been HMS *Balta* which became the mercantile SS *Ching Hai* on 12.7.46. One ex-Canadian *Basset* class patrol trawler (dimensionally identical to the 'Isles' class) was also rearmed. This was either SS *Sung Ming* (ex-HCMS *Comox*), SS *Sung Li* (ex-HCMS *Gaspe*) or SS *Sung Ling* (ex-HCMS *Nanoose*, ex-*Nootka*). All three units were deleted in 1967.

Ex-Soviet 'KOMAR' class *fast attack craft (missile)*

Seven or eight transferred in the early 1960s. Two or four reported as in service 1982.

'HOKU' class *fast attack craft (missile)*

Displacement:	68t standard; 80t full load
Dimensions:	91ft 10in × 21ft × 6ft
	28m × 6.3m × 1.8m
Machinery:	4 shafts, 4 M50 diesels, 4800bhp = 39kts. Range 400nm/500nm at 30kts/25kts
Armament:	2 SS-N-2 SSM (2×1), 2–25mm (2×1)
Sensors:	Radar Square Tie
Complement:	18

Class:
1109 series, *3125* series

Chinese-built development of the Soviet 'Komar' with a steel rather than a wooden hull. The SSM launchers are farther inboard and they have a pole mast. Otherwise they are very similar apart from a slightly modified hull form. Anything from 80 to 110 'Hokus' have been built since the late 1960s, and they are still in production at ten a year. Their value has gradually been eroded by the widespread adoption of ECM by potential enemies. Four transferred to Albania, 1976–77. A single hydrofoil variant of this class, the *Homa* (c100t, 95ft/*29m*, 4–25mm), was built in the 1970s but not repeated.

Soviet 'OSA I' class *fast attack craft (missile)*

Class:
3100 series

Chinese version of the Soviet 'Osa I' class. Anything from 80 to 112 'Osa I' class have been built in Chinese shipyards (Kiangnan, Shanghai) since c1966–67. The first four (Soviet transfers 1965–67) differed in having 4–30mm (2×2) in place of 25mm. They are still being built at about ten a year, and form the backbone of China's coast defence force. Their electronics differ slightly from the Soviet vessels. Chinese top speed is given as 41kts instead of 35kts. As with the smaller 'Hokus', their effectiveness has been reduced in recent years by the widespread adoption of suitable ECM by potential enemies.

'Hola' class
NB 1/750 scale

'HOLA' class *fast attack craft (missile)*

Displacement:	185t standard; c200t standard
Dimensions:	137ft 10in oa × 26ft 6in × 6ft 6in
	42m × 8.1m × 2m
Machinery:	3 shafts, 3 diesels, 12,000bhp = 36kts
Armament:	4 or 6 SS-N-2 SSM (6×1 or 4×1), 4–25mm (2×2)
Sensors:	Radar Square Tie

Enlarged and lengthened version of 'Osa I' class with greater striking power. Built c1970 and numbered *5100*. She can be distinguished by her aft mounted radome and folding mast. Only one has been built.

Chinese 'P 4' class
NB 1/750 scale

Ex-Soviet 'P 4' class *fast attack craft (torpedo)*

Class:
5220 series

Over 70 Soviet 'P 4s' were supplied to China from 1952. Six were transferred to Albania in 1956 followed by 6 Chinese-built units in 1965. Very few of these aluminium hulled boats remain operational, approx 50 in reserve. Deletions: 10 in 1976, 20 in 1977 and 5 each in 1978 and 1981.

Chinese 'P 6' class
NB 1/750 scale

Soviet 'P 6' class *fast attack craft (torpedo)*

Class:
5200 series
About 80 built in China (mainly Shanghai) 1956–66. Six transferred to N Vietnam 1967, rest extant 1982.

'Huchwan' class
NB 1/750 scale

'HUCHWAN' class *torpedo hydrofoils*

Displacement:	39t standard; 45t full load
Dimensions:	71ft 6in oa × 16ft 6in × 3ft 3in
	21.8m × 4.9m × 1m
Machinery:	3 shafts, 3 M50 12-cyl diesels; 3600hp = 55kts. Range 500nm at 20kts
Armament:	2–533mm TT (2×1), 4–14.5mm MG (2×2)
Sensors:	Radar Skin Head
Complement:	20

Class:
205, 207, 209, 248, 3206, 3214, 6218, 7230 and many more.
Nearly 200 of these successful torpedo armed hydrofoils, the world's first operational foil borne warships, have been built since 1966 by Hutung of Shanghai. By 1968 at least 25 were in service with S Sea Fleet. There are two versions, one with the bridge well forward and both twin MG mountings aft, and the other version with the bridge farther aft and the MGs fore and aft. Transfers: 32 to Albania (1968–74), 4 to Pakistan, 4 to Tanzania (1975) and 3 to Romania which has also built her own version. Anything from 120 to 140 are currently in service with the Chinese Fleet.

Ex-Soviet BO 2 type *submarine chasers*

Six of these World War II 'Artillerist' class units transferred in the mid-1950s. Replaced by Chinese 'Hainan' class in mid-1960s and deleted 1967.

Soviet 'KRONSTADT' class *large patrol craft*

Class (deployment):
251–258 (N Sea Fleet at Tsingtao and Lushin), *262, 263, 633–635* (E Sea Fleet in Chou Shan Islands), *651–656* (S Sea Fleet in Hainan)
Six transferred from the USSR in 1956–57. Fourteen more were built at Shanghai and Canton from Soviet components in 1956–57. Armed in Chinese service with 6–14.5mm MG (3×2) instead of 2 MG. They are now very old and will soon need to be taken out of service.

Ex-Soviet 'SO 1' class *submarine chasers*

Two transferred 1960. Neither remains in service.

'Hainan' class

'HAINAN' class *large patrol craft*

Displacement:	360t standard; 400t full load
Dimensions:	193ft 8in oa × 24ft × 7ft 10in
	59m × 7.3m × 2.4m
Machinery:	4 shafts, 4 diesels, 8000bhp = 30.5kts. Range 1300nm at 15kts
Armament:	4–57mm (2×2) (some 2–76mm (2×1)), 4–25mm (2×2), 4-MBU 1800 ASW RL, 2 DCT, 2 DC rails, mine rails
Sensors:	Radar Pot Head (most), Skin Head (remainder)
Complement:	*c*60

Class:
267–285, 290, 302, 641, 642, 677, 678, 680
Developed from the Soviet 'SO 1' class but have a considerably larger hull. More than 20 have been built at Shanghai since 1963. They are still being built at 4 a year and are the standard Chinese large patrol craft. Transfers: 6 to N Korea and 4 to Pakistan (1976 and 1980). Early ships were armed with single US Mk 26 76mm guns fore and aft, but on later vessels twin 57mm are standard.

Chinese 'P 6' class 21.7.77   *Xinhua News Agency*

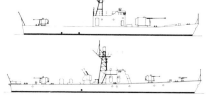

'Shanghai I' class
NB 1/750 scale

'Shanghai II' class
NB 1/750 scale

'SHANGHAI' class *large patrol craft*

Displacement:	120t standard; 155t full load
	Shanghai I: 100t standard)
Dimensions:	128ft oa × 18ft × 5ft 8in (Shanghai I 120ft oa/*35.1m*)
	39m × 5.5m × 1.7m
Machinery:	4 shafts, 4 M50 F-4 diesels, 4800hp = 28kts. Range 800nm at 17kts
Armament:	(Type II – see notes) 4–37mm (2×2), 4–25mm (2×2), 1-ASW RL
Sensors:	Radar Pot Head or Skin Head; sonar hull mounted (some have VDS)
Complement:	25

Class:
1300 series, *4300* series, *8300* series
Very simple and economical coast patrol vessels. 25 Shanghai I were built from 1959, of which 8 were transferred to N Korea and 10 deleted in 1978. Only a few remain in service. These had a shorter hull than later versions and were armed with 2–57mm (1×2) forward and 2–37mm (1×2) aft. Some had 2–457mm TT (1×2) but these were later removed. The longer-hulled Types II, III, IV and V were built from 1961. The Type III have 57mm in place of the 37mm and the other two Types have more minor differences. Some have 2–75mm Army RRs (1×2) mounted forward. Over 350 have been built. Transfers: Albania (6), Bangladesh (6), Cameroons (2), Congo (3), Guinea (6), Pakistan (12), Sierra Leone (3), Sri Lanka (5), Tanzania (7) and N Vietnam (8). In addition the Romanians have built their own versions. About 290–315 remain in service with the Chinese Fleet, but the first to be built are being rapidly discarded (50 deleted in 1979).

'HAIKOU' class *large patrol craft*

Displacement:	160t standard; 175t full load
Dimensions:	150ft oa × 21ft × *c*7ft
	45.7m × 6.4m × 2.1m
Machinery:	4 shafts, 4 diesels = *c*30kts. Range 850nm at 20kts (est)
Armament:	4–37mm (2×2), 4–25mm (2×2)
Other particulars:	not known

Enlarged 'Shanghai' class. Six built in the late 1960s. Only 3 extant in 1982.

'Shantung' class hydrofoil
NB 1/750 scale

'SWATOW' class *coastal patrol craft*

Displacement:	*c*70t standard; 80t full load
Dimensions:	84ft oa × 20ft × 6ft 6in
	25.7m × 6.1m × 2m
Machinery:	4 shafts, 4 diesels, 3000hp = 28kts. Range 500nm/750nm at 28kts/15kts
Armament:	4–37mm (2×2), 2–12.7mm (2×1), 8-DC
Sensors:	Radar Pot Head or Skin Head
Complement:	17

Steel hull, gun armed Chinese version of Soviet 'P 6' torpedo FAC. About 80 were built during 1956–60 but since the mid-1970s over half have been deleted (10 in 1976, 10 in 1977, 5 in 1978, 5 in 1979, 12 in 1981). Eight transferred to N Korea and 12 to N Vietnam. Fleet deployments 1982: E Sea 24; S Sea 16; N Sea 14 or 18. Hydrofoil 'Shantung' class variants were built in the 1960s (2 shafts, 2 diesels, 3800bhp = 40kts) armed with 4–37mm (2×2). Only 2 or 3 extant in 1982.

'HUANGPU' ('WHAMPOA') class *river patrol craft*

Displacement:	42t standard; 50t full load
Dimensions:	88ft 7in × 13ft × 5ft
	27m × 4m × 1.5m
Machinery:	2 shafts, 2 diesels, 1000bhp = 14kts. Range 400nm at 9kts
Armament:	4–25mm (2×2) see notes
Sensors:	Radar Skin Head
Complement:	25

Built in Shanghai and Canton 1950–55. Low freeboard and inadequate propulsion, 10 deleted 1977, 5 in 1978 and 7 in 1981. Some armed with 2–37mm (1×2) and 2–12.7mm MG (1×2). Remainder deployed in 1982: 25 in E Sea, 8 in N Sea and 7 S Sea.

'YULIN' class *river patrol craft*

Displacement:	10t full load
Dimensions:	40ft × 9ft 6in × 3ft 6in
	12.8m × 2.9m × 1.1m
Machinery:	1 shaft, 1 diesel, 300bhp = 20–24kts
Armament:	2–12.7mm MG (2×1)
Complement:	10

Built in Shanghai 1964–68. Transfers: 4 to Congo (1966), 3 to Cambodia and 4 to Tanzania. In 1982 40 were extant.

OTHER COASTAL PATROL CRAFT
Thirty 'Behai' or 'Pen Hai' class (80t full load, 90ft, 3 diesels, 900bhp = 18kts, 4–25mm in twin mounts), built in 1950s, most manned by Naval Militia and soon to be deleted.

Thirty 'Fukien' or 'Fuijan' class (65ft, 2–12.7mm MG, 1–7.62mm MG): river patrols in E Sea Fleet area.

'Ying Kou' class (30t, 70ft, 1 diesel, 300bhp = 16kts, 4–12.7mm MG in twin mounts); built early 1960s.

Four 'Taishan' class (60t, 95ft, diesels, 2–37mm, 2–12.7mm); built 1950s and 1960s.

MINE WARFARE VESSELS

Soviet 'T 43' class *ocean minesweepers*

Class (deployment):
341 (E Sea), *342* (E Sea), *364–366* (N Sea), *375–380* (E Sea), *386–389* (S Sea), *396–399* (S Sea), *801–803* (N Sea), *807* (N Sea)

Four Soviet units were transferred in 1954–55, two of which were returned in 1960. Another 21 were built in Chinese shipyards at Shanghai and Canton from 1956. Last pair completed in 1966. Some early ships had a slightly smaller hull. In the late 1970s three ships were converted to survey vessels and three more to civilian research ships. The remainder are still in service.

WOOSUNG class *ocean minesweeper*

One *c*250t–300t ship (2–37mm, 4–14.5mm MG) was built in 1970–72, but she (pennant number 535) was unsuccessful. No more were built and she was transferred to N Vietnam in 1974.

NOTE:
At least 60 auxiliary minesweepers including trawlers are reported as well as 20 'Fushin' class (no details available).

Fiji

Fiji was annexed by Britain in 1874 and this South Pacific archipelago became an independent dominion of the Commonwealth in 1970. The Fijian Naval Force was created on 12 June 1974 for coastal patrol, fishery protection, coastguard and survey duties. It is trained in Australia. It consists of 160 sailors with three ex-USN coastal minesweepers based at the Fiji capital of Suva. There are also two 130–140ft (40–42m) landing craft used for supply work and a survey ship.

Ex-US 'BLUEBIRD' class *coastal minesweepers*

Class (no, former name/no):
Kikau (204, ex-*Woodpecker*/MSC 209), *Kula* (206, ex-*Vireo*/MSC 206), *Kiro* (205, ex-*Warbler*/MSC 205)

First two transferred on 14.10.75 having served with USN since 3.2.56 and 7.6.55 respectively. Third unit transferred June 1976 having first been commissioned on 23.7.55. Magnetic sweeper gear removed for deckhouse installation with helicopter platform. Extant 1982 as large if slow patrol craft.

FIJI-built *landing craft*

Class:
Vasua, Yaubula

Both built at Suva and in service since 1978. Both powered by 2 GM diesels at a maximum of 8kts but displacement and dimensions differ. *Yaubula* is 500t full load. Both able to carry 200 or 220t of cargo.

Hong Kong

Hong Kong was seized by the British from China in 1839 during the First Opium War, and British ownership was confirmed in 1842 by the Treaty of Nanking. Kowloon was acquired in 1860, and in 1898 a 99-year lease was taken on the New Territories. Hong Kong remains a British Crown Colony, and its force of 63 small patrol boats are operated by 1291 volunteers of the Marine District of the Royal Hong Kong Police Force. The Royal Navy also maintains a presence at Hong Kong. This diminished from a cruiser squadron in the early 1950s to the frigate HMS *Mermaid* in the mid-1970s. In 1982 it consisted of 5 'Ton' class large patrol craft and 2 SRN–6 hovercraft and from 1984 these will be replaced by the 5 *Peacock* class patrol vessels being 75 per cent funded by the Hong Kong Government. The main duties of both the RN Squadron and the Hong Kong police boats are to prevent smuggling of goods and illegal immigrants.

Two Command vessels (222t full load, 111ft 4in × 24ft × 10ft 6in *33.9m × 7.3m × 3.2m*, 2 Cummins diesels, 6746bhp = 11.8kts, 5200nm range, crew 25 or 29 plus 2 platoons of troops, 1–12.7mm MG): *Sea Lion* (PL 1), *Sea Tiger* (PL 2), built HK United DYd 1965 for 1,778,550 HK dollars and extant 1982.

Ten Damen type coastal patrol craft (86t standard, 85ft 10in × 19ft 5in × 5ft 10in, *26.2m × 5.9m × 1.8m*, 2 MTU 12V 396 TC 82 diesels, 2600bhp = 23kts, 1 MAN D2566, 1956hp = 2–8kts cruising, 1400nm at 8kts, 1–12.7mm MG, Decca 150 radar, crew 14): PL 60–69 built by Chung Wah of Kowloon. First 3 in service Feb 1980, next 4 by 8.9.80, last 3 by early 1981. PL 65 named *Cetus*, PL 66 *Dorado*.

Eight 78ft Vosper Thornycroft type (82t full load, 78ft 6in × 17ft 2in × 5ft 6in, *23.9m × 5.2m × 1.7m*, 2 Cummins diesels, 1500bhp = 20.7kts, 4000nm at 20kts, 1–12.7mm MG, crew 16): *Sea Cat* (PL 50), *Sea Puma* (PL 51), *Sea Leopard* (PL 52), *Sea Eagle* (PL 53), *Sea Hawk* (PL 54), *Sea Lynx* (PL 55), *Sea Falcon* (PL 56); all built at Singapore and in service since May 1972–May 1973. *Sea Horse* (PL 4) is a 1958, 15.5kt, 21-man predecessor still in service.

Nine 70ft HK-built patrol craft (52t full load, 70ft × 17ft × 5ft 2in, *21.3m × 5.2m × 1.6m*, 2 diesels, 215bhp = 10kts, 1600nm range, 1–12.7mm MG, crew 12): *Sea Rover* (PL 26), *Sea Farer* (PL 27), *Sea Roamer* (PL 28), *Sea Rider* (PL 29), *Sea Nomad* (PL 30), *Sea Wanderer* (PL 31), *Sea Raker* (PL 32), *Sea Rescuer* (PL 33), *Sea Ranger* (PL 34). PL 26–28 built 1954, rest 1955. All extant 1982.

One 65ft patrol craft (48t full load, 1 diesel, 152hp = 10.5kts, 1400nm at 9kts, crew 11): *Islander* (PL 6), built *c*1960.

Ten 45ft converted wooden tugs built in Australia 1944–45, two discarded 1975 rest in service 1982 with small arms only.

Three 40ft *Jetstream* class (17t, 2 diesels, 740bhp = 24kts, 380nm range, 5 men), built by Cheoy Lee SY 1971.

Nine 30ft Fairey Marine 'Spear' class in service since 1981 with 1–7.62mm MG.

Eleven 22ft personnel launches built by Cheoy Lee SY 1970.

There are two other logistic craft.

India

'The future of India will undoubtedly be decided on the sea' wrote K M Panikkar in 1945. This lone oceanic visionary was striving even before the subcontinent's independence to counteract the overwhelmingly land-based attitudes and preoccupations of its rulers. India lacks a continuous or general maritime tradition yet it was Europeans coming by sea who came to dominate her. The evolution of the Indian Navy to its present status of seventh largest in the world and third largest in Asia (with the region's only aircraft carrier) is inseparable from its pre-independence background.

In 1939 the Royal Indian Navy, having almost disappeared in the economies of the 1920s, stood at 8 ships and 1600 men all based at Bombay. By the end of 1944 the Fleet consisted of 117 warships including 7 sloops, 9 corvettes, 14 ocean minesweepers and 49 coastal craft as well as the Landing Craft Wing. Shore establishments included six ports, gunnery, radar, torpedo, signals, engineering and tactical training schools while personnel including nearly 1000 Indian Wrens (WRINS) totalled almost 35,000. The RIN contribution to Allied victory was at least comparable with the Royal Australian Navy's. Four of the major ships had Indian captains in 1945 but expansion had been so headlong that British officers were needed long after independence. The unexpected early defeat of Japan led to rapid demobilisation down to 11,000 men by the end of 1946. Poor shore conditions and Nationalist agitation sparked a five-day mutiny at Bombay in February 1946. It spread to the Andamans, Hong Kong and Aden but was over almost as soon as it started after 10 sailors were killed. Only the sloop *Hindustan* exchanged fire with the Indian Army at Karachi.

Partition split the Navy as it did all other institutions. Before 1939 most sailors had been Muslim and only wartime expansion brought in large numbers of Hindus. Over half the Fleet's ships sailed to the two halves of Muslim Pakistan. Neither force took part in the 1948–49 war between the new states, nor indeed in the 1965 fighting which was again a localised frontier dispute. Ambitious expansion plans went ahead. Postwar acquisition of cruisers and destroyers had been proposed as early as mid-1943 and these were acquired in 1948–49 despite the manning problem. On 26 January 1950 the Royal Indian Navy was officially retitled the Indian Navy and in 1952 the first Indian admiral took command. Three classes of the latest British frigates were ordered in 1954–56 and new minesweepers acquired. Most ambitiously of all, India bought the light fleet carrier HMS *Hercules* in 1957 and had her rebuilt as the *Vikrant*. The Fleet Air Arm trained a new naval aviation service to operate from her with Sea Hawk jets and helicopters. The 'Indian Flotilla' became the Indian Fleet on 30 December 1957.

In 1961 the Navy played its part in the almost bloodless annexation of Portuguese Goa, from which European seapower had first dominated the Indian Ocean. By 1964 manpower had reached 19,500 when it had been only 8800 in 1958. The Navy now shared in the general defence expansion after the shock of China's limited invasion in 1962. Between 1966 and 1970 manpower doubled and the Fleet expanded from 32 warships to 55. Traditional reliance on Britain was supplemented by the purchase of cheap Soviet ships on easy terms from 1967. The Soviet Union also helped to expand the naval base at Vishakhapatnam. India had her first submarines (four) by the time she went to war for a third time with Pakistan and now the Navy could show its teeth.

The carrier *Vikrant* headed a task force of 7 destroyers and frigates, 2 submarines, a minesweeper, 5 fast attack craft and 3 landing ships in the Bay of Bengal during December 1971. Their blockade of doomed East Pakistan was totally effective. More than that, the Navy trained *Mukhti Bahini* Bengali guerrillas to plant limpet mines on ships and bridges in the waterways of the Pakistan state before Indian's conventional invasion. The Indian Western Fleet also demonstrated its superiority over Pakistan's main force. The submarine *Ghazi* was sunk by ASW surface forces off Vishakhapatnam while trying to ambush *Vikrant*.

Bangladesh's creation meant that the Navy need no longer worry about a two-sea war and could concentrate on long term expansion and indigenous warship building. The August 1971 mutual assistance treaty with the USSR has not meant a Soviet predominance in naval matters. Bombay's Mazagon Dockyard built 6 British *Leander* type frigates between 1966 and 1981 fitting Western electronics and expanding their helicopter facilities. The yard's new *Godavari* class combines a *Leander* hull with Soviet missiles, West Germany will supply India's second generation submarines. A new type of landing craft is being built at Calcutta and Goa.

An Indian Coast Guard to patrol the country's 200-mile EEZ was formed on 1 February 1977 as part of the Navy. It became independent in August 1978 with a rear-admiral as director-general. The force started with two former Navy frigates but two home-built classes of armed patrol vessels are in service. Oil is being drilled more than 100 miles off Bombay and India's merchant marine expanded by 165 ships or almost 2.5 million tons between 1974 and 1980.

India's prompting of the UN declaration of the Indian Ocean as 'a zone of peace' in 1971 has not reduced 'outside' naval activity since Britain's withdrawal. The US Navy, based mainly on Diego Garcia, has come into South Asian waters for the first time in a permanent way to counter the Soviet Indian Ocean Squadron, but the eclipse of Iran leaves India unchallenged as the main regional sea power. *Vikrant*'s life is being extended by the acquisition of Sea Harriers.

Since 1977 the Navy has had 46,000 volunteer sailors including a naval air arm of 2000 men with 35 combat aircraft and 36 helicopters. In 1982 they manned an active fleet of 86 warships and 30 auxiliaries.

FLEET STRENGTH 1947

FRIGATES (ex-sloops)

Name	Fate	Name	Fate
Modified Hastings class			
HINDUSTAN	To Pakistan 1948		
Modified Bittern class			
JUMNA	Extant 1982	GODAVARI	To Pakistan 1948
SUTLEJ	Extant 1982	NARBADA	To Pakistan 1948
Modified Black Swan class			
CAUVERY	Paid off 1979	KISTNA	Extant 1982
'River' class			
TIR (ex-*Bann*)	Paid off 1979	SHAMSHER (ex-*Nadder*)	To Pakistan 1948
DHANUSH (ex-*Deveron*)	To Pakistan 1948	KHUKRI (ex-*Trent*)	Survey ship 1951

Hindustan was transferred from the former Royal Indian Navy but was worn out and of little military value. *Godavari* and *Narbada* became the Pakistani *Sind* and *Jhelum*, having previously been handed over from the ex-RIN; *Jumna* and *Sutlej* formed the 12th Frigate Squadron but from 1955 *Sutlej* served as a surveying vessel, followed by *Jumna* in 1957. *Jumna* was renamed *Jumuna* c1976.

Kistna had her after 4in guns replaced by a deckhouse c1962; she is unlikely to remain in service much longer. *Cauvery* acted as temporary Fleet Flagship in the mid-1950s.

Neza (ex-*Trent*) was returned to the RN in April 1947 but four sisters were retained. *Dhanush* and *Shamsher* went to Pakistan in 1948, the former retaining her name but the latter becoming *Zulfiquar*. *Tir* was converted to a midshipmen's training ship in 1948; *Khukri* was refitted as a survey ship in 1951 and renamed *Investigator*.

MINESWEEPERS

Name	Fate	Name	Fate
Ex-Bangor class			
ROHILKAND	For disposal 1960	KATHIAWAR	To Pakistan 1948
KONKAN	For disposal 1973	OUDH	To Pakistan 1948
RAJPUTANA	For disposal 1960	MALWA	To Pakistan 1948
BALUCHISTAN	To Pakistan 1948		
Ex-Bathurst class			
BENGAL	BU 1967	MADRAS	For disposal 1962
BOMBAY	For disposal 1962		

Kathiawar, *Oudh* and *Malwa* became the Pakistani *Chittagong*, *Dacca* and *Peshawar* in 1948.

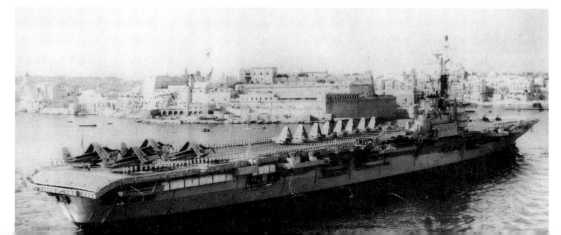

Vikrant 1961　　*Navarret Collection*

MAJOR SURFACE SHIPS

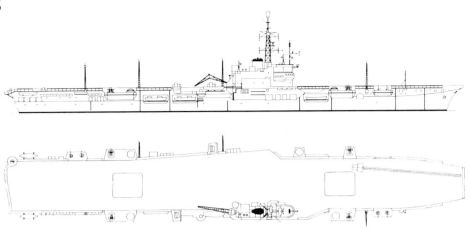

Vikrant as completed
NB 1/1750 scale

The last of the light fleet carriers to be completed was HMS *Hercules*, bought in Jan 1957 by the Indian Navy, building to a recast design resumed at Harland & Wolff's yard in Belfast three months later. When she was ready in 1961 she had received a steam catapult, an angled deck, air conditioning and new radar, similar to HMAS *Melbourne*.

The air group comprised 10 Sea Hawk jet fighters, 4 Alizé ASW aircraft and 2 Alouette helicopters, but in 1979 it was announced that re-equipment with Sea Harrier V/STOL aircraft would take place. Delivery of 8 began in Jan 1983. During the 1971 Indo-Pakistan War *Vikrant* operated in the Bay of Bengal and flew off several strikes against naval and military targets including Chittagong. In

Delhi arrived at Bombay in Sept 1948, having been refitted. Apart from playing herself (*Achilles*) in a 1953 film of the Battle of the River Plate, the only further action she saw was in 1961, when Goa was seized by a small naval force. Although on the active list at the time of the Indo-Pakistan War in 1971 she did not get to sea, having been replaced by the *Mysore* as Fleet Flagship in 1957. TT were removed in 1958. In 1969 she visited Australia, New Zealand and Fiji; thereafter she was based at Cochin as a harbour TS, with the 40mm and 4in guns removed to provide additional space for cadets. In July 1977 she returned to Bombay under her own power to pay off. Although preservation was out of the question steps were taken to display a twin 6in turret at the Defence Academy in Poona.

Brought from Britain on 8.5.54 for £300,000. Refitted and rebuilt by Cammell Laird. 'X' 6in turret and all 6 TT were removed, the bridge was modified, two lattice masts stepped, electrics were renewed and machinery refitted. Handed over at Birkenhead on 29.8.57 and relieved *Delhi* as flagship. She took part in the 1971 Indo-Pakistan War and in May 1978 relieved *Delhi* once more, this time as flagship of the Training Squadron. She has been in two major collisions, the more recent being in 1972 with the frigate *Beas* which caused two months of repairs. *Mysore* was decommissioned at the end of 1981.

VIKRANT *aircraft carrier*

Displacement:	16,000t standard; 19,500t full load
Dimensions:	700ft oa × 128ft max × 24ft
	213.4m × 39.0m × 7.3m
Machinery:	2-shaft geared steam turbines: 40,000shp = 23kts. Oil 3200t. Range 12,000nm/6200nm at 14kts/23kts
Armour:	Mantlets over magazines
Armament:	15–40mm/60 Bofors (4×2, 7×1), 16 aircraft
Sensors:	Radar Types 960, 278, 293, 963
Complement:	1075 (peace), 1345 (war)

No	Name	Builder	Acquired	Fate
R 11	VIKRANT (ex-*Hercules*)	Vickers-Armstrong, Tyne	4.3.61	Extant 1982

1973–74 she was extensively overhauled but her appearance remains unaltered. An Indian-built replacement is being designed.

Ex-British LEANDER class *cruiser*

Displacement:	7114t standard; 9740t full load
Dimensions:	522ft pp, 554ft 6in oa × 55ft 8in × 20ft
	159.1m, 169.0m × 17.0m × 6.1m
Machinery:	4-shaft Parsons geared turbines: 6 Admiralty 3-drum boilers, 72,000shp = 32.5kts. Oil 1800t. Range 12,000nm at 14kts
Armament:	6–6in/50 (3×2), 8–4in/45 Mk 16 (4×2), 8–40mm/60 Mk 5 (4×2), 6–40mm/60 Mk 7 (6×1), 4–3pdr saluting, 6–21in TT (2×3)
Sensors:	Radar types 274, 285, 277Q, 960, 293
Complement:	680 (800 as TS)

No	Name	Builder	Acquired	Fate
C 74	DELHI (ex-*Achilles*)	Cammell Laird	Sept 1948	For disposal May 1978

Ex-British FIJI class *cruiser*

Displacement:	8700t standard; 11,040t full load
Dimensions:	As British *Fiji* class
Machinery:	As British *Fiji* class
Armament:	9–6in/50 Mk 23 (3×3), 8–4in/45 Mk 16 (4×2), 10–40mm/60 Mk 5 (5×2), 2–40mm/60 Mk 7 (2×1)
Sensors:	Radar Types 274, 275, 960, 277Q, 293
Complement:	800

No	Name	Builder	Acquired	Fate
C 60	MYSORE (ex-*Nigeria*)	Vickers-Armstrong, Tyne	29.8.57	Extant 1982

All given lattice foremast in place of tripod, new funnel ventilating trunks for tropical service, retubed boilers, TT removed and new radar prior to transfer. The new top hamper was counterweighted with 30t of permanent pig iron ballast. Arrived in Indian waters Jan 1950 as 11th Destroyer Flotilla.

Rajput 1981

New construction and unlike in modified Soviet units the SS-N-2C SSM are mounted fwd. The stern 76mm turret has been deleted to provide a helicopter hangar reached by a ramp. They have twin 30mm instead of singles.

Lent by RN initially for 3 years and rerated as escort destroyers.

Slightly modified Type 14, ordered in 1954. The 4–21in TT were not fitted. *Khukri* was torpedoed and sunk by the submarine *Hangor* during the 1971 Indo-Pakistan War, the first warship so sunk since 1945, 191 of the 288 crew were lost. *Kirpan* (means 'Sword') and *Kuthar* were transferred to the new Coast Guard Service in 1978.

Talwar 1976

Two slightly modified Type 12 frigates were ordered in 1956. They differed mainly in having a twin 40mm Bofors Mk 5 with a CRBF director in place of the STAAG Mk 2. In 1974–75 *Talwar* had her 4.5in Mk 6 replaced by three SS-N-2 'Styx' SSM with 'Square Tie' radar above the bridge. In 1977–78 *Trishul*, flagship of 15th

Three Type 41 frigates were ordered in 1954 and the RN made the *Panther* available from its own programme. *Brahmaputra* is now a TS, with the after 4.5in guns and CRBF director replaced (1978) by classrooms. *Beas* modernised in 1980, her 40mm GFCS radar being removed.

Ex-British 'R' class *destroyers*

No	Name	Builder	Acquired	Fate
D 115	RANA (ex-*Raider*)	Cammell Laird	Sept 1949	For disposal 1976
D 41	RAJPUT (ex-*Rotherham*)	John Brown	29.7.49	For disposal 1976
D 209	RANJIT (ex-*Redoubt*)	John Brown	4.7.49	For disposal 1979

Soviet 'KASHIN II' class *destroyers*

No	Name	Builder	Acquired	Fate
D 51	RAJPUT	Nikolayev	Oct 1980	Extant 1982
D 52	RANA	Nikolayev	1981	Extant 1982
D 53	RANJIT	Nikolayev	1982	Extant 1982

Ex-British 'HUNT' class (Type 2) *frigates*

No	Name	Builder	Acquired	Fate
D 94	GANGA (ex-*Chiddingfold*)	Scotts	Apr/May 1953	For disposal 1975
D 92	GODAVARI (ex-*Bedale*)	Hawthorn Leslie	Apr/May 1953	For disposal 1979
D 93	GOMATI (ex-*Lamerton*)	Swan Hunter	Apr/May 1953	For disposal 1975

British BLACKWOOD class *frigates*

No	Name	Builder	Laid down	Launched	Comp	Fate
F 49	KHUKRI	White	29.12.55	20.11.56	15.7.58	Sunk 9.12.71
F 44	KIRPAN	Stephen	5.11.56	19.8.58	Jul 1959	Extant 1982
F 46	KUTHAR	White	19.9.57	14.10.58	Nov 1959	Extant 1982

British WHITBY class *frigates*

No	Name	Builder	Laid down	Launched	Comp	Fate
F 40	TALWAR	Cammell Laird	7.6.57	18.7.58	26.4.59	Extant 1982
F 43	TRISHUL	Harland & Wolff	19.2.57	18.6.58	13.1.60	Extant 1982

Frigate Squadron, was similarly refitted.

British LEOPARD class *frigates*

No	Name	Builder	Laid down	Launched	Comp	Fate
F 31	BRAHMAPUTRA (ex-*Panther*)	John Brown	20.10.55	15.3.57	31.3.58	Extant 1982
F 37	BEAS	Vickers, Tyne	29.11.56	9.10.58	24.5.60	Extant 1982
F 38	BETWA	Vickers, Tyne	29.5.57	15.9.59	8.12.60	Extant 1982

Udaygiri June 1977   *G Arra*

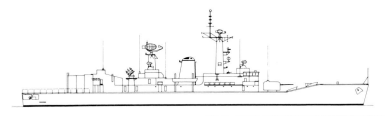

Taragiri 1980

Although originally intended to be repeats of the *Leander* design, progressive improvements have been made, and the later ships are a hybrid Anglo-Dutch design. Only *Nilgiri* and *Himgiri* have British electronics; the other two have Dutch Signaal radars built under licence by Bharath Electronics in India, and all but *Nilgiri* have M-4 directors for the Seacat SAMs. The Alouette III helicopter is too long for the original *Leander* hangar and so a telescoping type is fitted. The last two have been completed to a modified design, with a longer flight deck to permit a Sea King helicopter to be carried. This involved removing the Mk 10 mortar (replaced by 1–375mm Bofors ASW RL on fo'c'le) and installing a larger telescopic hangar much nearer the stern. The hull side beneath the flight deck is open to facilitate the handling of mooring wires etc. The 6 ships form 14th Frigate Squadron.

British 'broad beam LEANDER' type *frigates*

No	Name	Builder	Laid down	Launched	Comp	Fate
F 33	NILGIRI	Mazagon Dock, Bombay	Oct 1966	23.10.68	3.6.72	Extant 1982
F 34	HIMGIRI	Mazagon Dock, Bombay	1967	6.5.70	23.11.74	Extant 1982
F 36	DUNAGIRI	Mazagon Dock, Bombay	14.9.70	24.10.72	18.2.76	Extant 1982
F 35	UDAYGIRI	Mazagon Dock, Bombay	Jan 73	9.3.74	1.2.77	Extant 1982
F 37	TARAGIRI	Mazagon Dock, Bombay	1974	25.10.76	Sept 1979	Extant 1982
F 38	VINDHYAGIRI	Mazagon Dock, Bombay	1975	12.11.77	8.7.81	Extant 1982

By broadening and lengthening the basic *Leander* hull the designers at Mazagon Dock were able to incorporate an extra Sea King helicopter. With four 'Styx' missiles and SAN-4 missiles forward they are the first examples of a Western hull design incorporating Russian weapons. Although Russian twin 57mm were planned, an OTO-Melara 76mm Compact has been substituted. Two 30mm 'Gatlings' are mounted on the hangar roof. A second group of 3 will have 30kt machinery.

GODAVARI class *frigates*

Displacement:	3350t normal; 3850t deep load
Dimensions:	397ft wl, 414ft 9in oa × 47ft 11in × 29ft 6in
	121.0m, 126.4m × 14.6m × 9.0m
Machinery:	2-shaft Spey gas turbines, 30,000shp = 27kts. Range 4500nm at 12kts
Armament:	4 SS-N-2C 'Styx' SSM, 1 twin SA-N-4 SAM, 1–76mm/62 DP, 4–30mm (2×2), 2 helicopters
Sensors:	Radar LW-05, Head Net-C, Pop Group, Drum Tilt; sonar type 184M
Complement:	250

Name	Builder	Laid down	Launched	Fate
GODAVARI	Mazagon Dock, Bombay	2.6.78	15.5.80	Extant 1983
GANGA	Mazagon Dock, Bombay	1981	Oct 1981	Fitting out
GOMATI	Mazagon Dock, Bombay	1980	21.10.81	Building

SUBMARINES

Ex-Soviet 'FOXTROT' class *submarines*

Class (no, transfer):
Kursura (S 20, Dec 1970), *Karanj* (S 21, Oct 1970), *Kandheri* (S 22, Jan 1969), *Kalvari* (S 23, 16.7.68), *Vela* (S 40, 31.8.73), *Vagir* (S 41, 3.11.73), *Vagli* (S 42, 10.8.74), *Vagsheer* (S 43, 26.12.74)

India's first submarines, another pair may be transferred. Their base is at Vishakhapatnam.

German Type 1500 *submarines*

Displacement:	1150t standard; 980t surfaced; 1440t submerged
Dimensions:	200ft 1in × 20ft 4in × 18ft
	61.0m × 6.2m × 5.5m
Machinery:	1 shaft, 4 MTU 820Db diesels, 2400bhp = 11kts/21.5kts. Oil 118t. Range 8200nm at 8kts (snorkel)
Armament:	8–533mm TT (bow, 14 torpedoes)
Complement:	32

A variant of the Howaldswerke Type 209 export design. The Indian Navy finally signed a contract for 4 boats on 11.12.81, first pair to be built in Hamburg and the second pair to be assembled at Mazagon D Yd, Bombay, after training for Indian builders. The Type 1500 will have the IKL rescue system. The order is worth 350 million dollars and delivery is expected in 1985–86.

AMPHIBIOUS WARFARE VESSELS

Ex-British LST 3 class *tank landing ship*

HMS *Avenger* (*LST 3001*) became INS *Magar* (L 11) in 1951 and still extant 1982.

Ex-Soviet 'POLNOCNY' class *landing ships*

Class (no, transferred):
Gharial (L 12, 1966), *Guldar* (L 13, 1966), *Ghorpad* (L 14, 1975), *Kesari* (L 15, Sept 1975), *Shardul* (L 16, Dec 1975), *Sharab* (L 17, March 1976)

First two 'A' class ships sailed direct from Poland. The 4 'C' class units do not have export helicopter platform. Another 6 may have been ordered.

VASCO DA GAMA class *utility landing craft*

Displacement:	500t full load
Dimensions:	175ft 10in × 26ft 2in × 4ft
	53.6m × 8m × 1.2m
Machinery:	3 shafts, 3 Kirlasker-MAN W8V 17.5/22 AMAL diesels, 1245bhp = 9kts. Range 1000nm at 8kts
Armament:	2–40mm (2×1)
Complement:	? + 120 troops or 250t cargo

Class (no, launched/in service):
Vasco da Gama (L 34, 29.11.78/28.1.80), L 35 (13.1.79/1.12.80), L 36 (16.3.80), L 37

New design, first 2 built by Goa S Yd, next two by Hooghly of Calcutta.

SMALL SURFACE COMBATANTS

Soviet 'PETYA II' class *frigates (corvettes)*

Class (no):
Arnala (P 68), *Androth* (P 69), *Anjadip* (P 73), *Andaman* (P 74), *Amini* (P 75), *Kamorta* (P 77), *Kadmath* (P 78), *Kiltan* (P 79), *Kavaratti* (P 80), *Katchal* (P 81), *Kanjar* (P 82), *Amindivi* (P 83)

New export-version ships, the 5 'K' names being delivered in 1969 followed by 5 more with 'A' names in 1974 and, slightly later, by *Amindivi* and *Kanjar*.

Unlike Soviet ships have 4 RBU-2500 ASW RL and 3–21in TT as well as simpler radio equipment. It is reported that some of them needed attention to their machinery en route from Vladivostok to India. Despite having 'P' (patrol) pennant numbers the 12 ships form 32nd Frigate Squadron.

Soviet 'NANUCHKA II' class *missile corvette*

Class (no, acquired):
Vijaydurg (K 71, Dec 1976), *Sindhurdurg* (K 72, May 1977), *Hosdurg* (K 73, Jan 1978)

Export ships that arrived in India from Leningrad in March 1977, Aug 1977 and March 1978 respectively. Virtually identical to Soviet ships except for SS-N-2 'Styx' missiles in place of SS-N-9; the radar outfit is also slightly different, with no 'Fish Bowl' antenna. India is designing a new larger missile corvette to take the same weapon but be more seaworthy.

Ex-Soviet 'OSA I and II' class *fast attack craft (missile)*

Class (no):
'Osa I': *Veer* (K 82), *Vidyut* (K 83), *Vijeta* (K 84), *Vinash* (K 85), *Nipat* (K 86), *Nashat* (K 87), *Nirbhik* (K 88), *Nirghat* (K 89).

'Osa II': *Prachand* (K 90), *Pralaya* (K 91), *Prabal* (K 92), *Pratap* (K 93), *Chamak* (K 94), *Chapal* (K 95), *Chapak* (K 96), *Charag* (K 97)

First 8 boats transferred 1971, K 84 and K 87 lost their missile tubes (3 each) to the frigates *Talwar* (late 1975) and *Trishul* (1978), and used as patrol craft. K 87 converted to carry frogmen in 1980. 'Osa II' boats in service 17.2.76 and 5.11.76 (4 each). All to be modernised with ECM and perhaps new engines.

SDB Mk 2 class *large patrol craft*

Displacement:	160t full load
Dimensions:	123ft × 24ft 7in × 5ft 10in
	37.5m × 7.5m × 1.8m
Machinery:	2 shafts, 2 Deltic 18–42K diesels, 7,000bhp = 32kts, 1 Cummins NH-220 cruise diesel = 14kts. Range 1000nm at 14kts
Armament:	1–40mm/60 Bofors, 2 DCT, 2 DC rails (18 Mk 7 and 10 Mk 12 DCs)
Complement:	30

Class (in service):
T 51 (17.11.78), *T 52* (3.9.77), *T 53* (12.4.78), *Rajhans* (T 54, Jan 1981), *T 55* (Feb 1981), *T 56* (Feb 1981)

Indian design derived from the RN 'Ford' class. Built by Garden Reach SYd of Calcutta for the new Coast Guard. *T 51* launched 31.12.75 and began trials Sept 1977. Construction way behind schedule. *T 57* and 3 more may be built.

British 'FORD' class *seaward defence boats*

Class (no, in service):
Abhay (P 3135, 13.11.61), *Ajay* (?, 21.9.60), *Akshay* (P 3136, 8.1.62), *Amar* (P 3137)

Built by Hooghly Docking & Eng Co, Calcutta. *Amar* transferred to Mauritius in 1974. *Akshay* and *Ajay* transferred to Bangladesh 1973 and 1974. Larger crew (35) than RN vessels. Only *Abhay* (now T 35) extant 1982.

Ex-Soviet 'POLUCHAT I' class *coastal patrol craft*

Class (no):
Panaji (501/P 249), *Panvel* (502/P 246), *Pamban* (503/P 247), *Puli* (504/P 248), *Pulicat* (505/P 250)

Transferred 1967–69. Originally numbered in P sequence. Originally Home Dept units in service with the Coast Guard since 1977.

NEW Type P 957 *offshore patrol vessels*

Vikram, first of a class of 3 for the Coast Guard was laid down in March 1981 and launched in Sept. This 1040t full load, 21kt design was ordered in 1979 from Mazagon DYd, Bombay, as stretched version of the Dutch NEVESBU 750t OPV. Machinery is 2 SEMT-Pielstick 16 PA 6 diesels (2 CP propellers) giving 12,800bhp. Armament is 2–40mm and 2–7.62mm MG plus Alouette III helicopter and hangar. Three Type 956 200t OPVs were ordered from Garden Reach, Calcutta in 1979 notionally for 1982–83 delivery.

MINE WARFARE VESSELS

Ex-British 'TON' class *coastal minesweepers*

Class (no, former name, fate):
Cuddalore (M 90, ex-*Wennington*, stricken 1980), *Cannamore* (M 91, ex-*Whitton*, stricken 1981), *Karwar* (M 92, ex-*Overton*, stricken 1981), *Kakinada* (M 93, ex-*Durweston*, stricken 1980)

Transferred from RN in 1956 and named after small Indian ports. In reserve from early 1978 when Soviet 'Natya' class arrived.

Ex-Soviet 'NATYA' class *ocean minesweepers*

Class (no, transfer):
Pondicherry (M 61, early 1978), *Porbandar* (M 62, 1979), *Bedi* (M 63, 1979), *Bhavnagar* (M 64, 1979), *Alleppy* (M 65, 1980), *Ratnagiri* (M 66, 1980)

Last pair sailed from Baltic in July 1980. Lack stern ramp of Soviet ships.

British 'HAM' class *inshore minesweepers*

Class (no, former name):
Bimlipathan (M 79, ex-*Hildersham*), *Bassein* (M 80, ex-*Littleham*), *Bhatkal* (M 81), *Bulsar* (M 82)

First two transferred from RN in 1955. Last two built by Mazagon of Bombay being launched May 1967 and 17.5.69 respectively. All extant 1982.

Indonesia

After Indonesia finally gained independence from the Netherlands on 27 December 1949 the young republic started with a moderate build-up of her own naval forces. The first vessels of the Indonesian Navy were two former Australian *Bathurst* class minesweepers which were commissioned as corvettes in December 1949. In 1950 two sister ships and two former US subchasers as well as several Dutch customs and governmental vessels which had survived the war in the Dutch Indies were added to the Fleet. During 1949–52 17 patrol boats of the *Alkai* class were built by Dutch shipyards for Indonesia and from 1951 the former Dutch destroyer *Tjerk Hiddes* served for many years as the flagship. She was named *Gadjah Mada*.

In 1954 a programme for new construction was set up which included two destroyers and two corvettes ordered in Italy. Ten minesweepers and sail training vessel *Dewarutji* were built by German shipyards and in 1958 six patrol boats were received from Yugoslavia. Indonesia's approach to the Eastern Bloc led to a massive naval build-up. From 1959 to 1964 about 100 naval vessels, including a cruiser, 7 destroyers, 7 frigates and 14 submarines were received from the Soviet Union. None of these ships were involved in the 1963–66 Borneo Confrontation with Britain and Malaysia; only Indonesian marines and river craft took part.

In October 1965 when a military coup in Indonesia led by General Raden Suharto ended President Sukarno's pro-Soviet policy, the situation changed completely. As the new regime refused to pay the 800 million debt to Russia and many thousands of Communists were massacred, supply of spares for the above mentioned ships was ended. For this reason and the lack of funds for maintenance, the Indonesian government in July 1970 announced its decision to sell all ships of Russian origin for scrapping. In 1973 a decision was taken to reduce Indonesia's armed forces: the Army from 300,000 to 200,000, Air Force and Navy from 100,000 to 30,000 each. The Marine Corps which had been reduced from 16,000 to 5000 was however increased in recent years to 12,000.

During this period of rundown the Navy found itself enlarging the state. In August 1975 civil war broke out in the Portuguese colony of East Timor. By mid-September 30 Indonesian warships, including 3–5 frigates, were offshore and on 7 December they bombarded in support of marine and paratroop (1000 men each) landings to seize the island capital Dili. With the aid of local anti-Communist guerrillas the coastal towns of Maubara and Baucau, the Ocussi Ambeno enclave and the offshore island of Atauro were all occupied before the year was out. East Timor became the sprawling archipelago's 27th province.

After all ex-Soviet destroyers and most frigates had been sold for scrap new ships were ordered. From 1977–79 three new corvettes (light frigates) of the *Fatahillah* class were built in Dutch yards. Four frigates, 12 minesweepers and several auxiliary ships were bought from the United States. The South Korean shipyard Tacoma, Masan won a contract for four missile-armed fast attack craft with more to follow. Over the next 20 years it is planned to reorganise the Navy into a modern force with a total strength of 30,000 men, including 5000 marines. The Fleet will probably be composed of 4 modern ASW frigates, 4–5 corvettes, 6 modern submarines, several fast attack craft, numerous minesweepers, patrol craft and a fast supply ship.

Its principal bases are Gorontalo, Kemayoran (Jakarta) and Surabaya on Java. A new naval base is planned at Teluk Ratai on S Sumatra, costing a reported £3bn to replace that at Surabaya and due for completion in the late 1980s. The nine local shipyards are able to build small surface units. Some 1000 men serve in a naval air arm with 23 aircraft and 28 helicopters.

MAJOR SURFACE SHIPS

Ex-Soviet SVERDLOV class *cruiser*

No	Name	Builder	Acquired	Fate
201	IRIAN (ex-*Ordzonikidze*)	Admiralty	Oct 1962	BU

Sold to Indonesia in 1962 where she arrived in Oct 1962 with pennant no 201. A second Soviet cruiser was to have been acquired by the end of 1963 according to Indonesian sources but was never delivered. There were also talks about an aircraft carrier built on the *Sverdlov* class hull but eventually nothing came out of it. *Irian* was modified to serve in the tropical climate but still was ill suited to the tasks of the Indonesian Navy. She was put in 1972 on a disposal list because of lack of spare parts needed to keep this impressive ship running.

Ex-British 'N' class *destroyer*

No	Name	Builder	Acquired	Fate
	GADJAH MADA (ex-*Tjerk Hiddes*, ex-*Nonpareil*)	Denny	1.3.51	BU 1961

RN 1941-built destroyer transferred to the Royal Netherlands Navy in 1942. Served as Indonesian flagship. Stricken and scrapped in 1961.

Ex-Soviet SKORY class *destroyers*

No	Name	Builder	Acquired	Fate
201	SILIWANGI	USSR	1959	Deleted 1971
202	SINGAMANGA-RADJA	USSR	1959	Deleted 1971
203	SANDJAJA	USSR	1959	Deleted 1971
204	SAWUNGGALING (ex-*Srawadjala*)	USSR	1959	Deleted
304	SULTAN ISKANDARMUDA	USSR	1962	Deleted 1971
306	DIPONEGORO	USSR	1964	Deleted 1973
307	BRAWIDJAJA	USSR	1964	Deleted 1973

All 1950–53 built warships. *Sandjaja*, *Siliwangi*, *Singamangaradja* (means 'gannet') and *Sultan Iskandarmuda* were deleted from the list in 1971 and used for spare parts for remaining vessels; *Brawidjaja* and *Diponegoro* (named after the prince who fought the 1825–30 Great Java War against the Dutch) deleted in 1973. *Diponegoro* was probably renamed *Sultan Badarudin*.

ALMIRANTE CLEMENTE type *frigates*

No	Name	Builder	Launched	Fate
250	IMAN BONDJOL	Ansaldo Leghorn	5.5.56	Stricken 1978
251	SURAPATI	Ansaldo, Leghorn	5.5.56	Stricken 1978

Surapati as completed   *Navarret Collection*

Two fast frigates of the type designed and built (both laid down 8.1.56, completed 19.5. and 28.5.58) earlier for Venezuela as *Almirante Clemente* class. The light AA armament differed in being 6–30mm (3×2) and 6–20mm (3×2). They were never really modernised and were deleted in 1978. Pennant numbers 355 and 356 replaced 250 and 251.

Ex-Soviet 'RIGA' class *frigates*

No	Name	Builder	Acquired	Fate
351	JOS SUDARSO	USSR	1964	Extant 1982
352	SLAMET RIJADI	USSR		Deleted 1973
353	NGURAH RAI	USSR		Deleted 1974
355	MONGINSIDI	USSR		Deleted 1971
357	LAMBUNG MANG-KURAT	USSR	1964	Extant 1982
539	KALIALI	USSR		
360	NUKU	USSR		Stricken 1981
358	HANG TUAH	USSR		Deleted 1971

These 7 ships of the 'Riga' class (built 1954–57) were transferred from the USSR in the early 1960s: two (original pennant nos 405 and 406) in 1962 with cruiser *Irian*, two in 1963 and the last three in 1964. *Monginsidi* was placed in reserve in 1969.

Ex-US CLAUD JONES class *frigates*

No	Name	Builder	Acquired	Fate
341	SAMADIKUN (ex-*John R Perry*)	Avondale	20.2.73	Extant 1982
342	MARTADINATA (ex-*Charles Berry*)	Avondale	31.1.74	Extant 1982
343	MONGINSIDI (ex-*Claud Jones*)	Avondale	16.12.74	Extant 1982
344	NGURAH RAI (ex-*McMorris*)	Avondale	16.12.74	Extant 1982

These four ships modelled on *Dealey* class destroyer (ocean) escorts were fitted with diesel propulsion instead of steam plant and were considered not too successful by US Navy and as surplus to their needs were sold to Indonesian Navy. *Monginsidi* took part in the 1975 E Timor operations. In 341 and 342 2 Soviet 37mm (1×2) replaced a US 76mm and 2–25mm (1×2) were added to the fo'c'sle break. No 341 lost her ESM domes. SPS-10 and SPG-52 radar have been added. Sonar is now SQS-42. *Samadikun* has been Fleet flagship. All refitted at Subic Bay, Philippines, 1979–82.

Malahayati as completed

FATAHILLAH class *frigates*

Displacement:	1200t standard; 1450t full load
Dimensions:	276ft oa × 36ft 5in × 10ft 9in *83.9m oa × 11.1m × 3.4m*
Machinery:	2-shaft CODOG (2 CP propellers): 1 gas turbine Rolls-Royce TM 3B Olympus 28,000shp = 30kts, plus 2 diesels MTU 16V956 TB91, 6000bhp = 21kts. Range 4250nm at 16kts
Armament:	4 MM38 Exocet SSM (2×2), 1–120mm/46 Bofors (400rds), 1–40mm/70 Bofors (3000rds), 2–20mm (2×1), 2–375mm Bofors SR-375A ASW RL (1×2); 54 Neilli and Erica rockets) Mk 32 324mm ASW TT (2×3, 6 spare torpedoes)
Sensors:	Radar Decca AC 1229, HSA DA-05/2, WM-28; sonar PHS-32; ECM SUSIE-1 system, 2 Vickers Mk 4 chaff RL (50rds)
Complement:	89

No	Name	Builder	Launched	Fate
361	FATAHILLAH	Wilton-Fijenrood	22.12.77	Extant 1982
362	MALAHAYATI	Wilton-Fijenrood	19.6.78	Extant 1982
363	NALA	Wilton-Fijenrood	11.1.79	Extant 1982

These compact ships of small frigate type were ordered from Netherlands in Aug 1975 and designed by NEVESBU which belong to Rhine-Schelde-Verolme. *Fatahillah* laid down 31.1.77 and completed 16.7.79. *Malahayati* laid down 28.7.77, completed 21.3.80. Air-conditioned living spaces and NBC warfare citadel. DAISY computer system. Officially they are classed as corvettes. *Nala* (laid down 21.1.78, completed Aug 1980) differs from sisters having a helicopter (BO 105) facility and collapsible hangar for one small helicopter and her light AA consists of two Bofors 40mm/70 abreast the hangar.

Nala 27.3.80   *L & L van Ginderen*

HSAR DEWANTARA *training frigate*

Particulars: As Iraqi *Ibn Khaldoum*

No	Name	Builder	Launched	Fate
364	HSAR DEWANTARA	Titograd, Yugoslavia	11.10.80	Extant 1982

Ordered 14.3.78 from Yugoslavia, where the hull (laid down 11.5.79) was built and engines fitted. Armament and electronics were fitted in the Netherlands and Indonesia. She was completed 20.8.81. In peacetime used for training and troop transport.

SUBMARINES

Ex-Soviet 'WHISKEY' class *submarines*

Class (no):
Tjakra, *Trisula* (402), *Nagabanda* (403), *Nagarangsang* (404), *Hendradjala* (405), *Alugoro*, *Nanggala*, *Tjandrasa* (408), *Widjajadanu* (409), *Pasopati* (410), *Tjundamani*, *Bramastra* (412); two without Indonesian names.
Nanggala and *Tjakra* (bought from Poland) were transferred in 1959, the former being overhauled at Surabaya, and others followed. The four additional submarines which arrived in Indonesia on 28.6.62 brought the total number of this class transferred to 14 units. Some were to be used only for spare parts and others kept in reserve. *Nanggala* and *Tjakra* were deleted from the list in 1972; *Alugoro*, *Hendradjala*, *Nagarangsang*, *Tjandrasa*, *Tjundamani*, *Trisula*, *Widjajadanu* in 1974, *Naga Banda* in 1976. *Bramastra* stricken 1981. *Pasopati*, the sole named survivor, has new British batteries.

German Type 209 *submarines*

No	Name	Builder	Launched	Fate
401	CAKRA	Howaldswerke, Kiel	10.9.80	Extant 1982
402	NANGGALA	Howaldswerke, Kiel	10.9.80	Extant 1982

German export boats ordered on 2.4.77, and laid down 25.11.77 and 14.3.78 respectively. They were completed 18.3.81 and Aug 1981. There were plans to build two more boats. Some sources cite the name of second boat (No 402) as *Candrasa*.

AMPHIBIOUS WARFARE VESSELS

Ex-US LST 511 class *landing ships*

Class (no, former names):
Teluk Bajur (502, ex-*LST 616*), *Teluk Bone* (511, ex-*Iredell County* LST 839), *Teluk Kau* (504, ex-*LST 562*), *Teluk Langsa* (501, ex-*LST 1128*), *Teluk Manado* (505, ex-*LST 657*), *Teluk Ratai* (509, ex-*Inagua Shipper*, ex-*LST ...*), *Teluk Saleh* (510, ex-*Clarke County/LST 601*), *Teluk Tomini* (508, ex-*Bledsoe County*, LST 356), *Tandjung Nusanive* (ex-*Lawrence City*, LST 889), *Tandjung Radja* (ex-*LST 1090*), *Teluk Mentawi* (595, ex-*LST ...*)
Former US LST type landing ships transferred in March 1960 (505), June 1961 (502, 510, 511) and July 1970 (504 and 501). Built in 1943. 'Teluk' means 'bay'. *Tandjung Nusanive* deleted in 1974. Some armed with ex-Soviet 37mm guns. *Tandjung Radja* stricken 1966. Nos 502 and 508 have been in Military Sealift Command since 1978.

Japanese type LST *landing ship*

Class:
Teluk Amboina, no 869 (changed to 503)
Built in Sasebo, Japan, launched 17.3.61 and transferred to Indonesian Navy in June 1961. A copy of US LST 511 class.

Korean LST type *landing ships*

Class (no, in service):
Teluk Semangka (512, 20.1.81), *Teluk Penyu* (513, 20.1.81), *Teluk Mandarg* (514, July 1981), *Teluk Sampit* (515, 1981), *516*, *517*
All built by Tacoma, Korea and first 4 (ordered June 1979) were delivered in 1981 and the last 2 (ordered June 1981) in 1982. Technical details are lacking, but they are copies of the US LST 542 type. There are also *c*25 LCM type landing craft and *c*20 LCVP, and 13 LCMs built in Indonesia since 1976.

Ex-Yugoslav LCT type

Class:
Teluk Katurai, *Teluk Wadjo*, *Teluk Weda*, *Teluk Wori*
Transferred from Yugoslavia on 1.11.58. Nos 862, 860, 861 and 863 respectively. *Teluk Wadjo* and *Teluk Weda* in reserve in 1969. All stricken by 1974.

Ex-US LCI type *infantry landing craft*

Class (former names):
Amahai (864, ex-*Tropenvogel*, ex-*LCI 467*), *Marich* (866, ex-*Zeemeeuw*, ex-*LCI ...*), *Piru* (868, ex-*Zeearend*, ex-*LCI 420*), *Baruna* (ex-*Vogel*, ex-*LCI 948*), *Namlea* (ex-*Stormvogel*, ex-*LCI 588*)
Former US infantry landing craft, built in 1943. Handed over by the Netherlands East Indies Government on formation of Indonesian Navy in 1950. *Baruna* and *Namlea* were rerated as pilot ship and lightship in 1961. Remaining 3 deleted in 1974.

Ex-US LCU type *infantry landing craft*

Class:
Dore, *Amurang*, *Banten*
Transferred from USN. Built by Korneuburg SY, Austria, in 1968.

Banten   *Courtesy John Mortimer*

KRUPANG class *utility landing craft*

Displacement:	200t full load
Dimensions:	99ft 5in × 32ft 1in × ?
	30.2m × 9.8m × ?m
Machinery:	2 diesels, ? hp = 11kts. Range 700nm at 11kts
Armament:	Nil
Complement:	17

Class (in service):
Kupang (3.11.78), *Dili* (27.2.79), *Nusantara* (1980)
Indonesian-built and designed small landing craft type based on US LCU 1610 class. Built in Surabaya by Naval Training Centre. All in Military Sealift Command.

SMALL SURFACE COMBATANTS

Ex-Australian BATHURST class *minesweepers (corvettes)*

Class (former names):
Banteng (ex-*Ambon*, ex-*Cairns*), *Hang Tuah* (ex-*Morotai*, ex-*Ipswich*), *Pati Unus* (ex-*Tidore*, ex-*Tamworth*), *Radjawali* (ex-*Banda*, ex-*Wollongong*)
Built in Australia as ocean minesweepers and launched in 1941–42. *Hang Tuah* and *Pati Unus* transferred from Royal Netherlands Navy, 28.12.49, *Banteng* and *Radjawali* transferred 6.4.50. *Hang Tuah* was reported sunk by rebel aircraft off Balikpapan, E Borneo on 28.4.58; *Banteng* and *Randjawali* arrived at Hong Kong for scrapping in April 1968; and *Pati Unus*, latterly as TS, was disposed of in 1969.

Pattimura as completed

PATTIMURA class *corvettes*

Displacement:	950t standard; 1200t full load
Dimensions:	270ft 2in oa, 246ft pp × 34ft × 9ft
	82.4m, 75.0m × 10.4m × 2.7m
Machinery:	3 shafts, 3 Ansaldo-Fiat diesels, 6900bhp = 22kts. Oil 100t. Range 2400nm at 18kts
Armament:	2–76mm/40 (2×1), 2–30mm/70 (1×2), 2 Hedgehogs, 4 DCT, DC rail
Complement:	110

No	Name	Builder	Launched	Fate
252	PATTIMURA	Ansaldo	1.7.56	Extant 1982
253	SULTAN HASANUDIN	Ansaldo	24.3.57	Stricken 1979

Italian *Albatros* class corvettes with diesel engines. Such ships were built for Denmark, 1 for Netherlands and 3 for Italy. All sub-types vary in details. Indonesian ships were ordered together with fast frigates of *Surapati* class. Rearmed with Soviet 2–85mm and 4–25mm (2×2), 4–14.5mm MG (2×2) from deleted FAC 1976–77. New Pt. Nos 371 and 372 from *c* 1975 instead of 252, 263. Both laid down 8.1.56 and completed 28.1.58 and 8.3.58 respectively.

German JAGUAR type *fast attack craft (torpedo)*

Class:
Adjak, Anoa, Biruang, Harimau, Madjan Kumbang, Madjan Tutul, Serigala, Singa

'TNC 45' boats built by Lürssen, Vegesack, in 1959–60. The first four boats had wooden hulls, but the second four were built of steel. Pennant nos 601–608. *Madjan Tutul* sunk on 15.1.62 by Dutch warships off Borneo while trying to land infiltrators in New Guinea, her 2 sisters fled. *Adjak* and *Singa* deleted in 1974; *Serigala* in 1977, *Madjan Kumbang* in 1979. *Biruang* (652) and *Harimau* (654) extant 1982.

Ex-Soviet 'P 6' type *fast attack craft (torpedo)*

Class:
Angin Bohorok, Angin Badai, Angin Taufan, Angin Gending, Angin Prahara, Angin Pujuh, Angin Pasat, Angin Wambrau, Angin Brubu, Angin Tonggi, Angin Grenggong, Angin Wamandais, Angin Kumbang, Angin Ribut and ten boats without names.

Former Soviet interchangeable gun/torpedo boats. A total of 24 reported delivered since 1961, including 8 in 1961 and 6 in 1962. Pennant numbers in the 1600 range. Probably the last 10 were intended for cannibalisation to provide spare parts for operational boats. All stricken by 1975.

Ex-Soviet KOMAR class *fast attack craft (missile)*

Class (no):
Guawidjaja (612), *Hardadali, Kalamisani* (602), *Kalanada, Katjabola, Kelaplintah, Pulanggeni* (605), *Nagapasa* (611), *Surotama* (608), *Sarpamina, Sarpawasesa* (603), *Tritusta*

Transferred in three batches: 6 in 1961–63, 4 in Sept 1964 and 2 in 1965. Ten ships were in commission and two in reserve. Missiles now of probably doubtful capability. *Hardadali* sank early 1976 after hitting an underwater obstacle. *Surotama, Kalamisani, Nagapasa* deleted in 1979, *Pulanggeni* in 1974, *Katjabola, Tritusta* in 1976. Last 5 stricken 1979–81.

PSK Mk 5 class *fast attack craft (missile)*

Displacement:	290t full load; 250t standard
Dimensions:	175ft 10in × 26ft 2in × 5ft 2in
	53.6m × 8.0m × 1.6m
Machinery:	2-shaft CODOG (2 CP propellers): 1 gas turbine GE LM 2500, 25,000shp = 41kts, 2 diesels MTU 12V331 TC81, 2240bhp = 17kts. Range 2000nm at 17kts
Armament:	4 MM38 Exocet SSM (4×1), 1–57mm/70 Bofors Mk 1, 1–40mm/70 Bofors, 2–20mm (1×2)
Sensors:	Radar Decca AC 1229, HSA WM-28
Complement:	32

Class (no, completed):
Mandau (621, 20.7.79), *Rencong* (622, 20.7.79), *Badek* (623, Feb 1980), *Keris* (624, Feb 1980)

All built by S Korea-Tacoma SYd. First ship laid down May 1977. Modified US *Asheville class* FAC design. Another 4 ordered in 1980.

Ex-Soviet KRONSTADT class *large patrol craft*

Class (no):
Barakuda (817), *Kakap* (816), *Katula* (811), *Landjuru, Lapai, Lumba-Lumba, Madidihang, Momare, Palu* (818), *Pandrong* (814), *Sura* (815), *Tohok* (829), *Tongkol, Tjutjut.*

Fourteen former Soviet submarine chasers. Built 1951–54 and transferred to the Indonesian Navy on 30.12.58 (8) and later *Landjuru, Lapai, Lumba-Lumba, Madidihang, Momare* and *Tongkol* were withdrawn from active service in 1970 and used for spares for the rest of the type. Deletions: 1975 – *Landjuru, Lapai, Lumba-Lumba, Madidihang, Tongkol, Tjutjut;* 1976 – *Katula, Momare, Tohok;* 1981 – *Kakap.*

Ex-US PC (173ft) type *submarine-chasers*

Class (no, former name):
Hui (805, ex-*Malvern* PC 580), *Tenggiri* (ex-*PC 1183*), *Tjakalang* (807, ex-*Pierre* PC 1141), *Torani* (ex-*Manville* PC 581), *Alu Alu* (ex-PC 787)

Former US submarine chasers of the steel-hulled PC type built in 1942–43. *Pierre* transferred in 1958, *Malvern* and *Manville* in 1960. *Alu Alu* was removed from the the effective list in 1961. *Tenggiri* later had letters TGR painted on her bows instead of the no 309. Probably other boats had their markings also changed. *Torani* deleted in 1979, *Tenggiri* in 1974.

Carpentaria type patrol craft 26.12.76   *Ross Gillett*

Ex-Yugoslav Type 509 'KRALJEVICA *large patrol craft*

Class (no, former name):
Lajang (819, ex-*PBR 515*), *Lemadang* (820, ex-*PBR 517*), *Krapu* (821, ex-*PBR 518*), *Dorang* (822, ex-*PBR 513*), *Todak* (823, ex-*PBR 514*), *Bubara* (ex-*PBR 516*)

Six bought and transferred on 27.12.58. Original pennant nos 310–312, 314, 316 until *c* 1976. *Bubara* and *Lajang* deleted in 1970, *Krapu* in 1976.

KELABANG class *large patrol craft*

Class:
Kalahitam, Kelabang, Kompas

So called 'Mawar' class submarine-chasers built in 1966–70 in Indonesia at Surabaya; 150t, 127ft 11in × 18ft 8in × 5ft 10in, *39m × 5.7m × 1.8m*, 1–40mm, 1–20mm, 21kts. *Kompas* since deleted. Early armament: 4–12.7mm MG (2×2).

3 Ex-US PGM 39 class *patrol craft*

Class (no, former names):
Bentang Silungkang (572, ex-*PGM 55*), *Bentang Waitatiri* (571/841, ex-*PGM 56*), *Bentang Kalakuan* (570/843, ex-*PGM 57*)

Originally intended as amphibious control craft but now used for normal patrol duties. All transferred in Jan 1962. Built in 1958–60 by Petersen Boatbuilders. *Silungkang* deleted 1981, other 2 extant 1982.

Ex-Australian ATTACK class *patrol craft*

Class (no, former name, transfer):
Sibarau (870, ex-*Bandolier*, 16.11.73), *Silinan* (831, ex-*Archer*, 1974), *Sigalu* (832, ex-*Barricade*, 1982)

Transferred from RAN after refit. Renumbered 847, 848 and 849. Two more are to be transferred in 1983.

Australian CARPENTARIA type *coastal patrol craft*

Class (no, in service):
Sabola (853, Oct 1976), *Sadarin* (855, Dec 1976), *Salmaneti* (856, July 1977), *Samadar* (851, Aug 1976), *Sasila* (852, Sept 1976), *Sawangi* (854, Nov 1976)
Built by de Havilland Marine, Australia in 1975–77. Grant-aided purchase. All 6 extant 1982. See under Burma for data.

MINE WARFARE VESSELS

Ex-Dutch DJEMBER class *coastal minesweepers*

Class:
Djombangh, Djampea, Enggano, Flores
Four transferred to Indonesia in 1951. They were scuttled in 1942 at Tandjong Priok (where built) and repaired by Japanese. After the war returned and transferred to Indonesia. All stricken in 1974.

German R-BOAT type *inshore minesweepers*

Class:
Pulau Rangsang, Pulau Rau, Pulau Rindja, Pulau Raas, Pulau Rempang, Pulau Rengat, Pulau Rupat, Pulau Rusa, Pulau Roma, Pulau Roti
Built by Abeking & Rasmussen Yacht und Bootswerft, Lamwerder in 1954–57. These boats had a framework of metal covered with wood. *Pulau Ras* and *Pulau Roti* deleted in 1969; *Pulau Rau, Pualu Rempang, Pulau Rusa, Pulau Roma* deleted in 1974 and *Pulau Rindja* in 1975, *Pulau Rengat* in 1979, *Pulau Rupat* in 1981.

Ex-Soviet 'T 43' type *ocean minesweepers*

Class (no):
Pulau Rani (701), *Pulau Roon* (703), *Pulau Radja* (705), *Pulau Ratewo* (702), *Pulau Rorbas* (704), *Pulau Rondo* (706)
Four transferred in 1962 and two in 1964. *Pulau Roon* deleted in 1979 and *Pulau Rondo* deleted in 1976. Four extant 1982, some with Decca 110 radar.

Ex-US BLUEBIRD class *coastal minesweepers*

Class (no, former name):
Pulau Alor (717, ex-*Meadowlark*), *Pulau Anjer* (719, ex-*Limpkin*), *Pulau Atang* (721, ex-*Frigate Bird*), *Pulau Aru* (722, ex-*Falcon*), *Pulau Aruan* (718, ex-*Jacana*), *Pulau Impalasa* (720, ex-*Humming Bird*)
Transferred from USN in 1971; all have wooden hulls with low magnetic signature. Stricken from the list in 1976.

MISCELLANEOUS
Two Fairey Marine 'Spear' class patrol craft bought in 1973–74.
One Boeing Jetfoil hydrofoil, *Bima Samudera 1*, launched 22.10.81. Arrived Indonesia 1982 for naval/civil evaluation.
In 1982 the Indonesian Customs service had 58 patrol boats of French, German and Japanese construction, some armed with 20mm guns or MGs. Another 12 were building.
The Maritime Police operated the following *armed* large patrol craft:
Four *Bango* class (built Netherlands 1952–53, 194t, 11kts, 1–40mm, 4-MG): all deleted after 1976.
Eight 'Atang' class (built Netherlands 1949–50, 247t, 12kts, 1–37mm, 4-MG, 20 men): all deleted after 1976.

Kiribati (Gilberts)

This Central Pacific island group, formerly the British Gilberts, achieved independence as a Commonwealth republic in 1979. The 33 islands, half uninhabited, dot 2 million square miles of the SW Central ocean. Tarawa, the capital, has 40 per cent of the population (56,452 in 1978) and its Marine Training School teaches seamen for employment with overseas shipping companies. Kiribati acquired a 17-metre GRP patrol craft of 22t (23.6kts, 1–7.62mm MG, 7 men) from Cheverton of Cowes (UK) in 1980.

Korea

Allied troops entered Korea – Soviets from the North and Americans from the South to take the Japanese surrender in 1945. Korea was divided into Soviet and US areas at the 38th Parallel. This resulted finally in the establishment of two Korean states – the Communist-North and the anti-Communist South. Soviet troops were reportedly withdrawn in 1948 and US in 1949. South Korea was invaded from the North on 25 June 1950 and this started the Korean War which lasted more than three years. Most of the North's 16 patrol craft were sunk or run aground within a week by US and British warships. More than a million people were killed, 2.5 million were left homeless and property damage was estimated at over a billion dollars. Hostilities did not end until 27 July 1953. South Korea was helped by troops and ships from 15 UN countries and North Korea got help from China and the Soviet Union. South Korea, originally the more agricultural and less skilled part of the country, is officially called the Republic of Korea, and the 20 per cent larger but half as populous North became the Democratic People's Republic of Korea.

Korea's naval traditions are far older, preceding the Nelsonian victories of Admiral Yi Sung Sin's 'tortoise' ironclads against Japan in 1592–98. The North Korean Navy has as its mainstay a force of 'Romeo' and 'Whiskey' class patrol submarines. At least 16 of these boats are in service and they would be major offensive weapon in the event of another war with South Korea. In 1969, 1974 and 1979 'spy' ships of either side were sunk by the other's warships. The surface forces comprise a nucleus of four locally built frigates of the 'Najin' class and fast missile craft supported by several hundred gun/torpedo units of various types. Four of these made headlines on 23 January 1968 firing at and arresting the intelligence ship USS *Pueblo* in international waters. The ship was taken into Wonsan and 82 crew endured 11 months captivity before being released on North Korea's terms. These units are probably intended for coastal operations against more numerous South Korean large surface ships. A most interesting development is the reported construction of a number of small coastal submarines. Principal bases are Wonsan (E coast) and Nampo (W coast) with 14 minor harbours. Two 'Samlet' coast defence missile sites exist. North Korean sailors (33,000 with 40,000 reserves in 1982) have to serve five years. Their southern counterparts (49,000 including a 2-division Marine Corps of 24,000 and 60,000 reserves) do three years service.

The South Korean Navy had 7500 men by September 1949 and about 34 small ex-US and Japanese ships had been acquired before the Korean War began though many had not been delivered. Five frigates and landing ships were added during hostilities and in July 1954 took the disputed Takeshima islands. They were active afterwards seizing Japanese fishing boats infringing the 'Rhee Line' in a two-year dispute. The first two destroyers were received in 1963.

South Korea is, in terms of indigenous naval construction, one of the most advanced maritime nations in Asia. The merchant fleet was doubled in numbers and quadrupled in tonnage since 1974. Many warship designs are being produced, with an eye not only on home requirements, but also for increasing export in the region to Thailand, Indonesia, Taiwan, and the Philippines. Current construction programmes range from *Ulsan* class frigates and large sophisticated missile-armed fast attack craft to small patrol boats. For its part the South Korean Navy seems to be emphasising large missile craft designed for defence against larger ships or small fast patrol boats. At least eight *Paek Ku* type missile boats (called PSMM-5) have been constructed, and they will probably be followed by more. The *Ulsan* class are very important as they are to replace old, worn out ex-American destroyers as the chief surface units. However their high cost is prohibitive and so far only three are to be built although South Korean defence spending between 1975 and 1981 took 29–36 per cent of government expenditure, a higher proportion than anywhere in Asia except Taiwan.

Fleet HQ is at Chinhae with 100 active ships under command in 1982. The six naval commands (under a rear-admiral or commodore) are based at Inchon, Mokpo (both W Coast), Cheju island south of the peninsula, Mukho Pohang and Pusan (both E coast). The Navy flies 23 US Tracker ASW aircraft from Kimhae near Pusan. Since October 1973 the Marine Corps has been under the direct command of the Vice Chief of Naval Operations.

South Korea

MAJOR SURFACE SHIPS

Ex-US FLETCHER class *destroyers*

No	Name	Builder	Acquired	Fate
911	CHUNG MU (ex-*Erben*)	Bath Iron Wks	1.5.63	Extant 1982
912	SEOUL (ex-*Halsey Powell*)	Bethlehem, Staten I	27.4.63	Extant 1982
913	PUSAN (ex-*Hickox*)	Federal, Kearny	15.11.68	Extant 1982

Former USN destroyers built in 1942–43 and bought on 31.1.77. Original Korean pennant nos 91–93.

Ex-US GEARING (FRAM II) class *destroyers*

No	Name	Builder	Acquired	Fate
915	CHUNG BUK (ex-*Chevalier*)	Bath Iron Wks	5.7.72	Extant 1982
916	JEONG BUK (ex-*Everett F Larsen*)	Bath Iron Wks	5.7.72	Extant 1982

Built in 1944–45 and converted in American service to radar picket destroyers (DDR) in 1949 and subsequently modernised under the FRAM II programme in the 1960s. Fitted with a small hangar and flight deck. Armament includes an Alouette III helicopter. *Chung Buk* received reportedly in 1976 a 20mm Vulcan-Phalanx CIWS which was fitted on the hangar roof. *Jeong Buk* was armed with a twin 30mm Emerlec gun mounting. Both are to get 8 Harpoon SSM (2×4). Both loaned in 1972 and bought on 31.1.77. Originally had Korean pennant nos 95 and 96.

Ex-US ALLEN M SUMNER (FRAM II) class *destroyers*

No	Name	Builder	Acquired	Fate
917	DAE GU (ex-*Wallace L Lind*)	Federal, Kearny	Dec 1973	Extant 1982
918	IN CHEON (ex-*De Haven*)	Bath Iron Wks	Dec 1973	Extant 1982

Fitted with small flight deck and hangar intended for DASH drone but now are to be fitted with LAMPS (with light helicopter). Transferred in 1973 and sold in Jan 1977. To get 8 Harpoon SSM (2×4).

Ex-US GEARING (FRAM I) class *destroyers*

No	Name	Builder	Acquired	Fate
922	KANG WON (ex-*William R Rush*)	Federal, Kearny	1974	Extant 1982
921	KWANG JU (ex-*Richard E Kraus*)	Bath Iron Wks	23.2.77	Extant 1982
919	TAEJON	Consolidated, Orange	23.2.77	Extant 1982
925	CHANG JO (ex-*Rogers*)	Consolidated, Orange	11.8.81	Extant 1982
923	KYONG KAI (ex-*Newman K Perry*)	Consolidated, Orange	27.7.81	Extant 1982

Former US *Gearing* FRAM I class destroyers built in 1944–46. All modernised in 1960s under FRAM I programme. Fitted with enlarged helicopter hangar and landing deck for a small Alouette III helicopter. It is planned to fit them with 8 Harpoon SSM (2×4). *Kang Won* was loaned initially and bought on 1.7.78 or 1.7.79.

Ex-US TACOMA class *patrol frigates*

No	Name	Builder	Acquired	Fate
61	DU MAN (ex-*Muskogee*)	Consolidated Steel, San Pedro	5.11.50	Stricken c 1974
62	APNOK (ex-*Rockford*)	Consolidated Steel, San Pedro	5.11.50	Sunk as target 1963
63	TAE TONG (ex-*Tacoma*)	Kaiser, Richmond	8.10.51	Stricken c 1974
65	NAK TONG (ex-*Hoquiam*)	Kaiser, Richmond	8.10.51	Stricken c 1974
66	IM CHIN (ex-*Sausalito*)	Kaiser, Richmond	Sept 1952	Stricken c 1974

Former USN frigates modelled on the British 'River' class. Built in 1943–44. These ships were amongst the 28 ships of this class transferred to USSR during summer 1945. Survivors were returned to US Navy in Japan in 1949. First large ships loaned to Korean Navy. Two more, ex-*Pasco* (PF 6) and *Gloucester* (PF 22), were towed from storage in Japan to Korea for spare part cannibalisation in Jan 1969. *Apnok* was damaged in collision on 21.5.52; returned to USA and sunk as target in 1963. Replaced by *Im Chin* transferred in Sept 1952. Note that pennant no 64 was not assigned as Koreans consider 'four' as an unlucky number. Second pair transferred at Yokosuka.

Ex-US CANNON ('DET') class *frigates*

No	Name	Builder	Acquired	Fate
71	KYONG KI (ex-*Muir*)	Tampa SB	Feb 1956	Stricken 28.12.77
72	KANG WON (ex-*Sutton*)	Tampa SB	Feb 1956	Stricken 28.10.77

Former US destroyer escorts of Cannon ('DET') class. Built in 1944 and transferred at Boston to Korean Navy. Named after Korean states. Taken over by the Philippines.

Ex-US APD type *frigates/high-speed transports*

No	Name	Builder	Acquired	Fate
822	KYONG NAM (ex-*Cavallaro*)	Defoe, Bay City	Oct 1959	Extant 1982
823	AH SAN (ex-*Harry L Corl*)	Bethlehem, Hingham	June 1966	Extant 1982
825	UNG PO (ex-*Julius A Raven*)	Bethlehem, Hingham	June 1966	Extant 1982
826	KYONG PUK (ex-*Kephart*)	Charleston N Yd	Aug 1967	Extant 1982
827	JONNAM (ex-*Hayter*)	Charleston N Yd	Aug 1967	Extant 1982
828	CHI JU (ex-*William M Hobby*)	Charleston N Yd	Aug 1967	Extant 1982

Former US high-speed transports (APD) begun as destroyer escorts (DE) and converted during construction. Built in 1943–45. In Korean service four latter ships were originally rated as gunboats (PG 83, 85–87); changed in 1972 to APD. First pair originally APD 81 and 82. Fitted for about 160 troops and can carry four LCVPs. These ships are in two different configurations with high and low bridges. Fitted with tripod masts. All finally bought outright 15.11.74.

Ex-US RUDDEROW ('TEV') class *frigate*

No	Name	Builder	Acquired	Fate
827	CHUNG NAM (ex-*Holt*)	Defoe, Bay City	19.6.63	Extant 1982

Built in 1943–44 and bought outright on 15.11.74.

ULSAN class *frigates*

Displacement:	1600t standard; 1970t full load
Dimensions:	334ft 7in × 37ft 8in × 11ft 9in *102.0m × 11.5m × 3.6m*
Machinery:	2-shaft CODOG (CP propellers): 1 GE LM 2500 gas turbine, 46,000shp = 35kts, plus 2 MTU 12V 956 diesels, 9600bhp = 25kts
Armament:	8 Harpoon SSM (2×4), 2–76mm/62 OTO Melara (2×1), 8–30mm/85 Emerlec (4×2), 6–324mm Mk 32 ASW TT (2×3)
Sensors:	Radar HSA DA-05, HSA ZW-06, HSA WM-28; sonar PAS 32
Complement:	123

No	Name	Builder	Launched	Fate
951	ULSAN	Hayundai S Yd	8.4.80	Extant 1982

Korean designed fast frigate built locally by Hayundai at Ulsan. Originally four planned but eventually three were cancelled owing to the relatively high cost. Well armed with light AA weapons (8–30mm). Modern Dutch electronics. A ship put together from the off-the-shelf equipment offered by European makers. *Ulsan* previously listed as *Ulsan Ham*.

AMPHIBIOUS WARFARE VESSELS

Ex-US LST type *tank landing ships*

Class (no, former names, transfer):
Ex-LST 120, ex-LST 213, *Dan Yang* (ex-LST 343), ex-LST 378, ex-LST 380, *Ryong Pi* (ex-LST 388), *An Tong* (ex-LST 491), ex-LST 536, ex-LST 594, *Chon Po* (ex-LST 595), *Ulsan* (ex-*LST 608*), ex-LST 624, *Ryong Hwa* (ex-LST 659), *Lyung Wha* (ex-LST 805), *Un Bong* (LST 671, ex-LST 1010, Feb 1955), *Duk Bong* (LST 672, ex-LST 227, March 1955), *Bi Bong* (LST 673, ex-LST 218, May 1955), *Kae Bong* (LST 675, ex-*Berkshire County* LST 288, March 1956), *Wee Bong* (LST 676, ex-*Johnson County* LST 849, Jan 1959), *Su Yong* (LST 677, ex-*Kane County* LST 853, Dec 1958), *Buk Han* (LST 678, ex-*Lynn County* LST 900, Dec 1958), *Hwa San* (LST 679, ex-*Pendar County*, LST 1080, Oct 1958).

All 22 transferred in 1950s. *An Tong* was wrecked and scrapped on 24.1.52. All ships except the last 8 were discarded by the end of 1959. Some never got Korean names. Some were probably renamed while in Korean service: *Ryong Hwa* (ex-*Chong Ho*), *Chon Po* (ex-*Chochiwan*), *Ryong Pi* (ex-*Samlangjin*). There was also *Jung Su* (ex-*APL 59*, ex-*LST 53*), a barrack ship transferred in 1955 and since deleted.

Ex-US LSM type *medium landing ships*

Class (no, former no):
Tae Cho (LSM 601, ex-LSM 546), *Tyo To* (LSM 602, ex-LSM 268), *Tok To* (LSM 603, ex-LSM 419), *Ka Tok* (LSM 605, ex-LSM 462), *Ko Mun* (LSM 606, ex-LSM 30), *Pian* (LSM 607, ex-LSM 96), *Pung To* (LSM 608, ex-LSM 54), *Wol Mi* (LSM 609, ex-LSM 57), *Ki Rin* (LSM 611, ex-LSM 19), *Nung Ra* (LSM 612, ex-LSM 84), *Sin Mi* (ex-LSM 316), *Ul Rung* (ex-LSM 17)

Twelve former USN ships, built in 1944–45. First 4 transferred in 1955 and the rest in 1956. *Sin Mi* and *Ul Rung* had served as French L 9014 and L 9017 in Indo-China 1954–55. All finally bought 15.11.74. *Tok To* was deleted and scrapped in 1963, *Pung To* serves as mine force flagship, fitted with mine-laying rails and designated LSML, others LSM. The number LSM 604 was not assigned.

Ex-US LSSL type *large support landing ships*

Class (no, former no):
Chung Jin (LSSL 105, ex-LSSL 1056), *Yung Huang Man* (LSSL 107, ex-LSSL 77), *Kang Hwa Man* (LSSL 108, ex-LSSL 91), *Po Song Man* (LSSL 109, ex-LSSL 54), *Yong II Man* (LSSL 110, ex-LSSL 84)

Chung Jin was a former US infantry landing ship large (LSIL, ex-LCI/L). The rest were employed as gunboats. Transferred in 1950s; *Chung Jin* and *Yong II Man* were deleted in 1962; *Yung Huang Man* and *Kang Hwa Man* were decommissioned in 1960 and *Po Song Man* in 1962.

Ex-US LSMR type *fire support landing ship*

Class:
Si Hung (LSMR 311, ex-*St Joseph River* LSMR 527)
Transferred on 15.9.60. Renumbered LSMR 650. Extant 1982.

US LCU 501 type *utility landing craft*

Class:
Mulkae 71 (LCU 1, ex-LCU 531), *Mulkae 72*, *Mulkae 73*, *Mulkae 75*
First unit built in 1943 as LCT(6) 631 and transferred to Korea in 1960. Renamed LCU 1 in Korean service. The other 3 were built in Korea. All extant 1982.

US LCU 1610 type *utility landing craft*

Six copies of this design were built in S Korea and brought into service 1979–81.

Ex-US LCM(8) class *landing craft*

Ten ex-US Army units transferred Sept 1978.

SMALL SURFACE COMBATANTS

Ex-US AUK class *corvettes (former ocean minesweepers)*

Class (no, former name):
Shin Song (PCE 711, ex-*Ptarmigan* MSF 376), *Sunchon* (PCE 712, ex-*Speed* MSF 116), *Koje* (PCE 713, ex-*Dextrous* MSF 341)

Former USN fleet minesweepers built in 1941–44. Originally designated AM in USN. Original Korean numbers PCE 1001–1003. The minesweeping gear was removed before the transfer and the second 76mm gun was fitted aft, ASW was augmented. *Shin Song* was transferred in July 1973, *Suchon* in Nov 1967 and *Koje* in Dec 1967. All extant 1982.

Ex-US PCE (185ft) type *patrol vessels*

Class:
Ko Jin (ex-*Report* MSF 289), *Ro Ryang* (ex-PCEC 882), *Myong Ryang* (ex-PCEC 896), *Han San* (ex-PCEC 873), *Ok Po* (ex-PCEC 898), *Tang Po* (ex-*Maria* PCE 842), *Pyok Pa* (ex-*Dania* PCE 870), *Ryul Po* (ex-*Somerset* PCE 892), *Sa Chon* (ex-*Batesburg* PCE 903); No PCEC 50–53, 55, PCE 56–59.

Nine USN patrol craft based on the *Admirable* class minesweeper hull built in 1943–44. Four were modified in US service as control ships (PCEC for operation with landing craft, being fitted with additional radio equipment in an enlarged bridge area. Transfers: *Ro Ryang* and *Myong Ryang* in Feb 1955, *Han San* and *Ok Po* in Sept 1955 and the rest in 1961. *Tang Po* was sunk by N Korean coastal guns on 19.1.67. *Han San*, *Ok Po*, *Ro Ryang*, *Myong Ryang* deleted in 1977 and the rest in 1979.

Ex-US PC (173ft) type *submarine chasers*

Class:
Pak Tu San (ex-*Ensign Whitehead*, ex-PC 823), *Kum Kang San* (ex-PC 810), *Sam Kak San* (ex-PC 802), *Chiri San* (ex-PC ?), *Han La San* (ex-*PC* 485), *Myo Hyang San* (ex-PC 600), *O Tae San* (ex-*Winnemussa* PC 1145), *Kum Chong San* (ex-*Grosse Point* PC 1546), *Sol Ak* (ex-*Chadron* PC 546)

Nine USN units built in the Second World War. *Pak Tu San*, the Navy's first ship, was purchased in Sept 1949 for 18,000 dollars and delivered in early 1950; next 4 (3 at Honolulu when war began) transferred during Korean War; *Chiri San* was mined and sunk off Wonsan, Korea on 26.12.51; *Kum Chong San* and *O Tae San* transferred in 1960; *Sol Ak* transferred in 1964. Korean pennant numbers PC 701–709. *Han La San* was sunk in a typhoon at Guam in Nov 1962 and although raised was scrapped in 1964. *Kum Kang San* and *Sam Kak San* were decommissioned in 1960 and scrapped; *Myo Hyang San* scrapped in 1968; *O Tae San*, *Sol Ak* and *Kum Chong San* deleted in 1970s.

Ex-US PT type *fast attack craft (torpedo)*

Class (no, former no):
Kalmaeki (PT 23, ex-PT 616), *Kiroki* (PT 25, ex-PT 619), *Olpamei* (PT 26, ex-PT 613), *Jebi* (PT 27, ex-PT 620)

Former US MTB of plywood hull construction built by Electric Boat Co in 1945 and transferred in Jan 1952. *Olpamei* destroyed in Sept 1952. The rest deleted in 1969. Former PT 616 was returned to USA for use as a memorial.

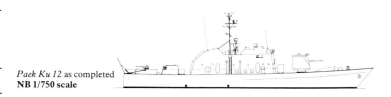

Paek Ku 12 as completed
NB 1/750 scale

PAEK KU (PSMM type) class *fast attack craft (missile)*

Displacement:	240t standard; 268t full load
Dimensions:	165ft × 24ft × 9ft 6in *50.3m × 7.3m × 2.9m*
Machinery:	COGAG, 2 shafts, (2 CP propellers): 6 Avco Lycoming TF 35 gas turbines, 16,800hp = 40+kts. Range 2400nm at 18kts
Armament:	4 Standard SSM (1 reload each), 1–76mm/50 Mk 34, 1–40mm, 2–12.7mm MG. See notes
Sensors:	LN-66HP, SPG-50
Complement:	32

Class (no, former name, completed):
Paek Ku 52 (PGM 352, ex-*Paek Ku 12*, 14.3.75), *Paek Ku 53* (PGM 353, ex-*Paek Ku 13*, 14.3.75), *Paek Ku 55* (PGM 355, ex-*Paek Ku 15*, 1.2.76), *Paek Ku 56* ((PGM 356, ex-*Paek Ku 16*, 1.2.76), *Paek Ku 57* (PGM 357, ex-*Paek Ku 17*, 1.2.76), *Paek Ku 58* (PGM 358, ex-*Paek Ku 18*, 1977), *Paek Ku 59* (PGM 359, ex-*Paek Ku 19*, 1977), *Paek Ku 61* (PGM 361, 1978)

Based on the US *Asheville* design and built for Korean Navy. Considered as multi-mission patrol ships (PSMM) by their builders. First 3 Tacoma, USA, the other 5 at Tacoma, S Korea. Aluminium hulls. Korean name *Paek Ku* means 'seagull'. The six TF 35 gas turbines turn two propeller shafts and one or two or three turbines can be selected to provide each shaft with variety of power settings. All are to get 8 Harpoon SSM (2×4). Prototype launched on 17.2.75 and others in 1975–77. All 8 extant 1982.

Ex-US ASHEVILLE class *fast attack craft (missile)*

US FAC (gun) ex-*Benicia* (PG 96), fitted in Korean service with Standard SSM. Built in 1969–70. Transferred to Korea on loan 15.10.71, became *Paek Ku 2*. Now *Paek Ku 5* (PGM 351, formerly 11 and 101). Arrived S Korea Jan 1972. No ASW weapons fitted. Missiles fitted in 1975–76. Extant 1982.

Kilurki class
NB 1/750 scale

KILURKI class *fast attack craft (gun)*

Particulars:	As US CPIC type

Class:
Kilurki 11 (ex-*Gireogi*), *Kilurki 12, 13, 15, 71, 72*
Built in USA and designated CPIC (Coastal Patrol and Interdiction Craft). *Gireogi* conducted extensive trials in US Navy. She was launched in 1973 by Tacoma Boatbuilding Co, Tacoma, Wash.; other 5 constructed in Korea by Korea Tacoma International. Pennant numbers PKM 211–213, 215, 271, 272. First commissioned in Korean Navy in 1975 and the rest in 1979. Of the planned next five boats none will be built.

Ex-US PCS (136ft) type *large patrol craft*

Class:
Su Song (ex-*PCS 1426*), *Kum Seong* (ex-*PCS 1445*), *Mok Seong* (ex-*PCS 1446*), *Hwa Seong* (ex-*PCS 1448*), *Kae Seong* (ex-Korean AMS 504), *Kilchu* (ex-Korean AMS 514), *Yong Kung* ex-AMS 518)
Seven former USN submarine chasers of wooden construction built on YMS type hull in 1941–44. Acquired from USN in 1952. *Su Song* returned to USA in 1963, *Kae Seong, Kil Chu* decommissioned in 1955–56; the rest were returned to US custody and scrapped in 1970s.

Ex-US 95ft type *coast guard large patrol craft*

Class (former name, no):
PB 3 (ex-*Cape Rosier*, WPB 95333), *PB 5* (*Cape Sable*, WPB 95334), *PB 6* (*Cape Providence*, WPB 95335), *PB 7* (*Cape Florida*, WPB 95325), *PB 8* (*Cape Porpoise*, WPB 95327), *PB 9* (*Cape Falcon*, WPB 95330), *PB 10* (*Cape Trinity*, WPB 95331), *PB 11* (*Cape Darby*, WPB 95323), *PB 12* (*Cape Kiwanda*, WPB 95329)
Nine former USCG steel-hulled patrol craft transferred to Korean Navy in Sept 1968. *PB 7* was stricken after grounding in May 1971.

PK type *large patrol craft*

Displacement:	120t
Dimensions:	100ft
	30.5m × ? × ?m
Machinery:	3 shafts, 3 MTU diesels, 10,200hp = 35kts
Armament:	1–40mm, 1–20mm
Complement:	

Class:
PK 10, PK 11
Two built in Korean shipyard in 1971–72 launched in 1969? Extant 1982.

CHEBI class *coastal patrol craft*

Displacement:	30t
Dimensions:	72ft × 11ft 6in × 3ft 7in
	21.9m × 3.5m × 1.2m
Machinery:	2 shafts, 2 MTU diesels, 1600hp = ?kts
Armament:	2–20mm (2×1)
Complement:	?

Class:
Chebi 51, 52, 57
Nine small patrol boats. First 3 belong to *Chebi* ('Schoolboy') Type I and were completed in 1973; 6 building as Type II.

Ex-US 40ft Sewart type *coastal patrol craft*

Class:
SB 1–3, 5
Aluminium-hulled boats built in USA by Sewart and transferred to Korean Navy in 1964. No 4 was not assigned.

Ex-US 65ft Sewart type *coastal patrol craft*

Class:
FB 1–3, 5–10
Built in USA by Sewart and transferred to Korean Navy in 1967. Referred to as Toksuuri No 1 etc by Koreans. No 4 being considered unlucky was not assigned.

MINE WARFARE VESSELS

Ex-US YMS type *coastal minesweepers*

Class:
Kang Jim (ex-*YMS 354*), *Kyoung Chu* (ex-*YMS 358*), *Kwang Chu* (ex-*YMS 413*), *Kae Song* (ex-*YMS ?*), *Kimhae* (ex-*YMS ?*), *Kangkae* (ex-*YMS ?*), *Kang Nung* (ex-*YMS 463*), *Kang Wha* (ex-*YMS 245*), *Ka Pyong* (ex-*YMS 210*), *Kang Kyong* (ex-*YMS 330*), *Kaya San* (ex-*YMS 423*), *Kupo* (ex-*YMS 323*), *Kim Chon* (ex-*YMS 258*), *Kil Chu* (ex-*BYMS 5*), *Ko Yung* (ex-*Ue Nam*, ex-*BYMS 55*), *Kong City* (ex-*BYMS 6*), *Ko Won* (ex-*YMS ?*), *Yong Kung* (ex-*BYMS 8*), *Kum Hwa* (ex-*Curlew* MSCO 8, ex-*AMS 8*, ex-*YMS 218*), *Kim Po* (ex-*Kite* MSCO 22, ex-*AMS 22*, ex-*YMS 375*), *Ko Chang* (ex-*Mockingbird* MSCO 27, ex-*AMS 27*, ex-*YMS 419*)
Twenty-one wooden Second World War-built units transferred 1948–56. Korean pennant numbers MSC 501–521. Fate: MSC 501 BU 1959, MSC 502 BU 1962, MSC 503 deleted 1972, MSC 504–506 (not known). MSC 507 BU 1959, MSC 508 lost 1959, MSC 509 sunk 1950, MSC 510 BU 1963, MSC 511 lost 1945, MSC 512 BU 1956, MSC 513 BU 1968, MSC 514 BU 1959, MSC 515 BU 1959, MSC 516 sunk 1950, MSC 517 lost 1948, MSC 518 BU 1955, MSC 519, 520 and 521 deleted in 1977.

US BLUEBIRD class *coastal minesweepers*

Class (no, former no, transfer):
Ha Dong (MSC 556, ex-*MSC 296*, Aug 1963), *Ko Hung* (MSC 552, ex-*MSC 285*, Sept 1959), *Kum Kok* (MSC 553, ex-*MSC 286*, Oct 1959), *Kum San* (MSC 551, ex-*MSC 284*, June 1959), *Nam Yang* (MSC 555, ex-*MSC 295*, Aug 1963), *Sam Kok* (MSC 557, ex-*MSC 316*, July 1968), *Yong Dong* (MSC 558, ex-*MSC 320*, 2.10.75), *Ok Cheon* (MSC 559, ex-*MSC 321*, 2.10.75).
Built by Peterson, Wisconsin, USA specially for transfer to Korea under MAP. Wooden hulled with non-magnetic metal fittings. Used to be numbered MSC 522–530. All 8 extant 1982.

Ex-US MSB type *minesweeping boat*

Former USN MSB 2 transferred 1.12.61, renamed *Pi Bong* (MSB 1) and bought 2.7.75.

North Korea

MAJOR SURFACE SHIPS

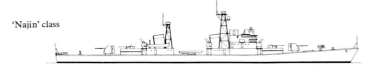

'Najin' class

'NAJIN' class *frigates*

Displacement:	1200t standard; 1500t full load
Dimensions:	328ft × 32ft 6in × 8ft 10in
	100.0m × 10.0m × 2.7m
Machinery:	3 shafts, 2 diesels, 15,000hp = 26kts. Range 4000nm at 14kts
Armament:	2–100mm/50 (2×1), 4–57mm (2×2), 4–25mm (2×2), 8–14.5mm (4×2), 3–533mm TT (1×3), 1 MBU-1800, 2 DC racks, 2 ASW mortars
Sensors:	Radar Skin Head, Pot Head; IFF: Ski Pole and hull sonar
Complement:	155 or 180

Name	Builder	Launched	Comp	Fate
3025	N Korea	1972	1973	Extant 1982
3025	N Korea		1975	Extant 1982
3027	N Korea		1976	Extant 1982
	N Korea	1977	1979	Extant 1982

Korean designed two-funnel light frigates fitted with Chinese produced electronics and armament based on Soviet types and technology of the 1950s. First laid down 1971 and last 1976. Very rough and ready ships.

SUBMARINES

Ex-Chinese 'ROMEO' class *submarines*

Twelve Chinese-built Soviet design boats. Pairs transferred 1973, 1974 and 1975. Two built in local shipyard Mayang Do. Continuing programme. Stationed in Yellow Sea (W coast).

Ex-Chinese 'WHISKEY' class *submarines*

Four Chinese-built Soviet design boats. Stationed in Sea of Japan (E Coast). Reportedly there are also up to five small submarines built in N Korea since 1974; length 40–45m.

AMPHIBIOUS WARFARE VESSELS

'NAMPO' class *fast assault landing craft*

Displacement:	82t full load
Dimensions:	84ft 2in × 20ft × 6ft
	27.7m × 6.1m × 1.8m
Machinery:	4 shafts, 4 M50 diesels, 4800bhp = 40kts. Range 375nm at 40kts
Armament:	6–14.5mm MG (3×2)
Complement:	20

A large class of 70–80 small fast assault ships based on the P 6 type MTB hull. Built in Korea since *c* 1975. All have retractable bow ramp for landing operations. Nine 'Hanchon' class LCU are also in service and 18 home-built LCM.

SMALL SURFACE COMBATANTS

Ex-Soviet TRAL class *coastal minesweepers (corvettes)*

Class:
Ex-*Strela, Tros, Provodnik, Podsekatel, Paravan, Kapsul, Viecha, Čeka* (T1–8)
Eight old Soviet ships built in 1938–42, transferred in 1950s and used as patrol vessels. There were only 2 left in service (ex-*Strela, Paravan*) by 1982.

'Sariwan' class

'SARIWAN' class *corvettes*

Displacement:	600t standard; 650t full load
Dimensions:	203ft 8in × 23ft 11in × 7ft 10in
	62.1m × 7.3m × 2.4m
Machinery:	2 shafts, 2 diesels, 3000bhp = 21kts
Armament:	1–100mm, 2–37mm (1×2), 16–14.5mm MG (4×4), DC rails, 30 mines
Sensors:	Radar Skin Head, Dori 2, IFF Ski Pole or Yard Rake
Complement:	65

Class:
725, 726, 727
Large patrol craft/escort ships built in Korea in the mid-1960s and closely modelled on the ex-Soviet *Tral* class minesweepers. They had the same silhouette. Displacement 475t (?). Armament also given as 1–76mm, 2–57mm, 4–2mm (2×2). Four units sometimes reported. There is also another class of patrol craft called *Tae Chong* built since 1975. Details are lacking.

Ex-Soviet 'OSA 1' class *fast attack craft (missile)*

Eight armed with somewhat obsolete missiles of Styx type. Some built in China.

Soviet 'KOMAR' type *fast attack craft (missile)*

Six delivered by Soviets and four built locally. There are reports of the existence of 'Sohung' class, which may be Korean version of 'Komar'.

'SIN HUNG' and 'KU SONG' class *fast attack craft (torpedo)*

Displacement:	25t full load
Dimensions:	60ft × 11ft × 5ft 6in
	18.3m × 3.4m × 1.7m
Machinery:	2 shafts, 2 diesels, 2400hp = ?kts
Armament:	2–14.5mm MG, 2–533mm or 457mm TT
Sensors:	Radar navigation
Complement:	

MTBs built in N Korea from mid-1950 to 1970. They resemble Soviet D-3 class MTBs of 25 years ago, 72 active in 1982.

Ex-Soviet 'P 6' type *fast attack craft (torpedo)*

These boats built in the late 1950s in USSR (45) and China were transferred upon completion to Korea. Remainder built of steel in N Korea and called 'Sinpo' class, 6 of which have no TT. Some are armed with 2–37mm (2×1) guns instead original 4–25mm (2×2), 64 extant in 1982. Pennant numbers in 400 sequence.

Ex-Soviet 'P 4' type *fast attack craft (torpedo)*

Small MTBs with aluminium hulls built in Korea and China in 1951–57, 12 possibly extant in 1982.

'IWON' class *fast attack craft (torpedo)*

MTBs built in Korea in late 1950s. Modelled on the Soviet 'P 2' type, 15 extant in 1982.

Ex-Soviet 'SHERSHEN' class *fast attack craft (torpedo)*

Four transferred in 1973–74.

'AN JU' class *fast attack craft (torpedo)*

Displacement:	35t full load
Dimensions:	65ft × 12ft × 6ft
	19.8m × 3.7m × 1.8m
Machinery:	4 shafts, 4 M50 diesels, 4800bhp = 50kts. Range 1200nm at 20kts
Armament:	2–25mm (1×2), 2–533mm TT
Sensors:	Radar navigation set
Complement:	20

MTBs designed and built in Korea in 1960s, 6 extant in 1982.

Ex-Soviet 'MO IV' type *fast attack craft (gun)*

Twenty of these 1945–47 built units transferred to Korea in 1957–60 and extant 1982. Four MO-I type submarine chasers transferred in 1954 were deleted 1971–72.

'Chaho' class
NB 1/750 scale

'CHAHO' class *fast attack craft (gun)*

Displacement:	80t full load
Dimensions:	90ft 11in × 20ft × 6ft
	27.7m × 6.1m × 1.8m
Machinery:	4 shafts, 4 M50 diesels, 4800bhp = 38kts
Armament:	8–23mm (4×2), 40-tube RL, 4–14.5mm MG (2×2)
Sensors:	Radar navigation set
Complement:	*c* 25

Korean designed FAC built since 1974 on 'P 6' type wooden hulls, 60 extant 1982. There are also 30 'Hong Jin' class FAC similar to 'Chaho' built since 1975; armed with 1–85mm tank gun and 4–14.5mm MG (2×2).

'K 48' class *large patrol craft*

Displacement:	110t full load (est)
Dimensions:	125ft × 18ft 1in × 4ft 11in
	38.1m × 5.5m × 1.5m
Machinery:	2 shafts, 2 diesels, 4000bhp = 24kts
Armament:	1–76mm/50, 3–37mm (3×1), 6–14.5mm MG (3×2)
Sensors:	Radar Skin Head
Complement:	

Korean designed ships built in Korea in late 1950s, 4 extant in 1982.

Ex-Soviet 'ARTILLERIST' class *large patrol craft*

Two transferred in 1950s and deleted in 1971–72. Built in 1943–44.

Soviet 'SO 1' class *submarine chasers*

Six transferred from USSR in 1957–61 and the remaining 9 were built in N Korea. All extant 1982.

'CHODO' class *large patrol craft*

Displacement:	130t (est)
Dimensions:	140ft × 19ft × 8ft 6in
	42.7m × 5.8m × 2.6m
Machinery:	2 shafts, 2 diesels, 6000bhp = 25kts. Range 2000nm at 10kts
Armament:	4–37mm (4×1), 4–25mm (2×2)
Sensors:	Radar Skin Head, Don
Complement:	40

Korean built in mid-1960s, 4 extant 1982 one numbered 971.

Ex-Chinese 'SHANGHAI II' class *large patrol craft*

Fifteen transferred from China since 1967.

Ex-Chinese 'HAINAN' class *large patrol craft*

Six transferred in pairs in 1975, 1976 and 1978.

Ex-Chinese 'SWATOW' class *coastal patrol craft*

Eight transferred from China in 1968. All extant 1982.

Soviet 'KM 4' class *coastal patrol craft*

Small coastal patrol boats of 10t built in Korea to Soviet design, 10 extant in 1982.

Ex-Soviet 'T 43' class *ocean minesweepers*

Built in 1954. Transferred from USSR in 1960s.

Laos

Laos has no coastline and her Navy consists of small gunboats and landing craft operating mainly on the Mekong River. Laos was formed from several different parts of French Cochin China as an independent member of the French Union in 1949 and achieved true independence in 1954. She had already been invaded by the Vietminh in 1953 and was soon split between the Communist Pathet Lao in the East and the Royal Laotian Government in the West. In 1962 a 14-nation conference at Geneva decided to recognise this split and neutralise Laos, but the fighting continued with the Pathet Lao gradually winning. During the 1950s and 1960s the United States and France supplied enough gunboats and landing craft to make up four squadrons, and in the early 1970s there were 7 ex-USN LCM 6 and 28 gunboats of 6–21t, plus 7 small transports.

After the fall of South Vietnam the Pathet Lao took over Laos and on 2 December 1975, the King having abdicated, declared a People's Democratic Republic, which was then completely overrun by Viet-namese troops (about 45,000 deployed in 1982). As a result, the state of the riverine navy is uncertain though anything from 500 to 1700 sailors (18 months compulsory service) are reported.

Malaysia

In 1950 the Malayan Naval Force consisted of the minelayer *Laburnum* (ex-Japanese *Wakataka* transferred to the Royal Navy at Singapore on 17 October 1947), the tank landing craft *Pelandok*, 3 seaward defence motor launches with 4 more awaiting transfer, the motor fishing vessel *Panglima* and the torpedo recovery vessel *Simbang*. No additions were made while the Royal Navy shielded the new Malayan Federation during the long years of the 'Emergency' till 1960 even though independence came in 1957. On 16 September 1963 the Federation was enlarged by the addition of Singapore, Sabah and Sarawak (both states of N Borneo) and became Malaysia.

The Royal Malaysian Navy now had the role of patrolling a 3000-mile coastline and the vital 500-mile South China Sea link between the two halves of the Federation; a task complicated by Singapore's secession in 1965. Fortunately for the fledgling service the Royal Navy maintained a massive deployment for the Borneo 'Confrontation' with Indonesia as new warships were delivered and worked up. In 1964 the first frigate joined the minesweepers and the 103ft Vosper patrol craft that were the simple and reliable basis of the Federation's new fleet. Fast attack craft were added in 1967 and by the early 1970s missile boats and landing craft were joining in numbers. In 1970 volunteer personnel numbered 4000. Defence spending increased sixfold between 1975 and 1981 in the uncertain era after Britain's final withdrawal and the fall of S Vietnam although Malaysia remains covered by the Five-Power Defence Arrangement of 1 November 1971 in which Britain and Australasia would consult about aid if her security or Singapore's are threatened. RAAF fighter squadrons are still based in the Federation.

In 1982 the service numbered 6000 with 1000 regular reserves and an RMNVR of 800 men and women with ambitious expansion plans after a decade that has seen a tripling of the Malaysian merchant fleet and a revival of piracy in the South China Sea. Shore bases are principally KD (*Kapal Diraja* = 'royal ship') *Malaya* at Woodlands on the Johore Straits and KD *Labuan* in Borneo. A new port was completed at Kuantan on the east coast in 1981 and Lumut (Telok Muroh) is due to become KD *Pelandok* in 1984, main Fleet base, dockyard and training centre on the Straits of Malacca. Commodores head Malaysia's two naval areas, covering the mainland and Borneo.

Warship acquisition plans include 4 Type FS 1500 frigates from Howaldswerke of Kiel. Two were ordered in February 1981 and two more, similar to Colombia's ships, will follow. Four Italian *Lerici* class minehunters were ordered at the same time and further units may be added. The Royal Malaysian Marine Police are taking delivery of 12 'PZ' class 221t locally-built fast patrol craft ordered in 1979 while Customs and Excise will receive 6 Vosper 105ft patrol craft ordered in February 1981.

MAJOR SURFACE SHIPS

Ex-British 'LOCH' class *frigate*

No	Name	Builder	Acquired	Fate
	HANG TUAH (i) (ex-*Loch Insh*)	Robb	1964	Stricken 1977

In 1964 HMS *Loch Insh* was transferred from the RN, refitted at Portsmouth DY and renamed *Hang Tuah* after a fifteenth century Malay admiral. She was stricken in 1977 when replaced by HMS *Mermaid*, and scrapped.

Ex-British MERMAID *frigate*

No	Name	Builder	Acquired	Fate
F 76	HANG TUAH (ii) (ex-*Mermaid*)	Yarrow	May 1977	Extant 1982

In May 1977 the RN frigate *Mermaid* was bought to replace the elderly *Hang Tuah*, and took over the same name when commissioned on 22 July the same year. A 1981–82 Singapore refit replaced her twin 4in with a French 100mm Compact plus fire control radar.

Rahmat 1972

RAHMAT (Yarrow type) *frigate*

Displacement:	1250t standard; 1600t full load
Dimensions:	300ft pp, 308ft oa × 34ft 1in × 14ft 10in *91.4m, 93.8m × 10.3m × 4.5m*
Machinery:	2-shaft CODOG (CP propellers): 1 Rolls-Royce Olympus TMIB gas turbine, 19,500shp = 26kts, plus Crossley-Pielstick diesels, 3850bhp = 16kts. Range 6000nm/1000nm at 16kts/26kts
Armament:	1–4.5in/45 Mk 5, 2–40mm/70 Bofors (2×1), 4 Seacat SAM (1×4), 1 Limbo Mk 10
Sensors:	Radar Decca 626, Signaal M-20, M-44, LW-02; sonar Type 170B, 174
Complement:	140

No	Name	Builder	Launched	Fate
F 24	RAHMAT (ex-*Hang Jebat*)	Yarrow, Scotstoun	18.12.67	Extant 1982

On 11.2.66 Malaysia ordered a new frigate from Yarrow to be called *Hang Jebat*. She was laid down on 1.6.67 and completed on 13.9.71. Emphasis was laid on simplicity, with a hand-loaded gun forward, single Bofors guns amidships and a depth-charge mortar and a Seacat close-range missile system aft. There is also provision for a helicopter, with hatch covers over the Limbo well forming the flight deck. She has an unusual machinery layout, with three engines driving into one gearbox which, in turn, drives two propeller shafts.

The ship was renamed *Rahmat* before completion and is similar to the Thai Navy's *Makut Rajakumarn*.

AMPHIBIOUS WARFARE VESSELS

Ex-US LST type *tank landing ships*

Class (no, former name/nos):
Sri Langkawi (A 1500, ex-*Hunterdon County*, AGP 838, ex-LST 838), *Sri Banggi* (A 1501, ex-*Henry County*, LST 824), *Rajah Jerom* (A 1502, ex-*Sedgwick County*, LST 1123)

A 1500 loaned by USN on 1.1.71, sold 1.8.74, other 2 sold 7.10.76. A 1500 was converted to small craft tender in US service. All have midships helicopter pad. Being re-engined 1981–82. Used as transports and FAC tenders.

SRI INDERA SAKTI class *logistic support ships*

Displacement:	1800dwt; 4300t full load
Dimensions:	328ft × 49ft 2in × 15ft 8in *100m × 15m × 4.8m*
Machinery:	2 shafts, 2 Deutz S/BMV6 540 diesels, 5986bhp = 16.5kts. Endurance 60 days
Armament:	1–40mm
Sensors:	Radar navigation set
Complement:	215

No	Name	Builder	Launched	Fate
A 1503	SRI INDERA SAKTI	Bremer Vulcan	1.7.80	Extant 1982

Ordered 24.10.79, laid down 15.2.80 and completed 24.10.80 as multi-purpose ship. Two more ordered Feb 1981. Usable as TS, FAC/MCM tender, C & C ship and troop transport. Bow thruster, stern helicopter deck and midships 15t crane all fitted. Large ops room, vehicle holds and divers' compression chamber are included. Up to 1300t of fuel and 200t water can be loaded with 3230sq ft (300sq m) of provisions. Ten 20ft containers can be carried on deck.

MINOR LANDING CRAFT

Five US LCM (6) class: *LCM 1–5* built in Australia and transferred *c* 1970.

Nine RCP class LCVP (15t std, 30t full load, 17kts, 1–20mm, 35 troops or vehicle): *RCP 1–9* built Hong Leong–Lürssen SY, Butterworth, Malaysia. All in service 1974.

Fifteen LCP class (19t full load, 48ft 4in × 14ft × 3ft 3in *14.6m × 4.3m × 1.0m*; 2 Cummins diesels, 400bhp = 16kts): built in Australia and transferred 1965–66. Light armour on midships pilot house.

Two *Jernih* class LCU (290t full load, 124ft 8in/*38m*, 2 Caterpillar D343 T diesels, 730bhp = 8kts: *Jernih* and *Terijah* built at Brooke DY, Malaysia 1977–78 to supply Sarawak. Another longer LCU, *Meleban* was launched at the same yard 15.10.77.

Rahmat on trials   *Yarrow*

SMALL SURFACE COMBATANTS

PERKASA class *fast attack craft (gun)*

Displacement:	95t normal; 114t deep load
Dimensions:	90ft wl, 99ft 9in oa × 24ft × 7ft max *27.4m, 30.4m × 7.3m × 2.1m*
Machinery:	3-shafts: Proteus gas turbine plus 6cyl GM diesels, 12,750shp + 380bhp = 54kts. Fuel 24.25kt
Armament:	1–40mm/60 Bofors Mk 9, 1–20mm Oerlikon, 4–21in side-launched torpedoes or 10 mines
Sensors:	Radar navigation set only
Complement:	24

Class (no, launched):
Perkasa (P 150, 26.10.65), *Handalan* (P 151, 18.1.66), *Gempita* (P 152, 6.4.66), *Pendekar* (P 153, 24.6.66)

Four modified versions of the RN 'Brave' class were ordered in Oct 1964 and shipped out from England in 1967. P 150 achieved 57kts on trials. Generally similar to the RN craft but the hull was made of bonded wood, as in the private-venture boat *Ferocity*. Air conditioned quarters. Armed with 8 SS 12 SSM (2×4) in 1972. Another improvement was the provision of cruising diesels on the wing shafts to improve endurance. All were built by Vosper at Southampton and all were stricken in 1977.

Perdana and *Serang*, with *Jerong* and *Yu* (of the *Jerong* class) beyond *Courtesy Ross Gillett*

French 'LA COMBATTANTE II' type *fast attack craft (missile)*

Armament:	4 MM38 Exocet SSM (4×1), 1–57mm Bofors, 1–40mm/70 Bofors, 6–103mm RFL on 57mm mount
Complement:	35
Other particulars:	As under Greece Part I

Class (no, launched, in service):
Perdana (P 3501, 31.5.72–31.12.72), *Serang* (P 3502, 22.12.71–31.2.73), *Ganas* (P 3503, 26.10.72–28.2.73), *Ganyang* (P 3504, 16.3.72–20.3.73)

Four missile strike craft were ordered from CMN, Cherbourg in 1970. Although equipped with Swedish guns the fire control is the French Vega type normally associated with the 'Combattante II' 4AL series. All four were launched in 1971–72 and delivered in 1973 after sailing for Malaysia on 2 May. They are still in service.

Modified SPICA class *fast attack craft (missile)*

Displacement:	240t normal; 268t full load
Dimensions:	143ft 1in oa × 23ft × 12ft 2in aft *42.6m × 7.0m × 2.3m*
Machinery:	3 shafts, 3 MTU diesels, 10,800bhp = 34.5kts. Range 1850nm at 14kts
Armament:	4 MM38 Exocet SSM (4×1), 1–57mm/70, 1–40mm/70 Bofors
Sensors:	Radar PEAB 9LV200
Complement:	39

Class (no, laid down):
Handalan (P 3511, 24.5.77), *Perkasa* (P 3512,　), *Pendikar* (P 3513), *Gempita* (P 3514,　)

Four modified versions of the Swedish *Spica* class were ordered on 13.8.76 to replace the *Perkasa* class torpedo-boats, whose names were transferred. The bridgework is farther forward than in the original *Spica* design, no torpedoes are mounted, and diesels replace the gas turbines. All four built by Karlskrona and in service from 26.10.79.

Jerong as completed
NB 1/750 scale

JERONG class *fast attack craft (gun)*

Displacement:	210t normal; 255t full load
Dimensions:	147ft 8in oa × 23ft × 8ft 2in aft *44.9m × 7.0m × 2.5m*
Machinery:	3 shafts, 3 MTU diesels, 9900bhp = 32kts. Range 2000nm at 15kts
Armament:	1–57mm Bofors, 1–40mm/70 Bofors
Sensors:	Radar Decca 1226
Complement:	35

Class (no, launched–in service):
Jerong (P 3505, 28.7.75–27.3.76), *Tudak* (P 3506, 16.3.–16.6.76), *Paus* (P 3507, 2.6.–18.8.76), *Yu* (P 3508, 17.7.–15.11.76), *Baung* (P 3509, 5.10.76–11.7.77), *Pari* (P 3510, Jan.–23.3.77)

Six fast gunboats were ordered in 1973 from Lürssenwerft in Bremen-Vegesack but to be built at a new yard (Hong Leong) at Butterworth near Singapore. They are a Lürssen design somewhat smaller than the 'Combattante II' type, with Swedish armament (CSEE Naja optronic detector).

Sri Trengganu as completed　　　　　　　　*Vosper Thornycroft*

SRI KEDAH class *large patrol craft*

Displacement:	96t normal; 109t deep load
Dimensions:	95ft wl, 103ft oa × 19ft 10in × 5ft 6in *31.4m × 6m × 1.7m*
Machinery:	2 shafts, 2 Bristol Siddeley MTU MD665/18 diesels, 3500bhp = 27kts. Range 1400nm at 14kts
Armament:	2–40mm/70 Bofors (2×1)
Sensors:	Radar
Complement:	22

Class (no, launched–in service):
Sri Kedah (P 3138, 4.6.62), *Sri Selangor* (P 3139, 17.7.62–25.3.63), *Sri Perak* (P 3140, 30.8.62–June 1963), *Sri Pahang* (P 3141, 15.10.62), *Sri Kelantan* (P 3142, 8.1.–12.11.63), *Sri Trengganu* (P 3143, 12.12.62–16.12.63).
Sri Sabah (P 3144, 30.12.63–2.9.64), *Sri Sarawak* (P 3145, 20.1.–30.9.64), *Sri Negri Sembilan* (P 3146, 17.9.–28.9.64), *Sri Melaka* (P 3147, 25.2.–2.11.64).

Kris (P 3148, 1.1.1–11.3.66), *Sundang* (P 3149, 22.5.–29.11.66), *Badek* (P 3150, 8.5–15.12.66), *Renchong* (P 3151, 22.6.–17.1.67), *Tombak* (P 3152, 20.6.66–2.3.67), *Lembing* (P 3153, 22.8.66–12.4.67), *Serampang* (P 3154, 15.9.66–19.5.67), *Panah* (P 3155, 10.10.66–27.7.67), *Kerambit* (P 3156, 20.11.66–28.7.67), *Beladu* (P 3157, 11.1.–12.9.67), *Kelawang* (P 3158, 31.1–4.10.67), *Rentaka* (P 3159, 15.3–22.9.67), *Sri Perlis* (P 3160, 26.5.67–24.1.68), *Sri Johore* (P 3161, 21.8.67–14.2.68)

Six patrol craft were ordered from Vosper, Portsmouth, in Sept 1961 for delivery in 1963; the next four were ordered in March 1963 for delivery in 1965, followed by 14 more in 1965 for delivery in 1966–68. Various minor improvements have been made in each group (Second greater range of 1660nm at 14kts) but the basic design is the same – an all-welded steel hull with aluminium superstructure. All named after states of the Malaysian Federation. The last group were subsequently renumbered P 34, 36–47 and 49 respectively. *Sri Kedah* and *Sri Pahang* were stricken in 1976.

'P Z' class *large patrol craft*

Displacement:	221t full load
Dimensions:	126ft 4in × 22ft 10in × 5ft 10in *38.5m × 7m × 1.8m*
Machinery:	2 shafts, 2 MTU 20V 538 TB92 diesels, 10,000bhp = 31kts. Range 550nm/1200nm at 31kts/24kts
Armament:	1–40mm (1000rds), 1–20mm (2000rds), 2–7.62mm MG, 2 RFL
Sensors:	Radar Kelvin Hughes
Complement:	38

Class (no):
Lang Hitam (PZ 1), PZ 2–12

Ordered from Hong Leong–Lürssen, Butterworth, Malaysia in 1979. First delivery Aug 1981, 5 in late 1981 and remainder by mid-1982. Royal Malaysian Marine Police ships.

Ex-British *seaward defence motor launches*

Class (former no, fate):
Sri Kedah (SDML 3501, BU 1959), *Sri Trengganu* (SDML 3502), *Sri Pahang* (SDML 3505, BU 1965), *Sri Negri Sembilan* (SDML 3506), *Sri Perak* (SDML 3507), *Sri Kelantan* (SDML 3508, BU 1965), *Sri Selangor* (SDML 3509, BU 1961)

Originally 7 SDMLs made up the 200th Seaward Patrol Craft Squadron based at Singapore. Only SDML 3502 remained in service by 1970. SDML 3506 and SDML 3507 were offered for sale in 1966.

'PX' class *coastal patrol craft*

Displacement:	85t full load
Dimensions:	87ft 6in × 19ft × 4ft 10in *26.7m × 5.8m × 1.5m*
Machinery:	2 shafts, 2 MB820Db diesels, 2460bhp = 25kts. Range 700nm at 15kts
Armament:	2–20mm (2×1)
Complement:	15

Class (no):
Mahkota (PX 1), *Temenggong* (PX 2), *Hulubalang* (PX 3), *Maharajasetia* (PX 4), *Maharajalela* (PX 5), *Pahlawan* (PX 6), *Bentora* (PX 7), *Perwira* (PX 8), *Pertanda* (PX 9), *Shahbandar* (PX 10), *Sangsetia* (PX 11), *Laksamana* (PX 12), *Pekan* (PX 13), *Kelang* (PX 14), *Kuala Kangsar* (PX 15), *Arau* (PX 16), *Sri Gumantong* (PX 17), *Sri Labuan* (PX 18)

Eighteen built by Vosper of Singapore 1963–70. Named after islands. All extant 1982 and operated by Royal Malaysian Marine Police except last 2 which are in Sabah government use.

Improved 'PX' class *coastal patrol craft*

Class (no):
Alor Star (PX 19), *Kota Bahru* (PX 20), *Kuala Treggganu* (PX 21), *Johore Bahru* (PX 22), *Sri Menanti* (PX 23), *Kuching* (PX 24)

Six built by Vosper of Singapore 1972–73 as 92t units, 91ft long (*27.8m*) with longer range (750nm) and larger crew (18). All extant 1982 in police service.

PX 26 class *coastal patrol craft*

Displacement:	62.5t
Dimensions:	91ft 10in × 17ft 8in × 5ft 3in *28.0m × 5.4m × 1.6m*
Machinery:	2 shafts, 2 MTU MB 820 Db diesels, 2460bhp = 25kts. Range 1050nm at 15kts
Armament:	1–20mm
Complement:	19

Class (no):
PX 25, *Sri Kudat* (PX 26), *Sri Tawau* (PX 27), PX 28–30
Six built by Hong Leong-Lürssen of Butterworth, Malaysia, in 1973. All extant 1982 in police service.

MINE WARFARE VESSELS

Ex-British 'TON' class *coastal minesweepers*

Class (no, former name, transferred):
Mahamiru (M 1127, ex-*Darlaston*, 1960), *Kinabulu* (M 1134, ex-*Essington*, 1964), *Ledang* (M 1143, ex-*Hexton*, Oct 1963), *Tahan* (M 1163, ex-*Lullington*, April 1966), *Jerai* (M 1168, ex-*Dilston*), *Brinchang* (M 1172, ex-*Thankerton*, May 1966)
Six coastal minesweepers were transferred from the RN in 1960–66 starting with *Mahamiru*. All underwent modernisation at Singapore in 1972–73, but in 1977 *Jerai* was stricken.

Ex-British 'HAM' class *inshore minesweepers*

Class (no, former name, in service):
Langka Suka (M 2606, ex-*Bedham*, 1958–67), *Sri Johore* (M 2602, ex-*Altham*, 1959–67), *Sri Perlis* (M 2604, ex-*Asheldham*, 1959–67), *Temasek* (M 2612, ex-*Brantingham*, 1958–66), *Jerong* (M 2627, ex-*Boreham*, Jan 1966), *Todak* (M 2610, ex-*Felmersham*, March 1966)
Six RN units transferred in two groups, 4 in 1958–59 and 2 in 1966. Some had 2–20mm aft instead of sweeping gear.

Maldives

This republic of about 2000 coral islands and islets (only 210 inhabited) lies 450 miles SW of Sri Lanka and extends more than that distance in 12 major atolls from north to south. No island is larger than 5 square miles or higher than 8ft above sea level. Britain granted independence in July 1965. The hereditary sultanate became a republic by referendum in November 1968. Britain retained an RAF staging post on Gan in the southernmost Addu Atoll until March 1976. The almost entirely Muslim population (143,469 in 1978) are expert fishermen and traders with a merchant marine totalling 43 ships of 180,117 grt in 1982.

The republic's Navy was created in 1976 by the departing RAF handing over a 68ft target towing launch, a 63ft pinnace and 4 utility landing craft. A 45ft Fairey Marine customs launch had been bought the year before. Three ex-Soviet trawlers (2–25mm guns) were handed over by the USSR after being confiscated for illegal fishing, but an attempt to rent Gan in 1977 as a fishing base was rejected. About 150 sailors manned this force in 1982.

Mauritius

Mauritius became independent within the Commonwealth in March 1968. The densely populated main island has 90 per cent of the million inhabitants with 30,000 more on Rodrigues 350 miles to the east and a few hundred on the satellite islands. A defence agreement with Britain was not renewed when it expired in 1976, and the British naval communication base was closed down. The Mauritius Naval Volunteer Force, 111 strong, was disbanded in June 1968. Instead of a regular army, there is a security force of about 3500 men, including paramilitary elements trained by French advisers. Defence spending was only 4 million dollars in 1980.

In April 1974 India transferred as a gift a large patrol craft of the *Abhay* class (Indian-built version of the British 'Ford' class seaward defence boats); this ship kept her name of *Amar* and is Mauritius' sole warship. A crew of ten were trained in India. The future of this strategically important island group is uncertain. She claims Diego Garcia in the Chagos Archipelago leased by Britain to the US as an air and naval base for 50 years from 1966 and the French weather station island of Tromelin, halfway to Malagasy 500 miles to the west. The Soviet Union has laid naval mooring buoys near Mauritius and uses Port Louis as a fishing base. This fine harbour was also the seventh most visited by the Soviet Indian Ocean Squadron in the period 1962–80. Warships of all the great powers and India helped with cyclone relief operations in February 1975.

Pakistan

For the first 24 years of its existence the Navy of Pakistan faced the impossible task of maintaining maritime links between the two halves of history's most geographically absurd state, round 3500 miles of hostile coastline. It inherited only two of the old RIN training establishments in August 1947. If that was not bad enough, the service most definitely came last in the line of the new Muslim state's defence priorities. In the air and on the ground Pakistan might hope to offset India's permanent numberical advantage, never at sea. The Royal Pakistan Navy's warships, like India's, were Royal Navy transfers until the early 1960s. A smaller cruiser acquired in 1956 was joined by a pair of 'Battle' class destroyers, more powerful and less old than India's units, but on the other hand Pakistan could not match her neighbour's seaborne air power. She did acquire the subcontinent's first submarine in 1964, an ex-US *Tench* class

There was no maritime dimension to the 1965 Indo-Pakistan War though, according to the then Pakistan Air Force C-in-C, *Indonesia* offered to launch diversionary naval attacks. The service grew steadily in manpower from 7700 in 1963 to 9870 in 1970. But this build-up, including 4 submarines, could not match India's and in the hectic days of December 1971 the Navy's strategic and numerical inferiority was glaringly revealed. In East Pakistan Rear-Admiral Shariff's 4 large patrol craft and 17 MG-armed civilian boats were neutralised by Indian carrier and land-based aircraft on the first day. Thereafter the sailors became soldiers in a lost cause. Off Karachi on the same day India's Western Fleet sank the destroyer *Khaibar* and a minesweeper in the largest surface action since 1945 before shelling and rocketing the naval base. This treatment was repeated on 9 December with 3 foreign merchant ships being hit as well. Pakistan's only naval consolation was her submarine *Hangor*'s sinking of the Indian frigate *Khukri* in the Arabian Sea.

In defeat the Navy turned to China for fast attack and patrol craft, receiving 16 in 1972–73. By the end of 1980 the submarine force had been doubled and modernised US destroyers were being acquired. Volunteer manpower reached 11,000 in that year with 5000 reserves. A naval air arm of three Breguet Atlantic patrol aircraft and 10 helicopters (both armed with AM-39 Exocet) was set up in 1975. The ageing cruiser *Babur* was replaced by the former HMS *London* in March 1982. This is probably the limit of expansion given Pakistan's overwhelmingly land and air requirements in the wake of the Soviet invasion of Afghanistan. The ports of Pakistan's troubled province of Baluchistan are a tempting prize.

MAJOR SURFACE SHIPS

Ex-British BELLONA class *cruiser*

No	Name	Builder	Acquired	Fate
C 84	BABUR (ex-*Diadem*)	Hawthorn Leslie	29.2.56	Extant 1982

Refitted at HM Dockyard, Portsmouth, with new bridge, radar and lattice masts. Renamed *Babur* 5.7.57 after the Moghul emperor. Adapted to be TS during 1961 refit and now used mainly as floating AA battery. C prefix dropped from pennant number in 1963.

Ex-British 'O' class *destroyers*

No	Name	Builder	Acquired	Fate
	TARIQ (i) (ex-*Offa*)	Fairfield	30.11.49	BU 1959
260	TIPPU SULTAN (i) (ex-*Onslow*)	John Brown	30.9.49	Stricken 1980
261	TUGHRIL (i) (ex-*Onslaught*)	Fairfield	3.3.51	Stricken 1977

Refit and conversion of *Tippu Sultan* and *Tughril* to Type 16 frigates with US MDAP funds agreed in London 29.4.57. Both ships were converted at Liverpool but *Tariq* was handed back to RN in 1959. *Tughril* was disarmed in 1977 and used as midshipmen's naval academy TS. *Tippu Sultan* was stripped 1980 with her hulk being used as a work platform.

Ex-British 'Ch' and 'Cr' class *destroyers*

No	Name	Builder	Acquired	Fate
	TAIMUR (i) (ex-*Chivalrous*)	Denny	29.6.54	BU 1960–61
D 160	ALAMGIR (ex-*Creole*)	White	29.2.56	Extant 1982
D 162	JAHANGIR (ex-*Crispin*, ex-*Craccher*)	White	29.2.56	Extant 1982
D 164	SHAH JAHAN (ex-*Charity*)	Thornycroft	16.12.58	Extant 1982

Taimur was loaned by RN after 22.10.53 agreement, handed over at Liverpool, and returned to UK in 1960. *Alamgir* and *Jahangir* bought in 1956 and modernised with US MDAP funds by Thornycroft being handed over to the Pakistan Navy on 18.3.58 and 20.6.58 respectively at Southampton. *Shah Jahan* bought by US under MDAP and handed over at Cowes after refit by White.

Ex-British 'BATTLE' class *destroyers*

No	Name	Builder	Acquired	Fate
D 161	BADR (ex-*Gabbard*)	Swan Hunter	29.2.56	Extant 1982
D 163	KHAIBAR (ex-*Cadiz*)	Fairfield	29.2.56	Sunk 5.12.71

Modernised and refitted with US MDAP funds, *Badr* at Yarrow being handed over on 24.1.57 and sailing for Karachi from Portsmouth on 17.2.57. *Khaibar* refitted by Gowan, Glasgow, and handed over 1.2.57. Both named after early Islamic victories. *Khaibar* sunk off Karachi by Indian 'Osa' FAC 5.12.71.

Ex-US GEARING (FRAM I) class *destroyers*

No	Name	Builder	Acquired	Fate
D 165	TARIQ (ii) (ex-*Wiltsie*)	Federal, Kearny	29.4.77	Extant 1982
D 166	TAIMUR (ii) (ex-*Epperson*)	Federal, Kearny	29.4.77	Extant 1982
D 167	TUGHRIL (ii) (ex-*Henderson*)	Todd-Pacific, Seattle	30.9.80	Extant 1982
D 168	TIPPU SULTAN (ii) (ex-*Damato*)	Bethlehem, Staten I	30.9.80	Extant 1982

First pair refitted by Campbell Industries, San Diego, for 7.43 million dollars 1977–78. Two more to be transferred in 1982. *Tariq* finished 2.6.78, *Taimur* 16.2.78.

Ex-British 'COUNTY' class *guided missile destroyer*

No	Name	Builder	Acquired	Fate
?	BABUR (ex-*London*)	Swan Hunter	Feb 1982	Extant 1982

Bought Feb 1982 and refitted, Seaslug SAM system removed from stern. Handed over 24.3.82.

Ex-British modified BITTERN class *frigates*

No	Name	Builder	Acquired	Fate
F 40	JHELUM (ex-*Narbada*)	Thornycroft	1948	For disposal c1960
F 52	SIND (ex-*Godavari*)	Thornycroft	1948	For disposal c1960

Transferred by India 1948. *Sind* refitted by original builders at Southampton 1949–50 touring Australasian ports 1951. *Jhelum* refitted 1950–51, retained her tripod mast until also replaced by lattice in Karachi 1955. Also fitted as flagship.

Ex-British 'RIVER' class *frigates*

No	Name	Builder	Acquired	Fate
F 392	SHAMSHER (ex-*Nadder*)	Smiths Dock	1948	Stricken 1960
F 265	ZULFIQUAR (ex-*Dhanush*, ex-*Deveron*)	Smiths Dock	1948	Extant 1982

Transferred by India in 1948. *Shamsher* became a TS. *Zulfiquar* became a survey ship in 1951 with her aft 4in removed to fit a charthouse. She surveyed for the new port of Chalna, E Pakistan. Renumbered 262 in 1963.

SUBMARINES

Ex-US TENCH class *submarine*

No	Name	Builder	Acquired	Fate
S 130	GHAZI (i) (ex-*Diabolo*)	Portsmouth N Yd	1.6.64	Sunk 4.2.71

Loaned by USN after Fleet Snorkel conversion at Philadelphia N Yd. Commissioned *Ghazi* ('Defender of the Faith') at USN Submarine Base, New London, Connecticut. Sunk by Indian ASW surface ships off Vishakhapatnam while trying to torpedo the carrier *Vikrant* at the start of the third Indo-Pakistan War.

French DAPHNE type *patrol submarines*

No	Name	Builder	Launched	Fate
S 131	HANGOR	Arsenal de Brest	28.6.69	Extant 1982
S 132	SHUSHUK	CN Ciotat	30.7.69	Extant 1982
S 133	MANGRO	CN Ciotat	7.2.70	Extant 1982
S 134	GHAZI (ii) (ex-*Cachalote*)	A C Dubigeon	23.9.68	Extant 1982

Some internal modification for Pakistani service. First pair laid down 1.12.67 and in service 12.1.70. *Mangro* laid down 8.7.68 and in service 8.8.70. *Ghazi* bought from Portugal in Dec 1975. *Hangor* torpedoed and sank the Indian frigate *Khukri* on 9.12.71, the first such attack since 1945.

French AGOSTA type *attack submarines*

No	Name	Builder	Launched	Fate
S 135	HASHMAT (ex-*Astrant*)	A C Dubigeon	14.12.77	Extant 1982
S 136	HURMAT (ex-*Adventurous*)	A C Dubigeon	1.12.78	Extant 1982

When France cancelled an order for submarines destined for South Africa they were quickly bought by Pakistan in Nov 1978. They had been built in 1976–79, and *Hashmat* (completed 17.2.79) arrived at Karachi 31.10.79. *Hurmat* was completed on 17.2.80, and arrived Karachi 11.8.80.

Italian SX 404 type *midget submarines*

Displacement:	40t
Dimensions:	52ft 5in oa × 6ft 7in 16.97m × 2.0m
Machinery:	1-shaft electric = 11kt/6½kts. Range 1200nm surface, 60nm underwater
Complement:	4

A commercial rather than naval design of midget submersible, capable of carrying 12 passengers. Built 1972–73 by Cosmos, Livorno, and 5 out of 6 still in service. Diving depth 330ft (*100m*). One lost at sea 27.12.76. See under Taiwan.

SMALL SURFACE COMBATANTS

Ex-British BASSET class *trawlers*

Class (no, former name, builder, fate):
Bahawalpur (P 149, ex-*Baroda*, ex-*Lucknow*, Shalimar, for disposal c1960), *Lahore* (P 12, ex-*Rampur*, ex-*Barisal*, Burn, for disposal c1960)
Two transferred from India 1948.

Ex-Chinese 'HUCHWAN' class *torpedo hydrofoils*

Class:
HDF 01–04
Transferred to China 1973 and all 4 extant 1982.

Ex-Chinese 'HOKU' class *fast attack craft (missile)*

Four transferred mid-1981.

'TOWN' class *large patrol craft*

Displacement:	115t standard; 143t full load
Dimensions:	107ft × 20ft × 11ft
	32.6m × 6.1m × 3.4m
Machinery:	2 shafts, 2 MTU 12V 538 diesels, 3400bhp = 24kts
Armament:	2–40mm/70 (600rds)
Complement:	19–24

Class (no):

Rajshahi (P 140), *Jessore* (P 141), *Comilla* (P 142), *Sylhet* (P 143)

Ordered from Brooke Marine 5.10.63 and named after E Pakistan towns. *Jessore* and *Comilla* commissioned 20.5.65, *Rajshahi* and *Sylbet* 2.8.65. Specially strengthened hulls with sea resistant aluminium alloy superstructures. All were attacked by Indian aircraft on 4.12.71. Off Chittagong *Rajshahi* was hit 6 times by 4 Hunter jets, set on fire, losing 1 killed and 6 wounded but regained port after the crew checked flooding and fire in the engine room. Extant 1982. Nine aircraft sank *Comilla* in the same action. *Jessore* and *Sylhet* destroyed in air strikes from the carrier *Vikrant* the same day at Khulna to the W. *Jessore* salvaged by Bangladeshi Navy.

Ex-Chinese 'SHANGHAI II' class *large patrol craft*

Class (no):

Lahore (P 140), *Quetta* (P 141), *Mardan* (P 143), *Gilgit* (P 144), *Pishin* (P 145), *Sukkur* (P 147), *Sehwan* (P 148), *Bahawalpur* (P 149), *Bannu* (P 154), *Kalat* (P 156), *Larkana* (P 159), *Sahival* (P 160)

Eight transferred 1972, 4 in 1973. All named after Pakistani cities and extant 1982.

Ex-Chinese 'HAINAN' class *large patrol craft*

Class (no):

Baluchistan (P 155), *Sind* (P 159), *Punjab*, *Sarhad*

First pair transferred mid-1976, second April 1980. Extant 1982.

COASTAL PATROL CRAFT

Eighteen MC 55 class (22.8t full load, 54ft 1in × 17ft × 2ft 10in, *16.5m × 5.2m × 0.8m*, 2 V6 diesels, 1600hp = 30kts, 1–14.5mm MG, 5 crew): *P 551–568* built by Crestitalia and delivered 1979–80. GRP units, *P 553* named *Vaqar*.

One Fairey Marine 'Spear' class.

Four ex-British SDMLs: SDML 3518 and 2519 BU 1965. SDML 3517 and 3520 deleted 1975–77.

MINE WARFARE VESSELS

Ex-British BANGOR class *minesweepers*

Class (no, former name):

Dacca (M 245, ex-*Oudh*), *Peshawar* (M 55, ex-*Malwa*), *Baluchistan* (M 182, ex-*Greenock*), *Chittagong* (ex-*Kathiawar*, ex-*Hartlepool*)

Transferred from India 1948, second pair were turbine-powered. All marked for disposal *c* 1960 except *Chittagong* 1956.

Ex-US BLUEBIRD class *coastal minesweepers*

Class (no, former no, transfer):

Mahmood (M 160, MSC 267, April 1957), *Momin* (M 161, MSC 293, July 1962), *Mubarak* (M 162, MSC 262, Jan 1957), *Muhafiz* (M 163, AMS 138, 25.2.55), *Mujahid* (M 164, MSC 261, Oct 1956), *Mukhtar* (M 165, MSC 274, 25.6.59), *Munsif* (M 166, MSC 273, 25.6.59), *Moshal* (M 167, MSC 294, 13.7.63)

Momin and *Moshal* have lower bridges than the other 6. All built under MAP. *Mujahid* and *Mubarak* arrived Karachi 5.6.57. *Munsif* stricken 1979. *Muhafiz* sunk off Karachi by Indian Navy 5.12.71.

Papua New Guinea

Papua New Guinea (PNG) received her independence from Australia in September 1975, but strong links remain and all the Navy has been transferred from and trained by the RAN. HQ is at Port Moresby with the patrol boat base at Lombrun on Manas in the Admiralties. It is a very small force to patrol the 3200 mile coastline and rivers as well as six island groups. The 410 volunteer sailors are part of the Defence Force.

Five ex-Australian *Attack* class large patrol craft: *Aitape* (P 84), *Samarai* (P 85), *Ladava* (P 92), *Lae* (P 93), *Madang* (P 94). *Aitape* stricken 1981 for spares. All named after Papuan towns.

Two ex-Australian *Balikpapan* utility landing craft: *Salamaua* (31) and *Buna* ((32).

Seven Australian personnel landing craft: *Kokuba*, *Kaiapit*, *Kandep*, *Kiunga*, *Kuniawa*, *Kukipi*, *Kiunga*. Built and delivered 1975.

Two landing craft: *Burfoam* (launched May 1981), *Burcrest* (launched 20.7.81) and 2 more being built by Sing Koon Seng of Singapore.

Philippines

The Philippines like Indonesia are an extensive archipelago of 11 large and 7079 other islands spreading over an area of some 115,800 square miles with a total coastline of about 14,000 miles. The archipelago (population 50,350,000 in 1982) lies to the north of the Indonesian archipelago and bisects the sea routes between China, Japan, Korea, Asian Russia and Indonesia and routes to the Indian Ocean. Strategically, therefore, the Philippines hold an important position as regards maritime strategy in South East Asia. The country has 93 ports and 12,049 vessels involved in inter-island traffic.

The Filipino Government has always maintained close ties with the USA since the republic's full independence on 4 July 1946. The US Navy has a 25-year lease on its major base at Subic Bay. This has resulted in extensive military aid, the majority of warships being fairly sizeable, but now greatly overage, ex-American units (over 49 acquired by 1950). Certainly the age of the present 17-ship escort force indicates a definite need for reliefs, particularly following the loss of the frigate *Datu Kalantiaw* in the September 1981 typhoon.

As part of a general 15-year modernisation programme due for completion in about 1982–83 the Navy is to replace some of the overage ships with 12 missile-armed craft. Three missile-armed fast attack craft of Korean PSMM-5 type (*Paek Ku* 12) already supposed to be under construction and it is probable that all 12 planned under 5-year programme will be fast missile attack craft. In addition to these 12 vessels, which will probably replace the old ex-US frigates, the Navy is said to be interested in acquiring two submarines, probably German Type 209s. Nothing was however done in that direction.

There are many coastal patrol craft and larger patrol vessels (the Coast Guard was formed as a branch of the Navy in October 1967) designed and used to patrol the large territorial seas as the Filipino Government claimed a 300nm limit. The Philippines Navy has also a very large fleet of old landing ships used mainly as transports for landing stores on harbourless coasts or in small fishing ports. Both these categories have been used against Muslim secessionists on Mindanao and in the Sulu Archipelago since 1965 in the bloody and still continuing Moro Rebellion. There are only two small coastal motor minesweepers (US *Bluebird* class) probably only for training purposes.

Selective service manpower, for an active Fleet of 91 surface combatants and 102 amphibious vessels, totalled 14,672 (12,000 reserves) in 1982 (4000 in 1958, 8000 in 1970) with a marine corps of 6838 organised in two seven-battalion brigades. The main base is Sangley Point. There are six main commands held by captains or commodores; Naval Defence Forces; Coast Guard Sealift; Amphibious Command; Training; Ready Force and Fleet Support.

MAJOR SURFACE SHIPS

Ex-US BUCKLEY ('TE') class *frigate*

No	Name	Builder	Acquired	Fate
PF	RAJAH SOLIMAN (ex-*Bowers*)	Bethlehem, San Francisco	21.4.61	BU 1966

Former US high speed transport converted from destroyer escort built in 1943. Transferred under MAP. Fitted as command ship for the Philippine Navy. Sunk in typhoon in June 1962, raised but stricken on 3.12.64.

Ex-US EDSALL ('FMR') class *frigate*

No	Name	Builder	Acquired	Fate
PF 4	RAJAH LAKANDULA (ex-*Tran Hung Dao*, ex-*Camp*)	Brown SB, Houston	5.4.76	Extant 1982

USN destroyer escort converted to radar picket after the Second World War, redesignated DER instead. Transferred to South Vietnamese Navy on 6.2.71. Acquired by Philippines in 1975 and formally transferred the next year.

Ex-US CASCO class *cutters*

Class (no, former names):
Andres Bonifacio (PF 7, ex-*Ly Thoung Kiet*, ex-*Chincoteague* WHEC 375, ex-*AVP 24*), *Georgio de Pilar* (PF 8, ex-*Ngo Kuyen*, ex-*McCulloch* WHEC 386, ex-*Wachapreague* AGP 8, ex-*AVP 56*), *Diego Silang* (PF 9, ex-*Tran Quang Khai*, ex-*Bering Strait* WHEC 382, ex-*AVP 34*), *Francisco Dagohoy* (PF 10, ex-*Tran Binh Trong*, ex-*Castle Rock* WHEC 383, ex-*AVP 35*)

Built by L Washington S Yd as *Barnegat* class seaplane tenders for USN. All 4 transferred to Coast Guard in 1946–48, initially on loan designated WAVP and then on permanent transfer except ex-*McCulloch* transferred outright from USN to CG, subsequently redesignated as high endurance cutters (WHEC). Transferred from CG to S Vietnam in 1971–72 and officially transferred to Philippines in 1976. *Francisco Dagohoy* commissioned in Philippines Navy in 1979. Two other cutters *Yakutat* WHEC 380 (ex-*AVP 32*) and *Cook Inlet* WHEC 384 (ex-*AVP 36*) transferred in 1976 for spares.

Ex-US CANNON ('DET') class *frigates*

Class:
Datu Kalantiaw (PF 76, ex-*Booth*), *Datu Siratuna* (PF 77, ex-*Asahi*, ex-*Amick*), *Rajah Humabon* (PF 78, ex-*Hatsuhi*, ex-*Atherton*), I (ex-*Kyong Ki*, ex-*Muir*), II (ex-*Kang Won*, ex-*Sutton*)

USN destroyer escorts type built in 1943–44. *Datu Kalantiaw* transferred 15.12.76, and sold on 31.8.78; *Datu Siratuna* and *Rajah Humabon* served in Japanese Navy in 1955–75 and were transferred to Philippines in 1976 and purchased at scrap value, towed to S Korea in Oct 1978 for overhaul and modernisation. The last two ships without new names were taken over from Korean deletion list and will be probably cannibalised for spares for active units. *Datu Kalantiaw* lost on 20.9.81 in Typhoon 'Clara'.

AMPHIBIOUS WARFARE VESSELS

Ex-US LST type *landing ships*

Class (no, former names, transferred):
Cutabato (ex-*LST 75*), *Pampanga* (ex-*LST 842*), *Bulacan* (ex-*LST 843*), *Albay* (ex-*LST 865*), *Misamis Oriental* (ex-*LST 875*). *Bataan* (ex-*Caddo Parish*, LST 515), *Cagayan* (LT 86, ex-*Hickman County*, LST 825), *Ilcos Norte* (LT 97, ex-*Madera County*, LST 905), *Zamboanga del Sur* (LT 86, ex-*Cam Ranh*, ex-*LST 975*), *Mindoro Occidental* (LT 93, ex-*LST 222*), *Surigao del Norte* (LT 94, ex-*LST 488*), *Surigao del Sur* (LT 95, ex-*LST 546*, 15.7.72), *Tarlac* (LT 500, ex-*LST 47*), *Laguna* (LT 501, ex-*LST 230*), *Samar Oriental* (LT 502, ex-*LST 287*), *Lanao del Sur* (LT 503, ex-*LST 491*), *Lanao del Norte* (LT 504, ex-*LST 566*), *Leyte del Sur* (LT 505, ex-*LST 607*), *Davao Oriental* (LT 506, ex-*Daggett County*, LST 689), *Benguet* (LT 507, ex-*Davies County*, LST 692), *Sierra Madre* (AL 57, ex-*Dumagat*, ex-*My Tho*, ex-*Harnett County* APG 821, ex-*LST 821*), *Aurora* (LT 508, ex-*Harris County*, LST 822), *Cavite* (LT 509, ex-*Hillsdale County*, LST 835), *Samar del Norte* (LT 510, ex-*Nansemond County*, LST 1064), *Cotabato del Norte* (LT 87, ex-*Orleans Parish*, LST 1069, ex-*MCS 6*), *Tawi-Tawi* (LT 512, ex-*LST 1072*), *Agusan del Sur* (ex-*Nha Trang*, ex-*Jerome City*, LST 848).

Twenty-three US tank landing ships built in 1942–45. Named after Filipino islands and straits. Several have undergone major refits including replacement of frames and plating as well as engines and electrics. First 5 ships transferred in 1948 and the next 3 in Nov 1969. Other ships acquired from S Korea and S Vietnam in the 1970s (LT 93–95 unarmed July 1972) especially after the fall of S Vietnam (LT 54 and 87). LT 510 bought 24.9.77. Vietnamese ships were bought at scrap value on 5.4.76. LT 500 series recommissioned 8.8.78 and 18.10.78 after Japan refits. *Cutabato* and *Pampanga* were scrapped. *Bataan* renamed *Maquindanao*. Twelve new LSTs were on order in 1982.

Ex-US LSM type *medium landing ships*

Class (no, former names, transfer):
Isabela (LP 41, ex-*LSM 463*, March 1961), *Batanes* (i) (ex-*LSM 236*), *Oriental Mindoro* (LP 68, ex-*LSM 320*, April 1962), *Batanes* (ii) (ex-*Huong Giang*, ex-*Oceanside*, ex-*LSM 175*), *Western Samar* (LP 66, ex-*Hat Giang*, ex-*LSM 9011*, ex-*LSM 335*)

Two transferred to the Philippines in 1961–62. *Batanes* (i) ran aground 1971, stricken 1972. LSM 175 acquired from S Vietnam in 1975. Also LSM 110 (17.11.75) for spares cannibalisation.

Ex-US LSSL 1 class *fire support landing ships*

Class (no, former names):
Camarines Sur (LF 48, ex-*Nguyen Duc Bong*, ex-*LSSL 129*), *Sulu* (LF 49, ex-*LSSL 96*), *La Union* (LF 50, ex-*Doan Ngoc Tang*, ex-*LSSL 9*)

La Union was transferred to France in 1951 (*Hallebarde* L 9023) transferred to Japan 1956–64; returned and transferred to S Vietnam in 1965 for spares. Acquired by Philippines in 1975 as was *Lulu Phu Tho* (ex-*LSSL 101*) for spares. *Camarines Sur* and *Sulu* transferred on 17.11.75. Ex-US LSSL 68 and 87 transferred from Japan Sept and Nov 1975 but not commissioned. Armament: 1–76mm, 4–40mm, 4–20mm, 4 MG.

Ex-US LSIL type *infantry landing ships*

Class:
Marinduque (LF 36, ex-*LSIL 875*), *Seorsogon* (LF 37, ex-*Thien Kich*, ex-L 9038, ex-*LSIL 872*), *Camarines Norte* (LF 52, ex-*Loi Cong*, ex-L 9034, ex-*LSIL 699*), *Misamis Occidental* (LF 53, ex-*Tam Set*, ex-L 9033, ex-*LSIL 871*).

Transferred to France and later to S Vietnam and in 1975 acquired by Philippines. There is also LSIL 476 transferred at the same time for spares. First 3 stricken 1980, last unit 1979.

MINOR LANDING CRAFT
Eleven ex-US LCM (8) type transferred 1973–75.
Fifty ex-US LCM (6) type transferred 1955 (1), 1971–73 (13), 1973–75 (36).
Seven ex-US LCVP type transferred in 1955–56 (2), 1965 (1), 1971 (2), 1973 (2).
Three ex-US LCU 1466 type transferred from Japan 17.11.75.

SMALL SURFACE COMBATANTS

Ex-US ADMIRABLE class *ocean minesweepers (corvettes)*

Class (no, former names):
Pagasa (ex-APO 21, ex-*Quest* AM 281), *Samar* (ex-*Project* AM 278), *Magat Salamat* (PS 20, ex-*Chi Lang II*, ex-*Gayety* MSF 239)

Minesweeping gear removed upon transfer in 1948. *Pagasa* renamed several times: *Santa Maria*, *Corregidor* and *Mount Samat*; served as presidential yacht and had her stern rebuilt, later used as command vessel. *Samar* later served as patrol vessel, armament: 1–76mm, 4–40mm (2×2), 4–20mm; APO 21: 1–76mm, 4–20mm. *Samar* later served as survey vessel. *Magat Salamat* was built in 1943–45 and transferred to S Vietnam in April 1962 and to Philippines in Nov 1975. Minesweeping gear removed and ship used as large patrol ship (1–76mm, 2–40mm, 6–20mm).

Ex-US PCE type (185ft) *patrol craft (corvettes)*

Class:
Cebu (PS 28, ex-*PCE 881*), *Negros Occidental* (PS 29, ex-*PCE 884*), *Leyte* (PS 30, ex-*PCE 885*), *Pangasinan* (PS 31, ex-*PCE 891*), *Iloilo* (PS 32, ex-*PCE 897*), *Miguel Malvar* (PS 19, ex-*Ngoc Hoi*, ex-*Brattleboro* PCER 852), *Sultan Kundarat* (PS 22, ex-*Dong Da II*, ex-*Crestview*, PCER 895). *Datu Marikudo* (PS 23, ex-*Van Kiep II*, ex-*Amherst* PCER 853)

Built in 1943–45 and transferred in July 1948. Originally numbered E 28–32. Armament: 1–76mm/50, 3 or 6–40mm, 4–20mm (4×1), 2–324mm Mk 32 ASW TT (3×1), DC, Hedgehog. *Leyte* ran aground in 1979. Last 3 transferred from Vietnamese Navy in 1975–76. PCER 852, 895, 853 originally fitted as rescue ships. Seven extant 1982.

Ex-US AUK class (MSF type) *ocean minesweepers (corvettes)*

Class:
Rizal (PS 69, ex-*Murrelet*, MSF 372), *Quezon* (PS 70, ex-*Vigilance*, MSF 324)

Former US Navy minesweepers (originally designated AM) built in 1943–45 and transferred to Philippines on 18.6.65 and 19.8.67 respectively. Upon transfer the minesweeping gear was removed and a second 76mm gun fitted aft until replaced by raised helicopter pad. SPS-5 radar and SQS-17B sonar; armament: 2–76mm/50 (2×1), 4–40mm (2×2), 4–20mm (2×2), 3–324mm Mk 32 ASW TT, 1 Hedgehog, 2 DCT, 2 DC rails. Used as patrol vessels. Both extant 1982.

Korean PSK 5 type *fast attack craft (missile)*

Particulars: As Indonesia

Three ordered from S Korea-Tacoma S Yd, Masan, in 1980. Another 3 on order.

Ex-US PC (173ft) type *submarine-chasers (large patrol craft)*

Class:

Camarines Sur (PS 21, ex-*PC 1121*), *Bohol* (PS 22, ex-*PC 1131*), *Zamboango del Sur* (PS 23, ex-*PC 1133*), *Batangas* (PS 24, ex-*PC 1134*), *Nueva Ecija* (PS 25, ex-*PC 1241*), *Negros Oriental* (PS 26, ex-*PC 1563*), *Capiz* (PS 27, ex-*PC 1564*), *Nueva Viscaya* (PS 80, ex-*Altus*, ex-*PCE 568*), *Negros Oriental* (PS 26, ex-*E 312*, ex-*L'Inconstant*, ex-*PC 1171*)

Eight transferred in 1947–48, 1958 and March 1968. *Camarines Sur* stricken in 1953, *Negros Oriental* sunk in typhoon at Guam in Nov 1962 (raised and stricken in 1963), *Bohol* scrapped in 1969, *Capiz* and *Batangas* deleted in 1979. Others: *Nueva Ecija* (1977) and *Zamboango del Sur* also deleted (16.10.56). PC 1171 escaped from Cambodia to the Philippines and was bought by the latter in Dec 1976. Two extant 1982.

Ex-US PCS type *submarine-chasers (large patrol craft)*

Class:

Tarlac (PG 11, ex-*PCS 1399*, ex-*YMS 450*), *Laguna* (LG 12, ex-*PCS 1403*)

Built in 1942 and transferred in Jan 1948. Both scrapped in 1969. Armament: 1–76mm, 1–40mm, 4–20mm.

Ex-US SC (110ft) type *submarine-chasers (large patrol craft)*

Class:

Cagayan (ex-*SC 731*), *Mountain Province* (ex-*SC 736*), *Ilocus Sur* (ex-*SC 739*), *Alert* (ex-*SC 1267*), *Surigao* (ex-*SC 747*), *Isabella* (ex-*SC 750*), *Cavite* (ex-*SC 981*), *Ilocus Norte* (ex-*SC 1274*)

Built in 1942–43 and all 8 transferred in 1946–48. *Ilocus Norte* renamed *Malampay Sound*. *Ilocus Sur*, *Cagayan* and *Isabella* stricken in 1956. *Alert* was sunk in 1956. Others since deleted.

US SC type (110ft) *large patrol craft*

Class:

Antique (ex-*PGM 36*), *Camarines Sur* (ex-*PGM 33*), *La Union* (PGM 35), *Masbate* (ex-*PGM 37*), *Misamis Occidental* (ex-*PGM 38*), *Sulu* (ex-*PGM 34*)

Six built under MAP for Philippines; four transferred in 1955 and two (*Masbate* and *Misamis Occidental*) in 1956. Design based on the 110ft wooden submarine chasers of the Second World War. *Masbate* sunk 1965. *Camarines Sur*, *Sulu*, *La Union*, *Antique*, *Misamis Occidental* decommissioned in 1973–74.

US PGM type *large patrol craft*

Class:

Agusan (ex-*PGM 39*), *Catanduanes* (ex-*PGM 40*), *Palawan* (ex-*PGM 42*), *Romblon* (ex-*PGM 41*), *Yachi* (ex-*PGM 60*), *Yanga* (ex-*PGM 59*), *Yundi* (ex-*PGM 57*), *Basilan* (ex-*Hon Troc*, ex-*PGM 83*)

Steel-hulled patrol gunboats, longer versions of the US Coast Guard 95ft 'Cape' class built under MAP in US by Tacoma Boatbuilding for Philippines and transferred upon completion in 1960 (first pair in service March; second in June). *Yachi*, *Yanga* and *Yundi* intended for Indonesia transferred to Philippines in 1965. *Basilan* acquired from S Vietnam in Dec 1975. All 5 extant 1982.

KATAPANGAN class *large patrol craft*

Displacement:	135t standard; 150t full load
Dimensions:	100ft 4in × 18ft 7in × 5ft
	30.6m × 5.7m × 1.5m
Machinery:	2 shafts, 2 MTU MB 820 D61 diesels, 2050bhp = 16kts
Armament:	4–30mm Emerlec (2×2), 2 MG

Class (no):

Katapangan (P 101), *Bagong Lakas* (P 102)

Designed and built by W Müller, Hameln, W Germany. Prototype delivered for trials 11.10.78. Both in service 9.2.79 but plans to build more at Cavite Navy Yd and Boseco, Bekan, in the Philippines abandoned due to their inadequacy.

Ex-British *seaward defence motor launches*

Class:

SDB 1323, 1326, 1328, 1329

Former British HDML type motor launches acquired from Australia in 1959 and commissioned without name change. Deleted in *c* 1963.

Ex-US 'SWIFT' Mk 1 and 2 type *coastal patrol craft*

Class:

PCF 300–317 (ex-US *PCF 6633, 6634, 35–38, 681–688, 6911–6913*)

Eighteen inshore patrol craft built in the USA. *PCF 302–305* served in USN prior the transfer, rest built under MAP. *PCF 300–305* transferred in March and Aug 1966, *PCF 306–313* in Feb 1968 and *PCF 314–316* in July 1970, *PCF 317* was Filipino built (ferro concrete) and used as a yacht for the president's wife until discarded 1976. *PCF 304* and *305* and one other stricken then. *PCF 308* stricken 1979, 13 extant in 1982.

ABRA class *coastal patrol craft*

Displacement:	40t standard; 72t full load
Dimensions:	87ft × 9ft × 5ft
	26.5m × 2.7m × 1.5m
Machinery:	2 shafts, 2 MTU diesels, 2400bhp = 25kts
Armament:	2–20mm (2×1), 1–12.7mm MG
Complement:	15 or 16

Class (no, in service):

Abra (FB 83, 8.1.70), *Bukindon* (FB 84, 1971), *Tablas* (FB 85, 1975)

First ship built by Vosper at Singapore, other 2 at Cavite N Yd in the Philippines. Similar to Malaysian 'PX' class. All extant 1982.

US 'SWIFT' Mk 3 type *coastal patrol craft*

Displacement:	33t full load
Dimensions:	65ft × 16ft 1in × 3ft 3in
	19.8m × 4.9m × 1.0m
Machinery:	3 shafts, 3 GM 8V 71 TI diesels, 1590bhp = 25kts. Range 500nm at 30kts
Armament:	2–12.7mm MG (2×1), 2–7.62mm (2×1)
Sensors:	Radar LN-66
Complement:	8

Class:

PCF 318–323, 333, 334, 336–340

Built in USA by Sewart for Philippine Navy. First 6 delivered Jan–June 1972, *PCF 333* and *334* in April 1975, *PCF 338* in July, *336* in Nov, *339* and *340* in Dec. All 13 extant 1982, 25 more ordered in early 1980. Some serve with Coast Guard.

De Havilland Marine series 9209 *coastal patrol craft*

Displacement:	16.5t full load
Dimensions:	45ft 10in × 14ft 6in × 3ft 4in
	14m × 4.4m × 1m
Machinery:	2 shafts, 2 Caterpillar D348 diesels, 740bhp = 25kts. Range 500nm at 12kts
Armament:	2–12.7mm MG (2×1)
Complement:	8

Class:

PC 326–331

Built by De Havilland Marine of Sydney, Australia with GRP hulls. In service 20.11.74–8.2.75. All 6 extant 1982.

MARCELO type *coastal patrol craft*

Displacement:	21.75t full load
Dimensions:	46ft × 14ft 1in × 3ft 4in
	14m × 4.3m × 1m
Machinery:	2 shafts, 2 MTU 8V-331 TC80 diesels, 1800bhp = 46kts. Range 200nm at 36kts
Armament:	4–12.7mm MG (1×2, 2×1)
Sensors:	Radar LN-66

Class:

PSB 411, PSB 414, PSB 417–434

Eighty ordered Aug 1975 from Marcelo of Manila but 15 of 25 completed that year destroyed by fire, halting production. Turin MG set into fo'c'sle. Ten extant 1982.

MINE WARFARE VESSELS

Ex-US BLUEBIRD class *coastal minesweepers*

Class (no, former no):
Zambales (PM 55, ex-*MSC 218*), *Zamboanga del Norte* (PM 56, ex-*MSC 219*)
Built by the US yards specifically for transfer under MAP. Transferred 7.3.56 and 23.4.56. Wooden hull with non-magnetic metal fittings. Deleted in 1979.

Ex-US AGILE class *ocean minesweepers*

Class (no, former name):
Davao del Norte (PM 91, ex-*Energy* MSO 436), *Davao del Sur* (PM 92, ex-*Firm* MSO 444)
Built in 1953–54 and transferred on 5.7.72. Designated PM (patrol minesweepers). Wooden hull. Deleted in 1976. To US for disposal 1977.

MISCELLANEOUS

Two Italian 68ft Rodriguez type patrol hydrofoils (28t, 38kts, 400nm range, 1–20mm, 1–TT, 15 men): *Camiguin* (H 72), and *Siquisor* (H 73) completed at Messina April 1965. Deleted 1979.
Two Japanese 68ft Hitachi *Zozen* type patrol hydrofoils (32t, 37.8kts, 400nm range, MG fore and aft, 15 men): *Bontoc* (M 74) and *Balek* (M 75) built at Osaka in 1966. Deleted 1979.

Seychelles

The Seychelles Indian Ocean archipelago of 92 granite and coral islands, independent in 1976 and with a left-wing non-aligned government from June 1977, has a 1000-strong defence force trained by Tanzanian military advisers, and an embryo naval force (organic to the Army) consisting of 150 sailors, the ex-French *Sirius* class coastal minesweepers *Croix du Sud*, transferred as a gift on 20 January 1979 as a patrol boat (without sweeping gear) and renamed *Topaz* (for particulars, see French section), and the 350t LCT *Cinq Juin* (ordered 12 December 1977) used as an inter-island transport. A Soviet 'Zhuk' type coastal patrol craft was delivered from the Black Sea on 11 October 1981 and an Italian 42m, 25kt patrol boat was ordered from CN, La Spezia, the same month. They are based at Port Victoria, the capital on Mahé, the largest island.

Singapore

Singapore became independent in 1958. She had been a British possession almost uninterruptedly since 1819; first ruled by the British East India Company, then controlled from India from 1826–67, and finally as the separate colony of the Straits Settlements. Britain retained control of the naval base until a final withdrawal in March 1976. Singapore joined the Malaysian Federation when it was set up in September 1963, but pulled out following disputes and Chinese-Malay clashes in August 1965. She then set up her own armed forces, replacing expatriates with islanders, but retains links with Malaysia. Singapore is now a member of ASEAN (the Association of South East Asian Nations), which is gradually taking on aspects of a military alliance. In 1980 the Soviet Pacific Fleet lost the Singapore repair facilities it had used heavily in the 1970s, indeed more than any other foreign Asian port.
Almost all the trade to and from the Far East passes the port of Singapore, giving it great strategic significance and making it one of the world's major trading centres. Her spectacular economic growth is today attested by a merchant fleet of 988 ships worth 7,664,229 grt. This has assisted Singapore's drive to self-sufficiency – most of her warships have been built in the two specialist warship yards, and she now exports warships to other navies. Defence spending has doubled since 1975 (to 707 million US dollars) while naval manpower has tripled. The country only consists of Singapore Island itself, the size of the Isle of Wight, plus a small archipelago of 54 other islands, but despite her small size she has a powerful and efficient force of gun and missile-armed patrol boats. These are well suited to policing the restricted waters around Singapore, and coping with pirates and infiltrators, but other navies would have to be called on to cope with large scale mining or submarines. In 1982 the service's 3000 men (2–3 year conscripts and regular volunteers) were commanded by a colonel.

Ex-US LST 542 type *tank landing ships*

Class (no, former no):
Endurance (L 201, ex-*Holmes County*, LST 836), *Excellence* (L 202, ex-LST 629), *Intrepid* (L 203, ex-*LST 759*), *Perseverance* (L 206, ex-*LST 623*), *Persistence* (L 205, ex-*LST 613*), *Resolution* (L 204, ex-*LST 649*)
Nine ex-USN LSTs, all 1944-built, have been acquired by Singapore, but three have been sold. *Endurance* was loaned from the USN on 1.7.71 and purchased on 5.12.75. Ex-USS LST 276 and ex-USS LST 532 were transferred in June 1974 but sold commercially. The rest and ex-USS LST 117 were acquired on 4.6.76, but the latter was sold commercially. The other 6 originally numbered A 81 to A 86. *Endurance* has been leased commercially since 1976. *Excellence*, *Intrepid* (only a stern 40mm gun each, former has helicopter pad) and *Resolution* were rebuilt in 1977 with a derrick forward of the bridge and a pole mast in place of the lattice mast. The six named ships are in service in 1982.

AYER CHAWAN class *landing craft*

Displacement:	150t full load
Dimensions:	88ft 6in × 22ft × 4ft
	27m × 6.9m × 1.3m
Machinery:	2 shafts, 2 diesels, 650bhp = 10kts
Armament:	None
Complement:	?

Class:
Ayer Chawan, *Ayer Merban* and 2 others
Built by Vosper Thornycroft, Singapore 1968–69 and extant 1982.

MINOR LANDING CRAFT

Two *Brani* class LCU (56t full load, 55ft 8in × 14ft × 4ft 7in, *17m × 4.3m × 1.4m*, 2 diesels, 460bhp = 9kts): *Brani* and *Berlayer* built in Australia 1955–56 and extant 1982.

Sea Dragon as completed
NB 1/750 scale

Lürssen 'TNC 45' type *fast attack craft (missile)*

Armament:	5 Gabriel SSM (1×3, 2×1), 1–57mm (504rds), 1–40mm/70 (1008rds), 2 RFL on 57mm
Other particulars:	As Bahrein and Kuwait

Class (no):
Sea Wolf (P 76), *Sea Lion* (P 77), *Sea Dragon* (P 78), *Sea Tiger* (P 79), *Sea Hawk* (P 80), *Sea Scorpion* (P 81)
Six 48m Lürssen type FAC were ordered in 1970. Apart from the machinery and armament, they are similar to those supplied since to the Gulf navies. Armed with the first Israeli Gabriel missiles to be exported. *Sea Wolf* and *Sea Lion* were built by Lürssen in W Germany. They were commissioned in 1972. *Sea Dragon*, *Sea Hawk*, *Sea Serpent* and *Sea Tiger* were all built at Singapore with assistance from Lürssen. First pair commissioned 1974 and other two 1975. Two more ordered in 1977. All six in service in 1982.

Vosper 110ft Type A and B *fast attack craft (gun)*

Displacement:	100t standard; 130t full load
Dimensions:	103ft 8in wl, 109ft 8in oa × 21ft × 5ft 8in
	31.6m, 33.5m × 6.4m × 1.8m
Machinery:	2 shafts, 2 MTU 16V 538 diesels, 7200hp = 32kts. Range 1100nm at 15kts
Armament:	Type A: 1–40mm/70, 1–20mm
	Type B: 1–76mm/50, 1–20mm
Sensors:	Type A: Radar Type Decca TM 626
	Type B: Radar Types HSA M 26, Decca TM 626
Complement:	Type A: 22
	Type B: 19

Sovreignty (Type B) as completed   *Vosper Thornycroft*

Independence (Type A) as completed   *Vosper Thornycroft*

Class (no, launched):

Independence (P 69, 15.7.69), *Freedom* (P 70, 18.11.69), *Sovereignty* (P 71, 25.11.69), *Justice* (P 72, 20.6.70), *Daring* (P 73, 1970), *Dauntless* (P 74, 6.5.71)

Six Vosper Thornycroft 110ft patrol boats were ordered on 21.5.68. Three have a 40mm gun forward (Type A) and three a 76mm set further aft (as in Norwegian *Storm* class FAC) with a shorter superstructure (Type B). Latter also have Signaal M 26 radome atop the short lattice mast. The first of each type was built at Vosper Thornycroft's Portsmouth yard; *Independence*, Type A, delivered on 8.7.70, and *Sovereignty*, Type B, delivered in Feb 1970. The other four were built at Vosper Thornycroft's Singapore yard. *Freedom* and *Justice*, Type A, were delivered on 11.1.71 and 23.4.71 respectively, and *Daring* and *Dauntless*, Type B, in Sept and Dec 1971 respectively. Developed from the Malaysian 103ft type, and have a steel hull and aluminium alloy superstructure. All are in service in 1982.

Lürssen 'FPB 57' type *fast attack craft*

Particulars:	As Kuwait

Three ordered in 1980 from Singapore SB, Jurong. First laid down June 1980. Armament of 1–76mm OTO Melara (300rds) and 2–35mm Oerlikon GDM-A (1×2, 2750rds) possibly SSM as well. Three more may be built for export. SUSIE-1 passive intercept ECM. Similar to W German Type 143 (S 61) class.

British 'FORD' type *large patrol craft*

Panglima (P 68) was built at United Engineers, Signapore and launched on 14.1.56 to the design of the British 'Ford' class seaward defence boats, but crew 15 and 1–20mm as well. Delivered to the Singapore Government but (commissioned May 1956) transferred to the Royal Malaysian Navy in 1963 when the Federation was created. Transferred back to Singapore in 1967, and is now used as TS.

ENDEAVOUR *large patrol craft*

Displacement:	250t full load
Dimensions:	135ft × 25ft × 8ft
	40.9m × 7.6m × 2.4m
Machinery:	2 shafts, 2 Maybach diesels, 2600bhp = 20kts. Range 800nm at 8kts
Armament:	2–20mm (2×1)
Complement:	24

Endeavour (P 75) was built by Schiffswerft Oberwinter, W Germany, in 1955 and purchased from the Netherlands on 30.9.70. In service 1982 and used as TS and diving tender.

Ex-US BLUEBIRD class *coastal minesweepers*

Class (no, former name, launched):

Jupiter (M 101, ex-*Thrasher*, MSC 203, 6.10.54), *Mercury* (M 102, ex-*Wippoorwill*, MSC 207, 13.8.54)

Commissioned into USN 16.8.55 and 20.10.55 respectively. Bought by Singapore 5.12.75. Rearmed with new 20mm Oerlikon in 1980. Both extant 1982.

MISCELLANEOUS

The Singapore Marine Police operate 12 45t 'Swift' class fast patrol craft (P 10–P 21 built 1980–81 by Singapore SB, Jurong) based on the Australian De Havilland 'Capricornica' design. These 34kt craft carry 1–20mm, 1–7.62mm MG and 13 men. All formally commissioned 20.10.81. Four Vosper 'PX' type coastal patrol craft (sisters to Malaysia's) have been in service since 1969. Twenty PC 32 class speed boats have been in service since 1978–79 and 19 larger craft (PX 14–33) are building at Sembawang SY.

Solomons

The Solomons, despite being best known for the 1942–43 US-Japanese naval campaign, remain a British colony covering 249,000 sq nm in the SW Pacific with 6 major islands in the 900-mile chain. A solitary Australian-built *Carpentaria* class coastal patrol craft, the *Tulagi*, has policed the archipelago since 30 March 1979.

Sri Lanka

The Royal Ceylon Navy was established on 9 December 1950 with its principal base at the historic port of Trincomalee. No part of this island paradise, less than a third the size of Britain, is further than 80 miles from the sea and India lies 35 miles across the Palk Strait. Independence came on 4 February 1948 and on 22 May 1972 Ceylon became a republic being renamed Sri Lanka ('Resplendent Island'), the Navy likewise.

Until 1971 Ceylon relied on the British presence East of Suez for external security under the 1947 Defence Agreement (still valid today). A very modest military expansion began after an internal revolt that year and the Navy began adding some Chinese patrol craft to its all British fleet. Manpower totals have hardly changed since 1963 (2000) being 2960 today with 713 volunteer reserves under a rear-admiral. Secondary bases are at Karaingar, Colombo, Welisara, Tangalla and Kalpitiya. Coastal craft for anti-illegal immigration patrols are being locally built, but it is hard to see where many offshore patrol vessels for the 200-mile EEZ are coming from out of a 29.4 million dollar defence budget (1981).

Ex-British 'RIVER' class *frigates*

No	Name	Builder	Acquired	Fate
	GAJABAHU (ex-*Misnak*, ex-*Hallowell*)	Canadian Vickers	1959	For disposal 1978
	MAHASENA (ex-*Mivtakh*, ex-*Violetta*, ex-*Orkney*)	Canadian Yarrow	1959	BU 1964

Two elderly ex-Canadian 'River' class frigates were bought from Israel in 1959. The former armament of three 4.7in was replaced by a single RN-pattern 4in/45 Mk 5 HA in 'B' position. *Mahasena* sold to Hong Kong breakers for £20,000 in June 1964. About 1972 *Gajabahu* was reported to be non-operational.

Ex-British 'FORD' class *seaward defence boat*

Class (former name, fate):

Kotiya (ex-*Desford*, wrecked 22.12.64)

Transferred from the RN 1955; later wrecked off Colombo.

Ex-Chinese 'SHANGHAI II' class *large patrol craft*

Class:

Balawatha, Daksaya, Ramakami, Sooraya, Weeraya, Jagatha, Pakshaka

Transferred Feb 1972 and 1975 (first 5). Last 2 in 1980 commissioning 30.11.80. All 7 extant 1982.

Ex-Soviet 'MOL' class *fast attack craft*

Samudra Devi handed over Dec 1975 without TT, radar of IFF.

Vosper Type 101 *coastal patrol craft*

Displacement:	15t full load
Dimensions:	45ft 3in × 11ft 6in × 2ft 11in
	13.8m × 3.6m × 0.9m
Machinery:	2 shafts, 2 GM 6-71 diesels, 500bhp = 25kts
Armament:	1 MG
Complement:	6

Class:
P 102–110, P 201–211

Two ordered 1965, 7 in 1966; hard chine construction with double teak planking, 21 built by Vosper Thornycroft of Singapore and assembled in Sri Lanka by Sept 1968. Radar, radio and searchlight equipped. *P 102* lost 1979, *P 106, 109, 201, 204, 205, 207, 208, 210* stricken 1978–79, 11 extant 1982, in 2 squadrons at Kalpitiya and Kavainagar, *103, 104, 108* and *109* only on harbour duties.

BELIKAWA class *coastal patrol craft*

Displacement:	22t full load
Dimensions:	55ft 11in × 14ft 9in × 3ft 11in
	17m × 4.5m × 1.2m
Machinery:	2 shafts, 2 GM 8V-71 T1 diesels, 800bhp = 23.6kts. Range 1000nm/790nm at 18kts/12.2kts
Armament:	3–7.62mm MG
Sensors:	Radar Decca
Complement:	7

Class (no, in service):
Belikawa (P 421, April 1977), *Diyakawa* (P 422, June 1977), *Korawakka* (P 423, July 1977), *Seruwa* (P 424, Sept 1977), *Tarawa* (P 425, Oct 1977)

Five built by Cheverton Workboats of Cowes (UK) for Customs work but transferred to general naval patrol duties.

PRADEEPA class *coastal patrol craft*

Displacement:	40t standard; 44t full load
Dimensions:	66ft × 10ft × 7ft
	20m × 5.5m × 2.1m
Machinery:	2 shafts, 2 GM 8V 71 TI diesels, 800bhp = 19kts. Range 1200nm at 14kts
Armament:	2–20mm (2×1)
Complement:	10

Class (no, in service):
Pradeepa (P 431, 1980), P 432 (1980), P 433 (30.9.80), P 434 (9.10.80), P 435 (11.2.81), P 436 (11.4.81)

First pair ordered June 1976 from Colombo D Yd, second in Nov. Very slow building programme. Five more 22kt, 1240bhp, beamier units ordered in 1979.

Ex-British ALGERINE class *minesweepers*

Class (former name, acquired, fate):
Parakrama (ex-*Pickle*, July 1958, BU 1964), *Vijaya* (ex-*Flying Fish*, ex-*Tillsonburg*, Sept 1949, returned to RN 1964)

Parakrama was sold for scrapping in Hong Kong but *Vijaya* was returned to RN for scrapping.

MISCELLANEOUS

Two unarmed *Hansaya* class coastal patrol craft (36t, 66ft, 16kts) built by Korody Marine Corporation of Venice in 1956 are still extant 1982.

Two large patrol craft (330t, 130ft 6in × 23ft × 7ft, *39.8m × 7m × 2.1m*, 2 MAN diesels, 2100bhp = 15kts. Range 3200nm at 13kts, 2–20mm, 37 crew) ordered from Colombo D Yd 31.12.81.

Taiwan

After the failure to stop the Communist forces crossing the Yangtze in April 1949, the Kuomintang commanders met on 16 July and decided to evacuate their remaining troops and ships 90 miles from the mainland to Taiwan and the other offshore islands. This was completed by 8 December to the tune of 2 million people, and, although Hainan Island fell to Lin Piao's Communists in 1950, Quemoy and Matsu remained under Kuomintang (Nationalist) control with the help of the US Seventh Fleet. Since then Taiwan, from her capital Taipei, has never ceased to claim to be the lawful ruler of all China (similarly the mainland claims sovereignty over Taiwan). With American help, Taiwan retained China's seat in the United Nations and it was not until the American *rapprochement* with Peking that Taiwan was expelled from the UN and the People's Republic took her place on 26 October 1971.

Although about half the Chinese Navy either defected to the Communists or was captured by them, Taiwan retained all the larger ex-USN warships, and these formed the basis of her fleet for the early 1950s. Unlike the Communists, who rearmed all their ex-Japanese vessels, Taiwan only rearmed those in the best condition, and the others were left to rot until they were finally scrapped. A few ex-British and Canadian vessels that had been demilitarised and sold to Chinese owners were also rearmed at this time.

After the end of the Korean War the Americans began building up the armed forces of their client states in the Far East, and Taiwan received several ex-World War II US destroyers, destroyer escorts and smaller craft. Her amphibious forces were also built up at this time, so that they would be able to invade the mainland if a suitable opportunity offered. There were a number of small clashes with the Communist Navy in which the Nationalists usually came off badly, but the US Seventh Fleet provided protection against a major offensive. This was demonstrated in 1958, when the Communists made a second major attempt to take over the offshore islands of Quemoy (which dominates the mainland port of Amoy) and Matsu. The US involvement in the Vietnam War, and the logistic support offered by Taiwan, led to an increase in the numbers of warships transferred from the USN.

In the aftermath of the Vietnam War US foreign policy swung from supporting Taiwan to developing relations with Peking, and this was reflected in Taiwan losing her seat in the UN. However, to counterbalance this, military support increased and the island state received large numbers of ex-World War II US warships, from destroyers downwards. Chiang Kai-Shek died in April 1975 and his son took over the presidency. Up to this point Taiwan had relied almost completely on US arms supplies, but attempts were now made to obtain arms elsewhere. This proved difficult because most countries were unwilling to offend Peking by supplying arms to Taiwan, but the Navy has been able to build under licence the highly effective Gabriel anti-ship missile from Israel, and in 1980 ordered two new *Walrus* class submarines from the Netherlands. These submarines are not likely to be delivered till after 1985 but will be the first modern major warships possessed by Taiwan. Virtually all of her ships, including all the destroyers and frigates, date from World War II, and although they have mostly been modernised or rebuilt in Taiwan, they will all need replacing in the not too distant future. In addition, some of the ships transferred were in very bad condition, and this has made the Navy's re-equipment problem worse. Not only does Taipei find it difficult to obtain new warships abroad, but also Taiwan's own shipbuilding industry, though launching large numbers of merchant ships (numbers and tonnage quadrupled since 1964), is completely inexperienced in designing and building major warships. So far, the only ones actually built in Taiwan have been two US-designed missile fast attack craft. In any case, the Taiwanese economy, though relatively buoyant, cannot afford to buy all the ships that would be necessary to re-equip the Navy even though nearly half government spending is devoted to defence.

The Navy's role has been conditioned by the strengths and weaknesses of the Communist Navy. Because the mainland has large numbers of submarines but relatively few large surface vessels, Taiwan concentrated on anti-submarine warfare, though the growth of the Communist surface fleet in recent years has caused the Nationalists to equip their ships with effective missiles and to acquire their own submarines. A relatively large amphibious force (two landing ship squadrons) has been maintained, both to resupply the offshore islands (over 100 miles from Taiwan) and to be able to invade the mainland if opportunity offered. Taiwan has the world's second largest marine corps, 39,000 men organised in three divisions, bigger than the 38,000-strong Navy itself. All are two-year conscripts. The Fleet is divided into amphibious forces, two destroyer squadrons, and squadrons for mine warfare, patrol, fast attack craft, logistic support and transport. Tsoying in the south is its main base and HQ. Kaohsiung also has a shipyard, while Makung in the Pescadores covers Quemoy. Keelung is the northern harbour serving Matsu. Taipei received its rudest shock in 1978 when the US Carter Administration withdraw diplomatic recognition and abrogated the 1955 Mutual Defence Treaty. After the American technological aid agreement with Peking was also signed in 1978, and the US Government in the same year decided to make Taiwan buy military equipment rather than having most of it transferred more or less free (2.64 billion dollars since 1950), the Navy's outlook became bleak. The Reagan Administration has since gone back somewhat on the decision to concentrate on the People's Republic rather than Taiwan, and some military aid has been forthcoming, but the Navy can no longer rely on the US Fleet as it could before. Taiwan currently has a highly effective naval force which has only to counter one of China's three fleets, the E Sea Fleet, albeit the largest, as long as Vietnam and the Soviet Union pre-occupy the other two, but it is unlikely its present strength will be maintained until the end of the 1980s.

MAJOR SURFACE SHIPS

Ex-Japanese KAGERO class *destroyer*

Armament:	(1952) 6–127mm/50 (3×2), 8–25mm (4×2)
	(1959) 3–127mm/38 (3×1), 2–76mm (2×1), 17–40mm
Sensors:	Radar, Sonar
Complement:	290
Other particulars:	As Japanese *Kagero* class

Name	Builder	Acquired	Fate
TAN YANG (ex-*Yukikaze*)	Sasebo DY	1947	BU 1971

After being disarmed from 1945–51, *Tan Yang* was given an extensive refit between 1951–52, being rearmed with three twin 127mm mounts (one forward and two aft), her main gun armament when she was the IJN *Yukikaze*. Her machinery was refurbished, but the maximum speed that she achieved on trials in Feb 1953 was 27.5kts. She was refitted with US weapons and sensors in 1959. At the same time the forecastle was extended slightly aft. For many years she was Taiwan's largest operational warship. She ran aground during a typhoon in May 1970, and because of her age and the damage it was decided to scrap her.

Ex-US BENSON/GLEAVES class *destroyers*

Armament:	4–127mm/38 (4×1) (*Hsien Yang* 3–127mm/38 (3×1)), 4–40mm, 4–6–20mm, 5–533mm TT (1×5) (*Nan Yang* only)
Sensors:	Radar SC, SG, Mk 4; sonar
Complement:	250
Other particulars:	As US *Benson/Gleaves* class

Name	Builder	Acquired	Fate
LO YANG (ex-*Benson*)	Bethlehem, Quincy	26.2.54	Deleted 1975
HAN YANG (ex-*Hilary P Jones*)	Charleston NY	26.2.54	Deleted 1975
NAN YANG (ex-*Plunkett*)	Federal, Kearny	16.2.59	Deleted 1975
HSIEN YANG (ex-*Rodman*)	Federal, Kearny	28.7.55	Expended 1976

Lo Yang and *Han Yang* were presented to Taiwan. *Hsien Yang* and *Nan Yang* were transferred on loan from the USN. In addition the ex-Japanese destroyers *Hatakaze* and *Asakaze* were transferred to Taiwan in Aug 1970 to provide spares for the first four. Neither saw service, being immediately cannibalised. *Hsien Yang* and ex-*Hatakaze* were both rebuilt as destroyer minesweepers in 1944, losing a 127mm gun and the TT to provide space for the minesweeping gear. They were reclassified as destroyers in 1954. The others were all standard units of their class. *Nan Yang* was the only one to retain TT, otherwise they were unmodernised. They were replaced by larger modernised ex-US destroyers. *Hsien Yang* was sunk for a film.

Ex-US FLETCHER class *destroyers*

Armament:	5–127mm/38 (5×1), 6–40mm (3×2), 6–20mm (3×2), 5–533mm TT (1×5), 2 Hedgehog Mk 2. See notes
Sensors:	Radar SPS-6, SPS-10, Mk 25, Mk 37. See notes. Sonar SQS-4 or SQS-29; ECM BLR-1, 4 chaff RL
Complement:	250–275

No	Name	Builder	Acquired	Fate
997	AN YANG (ex-*Kimberly*)	Bethlehem, Staten Island	2.6.67	Extant 1982
947	CHIANG YANG (ex-*Mullany*)	Bethlehem, San Francisco	6.10.71	Extant 1982
934	KUN YANG (ex-*Yarnell*)	Bethlehem, San Francisco	10.6.68	Extant 1982
956	KWEI YANG (ex-*Twining*)	Bethlehem, San Francisco	16.8.71	Extant 1982

An Yang and *Kun Yang* were transferred on loan. Both were purchased in Jan 1974. *Chiang Yang* and *Kwei Yang* were bought direct. The ex-USS *Sproston* was transferred in 1968 to provide spare parts for the other ships and was immediately cannibalised. Their armament varies. Armament details in data apply to *Kun Yang* as transferred. Her twin 40mm mounting between Q and X 127mm guns has since been replaced by a twin Sea Chaparral close-in SAM launcher (16 missiles). *An Yang* and *Kwei Yang* have been modified similarly, but they also have had their 533mm TT replaced by two Mk 32 triple 324mm ASW TT. *Chiang Yang* was transferred with a modified armament and sensors. She has 4–127mm/38 (4×1) in A, B, X and Y positions, 6–76mm (3×2) in Q position and between the funnels, 2 Hedgehog and two Mk 32 triple 324mm ASW TT. She is fitted with SPS-10, SPS-12, Mk 25, Mk 37, Mk 56 and Mk 63 radars.

Ex-US ALLEN M SUMNER class *destroyers*

Armament:	6–127mm×38 (3×2), 6–76mm (2×2, 2×1), 2 Hedgehog Mk 2, 6–324mm Mk 32 ASW TT (2×3), DC in some ships. See notes
Sensors:	Radar SPS-10, SPS-6C, Mk 25. See notes. Sonar SQS-29. See notes; ECM WLR-1, 4 chaff RL
Complement:	c275

No	Name	Builder	Acquired	Fate
976	HENG YANG (ex-*Samuel N Moore*)	Bethlehem Staten Island	Feb 1970	Extant 1982
986	HSIANG YANG (ex-*Brush*)	Bethlehem, Staten Island	9.12.69	Extant 1982
988	HUA YANG (ex-*Bristol*)	Bethlehem, San Pedro	9.12.69	Extant 1982
972	HUEI YANG (ex-*English*)	Federal, Kearny	11.8.70	Extant 1982
949	LO YANG (ex-*Taussig*)	Bethlehem, Staten Island	6.5.74	Extant 1982
954	NAN YANG (ex-*John W Thomason*)	Bethlehem, San Francisco	6.5.74	Extant 1982
928	PO YANG (ex-*Maddox*)	Bath Iron Wks	6.7.72	Extant 1982
944	YUEN YANG (ex-*Haynsworth*)	Federal, Kearny	12.5.70	Extant 1982

These ex-USN units had been modified in the 1950s with 76mm guns, ASW TT and improved sensors. They now have a variety of armaments. *Huei Yang* and *Po Yang* have landed the two single 76mm, they have a quadruple 12.7mm MG mounting and Mk 37 fire control radar. *Po Yang* has SPS-40 radar. *Heng Yang* has landed all her 76mm. These have been replaced by two twin and one quadruple 40mm mounting and one quadruple 12.7mm MG mounting. *Hsiang Yang*, *Hua Yang* and *Yuen Yang* also landed all their 76mm and had them replaced by 40mm guns, but they are now fitted with two twin 40mm mountings and one quadruple 12.7mm MG mounting. They also have one triple and one twin Gabriel SSM mounting (this missile is known as the *Hsiung Feng* in Taiwanese service) with a Selenia Orion RTN-10X radar on an additional mast. All retain their 127mm guns and ASW armament. *Lo Yang* and *Nan Yang* were converted to FRAM II configuration in Sept 1962 and Jan 1961 respectively, giving improved ASW performance. Since their transfer with armament as in data excluding 76mm they have been fitted with a quadruple 12.7mm MG mounting and a Hughes 500 ASW helicopter, which is small enough to use the existing DASH ASW drone helicopter landing pad and hangar. They have SPS-10, SPS-29, Mk 25 and Mk 37 radar, an SQS-29 hull mounted sonar and SQS-10 VDS. This gives them a reasonable, though by no means excellent ASW capability.

Ex-US GEARING class *destroyers*

Armament:	4–127mm/38 (2×2), 1-ASROC ASW system (1×8), 6–324mm Mk 32 ASW TT (2×3). See notes
Sensors:	Radar SPS-10, SPS-37, Mk 37; sonar SQS-23; ECM WLR-1 or WLR-3, ULQ-6 in some, 4 chaff RL. See notes
Complement:	c275

No	Name	Builder	Acquired	Fate
	CHAO YANG (ex-*Rowan*)	Todd, Seattle	10.6.77	Cannibalised 1977
921	CHIEN YANG (ex-*James E Kyes*)	Todd, Seattle	18.4.73	Extant 1982
966	DAN YANG (ex-*Lloyd Thomas*)	Bethlehem, San Francisco	12.10.72	Extant 1982
963	FU YANG (ex-*Ernest G Small*)	Bath I W	19.2.71	Extant 1982
978	HAN YANG (ex-*Herbert J Thomas*)	Bath I W	19.2.71	Extant 1982
915	KAI YANG (ex-*Richard B Anderson*)	Todd, Seattle	10.6.77	Extant 1982
981	LAI YANG (ex-*Leonard F Mason*)	Bethlehem,	10.3.78	Extant 1982

No	Name	Builder	Acquired	Fate
	LAO YANG (ex-*Shelton*)	Todd, Seattle	18.4.73	Extant 1982
938	LIAO YANG (ex-*Hanson*)	Bath I W	18.4.73	Extant 1982
932	SHEN YANG (ex-*Power*)	Bath I W	1.10.77	Extant 1982
925	TE YANG (ex-*Sarsfield*)	Bath I W	1.10.77	Extant 1982
912	CHAO YANG (ex-*Hamner*)	Federal, Kearny	Dec 1980	Extant 1982

Fu Yang (ex-DD 7, earlier Taiwan pennant number) had been converted into a radar picket destroyer in 1952 and had been given a FRAM II conversion in Aug 1961. Her SPS-30 radar was removed before transfer. In Feb 1971 she was armed with 6–127mm/38 (3×2), 2 Hedgehog and 6–324mm ASW TT (Mk 32, 2×3). Since then she has also received 8–40mm (4×2) and 4–12.7mm (1×4). Her sensors are as in data with the addition of SQA-10 VDS. The other Taiwan *Gearings* are all in FRAM I configuration. When they were transferred, most were armed as in data. They all now operate a Hughes 500 ASW helicopter, which is small enough to use the DASH landing pad and hangar, and have Hsiung Feng (Gabriel) SSM (1×3). *Dang Yang* (ex-DD 11) was completed as a specialist ASW destroyer, and was given the FRAM I conversion in Nov 1961. She has a Mk 15 trainable Hedgehog instead of ASROC and as well as the SSM and helicopter has received 4–40mm (2×2) and 4–12.7mm (1×4). *Chien Yang* (ex-DD 12) has SPS-40 rather than SPS-29. *Han Yang* had been converted for use as an NBCW trials ship in 1963–64 and retains the additional superstructure. When transferred she had no ASROC, and received 4–40mm (2×2) and 4–12.7mm (1×4) in its place. *Kai Yang* also had no ASROC when she was sold to Taiwan. *Chao Yang* was sold to Taiwan on the same date but ran aground on 22.8.77 whilst on tow to Taiwan. She was so badly damaged that she was stripped to provide spares for the other *Gearings*. *Te Yang*, like *Chien Yang*, has SPS-40 radar in place of SPS-29. Those ships without 40mm will be fitted with them, and these may replace ASROC, *Kai Yang* and *Lao Yang* (ex-DD 20) differ from the other FRAM I conversions in having both 127mm gun mountings forward, instead of one forward and one aft. Some of these ships were in very bad condition when they were transferred. *Chien Yang*, *Lao Yang* and *Liao Yang* (ex-DD 21) were all offered to Spain in 1973 before they went to Taiwan, but the Spanish Navy refused them because of their bad condition. The ex-USS *Warrington*, also a FRAM I conversion, was transferred for cannibalisation in 1972 and like *Chao Yang* was stripped to provide parts for her sisters. The ex-USS *Johnston* was bought on 27.2.81 possibly for the same purpose.

Ex-British 'CASTLE' class *frigates*

Name	Builder	Acquired	Fate
TE AN (ex-*Shih Lin*, ex-*Hsi Ling*, ex-*Ta Tung*, ex-*Orangeville*, ex-*Hedimgham Castle*)	Robb	1.6.51	Deleted *c*1970
KAO AN (ex-*Chiu Chin*, ex-*Ta Ting*, ex-*Tillsonburg*, ex-*Pembroke Castle*)	Ferguson	1.6.51	Deleted 1963

RN corvettes built in 1944 that had served in the RCN and were sold as merchant ships to China in 1947. Two were rearmed with 1–120mm, 1–76mm, 4–40mm (2×2), 4–20mm (2×2) by Taiwan on 1.6.51 at much the same time that Communist China also rearmed two.

Ex-US BUCKLEY and RUDDEROW (TE and TEV type) class *destroyer escorts (frigates)*

Armament:	1–127mm/38, 6–40mm (3×2), 4–LCVP. See notes (*Tai Yuan* 2–127mm/38 (2×1), 4–40mm (2×2), 4–20mm (4×1), 1 Hedgehog Mk 2, 6–324mm Mk 32 ASW TT (2×3), 2 Mk 9 DC racks
Sensors:	Radar SPS-5 (*Tai Yuan* SPS-5, SPS-6, Mk 26); sonar
Complement:	200 + 160 troops (except *Tai Yuan*)

No	Name	Builder	Acquired	Fate
845	CHUNG SHAN (ex-*Blessman*)	Bethlehem, Hingham	Aug 1967	Extant 1982
838	FU SHAN (ex-*Truxtun*)	Charleston NY	March 1966	Extant 1982
322	HENG SHAN (ex-*Raymond W Herndon*)	Bethlehem, Quincy	11.7.66	Discarded 1976
854	HUA SHAN (ex-*Donald W Wolf*)	Defoe, Bay City	May 1965	Extant 1982

No	Name	Builder	Acquired	Fate
323	KANG SHAN (ex-*George W Ingram*)	Bethlehem, Ingram	19.5.67	Discarded 1978
821	LU SHAN (ex-*Bull*)	Defoe, Bay City	Aug 1966	Extant 1982
325	LUNG SHAN (ex-*Schmitt*)	Bethlehem, Quincy		Discarded 1976
893	SHOU SHAN (ex-*Kline*)	Bethlehem, Quincy	March 1966	Extant 1982
878	TAI SHAN (ex-*Register*)	Charleston NY	Oct 1966	Extant 1982
959	TAI YUAN (ex-*Riley*)	Bethlehem, Hingham	10.7.69	Extant 1982
615	TIEN SHAN (ex-*Kleinsmith*)	Defoe, Bay City	June 1967	Extant 1982
834	WEN SHAN (ex-*Gantner*)	Bethlehem, Hingham	May 1966	Extant 1982
826	YU SHAN (ex-*Kinzer*)	Charleston NY	April 1962	Extant 1982

Chung Shan (ex-PF 43), *Kang Shan* (ex-PF 43), *Lu Shan* (ex-PF 36) and *Wen Shan* (ex-PF 34) are ex-USN 'TE' class DEs. They have higher bridges than the others which are ex-USN 'TEV' class DEs. Apart from that, they are almost identical. All except *Tai Yuan* (ex-PF 27) were converted into high speed transports (APD) either before or just after completion. *Tai Yuan* was never converted, and differs from the others by having a tripod mast, no davits for LCVP or troop quarters, and more sophisticated sensors. She was finally bought in March 1974. Since then she has been fitted for minelaying.

Wen Shan collided with ex-*Walter B Cobb* whilst under tow to Taiwan on 17.4.66, and the latter foundered four days later. She was replaced by *Lu Shan*. *Tien Shan* (meaning 'Heavenly Mountain') was not bought by Taiwan until 1974. Whereas the other APDs were fitted with a second 127mm/38 gun aft instead of from 1970, *Tien Shan* was not given it until she was actually bought. *Hua Shan* (ex-PF 33) now has 8–40mm (4×2) and 8–20mm (4×2). Some of the others may have been fitted similarly. A few have Decca 707 radar, but they are very sparsely equipped with sensors, having only optical directors for their guns. Because of the extra topweight caused by the second 127mm/38 gun, they only carry 2-LCVP. Taiwan rates them as frigates rather than high speed transports and uses them accordingly. Pennant numbers changed in 1976. *Yu Shan* was PF 32, *Tai Shan* PF 38 and *Shou Shan* PF 37.

SUBMARINES

Ex-US 'GUPPY II' type *attack submarines*

No	Name	Builder	Acquired	Fate
736	HAI SHIH (ex-*Cutlass*)	Portsmouth NY	12.4.73	Extant 1982
794	HAI PAO (ex-*Tusk*)	Cramp, Philadelphia	18.10.73	Extant 1982

Formerly USN *Tench* class submarines, launched 1944–45. Both converted to GUPPY II configuration in 1948 with increased battery capacity, a streamlined fin and bow and improved sonar. The US intended that they should only be capable of being used for ASW training, so the TT were sealed up before they were transferred. However, Taiwan has no other submarines, so both have since been made operational with modern Italian torpedoes (sold in 1976), but must be considered obsolescent. They are to be replaced by two Dutch-built submarines.

Dutch WALRUS type *attack submarines*

Two 2365t submarines were ordered from the Netherlands in September 1981 despite mainland China's protests. These will be the first new major warships built for Taiwan since 1949. See Part I under Netherlands for details.

Italian SX 404 class *midget submarines*

Three were used to land agents on the Chinese mainland. All discarded 1974–75. See Pakistan for data.

AMPHIBIOUS WARFARE VESSELS

Ex-US *dock landing ships*

No	Name	Builder	Acquired	Fate
639	CHUNG CHENG (ex-*White March*)	Moore, Oakland	17.11.60	Extant 1982
618	CHEN HAI (ex-*Fort Marion*)	Gulf SB	15.4.77	Extant 1982

Chung Cheng (ex-191) formerly *Tung Hai*, finally bought in May 1976. *Chen Hai* stricken from USN Oct 1974 having received FRAM II modernisation Dec 1959–April 1960. Has a helicopter platform over docking well and SPS-5 radar.

Ex-US LST class *tank landing ships*

Class (former name/no, new nos, transfer):
Chung Hai (ex-*LST 755*, 697/201, April 1946), *Chung Ting* (ex-*LST 537*, 673/203, March 1946), *Chung Hsing* (ex-*LST 557*, 684/204, March 1946), *Chung Chien* (ex-*LST 716*, 679/205, June 1946), *Chung Chi* (ex-*LST 1017*, 626/206, Dec 1946), *Chung Shun* (ex-*LST 732*, 624/208, March 1946), *Chung Lien* (ex-*LST 1050*, 691/209, Jan 1947), *Chung Yung* (ex-*LST 574*, 657/210, March 1959), *Chung Kuang* (ex-*LST 503*, 646/216, June 1960), *Chung Suo* (ex-*Bradley County*/*LST 400*, 667/217, Sept 1958), *Chung Chih* (ex-*LST 279*, 218, June 1960), *Chung Chuan* (ex-*LST 1030*, 651/221, Feb 1948), *Chung Sheng* (ex-*LST 1033*, 686/222, Dec 1947), *Chung Fu* (ex-*Iron County*/LST 840, 619/223, July 1955), *Chung Cheng* (ex-*Lafayette County*/LST 859, 676/224, Aug 1958), *Chung Chiang* (ex-*San Bernadino County*/LST 1110, 635/225, Aug 1958), *Chung Chih* (ex-*Sagadahoh County*/LST 1091, 655/226, Oct 1958), *Chung Ming* (ex-*Sweetwater County*/LST 1152, Oct 1958), *Chung Shu* (ex-*LST 520*, 228, Sept 1958), *Chung Wan* (ex-*LST 535*, 654/229, Sept 1958), *Chung Pang* (ex-*LST 578*, 629/230, Sept 1958), *Chung Yeh* (ex-*Sublette County*/LST 1144, 699/231, Sept 1961)

Fifteen were transferred from the USN between 1957–61 to complement those surviving from before 1949. All were built between 1942–45. A number were scrapped in the 1950s and 1960s and one was sunk by Communist MTBs off Quemoy on 25.8.58. Four others were transferred from the mercantile service. One was used as a workshop by the CIA-run Air America in Taiwan during the early 1950s. The survivors were extensively rebuilt during the late 1960s and are now the equivalent of new ships. They have davits for 2–6 LCVP. Most are armed with up to ten 40mm and six 20mm, but others have been rearmed with 2–76mm (2×1) and 6–40mm (3×2). *Chung Chih* (218) was deleted in 1978. Twenty-one were in service in 1982, as well as an ex-repair ship *Tai Wu* (520, ex-*Sung Shan*, ex-French *Vulcain*, ex-USS *Agenor* ex-LST 490), which was transferred to Taiwan on 15.9.57, has been reconverted between 1973–74 into a troop transport, and *Kao Hsiung* (ex-*Chung Hai*, ex-USS *Dukes County*, ex-*LST 735*) which was transferred as an LST in May 1957, converted into an amphibious flagship with additional radar and radio equipment in 1964, and purchased in Nov 1974.

Ex-US LSM 1 class *landing ships*

Class (no, former name, transfer):
Mei Chin (241, ex-*LSM 155*), *Me Heng* (245, ex-*LSM 456*), *Mei Ho* (248, ex-*LSM 13*), *Mei Hung* (246, ex-*LSM 442*), *Mei I* (243, ex-*LSM 76*), *Mei Chien* (249, ex-*LSM 76*), *Mei Hwa* (250, ex-*LSM 256*), *Mei Chen* (251, *LSM 422*), *Mei Kun* (252, ex-*LSM 478*), *Mei Ping* (253, ex-*LSM 471*), *Mei Wen* (254, ex-*LSM 472*), *Mei Han* (255, ex-*LSM 474*), *Mei Lo* (637/256, ex-*LSM 362*, May 1962), *Mei Ping* (659/253, ex-*LSM 471*, Nov 1956), *Mei Sung* (694/247, ex-*LSM 457*, 1946), *Mei Tseng* (649/244, ex-*LSM 431*, 1946)

Mei Tseng also formerly numbered 341. Rebuilt in Taiwan late 1960s and have SO-8 radar. *Mei Lo* replacement for namesake (ex-*LSM 157*) damaged by Communist artillery and beached on Quemoy Island 8.9.58. Only last four extant 1982, rest deleted 1970–75.

Ex-US LSIL and LSSL type *landing craft*

Class (no, former name):
Mei Chien (249, ex-*LSM 76*), *Mei Hwa* (250, ex-*LSM 256*), *Lien Chu* (261, ex-*LSIL 233*), *Lien Li* (262, ex-*LSIL 417*), *Lien Sheng* (263, ex-*LSIL 418*), *Lien Chang* (466, ex-*LSIL 1017*)

First five transferred on 19.2.54 after being on loan to the French in Indo-China. Another five transferred to provide spare parts. All deleted in early 1970s. *Lien Chang* transferred in 1958 and serves as survey ship with 1–40mm and 4–20mm (4×1).

Ex-US LCT (6) class *tank landing craft*

Class (no, former name):
Ho Chang (485, ex-*LCU 512*), *Ho Chao* (406, *LCU 1429*), *Ho Cheng* (486, ex-*LCU 1145*), *Ho Chi* (401, ex-*LCU 1212*), *Ho Chie* (SB 1, ex-*LCU 700*), *Ho Chien* (496, ex-*LCU 1278*), *Ho Chun* (494, ex-*LCU 1225*), *Ho Chung* (484, ex-*LCU 849*), *Ho Deng* (404, ex-*LCU 1367*), *Ho Feng* (405, ex-*LCU 1397*), *Ho Hoei* (402, ex-*LCU 1218*), *Ho Shun* (494, ex-*LCU 1225*), *Ho Teng* (407, ex-*LCU 1452*), *Ho Tsung* (482, ex-*LCU 1213*), *Ho Yao* (403, ex-*LCU 1244*), *Ho Yung* (495, ex-*LCU 1271*)

Ex-USN units later reclassified as LCU 501 class. Three transferred in Jan–Feb 1958 and six more in Nov–Dec 1959 to add to the six left in Nationalist hands after 1949. Ex-LCUs *1212*, *1218*, *1367*, *1397* and *1452* transferred under MAP in 1964. All rearmed with 2–12.7mm in addition to existing 2–20mm, all still in service in 1982. Built between 1942–43, and finally bought on 3.4.78.

US LCU 1466 class *utility landing craft*

Displacement:	130t, light; 268t full load
Dimensions:	115ft 2in oa × 34ft × 4ft 2in
	35.1m × 10.7m × 1.2m
Machinery:	3-shafts, Gray Marine 64/65 YTL diesels; 675bhp = 10kts. Oil 11t. Range 1200nm at 6kts
Armament:	3–20mm (3×1) (some also have 2–12.7mm)
Complement:	15

Class (no, former name):
Ho Shan (488, ex-*LCU 1596*), *Ho Chuan* (489, ex-*LCU 1597*), *Ho Seng* 490, ex-*LCU 1598*), *Ho Meng* (491, ex-*LCU 1599*), *Ho Mou* (492, ex-*LCU 1600*), *Ho Shou* (493, ex-*LCU 1601*)

All six built by Ishikajima, Harima, Tokyo, Japan under US Offshore Procurement Program for transfer to Taiwan. In service March 1955 and all extant 1982. Can carry 167t of cargo. All originally numbered in 200 series eg *Hou Mou* (292)

MINOR LANDING CRAFT
About 250 US LCM (6) class built in Taiwan.
Eight ex-US LCM (3) class.
About 100–120 US LCVP class most attached to the LSTs.
Some 25–30 Taiwan Type 272 (5t full load, some 2 MG, 3 crew, built 1970s).

SMALL SURFACE COMBATANTS

Ex-US RAVEN and AUK class *fleet minesweepers (now corvettes)*

No	Name	Builder	Acquired	Fate
896	CHU YUNG (ex-*Waxwing*)	American SB, Cleveland	18.11.65	Extant 1982
867	PING JIN (ex-*Steady*)	American SB, Cleveland	March 1968	Extant 1982
884	WU SHENG (ex-*Redstart*)	Savannah Machine & Foundry, Georgia	22.7.65	Extant 1982
	CHEIN MEN (ex-*Toucan*)	American SB, Cleveland	22.12.64	Sunk 6.8.65

After transfer to Taiwan all sweeping gear removed and second 76mm gun mounted aft. *Chein Men* sunk by Communist warships S of Quemoy and replaced by *Ping Jin*. *Chu Yung* fitted for minelaying (80 mine capacity?) 1975. Fitted with SPS-5 radar and SQS-17 sonar. ASW Hedgehog and 2 Mk 9 DC racks supplemented by triple Mk 32 324mm TT.

FUH CHOW class *fast attack craft (torpedo)*

Displacement:	33t light; 40t full load
Dimensions:	69ft oa × 19ft 10in × ?
	22.6m × 6.5m × ?m
Machinery:	3 shafts, 3 petrol engines; ? hp = 40kts, 27kts cruising
Armament:	1–40mm, 2–20mm (2×1), 2–457mm TT (2×1)
Complement:	12

Class (no, transfer):
Fuh Chow (PT 1/PT 511, 1.6.57), *Hsueh Chih* (PT 2/PT 512, 6.11.57)

Both built by Mitsubishi SB Co, Japan. They are conventional torpedo-armed FAC with Italian Type 184 weapons.

Ex-US 'Vosper' type 70ft *fast attack craft (torpedo)*

Class (no, former name, transfer):
Fan Kong (PT 513, ex-*PTC 32*, 19.8.57), *Sao Tong* (PT 514, ex-*PTC 33*, 1.11.57)

Both PT boats built by Annapolis Yacht Yd, Annapolis 1943. Wooden hulls, extant 1982. Armament 1–20mm, 4–12.7mm (2×2), 2 TT.

Ex-US 'Elco' type 80ft *fast attack craft (torpedo)*

Class (former name, transfer):
Fu Kuo (ex-*PTC 34*, 1.9.57), *Tian Kuo* (PT 516, 1.9.57)

Both Second World War PT boats built by Hutchins Yacht Co, Jacksonville, Florida.

LUNG CHIANG class *fast attack craft (missile)*

Displacement:	218t standard; 250t full load
Dimensions:	154ft pp, 164ft 6in oa × 23ft 9in × 7ft 5in
	46.9m, 50.1m × 7.2m × 2.2m
Machinery:	3 shafts CODOG: (3 CP propellers), 3 AVCO-Lycoming TF-40A gas turbines, 15,000shp = 40kts plus 3 GM 12V149 TI diesels, 3600bhp = 20kts. Range 700nm at 40kts (gas), 2700nm at 12kts (diesel), 1900nm at 20kts (3 diesels)
Armament:	4 Hsiung Feng SSM (4×1), 1–76mm OTO Melara Compact, 2–30mm Emerlec (1×2), 2–12.7mm (2×1)
Sensors:	Radar Selenia RAN 11 LX, IPN 10
Complement:	35

Class (no, in service):
Lung Chiang (PGG 581, 15.5.78), *Sui Chiang* (PGG 582, 1979)

The first of this class was built to Tacoma's design at their yard in Washington State, USA. The PSMM-5 design is developed from the US *Asheville* class FAC and is the same as the Korean *Paek Ku* class. There were 13 more planned from Taiwanese yards but they have been cancelled because of the unavailability of US or Italian missiles. The two ships built have been armed with the shorter-ranged Israeli Gabriel SSM, which Taiwan calls the Hsiung Feng. Two more laid down at Tsoying SY, Taiwan, in 1981.

Israeli DVORA type *fast attack craft (missile)*

This small Israeli aluminium design is being copied by Taiwan's Sun Yatsen Scientific Research Institute in large numbers. The first unit *Tzu Chiang*, was completed at Tsoying SY, Kaohsung, in 1980. Reached 45kts on trials. An initial order for 12 was increased to 26. Either 19 or 26 (+4 building) were extant in 1982.

Ex-US PC (173ft) class *submarine chasers (large patrol craft)*

Class (former name):
Pei Kiang† (ex-*Hanford*, PC 1142), *Po Kiang** (ex-*PC 1254*), *To Kiang* (ex-*Milledgeville*, PC 1263), *Tung Kiang*† (ex-*Placerville*, PC 1087), *Yuan Kiang** (ex-*PC 1182*), *Chang Kiang** (ex-*PC 1232*), *Chih Kiang** (ex-*PC 1078*), *Ching Kiang** (ex-*PC 1168*), *Chu Kiang** (ex-*PGM 31*, ex-*PC 1567*), *Chung Kiang** (ex-*PC 1262*), *Han Kiang*† (ex-*Vandalia*, PC 1175), *Hsi Kiang*† (ex-*Susanville*, PC 1149), *Hsiang Kiang** (ex-*PC 786*), *Li Kiang** (ex-*PC 1208*), *Lin Kiang*† (ex-*Escondido*, PC 1169)

These 15 ex-USN units (launched 1942–44), named after rivers, were added to those left in Nationalist service from before 1949. * = 1954 transfers (9). † = 15.7.57 transfers (5). *To Kiang* was transferred in July 1959. *Chang Kiang* was sunk by Communist warships south of Quemoy on 6.8.65. Most other units were discarded in the early 1970s, except *Yuan Kiang* (deleted 1966), but *Hsi Kiang*, *Pei Kiang* and *Tung Kiang* were transferred to the Customs *c*1973. They were sold in 1976.

COASTAL PATROL CRAFT
Two ex-US 'AVR' type (32.3t full load, 63ft, 22kts, 4 MG, 8 crew, transferred 1.6.69), *Chie Kuo* (PTC 35) and PTC 36.

Fifteen Type 42 (10.5t standard, 40kts, 1–40mm) *PB 60–74* built in Taiwan late 1960s and early 1970s.
PTC 38 (30t, 21kts, 1–40mm, 1–20mm) unsuccessful design built at Chien Hwa SY 1962.

Ten or more 15m new patrol craft (12t, 25kts, 1–40mm, 2 diesels and water jet) built at China SB Kahosung (Taiwan) since 1971.

MINE WARFARE VESSELS

US ADJUTANT class *coastal minesweepers*

Class (former names, nos, in service):
Yung An* (ex-*MSC 123*, 449, 4.6.55)
Yung Chen (ex-*Maaseick*, ex-MSC 78, 441, July 1953)
Yung Chi (ex-*Charleroi*, ex-MSC 152, 497/166, Feb 1954)
Yung Ching (ex-*Eakloo*, ex-MSC 101, May 1953)
Yung Chou (ex-*MSC 278*, 423/158, 10.6.59)
Yung Fu* (ex-*Diest*, ex-*Macaw* MSC 77, May 1953)
Yung Hsin† (ex-*MSC 302*, 488, 5.3.65)
Yung Ju† (ex-*MSC 300*, 457, 15.4.65)
Yung Jen (ex-*St Nicholas*, ex-MSC 64, 485, Feb 1954)
Yung Lo† (ex-*MSC 306*, 469/161, 18.3.66)
Yung Nien* (ex-*MSC 277*, 479, 10.6.59)
Yung Ping* (ex-*MSC 140*, 4.6.55)
Yung Shan (ex-*Lier*, ex-*MSC 63*, 476, July 1953)
Yung Sui (ex-*Diksmunde*, ex-MSC 65, Feb 1954)

US-built wooden minesweepers for transfer to friendly navies. * = MSC 268 with less powerful machinery. † = MSC 289 with lower bridges and taller funnels. The other 6 were built for Belgium during 1953–56 as part of the *Adjutant* class. They were transferred to Taiwan in Nov 1969 and can be

distinguished from their sisters by the pole mast aft. Original armament of 1–40mm was replaced by 2–20mm (2×1) on transfer. Decca 45 or 707 radar is carried and UQS-1D sonar. A further unit, *De Panne*, was transferred for cannibalisation and has been stripped for parts.

Ex-US *minesweeping boat*

MSB 12 (ex-*MSB 4*) transferred in Dec 1961 and extant 1982.

Ex-US *minesweeping launches*

MSML 1–12 transferred in March 1961 (built 1943–45) and extant 1982.

Thailand

The Kingdom of Thailand, an ancient and uncolonised country the size of Spain lying between Burma to the West, Cambodia (Kampuchea) and Laos to the East has many difficult internal and external defence problems to resolve with limited means. She has nearly 700 miles of navigable waterways, increased by half in the monsoon. Up to 1949 Thailand was known in the English-speaking world as Siam. The existence of an anti-Japanese underground movement won Thailand moderate treatment at the end of the war, though she was forced to return the territories acquired in 1941 and 1943 to French and British control. The Royal Thai Navy was left unmolested and the ships served the new Thai state for many years. One coast defence ship *Sri Ayuthia* was lost during the 1951 rebellion. Manpower rose from 10,000 to 18,000 in the 1950s.

Thailand was one of the original signatories of the 1954 SEATO Manila Pact agreement, having already lost a frigate in the Korean War, later provided troops, air bases and equipment to assist American forces in Vietnam. Currently Thailand, one of the instigators of the ASEAN agreement, has formed close ties with both Malaya and the Philippines. A Burmese gunboat sank a Thai fishing vessel in an October 1977 dispute. The Thai Navy is presently modernising both its fighting and patrol components. Apart from the three ex-US frigates of World War II vintage (obsolete and possibly non-operational), the only modern frigates are two American-built *Tapi* class vessels completed in 1971 and 1974 and the British-built *Makut Rajakumarn* completed in 1973. These three frigates are quite modern and relatively well-armed vessels, but there is a need for more craft with an extended range, modern fire control and weapons. The construction of modified Spanish *Descubierta* class missile frigates has been discussed.

The Thai Navy received its first six modern missile-armed fast attack craft of the *Ratcharit* and *Prabparapak* classes in the late 1970s. Three more of the *Dhonburi* class are building in Italy. Thailand is also developing a capability to build smaller combatant craft; and it has recently built a new amphibious support craft and small auxiliaries.

In 1982 the Navy's manpower totalled 30,000 (2 year conscripts) including a marine brigade of 10,000 and a naval air arm of 9 S-2F Grumman ASW aircraft, 2 HU-16B seaplanes, and 59 light aircraft/helicopters. Their bases are at Bangkok, Sattahip, Songkhia (formerly Singora on the Malayan Peninsula), Paknam, and a new one at Phang-Nga on the W Coast (Indian Ocean). The Fleet mustered 67 surface combatants, 52 amphibious units, and 45 river craft. In addition there are 1700 Marine Police with at least 15 armed patrol craft of all sizes in a coast guard role.

FLEET STRENGTH 1947

DESTROYER

Name	Launched	Disp (std)	Fate
PHRA RUANG (ex-*Radiant*)	1916	1035t	Discarded 1959

FRIGATE

Name	Launched	Disp (std)	Fate
MEKLONG	1936	1400t	TS 1976

Meklong 6.3.82

RAN, courtesy Ross Gillett

COAST DEFENCE SHIPS

Name	Launched	Disp (std)	Fate
SRI AYUTHIA	1937	2265t	Sunk 3.7.51
RATANAKOSINDRA	1925	886t	Discarded 1968
SUKHOTHAI	1929	886t	Discarded c1972

TORPEDO-BOATS

Name	Launched	Disp (std)	Fate
CHANDRABURI	1937	318t	Discarded 1978
CHUNPHORN	1937	318t	Discarded c1976
PATANI	1936	318t	Discarded 1978
PUKET	1935	318t	Discarded c1976
RAYONG	1937	318t	Discarded 1978
SURASDRA	1936	318t	Discarded 1978
TRAD	1935	318t	Discarded c1976
KANTAN	1937	110t	Discarded 1976
KYLONGYAI	1937	110t	Discarded 1976
TAKBAI	1937	110t	Discarded c1973

SUBMARINES

Name	Launched	Disp (std)	Fate
BALAJUNBOL	1936	370/430t	Decommissioned 1955
MACHANU	1936	370/430t	Decommissioned 1955
SINSAMUDAR	1936	370/430t	Decommissioned 1955
VILUN	1936	370/430t	Decommissioned 1955

MINELAYERS

Name	Launched	Disp (std)	Fate
BANGRACHAN	1936	368t	Extant 1982
NHONGARHAI	1936	368t	Extant 1982

MINESWEEPER

Name	Launched	Disp (std)	Fate
CHOW PHRAYA (ex-*Havant*)	1918	840t	Stricken 24.8.71

COASTAL CRAFT

Name	Launched	Disp (std)	Fate
CMB 6–17	1935–37	16t	Discarded 1950s
SARASINDHU	1936	50t	Discarded 1960s
THIEW UTHOCK	1936	50t	Discarded 1960s
TRAVANE VARI	1936	50t	Discarded 1960s
SAMET (ex-*Pi Sua Nam*)	1906	150t	Discarded 1960s

MAJOR SURFACE SHIPS

Ex-British Modified 'FLOWER' class *frigates*

No	Name	Builder	Acquired	Fate
PF 4	BANGPAKONG (ex-*Gondwana*, ex-*Burnet*)	Ferguson	15.5.47	Extant 1982
	PRASAE (i) (ex-*Sind*, ex-*Betony*)	Hall	15.5.47	Sunk 13.1.51

Both 1943-built units. Served in Royal Indian Navy from 1945 before transfer to the Royal Thai Navy on 15.5.47. *Prasae* lost in Korean War on 13.1.51. On *Bangpakong* 76mm replaced the old 102mm gun and 40mm guns replaced 20mm. *Bangpakong* now TS.

Ex-US TACOMA class *patrol frigates*

No	Name	Builder	Acquired	Fate
1	TAHCHIN (ex-*Glendale*)	Consolidated Steel, San Pedro	29.10.51	Extant 1982
2	PRASAE (ii) (ex-*Gallup*)	Consolidated Steel, San Pedro	29.10.51	Extant 1982

Similar to the British-designed 'River' class frigates. Built in 1943–44. Refitted early 1970s. *Prasae* has never been fully repaired since she sustained collision damage in Jan 1972. Both extant 1982 as last survivors of their class.

Ex-US CANNON ('DET') class *destroyer escort*

No	Name	Builder	Acquired	Fate
3	PINKLAO (ex-*Hemminger*)	Western Pipe & Steel, San Pedro	Jul 1959	Extant 1982

Built in 1943–44 and transferred at New York Navy Yd July 1959, under MDAP and finally purchased on 6.6.75. The 3–533mm TT were removed and the 4–20mm were replaced by 4–40mm. The 6–324mm Mk 32 ASW TT (2×3) were fitted in 1966. Extant 1982.

Khirirat 20.2.80   *L & L van Ginderen*

Tapi 1975

TAPI class (US PF 103 class) *frigates*

Armament:	2–76mm/50 Mk 34 (2×1), 2–40mm/60 (1×2), 6–324mm Mk 32 ASW TT (2×3), 1 Hedgehog Mk 2, 1 DC rack Mk 9
Complement:	150

Other particulars: As Iranian *Bayandor* class

No	Name	Builder	Launched	Fate
5	TAPI (ex-*PF 107*)	American SB Co, Toledo	17.10.70	Extant 1982
6	KHIRIRAT (ex-*PF 108*)	Norfolk SB	2.6.73	Extant 1982

Sisters to the Iranian *Bayandor* class frigates. *Tapi* ordered on 27.6.69 (laid down 1.4.70) and *Khirirat* on 25.6.71 (laid down 18.2.72). Completed 1.11.71 and 10.8.74 respectively.

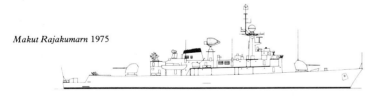

Makut Rajakumarn 1975

MAKUT RAJAKUMARN (Yarrow type) *frigate*

Displacement:	1650t standard; 1900t full load
Dimensions:	320ft oa, 305ft 1in pp × 36ft × 18ft 1in *97.6m, 93.0m × 10.97m × 5.5m*
Machinery:	2-shaft CODOG (CP propellers): 1 Rolls-Royce Olympus TM 3B gas turbine, 23,000shp = 26kts plus 1 Crossley-Pielstick 12 PC2V diesel 6000bhp = 18kts. Range 5000nm/1200nm at 18/26kts
Armament:	2–4.5in/55 Mk 8 (2×1), 2–40mm/60 Bofors (2×1), 4 Seacat SAM (1×4), 1 Limbo, 1 DC rack, 2 DCT
Sensors:	Radar HSA LW-04, HSA WM-22, Seacat control M 44, Decca 626; sonar type 170B, 162 and Plessey MS 27
Complement:	140

No	Name	Builder	Launched	Fate
7	MAKUT RAJAKUMARN	Yarrow	18.11.71	Extant 1982

A general purpose frigate was ordered from Yarrow on 21.8.69 similar to the earlier, shorter and move lightly armed Malaysian *Rahmat*. Laid down 11.1.71 and completed 7.5.73. The ship is highly automated and proved successful in service. Fitted as flagship.

AMPHIBIOUS WARFARE VESSELS

Ex-US LST type *tank landing ships*

Class (former name, transferred):
Angthong (ex-*LST 294*, 1950s), *Chang* (ex-*Lincoln County*, LST 898, Aug 1962), *Pangan* (ex-*Stark County*, LST 1134, May 1966), *Lanta* (ex-*Stone County*, LST 1141, 12.3.70), *Prathong* (ex-*Dodge County*, LST 722, 17.12.75)
    Five USN units built in 1943–45. Numbered LST 1–5 in Thai service. *Angthong* employed as TS since 1978. *Chang* has reinforced bow and hull for previous arctic service. All extant 1982.

Ex-US LSM 1 type *medium landing ships*

Class:
Kut (ex-*LSM 338*), *Phai* (ex-*LSM 333*), *Kram* (ex-*LSM 469*)
    Built in 1944–45. Transfers: *Kram* under MAP at Seattle, Washington 25.5.62, *Kut* and *Phai* in Oct 1946. Have SO-8 or SPS-5 radar. All 3 extant 1982.

Ex-US LCI type *infantry landing craft*

Class:
Prab (ex-*LCI 670*), *Satakut* (ex-*LCI 739*)
    Built in 1944 and transferred in 1950. SO-8 radar. *Prab* deleted in c1980, extant as hulk.

Ex-US LCT(6) type *tank landing craft*

Class:
Ardang (ex-*LCU 10*), *Kolum* (ex-*LCU 12*), *Mataphon* (ex-*LCU 8*), *Phetra* (ex-*LCU 11*), *Rawi* (ex-*LCU 9*), *Talibong* (ex-*LCU 13*)
    All built 1944. Transferred Oct 1946–Nov 1947. Employed as transport ferries on the Chao Phyra river, all 6 extant 1982.

Ex-US LSSL type *support landing craft*

Nakha (LSSL 3, ex-*LSSL 102*) acquired in Oct 1966 when Japan returned her as *Himawari* to USA and classed as support gunboat. Modified LCI with following armament: 1–76mm, 4–40mm, 2–20mm, 4–81mm mortars (4×1). Raytheon 1500B Pathfinder radar. Used mainly as small craft tender.

New Thai LCT type *tank landing craft*

Displacement:	200t standard; 375t full load
Dimensions:	134ft 6in × 28ft 11in × 6ft 2in *41.0m × 8.8m × 1.9m*
Machinery:	2-shaft GM16Y 71N diesels, 2000bhp = 10kts. Range 1200nm at 10kts
Armament:	2–20mm, 2–12.7mm MG
Complement:	32 plus 16 troops

A class of four new Thai designed landing craft building in Bangkok Dock, Laid down 1980 and 1981. *Thong, Kaeo* (7) completed 23.12.82.

MINOR LANDING CRAFT

There are also 26 ex-US LCM 6 type landing craft (*14–16, 61–68, 71–78, 81–82, 85–87*) of which 21 were delivered in Feb–April 1969 and 8 LCVP transferred in March 1963 and carried by the 4 LSTs. Also one Thai-built LCA with glass fibre hull and a bow ramp (10t, 39ft 5in × 9ft 9in, *12.0m × 3.0m*, 2 Chrysler diesels, 25kts, 35 troops).

SMALL SURFACE COMBATANTS

Lürssen 'TNC 45' type *fast attack craft (missile)*

Particulars:	As Singapore

Class (no, launched, in service):

Prabparapak (1, 29.7.75, 28.7.76), *Hanhak Sattru* (2, 28.10.75, 6.11.76), *Suphairin* (3, 20.2.76, 1.2.77)

Ordered in June 1973. Of basic Lürssen TNC 45 type but very similar to Singapore's *Sea Wolf* FAC (also built by Lürssen's Hong Leong, Singapore subsidiary). Fitted with HSA WM 28 fire control and one navigation radar. All 3 extant 1982.

Ratcharit as completed
NB 1/750 scale

RATCHARIT class *fast attack craft (missile)*

Displacement:	235t standard; 270t full load
Dimensions:	163ft 5in × 24ft 6in × 7ft 6in *49.8m × 7.5m × 1.7m*
Machinery:	3 shafts (CP propellers), 3 MTU MD 20V538 TB91 diesels, 13,500hp = 37kts. Range 2000nm at 15kts, 650nm at 36kts
Armament:	4 MM38 Exocet SSM (4×1), 1–76mm/62 OTO Melara, 1–40mm/70 Breda-Bofors
Sensors:	Radar WM-20, navigation
Complement:	45

Class (no, launched, in service):

Ratcharit (4, 30.7.78, 10.8.79), *Witthayakhom* (5, 2.9.78, 12.11.79), *Udomet* (6, 28.9.78, 21.2.80)

Ordered 23.7.76. Built by CN Breda of Venice. Belong to Breda's MV 250 type. Can make 20kts on one engine. All 3 extant 1982.

Dhonburi class design

DHONBURI class *fast attack craft (gun)*

Displacement:	400t standard; 450t full load
Dimensions:	198ft oa, 188ft 7in pp × 29ft × 15ft *60.4m, 57.5m × 8.8m × 2.0m*
Machinery:	3 shafts (CP propellers), 3 MTU 20V 538 TB91 diesels, 12,600hp = 29kts. Range 2500nm at 18kts, 900nm at 29kts
Armament:	2–76mm/62 OTO Melara (2×1), 2–40mm/70 Breda-Bofors (1×2), 4 Hycor Mk 135 chaff RL
Sensors:	Radar 3RM-series WM-22/61, Elsag-Selenia Dando; ECM passive intercept
Complement:	45

Class (no, launched):

Dhonburi (7, 7.6.82), *Songkhla* (8, 6.9.82)

First pair ordered from CN Breda of Venice in Nov 1979, third in 1981 for 1982–83 delivery. Italian MV 400 TH type FAC (gun) design. Will be able to have SSM.

PSMM Mk 5 type *fast attack craft (missile)*

Four ordered 9.9.81 from Ital-Thai S Yd, Bangkok to be built under licence and with help from Korea-Tacoma S Yd. First delivery 1983, last 1985.

Ex-US PC 461 (173ft) type *submarine-chasers (large patrol craft)*

Class:

Khamronsin (ex-*PC 609*), *Liulom* (7, ex-*PC 1253*), *Longlom* (8, ex-*PC 570*), *Phali* (4, ex-*PC 1185*), *Sarasin* 1, ex-*PC 495*), *Sukrip* (5, ex-*PC 1218*), *Thayanchon* (2, ex-*PC 575*), *Tongpliu* 6, ex-*PC 616*)

Eight transferred to Thai Navy March 1947 to December 1952. *Khamronsin* stricken 1956. SPS-25 radar in some. All except *Sarasin* have 2–324mm Mk 32 ASW TT (2×1). Larger crews (62–71) than original USN complement.

Makut Rajakumarn as completed

Yarrow

Ex-US SC (110ft) type *submarine-chasers (large patrol craft)*

Class:
SC 31 (ex-*SC 1632*), *SC 32* (ex-*SC 1633*), *SC 33* (ex-*SC 1634*)

Three built in 1945 and transferred in 1950s. Renamed *SC 7* and *SC 8* (ex-*SC 31, 32*). *SC 33* BU 1962 and *SC 7* (ex-*SC 31*) in 1973.

US 'CAPE' class *coast guard cutters (large patrol craft)*

Class:
T 81–84 (ex-*CG 13–16*)

New Coast Guard cutters transferred from USA to Thailand in 1954. Built in 1953. Cost 475,000 dollars each. Similar to USCG 95ft type. Built by US Coast Guard Yard, Curtis Bay. Renamed *CGC 3–6* and later *T 81–84*. All 4 extant 1982.

US PGM 71 type *large patrol craft*

Class (former no, launched, in service):
T 11 (ex-*PGM 71*, 22.5.65–1.2.66), *T 12* (ex-*PGM 79*, 18.12.65–1967), *T 13* (ex-*PGM 107*, 13.4.–28.8.67), *T 14* (ex-*PGM 116*, 13.6.–18.8.69), *T 15* (ex-*PGM 117*, 24.6–18.8.69), *T 16* (ex-*PGM 115*, 24.4.69–12.2.70), *T 17* (ex-*PGM 113*, 3.6.69–12.2.70), *T 18* (ex-*PGM 114*, 24.6.69–12.2.70), *T 19* (ex-*PGM 123*, 14.5–25.12.70), *T 20* (ex-*PGM 124*, 22.6–Oct 1970)

Ten US PGM type launched May 1965–June 1970 by Peterson, Wisc, USA and on completion transferred to the Thai Navy. All 10 extant 1982.

COASTAL PATROL CRAFT

Two ex-US YP type: *CGC 11, CGC 12*. Former US Coast Guard cutters of YP type (44.5t, 20.5kts, 1–20mm). Renamed *CGC 1* and *CGC 2*. *CGC 12* deleted in 1978 and *CGC 11* in 1973.

Seven Thai-built T 91 type built by Naval Dockyard, Bangkok in 1970–81 in two batches. Characteristics: 88t, 104ft 4in × 17ft 6in × 5ft 6in *31.8m × 6.4m × 1.9m*, MTU diesels, 25kts, 1–40mm, 4–20mm (4×1), 2 MG (21 men). *T 93* deleted in 1976.

Six MPB built in Bangkok in 1940s (16t, 12.5kts, 1–20mm): *MPB 1, 3* deleted in 1956 and the rest in 1961.

Five ex-US 36ft RPC type transferred in March 1967; (10.4t, 14kts, 2 twin MG). Used on Mekong river. *T 21–23* extant 1982.

Thirty-seven ex-US PBR Mk 2 type, 20 transferred 1966–67, 10 in 1972. All extant 1982 and used on Mekong.

Twelve ex-US 'Swift' class: *T 27–35, T 210–212*, transferred 1967–75.

Twelve Thai-built 64ft units (34t full load, 1–20mm, 1–81mm mortar, 2 MTU diesels, 1300bhp = 22kts, 8 men); built by Ital-Thai Development Co, Bangkok 1980–81. *T 213–224*, first 3 in service 29.8.80, last 5 on 16.9.81. Fishery protection role.

MINE WARFARE VESSELS

Ex-British ALGERINE class *ocean minesweeper*

Phosamton (ex-*Minstrel*) transferred in April 1947. The 20mm guns were increased from 3 to 6 and DCTs from 2 to 4 in 1966. Extant 1982 as TS.

Ex-US YMS type *motor coastal minesweepers*

Class:
Bangkeo (ex-*YMS 334*), *Ladya* (ex-*YMS 138*), *Tadindeng* (ex-*YMS 21*)

Transferred to Thai Navy in 1947–51. Wooden construction. All 3 deleted from list in 1964–65.

US BLUEBIRD class *coastal minesweepers*

Class (no, former no):
Bangkeo (6, ex-*MSC 303*), *Donchedi* (8, ex-*MSC 313*), *Ladya* (5, ex-*MSC 297*), *Tadindeng* (7, ex-*MSC 301*)

Built by Peterson Builders Inc and Tacoma Boatbuilding Co in 1962–66. Similar to *Bluebird* class. In service: *Ladya* 14.12.63, *Bangkeo* 9.7.65, *Tadindeng* 26.8.65, *Donchedi* 17.9.65. All 4 extant 1982.

THALANG *mine countermeasures support ship*

Displacement:	1000t full load
Dimensions:	185ft 6in × 33ft × 10ft
	55.7m × 10m × 3.1m
Machinery:	2 shafts, 2 MTU diesels, 1310bhp = 12kts
Armament:	1–40mm, 2–20mm (2×1), 2–12.7mm (2×1), mines
Sensors:	Radar Decca TM 1226
Complement:	77

No	Name	Builder	Launched	Fate
1	THALANG	Bangkok Naval DY	1979	Extant 1982

Designed by Ferostaal of Essen, W Germany. In service 25.6.80. She carries 2–3t cranes and 4 spare MCM kits for minesweepers.

MINESWEEPING BOATS

Five *MSML 1–5* (25t, 2–20mm) built in Thailand and stricken 1980. Five ex-US 50ft MSB (21t full load, 8kts, MGs, 6 men) transferred 1963–66 and extant 1982.

Tonga

The Kingdom of Tonga or Friendly Islands, a collection of seven main groups of islands spread over nearly 300 square miles of the South Pacific, 450 miles ESE of Fiji, was annexed by Britain in 1899. It became independent in June 1970. King Taufa'ahau Tupou IV commissioned the 15t coastal patrol craft *Ngahau Koula* (P 101) into the Maritime Division of the Royal Tongan Defence Force on 10 March 1973. She was joined by her sister *Ngahau Siliva* (P 102) on 10 May 1974. They are both Brooke Marine-built 45ft vessels capable of 21kts (800–1000nm range) with 2 12.7mm Browning MGs, Decca 101 radar and 7 volunteer crew. 'Golden and Silver Arrow', as their names mean, have been joined by the Rolandswerft-built utility landing craft *Olovaha* (launched 24.6.81), a 600 grt vessel.

Vietnam

When South Vietnam was conquered by the armed forces of North Vietnam in April 1975 most of her Navy's sea-going warships escaped capture by sailing into foreign ports (mainly Philippine). They totalled 10 escorts, 7 landing ships, 3 patrol vessels and 3 repair ships. Other ships were destroyed or were captured by the North Vietnamese in a poor state of repair. For example, the frigate *Tran Khanh Du* (HQ 04) was captured in Saigon during refit; others were scuttled such as the LSM *Lam Giang* (HQ 402), *Keon Ngua* (HQ 604) or the oiler HQ 474.

It is rather impossible to give an accurate account of the fates of most South Vietnamese ships because of the lack of official information. We are left only with conjecture. Some fleet handbooks list all former South Vietnamese ships which did not leave Vietnam under the new united Vietnam but this is incorrect as many ships are not serviceable any longer because of their age, lack of spare parts or simply are worn out beyond repair so detailed fates are not given in this section. Those transferred to other navies (Philippines, Thailand or Korea) are listed under the relevant countries.

The Vietnam War (1946–75) is thought of mainly as a ground and air conflict but in both phases, French and American, naval operations, especially amphibious and river ones, were widespread. One whole theatre of war, the Mekong Delta, was a watery maze never dominated by one side or the other. American involvement was gravely increased by the Gulf of Tonkin Incident in August 1964. On 2 August three North Vietnamese ex-Soviet 'P 4' torpedo boats attacked the destroyer USS *Maddox* 30–60 miles off the coast because she had been violating territorial waters (Hanoi claimed 12 miles instead of 3) and more importantly because she had given distant cover to a South Vietnamese 31 July bombardment of the North Vietnamese islands of Hon Me and Hon Nieu, 3–5 miles from the mainland. Communist infiltration of the South was done by sea as well as by the Ho Chih Minh Trail. A second apparent attack (4 August) on *Maddox* and her sister destroyer *Turner Joy* in an atmosphere of considerable electronic confusion precipitated US carrier air strikes that claimed the destruction of 25 North Vietnamese warships and fuel bases for the loss of three planes and a pilot.

By this stage South Vietnam's Navy (established 1 January 1955) numbered 15,350 men including a marine corps whereas the North had 2200 sailors (given warships from 1958). Six years later the South's Navy had doubled to crew 39 surface combatants, 215 landing vessels, 12 mine launchers and 30 auxiliaries. Their role was increasingly active despite the US Navy's obvious predominance. Both services played a crucial part in blunting the North Vietnamese 1972 offensive into Quang Tri Province with gunfire support and amphibious landings.

The South's naval prowess was demonstrated in January 1974. A Chinese battalion-strong invasion of the Paracel Islands, 225 miles east of Vietnam, cost the Communist superpower two warships sunk and two heavily damaged for one Vietnamese vessel (23 survivors rescued by a Dutch cargo ship). Ten days later the South's warships put troops onto the Spratley Islands, several hundred miles to the south, to prevent their seizure. In April 1976 the Vietnamese Liberation Navy replaced the garrison.

The fall of South Vietnam in early 1975 began in the Central Highlands and her navy, short of fuel and spare parts though not ammunition, could not provide the firepower that had been available in 1972. Evacuation of Hue, Da Nang (6000 marines and 4000 other troops), Qui Nhon and other coastal towns degenerated into chaos and heralded the exodus since of 800,000 'Boat People'.

Today the Socialist Republic of Vietnam has 4000–5000 sailors (service is for 3 years or longer) maintaining its large but mainly old and probably unserviceable fleet of Communist and American warships together with a search and rescue force of 10 Soviet helicopters. The Soviet Pacific Fleet began an intensive presence during the brief Sino-Vietnamese War of early 1979. The American-built base of Cam Ranh Bay now reportedly hosts Russian nuclear submarines while the estimated 170,000 Vietnamese troops (of the million still under arms) in Kampuchea include two marine divisions.

South Vietnam

MAJOR SURFACE SHIPS

Ex-US EDSALL ('FMR') class *frigates*

Class (no, former name, transferred):
Tran Hung Dao (HQ 01, ex-*Camp* 6.2.71), *Tran Khanh Du* (HQ 04, ex-*Forster*. 25.9.71).

Former USN destroyer escorts. Built in 1943–44. Extensively converted to radar pickets after 1945. In 1965 large radar antennae was removed and the ships were employed in Indo-China as patrol frigates until transferred to S Vietnam.

Ex-US BARNEGAT class *seaplane tenders (frigates)*

Class (former names):
Tran Quang Khai (HQ 15, ex-*Bering Strait* WHEC 382, ex-*AVP 34*), *Tran Nhat Duat* (HQ 16, ex-*Yakutat* WHEC 380, ex-*AVP 32*), *Tran Binh Trong* (HQ 17, ex-*Castle Rock* WHEC 383, ex-*AVP 35*), *Tran Quoc Toan* (HQ 02, ex-*Cook Inlet* WHEC 384, ex-*AVP 36*), *Tham Ngu Lao* (HQ 03, ex-*Absecon* WHEC 374, ex-*AVP 23*), *Ly Thoung Kiet* (HQ 05, ex-*Chincoteague* WHEC 375, ex-*AVP 24*), *Ngo Kuyen* (HQ 06, ex-*McCulloch* WHEC 386, ex-*Wachapreague* AGP 8, ex-*AVP 56*)

Built 1942–44 as USN seaplane tenders and transferred in 1946–48 to US Coast Guard then to S Vietnam. First 2 pairs on 1.1.71 and 21.12.71. *Tham Ngu Lao* transferred on 15.7.72 and the last pair on 21.6.72. These ships were the largest combatants in the S Vietnamese Navy and the only ones to mount a 127mm gun battery. It is believed that all ASW weapons were removed before transfer.

AMPHIBIOUS WARFARE VESSELS

Ex-US LST type *tank landing ships*

Class (former names):
Cam Ranh (ex-*Marion County*, LST 975), *Da Nang* (ex-*Maricopa County*, LST 938), *Thi Nai* (ex-*Cayuga County* LST 529), *Vung Tau* (ex-*Cochino County* LST 603), *Qui Nhon* (ex-*Bullock County*, LST 509), *Hna Trang* (ex-*Jerome County*, LST 484)

Built in 1943–45, transferred to S Vietnam in 1962 and numbered in order above (HQ 500), HQ 501, 1963 (HQ 502, escaped 1975), 1969 (HQ 503), 1970 (HQ 504, 505).

Ex-US LSM type *medium landing ships*

Class (former nos):
Hat Giang (ex-*LSM 9011*, ex-*LSM 335*), *Han Giang* (ex-*LSM 9012*, ex-*LSM 110*), *Ninh Giang* (ex-*LSM 85*), *Huong Giang* (ex-*Oceanside*, LSM 175), *Tien Giang* (ex-*LSM 313*), *Hau Giang* (ex-*LSM 276*)

All 7 built in 1944. First 2 units transferred by USA to France in Jan 1954 for use in Indo-China and in Dec 1955 transferred to Vietnam (fitted as hospital ships, LSM-H). Numbered HQ 400–406. *LSM 175* transferred in 1961, *LSM 313* in 1962 and *LSM 276* in 1965. *HQ 401* and *HQ 404* escaped in 1975. *HQ 402* scuttled.

Ex-US LSSL type *landing support ships*

Class (former names):
Nguyen Van Tru (ex-*No Than*, ex-*Framée*, LSSL 105), *Le Trong Dam* (ex-*Linh Kiem*, ex-*Arquebuse*, ex-*LSSL 4*), *Le Van Binh* (ex-*Javeline*, ex-*LSSL 10*), *Doan Ngoc Tang* (ex-*Hallebarde*, ex-*LSSL 9*), *Lulu Phu Tho* (ex-*LSSL 101*), *Nguyen Ngoc Long* (ex-*LSSL 96*), *Nguyen Duc Bong* (ex-*LSSL 129*)

All 7 built in 1944–45. Numbered HQ 225–231 by S Vietnam. First 4 transferred to France in 1951 and 2 (HQ 225, 226) in 1955 and 1957. HQ 227–230 transferred in 1953 to Japan and retransferred to Vietnam in 1965. *Niguyen Duc Bong* transferred in 1966. First 3 officially stricken from the list in 1971. *Le Van Binh* sunk in 1966, *Nguyen Van Tru* sunk in 1970, *Le Trong Dam* sunk in 1970. Three (HQ 228, 229 and 231) escaped in 1975.

Ex-US LSIL type *landing ships*

Class (former nos):
Long Dao (ex-*LSIL 9092*, ex-*LSIL 698*), *Than Tien* (ex-*LSIL 9035*, ex-*LSIL 702*), *Thien Kich* (ex-*LSIL 9038*, ex-*LSIL 872*), *Lio Cong* (ex-*LSIL 9034*, ex-*LSIL 699*), *Tam Set* (ex-*LSIL 9033*, ex-*LSIL 871*)

All 5 built in 1944, transferred to France in 1951–53 and retransferred to Vietnam in 1956. Numbered HQ 327–331. HQ 329 escaped in 1975.

Ex-US LCU type *utility landing craft*

Class:
HQ 533 (ex-*LCU 1479*), HQ 534 (ex-*LCU 1480*), HQ 535 (ex-*LCU 1221*), HQ 536 (ex-*LCU 1446*), HQ 537 (ex-*LCU 1501*), HQ 538 (ex-*LCU 1594*), HQ 539 (ex-*1502*), HQ 540 (ex-*LCU 1475*), HQ 541 (ex-*LCU 1477*), HQ 542 (ex-*LCU 1494*), HQ 543 (ex-*LCU 1493*), HQ 544 (ex-*LCU 1445*), HQ 545, HQ 1484, HQ 546 (ex-*YFU 90*, ex-*LCU 1582*), HQ 547 (ex-*LCU 1481*), HQ 548 (ex-*LCU 1498*) HQ 549 (ex-?), HQ 560 (ex-*YLLC 1*, ex-*LCU 1348*), HQ 561 (ex-*YLLC 5*, ex-*YFU 2*, ex-*LCU 529*), HQ 562 (ex-*YLLC 3*, ex-*YFU 33*, ex-*LCU 1195*)

Eighteen former USN units 501 series were built during World War II with LCT (6) designation; 1466 series were built as LCU (7) during early 1950s. HQ 533–537 served as French *LCU 9076, 9089, 9086, 9074* and *9887* and were acquired in 1954 from French reparations and other transferred from USA up to 1971. Three units (ex-YLLC) converted while in US service for use as salvage lifting craft fitted with 20t capacity 'A' frame derrick, special anchors, divers' air compressors, welding equipment and salvage pumps.

SMALL SURFACE COMBATANTS

Ex-US PCE type *large patrol craft*

Class (no, former name):
Dong Da II (HQ 07, ex-*Crestview*, PCE 895), *Ngoc Hoi* (HQ 12, ex-*Brattleboro*, EPCER 852, ex-*PCER 852*), *Van Kiep II* (HQ 14, ex-*Amherst*, PCER 853)

Former US patrol vessels – escort (PCE), two of which were fitted as rescue ships (PCER) to pick up survivors of convoy sinkings. Built in 1943–44. *Brattleboro* for a time used as an experimental vessel (EPCER). Transferred to Vietnam on 29.11.61, 11.7.66 and in June 1970 respectively.

Ex-US ADMIRABLE class *minesweepers (large patrol craft)*

Class (no, former name):
Chi Lang II (HQ 08, ex-*Gayety*, MSF 239, ex-*AM 239*), *Ky Hoa* (HQ 09, ex-*Sentry*, MSF 299, ex-*AM 299*), *Nhut Tao* (HQ 10, ex-*Serene* MSF 300, ex-*AM 300*), *Chi Linh* (HQ 11, ex-*Shelter* MSF 301, ex-*AM 301*), *Ha Hoi* (HQ 13, ex-*Prowess*, IX 305, ex-*MSF 280*, ex-*AM 280*)

All 5 built in 1943–44 and later used as patrol vessels. *Prowess* was used as Naval Reserve TS 1962–71 (redesignated IX 305). Transferred to Vietnam in

April 1962 (*Chi Lang II*), Aug 1962 (*Ky Hoa*), Jan 1964 (*Nhut Tao, Chi Linh*) and June 1970 (*Ha Hoi*).

Ex-US PC (173ft) type *submarine-chasers (large patrol craft)*

Class (former names):
Chi Lang (ex-*Mausquet*, ex-*PC 1144*), *Dong Da* (ex-*L'Ardent*, ex-*PC 1167*), *Tay Ket* (ex-*Glaive*, ex-*PC 1143*), *Tuy Dong* (ex-*Trident*, ex-*PC 1146*), *Van Kiep* (ex-*L'Intrépide*, ex-*PC 1130*), *Van Don* (ex-*Anacortes*, ex-*PC 1569*)

Six former USN ships transferred to France after 1945. Subsequently transferred to Vietnam and numbered HQ 01–06; 1955 (*Chi Lang*), 1956 (next 4), 1960 (*Van Don*). *Dong Da* and *Chi Lang* deleted in 1961, *Tay Ket* and *Van Kiep* deleted in 1965, *Tuy Dong* deleted in 1971.

Ex-US SC type *submarine-chasers*

Class:
HQ 600 (ex-*GC 8*, ex-*SC 1020*), *HQ 601* ex-*GC 7*, ex-*SC 679*)

Transferred in 1951 to France and retransferred to Vietnam. Both deleted in 1960.

US PGM (100ft) type *large patrol craft*

Class:
Phu Du, Tien Moi, Minh Hoa, Kien Vang, Keo Ngua, Kim Qui, May Rut, Nam Du, Hoa Lu, To Yen, Dinh Hai, Truong Sa, Thai Binh, Thi Tu, Song Tu, Tat Sa, Hoang Sa, Phu Qui, Hon Troc, Tho Chau

Welded steel patrol boats built in the US yards specifically for foreign transfer and assigned PGM numbers (59–70, 72–74, 80–83, 91) for contract purposes.. Twenty transferred on completion and numbered HQ 600–629 in 1963–67. Built by J M Martinac SB Corp, Tacoma (HQ 600–605), and Marinette Marine Corp, Washington (the rest). *Phu Du* and *Hong Troc* escaped in 1975.

Ex-US 82ft 'POINT' class *large patrol craft*

Class (former name):
Le Phuoc Dui (ex-*Point Garnet 82310*), *Le Van Nga* (ex-*Point League 82304*), *Huynh Van Cu* (ex-*Point Clear 82315*), *Nguyen Dao* (ex-*Point Gammon 82328*), *Dao Thuc* (ex-*Point Comfort 82317*), *Le Ngoc Thanh* (ex-*Point Ellis 82330*), *Nguyen Ngoc Thach* (ex-*Point Slocum 82313*), *Dang Van Hoanh* (ex-*Point Hudson 82322*), *Le Dinh Hung* (ex-*Point White 82308*), *Thuong Tien* (ex-*Point Dume 82325*), *Pham Ngoc Chau* (ex-*Point Arden 82309*), *Dao Van Dang* (ex-*Point Glover 82307*), *Le Dgoc An* (ex-*Point Jefferson 82306*), *Huynh Van Ngan* (ex-*Point Kennedy 82320*), *Tran Lo* (ex-*Point Young 82303*), *Bui Viet Thanh* (ex-*Point Partridge 82305*), *Nguyen An* (ex-*Point Caution 82301*), *Nguyen Han* (ex-*Point Welcome 82329*), *Ngo Van Quyen* (ex-*Point Banks 82327*), *Van Dien* (ex-*Point Lomas 82321*), *Ho Dang La* (ex-*Point Grace 82323*), *Dam Thoai* (ex-*Point Mast 82316*), *Huynh Bo* (ex-*Point Grey 82324*), *Nguyen Kim Hung* (ex-*Point Orient 82319*), *Ho Duy* (ex-*Point Cypress 82326*), *Troung Ba* (ex-*Point Marmoc 82331*)

Twenty-six former US Coast Guard 82ft cutters designated WPB (actual length 83ft oa). Transferred to Vietnam in 1969 (HQ 700–707) and 1970 (HQ 708–725). *Huynh Van Cu* (HQ 702) escaped in 1975.

RIVERINE CRAFT
There were over 700 armed craft transferred to South Vietnam by the US Navy from 1965 for use in the riverine and coastal areas of Indo-China. There were also many former French craft which were widely used in the late 1950s and early 1960s. Some of them survived even into 1970s. The exact number of these small craft serving at any given time is difficult to determine. Below are listed all ex-American craft which were in existence in 1972. There were 107 'Swift' type patrol craft; 293 PBR river patrol boats; 28 RPC river patrol craft; 84 ASPB assault support patrol boats; 42 river monitors; 22 LCM-6 landing craft; 100 ATC armoured troop carriers; 9 CCB command and patrol boats; 4 CSB combat salvage boats; and 24 minesweeping launches. See US section of Part I for data and discussion.

A coastal force of motorised junks was organised with US assistance on 12 April 1960 with 100 junks, 28 groups of junks having been formed by June 1962. Mass production of improved design junks was undertaken to control infiltration of S Vietnamese coastal waters. The latest junks had diesel engines capable of reaching 15kts. They were fitted with armour plates and glass fibre to protect the wooden hull against marine borers and small arms fire. By 1969 about 500 junks were crewed by some 4000 men. Coastal Force (ex-Junk Force) become part of the Vietnamese Navy and no longer a paramilitary organisation in July 1965. Approximately 250 motor-propelled junks were pressed into naval service in Jan 1972 and these included 62 command junks, 31 Kien Giang junks, and 153 Yabuta junks. Some of the Yabuta junks were built of ferrous cement. The Yabuta junks usually had two .50 cal MGs; some also had a 60mm mortar. Diesel propulsion permitted them to overtake and search some of the thousands of coastal sailing craft in Indo-China waters.

MINE WARFARE VESSELS

Ex-US BLUEBIRD class *coastal minesweepers*

Class (no, former no):
Ham Tu (HQ 114, ex-*MSC 281*), *Chuong Duong II* (HQ 115, ex-*MSC 282*), *Bach Dang II* (HQ 116, ex-*MSC 283*)

Built in 1958–60 and transferred under MAP to Vietnam in 1959 (first two) and 1960. *Bach Dang II* grounded on 9.10.70, was stripped and destroyed.

Ex-US YMS type *coastal minesweepers*

Class (no, former name):
Ham Tu (HQ 111, ex-*Aubepine*, ex-*YMS 28*), *Bach Dang* (HQ 113, ex-*Belledone*, ex-*YMS 78*), *Choung Dong* (HQ 112, ex-*Digitale*, ex-*YMS 83*)

Transferred from the French Navy to Vietnam on 11.2.54. *Ham Tu* deleted in 1958, *Bach Bang* in 1963 and *Choung Dong* in 1964.

North Vietnam

Four ex-Soviet 'Petya II' type frigates: First two transferred in 1978, second pair April 1981. Same version as exported to Syria and India.

Three ex-Soviet 'Yurka' type ocean minesweepers: built in *c*1970 at Izora Shipyard, Leningrad. One transferred Dec 1979.

Ten ex-Soviet 'Osa II' type missile FAC: transferred in pairs Oct 1979, Sept 1980, Nov 1980 and Feb 1981.

Three ex-Soviet 'Komar' type missile FAC: transferred in 1972. One sunk on 19.12.72. Probably in poor condition.

Eight ex-Soviet 'Shershen' type torpedo FAC: transferred in pairs 16.4.79, 12.9.79, Aug 1980 and Oct 1980. First pair may lack TT.

Six Chinese-built Soviet 'P 6' torpedo FAC: built in 1956. Four transferred in 1967. In poor condition now.

Twelve ex-Soviet 'P 4' type torpedo FAC: Built *c*1955. Probably some built in China. Transferred in 1961 and 1964. Three of this class attacked US destroyers in the Aug 1964 Gulf of Tonkin Incident. Eight since deleted or sunk.

Seven ex-Soviet 'SO 1' type submarine-chasers used as patrol vessels: built in *c*1960. Two transferred in 1960–61 and next two in 1964–65 with the rest in 1966. One lost to US air attack 1.2.66.

Eight ex-Chinese 'Shanghai II' type large patrol boats: Built *c*1962 and transferred equally in 1966 and 1968.

Fifty ex-Chinese 'Swatow' type patrol craft: Built in *c*1957 and transferred in 1958 (30) and 1964 (20). First group had 600-series pennant numbers. Some 26 lost in action or deleted. Remaining probably in very poor condition.

Two ex-Soviet 'Poluchat type' patrol craft: Built in *c*1960 in Jaroslavl and transferred.

Six Soviet 'Zhuk' type coastal patrol craft. Built in *c*1975. Transferred equally 1978 and Nov 1979.

Three ex-Soviet 'Polnocny B' class landing ships: transferred May 1979, Nov 1979 and Feb 1980

Twelve ex-Soviet 'T 4' class landing craft: transferred 1979.

There are also 30 motor launches, 10 general utility service tenders, 7 ex-US LSM type landing ships, 5 ex-US LSSL type landing craft, 5 LCI, 1 LCT (6) and 6 LCT (7).

Albania

Albania, which is unique among the small nations, freed herself from the World War II Axis occupation using her own military forces. An underground army was set up and commanded by the Communists who seized power in 1944 after the country was liberated. With the government formed by Enver Hoxha, a totalitarian Communist state was set up and plans for rapid industrial development were drawn up, despite lack of capital, know-how and material wealth. The scale of industry proved to be inadequate to supply any kind of fighting craft and the status of the Albanian naval forces has reflected changes in the political sympathies of the regime since the end of the war. Until 1948 Albania was a satellite of Yugoslavia with a customs as well as a monetary union. The Albanian naval forces, part of the 'People's Army' at that time, were supplied by the Soviets with some minor craft while Yugoslavia helped the Albanians to restore two old minesweeping tenders. After the expulsion of Yugoslavia from the Cominform and the overpowering of the pro-Tito group by the Stalinist faction in Albania, the country became a close Soviet ally despite territorial isolation and had to rely on the Soviet Union for both technical advice and capital loans. Albania was valuable to the Soviet Union as she provided her with Mediterranean bases for the Soviet Navy. After joining the Warsaw Pact in 1955 Albania allowed the Soviet Union to begin construction of base facilities at Sazan (Saseno) Island in the Gulf of Valona. In exchange, cancellation of the large Albanian debt was announced by the Soviet Union in 1957 and large amounts of credit made available for the modernisation and expansion of the armed forces. During 1956–61 the Albanian Navy, which was separated from the Army at that time, purchased 2 'Whiskey' class submarines, 6 MTBs of the P 4 type, 2 minesweepers of the T 43 type, 6 inshore minesweepers of the T 301 class, 4 'Kronstadt' class patrol craft, 11 minesweeping boats and a number of auxiliaries.

The new Soviet credit dried up by the late 1950s which, together with Khrushchev's dislike of the strict Stalinist course maintained by the Albanian government, inclined Tirana to flirt with Red China. When a rift between the two Communist giants became evident, public disapproval of the Chinese viewpoint was disguised by the Soviet Communist Party as an attack on Albania. This resulted in diplomatic relations with the Soviet Union being severed in December 1961. Albania effectively withdrew from the Warsaw Pact and deprived the Soviet Union of her base at Sarzan Island seizing two 'Whiskey' class submarines there. The Soviet-made ships were commissioned and maintained with Chinese assistance giving the Albanians an effective task force of 3 submarines and 6 MTBs; however lack of spares soon decreased their efficiency.

Transfer of Chinese craft was initiated in 1965 with 6 MTBs of the P 4 type and provided Albania with an effective squadron of fast attack craft which by the late 1970s consisted of 4 missile craft of the 'Hoku' class, 32 torpedo hydrofoils of the 'Huchwan' class and 6 patrol craft of the 'Shanghai' class. This force of comparatively new craft – despite their somewhat obsolescent design – and favourable strategic location of bases gave the Albanians the ability to control traffic through the 50-mile wide Strait of Otranto, although the strained relations between Albania and China disclosed in the late 1970s may have affected the supply of spares for the Chinese-made craft.

The Albanian Navy, part of the People's Army whose ranks were abolished in 1966, has a total of 3000 men (three-year conscripts); main bases are Durazzo, Valona, Sazan Island, Sarande, Shingjin and Paşa Liman. There are over 5000 trained reservists and the Fleet is organised into a submarine brigade with the Durazzo and Valona sea defence brigades. Warships are controlled by the Coastal Defence Command of which the Navy's C-in-C is deputy commander.

FLEET STRENGTH 1947

The 1947 status of the Albanian naval forces cannot be described precisely but according to some sources the following craft were in service:

2 Italian-built motor boats of the *Tirane* class although they may be former Italian MAS-boats transferred from the Soviet Union.

2 ex-German *MFP*-craft (220t, built c 1943, deleted early 1970s).

2 minesweeping tenders (ex-Yugoslav *Marjan* and *Mosor*, 125t, built 1931, recovered after the war, deleted 1967).

SUBMARINES

Ex-Soviet 'WHISKEY' class *submarines*

Two transferred from the USSR in 1960 while an additional pair was seized in 1961 upon the withdrawal of the Soviets from their base at Sazan Island. Three were operational while the remaining boat was used for harbour training duties. One deleted in 1976 and cannibalised for spare parts; the others with numbers *512, 514* and *516* were extant in 1982.

SMALL SURFACE COMBATANTS

Ex-US 'VOSPER' type *fast attack craft (torpedo)*

Seven (Lend-Lease supplies) were transferred from the Soviet Union in 1950. Deleted in the mid-1960s.

Ex-Soviet 'P 4' type *fast attack craft (torpedo)*

Six transferred in 1956 and were augmented in 1965 by six others of Chinese construction. The latter were different in having additional twin 0.5in MG mount fitted and lacking radar which was to be installed later. Only three numbers are known: *111, 115* and *304*. All 12 were in service in 1982.

Ex-Chinese 'HUCHWAN' class *torpedo hydrofoils*

The first six boats came from China in 1968, 15 were delivered in 1969 and nine others by 1971. Purchase of two craft in 1974 may be proof of a second contract as transfer of a further four was probable. Numbers reported in 100 and 300 series. Extant 1982.

Ex-Chinese 'HOKU' class *fast attack craft (missile)*

Four of this class were transferred from China during 1976–77. Extant 1982.

Ex-Soviet 'KRONSTADT' class *patrol craft*

Four craft transferred in 1958. Two were sent for ASW updating to the Soviet Union shortly before the 1961 break and were claimed back by the Albanian government in mid-1965. Numbered *191, 192, 502, 504* at the beginning of 1960s, later being changed to *150, 151, 340, 341*. *151* deleted in 1979; all others extant in 1982.

Ex-Chinese 'SHANGHAI II' class *patrol craft*

Six craft transferred during 1974–75 and were commissioned with numbers *101* to *106*. Extant 1982.

MINE WARFARE VESSELS

Ex-Soviet 'T 43' type *ocean minesweepers*

Two of the short hull series were acquired in Aug 1960. Numbers recently reported were *152* and *342*. Extant 1982.

Ex-Soviet 'T 301' class *inshore minesweepers*

Three pairs transferred in 1957, 1959 and 1960 respectively. Reportedly fitted with navigation radar recently. Numbers of five of these boats became known in the late 1970s: *153, 154, 343* to *345*. No *343* and the one with number unknown were deleted in 1979, the others remained in service in 1982.

Ex-Soviet 'KM 4' type *minesweeping boats*

Three transferred after 1945. All deleted 1967.

Ex-Soviet 'PO 2' type *minesweeping boats*

Eleven bought in the Soviet Union during 1957–60. Used for general purposes, extant 1982.

Austria

Austria was divided into four occupied zones after World War II; Vienna – situated in the Soviet zone – being divided into four sectors as was Berlin. Through the untiring efforts of the Austrian politicians an international Treaty was signed on 15 May 1955, giving Austria self-control, a democratic constitution and perpetual neutrality. The treaty forbids her from owning nuclear weapons . . . submarines, assault craft, manned torpedoes and sea mines.

In accordance with Austria's strict neutrality and budget limitations, the Austrian Second Republic's riverine forces were small, consisting only of the equipment of the Army Engineering Corps. In 1968 a patrol boat detachment was formed consisting of the tiny 40ft boat *Oberst Brecht* (A 601) and an old self-propelled pontoon nicknamed 'flat-iron'. At the end of the 1960s the conservative government planned to build 10 armed patrol boats nicknamed 'Prader's Panzerkreuzer' after the then Minister of Defence. Of this group only *Niederösterreich* was built. Apart from her there are 10 US-built M 3 launches (normally unarmed, 4 delivered 1965 and 6 in 1976).

NIEDERÖSTERREICH *patrol craft*

Displacement:	73t full load
Dimensions:	97ft 4in × 17ft 5in × 3ft 7in
	29.67m × 5.41m × 1.1m
Machinery:	2 shafts, 2 MWM V16 diesels, 1620bhp = 22kts. Oil 9.3t. Range 1030nm
Armament:	1–20mm AA, 2–12.7mm MG, 2–7.62mm MG 42, 1–84mm Carl Gustav M2 AT launcher
Complement:	12

No	Name	Builder	Launched	Fate
A 604	NIEDERÖSTERREICH	Korneuberg	26.7.69	Extant 1982

This multipurpose boat was designed by Mayerform S A, an Austrian design bureau based in Geneva, Switzerland. She can be quickly changed into three different configurations: E meaning river patrol boat, K meaning rescue boat, R meaning dispatch boat.

Based at the harbour of the 'Pionierkaserne Wien Kuchelau' and maintained by the 27 Danube Flotilla personnel of the Engineering Corps ('Heerespioniere'); she is under command of 1st Panzer Brigade should she be needed for action.

Eire

Ireland officially left the Commonwealth in 1948 and the Republic of Eire was proclaimed in April 1949. She joined the EEC in January 1973 but has maintained the policy of neutrality adopted before World War II. The Irish Navy or Naval Service was created in 1947 from the disbanded Wartime Marine Service and Port Control Service. Until the 1970s the Irish Navy was a coastal Fishery Protection service, but the increased fishing of ever smaller fish stocks, the adoption of a 200-mile EEZ and the exploitation of offshore minerals and oil and gas have meant that the area the Irish Navy has to patrol has increased manyfold. Modern Irish warships have to be capable of carrying out long patrols in the extremely inclement North Atlantic in mid-winter. This has meant a considerable expansion in numbers and an emphasis on much larger, more capable vessels. Second-hand warships are no longer sufficient. The main base is Haulbowline Island, Cork which may be enlarged. The Navy is made up of about 1200 volunteers including reserves (500 in 1974).

FLEET STRENGTH 1947

FRIGATES

Name	Launched	Disp	Fate
CLIONA (ex-*Bellwort*)	11.8.41	1020t	Stricken Jan 1971
MACHA (ex-*Borage*)	22.11.41	1020t	Stricken Jan 1971
MAEV (ex-*Oxlip*)	28.8.41	1020t	Stricken March 1972

Three ex-RN 'Flower' class frigates (formerly corvettes) were acquired by the Irish Navy in 1946. *Cliona* and *Maev* were in the original short forecastle form. *Macha* had been fitted with an extended forecastle during World War II. One of her messdecks was converted into cabins for the flotilla commander, and she was used as leader. When purchased all were armed with 1–4in and 2–20mm (2×1), plus a Hedgehog ASW mortar in *Cliona* and *Maev* and a 2pdr (40mm) in *Cliona* and *Macha*.

Their pole masts were replaced by lattice masts in 1953, and in 1966–67 *Cliona* and *Macha* were refitted for fishery protection duties. Armament was reduced to 1–4in. *Maev* was placed in preservation in reserve and retained her original armament.

OTHER VESSELS

Name	Launched	Disp	Fate
FORT RANNOCH	1936	258t gross	Stricken 1947
MTBs 1–5	1939	32t	Stricken c1948

SMALL SURFACE COMBATANTS

Ex-British 'TON' class *coastal minesweepers*

Class (no, former name):
Banba (CM 11, ex-*Alverton*), *Fola* (CM 12, ex-*Blaxton*) and *Gráinne* (CM 10, ex-*Oulston*)

Ex-RN 'Ton' class coastal minesweepers, built between 1952–56. Purchased by the Irish Navy in 1971 to replace the worn out 'Flower' class frigates. Used for Fishery Protection duties. *Gráinne* had to use Bofors and small arms fire to arrest a 3272grt Soviet trawler in Sept 1976. Moveable minesweeping gear has been landed, but the fixed gear remains on board. All in service 1982.

DEIDRE *patrol vessel*

Displacement:	972t full load
Dimensions:	184ft 4in pp, 205ft 2in oa × 34ft 2in × 14ft 5in
	56.2m, 62.5m × 10.4m × 4.4m
Machinery:	1 shaft (CP propeller), 2 Polar SF 112 VS-F diesels, 4200bhp = 18kts. Oil 150t. Range 3000nm/5000nm at 15.5kts/12kts
Armament:	1–40mm, 2–2in RFL
Sensors:	Radar Decca type; sonar Simrad sidescan type
Complement:	46

No	Name	Builder	Launched	Fate
P 20	DEIDRE	Verolme, Cork	29.12.71	Extant 1982

The first warship designed and built in Eire. Intended to be the prototype for a number of fishery protection vessels (entered service 19.6.72), but her seakeeping, though adequate for most navies, was not as good as had been hoped. Subsequent vessels have been built to a slightly elongated and modified design. *Deidre* is fitted with Vosper stabilisers.

Deidre as completed
VCD via T A Adams

Emer 1979

EMER class *patrol vessels*

Displacement:	1020t full load
Dimensions:	192ft 1in pp, 213ft 11in oa × 33ft 6in × 15ft
	58.5m, 65.2m × 10.2m × 4.6m
Machinery:	1 shaft (CP propeller), 2 SEMT-Pielstick 6 PA6L-280 diesels, 4800bhp = 18kts. Oil 172t. Range 4500nm/6750nm at 18/12kts
Armament:	1–40mm, 2–20mm (2×1)
Sensors:	Radar Decca type; sonar Simrad sidescan type
Complement:	55

No	Name	Builder	Launched	Fate
P 21	EMER	Verolme, Cork	1977	Extant 1982
P 22	AOIFE	Verolme, Cork	12.4.78	Extant 1982
P 23	AISLING	Verolme, Cork	3.10.79	Extant 1982

This class was developed from *Deidre*; they completed on 18.1.78, 21.11.79 and 21.5.80 respectively. They have a 7ft 8in *(2.4m)* longer hull with a raised forecastle to improve seakeeping, more powerful machinery to maintain the speed, better watertight subdivision and improved accommodation. *Aoife* and *Aisling* differ from *Emer* by having a satellite navigation system, and improved noise levels in the control rooms and accommodation to make it easier for them to patrol the new 200 mile EEZ limit. They also have a bow thruster and a new Ka-Me-Wa propeller.

P 31 design

P 31 class *patrol vessels*

Displacement:	1800t full load
Dimensions:	265ft oa × 39ft 4in × 13ft 8in
	80.8m × 12.0m × 8.8m
Machinery:	2 shafts, 2 diesels, 7200hp = 20+kts. Range 7000nm at 15kts
Armament:	1–76mm OTO Melara, 2–20mm (2×1), 1 helicopter
Sensors:	Radar ?; sonar ?
Complement:	85

Two ships of this type have been ordered (P 31 laid down Nov 1981 and P 32 in 1982) from Verolme, Cork. Enlarged *Emers* with a longer range, a more powerful gun and a helicopter pad and hangar over the wide transom stern. Designed for long patrols at the limits of the 200-mile EEZ, leaving the inshore patrols to the *Emers* and *Deidre*. The 'P 31s' will have excellent seakeeping qualities. More may be built later.

MISCELLANEOUS

The Danish trawler *Ferdia* was temporarily hired by the Irish Navy to act as a fishery protection vessel until *Emer* entered service. In the mid-1970s the only other vessel the Irish Navy possessed that could police the extended EEZ was *Deidre*. *Ferdia* was returned to her owners in 1978.

Finland

The second armistice in 1944 and the following Treaty of Paris in February 1947 brought difficulties; a maximum of 10,000 tons and 4500 men were permitted to the Navy and submarines and torpedoes were forbidden.

The remaining coast defence ship *Väinämöinen* was taken as 'reparation' by the Soviet Union. The submarines were scrapped and the MTBs were deprived of torpedo tubes. They were reclassified as patrol boats.

Since then Finland has had a very difficult position, politically and geographically. But Finland has remained as a free nation, although her policy of course must take into consideration the Soviet Union.

All the three services have been reduced as has the training time for conscripts. The reparations to the Soviet Union badly affected the Finnish Navy and economy which has not yet the facilities to build up

Emer as completed   VCD via T A Adams

its former strong defence forces. This is reflected in the small grants which have been allotted to the Navy. The stress is laid upon minelayers, minesweepers, missile boats and patrol vessels. Consequently Finland's Navy in 1982 consists of these types with two corvettes as backbone for its 2500 men (8–11 month conscripts) and 8000 reservists. Most of the warships are of Finnish construction. The world famous Wärtsilä yard has been the world's most successful builder of icebreakers, delivered for example to the Soviet Union, Sweden and Argentina. The main Fleet Base is at Turku; training establishment at Upinniemi (Helsinki). The Fleet is organised into four flotillas; gunboats (Turku), missile craft, mine warfare vessels and patrol units (Helsinki).

FLEET STRENGTH 1947

The coast defence ship *Väinämöinen* was ceded to the Soviet Union as part of reparations and renamed *Vyborg*, capital of the conquered southeast province of Finland. The submarines *Vetehinen*, *Vesihiisi*, *Iku-Turso*, *Saukko* and *Vesikko* were all stricken, the last preserved as a museum boat at Sveaborg, outside Helsinki.

SLOOPS

Name	Launched	Disp	Fate
Hämeenmaa class			
HAMEENMAA	1917	400t	BU 1953
UUSIMAA	1917	400t	BU 1953
Karjala class			
KARJALA	1918	342t	BU 1953
TURUNMAA	1918	342t	BU 1953

MINELAYERS

Name	Launched	Disp	Fate
LOIMU, LIESKA	1915–16	60t	Stricken 1953
POMMI, MIINA	1917	80t	Stricken 1953
RUOTSINSALMI	1940	310t	Stricken 1975

PATROL VESSELS

Name	Launched	Disp	Fate
AURA	1907	350t	Stricken 1971
VMV 1, 2, 5, 6	1930–31	30t	Stricken 1950–60
VMV 9, 11, 13, 15, 16	1935	30t	Stricken 1960–70, VMV 11 museum boat
TURSAS	1938	360t	Stricken 1975
J 1–4 (ex-Italian MAS 526–529), JYLHA, JYRY, JYSKE, JYMY	1939	22t	Stricken 1961
H 1–5, HYOKY, HIRMU, HURJA, HYRSKY, HAIJY	1943	20t	Stricken 1963
T 2–8, TAISTO, TYRSKY, TUIMA, TUISKO, TUULI T 7, T 8	1942–46	22t	Stricken 1962–77
VMV 19, 20	1943	21t	Stricken 1970

EUROPE (NEUTRAL)

MINESWEEPERS

Name	Launched	Disp	Fate
RAUTU	1917	165t	Stricken 1950
Pukkio class			
PUKKIO, PORKKALA, PANSIO	1939–47	162t	Stricken 1974–79
Ahven class			
1 AHVEN, 2 KIISKI, 3 MUIKKO, 4 SARKI, 5 KUORE, 6 LAHNA	1936–37	17t	Stricken 1960–62
SM 1, 2, 4	1939–40	20t	Stricken 1951–54
AJONPAA KALLANPAA	1941	52t	Stricken 1960 and 1962
Ex-US (purchased 1946)			
DR 2 PYHTAA, DR 7 PIRTTISAARI, DR 10 PURHA	1943–44	150t	DR 2 stricken 1978, others 1980
KUHA 1, 2, 4, 5, 7–18	1941–46	17t	Stricken 1957–62

Porkkala sunk 28.11.41, was raised and rebuilt.

ICEBREAKERS

Name	Launched	Disp	Fate
MURTAJA	1898	1000t	Stricken 1959
SAMPO	1898	1850t	Stricken 1960
APU	1899	900t	Stricken 1959
TARMO	1907	2300t	Stricken 1969
OTSO	1936	800t	Stricken 1967
LOUHI (ex-*Sisu*)	1938	2012t	From 1975 HQ ship

Hämeenmaa c1975   *Author's Collection*

Karjala 1975   *Author's Collection*

Isku 1973   *Author's Collection*

MAJOR SURFACE SHIPS

Ex-British 'BAY' class *frigate*

No	Name	Builder	Acquired	Fate
–	MATTI KURKI (ex-*Porlock Bay*, ex-*Loch Seaforth*, ex-*Loch Muick*)	Charles Hill & Sons, Bristol	Mar 1962	Stricken 1975

Ex-Soviet 'RIGA' class *frigates*

No	Name	Builder	Acquired	Fate
01	UUSIMA	Soviet NYd	14.5.64	Stricken 1979
02	HAMEENMAA	Soviet NYd	14.5.64	Extant 1982

Hämeenmaa was converted to a minelayer 1978-79; no TT, 50 mines.

AMPHIBIOUS WARFARE VESSELS

Five *Kave* class LCUs (27t standard, 160t full load; 59ft × 16ft 5in × 4ft 4in, (*18m × 5m × 1.4m*); 2 Valmet diesels, 360bhp = 9kts; 1–20mm; 3 crew). Built by Hollming, Rauma, completed 19.12.60. *Kave 5* lost in tow 15.12.60. *Kave 1* completed by Haminan Konepaja 16.11.56
Six *Kala* class LCUs (60t standard, 200t full load; 88ft 7in × 26ft 2in × 6ft (*27m × 8m × 1.8m*); machinery and gun as *Kave* class; 10 crew). Built by Rauma Repola, *Kala 1* completed 16.11.56, *Kala 6* 4.12.59. Can lay up to 34 mines. *Kampela class* LCUs (90t standard, 260t full load; 106ft 7in × 26ft 2in × 4ft 10in, (*32.5m × 8m × 1.5m*); 2 Scania diesels, 460bhp = 9kts; 2–20mm, mines; 10 crew. *Kampela 1* (in service 29.7.76), *Kampala 2* (in service 21.10.76) built by Enso Gutzeit, Savonlinna *Kampala 3* (in service 23.10.79) built by Finnmekano, Teija. There are also five *Valas* class, six *Hauki* class and two *Pukkio* class, officially rated as artillery and personnel ferries.

SMALL SURFACE COMBATANTS

Turunmaa 1978

TURUNMAA class *corvettes*

Displacement:	650t standard; 770t full load
Dimensions:	229ft 7in oa, 243ft 1in wl × 25ft 7in × 7ft 11in 70.0m, 74.0m × 7.8m × 2.4m
Machinery:	3-shaft CODOG (3 CP propellers): 1 Olympus TM3B gas turbine, 16,180shp = 35kts, plus 3 MTU diesels, 4050bhp = 17kts. Oil 120t. Range 2500nm at 14kts
Armament:	1–120mm Bofors, 2–40mm Bofors, 2–23mm (1×2), 2 RBU 1200 ASW RL (2×5), 2 DCT, 6–103mm RFL on main gun
Sensors:	Radar HSA M22, navigation
Complement:	70

No	Name	Builder	Launched	Fate
03	TURUNMAA	Wärtsilä, Helsinki	11.7.67	Extant 1982
04	KARJALA	Wärtsilä, Helsinki	16.8.67	Extant 1982

Ordered 18.2.65. Laid down March 1967, completed 29.8.68 and 21.10.68 respectively, commissioned 1969. Engine exhausts taken astern either side of the quarterdeck to discharge as one 50ft astern, thus providing an IR decoy and allowing the ships to steam at 12kts without using the propellers. Can cruise 17kts on diesels alone.

ISKU *experimental missile patrol boat*

Displacement:	115t standard; 140t full load
Dimensions:	86ft 6in × 28ft 7in × 6ft 5in 26.4m wl, 28.0m × 8.7m × 1.8m
Machinery:	4 shafts, 4 Soviet M50 diesels, 3600bhp = 15kts
Armament:	2–30mm (1×2), 4 MTO/68 (SS-N-2A Styx) SSM
Sensors:	Radar 1 navigation, 1 Square Tie
Complement:	15

No	Name	Builder	Launched	Fate
16	ISKU	Reposaaren konepaja, Björneborg	4.12.69	Extant 1982

Laid down Nov 1968 and commissioned 1970 for training and trials. Landing craft hull designed for missile armament and more powerful engines.

Ex-Soviet 'OSA II' class *fast attack craft (missile)*

Class (no):
Tuima (11), *Tuisko* (12), *Tuuli* (14), *Tyrsky* (15).
Purchased 1974–75 from the USSR. Finnish electronics. Extant 1982.

Helsinki running trials 1980   *Author's Collection*

Helsinki as completed
NB 1/750 scale

HELSINKI class *fast attack craft (missile)*

Displacement:	280t standard; 350t full load
Dimensions:	147ft 7in × 29ft 3in × 9ft 9in
	45.0m × 8.5m × 3.0m
Machinery:	3 shafts, 3 MTU 16V 538 TB92 diesels, 11,000bhp = 32kts
Armament:	8 RBS 15 SSM (4×2), 1–57mm Bofors Mk 1, 2–23mm (1×2), 2 Philax chaff RL, mines
Sensors:	Radar
Complement:	30

No	Name	Builder	Launched	Fate
60	HELSINKI	Wärtsilä, Helsinki	5.11.80	Extant 1982

Ordered 5.10.78 as prototype for aluminium class of FAC. Laid down 3.9.80, delivered 1.9.81. Four more ordered early 1981, eight more planned. Optronic fire control system is Philips 9LV225. Swedish RBS 15 SSM ordered 7.3.83.

British 'DARK' class *fast attack craft (gun)*

Class:
Vasama 1 and *Vasama 2*.
Built 1955–57 by Saunders Roe, Anglesey, UK. Different from RN armament, 2–40mm, 4 DCs and mines. *Vasama 1* stricken 1977, *Vasama 2* stricken 1979.

Nuoli 2 c 1975   *Author's Collection*

NUOLI class *fast attack craft (gun)*

Displacement:	47t standard; 53t full load
Dimensions:	72ft 2in × 21ft 8in × 5ft
	22.0m × 6.6m × 1.5m
Machinery:	3 Soviet M50 diesels, 2700bhp = 40kts
Armament:	1–40mm, 1–20mm
Sensors:	Radar Decca 707
Complement:	15

Class (no, launched):
Nuoli 1–4 (31—34, 1961), *Nuoli 5–8 (35–38, 1962)*, *Nuoli 9 (39, 1963)*, *Nuoli 10–12 (40–42, 1964)*, *Nuoli 13 (43, 1966)*.
All built at Laivateollisuus, Åbo, (Turku). *Nuoli 9* deleted 1979, *Nuoli 4* in 1980. Six being modernised 1980–82, another 5 to be discarded. A 50t experimental prototype replacement FAC, the *Hurja* was completed in 1981. She has a 72ft × 16ft (*22m × 5m*) GRP hull. Intended to replace the 7 discarded *Nuoli* class in the 1980s.

Rymattyla 1975   *Author's Collection*

RIHTNIEMI class *large patrol craft*

Displacement:	90t standard; 110t full load
Dimensions:	101ft 8in × 18ft 8in × 5ft 11in
	31.0m, 33.0m × 5.6m × 1.8m
Machinery:	2 shafts, 2 MTU diesels, 2500bhp = 15kts
Armament:	1–40mm, 1–20mm (from 1976 4–23mm (2×2)), 2-RBU 1200 ASW RL (2×5)
Complement:	20

No	Name	Builder	Launched	Fate
51	RIHTNIEMI	Repola, Rauma	1956	Extant 1982
52	RYMATTYLA	Repola, Rauma	1956	Extant 1982

Ordered June 1955. Commissioned 21 Feb and 20 May 1957. Modernised 1980–81. Also minesweepers.

Ruissalo c 1970   *Author's Collection*

RUISSALO class *large patrol craft*

Displacement:	110t standard; 130t full load
Dimensions:	108ft 11in × 18ft 6in × 5ft 11in
	32.0m, 33.1m × 6.0m × 1.8m
Sensors:	Radar Decca, hull sonar
Other particulars:	As *Rihtniemi* class

No	Name	Builder	Launched	Fate
53	RUISSALO	Laivateollisuus, Turku	16.6.59	Extant 1982
54	RAISIO	Laivateollisuus, Turku	2.7.59	Extant 1982
55	ROYTTA	Laivateollisuus, Turku	2.6.59	Extant 1982

Ex-*R 3–5*, completed 11.8.59, 12.9.59, 14.10.59 respectively; 53 modernised 1976, other two 1980. Also minesweepers.

MINE WARFARE VESSELS

KEIHASSALMI class *minelayer*

Displacement:	290t standard; 360t full load
Dimensions:	184ft 9in × 25ft 4in × 6ft 6in
	56.0m × 7.7m × 2.0m
Machinery:	2 shafts, 2 Wärtsilä diesels, 1600bhp = 15kts
Armament:	2–40mm, 2–20mm (2×1), up to 100 mines
Complement:	60

No	Name	Builder	Launched	Fate
05	KEIHASSALMI	Valmet, Helsinki	16.3.57	Extant 1982

Commissioned 1958. The 2–40mm changed to Soviet 4–30mm (2×2) in 1975.

Pohjanmaa as completed

POHJANMAA class *minelayer*

Displacement:	1000t standard; 1100t full load
Dimensions:	255ft 9in × 37ft 8in × 9ft 10in
	78.0m × 11.5m × 3.0m
Machinery:	2 shafts, 2 Wärtsilä Vasa 16V22 diesels, 5800hp = 20kts. Range 3500nm at 17kts
Armament:	1–120mm, 2–40mm (2×1), 8–23mm (4×2), up to 120 mines, 2 RBU 1200 ASW RL (2×2)
Sensors:	Radar navigation, air search, Philips 9LV 100 fire control; sonar 2 sets; ECM
Complement:	77–90 (as training ship)

No	Name	Builder	Launched	Fate
01	POHJANMAA	Wärtsilä, Helsinki	28.8.78	Extant 1982

Designed in 1976 and laid down May 1978. Also TS, as such maximum 56 men in portacabins on mine deck. Commissioned 8.6.79. Helicopter pad on quarterdeck. Bow thruster.

Ex-US BYMS type *inshore minesweepers*

Class:
Katanpää (1), *Purunpää* (2), *Vahterpää* (3), *Tammenpää* (4)
  Ex-US BYMS 2049, 2032, 2044, 2047. Launched 1941–42, purchased 1948, scrapped 1958–60.

KUHA class *inshore minesweepers*

Displacement:	90t standard
Dimensions:	87ft 2in × 22ft 8in × 6ft 6in
	26.6m × 6.9m × 2.0m
Machinery:	1 shaft, 2 Cummins NT-380M diesels, 600bhp = 11kts
Armament:	2–20mm (2×1) or 2–23mm (1×2) and 1–20mm
Sensors:	Radar Decca
Complement:	15

Class:
Kuha 21–26
  Ordered 1972 and launched at Laivateollisuus, Turku, 1974–75. Hulls constructed of GRP. Active rudders.

ICEBREAKERS

All built by Wärtsilä, Helsinki, with pairs of propellers fore and aft. Extant 1982.
  Voima (4415t standard; 274ft × 63ft 8in × 23ft, *83.5m × 19.4m × 6.8m*; 6 diesels, 10,500bhp = 16.5kts; 58 crew). Launched 1952, in service 1953. Rebuilt and re-engined 1978–79 to serve until 1994.
  Four *Karhu* class (3540t standard; 243ft × 57ft × 21ft, *74.2m × 17.4m × 6.4m*; 4 diesels, 7500bhp = 16kts, 53 crew). *Karhu* (launched 22.10.57, in service Dec 1958), *Murtaja* (22.9.58, in service 1959), *Sampo* (launched and in service 1960), *Hansa* (W German-owned, in service 25.11.66) has a Finnish crew and summers off Finland.
  Three *Tarmo* class (4890t standard; 284ft × 71ft × 23ft, *86.5m × 21.7m × 6.8m*; 4 diesels, 12,000bhp = 16.5kts; 58 crew). *Tarmo* (in service 1963), *Varma* (1968), *Apu* (25.11.70).
  Two *Urho* class (as Swedish *Atle* class). *Urho* (launched 1974, in service 5.3.75), *Sisu* (1975, in service 28.1.76). A helicopter but no other armament, 45 crew.

Keihassalmi c1975   *Author's Collection*

Pohjanmaa 1981   *Author's Collection*

Kuha 22, 21 and 25 c1978   *Author's Collection*

Malta

A coastal patrol force of small craft was formed in 1973. It is manned by the marine section of the 800-volunteer Maltese Regiment and primarily employed as a coast guard. Malta achieved independence in 1964 but a Royal Navy presence was prolonged until 1979 under a NATO arrangement concluded in 1972. In September 1980 Malta declared her neutrality banning any foreign troops or bases, including Soviet warship docking facilities (the first Soviet Navy courtesy visit was in 1978). Italy, France and Algeria have all since guaranteed the island republic's status.

  Malta-built customs launch (25t, 19kts, 2–12.7mm MG, 8 crew). Launched 1969, bought 1973, deleted 1979.
  Three ex-W German customs launches (90–100t, 9–16kts, 1–12.7mm MG, 7–9 crew) bought 1974. *C 29* (ex-*Kondor*) built by Lürssen. Deleted 1979. *C 27* (ex-*Brunsbüttel*) built Buschmann, Hamburg, 1953, extant 1982. *C 28* (ex-*Geier*) built Bremen Burg, deleted 1979.
  Two ex-Libyan (Yugoslav-built) customs launches (100t, 21kts, 1–12.7mm MG, 12 crew). *C 25* (ex-*Arraid*) and *C 26* (ex-*Tariq*) transferred 16.1.74.
  Two ex-US 'Swift' class PCF type patrol boats (22.5t full load, 25kts, 1–81mm mortar, 4–12.7mm MG, 6–8 crew). *C 23* (ex-US *C 6823*), *C 24* (ex-US *C 6824*) built by Sewart Seacraft 1967, bought or donated Jan–Feb 1971.
  Three ex-Libyan *Farwa* class large patrol craft transferred 1978. *C 30* (ex-*Farwa*) sank 1981. *C 28* (ex-*Ar Rakib*) and *C 29* (ex-*Akrama*) extant 1982.
  Two ex-Yugoslav Type 131 coastal patrol craft transferred 31.5.82. *Dom Mintoff* (ex-*Cer*/P 138), *President Tito* (ex-*Durmitor*/P 139).
  Two new construction custom launches launched 1979. *Aphrodite, Kiklan* built by Guy Couacher. To be fitted with 2 MG and Decca 110 radar.

Sweden

Sweden's Fleet dominated the Baltic in 1947 and for some years after while her war-ravaged neighbours recovered. New ships and vessels, from heavily armed, very fast cruisers to small high speed MTBs were built, delivered and commissioned. New classes of destroyers, submarines, torpedo-boats and minesweepers joined the Royal Swedish Navy. Uniquely, it acquired nuclear weapon proof bunkers carved out of cliffsides to shelter and hide submarines and ships up to destroyer size.

The Baltic was never a 'sea of peace', as declared by some Eastern bloc regimes. It was – and is still in 1982 – an area of concentrated military activity on the sea and in the air. In June 1952 Soviet Mig fighters shot down two Swedish military aircraft, one intelligence and one sea rescue aircraft. And today many incidents occur every year inside Swedish territorial waters; foreign aircraft and warships and Communist government ships are spotted; Soviet submarines are hunted out of Swedish waters. No fewer than 40 such incidents took place in 1982. The Royal Swedish Navy was forced to depth charge these unwanted visitors – and even to set off ground mines – but all escaped.

From 1958 the five year defence plans changed to the disadvantage of the Navy – and later also of the Army and the Air Force. The idea of a 'light navy', no longer including coastal battleships or cruisers as backbones of the three task forces, was followed by a theory of light task forces of only one or two destroyers with one or two squadrons of large torpedo boats and, of course, submarines, coast defence flotillas of small MTBs, minesweepers etc. However, this 'lighter' navy could not be maintained. The last cruiser, *Göta Lejon*, was sold to Chile in 1971. Two missile destroyers and one ocean minelayer were cancelled. Destroyers were reclassified as frigates after or without being equipped with modern ASW weapons. The submarine force fell by half between 1975 and 1982.

At the beginning of the 1980s Sweden had only two destroyers – the non-Soviet world's first with surface-to-surface missiles – in the active fleet. But the light vessel navy has grown: a lot of large torpedo-boats, being rearmed with a new Saab-constructed anti-ship missile, 'RBS 15'; a number of smaller missile boats; a dozen submarines; three big minelayers; a growing fleet of small patrol boats and some 20 minesweepers. Work started in 1982 on a new series of missile vessels, an improved Spica type, a new class of attack submarines of the A 17 type and a modern type of minehunter and sweeper. Personnel fall into three categories, 3700 regulars, 7000 conscripts doing 7½–15 months service and 3500 reserves. Another 8000 conscripts receive annual naval training. These figures include a small helicopter-equipped naval air arm and the organic Coastal Artillery of 12 mobile and 45 static batteries (guns and missiles), six amphibious brigades, as well as small craft protecting the four main naval bases of Stockholm, Karlskrona, Göteborg and Härnösand.

The Swedish Navy of 1982 is a very 'light' navy and in the mid-1980s the last destroyers will be stricken. From a fairly strong, well proportioned navy of 1947 it has been reduced to a small navy while its larger neighbour, the Soviet Union, also in the Baltic, has built up an enormous offensive navy with large amphibious forces, supplemented by the satellite fleets of Poland and East Germany.

Ehrensköld as a frigate 1953　　　　　　　　Royal Swedish Navy

FLEET STRENGTH 1947

COASTAL BATTLESHIPS

Name	Launched	Disp (std)	Fate
Aran class			
ARAN	14.8.01	3800t	Stricken 13.6.47, BU 1955
TAPPERHETEN	7.11.01	3800t	Stricken 13.6.47, BU 1952
MANLIGHETEN	1.12.03	3850t	Stricken 24.2.50, pontoon pier at Gullmarsbasen naval base
Oscar II class			
OSCAR II	6.6.05	4320t	Stricken 24.2.50, school hulk, BU 1974
Sverige class			
SVERIGE	3.5.15	7850t	Stricken 30.1.53, BU 1958
DROTTNING VICTORIA	15.9.17	7920t	Stricken 1.4.57, BU 1959
GUSTAF V	31.1.18	7980t	Stricken 1.4.57, school hulk, BU 1970

CRUISERS

Name	Launched	Disp (std)	Fate
FYLGIA	20.12.05	4400t	Stricken 30.1.53, BU 1957
GOTLAND	14.9.33	4775t	Stricken 1.7.60, BU 1962
Tre Kronor class			
TRE KRONOR	16.12.44	8200t	Stricken 1.1.64, BU 1968
GOTA LEJON	17.11.45	8200t	Sold to Chile 18.9.71

Uppland 1955

DESTROYERS

Name	Launched	Disp (std)	Fate
Sigurd class (stricken 13.6.47)			
SIGURD	19.9.08	460t	Sold 1951, BU
RAGNAR	30.5.08	460t	Sold 1951, BU
VIDAR	9.6.09	460t	Sunk as target 1961
Hugin class (stricken 13.6.47)			
HUGIN	10.12.10	460t	BU 1949
Wrangel class (stricken 13.6.47)			
WRANGEL	25.9.17	587t	Research and target ship, BU 1960
WACHTMEISTER	19.12.17	587t	BU 1950
Ehrensköld class (rebuilt as frigates 1951, stricken 1.4.63)			
EHRENSKOLD	25.9.26	1050t	BU 1964
NORDENSKJOLD	19.6.26	1050t	BU 1964
Psilander class (stricken 13.6.47)			
PSILANDER (ex-Italian *Giovanni Nicotera*)	24.6.26	1250t	BU 1949
PUKE (ex-Italian *Bettino Ricasoli*)	29.1.26	1250t	BU 1949
Klas Horn class			
KLAS HORN	13.6.31	1020t	Stricken 15.8.58, school hulk, BU 1968
Romulus class (rebuilt as frigates 1953, stricken 15.8.58)			
ROMULUS (ex-Italian *Spica*)	11.3.34	870t	BU 1959
REMUS (ex-Italian *Astore*)	22.4.34	870t	BU 1959

EUROPE (NEUTRAL)

Name	Launched	Disp (std)	Fate
Göteborg class (rebuilt* 1961-63, or rerated† as frigates 1961)			
GÖTEBORG	14.10.35	1040t	Stricken 5.8.58, sunk as target 14.8.62
STOCKHOLM†	24.3.36	1040t	Stricken 1.1.64, BU 1965
MALMO*	22.9.38	1200t	Stricken 1.1.67, BU 1970
KARLSKRONA*	16.6.39	1200t	Stricken 1.7.74, BU 1979
NORRKOPING	5.9.40	1200t	Stricken 1.2.65, BU
GAVLE†	25.9.40	1200t	Stricken 6.12.68, from 1969 generator at Simpevarp nuclear power stn
Mode class (rebuilt as frigates 1954–55)			
MODE	11.4.42	750t	Stricken 1.7.70, school hulk, BU 1978
MAGNE	25.4.42	750t	Stricken 1.1.66, BU 1973
MJOLNER	9.4.42	750t	Stricken 1.4.66, sold 1969, civil hulk
MUNIN	27.5.42	750t	Stricken 6.12.68, BU 1970
Visby class			
VISBY	16.10.42	1150t	Rebuilt to frigate 1966, stricken 1.7.82
SUNDSVALL	20.10.42	1150t	Rebuilt to frigate 1968, stricken 1.7.82
HALSINGBORG	23.3.43	1150t	Rated frigate 1.1.65, stricken 1.7.78, BU 1979
KALMAR	20.7.43	1150t	Rated frigate 1.1.65, stricken 1.7.78, air force target
Oland class (rated frigates 1975)			
OLAND	15.12.45	2000t	Stricken 1.7.78
UPPLAND	15.11.46	2000t	Stricken 1.7.78, BU 1983

Karlskrona as a frigate 1965   *Royal Swedish Navy*

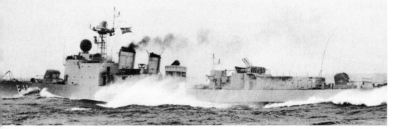

Visborg as a frigate 1966   *Royal Swedish Navy*

Mjölner as a frigate 1960   *Royal Swedish Navy*

Sjölejonet as reconstructed Oct 1952   *Royal Swedish Navy*

Abborren as reconstructed 1970   *Royal Swedish Navy*

SUBMARINES

Name	Launched	Disp (std)	Fate
Draken class			
DRAKEN	20.10.26	667t	Stricken 28.10.48, BU 1951
GRIPEN	21.8.28	667t	Stricken 13.6.47, BU 1957
Delfinen class (stricken 24.2.53)			
DELFINEN	20.12.34	540t	BU 1957
NORDKAPAREN	9.2.35	540t	BU 1958
SPRINGAREN	27.4.35	540t	BU 1956
Sjolejonet class			
SJOLEJONET	25.7.36	580t	Stricken 15.5.59, BU 1962
SJOBJORNEN	15.1.38	580t	Stricken 1.11.64, BU 1967
SJOHUNDEN	26.11.38	580t	Stricken 1.7.60, BU 1962
SVARDFISKEN	18.5.40	580t	Stricken 15.5.59, BU 1961
TUMLAREN	8.9.40	580t	Stricken 1.1.64, BU 1967
DYKAREN	17.12.40	580t	Stricken 1.12.59, BU 1962
SJOHASTEN	19.10.40	580t	Stricken 1.4.63, BU 1963
SJOORMEN	5.4.41	580t	Stricken 1.1.64, BU 1965
SJOBORREN	14.6.41	580t	Stricken 15.6.59, BU 1961
Neptun class (stricken 1.4.66)			
NEPTUN	17.11.42	550t	BU 1971
NAJAD	26.9.42	550t	BU 1971
NACKEN	26.9.42	550t	BU 1971
U 1 class			
U 1	14.6.41	367t	Stricken 1.7.60, experiment boat, BU 1964
U 2	16.5.42	367t	Stricken 1.12.1961, BU 1965
U 3	11.6.42	367t	Stricken 1.11.64, from 1965 museum boat at Malmö
U 4	5.6.43	367t	Stricken 1.7.70, BU
U 5	8.7.43	367t	Stricken 1.7.76, BU 1977
U 6	18.8.43	367t	Stricken 1.7.74, BU 1976
U 7	25.11.43	367t	Stricken 1.7.73, BU 1975
U 8	25.4.44	367t	Stricken 1.7.76, BU 1977
U 9	23.5.44	367t	Stricken 1.7.76, BU 1977

U 1 class
U 4–U 9 rebuilt 1963–64 as streamlined hunter killer boats of 388t with single hull and snorkel. Renamed *Forellen, Abborren, Siken, Gäddan, Laxen* and *Makrillen* respectively.

AMPHIBIOUS WARFARE VESSELS

Ane class landing craft (135t launched 1943–45)
Ane (J 324), *Balder* (J 325), *Loke* (J 326), and *Ring* (J 327). Extant 1982.

MINELAYERS

Name	Launched	Disp (std)	Fate
CLAS FLEMING	14.12.12	1735t	Stricken 1.1.59, BU 1961
ALVSNABBEN	19.1.43	4250t	Stricken 1.7.82, BU

Coastal minelayers: *Mul 3*, 99t, stricken 1956; *Mul 5*, 108t, stricken 1952; *Mul 6*, 108t, stricken 1951; *Mul 7*, 109t, stricken 1953; *Mul 8*, 109t, stricken 1953; *Mul 9*, 120t, stricken 1957; *Mul 10*, 166t, stricken 1970; *Mul 11*, 200t, launched 1946.

MOTOR TORPEDO-BOATS

T 11–14 (ex-Italian *MAS 506, 508, 511, 524*), launched 1937–38, purchased 1940, 17t. *T 11* stricken 28.6.46, target, sunk, salvaged, private motor yacht; *T 12* stricken 1.4.49, sold; *T 13* stricken 28.6.46, sold; *T 14* stricken 28.6.46, experiment boat, burned and sunk 1948.
T 3 and *T 4* Vosper boats, launched 1939, stricken 1.4.49, sunk as targets 1963; *T 4* salvaged, private motor yacht.
T 15–18, built at Kockums, launched 1941, 22.5t all stricken 1.10.56.
T 21–31, built at Kockums, launched 1942, 27t *T 21–24* stricken 1.1.59, *T 25, 26, 27* and *30* stricken 10.10.57, *T 28, 29* and *31* stricken 15.5.59.

MINESWEEPERS

Styrbjörn, Starkodder (ex-Norwegian whalers *Klo, Graham*) launched 1923 and 1925, 350t and 357t, stricken 1.12.59; *Styrbjörn* sold to tug company; *Starkodder* BU 1961.
Arholma, Landsort, launched 1937, 367t. *Arholma* stricken 1.4.60, target, sunk; *Landsort* stricken 1.1.64, BU 1965.
   Bremön class: *Bredskär, Bremön, Grönskär, Holmön, Koster, Kullen, Ramskär, Sandön, Ulvön, Ven, Vinga, Örskär*, launched 1940–41, 460t, stricken 1964–68. *Bredskär, Holmön, Sandön, Ven, Vinga* and *Örskär* targets, all scrapped except *Bremön*, school hulk and museum ship in Karlskrona.
M 1, M 2, launched 1937, 61t, stricken 1952 and 1953 respectively, both to the navigation administration, later BU.

M 3–M 14, launched 1940–41, 60t, stricken 1955–60. *M 3, 4, 5, 6, 9* and *10* surveying vessels, later BU, the last one in 1971. *M 7* and *M 8* training vessels, sold 1968 to private owners. *M 11, 12* and *14* transferred to Central Customs Authority. *M 13* transferred to Royal Science Academy as research vessel *Sagitta*.
M 15–26, launched 1941, 70t. *M 15, 16* and *21–26* from 1976 clearance diving tenders. *M 17* and *18* from 1961 tenders *Lommen* and *Spoven*. *M 19* stricken 1965 and transferred as tender to Central Torpedo Workshop. *M 20* rebuilt 1969 as mine research vessel *Skuld*.

PATROL BOATS

V 27, 28, 30 and *35*, ex-first class torpedo-boats, launched 1898–1903, 102–116t, all stricken 13.6.47. BU.
V 39 Iris, V 40 Thetis, V 41 Spica, V 42 Astrea, V 43 Antares, V 45 Altair, V 47 Polaris and *V 48 Perseus*, ex-first class torpedo-boats, *Plejad* type, launched 1908–10, 115–124t, all stricken 13.6.47, *Astrea* sunk as target, remaining BU.
V 5, 8, 11, 12, 14 and *15*, ex-second class torpedo-boats, launched 1906–09, 60t, stricken 1953, 1954, 1954, 1947, 1954 and 1947 respectively, successively BU.
V 19, launched 1914, 67t, stricken 1947, BU.
V 47 Sökaren (ex-*V 16*), *V 48 Sveparen* (ex-*V 17*, later A 253), *V 49 Sprängaren* (ex-*V 18*, later A 254), launched 1917–18, 226t. *Sökaren* sunk 1953. *Sveparen* stricken 1964, sold 1967. *Sprängaren* stricken 1961, civil harbour tug.
J 71 Kanon, J 72 Krut, ex-Norwegian whalers, launched 1924 and 1923 respectively, 300t, stricken 1958, BU.
J 21 Granat, J 22 Harpun, ex-Norwegian whalers, launched 1925, 440t, stricken 1963 and 1965 respectively, sold.
V 71 Asköfjärd, V 72 Baggensfjärd, V 73 Nämdöfjärd, launched 1931–32, 25t, stricken 1954.
V 74 Kanholmsfjärd, V 75 Lidöfjärd, V 76 Edöfjärd, launched 1933, 28t, stricken 1954.
V 41 (ex-*V 21*) *Jägaren, V 42* (ex-*V 22*) *Kaparen, V 43* (ex-*V 23*) *Snapphanen, V 44* (ex-*V 24*) *Väktaren*, launched 1932–34, 310t. *Snapphanen* sold 1959, rebuilt, sold to Guatemala as *José Francisco Barrundia*, remaining three stricken 1.1.59, later BU.
SVK 1–5, launched 1944, 19t. *SVK 2, 4* and *5* stricken 1980.
V 51–56, launched 1944–45, 145t. *V 51, 52, 53* and *56* stricken 16.11.66, *V 54* and *55* stricken 17.6.65.

ICEBREAKERS

Atle (ex-*Statsisbrytaren*), launched 1925, 1750t, stricken 23.9.66, sold 1967.
Ymer, launched 1932, 3465t, stricken 15.2.76.

MAJOR SURFACE SHIPS

Halland 1973

Halland and *Småland* voted 19.11.48. First non-Soviet destroyers with anti-ship missiles (1967), first Rb 315, then Rb 08 and later Rb 20. *Halland* modernised 1962 and 1969, *Småland* 1964 and 1967. Bofors 120mm guns fully automatic (40rpm) and also AA. *Lappland* and *Värmland* voted 1955. PEAB 9LV 200 Mk 2 fire control radar replaced original LW-03 air search and M 45 fire control sets. Missile magazine below aft superstructure with launcher above the aft triple TT. Two sisters built for Colombia.

HALLAND class *destroyers*

Displacement:	2630t standard; 3400t full load
Dimensions:	397ft 2in oa, 381ft wl × 41ft 4in × 18ft
	121.0m, 116.0m × 12.6m × 4.5m
Machinery:	2-shaft de Laval geared turbines, 2 Penhöet 40 atö boilers, 58,000shp = 35kts. Oil 524t. Range 3000nm/445nm at 20kts/35kts
Armament:	1 Saab Rb08A SSM (Mk 20 launcher), 4–120mm/50 (2×2), 2–57mm/60 AA (1×2), 6–40mm/70 AA (6×1), 8–533mm TT (1×5 + 1×3), 2–375mm ASW RL (2×4), mines, 6–103mm RFL on 120mm turret
Sensors:	Radar Scanter 009, Thomson-CSF Saturn, HSA M22; sonars search and attack sets
Complement:	290

No	Name	Builder	Laid down	Launched	Comp	Fate
J 18	HALLAND	Götaverken, Göteborg	1951	16.7.52	8.6.55	Extant 1982
J 19	SMALAND	Eriksberg, Göteborg	1951	23.10.52	12.1.56	Extant 1982
	LAPPLAND					Cancelled 1958
	VARMLAND					Cancelled 1958

Halland on trials 1955   *Author's Collection*

Ostergötland c1960   Royal Swedish Navy

Halsingland 1975

Voted 1953. Modernised: *Ostergöt-land* 1963 and 1971, *Södermanland* 1962 and 1967, *Gästrikland* 1965, *Hälsingland* 1968. From 1963 3–40mm were replaced by 1 Seacat SAM (1×4), known in Swedish service as Rb 07. Pennant numbers (J for *Jagare*, destroyer) painted on bows from 1966.

OSTERGOTLAND class *destroyers*

Displacement:	2150t standard; 2600t full load
Dimensions:	351ft wl, 367ft 6in oa × 36ft 10in × 12ft
	107.0m, 112.0m × 11.2m × 3.7m
Machinery:	2-shaft de Laval geared turbines, 2 Babcock & Wilcox 40 atö boilers, 47,000shp = 35kts. Oil 330t. Range 3000nm at 20kts
Armament:	4–120mm/50 (2×2), 7–40mm 6–533mm TT (1×6), 1 Squid ASW Mk 3 mortar, 60 mines
Sensors:	Radar Thomson-CSF Saturn, HSA M44 and M45; sonars search and attack sets
Complement:	244

No	Name	Builder	Laid down	Launched	Comp	Fate
J 20	OSTERGOTLAND	Götaverken, Göteborg	1.9.55	8.5.56	3.3.58	Stricken 1.7.82
J 21	SODERMANLAND	Eriksberg, Göteborg	1.6.55	28.5.56	27.7.58	Stricken 1.7.82
J 22	GASTRIKLAND	Götaverken, Göteborg	1.10.55	6.6.56	14.1.59	Stricken 1.7.82
J 23	HALSINGLAND	Eriksberg and Kockums, Malmö	1.10.55	14.1.57	17.6.59	Stricken 1.7.83

SUBMARINES

Ex-RN midget submarine sold to Sweden, used as training platform for attack divers. Stricken 27.1.70, used as experimental boat. Presented to Imperial War Museum, London, 1975.

First three voted 1949; last three voted 1952. Swedish design derived from German *U 3503*, a type XXI submarine sunk by own crew outside Göteborg 8.5.45, and salvaged by the Swedish Navy. Three-letter markings (Haj, Säl, Val, Bäv, Iln and Utn) on sail instead of pennant numbers.

Ex-British STICKLEBACK class *midget submarine*

Name	Builder	Acquired	Fate
SPIGGEN (ex-X 51 *Stickleback*)	Vickers-Armstrong, Barrow	15.7.58	Museum boat 1975

HAJEN class *submarines*

Displacement:	720t standard; 785t max; *c*900t submerged
Dimensions:	211ft 7in wl, 216ft 6in oa × 16ft 8in × 16ft 5in
	64.5m, 66.0m × 5.1m × 5.0m
Machinery:	2 shafts, 2 Pielstick diesels, 2 ASEA electric motors, 1660bhp/1700kW = 16/20kts
Armament:	4–533mm TT (bow, 8 torpedoes), mines
Complement:	44

Name	Builder	Laid down	Launched	Comp	Fate
HAJEN	Kockums	1953	11.12.54	28.2.57	Stricken 1.7.80
SALEN	Kockums	1953	3.10.55	8.4.57	Stricken 1.7.80
VALEN	Karlskrona NYd	1953	21.4.55	4.3.57	Stricken 1.7.80
BAVERN	Kockums	1955	3.2.58	29.5.59	Stricken 1.7.80
ILLERN	Karlskrona NYd and Kockums	1955	14.11.57	31.8.59	Stricken 1.7.80
UTTERN	Kockums	1955	14.11.58	15.3.60	Stricken 1.7.80

Hajen c1970   *Author's Collection*

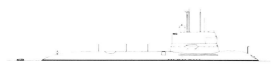

Draken as completed

First three voted 1956, last three voted 1957. *Draken* and *Gripen* modernised 1971 but not rebuilt later. *Vargen* modernised 1971, last three 1970. These four extensively modernised from 1981 and to remain until the A 17 type submarines are commissioned. The class is an improved *Hajen* type with only one, larger 5-blade propeller, giving reduced noise and higher speed. Pennant letters Dra, Gri Vgn, Del, Nor, Spr.

DRAKEN class *submarines*

Displacement: 770t standard; 835t max; c950t submerged
Dimensions: 211ft 6in wl, 226ft 6in oa × 16ft 9in × 17ft 5in
67.5m, 69.3m × 5.1m × 5.3m
Machinery: 1 shaft, 2 Pielstick type diesels, 2 ASEA electric motors, 1600bhp/1680kW = 17/22kts
Armament: 4–533mm TT (12 torpedoes), mines
Complement: 36

Name	Builder	Laid down	Launched	Comp	Fate
DRAKEN	Kockums	1957	1.4.60	4.4.62	Stricken 1.7.82
GRIPEN	Karlskrona NYd	1958	31.5.60	28.4.62	Stricken 1.7.82
VARGEN	Kockums	1958	20.5.60	15.11.61	Extant 1982
DELFINEN	Karlskrona NYd	1958	7.3.61	7.6.62	Extant 1982
NORDKAPAREN	Kockums	1959	8.3.61	4.4.62	Extant 1982
SPRINGAREN	Kockums	1960	31.8.61	7.11.62	Extant 1982

Sjöormen as completed
NB 1/750 scale

Voted 1961; two decks, bow planes on the sail and X-configured stern planes. Diving depth c150m. 'Teardrop' hull shape, 5-blade propeller. Attack submarines, A 11 type. Pennant letters Sor, Sle, Sbj Shu, and Shä.

SJOORMEN class *submarines*

Displacement: 1125t standard; 1400t submerged
Dimensions: 164ft wl, 165ft 7in oa × 20ft × 19ft
50.0m, 50.5m × 6.1m × 5.1m
Machinery: 1 shaft, 2 Pielstick 12 PA-4 diesels, 1 ASEA electric motor, 2200bhp/1270kW = 15/20kts. Endurance 21 days
Armament: 4–533mm TT (bow), 2–400mm TT (for Type 42 ASW torpedoes or mines)
Complement: 23

Name	Builder	Laid down	Launched	Comp	Fate
SJOORMEN	Kockums	1965	25.1.67	31.7.68	Extant 1982
SJOLEJONET	Kockums	1965	29.6.67	16.12.68	Extant 1982
SJOBJORNEN	Karlskrona NYd	1966	9.1.68	28.2.69	Extant 1982
SJOHUNDEN	Kockums	1966	21.3.68	25.6.69	Extant 1982
SJOHASTEN	Karlskrona NYd	1966	6.8.68	15.9.69	Extant 1982

Sjöormen 1975   *Royal Swedish Navy*

Näcken as completed
NB 1/750 scale

Voted 1972, contracted 22.3.73. They have a single Kollmorgen periscope, two decks, a diving depth c150m and 'tear-drop' hull shape. Data Saab NEDPS system uses two Censor 932 computers to give engine and tactical information. Attack submarines, A 14 type, with pennant letters Näk, Nep and Naj.

NACKEN class *submarines*

Displacement: 980t standard; 1150t submerged
Dimensions: 144ft 4in wl, 162ft 5in oa × 18ft 8in × 18ft
44.0m, 49.5m × 5.7m × 5.5m
Machinery: 1 shaft, MTU 16V 652 diesel, Jeumont-Schneider electric motor, 2100bhp/1150kW = 20/25kts
Armament: 6–533mm TT, 2–400mm ASW TT (all bow, 12 torpedoes)
Sensors: Large bow sonar
Complement: 18

Name	Builder	Laid down	Launched	Comp	Fate
NACKEN	Kockums and Karlskrona NYd	1976	17.4.78	25.4.80	Extant 1982
NEPTUN	Kockums and Karlskrona NYd	1976	6.12.78	5.12.80	Extant 1982
NAJAD	Kockums and Karlskrona NYd	1976	13.8.79	26.6.81	Extant 1982

EUROPE (NEUTRAL)

Näcken on trials   Author's Collection

URF Sept 1981   Author's Collection

Four ordered 1981 from Kockums (midships and assembly) and Karlskrona NYd (bow and stern) to be launched 1985–87. Improved *Näcken* type but more sophisticated electronics, data systems and other teletecnics. Attack submarines, A 17 type; names to be *Västergötland*, *Hälsingland*, *Södermanland* and *Östergötland*.

URF = 'Ubåtsräddningsfarkost' (submarine rescue vessel). Launched 24.8.78 at Kockums, commissioned 1978. Can be transported on trailer to launching place or be towed at 10kts. Television cameras and other equipment for finding submarines. Can take 26 men on board on each dive. Her HY 130 steel pressure hull can dive to 460m and has a collapse depth of 900m.

VASTERGOTLAND class *submarines*

Displacement:	950t standard; 1070t submerged
Dimensions:	159ft × 18ft 8in × 18ft
	48.5m × 5.7m × 5.5m
Machinery:	1 shaft, MTU diesels plus electric motors = 15/20kts
Armament:	3–533mm TT, 2–400mm ASW TT
Complement:	20

URF rescue *submarine*

Displacement:	52t standard
Dimensions:	44ft 3in × 14ft 9in × 9ft 6in
	13.5m × 4.5m × 2.9m
Armament:	None
Complement:	5

AMPHIBIOUS WARFARE VESSELS

GRIM class *landing craft*

Displacement:	327t standard
Dimensions:	124ft × 28ft 2in × 8ft 6in
	37.8m × 8.6m × 2.6m
Machinery:	2 shafts, 2 diesels, 800bhp = 12kts
Armament:	2–20mm

Name	Builder	Launched	Fate
BORE	Asiverken	1966	Extant 1982
GRIM	Kalmar varv	1961	Extant 1982
HEIMDAL	Asigeverken	1966	Extant 1982
SKAGUL	Hammarbyverken	1960	Extant 1982
SLEIPNER	Hammarbyverken	1959	Extant 1982

LCM type ships, all of car ferry design. *Bore* and *Heimdal* completed 1967, *Grim* 1961. *Skagul* and *Sleipner* completed 1960 (275t standard, 335t full load) slightly shorter and narrower with 640bhp diesels giving 10kts. Operated by the Coastal Artillery.

MINOR LANDING CRAFT

LCU type
The Coastal Artillery has 81 of this 31t type (nos *201–276* and *280–284*, launched 1957–77) and 12 of a 33t type (nos *401–412*). Five older 30t craft (*L 51–L 55*) built in 1968 are also extant in 1982.

LCA type
There are 54 craft (built 1956–73, nos *301–354*) of this 4t type, operated by the Coastal Artillery. All extant 1982. Fifteen older 10t craft (*L 1–L15*), launched 1949-50 were disposed of 1959-60.

SMALL SURFACE COMBATANTS

Ex-US 'HIGGINS' type *MTB*

Experimental boat *T 1*, launched 1945 at Annapolis Yacht Yard, USA, 50t standard, 72ft × 21ft 4in × 4ft (*22.0m × 6.5m × 1.2m*) wooden hull, 3 Packard petrol motors, 4050bhp = 40kts. 'Higgins' type bought 1950, burned 1957, sunk, salvaged, sold 1958.

T 32 1967
NB 1/750 scale

T 32 class *MTBs*

Displacement:	38.5t standard
Dimensions:	75ft 6in × 18ft 5in × 4ft 6in
	23.0m × 5.6m × 1.4m
Machinery:	3 shafts, 3 Isotta-Fraschini 184C petrol motors, 4500bhp = 45kts
Armament:	2–533mm TT, 1–40mm
Complement:	16

Class:
T 32–41.
Built 1951–52 with all-welded steel hulls at Kockums and Karlskrona N Yd, commissioned 1951–52. *T 32–37* stricken 1.7.72, *T 38–40* stricken 1.1.75. Hull of *T 41* used for building of patrol boat *Viken* (V 04) at Karlskrona 1966–67.

T 201 *experimental MTB*

Built at Fisksätra Varv, Saltsjöbaden, 1952; commissioned 1953; wooden hull, 17t. *16.3m × 3.8m × 1.5m*, 3 Isotta-Fraschini 184C petrol motors, 3 shafts 4500bhp = 44kts. Armament: 2–457mm TT, later changed to 2–533mm TT. Stricken 13.10.64. Target boat at missile experimental station at Karlsborg, Lake Vättern; sold 1980.

T 46 as completed
NB 1/750 scale

T 42 class *MTBs*

Displacement:	40t standard; 44.5t full load
Dimensions:	75ft 6in × 19ft 5in × 4ft
	23.0m × 5.9m × 1.4m
Machinery:	3 shafts, 3 Isotta-Fraschini 184C petrol motors, 4500bhp = 45kts
Armament:	2–533mm TT, 1–40mm
Complement:	16

Class:
T 42–T 56
Built 1955–57 at Kockums, hulls of *T 53, 54* and *55* at Karlskrona N Yd. Steel hulls of *T 42–44* used for building of patrol boats. *Skanör* (V 01), *Smyge* (V 02), *Arild* (V 03) at Karlskrona 1976–77. Hulls of *T 47, 48, 50* and *51* used for building of patrol boats V 05–V 08 (*Oregrund Slite*, *Sandhemn* and *Lysekil*), launched 1983 at Karlskronavarvet. Remaining 6 boats in reserve, but 4 earmarked to build V 09–V 12.

Astrea 1969
NB 1/750 scale

PLEJAD class *fast attack craft (torpedo)*

Displacement:	155t standard; 170t full load (*Perseus* 145t standard)
Dimensions:	148ft 3in wl, 157ft 6in oa × 19ft × 5ft 3in
	45.2m, 48.0m × 5.8m × 1.6m
Machinery:	3 shafts, MTU 20V 672 diesels (2 in *Perseus* and 1 Proteus gas turbine, 4500bhp + 6000shp), 9000bhp = 37.5kts. Range 600nm at 30kts
Armament:	6–533mm TT (4 in *Perseus*), 2–40mm, 4–103mm (4×1) and 12–57mm (1×12) RFL
Complement:	33

No	Name	Builder	Launched	Fate
T 101	PERSEUS	Karlskrona NYd	23.3.50	Stricken 1.1.67
T 102	PLEJAD	Lürssen-Karls-krona NYd	21.11.53	Stricken 1.7.77
T 103	POLARIS	Lürssen-Karls-krona NYd	18.1.54	Stricken 1.7.77
T 104	POLLUX	Lürssen-Karls-krona NYd	3.3.54	Stricken 1.7.77
T 105	REGULUS	Lürssen-Karls-krona NYd	15.4.54	Stricken 1.7.77
T 106	RIGEL	Lürssen-Karls-krona NYd	16.6.54	Stricken 1.7.77, sold 1978
T 107	ALDEBARAN	Lürssen-Karls-krona NYd	16.8.54	Stricken 1.7.81
T 108	ALTAIR	Lürssen-Karls-krona NYd	24.5.56	Stricken 1.7.77
T 109	ANTARES	Lürssen-Karls-krona NYd	14.8.56	Stricken 1.7.77
T 110	ARCTURUS	Lürssen-Karls-krona NYd	5.11.56	Stricken 1.7.81
T 111	ARGO	Lürssen-Karls-krona NYd	18.1.57	Stricken 1.7.77
T 112	ASTREA	Lürssen-Karls-krona NYd	15.3.57	Stricken 1.7.81

Perseus was a much altered prototype commissioned 1951 (145t standard). Frequently rebuilt for MTB experiment. First group of six commissioned 1954–55, rebuilt 1972, 1970, 1971, 1972, 1971 and 1965 respectively. Second group of five commissioned 1956–58, rebuilt 1965, 1964, 1964, 1964 and 1964 respectively. Could be fitted as minelayers if TT removed.

Nynäshamn, Västerås and *Norrtälje* 1977   *Royal Swedish Navy*

Arild, rebuilt from hull of *T 44,* on trials May 1977   *Author's Collection*

Perseus as completed   *Author's Collection*

Capella 1970
NB 1/750 scale

SPICA class *fast attack craft (torpedo)*

Displacement:	200t standard; 235t full load
Dimensions:	134ft 6in wl, 140ft 1in oa × 23ft 4in × 5ft 6in
	41.0m, 42.5m × 7.1m × 1.6m
Machinery:	3-shaft Bristol Proteus 1274 gas turbines (3 CP propellers), 12,750shp = 40kts
Armament:	6–533mm TT, 1–57mm/70, 4–103mm (4×1) and 6–57mm (1×6) RFL
Sensors:	Radar Scanter 009, HSA M22
Complement:	30

No	Name	Builder	Launched	Fate
T 121	SPICA	Götaverken	26.4.66	Extant 1982
T 122	SIRIUS	Götaverken	26.4.66	Extant 1982
T 123	CAPELLA	Götaverken	26.4.66	Extant 1982
T 124	CASTOR	Karlskrona NYd	25.10.65	Extant 1982
T 125	VEGA	Karlskrona NYd	12.3.66	Extant 1982
T 126	VIRGO	Karlskrona NYd	10.9.66	Extant 1982

Voted 1961, laid down 1964–65, commissioned 1966–68. Can be minelayers if TT removed.

Norrköping as completed
NB 1/750 scale

NORRKOPING ('SPICA II') class *fast attack craft (torpedo)*

Displacement:	220t standard; 255t full load
Dimensions:	137ft 9in wl, 143ft oa × 23ft 4in × 5ft 3in
	42.0m, 43.6m × 7.1m × 1.6m
Machinery:	3-shaft Rolls Royce Marine Proteus gas turbine (3 CP propellers), 12,750shp = 41kts
Armament:	6–533mm TT, 1–57mm/70
Sensors:	Radar Scanter 009, PEAB 9LV 200 Mk 1
Complement:	28

No	Name	Builder	Launched	Fate
T 131	NORRKOPING	Karlskrona	16.11.72	Extant 1982
T 132	NYNASHAMN	Karlskrona	24.4.73	Extant 1982
T 133	NORRTALJE	Karlskrona	18.9.73	Extant 1982
T 134	VARBERG	Karlskrona	2.2.74	Extant 1982
T 135	VASTERAS	Karlskrona	15.5.74	Extant 1982
T 136	VASTERVIK	Karlskrona	2.9.74	Extant 1982
T 137	UMEA	Karlskrona	15.1.75	Extant 1982
T 138	PITEA	Karlskrona	12.5.75	Extant 1982
T 139	LULEA	Karlskrona	19.8.75	Extant 1982
T 140	HALMSTAD	Karlskrona	17.10.75	Extant 1982
T 141	STROMSTAD	Karlskrona	26.4.76	Extant 1982
T 142	YSTAD	Karlskrona	3.9.76	Extant 1982

Laid down 1971–75. In service dates T 131 (11.5.73), T 132 (28.9.73), T 133 (1.8.74), T 134 (13.6.74), T 135 (25.10.74), T 136 (15.1.75), T 137 (15.5.75), T 138 (12.9.75), T 139 (28.11.75), T 140 (9.4.76), T 141 (24.9.76), T 142 (10.12.76). From 1982 all will be rebuilt and 4 of their TT exchanged for 8 Saab RBS 15 SSM (4×2). T 138 received SSM launchers in 1980. LM Ericson Giraffe GH band radar is to be added.

EUROPE (NEUTRAL)

HUGIN class *fast attack craft (missile)*

Displacement:	120t standard (*Jägaren* 115t); 150t full load (*Jägaren* 140t)
Dimensions:	118ft wl, 120ft oa × 20ft 8in × 5ft 7in (*Jägaren* 4ft 11in)
	36.0m, 36.4m × 6.2m × 2.0m (1.5m)
Machinery:	2 shafts, 2 MTU MB20V 672 TY90 diesels, 7200bhp = 35kts. Range 550nm at 35kts
Armament:	6 Penguin Mk 2 SSM (6×1), 1–57mm/70, 103mm RFL, 24 mines or 2 DC racks instead of missiles
Sensors:	Radar Scanter 009, PEAB 9LV200 Mk 2; sonar Simrad SQ 3D/SF; ECM Saab-Scania EWS-905
Complement:	18

No	Name	Builder	Launched	Fate
P 150	JAGAREN	Bergens Mekaniske Verksteder	8.6.72	Extant 1982
P 151	HUGIN	Bergens Mekaniske Verksteder	3.6.77	Extant 1982
P 152	MUNIN	Bergens Mekaniske Verksteder	5.10.77	Extant 1982
P 153	MAGNE	Bergens Mekaniske Verksteder	9.1.78	Extant 1982
P 154	MODE	Westermoen Hydrofoil, Mandal	8.8.78	Extant 1982
P 155	VALE	Westermoen Hydrofoil, Mandal	30.10.78	Extant 1982
P 156	VIDAR	Westamarin, Mandal	6.3.79	Extant 1982
P 157	MJOLNER	Westamarin, Mandal	12.6.79	Extant 1982
P 158	MYSING	Westamarin, Mandal	18.9.79	Extant 1982
P 159	KAPARARN	Bergens Mekaniske Verksteder	8.8.79	Extant 1982
P 160	VAKTAREN	Bergens Mekaniske Verksteder	12.11.79	Extant 1982
P 161	SNAPPHANEN	Bergens Mekaniske Verksteder	18.3.80	Extant 1982
P 162	SPEJAREN	Bergens Mekaniske Verksteder	13.5.80	Extant 1982
P 163	STYRBJORN	Bergens Mekaniske Verksteder	15.8.80	Extant 1982
P 164	STARKODDER	Bergens Mekaniske Verksteder	11.11.80	Extant 1982
P 165	TORDON	Bergens Mekaniske Verksteder	3.2.81	Extant 1982
P 166	TIRFING	Bergens Mekaniske Verksteder	14.9.81	Extant 1982

Built in Norwegian yards (order placed for P 151–P 160 on 15.5.75) for trade compensation reasons and similar to Norway's *Snögg* class FAC. *Jägaren* originally had the pennant number P 151 (till 1977) as prototype boat undergoing 3 years trials in Swedish waters. The missiles are a Swedish-Norwegian development of the original Penguin. The diesels are rebuilt and modernised diesels from Swedish *Plejad* class torpedo boats. The *Hugin* class boats are successors to the 'T 42' class MTBs as part of the coastal defence system. In service dates P 150 (24.11.72), P 151 and P 152 (3.7.78), P 153 (12.10.78), P 154 (12.1.79), P 155 (26.4.79), P 156 (10.8.79), P 157 (24.10.79), P 158 (14.2.80), P 159 (7.8.80), P 160 (19.9.80), P 161 (14.1.80), P 162 (2.3.80), P 163 (15.6.80), P 164 (24.8.81), P 165 (26.10.81), P 166 (21.1.82).

'Stockholm' class design
NB 1/750 scale

STOCKHOLM ('SPICA III') class *fast attack craft (missile)*

Displacement:	310t standard; 335t full load
Dimensions:	147ft 8 in wl, 157ft 5in oa × 24ft 7in × 7ft 10in
	45.0m, 48.0m × 7.5m × 2.4m
Machinery:	3-shaft CODOG: gas turbines, 15,000shp = 35kts; 2 Detroit Allison 501 diesels, 7200bhp = 20kts
Armament:	8 Rb 15 SSM (4×2), 1–57mm/70, 1–40mm 2–533mm TT
Sensors:	Radar Ericson Giraffe, PEAB 9LV 200 Mk 2; sonar VDS; ECM Saab-Scania EWS 905
Complement:	*c*25

Two ordered 25.6.81 from Karlskrona N Yd for 1984–85 delivery. The 40mm gun will be replaceable by a variable-depth sonar (VDS). The vessels will be prototypes for a new class of missile FAC, 'Robotbåt 90' (Missile boat 90). Launched in 1983; they were named *Stockholm* and *Malmö*.

Hugin 1978   *Royal Swedish Navy*

V 57 *patrol boat*

Displacement:	115t standard; 135t full load
Dimensions:	98ft wl, 106ft 7in oa × 17ft 4in × 6ft 10in
	29.9m, 32.0m × 5.3m × 2.3m
Machinery:	1 shaft, 1 Nohab diesel MG-8, 500bhp = 13.5kts
Armament:	1–20mm
Complement:	17

Built 1953, at Stockholm N Yd, commissioned 1954. Fitted for minelaying and attached to Coastal Artillery. Extant 1982.

BEVAKNINGSBAT 61 class *patrol boats*

Displacement:	28t full load
Dimensions:	69ft 2in × 15ft × 4ft 3in
	21.1m × 4.6m × 1.3m
Machinery:	3 shafts, 3 Volvo-Penta DSIR82 or Scania Vabis TIMD96B diesels, 535–705bhp = 18kts
Armament:	1–20mm
Sensors:	Radar navigation set
Complement:	8

Class:
Bevakningsbåt 61–77.
 Built at Bröderna Larsson, Varv & Verkstad, Kristinehamn (No *61–70*) in 1960–61 and Coastal Artillery Yard at Fårösund, Gotland (no *71–77*) in 1966–67. Extant 1982 with Coastal Artillery.

COASTAL PATROL BOATS
SVK 11 and *SVK 12* (ex-*Tv 228* and *226*), 12t, 2 Volvo-Penta diesels, 20kts, built 1956 and 1955 respectively. Acquired 1980 for the Volunteer Naval Corps (SVK = Sjövärnskåren).
 Muskö (ex-*Tv 316*), 9t, built 1965, acquired 1981; patrol boat for the Muskö naval base area.

MINE WARFARE VESSELS

Alvsborg as completed

ALVSBORG class *minelayers*

Displacement:	2500t standard; 2660t full load (2400t; 2540t *Visborg*)
Dimensions:	301ft 10in wl, 303ft 1in oa × 48ft × 13ft 2in
	92.0m, 94.4m × 14.7m × 4.0m
Machinery:	1 shaft (CP propeller), 2 Nohab-Polar 12cyl diesels, 4200bhp = 17kts
Armament:	3–40mm (3×1), 300 mines, 1 helicopter
Sensors:	Radar Scanter 009, Raytheon, HSA M22
Complement:	95

No	Name	Builder	Launched	Fate
M 02	ALVSBORG	Karlskrona N Yd	10.11.69	Extant 1982
M 03	VISBORG	Karlskrona N Yd	22.1.74	Extant 1982

Alvsborg ordered 1968 (after a predecessor of the same name was voted 1955 and cancelled 1958), laid down Nov 1968, commissioned 6.4.71. Also used as a submarine tender with accommodation for five crews (205 men). *Visborg* ordered 1972, laid down 16.10.73, commissioned 6.2.76. Also used as a command ship for C-in-C Baltic Fleet with accommodation for 155 staff members.

Visborg as completed   *Author's Collection*

Orust 1971   *Royal Swedish Navy*

Carlskrona on trials Dec 1981   *Author's Collection*

Carlskrona design

CARLSKRONA minelayer

Displacement:	3130t standard; 3300t full load
Dimensions:	321ft 6in wl, 346ft 8in oa × 49ft 10in × 13ft 1in
	98.0m, 105.7m × 15.2m × 4.0m
Machinery:	2 shafts (CP propellers), 4 Nohab-Polar F212-D825 12cyl diesels, 10,560bhp = 20kts
Armament:	2–57mm (2×1), 2–40mm (2×1), 105 mines, 1 helicopter
Sensors:	Radar Scanter 009, Raytheon, Thomson-CSF Saturn, 2 PEAB 9LV200 Mk 2; sonar Simrad SQ3D/SF
Complement:	186 (as training ship)

No	Name	Builder	Launched	Fate
M 04	CARLSKRONA	Karlskrona N Yd	28.5.80	Extant 1982

Ordered 25.11.77, laid down 8.2.79, commissioned 19.3.82. Reinforced hull and 14 watertight compartments. Also cadet training ship for the annual cruise when complement includes 136 cadets and conscripts. Also has a bow thruster. Two combat information centres on board for *Hugin* and 'Spica II' class FAC. A helicopter deck but no hangar.

Mul 19 1970
NB 1/750 scale

COASTAL MINELAYERS
Coastal minelayers (*Mul* = *minutläggare*): *Mul 12–19*, launched 1952–56, 245t standard, 102ft 4in oa × 24ft 4in × 10ft 2in, *31.2m × 7.4m × 3.1m*, 2 diesels, 460bhp = 10.5kts, 1–40mm, mines, 18 crew. All extant 1982. *Furusund* (*Mul 20*) laid down 1982, 200t standard, 95ft 1in × 26ft 10in × 5ft 7in, *29.0m × 8.2m × 1.7m*, 11kts, 1–20mm, 22t of mines, 10 crew. *Mul 21–23* will be built in the 1980s.

ORUST class inshore minesweepers

Displacement:	95t standard; 110t full load
Dimensions:	62ft 4in × 19ft 8in × 4ft 6in
	21.0m × 6.0m × 1.5m
Machinery:	1 shaft, 1 diesel, 210bhp = 9kts
Armament:	2–25mm
Complement:	10

Class:
Orust (M 41), *Tjorn* (M 42)
  Launched 1948, wooden hulls. Stricken 1.7.77.

Tjurkö 1969
NB 1/750 scale

HANO class coastal minesweepers

Displacement:	280t standard; 295t full load
Dimensions:	131ft 2in × 23ft × 8ft
	42.0m × 7.0m × 2.4m
Machinery:	2 shafts, 2 Nohab-Polar MG-7 diesels, 910bhp = 14.5kts
Armament:	2–40mm (2×1), (*Utö* 1–40mm), 6–57mm RFL
Complement:	25

Class:
Hanö (M 51), *Tärnö* (M 52), *Tjurkö* (M 53), *Sturkö* (M 54), *Ornö* (M 55), *Utö* (M 56)
  Launched 1952–53, commissioned 1953. Built at Karlskrona N Yd; *Hanö*, *Tärnö* and *Tjurkö* completed at Kalmar Varv. Steel hulls. All reclassified 1.7.79 as patrol boats ('vedettbåtar') with same numbers but M changed to V. *Hanö* and *Utö* stricken 1.7.82.

Skaftö 1966
NB 1/750 scale

ARKO class coastal minesweepers

Displacement:	272t standard; 300t full load
Dimensions:	131ft pp, 144ft 6in oa × 23ft × 8ft
	42.0m, 44.4m × 7.5m × 2.5m
Machinery:	2 shafts, 2 Mercedes-Benz diesels, 1600bhp = 14.5kts
Armament:	1–40mm, 6–57mm RFL
Complement:	25

Class (no, in service):
Arkö (M 57, 1958), *Spårö* (M 58, 1958), *Karlsö* (M 59, 1958), *Iggö* (M 60, 1961), *Styrsö* (M 61, 1962), *Skaftö* (M 62, 1962), *Aspö* (M 63, 1962), *Hasslö* (M 64, 1962), *Vinö* (M 65, 1963), *Vållö* (M 66, 1963), *Nämdö* (M 67, 1964), *Blidö* (M 68, 1964)
  M 57–M 59 were built at Oskarshamns Varv, M60–M62 at Kalmar Varv, M 63–M 65 at Karlskrona N Yd and M 66–68 at Helsingborgs Varv. M 57 to M 60 have one strake on the wooden hull, later units two. M 66 stricken 1.7.80, M 65 1.7.81.

EUROPE (NEUTRAL)

HISINGEN class *inshore minesweepers*

Displacement:	130t standard; 140t full load
Dimensions:	62ft 4in wl, 72ft oa × 21ft 4in × 7ft 10in
	19.0m, 22.0m × 6.4m × 2.4m
Machinery:	1 shaft (CP propeller), 1 Skandia F35T-4MA diesel, 400bhp = 9kts (*Hisingen* 2 Scania Vabis DSI 10R80 diesels, 370bhp)
Armament:	1–40mm
Complement:	10

Class:

Hisingen (M 43), *Blackan* (M 44), *Dämman* (M 45), *Galten* (M 46), *Gillöga* (M 47), *Rödlöga* (M 48), *Svartlöga* (M 49)

First four launched at different small yards 1960–61, commissioned 1960–61. Last three launched with higher bridges and bluffer bows at Karlskrona N Yd 1964, commissioned 1964. Wooden hulls. This class is a trawler type; used to train conscripts in the mobilisation of similar civil boats.

GASSTEN class *inshore minesweepers*

Displacement:	120t standard; 135t full load
Dimensions:	79ft × 21ft 4in × 11ft 6in
	(*Viksten* 83ft, *25.3m* long)
	24.0m × 6.5m × 3.7m
Machinery:	1 shaft (CP propeller), 2 Scania Vabis DSI 11R92 diesels, 460bhp = 9kts
Armament:	1–40mm
Complement:	10

Class:

Gåssten (M 31), *Norsten* (M 32), *Viksten* (M 33)

Wooden hull class similar to *Hisingen* boats. M 31 launched Knippla SY 17.11.72 and commissioned 16.11.73. M 32 launched Hällevikstrands Varv 24.4.73 and commissioned 12.10.73. M 33 launched Karlskrona 18.4.74 and commissioned 20.6.74 as GRP forerunner for new minehunters.

Gillöga 1965   *Royal Swedish Navy*

M 80 type design NB 1/750 scale

LANDSORT class *inshore minehunters*

Displacement:	270t standard; 340t full load
Dimensions:	155ft 10in oa × 31ft 6in × 7ft 4in
	47.5m × 9.6m × 2.2m
Machinery:	2 shafts, 4 TAMD 120B diesels, 1260bhp = 14kts
Armament:	1–40mm
Sensors:	Radar 9MJ 400; sonar Thomson-CSF TSM-2060
Complement:	24

Two ordered 25.2.81 at Karlskronavarvet for 1984 delivery. Combined minehunters and sweepers with the same type sandwich glass fibre hull as *Viksten*. Up to 12 may be built. They will be able to lay mines and operate 15t unmanned catamaran magnetic/acoustic sweepers. Launched in 1982 they were named *Landsort* and *Arholma*. Originally known as M 80 type.

Six 18m, 15t minehunting catamarans *Sam 01–Sam 06* were built at Karlskronavarvet 1981–83. They are self-propelled acoustic/magnetic minesweepers. 9 more are planned.

MISCELLANEOUS

THULE *icebreaker*

Displacement:	2280t standard; 2820t full load
Dimensions:	187ft wl, 204ft 4in oa × 52ft 10in × 20ft 4in
	57.0m, 62.0m × 16.1m × 6.2m
Machinery:	3 shafts (1 fwd), 3 Nohab K 58 M diesels, 5040bhp = 14kts
Armament:	(2–40mm), 1 helicopter
Complement:	43

Specially designed for the Sound and other narrow waters. Launched 12.10.51, commissioned 1953. Built at Karlskrona N Yd. Also used as a depot ship for minesweepers. Armament wartime only.

ODEN *icebreaker*

Displacement:	4950t standard; 5220t full load
Dimensions:	272ft 10in × 63ft 8in × 23ft 8in
	83.2m × 19.4m × 6.6m
Machinery:	4 shafts (2 fwd), 6 Nohab SN 19 diesels, 10,200bhp = 16kts. Oil 740t
Armament:	(4–40mm), 1 helicopter
Complement:	75

Launched 16.10.56 by Wärtsilä, Helsinki and similar to Finnish *Voima*. In service since 19.11.57.

TOR class *icebreakers*

Displacement:	4980t standard; 5290t full load
Dimensions:	277ft 2in × 69ft 6in × 22ft 8in
	86.5m × 21.2m × 6.9m
Machinery:	4 shafts (2 fwd), 4 Wärtsilä-Sulzer 8H51 (*Njord* 9MH51) diesels, 13,820shp = 18kts
Armament:	(4–40mm (2×1, 1×2)), 1 helicopter
Complement:	75

Norsten as completed   *Royal Swedish Navy*

Tor as completed   *Author's Collection*

Name	Builder	Launched	Comp	Fate
TOR	Wärtsilä, Turku	25.5.63	31.1.64	Extant 1982
NJORD	Wärtsilä, Helsinki	3.10.68	8.10.69	Extant 1982

Similar to *Oden* and the Finnish *Tarmo* class.

ALE *icebreaker*

Displacement:	1320t standard; 1488t full load
Dimensions:	154ft 2in × 41ft 8in × 17ft 4in
	47.0m × 12.7m × 5.3m
Machinery:	2 shafts, 4 Wärtsilä-Sulzer 824TS diesels, 5360bhp = 14kts
Armament:	(1–40mm)
Complement:	21

Specially designed for use on Lake Vänern in Central Sweden. Launched 1.6.73, commissioned 19.12.73. Built at Wärtsilä, Abo, completed in Helsinki. Also used as a surveying vessel.

ATLE class *icebreakers*

Displacement:	7300t standard; 9000t full load
Dimensions:	324ft 9in wl, 343ft 1in oa × 78ft 1in × 23ft 11in
	99.0m, 104.6m × 23.8m × 8.3m
Machinery:	4 shafts (2 fwd), 5 Wärtsilä-Sulzer 12 PC-2-2V diesels, 25,000bhp = 18kts
Armament:	(4–40mm), 2 helicopters
Complement:	54

Name	Builder	Launched	Fate
ATLE	Wärtsilä, Helsinki	27.11.73	Extant 1982
FREJ	Wärtsilä, Helsinki	10.12.74	Extant 1982
YMER	Wärtsilä, Helsinki	3.9.76	Extant 1982

Atle laid down 10.5.73 and commissioned 21.10.74; *Frej* commissioned 30.9.75. *Ymer* ordered 24.3.75 and laid down 12.2.76; commissioned 25.10.77. Sister ships of Finnish *Urho* class. Crew live and work above main deck.

A 1300t intelligence gathering ship, to be called *Orion* was ordered in 1981 from Karlskronavarvet; she will be launched in 1984.

Frej as completed   *Royal Swedish Navy*

Switzerland

From time to time, and particularly in the fifteenth and sixteenth centuries, the Swiss Confederation has maintained quite large fleets on the lakes. These all have the same purpose, to discourage unwelcome people and especially armies from crossing into Switzerland. The modern Swiss Navy has exactly the same purpose. Ten 8-ton 12-metre, 23kt diesel patrol craft (8 men and 2 MG) were built in 1942 to discourage the Germans and anyone else from crossing the lakes or Upper Rhine without permission, and they have been used since World War II against smugglers and illegal immigrants. They have now been worn out and are slowly being replaced by new 16-metre Type 80 boats equipped with radio and radar. These 27kt boats are operated by the Swiss Army. There are also a number of smaller powerboats and personnel transports.

Yugoslavia

The only real force in Yugoslavia able to rule the country after the expulsion of German forces, was the People's Liberation Army commanded by Tito, who formally became Prime Minister in March 1945. The monarchy was shortly abolished and a Federal People's Republic was proclaimed. A new constitution modelled on the Soviet one was adopted in 1946 and 'sovietization' of the country begun. Industry was nationalised and plans for economic development were introduced, aimed at rapid industrialisation based on Soviet advice and using Soviet credit.

Hostile at first to the West because of the Trieste incident and fears of a royalist counter-revolution, Tito remained closely allied to the Soviet Union. His political ambitions were aimed at the creation of a Communist Balkan federation. This was partially attained by Albania becoming a Yugoslav satellite while discussions with Bulgaria began and support was given to the Communist guerrillas in Greece. Such ambitious policies needed strong armed forces to support them. No wonder the first postwar naval estimate called for authorisation of 12 destroyers, 28 submarines, 120 MTBs, 130 patrol craft and 70 minesweepers. This was regarded as inadequate by the People's Assembly Presidium and a new programme had to be drawn up. It was approved in December 1946 and authorised the construction of 4 cruisers, 20 destroyers, 140 submarines, 200 MTBs, 100 patrol craft and 100 minesweepers. Such an enormous programme was impossible to complete in an industrially undeveloped country as Yugoslavia then was. Tito's plans failed to be realised when federation with Bulgaria did not materialise because of Soviet opposition. Stalin was unhappy with the foreign policy of Yugoslavia. In June 1948 Yugoslavia was expelled from the Cominform and all Communist countries denounced Tito and broke off relations. Stalin's attempts to unseat Tito failed, but the economic boycott had a devastating effect on the Yugoslav economy. This resulted not only in a lowering of living standards; no rearmament programme could be executed. In those years the Yugoslav Navy was strengthened by the commissioning of 4 ex-Italian torpedo boats and one recovered ex-Italian submarine, while the necessity of returning the single corvette to Britain was a painful blow.

Faced by economic collapse from one side and the threat of becoming a Soviet satellite from the other, Tito turned to the West for economic aid. Western credits and other innovations revived the Yugoslav economy in the early 1950s, and modernisation of the armed forces could be undertaken. In 1952 the first ten-year naval programme was initiated. Based on the design of the US Higgins PT boats, 96 MTBs were built in local yards as well as 24 'Kraljevica' class patrol craft, 44 landing craft and 32 minesweepers. Two 'W' class destroyers were purchased from Britain as well as a *Fougueux* class patrol craft and 3 *Sirius* class minesweepers from France as the US 'off-shore' procurement, while Yugoslav yards built 2 further patrol ships and one minesweeper to the above designs. The most impressive warship to join the Yugoslav Navy at that time was the destroyer *Split* begun in 1939 and completed with US assistance to a revised design. The Yugoslav yards' greatest achievement however was the completion of a pair of locally designed *Sutjeska* class submarines at the closing stage of the first programme.

After Stalin's death, Tito improved relations with the Soviet Union. As a result he was able to balance himself between the Soviet Union and the US – playing one off against the other and acquiring economic and military aid from both the great powers at once. In the longer term this policy led Tito to a doctrine of non-alignment while at the same time buying Soviet weapons. These purchases, together with building in Yugoslav yards enabled the second naval programme to take place during 1962–74. Soviet deliveries comprised 10 'Osa' class missile craft and 4 'Shershen' class torpedo craft. Licence production of the latter type began in Yugoslavia and 10 boats were finally completed. Four British *Ham* class inshore minesweepers were built in Yugoslavia under the US Military Aid Programme. Yugoslavia's own production consisted of 3 *Heroj* class submarines, 10 patrol boats and 7 inshore minesweepers. The emphasis in the Navy shifted to submarine and light forces as most of the war-built warships were deleted by the early 1970s.

The third naval programme which began in 1975 and reached its half-way point in 1980 was characterised by local yards taking a growing share in the supply of new vessels. Except for a 'Koni' class missile frigate bought from the Soviet Union in 1980 as a replacement for the obsolete *Split*, all other ships for the Yugoslav Navy were home built. By 1980 two *Sava* class submarines. 5 *Rade Koncar* class combined missile-gun attack craft, 20 landing craft and lesser ships were completed while further 5 missile craft and 2 landing ships of the LST type are under construction. Additionally Yugoslav yards won contracts to build training frigates for Iraq and Indonesia.

As can be seen, Yugoslavia was able to build up, with significant cooperation from both the West and the Soviet Union, a quite remarkable offensive naval force. The success of the third naval programme resulted from the balance between East and West initiated in the early 1960s. Despite a visit by Admiral Gorshkov in 1976 the Soviet Navy has not gained increased use of Yugoslav ports although lengthy paid for repair work makes Yugoslavia its fifth most visited country in the world.

The Fleet is under single command and there is a river flotilla based at Novi Sad on the Danube. A naval air arm was formed in 1974–75 with ASW helicopters and the Air Force maintains a 50-plane naval cooperation regiment. The main base is at Split; other bases are at Pula, Sibenik, Ploce and Gulf of Kotor (Cattaro). The Navy has 14,000 men (1500 officers; 12,500 men; national service is for 15 months) plus 1500 marines.

FLEET STRENGTH 1947

SUBMARINES

Name	Launched	Disp	Fate
Hrabri class			
TARA	1927	975t	Deleted 1958
Ex-Italian CB class			
MALISAN	1943	35.4t	Final fate unknown

Hrabri class
Ex-*Nebojsa* renamed after the war; one 4in gun was removed at the end of her career.

Ex-Italian CB class
Midget submarine *CB 20* laid down for the Italian Navy in 1943 and captured by the Germans the same year. Taken over by Yugoslavia in April 1945 and recommissioned.

CORVETTE

Name	Launched	Disp	Fate
Ex-British 'Flower' class			
PARTIZANKA	22.5.40	950t	Returned 1949

Transferred in 1944 and commissioned as *Nada*, then renamed *Partizanka* after the war. Returned to RN and reverted to her old name *Mallow*. Transferred to Egypt later in that year and commissioned as *Sollum*.

TORPEDO-BOATS

Name	Launched	Disp	Fate
T 1 class			
GOLESNICA	15.12.13	262t	Deleted Oct 1959
T 5 class			
CER	20.3.13	266t	BU 1962

Renamed and rearmed after the war with 2–40mm (2×1), 4–20mm (*Cer* 1–20mm) while the TT were removed.

MTBs

Name	Launched	Disp	Fate
Orjen class			
TC 5	1937	61.7t	Deleted 1963
TC 6	1938	61.7t	Deleted 1963
Ex-US Higgins 78ft type			
MT 1–8	1942	46t	Deleted 1966 (MT 8 deleted 1955)

Orjen class
Ex-*Durmitor* and *Kajmakcalan* renamed *TC 5* and *TC 6* respectively after the war, then changed to *TC 391* and *TC 392*.

Ex-US Higgins 78ft type
Lend-lease *PT 201, 204, 207–209, 211, 213, 217* transferred from the RN to the Royal Yugoslav Navy at Malta in mid-1944.

MINESWEEPERS

Name	Launched	Disp	Fate
Ex-Italian RD classes			
ML 301–307	1916–18	193–198t	Deleted 1960
Ex-German M-boat 1915 type			
ZELENOGORA	28.3.18	330t	Deleted 1962
Malinska class			
M 31–33	1931	130t	Deleted 1968 (M 32 in service 1978)

Ex-Italian RD classes
Small minesweepers of various types *RD 6, 16, 21, 25, 27–29* handed over to Yugoslavia in 1947–48 as war reparations.

Ex-German M-boat 1915 type
M 97 purchased in 1921 and commissioned as *Orao*, captured in company of 5 sisters by the Italians in April 1941 and commissioned by them as *Vergada*. Returned in 1943, renamed *Pionir* after the war, later changed to *Zelenogora*.

Malinska class
Mining tenders *Meljine, Malinska* and *Mljet* captured by the Italians in April 1941 and commissioned as *Solta, Arbe* and *Meleda*. Returned 1943–44, renamed *M 1* to *M 3* after the war, then *M 31* to *M 33*. Rearmed with one 47mm gun.

LANDING CRAFT

Name	Launched	Disp	Fate
Ex-German MFPs			
D 203, D 204	c1942	220t	Extant 1982
Ex-Italian MZ type			
D 206 (ex-*MZ 713*)	1942	239t	Deleted 1979
D 219 (ex-*MZ 717*)	1942	239t	Deleted 1979

There were also some ex-German *Siebel Fähres* in service at that time.

Split 1969   *Author's Collection*

MAJOR SURFACE SHIPS

Split as completed

Laid down in the Split Yd to the plans prepared by the French yard Chantiers de la Loire. The original design provided the armament of 5–140mm/50 (5×1), 10–40mm (5×2), 8–13mm MGs, 6–21in TT (2×3) and a speed of 37kts. The incomplete hull was seized by the Italians but they were not able to complete her and she fell into Yugoslav hands again in Oct 1944. The plans were redrawn to fit the US armament and sensors and the ship was commissioned in 1959. Fire control consisted of Mk 37 set with Mk 12 and Mk 22 radars for the 5in guns while Mk 51 set was provided for the 40mm guns. At the end of her career only one boiler was serviceable which enabled the power plant to produce 25,000shp = 24kts.

SPLIT *destroyer*

Displacement:	2400t standard; 3000t full load
Dimensions:	376ft 3in pp, 393ft 7in oa × 39ft 4in × 12ft 2in max
	114.7m × 120.0m × 12.0m × 3.7m
Machinery:	2-shaft Parsons geared turbines, 2 watertube boilers, 50,000shp = 31.5kts. Oil 590t
Armament:	4–5in/38 (4×1), 12–40mm (1×4, 2×2, 4×1), 5–21in TT (1×5), 2 Hedgehog, 6 DCT, 2 DC racks, 40 mines
Sensors:	Radar types SC, SG 1, Mk 12, Mk 22
Complement:	240

No	Name	Builder	Laid down	Launched	Comp	Fate
11	SPLIT (ex-*Spalato*, ex-*Split*)	3 Maj Yd, Rijeka	July 1939	Mar 1950	4.7.58	Deleted 1980

Two RN war built destroyers *Kempenfelt* (ex-*Valentine*) and *Wager* were purchased and towed to Yugoslavia in Oct 1956. They were refitted in a local yard and commissioned as *Kotor* on 10 Sept 1959 and *Pula* later in that year. Their appearance did not vary greatly from the original configuration.

Ex-British 'W' class *destroyers*

No	Name	Builder	Acquired	Fate
R 21	KOTOR (ex-*Kempenfelt*)	John Brown	Oct 1956	Deleted 1971
R 22	PULA (ex-*Wager*)	John Brown	Oct 1956	Deleted 1971

Identical to E Germany's two units.

Soviet 'KONI' class *frigate*

No	Name	Builder	Acquired	Fate
R 31	SPLIT	Zelenodolsk SY	April 1980	Extant 1982

One of two units laid down in 1981. Main diesels ordered June 1980 and delivered 31.3.81. Propulsion same as Soviet 'Koni' class. Design a modification of the training frigates delivered to Indonesia and Iraq.

NEW FRIGATES

Displacement:	1850t full load
Dimensions:	As Indonesian *Hasr Dewantara*
Machinery:	3-shaft CODAG (CP outboard): 1 Soviet gas turbine, plus 2 SEMT-Pielstick 12 PA6 V280 diesels, 15,000shp + 9600bhp = 27kts
Armament:	As Indonesian *Hasr Dewantara* ?
Complement:	*c*90

SUBMARINES

The former Italian war-built *Nautilo* of the *Flutto* class which sank in Pola when in German hands was raised and commissioned in 1949. Relegated to training duties in 1958 she completed a major refit in 1960 when the 100mm gun was removed and the conning tower streamlined. Deleted 1971.

SAVA *submarine*

Sutjeska 1964

The first submarines designed and built in Yugoslavia. Modernised later and equipped with Soviet sensors (bow sonar arrays added in early 1970s) and armament. Obsolete now and used for training duties only. P = *Podnornica* (submarine).

SUTJESKA class *submarines*

Displacement:	700t standard; 820t/945t
Dimensions:	196ft 8in oa × 22ft × 15ft 9in
	60.0m × 6.6m × 4.8m
Machinery:	2 (?) shafts, 2 Sulzer diesels electric motors, 1800hp = 14kts/9kts. Range 4800nm/8kts
Armament:	6–533mm TT (4 bow, 2 stern, 8 torpedoes)
Complement:	38

No	Name	Builder	Laid down	Launched	Comp	Fate
P 811	NERETVA	Uljanik Yd, Pula	1957	1959	1962	Extant 1982
P 812	SUTJESKA	Uljanik Yd, Pula	1957	28.9.58	16.9.60	Extant 1982

EUROPE (NEUTRAL)

Heroj as completed

Incorporated a number of improvements as compared with the earlier *Sutjeska* class, particularly in the shape of the hull and conning tower. Equipped with Soviet sensors and armament.

HEROJ class *submarines*

Displacement:	945t/1068t	
Dimensions:	210ft × 23ft 6in × 16ft 4in	
	64.0m × 7.2m × 5.0m	
Machinery:	1 shaft, 2 diesels, electric motors, 2400hp = 16kts/10kts. Range 9700nm at 8kts	
Armament:	6–533mm TT (bow)	
Complement:	55	

No	Name	Builder	Laid down	Launched	Comp	Fate
P 821	HEROJ	Uljanik Yd, Pula	1964	18.8.67	1968	Extant 1982
P 822	JUNAK	Uljanik Yd, Pula	1965	1968	1969	Extant 1982
P 823	USKOK	Uljanik Yd, Pula	1966	Jan 1970	1970	Extant 1982

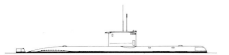

Sava 1979

Improved *Heroj* class, further boats planned. Soviet electronics and armament. Diving limit *c* 100ft.

SAVA class *submarines*

Displacement:	500t/964t	
Dimensions:	183ft 1in × 16ft 9in × 23ft	
	55.8m × 5.05m × 7.0m	
Machinery:	1 shaft, diesels, electric motors, 2400bhp = 16kts submerged. Endurance 28 days	
Armament:	6–533mm TT (10 torpedoes or 20 mines)	
Complement:	35	

No	Name	Builder	Laid down	Launched	Comp	Fate
P 831	SAVA	Split SY	1975	1977	1978	Extant 1982
P 832	DRAVA	Split SY			1982	Extant 1982

Apart from the large combat submarines there is one 25ft long submersible craft with a 2-man crew in service. Extant 1982.

MALA *midget submarine*

AMPHIBIOUS WARFARE VESSELS

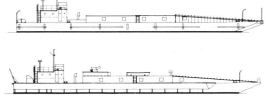

DTM 231 1959
NB 1/750 scale

DTM 233 1980
NB 1/750 scale

DTM 221 class *landing craft*

Displacement:	240t standard; 410t full load
Dimensions:	144ft 3in × 19ft 7in × 7ft
	47.3m × 6.4m × 2.3m
Machinery:	3 shafts, 3 Gray Marine 64HN9 diesels, 625bhp = 10.3kts. Range 500nm at 9.3kts
Armament:	3–20mm (3×1), 100 mines on 2 rails
Complement:	27 (+200)

Class:
DTM 211 to *DTM 234*

DTM = *Desantri Tenkonosac* (LST). Yugoslav built in the 1950s to the German wartime *MFP* design. Can carry 3 tanks (140t of vehicles) or 200 men. Widened by 1m sponsons for minelaying. Two sold to Sudan in 1969, one deleted in 1978. Remaining 7 extant in 1982.

Catamaran type *landing craft*

Ten 40t boats of the LCU type with a catamaran hull were built in the 1950s. Armed with 4–12.7mm MG (2×2), able to carry one light tank or one field gun. Could carry mines also. Deleted 1978.

TYPE 601 *landing craft*

Displacement:	32t
Dimensions:	70ft 2in × 15ft 1in × 2ft
	21.4m × 4.6m × 0.6m
Machinery:	2 shafts, 2 MTU 12V331 TC81 diesels, 2250 = 22kts
Armament:	1–20mm
Sensors:	Radar Decca 101
Complement:	?

Class:
DSC 601 to *DSC 612*

Fibreglass craft built by Gleben SY, Vela Luka, Korcula and in service since Sept 1976. DSC = *Desantni Jurisni Camac* (LCA). Can carry 40 troops in 32 sq metre cargo space. Twelve or even 21 extant in 1982 with more building.

NEW *tank landing ships*

Displacement:	2980t
Dimensions:	334ft 6in × 46ft 6in × 20ft 2in
	102.0m × 14.2m × 3.1m
Machinery:	2 Pielstick diesels, 6800bhp = ?18kts
Armament:	2–40mm/70 (2×1)
Complement:	?

Two landing ships of merchant ship appearance were under construction in 1980. Could carry several LCAs and 6 tanks (1500t of cargo). Fitted with a helicopter deck. Offered for export only.

SMALL SURFACE COMBATANTS

Ex-Italian CICLONE class *torpedo-boats*

Aliseo and *Indomito* were transferred to Yugoslavia in 1949 as war reparations and commissioned as *Biokovo* and *Triglav* respectively. Fitted with US sensors. Deleted 1971.

Ex-Italian ARIETE class *torpedo-boats*

The prototype of this class, *Ariete*, was transferred in 1949 as war reparations and commissioned as *Durmitor*. Two others of this class *TA 46* (ex-*Balestra*) and *TA 47* (ex-*Fionda*) seized incomplete by the Germans in 1943 were taken over by the Yugoslav Navy in 1948 and renamed *Ucka* and *Velebit* respectively. Only *Ucka* was finally completed in 1949 and unlike *Durmitor* her original armament was changed to 2–100mm/47 (2×1), 3–40mm (3×1), 2 DCT and 28 mines. *Durmitor* was deleted in 1963; *Ucka* in 1968.

Type 108 in early 1950s
NB 1/750 scale

TYPE 108 *fast attack craft (torpedo)*

Displacement:	55t standard; 60t full load
Dimensions:	69ft pp, 78ft oa × 21ft 3in × 7ft 8in
	21.0m, 23.8m × 6.5m × 2.4m
Machinery:	3 shafts, 3 Packard petrol engines, 5000bhp = 36kts
Armament:	1–40mm, 2–0.5in MG, 2–18in TT (see notes)
Complement:	14

Class:
P 101 to *P 199*

A total of 96 boats were built in Yugoslavia (1951–60) to the design of the US Higgins 78ft type PT boats. Six sold to Egypt in 1956, 2 to Ethiopia in 1960, 2 to Cambodia in 1964 and 6 to Sudan in 1970. In 1963 *c*24 boats were converted to MGBs by removal of the TTs and mounting one additional 40mm gun forward instead, being designated Type 158. Their speed did not exceed 24–26kts at that time and they could carry 2–4 mines in addition to the above arms. The unconverted boats were sold to civilian enterprises or subsequently scrapped. The last 6 converted boats were deleted in 1979.

Soviet 'SHERSHEN' class *fast attack craft (torpedo)*

Four were acquired in 1965 and commissioned as *Ivan*, *Jadran*, *Pionir* and *Partizan*. Licenced production of this class was begun at Tito SY, Kraljevica, in 1966 under designation *Type 201* and 10 boats were completed by 1971 (without DC racks unlike Soviet boats) and commissioned as *Biokovac* (TC 221), *Crvena Zvezda*, *Kornat*, *Partizan II*, *Proleter*, *Strjelko*, *Topcider*, *Pionir II*, *TC 223*, *TC 224*. TC = *Torpedni Camac*. Named after World War II partisan warships. Extant 1982.

Ex-Soviet 'OSA I' class *fast attack craft (missile)*

Ten transferred from the Soviet Union during 1965/70 and commissioned as *Mitar Acev* (RC 301), *Vlado Bagat* (RC 302), *Petar Drapsin* (RC 303), *Steven Filipovic* (RC 304), *Velimir Skorpik* (RC 305), *Nikola Martinovic* (RC 306), *Josip Mazar-Sosa* (RC 307), *Karlo Rojc* (RC 308), *Franc Rozman-Stane* (RC 309), *Zikaca Jovanovic-Spanac* (RC 310). RC = *Racetni Camac* ('Rocket boat'). Named after partisan war heroes. All extant 1982.

Nos 201, 203 *experimental MTBs*

Two experimental boats had been built under the first ten-year programme but further construction was abandoned because of design shortcomings. A *c*20t displacement *c*30kt speed (1 TT) applied to one of these boats at least.

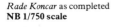

Rade Koncar as completed
NB 1/750 scale

RADE KONCAR class *fast attack craft (missile)*

Displacement:	240t full load
Dimensions:	147ft 6in × 27ft 6in × 8ft 2in
	45.0m × 8.4m × 2.5m
Machinery:	4-shaft CODAG (4 CP propellers): 2-shaft Rolls-Royce gas turbines, plus 2 MTU diesel engines, 11,600shp + 7200bhp = 40kts. Range 500nm at 35kts
Armament:	2 SS-N-2B Styx SSM (2×1), 2–57mm/70 Bofors (2×1)
Sensors:	Radar Decca 1226, Philips TAB, Square Tie
Complement:	30

Class (no, launched):
Rade Koncar (RT 401, 15.10.76), *Vlado Cetkovic* (RT 402, 28.8.77), *Ramiz Sadiku* (RT 403, 1978), *Hasan Zahirovic Laca* (RT 404, 1979), *Jordan Nikolov-Orce* (RT 405, 1979), *Ante Banina* (RT 406, 1979)

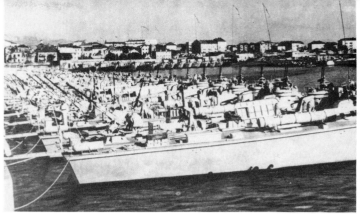

Type 108 MTBs   *Micinski Collection*

Borac 1969   *Author's Collection*

These combined missile-gun combatants were designed by the Naval Shipbuilding Institute of Zagreb and built by the Tito Yd, Kraljevica. Truly international boats close in design to the Swedish *Spica* class and equipped with Bofors guns, Soviet missile system (chosen in preference to Exocet), British turbines, German diesels and Dutch radar systems. RT = *Raketna Topovnjaca*. In service dates RT 401 April 1977, RT 402 March 1978, RT 403 10.9.78, RT 404 Nov 1979, RT 405 Aug 1979 and RT 406 Nov 1980. All extant 1982, three more building.

Ex-French FOUGUEUX class *submarine-chaser*

One unit (ex-US *PC 1615*) designated *P 6* (launched 21.12.54) was delivered by F C Méditerranée, Le Havre for the Yugoslav Government thanks to US 'offshore' procurement funds. She was completed and commissioned in Jan 1956 as *Udarnik* (PBR 51). Extant 1982.

Borac in 1970s
NB 1/750 scale

MORNAR class *large patrol craft*

Displacement:	330t standard; 430t full load
Dimensions:	170ft pp, 174ft 8in oa × 23ft × 6ft 6in
	51.8m, 53.3m × 7.0m × 2.0m
Machinery:	2 shafts, 4 SEMT-Pielstick diesels, 3240bhp = 24kts. Oil 55t. Range 3000/660nm at 24/12kts
Armament:	2–76mm (2×1), 2–40mm (2×1), 2–20mm (2×1), 4 MBU–1200 ASW RL (4×5), 2 Mk 6 DCT, 2 Mk 9 DC racks
Sensors:	Radar Decca 45; sonar Tamir-II
Complement:	60

Class (no, launched):
Mornar (PBR 551, 1958), *Borac* (PBR 552, 1965)

Built by the Tito Yd, Kraljevica to an improved design of the *Fougueux* class with increased armament. Both modernised during 1970–73 by the Naval Repair Yd in Trivat; with Soviet sonar and ASW equipment, the 76mm guns being removed. Extant 1982.

TYPE 501 'KRALJEVICA' class *large patrol craft*

Displacement:	195t standard; 220t full load
Dimensions:	134ft 5in × 20ft 7in × 5ft 7in
	41.0m × 6.3m × 1.7m
Machinery:	2 shafts, 2 diesels, 3000bhp = 17kts. Range 1000nm at 12kts
Armament:	1–3in Mk 22, 1–40mm, 4–20mm (4×1), 2 Mousetrap or 1 Hedgehog, 2 Mk 6 DCT, 2 DC racks
Sensors:	Radar Decca 45
Complement:	45

EUROPE (NEUTRAL)

Type 509 as completed
NB 1/750 scale

Class:
PBR 501 to *PBR 508*
    Built by the Tito Yd, Kraljevica (1953–56), this design was abandoned in favour of the improved Type 509 design. *PBR 502* and *PBR 505* were sold to Bangladesh in 1975. During the later 1970s the US 3in gun and the hedgehog were removed in favour of 2 RBU-1200 ASW RL (2×5) with Soviet Tamir-11 sonar. *PBR 504* and *PBR 506* reportedly carried names *Napred* and *Junak* respectively. The 6 remaining units were extant in 1982.

TYPE 509 'KRALJEVICA' class *large patrol craft*

Displacement:	210t standard; 235t full load
Dimensions:	141ft 5in × 20ft 7in × 6ft
	43.1m × 6.3m × 1.8m
Machinery:	2 shafts, 2 MAN W8V 30/38 diesels, 3300bhp = 19kts. Range 1000nm at 12kts
Armament:	1–76mm, 1–40mm, 4–20mm (4×1), 2 Mousetrap or 1 Hedgehog, 2 DCT, 2 DC racks
Sensors:	Radar Decca 45
Complement:	49

Class:
PBR 509 to *PBR 524*
    Built by the Tito Yd, Kraljevica (1957–59) to the improved and longer design of the Type 501. *PBR 513* to *PBR 518* were sold to Indonesia in 1958–59, *PBR 522* and *PBR 523* to Sudan in 1969 and *PBR 509* to Ethiopia in 1975. The remaining 8, including *Streljko* (PBR 520), *Marijan* (PBR 521) and *Proleter* (PBR 524), were extant in 1982.

TYPE 131 *coastal patrol craft*

Displacement:	85t standard; 120t full load
Dimensions:	105ft × 18ft × 8ft 3in
	32.0m × 5.5m × 2.5m
Machinery:	2 shafts, 2 MTU MB820 diesels, 900bhp = 17kts
Armament:	6–20mm Hispano Suiza HS831 (2×3)
Sensors:	Radar Kelvin-Hughes 14/9
Complement:	?

Class:
Bresice, Cer, Durmitor (PC 139), *Granica, Kalnik* (PC 132), *Kamenar, Kozuf, Lovćen* (PC 136), *Romanija, Triglav* (PC 135), *Kotor, Rudnik.*
    Built at Trogir Yd (1965–68). May be part of the coast guard style Maritime Border Brigade. Pennant numbers PC 131–140. All extant 1982.

MINE WARFARE VESSELS

GALEB *minelayer/training ship*

Displacement:	5182t standard; 5700t full load (3667grt)
Dimensions:	384ft 8in × 51ft 2in × 18ft 4in
	117.3m × 15.6m × 5.6m
Machinery:	2 shafts, 2 Burmeister & Wain diesels, 7200bhp = 17kts
Armament:	4–3.5in (4×1), 4–40mm (4×1), 24–20mm (6×4), mines
Complement:	?

    Former Italian banana carrier *Ramb III* completed by Ansaldo at Genoa in 1939, sunk as an auxiliary cruiser in 1944. Refloated and reconstructed after the war and commissioned in 1952. The guns were replaced by 6–40mm (6×1) in the late 1960s. Also used presidential yacht and fleet flagship. Extant 1982.

Ex-French SIRIUS class *coastal minesweepers*

Class (no, former name):
Vukov Klanac (M 151, ex-*Hrabri*), *Podgora* (M 152, ex-*Smeli*), *Blitvenica* (M 153, ex-*Slobodni*), *Gradac* (M 11, ex-*Snazhi*)
First three delivered under designation *D 25* to *D 27* to Yugoslavia by the A Normand Yd, Le Havre under the US Offshore Procurement Scheme. Commissioned in Sept 1957 as *Hrabri, Smeli* and *Slobodni* respectively.
    The fourth craft was built with French assistance by Mali Losinj Yd and commissioned as *Snazni*. She was experimentally fitted with a gas turbine propulsion. All four renamed *c*1976. Extant 1982.

TYPE 101 *inshore minesweepers*

Displacement:	90t standard; 95t full load
Dimensions:	82ft × 19ft 5in × 6ft 2in
	25.0m × 5.9m × 1.9m
Machinery:	1 shaft, 1 diesel, 135–175bhp = 12kts
Armament:	1–40mm, 1–20mm
Complement:	?

Class:
M 101 to *M 116, M 120, M 140*
    Built 1950–56. All deleted 1966–76.

British 'HAM' class *inshore minesweepers*

Four were built in Yugoslavia (1964–66) under the US MDAP. Commissioned as *Brsec* (M 142), *Iz* (M 143), *Olib* (M 144) and *M 141* (prototype). Extant 1982.

TYPE 117 *inshore minesweepers*

Displacement:	120t standard; 131t full load
Dimensions:	98ft 4in × 18ft × 4ft 9in
	30.0m × 5.5m × 1.5m
Machinery:	2 GM diesels, 1000bhp = 12kts
Armament:	1–40mm, 3–12.7mm MG (1×2)
Sensors:	Radar Decca 45
Complement:	25

Class:
Grajac, Ibet, Maun (M 118), *M 120* to *M 123*
    Yugoslav built 1964–68. One deleted 1980. *M 117* used for survey, others do coastal patrol as well. Six extant 1982.

MISCELLANEOUS

SAVA *river monitor*

Former Yugoslav monitor scuttled in 1944 by the Croatians and raised after the war. Recommissioned in 1952 and rearmed with 2–105mm (2×1), 3–40mm (3×1), 6–20mm. Deleted 1962.

RPC 200 type *river gunboats*

Two 30t craft (15kts and 2–3in guns) launched for the *Donauflotille* in 1945 were completed for the Yugoslav Navy after the war. Deleted in the late 1970s.

RLM 301 class *river minesweepers*

Class:
RLM 301–314, RLM 319–324
    Built by four Yugoslav yards 1951–53, 38t, 12kts, 1–20mm; 14 deleted 1980, 6 extant in 1982.

NESTIN class *river minesweepers*

Displacement:	65t
Dimensions:	88ft 7in × 20ft 8in × 5ft 3in
	27.0m × 6.3m × 1.6m
Machinery:	2 diesels, 520bhp = 18kts
Armament:	5–20mm Hispano Suiza (1×3, 2×1)
Sensors:	Radar Decca 101
Complement:	?

Class (no, launched):
Nestin (M 331, 20.12.75), *Motajica* (M 332, 18.12.76), *Belegis* (M 333, Jan 1977), *Bosut* (M 334, 1978), *Vucedol* (M 335, 1979), *Djerdap* (M 336, 1980), *Panonsko More* (M 337)
    Built of light metal alloy with very low freeboard by Brodotehnika, Belgrade. One unit exported to Hungary, 1981, three to Iraq. Programme continues.

Galeb in 1960s   *Author's Collection*

Argentina

The position of the Argentine Navy *vis-à-vis* its continental rivals was adversely affected by the political and naval changes wrought by World War II. From the late 1940s until the acquisition of the carrier *Independencia*, the Argentine Navy remained at numerical parity with the Brazilian Navy, and was only slightly superior to that of Chile. The acquisition of *Independencia*, followed by the *25 de Mayo*, gave the Navy a strike capability that neither of its neighbours could match, and thus returned superiority to the Argentine Fleet.

In the decades following World War II, the Argentine Navy was very active. In 1955, after a number of failures, the Navy deposed Juan Peron. On 16 September 1955, key sea and shore commands were seized, principally by using fictitious orders, although as anticipated, numerous naval shore facilities could not be protected and fell to Peron's forces. Rio Santiago, home of the Naval Academy, had to be evacuated, as well as the submarine base at Mar del Plata. The Navy then demonstrated its muscle. Naval aircraft bombed the ground forces, which were trying to attack Puerto Belgrano, the key naval base, and fleet units bombarded an oil storage area near the recently evacuated submarine base. The cruiser *9 de Julio* and two destroyers bombarded the area for four hours. Three frigates then landed 350 marines and sailors. The success of this attack proved the Navy's ability to bombard the capital. In the afternoon of 19 September, as the fleet appeared off Buenos Aires, Juan Peron resigned. This popularly supported victory strengthened the Navy's position nationally.

In recent decades, the Argentine Navy has been combating 'fish piracy' within its 200-mile limits. In 1966 the destroyer *Santa Cruz* fired on and holed a Russian trawler, which had refused to be escorted into Mar del Plata. A decade later, on 21 September 1977, the destroyers *Py*, *Rosales* and *Segui* caught nine Soviet fishing vessels, approximately 130 miles off Cabo dos Bahias; four were seized and five escaped. A week later *Rosales* caught the new Soviet factory ship *Herey*, whilst on 1 October the cruiser *General Belgrano* and the destroyers *Piedrabueno*, *Py* and *Segui* trapped four more trawlers, two Soviet and two Bulgarian; one poacher was killed by naval gunfire and three Argentine sailors drowned while attempting a boarding in rough seas. In the mid-1970s the Argentine Navy, along with sister services, fought against terrorists. The August 1975 bombing of *Santisima Trinidad* received international headlines.

In the spring of 1982, Argentina fought and lost the Falklands War over the Malvinas (Falklands). There can be little doubt that the initial decision to invade was the result of the diplomatic events that took place between January and the end of March. As with most countries, Argentina was unprepared for war. The Navy had no warning. The submarine force, the one potential wild card, was in a state of transition. Neither Type 209 was one hundred per cent worked up and only one of two old boats was operational. A few new naval attack aircraft were just becoming operational with almost a dozen more to arrive in the late spring.

Almost the entire Navy was used to support Operation 'Rosario' – the marine landings in the Malvinas (Falklands) and Georgias on 2–3 April, having put to sea on 28 March ostensibly for exercises with the Uruguayan Navy. Following the invasion, the Fleet withdrew to the principal Argentine naval base, Puerto Belgrano. Toward the end of April, the Fleet took up positions just outside the British 200-mile exclusion zone. Almost due north of the islands were the carrier *25 de Mayo*, and most of the Fleet, including the two Type 42s. To the SW of the islands was the cruiser *General Belgrano* and two destroyers supported by an oiler. Late on 1 May, the carrier aircraft located a British task force NE of the islands. The Argentine force attempted to close but were unable to do so. The Argentine northern force was now being shadowed by two Sea Harriers. Being aware that the United States was providing intelligence to the British, the Argentine fleet commander decided to withdraw to protected waters along the coast. Shortly after the Argentine force began to retire, the *General Belgrano* was torpedoed and sunk. The aircraft from the carrier were deployed from southern Argentina. The Fleet did not make another appearance.

In recent decades Argentina, like Brazil and Peru, has turned to bi-national shipbuilding agreements to acquire warships. These are construction agreements with developed European shipbuilders, which specify that part or all of the combatants are to be built or assembled in Argentina. For those ships built in Argentina, the European builders are required to supply some components, technical

Major units of the Argentine Navy in 1980: the *General Belgrano* with two A 69 type corvettes and the *Hercules* in the background
Author

aid and training, co-ordination and advice. The first bi-national agreement was with Howaldswerke Deutsche Werft for two Type 209 submarines; these boats joined the Fleet in the early 1970s. The second agreement was with Vickers for the construction of two Type 42 destroyers: *Hercules* commissioned on 12.7.76 and *Santisima Trinidad* joined the fleet in late 1981. The third was with Thyssen Nordseewerke for six Type TR1700 submarines, and the fourth is with Thyssen Reinstahl-Blohm und Voss for four Type MEKO 360 frigates and six Type MEKO 140 corvettes. These bi-national agreements mark the return of 'obtaining the best that money can buy' which was the policy of Latin American navies before World War II.

In 1982 for an active Fleet of 54 ships the personnel of the Argentine Navy numbered 31,000, including 2900 officers. Volunteers are supplemented by 12-month conscripts. There is also a Marine Corps of 6000 men. The main naval bases are Buenos Aires, Rio Santiago (La Plata), Mar de Plata (for submarines) and Puerto Belgrano, with a smaller facility at Ushaia on Tierra del Fuego. The main naval building yard is Astilleros y Fábricas Navales del Estado (AFNE) at Rio Santiago, but the Navy also holds a majority shareholding in Darsena Norte (Tandanou) and Darsena Este.

FLEET STRENGTH 1947

BATTLESHIPS

Name	Launched	Disp (normal)	Fate
Libertad class			
INDEPENDENCIA	26.2.1891	2300t	Discarded 1951
Rivadavia class			
MORENO	23.9.11	27,700t	Sold 8.2.56
RIVADAVIA	26.8.11	27,700t	Sold 8.2.56

Moreno and *Rivadavia* were inactive in the latter years of their careers.

CRUISERS

Name	Launched	Disp (normal)	Fate
LA ARGENTINA	16.4.37	6500t	Discarded 1974
Garibaldi class			
PUEYRREDON	25.7.1898	6800t	Discarded 2.8.54
Veinticinco de Mayo class			
ALMIRANTE BROWN	28.9.29	6800t	Discarded 27.6.61
VEINTICINCO DE MAYO	11.8.29	6800t	Discarded 24.3.60

La Argentina
Modified British *Arethusa* class. Designed as a training cruiser, *La Argentina* made numerous foreign cruises. In 1950, her aircraft catapult was removed and her 4–4in (4×1) AA guns were replaced by 12–40mm (4×2, 1×4) AA. This, plus the addition of radar and other electronics, increased full load displacement from 7500t in 1939 to over 8500t by 1974. In 1951 she was reclassified from a school ship to a cruiser, resuming her training role in 1961. She was disarmed and decommissioned in 1970.

LATIN AMERICA

Garibaldi class

In her closing days, the ageing armoured cruiser *Pueyrredon* was used as a coast defence ship and for training. She was converted to oil, had her secondary battery removed, and was fitted with a tripod mast and fire control director; she was renovated at Puerto Belgrano, Argentina. She was decommissioned on 4.1.55; her sisters *Garibaldi*, *San Marti* and *General Belgrano* were discarded 20.3.34, 18.12.35 and 8.5.47 respectively.

Veinticinco de Mayo class

Modified Italian *Trento* class ships, these cruisers were often criticised in British publications as being generally unsatisfactory; however, they were popular ships in the Argentine Navy. Their stacks were raised shortly before World War II, altering their appearance. Both cruisers took part in the 1948 Antarctic operation, and in 1959 they were placed in reserve.

DESTROYERS

Name	Launched	Disp (normal)	Fate
La Plata class			
CORDOBA	1911	890t	Discarded 10.1.56
LA PLATA	1911	890t	Discarded 10.1.57
Jujuy class			
CATAMARCA	1911	1010t	Discarded 10.1.56
JUJUY	15.4.12	1010t	Discarded 10.1.56
Churucca class			
CERVANTES	Jun 1925	1522t	Discarded 24.6.61
JUAN DE GARAY	2.11.25	1522t	Discarded 25.3.60
Mendoza class			
LA RIOJA	26.1.29	1570t	Discarded 30.4.62
MENDOZA	13.7.28	1570t	Discarded 30.4.62
TUCUMAN	10.10.28	1570t	Discarded 20.4.62
Buenos Aires class			
BUENOS AIRES	21.9.37	1375t	Discarded 1971
ENTRE RIOS	21.9.37	1375t	Discarded 1973
MISIONES	23.9.37	1375t	Discarded 3.5.71
SAN JUAN	24.6.37	1375t	Discarded 1973
SAN LUIS	23.8.37	1375t	Discarded 3.5.71
SANTA CRUZ	3.11.37	1375t	Discarded 1973

Churucca class

Built in Spain to the World War I British Admiralty Design Flotilla Leaders, this was a highly successful series. Following World War II, 1–4.7in and 1–3in gun were replaced by 6–40mm AA: two pairs were located between the funnels and one pair aft the second funnel. They were reclassified as *torpederos* (destroyer escorts) in 1952. In May 1961 *Cervantes* was placed in reserve. *Juan de Garay* was used for training 1952–59.

Mendoza class

Modified *Bruce* class. Reclassified as *torpederos* (destroyer escorts) in 1952, *La Rioja* and *Tucuman* were disarmed and laid up in that same year, although they continued to show up in naval annuals as being active. *Mendoza* was decommissioned in 1961.

Buenos Aires class

Modified *Greyhound* class. By the close of their careers, armament varied considerably throughout the class. *Buenos Aires* in 1969 is representative: 3–4.7in (3×1), 4–40mm (4×1) AA, 2 Hedgehog, 2 ASW torpedo launchers, 4 K-guns, 1 DC rack. *Buenos Aires* was disarmed in 1970, *Entre Rios* in 1972, *Misiones* in 1972, *San Juan* in 1972, *San Luis* in 1970 and *Santa Cruz* in 1971.

SUBMARINES

Name	Launched	Disp	Fate
Santa Fe class			
SALTA	17.1.32	775t/920t	Discarded 5.4.61
SANTA FE	28.7.31	775t/920	Discarded 23.4.59
SANTIAGO DE ESTERO	28.3.32	775t/920t	Discarded 23.4.59

Modified *Cavallini* class. *Salta* made her 1000th dive on 3.8.60. *Santiago de Estero* made a record dive for the class of 374ft (114m) in the South Atlantic.

Other vessels on strength in 1947 included the training ship *Presidente Sarmiento* (launched 31.8.1897, 2733t normal, decommissioned 1961); the *Rosario* class (river gunboats) *Parana* (28.4.08, 1050t, sold 14.9.56) and *Rosario* (27.7.08, 1050t, sold 23.7.59); the *Bouchard* class (minesweepers) *Bouchard*, *Drummond*, *Fournier*, *Granville*, *Parker*, *Py*, *Robinson*, *Seaver* and *Spiro* (launched 1936–39, 450t); and the *King* class (patrol vessels) *King* and *Murature* (launched 1943–44, 900t, in service 1982). *Presidente Sarmiento* currently lies at Buenos Aires as a museum. The *Bouchard* class were the first modern warship class constructed in Argentina. One unit, *Fournier*, struck an unchartered rock at the entrance of the San Gabriel Channel and sank on 22.9.49; *Parker* was ceded to Paraguay in 1964 and *Py* and *Bouchard* in 1968; the rest were discarded 1962–67.

MAJOR SURFACE SHIPS

Independencia 1963

Independencia, launched 20.5.44, was purchased from Great Britain in June 1958, in part with funds from the sale of the battleships *Moreno* and *Rivadavia* and of the armoured cruiser *Pueyrredon*. The carrier had been modernised in 1952–53 at which time she received a lattice mast and an enlarged bridge. Three years later she underwent another major refit, being fitted with a 5° angled deck. She was insulated for tropical service and partially air-conditioned. On 6.8.58 she was named *Independencia*; on 4.11.58

the Argentine flag was raised in Portsmouth; on 8.6.59 the first Argentine naval aircraft operated from her decks; and on 8.7.59 she commissioned. As transferred, she carried 12–40mm AA; however, this was reduced to 8–40mm shortly after

Ex-British COLOSSUS class *aircraft carrier*

No	Name	Builder	Acquired	Fate
V 1	INDEPENDENCIA (ex-*Warrior*)	Harland & Wolff	Jun 1958	Sold 17.3.71

going into service. In August 1963 the first jet aircraft, an F-9F Panther, operated from *Independencia*. She was capable of carrying 24 aircraft. Attack aircraft available in limited numbers for carrier operations included F-4U Corsairs, F9F Panthers, T-28 Trojans and TF-9J Cougars. At the end of her service she was carrying 6 S-2A Trackers and 14 T-28s. In 1970 she was disarmed and placed in reserve.

Independencia c1965   *Author*

Veinticinco de Mayo Dec 1978   *Argentine Navy*

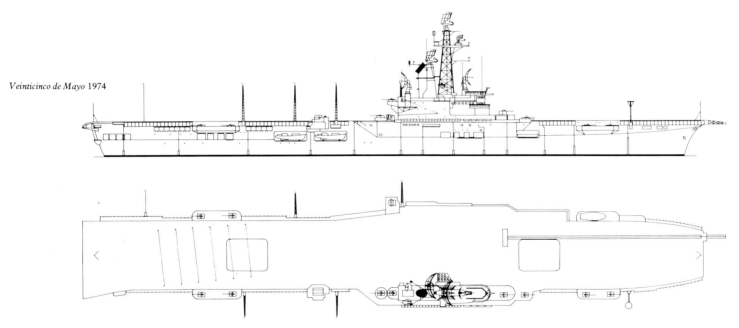

Veinticinco de Mayo 1974

An extensive boiler room fire caused this carrier to be prematurely decommissioned from Dutch service, but she was extensively rebuilt at Wilton Fijenoord Shipyard and purchased by Argentina. Her boilers were replaced with ones from an uncompleted near-sister, *Leviathan*. She commissioned in the Argentine Navy on 8.10.68 and embarked her first aircraft on 3.9.69.

Veinticinco de Mayo is air-conditioned. Her hangar deck is 455ft × 52ft × 17ft 6in (*138.7m × 15.9m × 5.3m*). Two 40mm guns have been removed. In 1972, Argentina acquired 16 A-4Q Skyhawks, which have been the backbone of the carrier's air complement, which also includes 4 S-2As and 2 SH-34J helicopters. In 1979, her flight deck was rebuilt and the area increased. In 1982 the carrier was used in the Falk-

Ex-British modified COLOSSUS class *aircraft carrier*

Displacement:	15,892t standard; 19,896t full load
Dimensions:	630ft pp, 693ft 2in oa, 690ft fd × 80ft, 121ft fd × 25ft
	192.0m, 211.1m, 210.3m × 24.4m, 36.9m × 7.6m
Machinery:	2-shaft Parsons geared turbines, 4 Admiralty 3-drum boilers, 42,000shp = 24kts. Fuel 3200t
Armament:	12–40mm (12×1), 22 aircraft
Complement:	1250

No	Name	Builder	Acquired	Fate
V 2	VEINTICINCO DE MAYO (ex-*Karel Doorman*, ex-*Venerable*)	Cammell Laird	8.10.68	In service 1982

lands War. A typical aircraft complement during the months from March through May was 8 Skyhawks, 4 Trackers, and a few general purpose helicopters. The Super Etendard attack aircraft, five of which had arrived in Argentina in the autumn of 1981, could not operate from the carrier. The *Veinticinco de Mayo* was not yet fitted with the essential electronics to provide the inertial guidance data to the aircraft. Following the war, the carrier was modified so that she could handle the Super Etendards. Electronics consist of Dutch LW-02, SGR-105 (DA-05), SGR-103 (ZW-0I), TACAN with the British CAAIS data automation system. See under the Netherlands for further details.

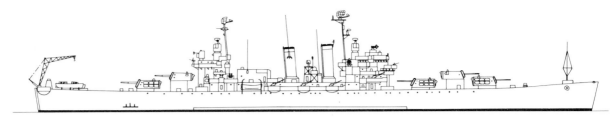

General Belgrano 1982

General Belgrano, launched 12.3.38, purchased by Argentina 12.4.51, and refitted at the Philadelphia Navy Yard. The superstructure was reduced, bulges were added, the beam was increased and mainmast derricks and catapults were removed. The hangar in *General Belgrano*'s hull could accommodate two helicopters with spare parts; the nearly flat counter and high freeboard aft provided an excellent helicopter platform. She commissioned 5.12.51, although numerous erroneous dates are cited. She was fitted with a Dutch search radar in the early 1960s, and in 1967 two Seacat SAM launchers were installed aft of the bridge. In 1980 she still mounted her full armament (including 20mm guns). She was retained for her amphibious support role and used as a gunnery training ship. During the Falklands War,

Ex-US BROOKLYN class *cruisers*

No	Name	Builder	Acquired	Fate
C 4	GENERAL BELGRANO (ex-*Diecisiete de Octubre*, ex-*Phoenix*)	New York SB	12.4.51	Sunk 2.5.82
C 5	NUEVE DE JULIO (ex-*Boise*)	Newport News	12.4.51	Decommissioned 1978

General Belgrano and 2 escorting *Allen M Sumner* class Exocet-armed destroyers were stationed to the southwest of the Falklands (Malvinas). She patrolled on a 200-mile line between Burwood Bank, S of the Falklands, and Isla de los Estados, E of Tierra del Fuego. On 2 May at 1600 local time she was torpedoed at a range of about 1400 yards by HMS *Conqueror*. At the time she was torpedoed, *General Bel-* grano was approximately 220 miles from the Falklands sailing at 10kts toward the mainland. Two Mk 8** torpedoes hit, the first under the aft 5in gun director and the second just forward of A turret. The first hit tore the emergency generators from their foundations. The ship was without power. *General Belgrano* sank at 1645; 321 lives were lost (95 per cent killed by the torpedo hits) with the cruiser and 880 rescued after 24 hours in life rafts.

Nueve de Julio launched 3.12.36, was commissioned 19.12.51. In the early 1960s, she, too, was fitted with a Dutch surface search radar. Decommissioned and stripped in 1978, she served as a parts reservoir for her sister-ship and was sold for scrap in 1981.

Brown and *Espora* commissioned on 10.8.61 and *Rosales* on 3.8.61. *Almirante Storni* fired across the bows of the British scientific survey ship *Shackleton* on 2.4.76 S of the Falklands.

Ex-US FLETCHER class *destroyers*

No	Name	Builder	Acquired	Fate
D 24	ALMIRANTE STORNI (ex-*Cowell*)	Bethlehem, San Pedro	17.8.71	Decommissioned 1982
D 20	BROWN (ex-*Heerman*)	Bethlehem, San Francisco	See notes	Decommissioned 1982
D 23	ALMIRANTE DOMECQ GARCIA (ex-*Braine*)	Bath Iron Wks	17.8.71	Extant 1982
D 21	ESPORA (ex-*Dortch*)	Federal, Kearny	See notes	Decommissioned 1977
D 22	ROSALES (ex-*Stembel*)	Bath Iron Wks	See notes	Decommissioned 1982

Bouchard was fitted with VDS, helicopter facilities and a hangar prior to transfer. *Piedra Buena* was originally acquired for spares, but she was actuated in 1977; the destroyer *Mansfield* was also originally transferred for spares, although for a while it was considered commissioning her as the *Espora*. Four MM38 Exocet (4×1) SSMs added to operational units in 1977-78. *Segui* did not receive FRAM II modernisation as other ships, although both have since had their VDS removed.

During the Falklands War *Bouchard* and *Piedra Buena* were used

Ex-US ALLEN M SUMNER class *destroyers*

No	Name	Builder	Acquired	Fate
D 26	HIPOLTO BOUCHARD (ex-*Borie*)	Federal, Kearny	1.7.72	Extant 1982
D 29	PIEDRA BUENA (ex-*Collett*)	Bath Iron Wks	Apr 1974	Extant 1982
D 25	SEGUI (ex-*Hawk*)	Federal, Kearny	1.7.72	Extant 1982
D 31	ESPORA (ex-*Mansfield*)	Bath Iron Wks	June 1974	BU 1978

to screen the cruiser *General Belgrano*, and delivered an unsuccessful depth charge attack following the torpedoing of that ship. *Segui* operated with the carrier during the conflict.

Four MM38 Exocet SSMs added 1977-78. Has SPS-40 and SPS-10 radar and SQS-23 sonar. During the Falklands conflict, she was part of the force working with the carrier. See under United States for further details.

Ex-US GEARING (FRAM II) class *destroyer*

No	Name	Builder	Acquired	Fate
D 27	COMODORO PY (ex-*Perkins*)	Consolidated, Orange	15.1.73	Extant 1982

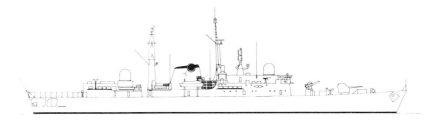

Hercules 1979

On 18.5.70 the Argentine Government announced the signing of a contract for two ships, one to be built in Argentina and the other in Great Britain. *Santisima Trinidad* has required a long time to build owing to delays caused by the technology transfer. She was sabotaged by terrorists on 22.8.75, causing moderate damage. *Hercules* was fitted with 2 MM38 Exocet above the hangar in 1979 and *Santisima Trinidad* commissioned with this system.

Both ships have since been fitted with 4 MM38, 2 either side of the funnel, rather than on top of the hangar. The Argentine Type 42s were part of the invasion force that captured the Falklands on 2 April. The 150 commandos that were landed at

British TYPE 42 (SHEFFIELD class) *destroyers*

No	Name	Builder	Laid down	Launched	Comp	Fate
D 1	HERCULES	Vickers, Barrow	16.6.71	24.10.72	10.5.76	Extant 1982
D 2	SANTISIMA TRINIDAD	AFNE, Rio Santiago	11.10.71	9.11.74	Dec 1982	Extant 1982

night on 1 April went ashore by helicopter from *Santisima Trinidad*. She was the flagship for the invasion force. During late April and early May, *Santisima Trinidad* provided a screen for the carrier. During this period, *Hercules* provided a screen for a destroyer force operating independently from the carrier forces. See under United Kingdom for further particulars.

Hercules, with Exocet fitted, 1982   *Author*

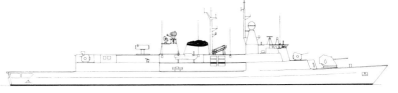

MEKO 360 H2 design

Initially to have been a class of six, four of which were to be built in Argentina, instead the Argentines decided to build four MEKO 360s and six MEKO 140s. Reloads are carried for the Aspide SAM magazine. The 40mm are controlled by 2 HSA LIROD optronic/radar directors. These ships were built on the modularised systems concept. Under construction during the War in the South Atlantic, the British-built gas turbines were embargoed for a while.

MEKO 360 H2 class *frigates*

Displacement:	3600t full load
Dimensions:	413ft oa, 390ft 5in pp × 49ft 3in × 19ft max
	125.9m, 119.0m × 15.0m × 5.8m
Machinery:	2-shaft COGOG: 2 Olympus TM 3B gas turbines, 51,800shp = 30.5kts; 2 Tyne RM-1C gas turbines, 10,200shp = 18kts. Range 4500nm at 18kts
Armament:	8 MM40 Exocet SSM missiles (4×2), 1 Albatros-Aspide SAM (1×8; 24 missiles), 1–127mm OTO Melara, 8–40mm Breda (4×2), 6–324mm ASW TT(2×3; 18 torpedoes), 2 Sea Lynx helicopters
Sensors:	Radar DA-08A, Decca 1226, WM 25 with STIR; sonar Atlas 80 hull-mounted; ECM AEG-Telefunken system, 2 SCLAR chaff RL (2×20)
Complement:	200

No	Name	Builder	Laid down	Launched	Comp	Fate
D 10	ALMIRANTE BROWN	Blohm & Voss, Hamburg	8.9.80	28.3.81	9.2.83	Extant 1983
D 11	LA ARGENTINA	Blohm & Voss, Hamburg	31.8.81	25.9.81	19.7.83	Extant 1983
D 5	HEROINA	Blohm & Voss, Hamburg	24.8.81	17.2.82	1984	Fitting out
D 13	SARANDI	Blohm & Voss, Hamburg	9.3.82	–	1984	Building

Launched 22.8.42. Armed in Argentina with 3–105mm (3×1), 4–47mm (4×1) AA, DC racks. Transferred to *Guardacostas* 1961 and renamed *Juan Batista Azopardo*.

Ex-British 'RIVER' class *frigate*

No	Name	Builder	Acquired	Fate
P 31	HERCULES (ex-*Asheville*, (ex-*Nadir*, ex-*Adur*)	Canadian Vickers	18.2.48	Sold 1969

Class (former name, comm, fate): *Heroina* (ex-*Reading*, 8.2.47, sold 5.8.64), *Sarandi* (ex-*Uniontown*, ex-*Chattanooga*, 18.2.48, sold 29.6.67), *Santisima Trinidad* (ex-*Caicos*, ex-*Hannam*, ?, sold 1971).

Ex-US TACOMA class *patrol frigates*

All units armed in Argentina with 2–105mm (2×1), 4–47mm (4×1) AA, DC racks. Pennant nos P 32–34 respectively. *Heroina* was converted 1961 to a meteorological vessel; *Santisima Trinidad* name often incorrectly cited as *Trinidad*) was converted to a hydrographic ship in 1962 and renamed *Comodoro Lasserre*.

Class (no, acquired):

Republica (P 35, 28.12.48)

British corvette *Smilax* launched on 24.12.42. Armed in Argentina with 1–105mm, 4–20mm (4×1), DC racks. See under Great Britain in the 1922–1946 volume for further details.

Ex-British modified 'FLOWER' class *frigate*

Drummond and *Guerrico* Apr 1980   *Author*

Good Hope and *Transvaal* were originally built for South Africa, but delivery was embargoed. They were purchased by Argentina on 25.9.78. For further details see under France. All three units were deployed extensively during the Falklands War. *Guerrico* supported the South Georgia operation on 3 April 1982. She was hit by an anti-tank rocket and heavy small arms fire. The hit was just below the Exocet launcher and the damage was modest. She spent three days in the yard being repaired. The other two ships supported the main invasion on 2 April. All three ships operated as an independent force to the north of the islands during late

March and the first two days of April. They retired to protected waters along with the rest of the fleet on 2 April.

French A 69 type *corvettes*

Armament: 4 MM38 Exocet SSM (4×1), 1–100mm, 1–40mm, 2–20mm (2×1), 6–324mm ASW TT (2×3)

Sensors: Radar DRBV-51A, DRBC-32C, Decca 1226; sonar Diodon

Other particulars: As French *D'Estienne D'Orves* class

No	Name	Builder	Laid down	Launched	Comp	Fate
F 701	DRUMMOND (ex-*Good Hope*)	Arsenal de Lorient	12.3.76	5.3.77	Oct 78	Extant 1982
F 702	GUERRICO (ex-*Transvaal*)	Arsenal de Lorient	1.10.76	Sept 77	Oct 78	Extant 1982
F 703	GRANVILLE	Arsenal de Lorient	late 78	28.6.80	22.6.81	Extant 1982

MEKO 140 basic design

This class was based on the Portuguese *Joao Coutinho* class. All six units are being built in Argentina. The first is scheduled to commission in 1985. Armament details not yet fixed.

MEKO 140 A16 class *corvettes*

Displacement: 1200t standard; 1470t full load

Dimensions: 299ft 3in oa, 283ft 6in pp × 40ft × 10ft 11in
91.2mm, 86.4m × 12.2m × 3.33m

Machinery: 2 shafts, 2 SEMT-Pielstick 16 PC2-5V400 diesels, 22,600bhp = 18kts. Range 4000nm at 18kts

Armament: 8 MM40 Exocet SSM (4×4), 1–76mm OTO Melara Compact, 2–40mm (1×2), 6–324mm ASW TT (3×2), 1 Sea Lynx helicopter

Sensors: Radar Decca 1226, DA-05/2, WM 28, LIROD gfcs; sonar ADS-4

Complement: 100

No	Name	Builder	Laid down	Launched	Comp	Fate
F 4	ESPORA	AFNE, Rio Santiago	3.4.81	23.1.82		Building
F 5	AZOPARDO	AFNE, Rio Santiago	Oct 81			Building
F 6	SPIRO	AFNE, Rio Santiago	Apr 82			Building
–		AFNE, Rio Santiago	Oct 82			Building
–		AFNE, Rio Santiago	Apr 83			Building
–		AFNE, Rio Santiago	Oct 83			Building

SUBMARINES

Santa Fe (i) was refitted at Mare Island Navy Yard, and commissioned 21.8.60; she was decommissioned in 1971. *Santa Fe* (ii) received a GUPPY II refit in 1948–50. The *Santa Fe* was employed in the initial invasion of the Falklands. On 2 April 1982 a small force of frogmen swam from the submerged submarine off Port Stanley and secured the landing site for the 600-plus Argentine Marine Corps

Ex-US BALAO class *submarines*

No	Name	Builder	Acquired	Fate
S 11	SANTA FE (i) (ex-*Lamprey*)	Manitowoc	27.7.60	BU for spares 1971
S 21	SANTA FE (ii) (ex-*Catfish*)	Electric Boat	7.1.71	Beached 25.4.82
S 12	SANTIAGO DEL ESTERO (i) (ex-*Macabi*)	Manitowoc	11.8.60	BU for spares 1972
S 22	SANTIAGO DEL ESTERO (ii) (ex-*Chivo*)	Electric Boat	Jan 1971	Extant 1982

invasion force. On 25 April *Santa Fe* was attacked by 3 British helicopters while on the surface after she had dropped supplies to the Argentine garrison of S Georgia. The submarine was hit by a Wasp AS 12 missile; she managed to reach King Edward Cove where she settled on the bottom. One petty officer was severely wounded during the attack and another killed by a British sentry after the crew had been taken prisoners. The hulk has since been moved out of the anchorage.

Santiago del Estero (i) was refitted at Mare Island Navy Yard and commissioned 21.8.60. A modernised fin was added in the United States in 1966; she was decommissioned in 1971. *Santiago del Estero* (ii) received a GUPPY IA refit in 1961. She was not operational during the Falklands War. Initially the submarine remained at Mar del Plata, the primary submarine base. During April she was moved to Puerto Belgrano in an attempt to keep the Royal Navy guessing.

Santiago del Estero outboard of the *Almirante Domecq Garcia* (*Comodoro Py* astern) 1982
Author

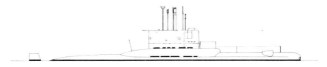

Salta as completed
NB 1/750 scale

These two units were built in sections in West Germany and assembled in Argentina. See Greek *Glavkos* class for details. Both units deployed for the Falklands War. *Salta* returned to base suffering from some mechanical problem. *San Luis* was stationed in a 'free fire' area north of the Falklands. She attacked British forces on two occasions. On the first, on about 5 May, she fired torpedoes at a British task force; none hit. *San Luis* was pinned down for about 20 hours by British forces before escaping. On 10 May *San Luis* attacked another target without result.

West German Type 209 *submarines*

No	Name	Builder	Laid down	Launched	Comp	Fate
S 31	SALTA	Howaldswerke, Kiel/AFNE, Rio Santiago	30.4.70	9.11.72	7.3.74	Extant 1982
S 32	SAN LUIS	Howaldswerke Kiel/AFNE, Rio Santiago	1.10.70	3.4.73	24.5.74	Extant 1982

TR 1700 design

Contracted on 30.11.77. Initially the Argentines were to acquire four Type 1700s and two TR 1400s (a smaller version), but in 1982 the order was changed to six of the larger type. The first two boats are being built in Emden and the remaining four in Argentina at Astilleros Domecq Garcia, Buenos Aires. One laid down 1982.

West German Type TR 1700 *submarines*

Displacement:	2100t surfaced; 2300t submerged
Dimensions:	213ft 3in pp × 23ft 11in × 21ft 4in max
	65.0m × 7.3m × 6.5m
Machinery:	1-shaft diesel-electric, 8970hp = 15kts surfaced, 13kts snorkeling, 25kts submerged. Range 20nm/110nm/460nm at 25kts/15kts/6kts submerged, or 15,000nm at 5kts surfaced
Armament:	6–533mm TT (bow, 22 torpedoes), 4 rocket launchers
Complement:	26

No	Name	Builder	Laid down	Launched	Comp	Fate
S 33	SANTA CRUZ	Thyssen Nordseewerke, Emden	6.12.80	Dec 1982	1983	On trials
S 34	SAN JUAN	Thyssen Nordseewerke, Emden				Building

AMPHIBIOUS WARFARE VESSELS

Modified US DE SOTO COUNTY type *tank landing ship*

Displacement:	4164t normal; 7100t full load
Dimensions:	445ft × 62ft × 17ft 6in
	135.6m × 18.9m × 5.3m
Machinery:	2 shafts; 6 diesels, 13,700bhp = 16kts
Armament:	12–40/60mm (3×4)
Sensors:	Plessey AWS-1 radar
Complement:	124

No	Name	Builder	Launched	Fate
Q 42	CABO SAN ANTONIO	AFNE, Rio Santiago	1968	Extant 1982

Very similar to US *De Soto County* LSTs; commissioned 2.11.78. Can carry up to 23 medium tanks and 700 men. She carried the reinforced 2nd Marine Battalion to the Falklands in April 1982 and laid mines off Port Stanley.

Ex-US LST 511 class *tank landing ships*

Class:
Cabo San Bartolome (ex-*BDT 1*), *BDT 2*, *Cabo San Francisco de Paula* (ex-*BDT 3*), *Cabo San Gonzalo* (ex-*BDT 4*), *BDT 5*, *Cabo San Isidro* (ex-*BDT 6*), *Dona Elora* (ex-*BDT 7*), *Dona Stella* (ex-*BDT 8*), *Dona Dorothea* (ex-*BDT 9*), *BDT 10*, *Dona Irma* (ex-*BDT 11*), *BDT 12*, *BDT 13*, *Cabo San Vicente* (ex-*BDT 14*)

Fourteen ex-US LSTs, built by Puget Sound DD in 1944, were transferred in the early 1950s. *BDT 5*, *8*, *9* and *12* were stricken 1958–60; *BDT 2*, *7*, *10*, *11* and *13* were broken up 1964; *BDT 1* was deleted 1971, *BDT 6* in 1978, *BDT 4* and *14* in 1980, and *BDT 2* in 1981

OTHER AMPHIBIOUS SHIPS
There were also two ex-US LSMs, *BDM 1* and *BDM 2* acquired after the war. *BDM 2* became the mine warfare support ship *Corrientes* in 1969, and *BDM 1* was stricken 1971. A number of troop transports have also been employed since 1947: *Bahia Aguirre* and *Bahia Buen Suceso* (3100t, built in Canada, 1950) were still in service 1982 the latter landing the Argentine scrap metal party on S Georgia; *La Pataia, Le Maire* and *Les Eclairseur* (3825t, built in Italy, 1949–50) were broken up in 1964, except *La Pataia* which was sold in 1971.

LATIN AMERICA

Ex-US ASHLAND class *dock landing ship*

No	Name	Builder	Acquired	Fate
Q 43	CANDIDO DE LASALA (ex-*Gunston Hall*)	Moore, Oakland	24.4.70	Extant 1982

War-built LSD armed with 12–40mm (2×4, 2×2). Doubles, when required, as a depot ship for small craft.

MINOR LANDING CRAFT
In 1982 these comprised:
Four ex-US LSM(6) type, numbered *EDM 1–4*, transferred 1971.
Ex-US LCVP type, variously reported as 8 and 14 strong, numbered between *EDVP 1* and *37*; the remainder of 37 craft transferred between 1946 and 1970
There is also an unknown number of Argentine-built LCVPs, constructed since 1971.
Fifteen US LCILs were transferred after the war, and numbered *BD 1* to *15*. These were withdrawn from service between 1958 and 1971.

SMALL SURFACE COMBATANTS

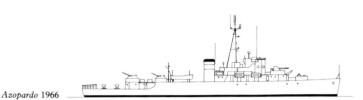

Azopardo 1966

AZOPARDO class *patrol escorts*

Displacement:	1220t standard; 1400t full load
Dimensions:	278ft 10in pp × 31ft 6in × 13ft 2in max 85.0m × 9.6m × 4.0m
Machinery:	2-shaft Parsons geared turbines, 2 watertube boilers, 5000shp = 20kts. Range 2300nm
Armament:	1–4.1in, 2–40mm (2×1) AA, 1 Hedgehog, 4 DC launchers
Complement:	170

Class (launched, comm):
Azopardo (11.12.53, Jan 1955), *Piedra Buena* (17.12.54, 16.12.58).
Both built by AFNE, Rio Santiago. Pennant nos P 35 and P 36 respectively. Originally, these units were to be *King* class patrol vessels, but they were redesigned to be a larger, follow-on type. They were discarded in 1973.

US 78ft HIGGINS type *torpedo boats*

Displacement:	36t; 50t full load
Dimensions:	78ft oa × 21ft × 5ft 23.8m × 6.4m × 1.5m
Machinery:	3-shaft Packard petrol engines, 4500bhp = 42kts
Armament:	2–40mm (2×1) AA, 4 torpedoes
Complement:	10 (est)

Class:
Alakush (P 82), *Towwora* (P 84); the last of LT 1–9
Commissioned in 1949, and built specifically for Argentina. Five were disposed of in 1963 and two in 1966; two remained in service 1982.

West German TNC 45 type *fast attack craft*

Displacement:	240t normal; 265t full load
Dimensions:	138ft 9in pp, 147ft 4in oa × 24ft 3in × 7ft 6in 42.3m, 44.9m × 7.4m × 2.3m
Machinery:	4 shafts, 4 MTU MD 872 diesels, 14,000bhp = 37kts. Range 640nm/1700nm at 36kts/16kts
Armament:	1–76mm OTO Melara Compact, 2–40mm (2×1), 2–533mm TT
Sensors:	Radar Decca 101, MSA M22
Complement:	42

Class (no, launched, comm):
Indomita (ELPR 2, 8.4.74, Dec 74), *Intrepida* (ELPR 1, 12.12.74, 20.7.74)
Both built by Lürssen, Vegesack, ordered in 1970. Two further projected units were cancelled. The TT fire German wire-guided T4 torpedoes.

Indomita 1980   *Author*

Israeli DABUR type *patrol craft*

Class (no):
Baradero (P 61), *Barranqueras* (P 62), *Clorinda* (P 63), *Concepcion del Uruguay* (P 64)
Built by IAI and delivered in 1978. Armed with 2–20mm (2×1) and 4–12.7mm MG (2×2).

OTHER PATROL VESSELS
The Argentine Navy also operates a number of armed tugs in the patrol role. Two 1235t ex-US *Achomawi* class ocean tugs, *Comandante General Irigoyen* (ex-*Cahuilla*, transferred 1961) and *Francisco de Churruca* (ex-*Luiseno*, purchased 1971) are armed with 4–40mm (1×2, 2×1). Three 570t ex-US *Sotoyomo* class tugs, *Yamana* (ex-*Maricopa*, transferred 1947), *Alferez Sobral* (ex-*Catawba*, transferred 1972) and *Comodoro Somellera* (ex-*Salish*, transferred 1972), are armed with 1–40mm and 2–20mm (2×1). A sister, *Daiquita* was sold in 1979; *Somellera* was sunk (on 3.5.82), and *Sobral* badly damaged, by Sea Skua missiles fired from British Lynx helicopters during the Falklands War.

MINE WARFARE VESSELS

Ex-British 'TON' class *minesweepers*

Class (former name, recomm):
Chaco (ex-*Rennington*, Dec 1969), *Chubut* (ex-*Santon*, 19.7.68), *Formosa* (ex-*Ilmington*, 19.7.68), *Neuquen* (ex-*Hicleton*, 13.9.68), *Rio Negro* (ex-*Tarlton*, 20.6.68), *Tierra del Fuego* (ex-*Bevington*, 23.12.68)
Pennant Nos M 5, M 3, M 6, M 1, M 2 and M 4 respectively. *Chaco* and *Formosa* have been converted to minehunters. All units are still in service.

Bahamas

The Bahamas archipelago of 700 islands (40 inhabited), which became independent within the Commonwealth in July 1973, has no navy as such; patrol boats are operated by the Marine Police and should stronger defences be called for the country would turn to Britain. The Bahamas serves as a base for a US naval underwater research and development station and thre are also US Navy and Coast Guard units on the islands. The patrol boats are based at Bay Shore Marina, Nassau. On 11.5.80 the patrol boat *Flamingo*, sister ship to *Marlin*, was hit by Cuban MiG-21 aircraft and sunk; Cuba subsequently paid out £2.5m in reparations.

One Vosper Thornycroft 103ft type patrol boat *Marlin* (P 01) (100t, ordered 1977, entered service 23.5.78) is operated. Extant 1982.
Seven Keith Nelson type patrol boats (30t, ordered 1977, glass fibre construction). Extant 1982. Specially designed for long patrols among the Bahamas group of islands.

Flamingo 1978   *C & S Taylor*

Barbados

Barbados operates a coastal patrol force; a 124-man volunteer coast guard (created early 1973) employs seven patrol boats (the 37.5m *Trident* in service November 1981, one 30t, British-built 'Guardian' class boat and three 11.5t Lewis type boats also British-built, plus 2 converted shrimp boats). As an independent state since 1966 within the Commonwealth Barbados would rely on Britain for military support. The Coast Guard, under a Royal Navy Commander, has its HQ at St Ann's Fort, St Michael and a new base (HMBS *Willoughby Fort*) at Bridgetown, the island capital.

Trident as completed   Brooke Marine

Belize

Belize (British Honduras until June 1973) became independent on 21 September 1981 after protracted negotiations; the 144,857 inhabitants were, and still are, wary of the Guatemalan threat to peace and security. Guatemala has consistently claimed a large area of Belize as her own territory. Security against an incursion by Guatamala remains upheld by a British military presence as well as by several states in the area, namely Jamaica, Barbados and Guyana.

Belize operates two 22kt patrol boats *Belize* and *Belmopan* (15t, Brooke Marine type, 3 MG built in 1972) along her 174-mile coastline (she has proven offshore oil reserves) and has a total of three merchant ships. Personnel amounts to 50 volunteers. A British frigate or destroyer is stationed off Belize and acts as Caribbean guard ship; she is backed up by a support ship.

Bolivia

An internally strife-torn country which has experienced numerous *coups*, Bolivia has less cause to fear external than internal aggression because of her mountainous and landlocked geographical location. Bolivia has been in dispute with Chile since the early 1960s over the Rio Lanca and outlets to the Pacific. The *Fuerza Naval Boliviana* with a total of 2600 men operates riverine (12,000 miles navigable) and lake patrol craft from bases at Tiquina, Puerto Suárez, Riberalta, Trinidad, Guaramerin and Puerto Villarroel. A rear-admiral commands the four naval districts and most training is done in Argentina.

One transport ship *Libertador Bolivar* is operated. Acquired from Venezuela in 1977 and employed commercially.
Seven river transport boats. Extant 1982.
Up to 30 river patrol boats in operation, including about 24 on Lake Titicaca, and 2 ex-US PBR Mk 2 boats.

Brazil

Out of World War II, the Brazilian Navy acquired the long-desired parity with that of Argentina. Brazil supported the Allied war against the Axis almost from the beginning: Allied planes patrolled the South Atlantic from Brazilian airfields; convoys were screened by Brazilian warships; and 25,000 Brazilian troops fought in Italy. It is not, therefore, surprising that, beginning in 1944, the United States began to transfer destroyer escorts to Brazil under Lend-Lease. Five years earlier, a proposed transfer of destroyers from the United States had created a furore in Argentina: the United States was accused of upsetting the balance of power and so the arrangement was cancelled. By the late 1940s, the theory of parity with Argentina had been established.

The Brazilian Navy has been the Latin American trend-setter in warship acquisitions. This navy was the first to obtain the submarine, the dreadnought, and the aircraft carrier. In 1956 Brazil purchased a *Colossus* class carrier, HMS *Vengeance*, from the Admiralty for $9 million, and the ship, renamed *Minas Gerais*, was extensively modernised. The acquisition of the carrier caused a major inter-service struggle within Brazil. At issue was the control of the aircraft to be flown from *Minas Gerais*. From the completion of her modernisation until 1963, the carrier was planeless and neither President Juseelino Kubitschek nor his two successors were able to resolve the problem. In 1963 the Navy purchased six T-28 trainers and four helicopters, but the Air Force, which was responsible for all military aircraft, refused to let the planes be assigned to the carrier. Ultimately, numerous high-ranking Air Force and Navy officials resigned. The final decision was that fixed-wing aircraft operating from the carrier would be flown by the Air Force, and rotary-wing aircraft by the Navy. A naval air arm was formed on 26 January 1965. The significance of this decision was that the Navy would not control attack aircraft and that the carrier would be exclusively an ASW platform. Thus, once again, the Argentine Navy, with *Independencia* and, later, *25 de Mayo* would be the most powerful in the South Atlantic.

Brazil has taken the greatest advantage of bi-national shipbuilding agreements of any country in Latin America. Since independence in the early nineteenth century, Brazil's struggle to develop a shipbuilding industry has been tenacious. One-third of the Brazilian fleet which participated in the War of the Triple Alliance (1864–70) was of indigenous construction, but from 1890 until the 1950s, Brazil struggled to re-establish her shipbuilding industry. In December 1958, a major breakthrough occurred: Ishikawa-Harima Heavy Industries of Japan founded a new shipyard in Brazil. By 1974 the labourers and skilled workmen were Brazilian, with a few Japanese filling technical and supervisory positions. In that year the yard employed 3250 persons, operated the two largest drydocks in Latin America, and had already constructed 426,906 grt tons. This, plus other maritime industries attracted into Brazil, provided the necessary industrial base for the bi-national agreement to construct frigates. In 1970 Brazil and the British company Vosper Thornycroft agreed to construct six Mk 10 frigates, four of which were to be built in England and two in Brazil. In mid-1981 Brazil ordered a modified Mark 10 frigate to be built in Brazil. The frigate will be classified as a training ship. Also, 12 corvettes of Italian design were ordered in 1982 and will be built in Brazil. The newly established shipbuilding industry, plus the bi-national construction agreement, have thus allowed Brazil to begin to meet much of its own shipbuilding needs. In 1982 46,000 officers and men (12-month conscripts, including 14,500 marines) serve with the Brazilian Navy; main bases are at Rio de Janeiro, Aratu, Belem, Natal, Ladario (river flotilla) and Sao Pedro (naval air arm) covering a 4655-mile coastline and the world's longest river system. The active Fleet totalled 102 warships.

FLEET STRENGTH 1947

BATTLESHIPS

Name	Launched	Disp (normal)	Fate
Minas Gerais class			
MINAS GERAIS	10.9.08	19,200t	Discarded 1953
SAO PAULO	19.4.09	19,200t	Discarded 1951

Minas Gerais was inactive in the latter years of her career. *Sao Paulo* had not been modernised in the 1930s as her sister had been, and she was no more than a stationary guard ship from that time until her sale.

CRUISER

Name	Launched	Disp (normal)	Fate
RIO GRANDE DO SUL	20.4.09	3000t	Discarded 1948

Mariz e Barros with Seacat SAM aft 1968   *USN*

DESTROYERS

Name	Launched	Disp (normal)	Fate
Marcilio Dias class			
GREENHALGH	8.7.41	1500t	Discarded 1966
MARCILIO DIAS	20.7.40	1500t	Discarded 1966
MARIZ E BARROS	28.12.40	1500t	Discarded 1972
Acre class			
ACRE	30.5.45	1340t	Discarded 1974
AJURICABA	30.5.45	1340t	Discarded 1964
AMAZONAS	29.11.43	1340t	Discarded 1973
APA	30.5.45	1340t	Discarded 1964
ARAGUARY	14.7.46	1340t	Discarded 1974
ARAGUAYA	29.11.43	1340t	Discarded 1974

Mariz e Barros was fitted with a Seacat SAM system in 1966 as a test platform; this system was transferred to *Mato Grosso*, an *Allen M Sumner* class unit, in the mid-1970s.

DESTROYER ESCORTS

Name	Launched	Disp (normal)	Fate
Ex-US Cannon class (DET type)			
BABITONGA (ex-*Alger*)	8.7.43	1240t	Discarded 1964
BAEPENDI (ex-*Cannon*)	25.5.43	1240t	Discarded 1974
BAURU (ex-*Reybold*)	22.8.43	1240t	Discarded 1975
BEBERIBE (ex-*Herzog*)	5.9.43	1240t	Discarded 1968
BENEVENTE (ex-*Christopher*)	8.7.43	1240t	Discarded 1975
BERTIOGA (ex-*Pennewill*)	8.8.43	1240t	Discarded 1964
BOCAINA (ex-*Marts*)	8.8.43	1240t	Discarded 1975
BRACUI (ex-*McAnn*)	5.9.43	1240t	Discarded 1974

*Minas Gerais c*1975   Brazilian Navy

SUBMARINES

Name	Launched	Disp	Fate
Humaita class			
HUMAITA	11.6.27	1390t/1884t	Discarded 1951
Tupi class			
TAMOIO	14.2.37	620t/853t	Discarded 1960
TIMBIRA	30.12.36	620t/853t	Discarded 1960
TUPI	28.11.36	620t/853t	Discarded 1960

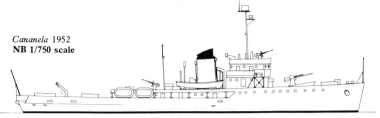

Cananela 1952
NB 1/750 scale

MINOR WARSHIPS

Name	Launched	Disp (normal)	Fate
Henrique Dias class trawlers			
BARRETO DE MENEZES (ex-*Paru*)	Feb 45	813t	Discarded 1960
FELIPE CAMARAO (ex-*Papaterra*)	Jul 42	813t	Discarded 1960
FERNANDES VIEIRA (ex-*Parati*)	11.6.42	813t	Discarded 1953
HENRIQUE DIAS (ex-*Pargo*)	26.8.42	813t	Discarded 1960
MATHIAS DE ALBUQUERQUE (ex-*Pampano*)	11.6.42	813t	Discarded 1952
VIDAL DE NEGREIROS (ex-*Pelegrime*)	1942	813t	Discarded 1951
Rio Pardo submarine chaser			
RIO PARDO	29.11.43	132t	Discarded 1974
Carioca class minelayers			
CABEDELO	16.9.39	552t	Discarded 1960
CAMOCIM	28.10.39	552t	Discarded 1960
CANANELA	22.10.38	552t	Discarded 1960
CARAVELAS	14.9.39	552t	Discarded 1960
CARIOCA	22.10.38	552t	Discarded 1960
Ex-US PC class submarine chasers			
GOIANA (ex-*PC 554*)	2.5.42	280t	Discarded 1952
GRAJAU (ex-*PC 1236*)	17.11.43	280t	Discarded 1960
GRAUNA (ex-*PC 561*)	6.12.43	280t	Discarded 1960
GUAIBA (ex-*PC 604*)	14.6.43	280t	Discarded 1952
GUAJARA (ex-*PC 607*)	22.10.43	280t	Discarded 1960
GUAPORE (ex-*PC 554*)	26.9.42	280t	Discarded 1958
GUAIPA (ex-*PC 605*)	14.6.43	280t	Discarded 1952
GURUPI (ex-*PC 547*)	26.9.42	280t	Discarded 1960
Ex-US SC 497 class submarine chasers			
JACUI (ex-*SC 1288*)	19.5.43	95t	Discarded 1951
JAGUARAO (ex-*SC 765*)	16.2.43	95t	Discarded 1951
JAGUARIBE (ex-*SC 767*)	16.2.43	95t	Discarded 1951
JAVARI (ex-*SC 763*)	7.12.42	95t	Discarded 1951
JUNDIAI (ex-*SC 1289*)	26.4.43	95t	Discarded 1951
JURUA (ex-*SC 764*)	31.12.44	95t	Discarded 1951
JURUENA (ex-*SC 766*)	31.12.42	95t	Discarded 1951
JUTAI (ex-*SC 762*)	31.12.42	95t	Discarded 1951

MISCELLANEOUS

Name	Launched	Disp (normal)	Fate
River gunboats			
PARNAIBA	2.9.37	595t	Extant 1982
PARAGUACU (ex-*Victoria*, ex-*Espiritu Santo*)	22.12.38	430t	Discarded 1972
PERNAMBUCO	1910	470t	Discarded 1948
Training ship			
ALMIRANTE SALDANHA	12.19.33	3325t	Extant 1982

Almirante Saldanha initially was a 4-masted schooner. In 1961 her masts were removed and she was refitted as an oceanographic research ship.

MAJOR SURFACE SHIPS

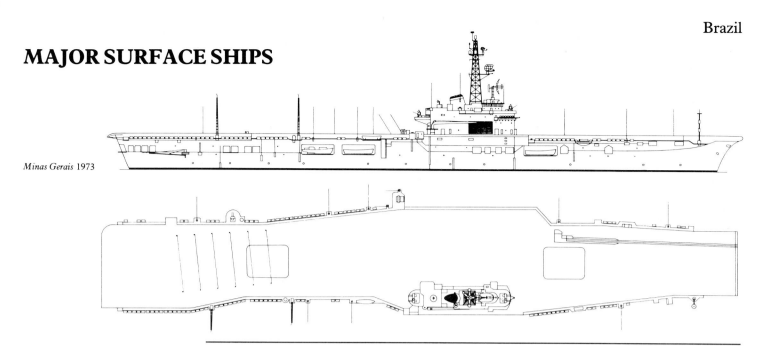

Minas Gerais 1973

Ex-British COLOSSUS class *aircraft carrier*

No	Name	Builder	Acquired	Fate
A 11	MINAS GERAIS (ex-*Vengeance*)	Swan Hunter, Wallsend	14.12.56	Extant 1982

Laid down 16.11.42 and launched 23.2.44, *Minas Gerais* was purchased by Brazil for $9 million and reconstructed for $27 million. She was reconstructed at Verolme Dock, Rotterdam from June 1957 to Dec 1960. She received an angled deck, steam catapult, mirror-sight deck landing system, new fire control equipment and radar. During reconstruction a 2500kW alternating current system was installed; current is supplied by 4 turbo-generators and one diesel generator. Hangar dimensions are 445ft × 52ft × 17ft 6in high (*135.64m*

× *15.85m* × *5.33m*). The flight deck and landing gear were reinforced to take aircraft up to 20,000lb. *Minas Gerais* was commissioned 6.12.60 at Rotterdam and arrived in Rio de Janeiro 13.1.61. A dispute between the Navy and Air Force delayed deployment until the mid 1960s. The compromise reached was that the Air

Force would fly the fixed wing aircraft and the Navy would fly the helicopters. *Minas Gerais* underwent a major refit 1976–80. She is used primarily for ASW. Currently armed with 10–40mm (2×4, 1×2) with SPG-34 radar on the quad mounts; 2 Mk 63 and 1 Mk 51 fire control systems. SPS-40B has replaced SPS-12 and the

rest of the radar fit comprises SPS-8B, SPS-4 and Raytheon 1402. Aircraft total about 15: up to 7 S2E Trackers, and 8 SH-3D Sea Kings (although 4 Sea Kings, 2 Jet Rangers and 2 Ecureuils is more common).

Two V/STOL carriers are reported to be under discussion.

Ex-US BROOKLYN class *cruiser*

No	Name	Builder	Acquired	Fate
C 11	BARROSO (ex-*Philadelphia*)	Philadelphia Yd	Jan 1951	BU 1973

Purchased by Brazil in Jan 1951, she commissioned 21.8.51. Bulges were added and the armoured conning tower was removed late during World War II to help improve stability. The mainmast derricks and catapults were removed prior to transfer. The hangar in the hull could accommodate 2 helicopters with spare parts. The nearly flat counter and high freeboard aft provide an excellent helicopter platform. Her 8–5in were in single mounts and AA weapons comprised 28–40mm and 20–20mm. *Barroso* was decommissioned in 1973 and scrapped.

Barroso date unknown   *Author*

Ex-US ST LOUIS class *cruiser*

No	Name	Builder	Acquired	Fate
C 12	TAMANDARE (ex-*St Louis*)	Newport News	29.1.51	Sold 1975

Purchased by Brazil 29.1.51 and commissioned 6.2.52. She underwent the same wartime alterations as *Barroso*. She differed substantially from the 5 ex-US *Brooklyn* class ships in Latin America. Her superstructure is placed closer together; her 8–5in guns were paired in gunhouses on high bases, and she had a small tripod abaft the aft funnel. Light AA comprised

28–40mm, 8–20mm. The remarks for *Barroso* concerning helicopter operations apply to *Tamandare*. *Tamandare* was offered for auction, Sept 1975.

LATIN AMERICA

Although sister-ships, these units possess many differences, explicable by the fact that they were completed over a 2 year period. *Para* and *Paraiba*, as early *Fletcher*s, have rounded bridges where later units have the angular fronts. Armament varies as follows: *Pernambuco* 4–5in (4×1), 6–3in (3×2), Hedgehog, DC racks; all others 5–5in (5×1), 10–40mm (4×2, 1×2), Hedgehog, DC racks.

Ex-US FLETCHER class *destroyers*

No	Name	Builder	Acquired	Fate
D 33	MARANHAO (ex-*Shields*)	Puget Sound N Yd	1.7.72	Extant 1982
D 27	PARA (ex-*Guest*)	Boston N Yd	5.6.59	Discarded 1978
D 28	PARAIBA (ex-*Bennett*)	Boston N Yd	15.12.59	Discarded 1978
D 29	PARANA (ex-*Franks*)	Bethlehem, Staten I	20.7.61	Extant 1982
D 30	PERNAMBUCO (ex-*Knapp*)	Seattle-Tacoma	20.7.61	Extant 1982
D 31	PIAUI (ex-*Lewis Hancock*)	Federal, Kearny	2.8.67	Discarded 1979
D 32	SANTA CATARINA (ex-*Irwin*)	Bethlehem, San Pedro	10.5.68	Discarded 1978

All except *Mato Grosso* had received FRAM II modernisation. *Mato Grosso* has 1 Seacat SAM (1×4) with M20 optical director. *Sergipe* and *Espirito Santo* have VDS as well as standard SQS-29/32 sonar.

Ex-US ALLEN M SUMNER class *destroyers*

No	Name	Builder	Acquired	Fate
D 34	MATO GROSSO (ex-*Compton*)	Federal, Kearny	27.9.72	Extant 1982
D 35	SERGIPE (ex-*James C Owens*)	Bethlehem, San Pedro	16.7.73	Extant 1982
D 36	ALAGAOS (ex-*Buck*)	Bethlehem, San Francisco	16.7.73	Extant 1982
D 37	RIO GRANDE DO NORTE (ex-*Strong*)	Bethlehem, San Pedro	29.10.73	Extant 1982
D 38	ESPIRITO SANTO (ex-*Lowry*)	Bethlehem, San Pedro	29.10.73	Extant 1982

FRAM I conversions. Transfer of one extra ship, *McKean* (DD 784) is under consideration.

Ex-US GEARING class *destroyers*

No	Name	Builder	Acquired	Fate
D 25	MARCILIO DIAZ (ex-*Henry W Tucker*)	Consolidated, Orange	3.12.73	Extant 1982
D 26	MARIZ E BARROS (ex-*Brinkley Bass*)	Consolidated, Orange	3.12.73	Extant 1982

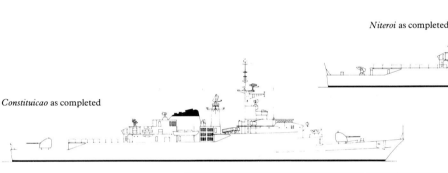

Niteroi as completed

Constituicao as completed

NITEROI class *frigates*

Designed by Vosper Thronycroft and designated Mk 10, this handsome class is unique to the Brazilian Navy. The contract between Vosper Thornycroft Ltd, Portsmouth, and the Brazilian government was announced on 29.9.70 for a value of £100 million. Under the terms, 4 ships were to be built in Great Britain and 2 in Brazil, with materials, equipment, and lead-yard services supplied by Vosper Thornycroft. These ships are comparable in size and complexity to the British Type 42, yet the Mk 10 requires a complement of 100 less men. Those ships built in Brazil required much more time to complete.

They are divided into two sub-types, for ASW and general purpose duties, the latter exchanging Ikara system (called Branik in Brazil) and VDS for SSMs and an extra gun. They are all fitted with CAAIS action data automation system and Decca ECM gear.

In June 1981 the Brazilian Navy ordered a training ship based on the design of the Mk 10 *Niteroi* from the Arsenal de Marinho, Rio de Janeiro.

Displacement:	3200t standard; 3800t full load
Dimensions:	400ft wl, 424ft oa × 44ft 2in × 18ft 2in max *121.9m, 129.2m × 13.5m × 5.6m*
Machinery:	2-shaft CODAG: 2 Rolls-Royce Olympus gas turbines, plus 4 MTU diesels, 56,000shp + 18,000bhp = 30kts (22kts diesels). Endurance 45 days
Armament:	2 Seacat SAM (2×3), 1 Ikara ASW missile, 1–4.5in, 2–40mm (2×1), 1–375mm Bofors ASW RL (1×2), 6–324mm Mk 32 ASW TT (2×3), 1 DC rack, 1 Lynx helicopter (except *Constituicao* and *Liberal* which have 1 extra 4.5in gun aft and 4 MM38 Exocet SSM instead of Ikara)
Sensors:	Radar AWS-2, ZW-06, RTN-10X fire control; sonar EDO 610, EDO 700E VDS (not in *Constituicao* and *Liberal*)
Complement:	200

No	Name	Builder	Laid down	Launched	Comp	Fate
F 42	CONSTITUICAO	Vosper Thornycroft, Ltd	13.3.74	15.4.76	31.3.78	Extant 1982
F 41	DEFENSORA	Vosper Thornycroft, Ltd	14.12.72	27.3.75	5.3.77	Extant 1982
F 44	INDEPENDENCIA	Arsenal de Marinho, Rio de Janeiro	11.6.72	2.9.74	3.9.79	Extant 1982
F 43	LIBERAL	Vosper Thornycroft, Ltd	2.5.75	7.2.77	19.11.78	Extant 1982
F 40	NITEROI	Vosper Thornycroft, Ltd	8.6.72	8.2.74	20.11.76	Extant 1982
F 45	UNIAO	Arsenal de Marinho, Rio de Janeiro	11.6.72	14.3.75	17.9.80	Extant 1982

She in fact will be considerably different from her near sisters. Her statistics are: 2333t light, 3345t full load; 430ft 9in oa × 44ft 4in × 13ft 9in max; *131.3m × 13.5m × 4.2m)*, 2 shafts, 2 diesels = 19kts; armed with 1–76mm OTO Melara Compact; complement of 150 plus cadets. She was laid down 18.9.81 and will be named *Brazil*.

Defensora June 1977

C & S Taylor

SUBMARINES

Both were refitted at Philadelphia N Yd before transfer, initially as a 5-year loan under MDAP. After return to the USN *Humaita* was sunk as a target.

Ex-US GATO class *submarines*

No	Name	Builder	Acquired	Fate
S 14	HUMAITA (ex-*Muskallunge*)	Electric Boat	Jan 1957	Returned 1969
S 15	RIACHVELO (ex-*Paddle*)	Electric Boat	Jan 1957	BU 1968

Both units were refitted at the Pearl Harbor N Yd and transferred in Sept 1963. They were overhauled in the early 1970s, at which time they received modern fins. *Rio Grande do Sul* was decommissioned in 1972 and sold for scrap, June 1975. *Bahia* was sold to the Brazilian Museum of Naval Technology, Santos.

Ex-US BALAO class *submarines*

No	Name	Builder	Acquired	Fate
S 11	RIO GRANDE DO SUL (ex-*Sand Lance*)	Portsmouth N Yd	Sept 1963	BU 1975
S 12	BAHIA (ex-*Plaice*)	Portsmouth N Yd	Sept 1963	Museum ship 1972

All modernised 1948–50 under GUPPY II programme (*Odax* had already received GUPPY I). *Rio Grande* and *Rio de Janiero* were decommissioned in 1978.

Ex-US GUPPY II type *submarines*

No	Name	Builder	Acquired	Fate
S 10	GUANA BARA (ex-*Dogfish*)	Electric Boat	28.7.72	Extant 1982
S 11	RIO GRANDE DO SUL (ex-*Grampus*)	Boston N Yd	13.5.72	BU 1981
S 12	BAHIA (ex-*Sea Leopard*)	Portsmouth N Yd	27.3.73	Extant 1982
S 13	RIO DE JANEIRO (ex-*Odax*)	Portsmouth N Yd	8.7.72	BU 1981
S 14	CEARA (ex-*Amberjack*)	Boston N Yd	17.10.73	Extant 1982

The first two units were ordered in 1969 and the third in 1972. Completion of *Toneleros* was delayed by a serious fire. She was towed to Chatham Dockyard where the centre 60ft section was replaced and she was rewired. This fire caused the recabling of all *Oberon* units then under construction. They carry 18 torpedoes, British Mk 8 and US Mk 37s.

British OBERON class *submarines*

No	Name	Builder	Laid down	Launched	Comp	Fate
S 20	HUMAITA	Vickers, Barrow	3.11.70	5.10.71	18.6.73	Extant 1982
S 21	TONELEROS	Vickers, Barrow	18.11.71	22.11.72	8.9.78	Extant 1982
S 22	RIACHUELO	Vickers, Barrow	26.5.73	6.9.75	12.3.77	Extant 1982

Both underwent Guppy III modernisations in 1948 followed by Guppy III reconstruction in 1961–62.

Early in 1983 Brazil decided in favour of the West German Type 209 design for 3 new submarines to be built in Rio de Janeiro, to replace the early Guppy types.

Ex-US GUPPY III type *submarines*

No	Name	Builder	Acquired	Fate
S 15	GOIAS (ex-*Trumpetfish*)	Cramp	15.10.73	Extant 1982
S 16	AMAZONAS (ex-*Greenfish*)	Electric Boat	19.12.73	Extant 1982

AMPHIBIOUS WARFARE VESSELS

Ex-US DE SOTO COUNTY class *tank landing ship*

No	Name	Builder	Acquired	Fate
G 26	DUQUE DE CAXAIS (ex-*Grant County*)	Avondale	15.1.73	Extant 1982

Launched 12.10.56. Stülken heavy lifting gear fitted.

Ex-US LST 511 class *tank landing ship*

No	Name	Builder	Acquired	Fate
G 28	GARCIA D'AVILA (ex-*Outagami County*)	Bethlehem, Hingham	1.12.73	Extant 1982

Originally transferred on loan 21.5.71.

Ex-US CABILDO class *dock landing ship*

The *Donner* (LSD 20) was reported to be on offer to Brazil in 1981, together with the *Rushmore* (LSD 14) which was to be purchased for spares.

MINOR LANDING CRAFT
Brazil also operates the following:
Four US *LCU 1610* type utility landing craft, named *Guarapari* (L 10), *Timbau* (L 11), *Comboriu* (L 12), *Tramandai* (L 13), built at Rio 1974–78.
Twenty-eight Japanese-built LCVPs, 1959–60.
Fifteen Brazilian-built 'EDVPs' (LCVPs), 1971.

SMALL SURFACE COMBATANTS

NEW CONSTRUCTION *corvettes*

Displacement:	1600t full load
Dimensions:	288ft 8in × 37ft 1in × 10ft 10in max
	88.0m × 11.3m × 3.3m
Machinery:	2 shafts, 4 diesels = 25kts
Armament:	8 MM40 Exocet SSM (2×4), 1–76mm OTO Melara Compact, 1–40mm, 6–324mm Mk 32 ASW TT (2×3), 1 helicopter
Complement:	100

This class is of Italian design and will be built at Arsenal de Marinho, Rio de Janeiro. Twelve units are planned. They are to be laid down in the mid-1980s and completed in the 1990s. The first four were ordered in Nov 1981.

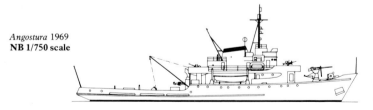

Angostura 1969
NB 1/750 scale

IMPERIAL MARINHEIRO class *tug/patrol ships*

Displacement:	911t standard
Dimensions:	183ft 7in pp × 30ft 6in × 11ft 7in max
	56.0m × 9.3m × 3.60m
Machinery:	2 shafts, 2 Sulzer diesels, 2160bhp = 16kts. 135t fuel
Armament:	1–3in, 4–20mm (4×1)
Complement:	60

Class (commissioned):
Angostura (1955), *Baiana* (1955), *Cabacia* (1954), *Forte de Coimbra* (1954), *Iguatemi* (1954), *Imperial Marinheiro* (1954), *Ipiranga* (1954), *Maerim* (1955), *Purus* (1955), *Solimoes* (1955)
Fleet tugs classified by Brazil as patrol ships, *Imperial Marinheiro* serves as a submarine tender and all are equipped for fire fighting. Pennant nos between V15 and V 24. All extant 1982.
The Brazilian Navy also uses three ex-US *Sotoyomo* class tugs in the patrol role (*Tritao* R 21, *Tridente* R 22, *Triunfo* R 23). They were purchased in 1947 and are extant 1982.

Raposo Tavares 1973

PEDRO TEIXEIRA class *river patrol ships*

Displacement:	700t standard
Dimensions:	203ft 5in pp × 30ft 9in × 6ft 1in max
	62.0m × 9.4m × 1.9m
Machinery:	2 shafts, 4 diesels = 18kts
Armament:	1–40mm, 2–81mm mortars
Complement:	80 (estimated)

Class (no, launched, commissioned):
Pedro Teixeira (P 20, 14.10.70, 17.12.73), *Raposo Tavares* (P 21, 11.6.72, 17.12.73)
Both units constructed by the Arsenal de Marinha, Rio de Janeiro. The design is indigenous. These ships have a helicopter platform and a hangar and carry 1 LCVP. Both extant 1982.

Roroima as completed
NB 1/750 scale

RORAIMA class *river patrol ships*

Displacement:	340t standard; 365t full load
Dimensions:	147ft 7in pp × 27ft 6in × 4ft 3in max
	45.0m × 8.4m × 1.3m
Machinery:	2 shafts, 2 diesels, 1814bhp = 14.5kts
Armament:	1–40mm, 2–81mm mortars
Complement:	54

Class (no, launched, commissioned):
Amapa (P 32, 9.3.73, Jan 1976), *Rondonia* (P 31, 10.1.73, 1974), *Roroima* (P 30, 9.11.72, 21.2.75)
A fourth unit was laid down in 1981. Constructed by Maclaren, Niteroi, these ships are of indigenous design. All in service 1982.

Parati 1972
NB 1/750 scale

PIRATINI class *large patrol craft*

Displacement:	105t standard
Dimensions:	95ft 2in pp × 19ft × 6ft 5in max
	29.0m × 5.80m × 2.0m
Machinery:	2 shafts, 4 diesels, 1100bhp = 17kts
Armament:	3–0.50cal MG, 1–81mm mortar
Complement:	15

Class (no, commissioned):
Pampeiro (P 12, May 1971), *Parati* (P 13, Jul 1971), *Penedo* (P 14, Sep 1971), *Piraja* (P 11, Mar 1971), *Piratini* (P 10, Nov 1970), *Poti* (P 15, Oct 1971)
All units were constructed by Arsenal de Marinha, Rio de Janeiro, under offshore agreement with the United States. Based on the US Coast Guard 95ft WPB type. All extant 1982.

PIRAJU class *submarine chasers*

Displacement:	130t
Dimensions:	128ft × 19ft 6in × 6ft
	39m × 6.0m × 1.8m
Machinery:	1 shaft, diesel, 890bhp = 20kts
Armament:	1–40mm, 3–20mm (3×1), 30 DC

Class (no):
Piraju (P 1), *Pirambu* (P 2), *Piranha* (P 3), *Piraque* (P 4), *Pirapia* (P 5), *Pirauna* (P 6)
All built, of wood, at Rio 1947–48. *Pirauna* was stricken 1960, *Pirambu* and *Pirapia* in 1964, *Piraju* and *Piranha* in 1971 and *Piraque* in 1973.

MINE WARFARE VESSELS

West German SCHUTZE class *minesweepers*

Displacement:	230t standard; 280t full load
Dimensions:	154ft 9in oa × 23ft 6in × 6ft 9in
	47.2m × 7.2m × 2.1m
Machinery:	2 shafts, 4 Maybach diesels, 4500bhp = 24kts
Armament:	1–40mm
Complement:	40

Class (no, ordered, commissioned):
Abrolhos (M 19, Nov 1973, 16.4.75), *Albardao* (M 20, Nov 1973, 21.7.75), *Anhatomirim* (M 16, Apr 1969, 30.11.71), *Aracatuba* (M 18, Apr 1969, 13.12.72), *Aratu* (M 15, Apr 1969, 5.5.71), *Atalaia* (M 17, Apr 1969, 13.12.72)

All units were built by Abeking and Rasmussen, Germany. They are wooden hulled and all are in service 1982.

Ex-US YMS type *minesweepers*

Class (former name, transfer date):
Javari (ex-*Cardinal*, 15.8.60), *Jurua* (ex-*Jackdaw*, 15.8.60), *Juruena* (ex-*Grackle*, Apr 1963), *Jutai* (ex-*Egret*, 15.8.60)

These units were reclassified as coastal minesweepers (old) in Feb 1955. Pennant nos M 11–14. All discarded in 1969, except *Juruena*, 1974.

Chile

The last ten years have been very stressful for the Chilean Navy. Chile has been beset by international and national problems. Relations with Argentina and Peru have become increasingly strained. Argentina and Chile have had a long-standing border dispute at the tip of the continent. Rumours that the disputed area might contain oil deposits have increased the tensions caused by this dispute. Oil is a critical problem for Chile. The nation can meet only a fraction of the national demand through indigenous production. Relations with Peru have been strained since the War of the Pacific (1879–83), when Chile crushed Peru. The significant increase in strength the Peruvian Navy *vis-à-vis* that of Chile in recent decades has added to the pressure upon the Chilean Navy. Thus, today the Chilean Navy faces reputedly strong fleets to both the north and south.

Chile's international problems, which directly affect the navy, do not end here. The fall of the Allende government in 1973 and the subsequent conflict between his exiled supporters and the new government have strained United States-Chilean relationships to the breaking point. Thus, the major supplier of warships and spare parts to Latin America has cut Chile off. This impacts very heavily on the maintenance of the *Fletcher* class destroyers and other US-built ships in the Chilean fleet. The reactivation of the cruiser *O'Higgins* in 1978 and the submarine *Simpson* in 1977 evidenced the need for fleet units. Also, Chile had been unable to purchase new warships from abroad or to secure a binational construction agreement as Argentina and Peru have done.

During the Falklands War, the Chilean fleet was moved South, adding pressure to the Argentine Navy. Chile's acquisition problems improved during the early 1980s. Chile was able to order two Type 209 submarines and built two small landing ships under a bi-national construction agreement with the French. The main naval base is at Talcahuano where there is also a major repair yard. Other bases are Puerto Montt, Punta Arenas, Iquique and Puerto Williams. In 1982 personnel numbered 28,600 including 2000 officers and 2700 Marines. Conscription is for a 12-month period. During 1982 there were persistent rumours that the British carrier *Hermes* was on offer to Chile for transfer after her final commission in the Royal Navy (1986).

For many decades the Chilean Navy, unit for unit, has been reported to be the best in Latin America. Evidence suggests that every effort is being made to retain this quality. Soon, however, the adverse material position of the Navy must have an impact.

FLEET STRENGTH 1947

BATTLESHIPS

Name	Launched	Disp	Fate
HUASCAR	1865	1130t	Extant 1982 as museum
ALMIRANTE LATORRE	17.11.13	28,000t	Discarded 1959

Huascar was captured from the Peruvians on 8.10.1879 during the War of the Pacific.

Almirante Latorre in 1950 had her main engines and auxiliary machinery overhauled and she was equipped with radar. In 1951 she suffered an engine room disaster; she remained inactive throughout the remainder of her career.

CRUISERS

Name	Launched	Disp	Fate
CHACABUCO	1898	4300t	Discarded 1959
O'HIGGINS	1898	8500t	Discarded 1958

Chacabuco was extensively rebuilt in 1942 and was actively employed in 1950.

DESTROYERS

Name	Launched	Disp	Fate
Serrano class			
ALDEA	29.11.28	1090t	Discarded 1957
HYATT	21.7.28	1090t	Discarded 1963
ORELLA	8.3.28	1090t	Discarded 1967
RIQUELME	28.5.28	1090t	Discarded 1963
SERRANO	25.1.28	1090t	Discaded 1967
VIDELA	16.10.28	1090t	Discarded 1960

SUBMARINES

Name	Launched	Disp	Fate
FRESIA	1915	364t/435t	Discarded 1953
GUACOLDA	1915	364t/435t	Discarded 1949
GUALA	1915	364t/435t	Discarded 1953
ALMIRANTE SIMPSON	15.1.29	1540t/2020t	Discarded 1957
CAPITAN O'BRIEN	2.10.28	1540t/2020t	Discarded 1957
CAPITAN THOMPSON	15.1.29	1540t/2020t	Discarded 1958

MINOR WARSHIPS

Name	Acquired	Disp	Fate
British 'River' class frigates			
COVADONGA (ex-*Seacliff*, ex-*Megantic*)	3.3.46	1445t	Sold 1968
ESMERALDA (ex-*Glace Bay*, ex-*Luzon*)	3.1.46	1445t	Sold 29.11.68
IQUIQUE (ex-*Joiliette*)	3.1.46	1445t	Sold 29.11.68
British 'Flower' class corvettes			
CASMA (ex-*Stellarton*)	1946	980t	Sold 2.7.69
CHIPANA (ex-*Strathray*)	1946	980t	Sold 2.7.69
PAPUDO (ex-*Thorlock*)	1946	980t	Sold 17.5.67

Both classes were Canadian wartime construction. *Esmeralda* was renamed *Baquedano* in 1952. *Chipana* was employed as a survey ship.

Other vessels on strength in 1947 included 3 ex-US tug type patrol craft *Lautaro*, *Lientur* (both extant 1982) and *Leucoton* (700t, 1944) and the depot ship *Araucano* (6438t, 1929). In 1947 Chile had just acquired 4 ex-US LSM type landing ships, named *Aspirante Goicolea*, *Aspirante Izaza*, *Aspirante Morel* and *Guardiamarina Contreras*; and 6 ex-US LCIL type landing craft: *Cabo Bustos*, *Grumete Diaz*, *Eduardo Llanos*, *Grumete Tellez*, *Grumete Bolados* and *Soldado Canaves*; they were also 8 LCPs, 22 LCVPs and 2 LCPLs transferred from the USN at the same time. The larger landing craft were withdrawn from service from 1958 onwards, the last vessel being stricken in 1967.

LATIN AMERICA

O'Higgins and *Prat* cost Chile $37 million apiece – ten per cent of the original cost. Both refitted in the US 1957–58. *O'Higgins* was damaged in a collision in 1974 and was laid up as an accommodation hulk; later repaired and recommissioned in 1978. Light AA comprised 28–40mm (6×4, 2×2) and 12–20mm (6×2), and the principal radars are SPS-6 and SPS-4. A Jet-Ranger helicopter is embarked.

Ex-US BROOKLYN class *cruisers*

No	Name	Builder	Acquired	Fate
02	O'HIGGINS (ex-*Brooklyn*)	New York N Yd	1951	Extant 1982
03	PRAT (ex-*Nashville*)	New York SB	1951	Decommissioned 1981

Göta Lejon before transfer as the *Latorre*   *Swedish Navy*

O'Higgins 1981 showing the camouflage recently adopted   *Chilean Navy*

Reconstructed 1951–52 and modernised 1958. 6in guns are high angle, automatic anti-aircraft weapons with 70 degrees elevation. AA armament comprises 4–57mm and 11–40mm (all single) and the main radars are Dutch LW-03 and British Types 277 and 293.

Ex-Swedish TRE KRONOR class *cruiser*

No	Name	Builder	Acquired	Fate
04	LATORRE (ex-*Göta Lejon*)	Eriksberg	15.7.71	Extant 1982

Initially to have been transferred in spring 1982 but the Falklands War delayed transfer until the summer. She was one of the last of the class to be completed, but contrary to some reports the Seaslug SAM as been retained. A second of the class (probably *Antrim*) may also be purchased.

Ex-British 'COUNTY' class *destroyer*

No	Name	Builder	Acquired	Fate
03	PRAT (ex-*Norfolk*)	Swan Hunter	1982	Extant 1982

Armed with 4–5in (4×1), 6–3in/50 (3×2), 5–21in TT (1×5), 2 Hedgehogs, 2 torpedo racks, 6 K-guns. Initially 3 more *Fletchers* were to have been transferred in 1966. However, 4 *Charles Lawrence* class units were substituted.

Ex-US FLETCHER class *destroyers*

No	Name	Builder	Acquired	Fate
14	BLANCO ENCALADA (ex-*Wadleigh*)	Bath Iron Wks	1963	Extant 1982
15	COCHRANE (ex-*Rooks*)	Seattle-Tacoma	1963	Extant 1982

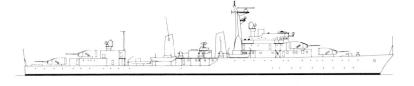

Almirante Williams as completed

Air conditioned quarters. 2 Seacat SAM (2×4) in lieu of 2–40mm fitted in 1964 at Talcahuano. Modernised in Britain between 1971–75 when 4 Exocet MM38 SSMs were fitted in place of the TT; 6–324mm Mk 32 ASW TT were fitted at the same time. Two of the Exocet SSMs were transferred to the *Allen M Sumner* class destroyers in 1980. Sensors now comprise Plessey AWS-1, Decca 629, Marconi SNW-10, SWW-20, SGR-102, SNG-20 with Dutch M-4 directors for Seacat. Sonar is Type 164B. The Vickers designed main armament is unique; max range is 12,500 yards (11,400m) and max elevation is 75°. Like many Chilean warships, they are now camouflaged.

ALMIRANTE class *destroyers*

Displacement:	2730t standard; 3300t full load
Dimensions:	402ft × 43ft × 13ft 4in
	122.5m × 13.1m × 4.0m
Machinery:	2-shaft Parsons Parmetrada geared turbines, 54,000shp = 34.5kts. Range 6000nm at 16kts
Armament:	4–4in/60 (4×1), 6–40mm/70 (6×1), 5–21in TT (5×1), 2 Squid ASW mortars
Sensors:	Radar Plessey AWS-1 (see notes)
Complement:	266

No	Name	Builder	Laid down	Launched	Comp	Fate
18	ALMIRANTE RIVEROS	Vickers, Barrow	12.4.57	12.12.58	31.12.60	Extant 1982
19	ALMIRANTE WILLIAMS	Vickers, Barrow	20.6.56	5.5.58	26.3.60	Extant 1982

Almirante Williams following 1970s refit

C & S Taylor

Both units received a FRAM II modernisation while in US service. VDS removed in 1980. Now carry 2 Exocet SSMs between the funnels.

Ex-US ALLEN SUMNER class *destroyers*

No	Name	Builder	Acquired	Fate
16	MINISTRO ZENTENO (ex-*Charles S Sperry*)	Federal, Kearny	8.1.74	Extant 1982
17	MINISTRO PORTALES (ex-*Douglas H Fox*)	Todd-Pacific, Seattle	8.1.74	Extant 1982

Riquelme was used for spare parts and was not commissioned. Constructed as destroyer escorts, these units were converted to high speed transports while in US service. Chile employed these ships as escorts. These four ships were transferred instead of three *Fletcher* class units. Only *Uribe* is active; the others survive as hulks.

Ex-US CHARLES LAWRENCE class *destroyer escorts*

No	Name	Builder	Acquired	Fate
27	ORELLA (ex-*Jack C Robinson*)	Dravo, Pittsburg	25.11.66	Extant 1982
28	RIQUELME (ex-*Joseph E Campbell*)	Bethlehem, Hingham	1.12.66	See notes
26	SERRANO (ex-*Odum*)	Consolidated, Orange	25.11.66	Extant 1982
29	VIRGILIO URIBE (ex-*Daniel Griffin*)	Bethlehem, Hingham	1.12.66	Extant 1982

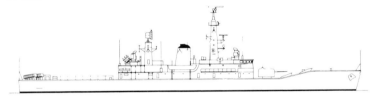

Condell 1977

Initially *Condell* was to have been named *Latorre*. These Chilean Leanders have taller foremasts than their British near-sisters. Exocet MM38 (4×1) fitted in the late 1970s, is mounted on the fantail as opposed to replacing the 4.5in gun as in the British Exocet-equipped *Leander*s. These Chilean units do not have VDS or Limbo ASW mortar. See under United Kingdom for full details.

British LEANDER type *frigates*

No	Name	Builder	Laid down	Launched	Comp	Fate
07	ALMIRANTE LYNCH	Yarrow, Scotstoun	6.12.71	6.12.72	25.5.74	Extant 1982
06	CONDELL	Yarrow, Scotstoun	5.6.71	12.6.72	21.12.73	Extant 1982

Condell 1979

USN

Two vessels of this type ordered in 1981, but possibly to a modified design with greater AA emphasis.

Spanish DESCUBIERTA type *corvettes*

SUBMARINES

Simpson served until 1975 when she was decommissioned; she was reactivated in 1977. *Thomson* had an overhaul in the US in 1966 when a new conning tower was installed; reduced to a training hulk in late 1970s.

Ex-US BALAO class *submarines*

No	Name	Builder	Acquired	Fate
21	SIMPSON (ex-*Spot*)	Mare Island N Yd	1962	Extant 1982
22	THOMSON (ex-*Springer*)	Mare Island N Yd	23.1.61	See notes

Both units were ordered in 1969. They suffered delays in fitting out due to recabling; see comments concerning *Oberons* in Brazilian service. *Hyatt* suffered a minor explosion in Jan 1966. Chile has developed the capacity to overhaul these units in her own yards. For further details see

These were the first modern units that Chile was able to contract for following the overthrow of the Allende government in 1973. Initially there was much public opposition in Germany to their construction.

British OBERON class *submarines*

No	Name	Builder	Laid down	Launched	Comp	Fate
23	HYATT (ex-*Condell*)	Scott-Lithgow	10.1.72	26.9.73	27.9.76	Extant 1982
22	O'BRIEN	Scott-Lithgow	17.1.71	21.12.72	Apr 76	Extant 1982

under United Kingdom.

West German Type 209 class *submarines*

No	Name	Builder	Laid down	Launched	Comp	Fate
21	SIMPSON	Howaldswerke, Kiel 1980		15.1.81		
20	THOMSON	Howaldswerke, Kiel 1981				

AMPHIBIOUS WARFARE VESSELS

Ex-US LST type *tank landing ships*

Class (no, former name/no):
Comandante Hemmendinger (88, ex-*New London County*), *Comandante Araya* (89, ex-*Nye County*), *Aguila* (91, ex-*Aventinus*, ex-*LST 1092*), *Comandante Toro* (97, ex-*LST 277*)
Transferred in 1973. *Comandante Toro* stricken 1977, *Aguila* 1980 (after grounding).

Ex-US LSM type *landing ship*

Class (no, acquired):
Aspirante Morel (92, 2.9.60)
Ex-US *Aloto*, ex-*LSM 444* transferred to replace earlier LSM of the same name. Stricken 1977.

Ex-US LCU type *landing craft*

Class (no, acquired):
Grumete Diaz (96, June 1970)
Ex-US *LCU 1396*, previously designated an LCT(6). Stricken 1977.

French BATRAL type *landing ships*

No	Name	Builder	Comp	Fate
91	MAIPO	Asmar, Talcahuano	1981	Extant 1982
92	RANCAGUA	Asmar, Talcahuano	1982	Extant 1982

French design and French equipment, armed with 2–40mm and 1–81mm mortar. Laid down 1980. See under France for further details.

ELICURA class *landing craft*

Displacement:	290t light; 750t full load
Dimensions:	145ft × 34ft × 12ft 9in
	44.2m × 10.4m × 3.9m
Machinery:	2 shafts, diesels, 900bhp = 10.5kts. Oil 77t. Range 2900nm at 9kts
Armament:	3–20mm
Complement:	20

No	Name	Builder	Comp	Fate
95	ELICURA	Talcahuano	10.12.68	Extant 1982
94	OROMPELLO	Dade Dry Dock Co, Miami	5.9.64	Extant 1982

Two further LCTs to be built in Chile likely to be similar to design.
In 1982 the Chilean Navy also operated 11 ex-US LCVPs.

SMALL SURFACE COMBATANTS

Ex-US CHEROKEE class *patrol vessel*

No	Name	Builder	Acquired	Fate
63	SERGENTO ALDEA (ex-*Arikara*)	Charleston SB	1.7.71	Extant 1982

Ex-US fleet tug, built 1943.

Ex-Israeli SAAR 4 class *fast attack craft (missile)*

Class (former name, transfer date):
Casma (ex-*Romach*, 1979), *Chipana* (ex-*Keshet*, 1979)
Both refitted before transfer. Pennant nos unknown. They are stationed in the Beagle Channel. Possibly 4 additional craft may be acquired. Harpoon missiles were removed prior to transfer. Both units extant 1982.

GUACOLDA class *fast attack craft (torpedo)*

Displacement:	134t full load
Dimensions:	111ft 6in wl, × 118ft 7in oa × 18ft 4in × 5ft 5in max
	34.0m, 36.2m × 5.6m × 1.68m
Machinery:	2 shafts, 2 Mercedes-Benz MB 839Bd diesels, 4800bhp = 32kts. Range 1500nm at 15kts
Armament:	2–40mm (2×1), 4–21in TT (4×1) British Mk IV
Complement:	20

No	Name	Builder	Launched	Fate
81	FRESIA	Bazan, Cadiz	9.12.65	Extant 1982
82	GUACOLDA	Bazan, Cadiz	30.7.65	Extant 1982
83	QUIBORA	Bazan, Cadiz	1966	Extant 1982
84	TEGUALDA	Bazan, Cadiz	1966	Extant 1982

Lürssen designed craft, these units serve in the Beagle Channel. The TT are British Mk 4.

PAPUDO class *large patrol craft*

Displacement:	313t normal; 417t full load
Dimensions:	173ft 6in × 23ft × 10ft 2in
	52.9m × 7.0m × 3.1m
Machinery:	2 shafts, 2 GM diesels, 2800bhp = 19kts. Range 5000nm at 18kts
Armament:	1–40mm, 4–20mm (2×2)
Complement:	69

Class (no):
Papudo (P 37, ex-*PC 1646*), *Abtao* (P 36), *Pisagua* (P 38)
Basically similar to the US PC design (and the postwar Turkish 'Hisar' class), the name ship was built with US 'offshore' funds by ASMAR, Talcahuano in Chile and was commissioned 27.11.71. The two other ships listed have been reported since. All are extant 1982.

MARINERO FUENTEALBA class *large patrol craft*

Displacement:	215t
Dimensions:	80ft × 21ft × 9ft
	24.4m × 6.4m × 2.7m
Machinery:	1 Cummins diesel, 340hp = 9kts. Range 2600nm at 9kts
Armament:	1–20mm, 3–12.7mm MG
Complement:	19

No	Name	Builder	Comp	Fate
75	MARINERO FUENTEALBA	ASMAR, Talcahuano	22.7.66	Extant 1982
76	CABO ODGER	ASMAR, Talcahuano	21.4.67	Extant 1982

Fishing boat type hull.

PILLAN class *coastal patrol craft*

Displacement:	40t		
Dimensions:	61ft × 17ft 4in × 5ft 7in		
	18.6m × 5.3m × 1.7m		
Machinery:	2 MTU diesels, 816hp = 30kts. Range 700nm at 15kts		
Armament:	2–20mm, 2 DCs		
Complement:	?		

Name	Builder	Comm	Fate
PILLAN	Maclaren, Niteroi	Aug 1979	Extant 1982
TRONCADOR	Maclaren, Niteroi	Aug 1980	Extant 1982
RANO KAU	Maclaren, Niteroi	Nov 1980	Extant 1982
CORCOVADO	Maclaren, Niteroi	Nov 1980	Extant 1982

Ten ordered in 1979; up to 20 projected. Numbered from GC 1801.

Colombia

Colombia has traditionally possessed one of the smallest navies in South America. The nation's river flotilla is as important as the deep water fleet. The short service time of many units suggests the Navy is experiencing maintenance problems. There are 7200 officers and men serving with the Colombian Navy and Colombia also has 2500 marines. National service is for a period of two years. The country's main naval base is at Cartagena which also has a naval training school. Balanguero, Barnquila, Santa Marta and Buenaventura, also naval bases, are less important.

MAJOR SURFACE SHIPS

Siette de Agosto 1961

Ordered in 1954, these units are modified *Halland* class destroyers. They mount a different armament, more electronics, and different interior arrangements than their near sisters in Sweden. In July 1957 *Trece de Junio*'s name was changed to *Siette de Agosto*. *Siette de Agosto* was extensively refitted in US in 1975–76, including a machinery overhaul – nevertheless 25kts reported as best recent speed, although they made 35kts on trials. Dutch electronics, with M4 type radar directors for gun armament.

Santander received a FRAM II modernisation while in US service.

FLEET STRENGTH 1947

DESTROYERS

Name	Launched	Disp	Fate
Vouga class			
ANTIQUOIS (ex-*Douro*)	1933	1383t	Discarded 1961
CALDAS (ex-*Tejo*)	1933	1383t	Discarded 1961

Both units were completely refitted 1952–53 and 1954–55 respectively.

RIVER GUNBOATS

Name	Launched	Disp	Fate
Cartagena class			
BARRANQUILLA	10.5.30	142t	Discarded 1970
CARTAGENA	26.3.30	142t	Extant 1982
SANTA MARIA	16.4.30	142t	Discarded Dec 1962

Also in service in 1947 were the gunboat *Mariscal Sucre* (125t, 1909), and the French-built coast guard patrol craft *Jumin*, *Carabobo* and *Pinchincha* (120t, 1925). The river flotilla operated 3 small gunboats, *Fernandez Madrid* (150t, 1926), *Demetrio Salamanca* (120t) and *Presidente Mosquera* (230t, 1912).

Siette de Agosto as completed   Navarret Collection

Swedish modified HALLAND class *destroyers*

Displacement:	2650t; 3300t full load					
Dimensions:	397ft 2in pp × 40ft 7in × 15in 4in max					
	121.1m × 12.4m × 4.7m					
Machinery:	2-shaft De Laval double reduction geared turbines, 2 Penhoët boilers, 55,000shp = 32kts. Range 450nm/3000nm at 32kts/18kts					
Armament:	6–120mm (3×2), 4–40mm (4×1), 4–533mm TT (1×4), 1–375mm Bofors ASW RL (1×4)					
Sensors:	Radar LW-03, DA-02					
Complement:	248					

No	Name	Builder	Laid down	Launched	Comp	Fate
D 06	SIETTE DE AGOSTO (ex-*Trece de Junio*)	Gotaverken, Goteborg	Nov 1955	19.6.56	31.10.58	Extant 1982
D 05	VEINTE DE JULIO	Kockums Mek Verkstads A/B, Malmö	Oct 1955	26.6.56	15.6.58	Extant 1982

Ex-US FLETCHER class *destroyer*

No	Name	Builder	Acquired	Fate
D 01	ANTIOQUIA (ex-*Hale*)	Bath Iron Wks	Dec 1960	Discarded 20.12.73

Ex-US ALLEN M SUMNER class *destroyers*

No	Name	Builder	Acquired	Fate
D 02	CALDAS (ex-*Willard Keith*)	Bethlehem, San Pedro	1.7.72	Discarded 1977
D 03	SANTANDER (ex-*Waldron*)	Federal, Kearny	30.10.73	Extant 1982

LATIN AMERICA

FS 1500 type

A letter of intention was signed with Howaldswerke Deutsche to build 4 units. The first ship was laid down in March 1981. *Antioquia* (53) laid down 22.6.81 and launched 28.8.82. *Intependiente* (54) launched 22.6.81. *Almirante Padilla* (51) launched 6.1.82 and completed early 1983. *Caldas* (52) laid down 23.4.82.

West German FS 1500 type *frigates*

Displacement:	1500t standard; 1800t full load
Dimensions:	295ft 3in × 37ft × 11ft 1in
	90.0m × 3.0m × 3.4m
Machinery:	2 shafts, 4 MTU 20V 1163 TB62 diesels, 15,600bhp = 26.5kts. Range 7000nm at 14kts
Armament:	8 MM40 Exocet (2×4), 1–76mm OTO Melara Compact, 2–40mm (1×2), 2–30mm (1×2), 6–324mm Mk 32 ASW TT (2×3)
Complement:	90

Cordoba was decommissioned in 1980 and is used as a museum. She was the only one of the above to receive a FRAM II modernisation.

Ex-US CROSLEY/BUCKLEY class *destroyer escorts/high speed transports*

No	Name	Builder	Acquired	Fate
DT 07	ALMIRANTE BRION (ex-*Barber*)	Norfolk N Yd	8.12.68	Discarded 1974
DT 03	ALMIRANTE PADILLA (ex-*Tollberg*)	Bethlehem, Hingham	14.8.65	Discarded 1973
DT 04	ALMIRANTE TONO (ex-*Bassett*)	Consolidated, Orange	6.9.68	Discarded 1977
DY 15	CORDOBA (ex-*Ruchamkin*)	Philadelphia N Yd	24.11.69	Museum 1980

An ex-US destroyer escort of the *Dealey* type, originally built 1955–57.

Ex-US DEALEY class *destroyer escort*

No	Name	Builder	Acquired	Fate
D 07	BOYACA (ex-*Hartley*)	New York SB	8.7.72	Extant 1982

All served in the Korean War.

Ex-US TACOMA class *patrol frigate*

No	Name	Builder	Acquired	Fate
FG 14	ALMIRANTE BRION (ex-*Burlington*)	Consolidated Steel, San Pedro	1953	Discarded 1968
FG 11	ALMIRANTE PADILLA (ex-*Groton*)	Walter Butler, Superior	Mar 1947	Discarded 1965
FG 12	CAPTAIN TONO (ex-*Bisbee*)	Consolidated Steel, San Pedro	Feb 1952	Discarded 1962

SUBMARINES

Both units ordered 1971; see Greek *Glavkos* class for details.

West German Type 209 *submarines*

No	Name	Builder	Laid down	Launched	Comp	Fate
SS 28	PIJAO	Howaldswerke, Kiel	1.4.72	10.4.74	17.4.75	Extant 1982
SS 29	TAYRONA	Howaldswerke, Kiel	1.5.72	16.7.74	18.7.75	Extant 1982

These units (similar to those ordered by Pakistan and Taiwan) can carry 2 submarine vehicles and 8 frogmen, with 2050kg of explosives.

Italian Type SX 506 *midget submarines*

Displacement:	58t/70t
Dimensions:	75ft 5in × 6ft 7in × 13ft 3in
	23.0m × 2.0m × 4.0m
Machinery:	Diesel-electric, 300bhp = 8kts/6kts. Range 1200nm at 7kts
Complement:	5

No	Name	Builder	Comp	Fate
SS 20	INTREPIDO	Cosmos, Livorno	1972	Extant 1982
SS 21	INDOMABLE	Cosmos, Livorno	1972	Extant 1982
SS 23	RONCADOR	Cosmos Livorno	1974	Stricken *c* 1981
SS 24	QUITO SUENO	Cosmos, Livorno	1974	Stricken *c* 1981

SMALL SURFACE COMBATANTS

Ex-US CHEROKEE class *patrol vessels*

Class (no, former name, acquired):
Pedro de Heredia (RM 72, ex-*Choctaw*, 1961), *Sebastian de Belalcazar* (RM 73, ex-*Carib*, 15.3.79), *Rodrigo de Bastedas* (RM 74, ex-*Hidatsa*, 15.3.79), *Bahia Solano* (RM 75, ex-*Jicarilla*, 15.3.79)
  Pedro de Heredia was purchased outright in 1978. Ex-US tugs used for patrol and rescue duties, armed only with 1–3in gun. All extant 1982.

Ex-US ASHEVILLE class *patrol gunboats*

The ex-*Tacoma* and ex-*Welch* were reported leased to Colombia in 1982.

Arauca 1957
NB 1/750 scale

ARAUCA class *river gunboats*

Displacement:	184t
Dimensions:	163ft 3in oa × 23ft 6in × 2ft 9in max
	49.8m × 7.2m × 0.8m
Machinery:	2 shafts, 2 Caterpillar diesels, 916bhp = 13kts
Armament:	2–76mm (1×2), 4–20mm (4×1)
Complement:	43

Class:
Arauca, *Leticia* and *Riohacha* built by Union Industrial de Barranquilla; launched 1955; completed 1956; extant 1982. *Leticia* converted to a hospital boat in the early 1970s and armament removed.

OTHER PATROL CRAFT
In 1982 Colombia also operates two coastal patrol craft (*Espartana*, 50t, commissioned 1950) and *Capitan R D Binney* (23t, commissioned 1947) both built by Ast Naval, Cartagena and six river patrol craft. Colombia also has a coast guard and a separate customs service.

Costa Rica

Although Costa Rica possesses both Pacific and Caribbean coastlines and covers an area of some 19,653 square miles she has no military forces to speak of. The Civil Guard, numbering about 1200 men, is responsible along with a police force of some 3000 for internal security, the Army having been abolished in 1948. In an area of political upheaval and uncertainty (Costa Rica is bordered by Nicaragua to the north and Panama to the south) the country remains stable and operates only nine patrol craft. These include a 105ft 'Swift' class fast patrol boat, five smaller 65ft 'Swift' class patrol boats, all six built in 1979 and three coastal patrol craft built in the mid-1950s (10t).

Cuba

The pre-Castro Cuban Navy was totally dependent upon the United States. Since independence at the turn of the century, Cuba, politically and militarily, had been dominated by American policies. The fleet reflected this. In 1959 the Cuban Navy was composed of ex-US warships, most of which had been built during World War II. Many of these were comparatively larger types such as *Tacoma* class frigates; their equipment was old and the ships were not well maintained. Many of these ships were built as ASW platforms and much of the US training aid was in this speciality. This force was ill-suited for a war against Castro's guerrilla forces and reflected the ultra-conservative

doctrines of both the Juan Batista military and the American advisers, although the Cuban Navy had a history of political involvement. The assumption and resumption of power by Juan Batista brought with it purges of the officer corps of all services and a resulting loyalty to the regime – as well as a lack of military professionalism and poor leadership. During the years immediately preceding Fidel Castro's emergence, the Navy was increasingly restless, and accordingly harassed by the Batista forces. Like all Latin American navies, the Cuban Navy was conservative. Officers were generally from the middle or lower upper class. Naturally, a group with this background must come to odds with the Castro leadership. In July 1959, Rual Castrol, Commander in Chief of the Armed Forces, assigned 36 politically indoctrinated Army officers to the Navy. In September the Marine Corps was ordered to be dissolved. The cohesiveness of the Navy was diluted by assigning personnel, including ships' crews, to various construction projects, mainly the improvement of transit facilities.

The new Cuban Navy is as dependent upon Russia as the old one had been upon the United States. Since 1962 the backbone of the fleet has been guided missile patrol boats. In fact, these were the first such craft in the Western Hemisphere. These missile boats have been supplemented by other patrol craft. Soviet naval aid took on far greater dimensions with the transfer of submarines, beginning in 1979 and continues with Soviet financial aid. A 'Koni' class frigate was transferred in 1981. Cuba's greatest maritime asset is her strategic location. The long-rumoured Soviet submarine base at Cienfuegos brings this painfully into focus. This key location married to Fidel Castro's professed desire to export revolution and his willingness to act as a Soviet surrogate, makes the Cuban Navy one of the most important in the Western Hemisphere, in spite of its relatively small size. Main naval bases are at Canasi, Cienfuegos, Havana, Mariel and Punta Ballenatos; 6000 officers and men serve with the Cuban Navy and there is a 3-year period of national service.

FLEET STRENGTH 1947

Name	Launched	Disp	Fate
Cuba (sloop)			
CUBA	10.8.11	2055t	Discarded 1971
Patria (sloop)			
PATRIA	10.8.11	1200t	Discarded 1955
Baire (gunboat)			
BAIRE	1906	500t	Discarded 1948

Patria operated as a training ship for the latter year of her service. There were also a number of coast guard patrol craft: the Cuban-built *Leoncio Prado* (80t, 1946); the ex-US SC type *Camaguey Habana*, *Las Villas*, *Oriente* and *Pinar del Rio*; and the 45t ex-US Coast Guard *GC 11–14*, *22*, *32–34*. The older *Donativo* (130t, 1932) and *Matanzas* (80t, 1912) were also on strength. Three US-built Vosper type MTBs (*R 41–R 43*) were employed on air-sea rescue vessels.

MAJOR SURFACE SHIPS

Soviet 'KONI' class *frigate*

Soviet export design, transferred 24.9.81. See under East Germany for details.

SUBMARINES

Ex-Soviet 'FOXTROT' class *submarines*

Names and numbers unknown. First unit transferred 7.2.79 and second Jan 1980. Extant 1982. These units operate from the large submarine base at Cienfuegos.

Ex-Soviet 'WHISKEY' class *submarine*

One unit transferred Mar 1979; probably not operational – used as a station ship for training and battery charging.

AMPHIBIOUS WARFARE VESSELS

Cuba operates seven 'T 4' class LCMs which are used for harbour duties.

SMALL SURFACE COMBATANTS

Ex-US TACOMA class *patrol escorts*

Class (transfer date):
Antonio Maceo (ex-*Peoria*, 1947), *Jose Marti* (ex-*Eugene*, 1947), *Maximo Gomez* (ex-*Grand Island*, 1947)
All units modernized 1956 at Key West, Florida; all discarded 1975. *Jose Marti* fitted as a flagship and sunk as a target 1975.

Ex-US PCE class *patrol escort*

Class (transfer date):
Caribe (ex-*PCE 872*, 1947), *Siboney* (ex-*PCE 893*, 1947)
Both units modernised 1956 at Key West, Florida. *Caribe* had box deckhouse removed 1953. Discarded 1976 and 1973 respectively.

Ex-Soviet 'KOMAR' class *fast attack craft (missile)*

18 units transferred – 12 in 1962, 4 between 1963–66, 2 in 1967; 4 discarded in 1979. 14 extant 1982.

Ex-Soviet 'OSA I' class *fast attack craft (missile)*

6 units transferred – 2 in 1972, 2 in 1973 and 2 in 1974. All extant 1982. Possibly one unit deleted in 1981.

Ex-Soviet 'OSA II' *fast attack craft (missile)*

13 units transferred – 2 in 1976, 1 in 1978, 4 in 1979, 2 in 1981, and 4 in 1982. All units extant 1982.

Ex-US PC type *submarine chaser*

Class:
Baire (ex-*Tribesman*, ex-*PC 790*). Acquired from Honduras in 1956 and rearmed; sank at dock, Isle de Pines, 17.4.61 during an abortive coup.

Ex-Soviet 'KRONSTADT' class *large patrol craft*

6 units towed by merchant ships to Cuba in Feb 1962; 2 units discarded in 1979. 4 extant 1982.

Ex-Soviet 'SO 1' class *large patrol craft*

12 units; 6 transferred in 1964 and 6 in 1967; 2 discarded 1979 and 1 in 1981; 9 extant 1982.

Ex-Soviet 'P 6' class *fast attack craft*

12 units towed by merchant ships to Cuba in 1962; 6 units discarded 1979; 6 extant 1982. Depth charge and mine carrying capabilities.

Ex-Soviet 'P 4' class *fast attack craft (torpedo)*

12 units transferred 1962–64; all extant 1982.

Ex-Soviet 'TURYA' *fast attack craft (hydrofoil)*

2 units transferred in 1979; 2 in 1980 and 2 in 1981; all extant 1982. They are not fitted with torpedo tubes.

Ex-Soviet 'ZHUK' class *coastal patrol craft*

12 units transferred 1972–80. All extant 1982.
The Cuban Navy also operates 12 SV type coastal patrol craft.

MINE WARFARE VESSELS

Ex-Soviet 'SONYA' class *minesweepers/hunters*

2 units transferred in Aug and Dec 1980. All extant 1982.

Ex-Soviet 'YEVGENYA' class *inshore minesweeper*

4 units transferred 1977, 1 in 1978, 2 in 1980, last 2 in 1981. All extant 1982.

Ex-Polish 'K 8' class *minesweeper*

1 unit transferred in 1978. Extant 1982.

Dominican Republic

During this era the numerical strength of the Dominican Navy peaked under the regime of Rafael Trujillo. Trujillo was assassinated in 1961, and many political changes took place. The Navy declined in size, and most of the units were renamed in 1962. There are just over 4000 officers and men serving with the Dominican Navy the main bases being at Santo Domingo, Las Calderas and Haina.

FLEET STRENGTH 1947

FRIGATES

Name	Launched	Disp	Fate
British 'River' class MELLA (ex-*Presidente Trujillo*, ex-*Carlplace*)	1944	1400t	Extant 1982
British 'Flower' class CRISTOBAL COLON (ex-*Lachute*)	1944	980t	Discarded 1978

Ex-Canadian units. *Mella* modified for use as a presidential yacht, renamed *Mella* in 1962; used for training and as a flagship. Transferred in 1946.
Cristobal Colon also cited as *Colon*. Transferred in 1946.
3 100t launches (*LR 101–103*; LR 102 lost 1956, survivors renamed *Capitan Alsina*.
The only other vessels on strength in 1947 were: 3 100t launches (*LR 101–103*); LR 102 lost 1956, survivors renamed *Capitan Alsina*, extant 1982, and *Capitan Maduro*, discarded 1968), launched in 1944; 3 47t patrol craft (*GC 9–11*) built in the USA in 1943, and 8 smaller launches.

MAJOR SURFACE SHIPS

Ex-British 'H' class *destroyer*

Class:
Duarte (ex-*Trujillo*, ex-*Hotspur*, 1936–48). Purchased Nov 1948; pennant no D 101. Renamed *Duarte* in 1962; discarded 1972.

A Cuban 'SO 1' class patrol craft, late 1960s   *US Coast Guard*

Ex-British 'F' class *destroyer*

Class:
Sanchez (ex-*Generalissimo*, ex-*Fame*, 1935–49). Purchased Feb 1949, pennant no D 102, renamed *Sanchez* in 1962; discarded 1968.

Ex-US ASHEVILLE class *frigate*

Class:
Juan Pablo Duarte (ex-*Natchez*, ex-*Annan*). Purchased Jul 1947; pennant no F 102; lost 1958.

Ex-US TACOMA class *frigates*

Class (former names):
Capitan General Pedro Santana (ex-*Presidente Peynado*, ex-*Pueblo*). Transferred Sep 1947; discarded 1979. *Gregorio Luperon*, ex-*Presidente Troncoso*, ex-*Knoxville*. Transferred Sep 1947; pennant nos F 104 and F 103; discarded 1979. Both renamed in 1962.

Ex-Canadian 'FLOWER' class *corvettes*

Class (former name, transfer date, fate):
Gerardo Jansen (ex-*Peterborough*, 1947, discarded 1972), *Juan Alejandro Acosta* (ex-*Louisbourg*, 1947, discarded 1978), *Juan Bautista Cambiaso* (ex-*Belleville*, 1947, discarded 1972), *Juan Bautista Maggiolo* (ex-*Riviere du Loup*, 1947, discarded 1972), *?* (ex-*Asbestos*, 1947, lost en route from Canada; Dominican Navy name not available). One additional unit, *Cristobal Colon*, had been transferred in 1946 and is listed among those ships on hand in 1947. She was discarded in 1978. They carried the pennant nos C 104, C 102, C 103, C 105 and C 101 respectively.

AMPHIBIOUS WARFARE VESSELS

Ex-US LSM type *landing ship*

Class (former name, transfer date, fate):
Sirio (ex-*LSM 483*, March 1958, extant 1982)
Two further vessels of this type were transferred after the war and served in an auxiliary capacity as the *San Rafael* and *Antares*; the former was discarded in 1960 and the latter was sold in 1959.

MINOR LANDING CRAFT
Three ex-US LCIL type served in the Dominican Navy: *BDI 101* and *102* were transferred c 1948; stricken 1957. A further unit was acquired from the merchant service in 1952, renamed *Paraiso* and served until 1960.
Two LCT(6) type were transferred from the USA c 1948 and served as the *17 de Julio* and *Maria Josefina* until stricken in 1956.
Two LCU type landing craft were built locally by the Astilleros Navales Dominicanos in 1957: *Enriquillo* (ex-*17 de Julio*), and *Samana*. The latter was lost in heavy weather, but replaced by a similar ship of the same name, and both of these were extant 1982.

SMALL SURFACE COMBATANTS

Ex-US PC type *submarine chasers*

Class (former names, transfer date, fate):
Patria (ex-*Capitan Wenceslao Arvelo*, ex-*PC 1207*, 1947, discarded 1962), *Constitucion* (ex-*Cibas*, ex-*PC 1497*, 1947, discarded 1968), *27 de Febrero* (ex-*PC 613*, 1947, discarded 1968).
Two units were renamed in 1962. Pennant nos P 102, P 103, P 101.

Ex-US COHOES class *corvettes*

Class (pennant number, former name, transfer date):
Cambiaso (P 207, ex-*Etlah*, 29.9.76), *Separacion* (P 208, ex-*Passaconaway*, 29.9.76), *Calderas* (P 209, ex-*Passaic*, 29.9.76)
Former net tenders, but now armed with 2–3in and 3–20mm guns and used as patrol craft. Pennant nos P 207–209. All extant 1982.

Ex-US ADMIRABLE class *corvettes*

Class (pennant number, former name, transfer date):
Prestol Botello (BM 454, ex-*Separacion*, 13.1.65), *Tortuguero* (BM 455, ex-*Signet*, 13.1.65)
Originally minesweepers. Both extant 1982.

Ex-US Coast Guard 165B class *large patrol craft*

Class (former names, transfer date, fate):
Independencia (ex-*Icarus*, 1948, extant 1982), *Libertad* (ex-*Rafael Atoa*, ex-*Thetis*, 1948, extant 1982), *Restauracion* (ex-*Galathea* 1948, extant 1982)
US Coast Guard *Argo* class 165ft cutters (335t full load), armed with 1–3in, 1–40mm and 1–20mm, *Libertad* was renamed in 1962.

US PGM 71 class *large patrol craft*

Class:
Betelgeuse (ex-US *PGM 77*), pennant number is GC 102, built by Petersen, USA and transferred under the Military Aid Programme (14.1.66).
In 1982 the Dominican Navy also operated eight coastal patrol craft, 4 being *Bellatrix* class, as well as 4 coastal patrol craft commissioned in 1975.

Ecuador

Until the acquisition of *Guayas* in 1947, Ecuador possessed a few ex-yachts and small coast guard units. Although Ecuador acquired a few frigate-sized units, most of the equipment remained obsolescent until the mid-1970s. Beginning in 1975, Ecuador began to acquire first class fighting units for the first time. Naval patrol boats are employed primarily for Ecuador's 200-mile coastal zone and it is a common occurrence for American fishing boats to be held up and fined. This action has affected the transfer of ships from the US, in particular, the *Gearing* class destroyer *Southerland* in 1981. Naval bases are at Guayaquil, Manta, San Lorenzo and the Galapagos Islands, Guayaquil being the main base. The Galapagos Islands are also the base for Ecuador's naval infantry (about 700 men); 3800 officers and men are employed by the Navy and national service is selective.

MAJOR SURFACE SHIPS

Ex-US GEARING class *destroyer*

No	Name	Builder	Acquired	Fate
DO 01	PRESIDENTE ELOY ALFARO (ex-*Holder*)	Consolidated, Orange	1.9.78	Extant 1982

Although a FRAM I reconstruction, ASROC was deleted before transfer. Overhauled at Norfolk Shipbuilding, Virginia, 1978–79.

Ex-US TACOMA class *frigate*

No	Name	Builder	Acquired	Fate
E 21	GUAYAS (ex-*Covington*)	Globe, Superior	Aug 1947	Discarded 1972

Pennant no originally E 01

Guayas c 1960   *Author*

Ex-British 'HUNT' class (Type 1) *frigates*

No	Name	Builder	Acquired	Fate
D 01	PRESIDENTE ALFARO (ex-*Quantock*)	Scotts	18.10.54	Discarded 1978
D 02	PRESIDENTE VELASCO IBARRA (ex-*Meynell*)	Swan Hunter	18.10.54	Discarded 1978

Both units refitted by J Samuel White, Cowes, Isle of Wight. Commissioned 16.8.55 and Aug 1955 respectively.

Ex-US CHARLES LAWRENCE class *destroyer escort*

Class:
Moran Valverde (ex-*Veinticinco de Julio*, ex-*Enright*).
Transferred 14.7.67; purchased 30.8.78. Constructed as a destroyer escort, this unit was converted to a high speed transport while in US service; she can carry 162 troops. Ecuador employs her primarily as an escort and carried the pennant no D 01. She had a small helicopter deck added in the late 1970s. Extant 1982.

SUBMARINES

West German Type 209 class *submarines*

No	Name	Builder	Launched	Fate
SS 12	HUANCAVILCA	Howaldtswerke, Kiel	18.3.77	Extant 1982
SS 11	SHYRI	Howaldtswerke, Kiel	8.10.76	Extant 1982

Similar to units sold to Greece, Turkey, Argentina and Peru, both were ordered in 1974 and completed 1.6.78 and 16.3.78 respectively. See Greek *Glavkos* class for details.

AMPHIBIOUS WARFARE VESSELS

Ex-US LST type *tank landing ship*

One unit, *Hualcopo* (ex-*Summit County*, LST 1148) transferred in Feb 1977 (1650t, 11.6kts, built by Chicago Bridge). Pennant no T 55. Extant 1982.

Ex-US LSM type *landing ship*

Two units, *Jambelli* and *Tarqui*, transferred in 1958 (513t, 12.5kts, built 1945). Pennant nos T 51 and T 52. Extant 1982.
Ecuador also operates 6 British Rotork 'Sea trucks', LF 91–96.

SMALL SURFACE COMBATANTS

Esmeraldas class design

Italian modified WADI M'RAGH class *corvettes*

Displacement:	605t standard; 685t full load
Dimensions:	189ft 7in pp, 204ft 5in oa × 30ft 6in × 9ft 3in max 57.8m, 62.3m × 9.3m × 2.8m
Machinery:	4 shafts, 4 MTU 20V956 TB92 diesels, 24,400bhp = 31kts. Range 1200nm/4000nm at 31kts/18kts
Armament:	6 MM40 Exocet SSM (2×3), 1 Albatros SAM (1×4), 1–76mm OTO Melara Compact, 2–40mm (1×2) 6–324mm Mk 32 ASW TT (2×3), 1 light helicopter
Sensors:	Radar SMA 3RM-20, RAN-105, Orion 10X; sonar Diodon; ECM Gamma system
Complement:	51

No	Name	Builder	Launched	Fate
CM 14	EL ORO	CNR, Tirreno	9.2.81	Extant 1982
CM 11	ESMERALDAS	CNR, Tirreno	1.10.80	Extant 1982
CM 15	GALAPAGOS	CNR, Tirreno	4.7.81	Extant 1982
CM 16	LOJA	CNR, Tirreno	Nov 1981	Extant 1982
CM 13	LOS RIOS	CNR, Tirreno	27.2.81	Extant 1982
CM 12	MANABI	CNR, Tirreno	9.2.81	Extant 1982

Ordered in 1978. Generally similar to the *Wadi M'Ragh* built for Libya. CM 11 and CM 13 were laid down in 1979, CM 16 on 6.2.81 and the remainder in 1980. They have more powerful engines and a helicopter deck, and more sophisticated electronics – Selenia IPN-10 data system, CO 3 directors and NA 21 fire control.

Ex-US PCE type *patrol vessel*

Class:
Esmeraldas (ex-*Eunice*), *Manabi* (ex-*Pascagoula*)
Transferred 29.11.60 and 5.12.60 respectively. Discarded 1970s. Pennant nos changed from E 03 and E 02 to E 22 and E 23 to P 22 and P 23.

MANTA class *fast attack craft*

Class (no, comp):
Manta (LM 24, 11.6.71), *Tulcan* (LM 25, 2.4.71), *Nueva Rocafuerte* (ex-*Tena*, LM 26, 23.6.71)
Similar to Chilean *Guacolda* class but 1 extra diesel makes them 3kts faster. Originally armed with 1–40mm gun, an Oerlikon twin RL, 2–21in TT, but rearmed in 1979 with 2–30mm Emerlec (1×2) and in 1981 4 Gabriel SSMs replaced the TT. All extant 1982.

Quito 1979 *USN*

QUITO class *fast attack craft (missile)*

Displacement:	250t; 265t full load
Dimensions:	154ft 2in × 23ft × 7ft 10in 47.0m × 7.0m × 2.4m
Machinery:	4 shafts, 4 MTU 16V538 diesels, 14,000bhp = 35kts. Range 600nm at 30kts
Armament:	4 MM38 Exocet SSMs, 1–76mm/62 OTO Melara Compact, 2–35mm (1×2)
Sensors:	Radar Triton, Vega fire control
Complement:	34

Class (no, comp):
Quito (LM 31, 13.7.76), *Guayaquil* (LM 32, 22.12.77), *Cuenca* (LM 33, 17.7.77)
All built by Lürssen, Vegesack. Named after cities. Extant 1982.

Ex-US PGM type *large patrol craft*

Class (no, acquired):
Veintecinco de Julio, ex-*Quito* (LC 71, 30.11.65), *Diez de Agosto*, ex-*Guayaquil* (LC 72, 30.11.65)
US *PGM 71* class patrol craft built by Peterson, Sturgeon Bay. Transferred to coast guard 1980.

OTHER SMALL CRAFT
Six 35t launches, *LP 7–12*, built in 1954 by Schürenstedt, Bardenfleth, West Germany, deleted 1960.
Six 64t full load launches, *LSP 1–6*, built 1954–55 by Schürenstedt. They were given the pennant nos *LP 81–86*, and *LSP 4–6* were stricken 1976. The survivors were renamed *10 de Agosto*, *9 de Octubre* and *3 de Novembre* respectively, and later *Baha Hoyo*, *Pichincha* and *Portoviejo*; they were all extant 1982.
Three 34t patrol craft built by Halter, New Orleans in 1976: *Comandancia de Balao*, *Comandancia de Guyaquil*, *Comandancia de Salinas*; all were extant 1982.
Two ex-US Coast Guard 10t utility boats: *Rio Napo*, *Isla Puna*; transferred 1971 and extant 1982.

El Salvador

A mountainous and densely populated state in which economic and social conditions are one of the main causes of the dissent and tension within the country. Successive repressive governments have encouraged the growth of guerrilla and terrorist groups and a string of *coups* has added to the republic's instability. In 1979 General Humberto Romero was overthrown by rebel officers and thus began a state of civil war which shows little sign of coming to an end. Much military aid comes to El Salvador from the United States although this is utilised mainly for the training and re-equipping of army and air force units. In 1982 the death toll from guerrilla activity fell to 6000 (between 1979 and 1982 30,000 lives were lost) and thus allowed Congress to mark an improvement in the country's strife-torn state; military aid from the United States continues.

El Salvador has a 160-mile Pacific coastline and operates a small navy (130 officers and men) employing patrol boats. The main operational ports are Acajutla, La Libertad and La Union.

One ex-British HDML patrol boat (46t, commissioned 1942, purchased 1959).
One American-built patrol craft (33t, commissioned 1967, 3 GM diesels, built by Sewart, Louisiana). Carries pennant no GC 5.
Three Camcraft type patrol boats (100t, 3 GM diesels), carry pennant nos GC 6, GC 7 and GC 8, commissioned Oct 1975, Dec 1975 and Nov 1975 respectively. Another US patrol craft was ordered in July 1981.
The Navy also operates 2 ex-US CG type patrol boats (10.5t, commissioned 1950), a tug *Libertad* and 25 small outboard-propelled craft.

Grenada

Independence for this tiny island state (133 square miles, population 109,000) came in 1974 and was followed in 1979 by a *coup* in which Maurice Bishop, heading the New Jewel Movement seized power from Sir Eric Gairy. The country operates a patrol force consisting of a Brooke Marine patrol craft (15t, 2 diesels, commissioned 1972) and three 'Spear' class patrol craft built by Fairey Marine.

Guatemala

The republic of Guatemala bordered by Mexico, Belize, Honduras and El Salvador covers an area of 42,042 square miles and is traversed by mountain ranges. The country's political turbulence is mirrored by its geographical location – afflicted, as it often is, by earthquakes; a major eruption in 1976 demolished several towns and caused about 25,000 deaths. In March 1982 Guatemala experienced a military *coup* and the country's constitution has been temporarily suspended. This is the most recent in a wave of overthrows which began in 1954; terrorist activity is rife throughout Guatemala. There have been several confrontations with the neighbouring state of Belize, over which Guatemala claims sovereignty. In 1972 and again in 1977 Guatemala sent troops to the border with Belize and Britain responded by reinforcing the existing military forces in Belize (then still a British colony).

The Guatemalan Navy was established in 1959 primarily for carrying out coast guard work. There are bases at Santo Tomas de Castillas on the Atlantic coast and Sipacate on the Pacific coast. There are 600 men serving with the Navy (including 200 Marines) and Guatemala operates a two-year period of national service. Most of the country's vessels come from the United States which paid out a total of 23.6 million dollars in military aid 1955–77.

Swedish JAGAREN class *patrol vessel*

The Swedish patrol vessel (ex-minesweeper) *Snapphanen* was transferred in 1959 to become the first Guatemalan warship. Renamed *José Francisco Barrundia*, she was rearmed with 2–3in (2×1) and 2–25mm guns, she was laid up in an inoperative state by 1964.

28ft *coastal patrol craft*

Class (no):
Xucuxuy (P 281), *Camalote* (P 282)
Transferred in 1961 and deleted in 1979.

'BROADSWORD' class *coastal patrol craft*

Displacement:	90.5t standard
Dimensions:	105ft × 20ft 5in × 6ft 4in
	32m × 6.2m × 1.9m
Machinery:	2 shafts, 2 GM 16V 149TI diesels, 3200hp = 32kts
Armament:	1–12.7mm, 1–75mm recoilless, 1–81mm mortar, 4 MGs
Complement:	20

No	Name	Builder	Comp	Fate
P 1051	KUKOLKAN	Halter Marine	4.9.76	Extant 1982
P 1052		Halter Marine	22.9.76	Extant 1982
P 1053		Halter Marine	1977	Extant 1982

Sewart 85ft type *coastal patrol craft*

Displacement:	60t
Dimensions:	85ft × 18ft 8in × 3ft
	25.9m × 5.7m × 0.9m
Machinery:	2 GM diesels, 2200bhp = 23kts. Range 400nm at 12kts
Armament:	2 MGs
Complement:	12

No	Name	Builder	Comp	Fate
P 851	UTATLAN	Sewart Louisiana	May 1967	Extant 1982
P 852	SUBTENIENTE USORIO SARAVIA	Sewart, Louisiana	1972	Extant 1982

Halter 'CUTLASS' class *coastal patrol craft*

Class (no, commissioned):
Tecunuman (P 651, 1972), *Kaibilbalam* (P 652, 1972), *Azumanche* (P 653, 1972), *Tzacol* (P 654, 10.3.76), *Bitol* (P 655, 4.8.76)
Built by Halter Marine, New Orleans. Extant 1982.

Ex-US AVR type *coastal patrol craft*

Class (no, commissioned):
Cabrakan (P 631, 1945), *Hunahpu* (P 632, 1945)
Transferred 1965 and 1964 respectively. US Coast Guard 63ft, 32t type.

In 1979 Guatemala ordered 3 coastal patrol craft from Abeking and Rasmussen, Lemwerder.
30 river patrol craft are being or have been built in Guatemala by Trabejos Baros SY. Wooden construction.

Ex-US LCM (8) type *landing craft*

Class:
Chinaltenango (E 81)
Transferred Dec 1965; 115t full load.

Ex-US LCU 1466 type *landing craft*

One craft of this type in service; 360t full load.

MACHETE class *transport craft*

Class no, commissioned):
Picuda (P 361, 4.8.76), *Barracuda* (P 362, 4.8.76)
Built by Halter Marine, 8.3t, 36ft × 12ft 6in × 2ft *(11m × 3.8m × 0.6m)*, can carry 20 troops.

Guyana

A poor country (although there are large bauxite and manganese deposits) bordered by Brazil, Surinam and Venezuela, Guyana has a 270-mile coastline and covers an area of 83,000 square miles, much of it rain forest and some areas have yet to be explored fully. The country was granted independence from Britain in 1966 (previously known as British Guiana). Guyana has had border clashes with all of her neighbours; Surinam has laid claim to 6000 square miles of Guyanan territory in which there is much bauxite to be mined. In 1969 there was a brief armed encounter with Surinam over this claim which was settled temporarily when both sides agreed to withdraw. Guerrilla activity took place along the Brazilian border in 1972 but again there was no serious confrontation.

Guyana operates a Defence Force, which is responsible for the operation of the country's patrol boats. The Defence Force itself numbers about 2000 volunteer personnel (including 60 women) and of these 150 are employed on naval duties. Bases are at Georgetown and New Amsterdam.

Two ex-North Korean patrol boats (names and numbers unknown) 35t, 40kts, armed with 2–14.5mm MGs, 2 shafts, 2 petrol engines, 9 crew. Both units transferred 1980. Extant 1982.
One 103ft Vosper Thonycroft type large patrol craft, *Peccari* (DF 1010), 96t standard, 27kts, armed with 2–20mm, 2 Paxman-Ventura diesels, 22 crew. Launched 26.3.76, commissioned 26.1.77. Extant 1982. Guyana ordered a second identical patrol craft in 1977; the order was subsequently cancelled. See Trinidad and Tobago for details.
Three 40ft Vosper Thornycroft coastal patrol craft, *Jaguar*, *Margay*, *Ocelot*. Numbers unknown. Commissioned 28.4.71, 21.5.71 and 22.6.71 respectively, 10t, 19kts, 1–7.62mm MG, 2 Cummins diesels, 6 crew. Constructed with glass fibre hulls. All extant 1982.
Four ex-US 45ft class coastal patrol craft, *Camoudie*, *Labana*, *Rattler* and one name unknown. Extant 1982.
One LCU; *Kimbla*, 600t, 14kts, 2 Caterpillar diesels, built by Damen, Netherlands. Launched 21.8.81. Extant 1982.
Guyana also operates two ex-shrimp boats, an ex-US tug (YTM 190) and a lighter (YFN 960).

Peccari on trials   *Vosper Thornycroft*

Haiti

Haiti occupies the Western section of the island of Hispaniola, the Eastern section being occupied by the more wealthy Dominican Republic, and together with several smaller offshore islands covers an area of 10,700 square miles, and has a population of 6,000,000. A former French colony, Haiti became an independent state in 1804. Deployment of US marines on the island came to an end in 1947, having begun in 1934. There have been attempts by Cuban guerrillas to overthrow the regime in Haiti; so far the president, Jean Claude Duvalier, who succeeded his father in 1971, has managed to maintain his position. The president commands all three armed forces in Haiti; there is no navy as such but a Coast Guard (300 men) which operates a number of small patrol craft. Main base is at Port au Prince.

Two ex-US *Sotoyomo* class tugs, *Henri Christophe* (MH 20, ex-*Samoset*), ? (MH 21, ex-*Keywadin*). Transferred 18.9.78 and 28.3.81 respectively. Latter unit to be employed in oceanographic research. Launched 14.7.44 and 9.4.45 respectively. Extant 1982.

Three 65ft commercial cruiser type coastal patrol craft, *Jean Claude Duvalier* (MH 21), *MH 22* and *MH 23*, 33t, 25kts, 2–12.7mm MG, 1–20mm, 3 shafts, 3 GM 8V71 diesels. Built by Sewart, Louisiana and in service 1976. Extant 1982.
Nine US 3812 VCF class patrol boats, *Le Maroon* (MH 11), *Oge* (MH 12), *Chavannes* (MH 13), *Capois* (MH 14), *Bauckman* (MH 15), *Makandal* (MH 16), *Charlemagne Perrault* (MH 17), MH 18 and MH 19. 8.5t, 2–7.62mm MGs, 1–12.7mm MG, 2 shafts, 2 GM 6V 71N diesels, 4 crew. Built by Monark, Monticello, Arkansas. These units came into service 1980–81.
Haiti also operates one, possibly two, US 'Enforcer' class patrol boats, *MH 5* (?) and *MH 6*, 9.5m, built by Bertram, Miami.

Honduras

Lying between Nicaragua and Guatemala with El Salvador to the west, Honduras is one of the larger of the Central American republics (43,277 square miles) and also the poorest. Her Caribbean coastline extends for roughly 375 miles while she has a 63-mile strip of Pacific coastline bordering the Gulf of Fonseca. Honduras has recently (1982) emerged from a long spell of military government during which time repressive action was taken by military leaders against agricultural unions; discontent was due to the slow pace with which agrarian reform was taking place. In 1982 a civilian government led by Roberto Suazo Cordora came into power. Honduras, like many Latin American countries, has experienced border disputes with all the countries adjacent to her. In 1969 the so-called 'Soccer War' took place with El Salvador, occasioned by disagreements over a football match. The dispute continued intermittently until 1976 when both countries agreed to talks. More recently Honduras has found herself the thoroughfare for arms supplies to El Salvadorian guerrillas coming from Nicaragua and consequently has been exposed to pressure from the US government in an effort to reduce these supplies of arms. The terrorist violence experienced by Honduras' neighbours now appears to be establishing itself in Honduras; in 1982 measures were taken by the military against terrorist groups.

The republic's Coast Guard force operates a total of 17 units and employs 100 men, a percentage of whom are carrying out the eight months national service. The main base is at Puerto Cortes on the Caribbean coast.

Three 'Swift' type 105ft class patrol boats, *Guaymuras* (FN 1051), *Honduras* (FN 1052), *Hibures* (FN 1053). Built by Swiftships, Morgan City, Louisiana, in service Apr 1977 (FN 1051) and Mar 1980 the latter units. 103t, 32kts, 2 shafts, 2 MTU diesels, 16 crew. Armament unknown. Extant 1982.
One US 85ft (commercial cruiser type patrol boat; *Chamelecon* (FN 8502); Built by Swiftships, Louisiana, in service date unknown. 50t, 23kts, 2 shafts, 2 GM diesels, 17 crew. Armament unknown. Extant 1982.
Five US 65ft commercial cruiser type patrol boats; *Aguan* (ex-*Gral*, (FN 6501), *Goascoran*, ex-*J T Cabanas* (FN 6502), *Petula* (FN 6503), *Ulua* (FN 6504), *Chuluteca* (FN 6505).
Built by Swiftships, Morgan City, Louisiana, in service Dec 1973 (FN 6501), Jan 1974 (FN 6502), 1980 remainder. 33t, 25kts, 3 shafts, 3 GM diesels, armed with 2–12.7mm MG, 5 crew. Haiti ordered FN 6501 and FN 6502 originally, transferred to Honduras 1977; 3 later units fitted with 3 MTU diesels (36kts).
Two inshore patrol craft; FN 2501 and FN 2502, names unknown, Built by Ampela Marine, Honduras, entered service 1981–82. 3t, 24kts, 25ft × 8ft 10in × 1ft 4in (7.6m × 2.7m × 0.4m), 1 Chrysler diesel, waterjet drive, armed with 1–7.62mm MG, 1–12.7mm MG, 4 crew.
Honduras also operates six ex-fishing boats: FN 7501, FN 7502, FN 7503, FN 7504, FN 7505, FN 7506.

Jamaica

The island state of Jamaica gained independence within the Commonwealth from Britain in 1962. Lying to the South of Cuba she covers an area of some 4411 square miles and has a population of approximately 2,223,400. A democratic country, following a foreign policy of non-alignment, Jamaica has remained a stable and untroubled nation since independence. The Jamaican Defence Force is headed nominally by the prime minister but in practice by a major general. The Coast Guard, Maritime Arm of the Defence Force, is based at HMJS *Cagway*, Port Royal; 18 officers command 115 men while the Coast Guard Reserve employs a total of 46 officers and men.

FORT CHARLES *patrol boat*

Displacement:	103t
Dimensions:	103ft 4in × 18ft 9in × 6ft 10in
	31.5m × 5.7m × 2.1m
Machinery:	2 shafts, 2 MTU MB 16V538 TB90 diesels, 7000hp = 32kts. Range 1200nm at 18kts
Armament:	2–12.7mm MG, 1–20mm
Complement:	16

Fort Charles (P 7) was built by Teledyne Sewart in 1974.

Refitted 1979–80 at Jacksonville, Florida. Capable of carrying 24 troops; converts to floating hospital.

There are also three 85ft commercial cruiser class patrol craft: *Discovery Bay* (P 4), *Holland Bay* (P 5), *Manatee Bay* (P 6). Built by Sewart Seacraft, Berwick, Louisiana, 60t, 30kts, *25.9m × 5.6m × 1.8m*, 3 shafts, 3 MTU diesels, 3–12.7mm MG, 11 crew. Engines refitted on two occasions, last time in 1975–77.

Mexico

Although the fifth largest navy in Latin America behind those of Argentina, Brazil, Chile and Peru, all of the large ships and most of the small craft are old, former US, equipment. Mexican naval forces are concerned mainly with patrolling fishing grounds as poaching is frequent; there have been brushes with Guatemala and the US. Mexico's offshore oilfields, recently developed, have necessitated greater vigilance by the Navy and the raising of the defence budget from 567m dollars in 1979 to 1150m dollars in 1981 is proof of this. The Navy operates a Gulf Command and a Pacific Command both of which are divided into zones. Main bases are at Veracruz, Tampico, Acapulco, Puerto Cortes, Manzanillo, Guaymas, Cuidad del Carmen and Islas Mujeres; 23,500 officers and men are employed – this figure includes 3800 marines and members of the naval air force.

FLEET STRENGTH 1947

CRUISER-TRANSPORT

Name	Launched	Disp	Fate
PROGESO	1907	1590t	Discarded 1947

PATROL SLOOPS

Name	Launched	Disp	Fate
GUANAJUATO	29.5.34	1300t	Discarded 1975
QUERETARO	29.6.34	1300t	Discarded 1975
POTOSI	24.8.34	1300t	Discarded 1975

GUNBOAT-TRANSPORT

Name	Launched	Disp	Fate
DURANGO	28.6.35	1600t	Extant 1982

GUNBOATS

Name	Launched	Disp	Fate
G 20	1922	130t	Discarded 1954
G 21	1922	130t	Discarded 1954
G 22	1922	130t	Discarded 1956
G 23	1922	130t	Discarded 1954
G 25	1922	130t	Discarded 1956
G 26	1922	130t	Discarded 1954
G 27	1922	130t	Discarded 1954
G 28	1922	130t	Discarded 1963
G 29	1922	130t	Discarded 1955

The only other significant vessels in service in 1947 were 3 trawler-type coast guard auxiliaries, *Mazatland, Acapulco* and *Veracruz* (486t, 1918). They were withdrawn from service after 1949.

MAJOR SURFACE SHIPS

Ex-US FLETCHER class *destroyers*

No	Name	Builder	Acquired	Fate
E 01	CUATHEMOC (ex-*Harrison*)	Consolidated, Orange	Aug 1970	Extant 1982
E 02	CUITLAHUAC (ex-*John Rodgers*)	Consolidated, Orange	Aug 1970	Extant 1982

Ex-US GEARING class *destroyers*

No	Name	Builder	Acquired	Fate
IE 03	QUIETZALCOATL, (ex-*Vogelgesang*)	Bethlehem, Staten I	Feb 1982	Extant 1982
IE 04	NETZAHUALCOYOTL (ex-*Steinaker*)	Bethlehem, Staten I	Feb 1982	Extant 1982

FRAM I modernisation in US service.

California 2.4.70   *USN*

Ex-US CHARLES LAWRENCE/CROSLEY class *destroyer escorts*

Class (former name, transfer date):

California (ex-*Belet*, 12.12.63), *Chihuahua* (ex-*Renour*, 1971), *Coahuila* (ex-*Barber*, 1971), *Papaloapan* (ex-*Earhart*, 12.12.63), *Tehuantepec* (ex-*Joseph M Auman*, 12.12.63), *Usumacinta* (ex-*Don O Woods*, 12.12.63)

Constructed as destroyer escorts, these units were converted to high speed transports while in US service. They could carry 162 troops. Used as patrol vessels while in Mexican service. *California* stranded and lost on Bahia, California, 16.1.72; *Papaloapan* discarded 1976; all others extant 1982.

Ex-US TACOMA class *frigates*

No	Name	Builder	Acquired	Fate
	CALIFORNIA (ex-*Hutchinson*)	Consolidated Steel, San Pedro	Nov 1947	Discarded Jun 1964
	PAPALOAPAN (ex-*Gladwyne*)	Globe, Duluth	Nov 1947	Discarded Jun 1974
	TEHUANTEPEC (ex-*Bangor*)	American SB, Lorain	Nov 1947	Discarded Aug 1964
	USUMACINTA (ex-*Annapolis*)	American SB, Lorain	Nov 1947	Discarded Aug 1964

Ex-US EDSALL class *frigate*

No	Name	Builder	Acquired	Fate
A 06	MANUEL AZUETA (ex-*Hurst*)	Brown SB, Houston	1.10.73	Extant 1982

Gulf Fleet command training ship.

AMPHIBIOUS WARFARE VESSELS

Ex-US LST type *tank landing ships*

Class (former name):
Panuco (ex-*Park County*), *Manzanillo* (ex-*Cleawater County*)
Transferred 20.9.71 and 25.5.72, and employed as rescue ships, numbered A 01 and A 02.

SMALL SURFACE COMBATANTS

Spanish B 119 type *corvettes*

Displacement:	767t normal; 844t full load
Dimensions:	219ft × 34ft 5in × 18ft
	67.0m × 10.5m × 5.5m
Machinery:	2 shafts, 2 MTU diesels, 9000bhp = 22kts. Range 4500nm at 18kts
Armament:	1–40mm Breda

Six ordered from Bazán, Cadiz, San Fernando, 1980. 1 light helicopter to be carried.

Ex-US AUK class *minesweepers (corvettes)*

Class (no, former name):
Leandro Valle (IG 01, ex-*Pioneer*), *Guillermo Prieto* (IG 02, ex-*Symbol*), *Mariano Escobedo* (IG 04, ex-*Champion*), *Ponciano Arriaga* (IG 03, ex-*Competent*), *Manuel Doblado* (IG 05, ex-*Defense*), *Sebastian Leido de Tejada* (IG 06, ex-*Devastator*), *Santos Degollado* (IG 07, ex-*Gladiator*), *Ignacio de la Llave* (IG 08, ex-*Spear*), *Juan N Alvarez* (IG 09, ex-*Ardent*), *Melchior Ocampo* (IG 10, ex-*Roselle*), *Valentin G Farias* (IG 11, ex-*Starling*), *Ignacio Altamirano* (IG 12, ex-*Sway*), *Francisco Zarco* (IG 13, ex-*Threat*), *Ignacio L Vallarta* (IG 14, ex-*Velocity*), *Jésus G Ortega* (IG 15, ex-*Chief*), *Gutierriez Zamora* (IG 16, ex-*Seater*), *Juan Aldarma* (IG 18, ex-*Pilot*), *Hermenegildo Galeana* (IG 19, ex-*Sage*).
All units transferred 1973. Reclassified as corvettes after minesweeping and ASW gear removed.

Ex-US ADMIRABLE class *minesweepers (corvettes)*

Class (no, former name):
DM 01 (ID 01, ex-*Jubilant*), *DM 02* (ID 02, ex-*Hilarity*), *DM 03* (ID 03, ex-*Execute*), *DM 04* (ID 04, ex-*Specter*), *DM 05* (ID 05, ex-*Scuffle*), *DM 06* (ID 06, ex-*Eager*), *DM 10* (ID 10, ex-*Instill*), *DM 11* (ID 11, ex-*Device*), *DM 12* (ID 12, ex-*Ransom*), *DM 13* (ID 13, ex-*Knave*), *DM 14* (ID 14, ex-*Rebel*), *DM 15* (ID 15, ex-*Crag*), DM 16 (ID 16, ex-*Dour*), *DM 17* (ID 17, ex-*Diploma*), *DM 18* (ID 18, ex-*Invade*), *DM 19* (ID 19, ex-*Intrigue*)
All units transferred 1.10.62, except DM 04, Feb 1973. Reclassified as corvettes after minesweeping and ASW gear removed.

Ex-US PCE type *submarine chasers*

Class (former no, fate):
Blas Godinez(ex-PCE 844, discarded 1965), *David Porter* (ex-PCE 847, discarded 1965), *Pedro Sainz de Baranda* (ex-PCE 868, discarded 1965), *Tomas Marin* (ex-PCE 871, discarded 1972), *Virgilio Uribe* (ex-PCE 875, discarded 1965).
All units purchased 1947. Armed with 1–3in, 6–40mm, 4–20mm, 4 DCT (*Uribe* no DCT; *Godinez* 3–40mm, 5–20mm)

Ex-US PC type *submarine chasers*

Class (former no, fate):
GC 30 (ex-*PC 820*, discarded 1966), *CG 31* (ex-*PC 608*, discarded 1964), *CG 32* (ex-*PC 614*, discarded 1964), *CG 33* (ex-*PC 813*, discarded 1966), *CG 34* (ex-*PC 794*, discarded 1964), *CG 35* (ex-*PC 824*, discarded 1966), *CG 36* (ex-*PC 1224*, discarded 1964), *CG 37* (ex-*PC 819*, discarded 1966), *CG 38* (ex-*PC 1210*, discarded 1971).
All units purchased 1947. Many were not armed while in Mexican service.

'AZTECA' class *patrol boats*

Displacement:	130t
Dimensions:	111ft 10in oa, 101ft 4in pp × 28ft 3in × 6ft 6in
	34.1m, 30.9m × 8.6m × 2.0m
Machinery:	2 shafts, 2 Ruston Paxman Ventura diesels, 7200bhp = 24kts. Range 2400nm at 12kts
Armament:	1–40mm, 1–20mm
Complement:	24

'Azteca' class patrol boat — *ABMTM*

Class (no):
Andres Quintana Roo (P 01), *Matias de Cordova* (P 02), *Miguel Ramos Arizpe* (P 03), *José Maria Izazago* (P 04), *Juan Bautista Morales* (P 05), *Ignacio Lopez Rayon* (P 06), *Manuel Crescencio Rejon* (P 07), *Antonio de la Fuente* (P 08), *Leon Guzman* (P 09), *Ignacio Ramirez* (P 10), *Ignacio Mariscal* (P 11), *Heriberto Jara Corona* (P 12), *José Maria Mata* (P 13), *Feliz Romero* (P 14), *Fernando Lizardi* (P 15), *Francisco J Mujica* (P 16), *Pastor Rouaix José Maria* (P 17), *José Maria del Castillo Velasco* (P 18), *Luis Manuel Rojas* (P 19), *José Natividad Macias* (P 20), *Esteban Baca Calderon* (P 21), *Ignacio Zaragoza* (P 22), *Tamaulipas* (P 23), *Yucatan* (P 24), *Tabasco* (P 25), *Veracruz* (P 26), *Campeche* (P 27), *Puebla* (P 28), *Margarita Maza de Juarez* (P 29), *Leona Vicario* (P 30), *Ortiz* (P 31)
Designed by a British agency and ordered from Associated British Machine Tool Makers which sub-contracted the construction of the first 21 (from 1974 onwards) and assisted with the building in Mexico of a further 10 (at Vera Cruz and Salina Cruz). Another 9 may be built in Mexico it was announced on 15.10.80, but this now seems unlikely. They are not entirely satisfactory in service, being subject to maintenance problems.

Mexico also operates an *Olmeca* class patrol craft (built Mexico 1979–80), of GRP construction, 6 small patrol craft (37t, 6kts) Mexican-built, 2 *Azueta* class (80t, 1959–60), and 4 *Polimar* class (57t, 1962–68), all locally built in Mexico.

Nicaragua

An unstable and strife-torn state, Nicaragua, a former Spanish colony, is the largest of the Central American republics. Government was, until 1979, in the hands of General Samoza, leader of the National Guard, who became president in 1936. Events following the earthquake of 1972 (which destroyed a large proportion of the capital Managua) led to the declaration of martial law by Samoza who earlier in the year had stepped down to allow a three-man junta to take over. By the late 1970s a strong anti-Samoza guerrilla force had emerged (Sandinista Liberation Organisation) with Communist backing and civil war broke out. American military aid was withdrawn as a solution was sought to the rifts developing within the country, but the Sandinista forces with aid from Panama, Venezuela and Costa Rica made many gains and by June 1979 Samoza was forced to resign. The way was now clear for Communist forces to establish a solid base in the region; in 1982 Nicaragua signed a 166.8m dollar deal with the Soviet Union. Arms supplies could now be shipped via Nicaragua to sympathetic rebel forces such as those in El Salvador although claims concerning this have been modified. Tension continues in the country and in 1982 a state of emergency was declared as growing anti-Sandinista forces became more openly hostile.

Nicaragua has no navy as such; patrol boats are operated by the Marine Section of the National Guard (200 officers and men). Main bases are at Corinto (the main port), Puerto Cabezas (Caribbean), Puerto Somaza and San Juan del Sur.

Fleet strength 1982 comprised. Four 'Dabur' class patrol craft, *GC 10*, *CG 11*, *GC 12* and *GC 13*. Delivered Apr 1978 (*GC 10–11*) and May 1978 (*GC 12–13*). *Dvora* class craft also ordered from Israel were embargoed by US.
One Sewart 65ft type patrol craft, *Rio Kuringwas* (GC 7), entered service 1972.
Two French patrol craft were ordered in Jan 1982.

Panama

Panama, the most southerly of the Central American republics, lies between Colombia (from which country independence was gained in 1903) and Costa Rica and is bisected by the Panama Canal. The canal, which the United States gained virtual control of in 1903 after Pananamian independence, came under the joint control of Panama and the United States in 1977–78. By 1999 Panama will assume sovereignty over the entire canal. A military coup in 1968 led by Omar Torrijos took the task of government out of civilian hands until 1978 when Dr Aristides Royo became president. There is a large US military presence (roughly 10,000 troops) in the Canal Zone on the Caribbean side of the canal, as the US Southern Command is based here. The Panamanian Coast Guard divided between the Pacific and Caribbean coastlines is responsible for maritime defence and employs approximately 500 officers and men.

Vosper 103ft type *large patrol craft*

Particulars:	See under Trinidad and Tobago		

No	Name	Builder	Comp	Fate
GC 10	PANQUIACO	Vosper, Portsmouth	Mar 1971	Extant 1982
GC 11	LIGIA ELENA	Vosper, Portsmouth	Mar 1971	Extant 1982

Launched 22.7.70 and 25.8.70 respectively. Armament varies from Trinidad and Tobago's units, being 2–20mm. Fitted with fin stabiliser equipment.

Ex-US AVR class *coastal patrol craft*

Class (no, commissioned, transfer date):
Ayanasi (GC 12, 1943, 1965), *Zarti* (GC 13, 1943, 1966)
Fitted with Raytheon 1500B radar. Have wooden hulls coated with fibre-glass.

Ex-US Coast Guard 40ft type *coastal patrol craft*

Class (no, commissioned, transfer date):
Marti (GC 14, 1950, 1962), *Jupiter* (GC 15, 1950, 1962). No radar fitted.

French 'BATRAL' type *landing ships*

Particulars:	See French *Champlain* class

Ordered from C de la Manche, France (probably 2 vessels).

Ex-US LSMR *fire support ship*

Class (former name, no):
Tiburon (ex-*Smokey Hill River*, GC 10)
Launched 7.7.45 and purchased by Panama 14.3.75 from a shipping company. Can carry 400t cargo. Employed on logistic support duties.

Panama also operates:
Three ex-US LCM(8) class landing ships; *GNT 1*, *GNT 2* and *GNT 3*. Transferred 1972. Employed on logistic support duties. Two deckhouses fitted in place of the wheelhouse.
One YF 852 class lighter (ex-*YF 886*), launched 25.5.45, by Defoe SB, Bay City, Michigan, transferred May 1975. Employed in logistic support duties.
One 65ft patrol craft, *GNT 8*, Panamanian-built, 60t, 8kts, 1 GM diesel, 6 crew.
One former shrimp boat, 65ft, 11kts, purchased 1976 also employed on logistics support duties.

Paraguay

Paraguay is one of two South American nations without a coastline. However, navigable rivers form part of her international boundaries and penetrate deep into her interior. Paraguay has traditionally maintained a small river force. Most of the Navy's ships are extremely old and in need of replacement. Bases are at Puerto Sajonia (Asuncion) where there are naval repair facilities, Chaco Island (naval air base) and Bahia Negra. Navy personnel includes 2000 officers and men as well as 500 marines.

FLEET STRENGTH 1947

Paraguay postwar

ARMOURED RIVER GUNBOATS

Name	Launched	Disp	Fate
HUMAITA	1930	745t	Extant 1982
PARAGUAY	1930	745t	Extant 1982

There were also 6 ex-US Coast Guard patrol craft, P 1–6 (45t, acquired 1944), the old *Capitan Cabral* (180t, 1907) and 3 smaller river craft.

SMALL SURFACE COMBATANTS

Ex-Argentine BOUCHARD class *minesweepers (patrol craft)*

No	Name	Builder	Acquired	Fate
M 1	NANAWA (ex-*Seaver*)	Rio Santiago, NY	5.3.68	Extant 1982
M 2	CAPITAN MEZA (ex-*Bouchard*)	Sanchez, San Fernando	Feb 1964	Extant 1982
M 3	TENIENTE FARINA (ex-*Py*)	Rio Santiago, NY	5.3.68	Extant 1982

Constructed as minesweepers, are being used as river patrol craft. Armament changed to 4–40mm/60 (1×4). There is some doubt as to which vessels were transferred since M 1 is often quoted as ex-*Bouchard* and M 2 as ex-*Parker*.

Paraguay also operates a large patrol craft, *Capitan Cabral* (A 1), (180t, launched 1907, wooden hull); 2 US-built CG type coastal patrol craft (*P 1*, *P 2*) and 6 ex-US 701 class coastal patrol craft, *P 101*–*P 106*.

Peru

During the early 1960s, the Peruvian Navy began to mature into a balanced force, once again comparable to those of Argentina, Brazil, and Chile. The decades of deprivation had forged a formidable submarine tradition. This was now complemented by the acquisition of powerful surface units.

The acquisition of elderly cruisers by the Peruvian Navy might mislead some into underestimating the capabilities of the fleet. Peru's chief rival is Chile. Should there be a conflict, the navy which can maintain station the longest might well be the victor. Large cruisers, armed with Exocet missiles, are formidable station platforms. Although many of the Navy's surface units are old, most are armed with Exocet missiles and they are kept in fighting trim.

Tension between Peru and the US has been brought about by the intrusion of American tuna boats into the 200-mile zone of waters extending from Peru's coastline. As a result of the impounding of tuna boats, arms and other military equipment being sold to Peru by America was curtailed for a time. A separate coast guard was formed in 1975 and a naval air arm earlier.

Personnel in 1982 totalled 2000 officers and 18,500 men, plus 1400 marines (2 years service). Main naval bases are at Callao and San Lorenzo (for submarines); Iquitos is the HQ of the Amazon flotilla and other inland bases are Puno (on Lake Titicaca) and Madre de Dios.

FLEET STRENGTH 1947

CRUISERS

Name	Launched	Disp	Fate
ALMIRANTE GRAU	1906	3200t	Discarded 1958
CORONEL BOLOGNESI	1906	3200t	Discarded 1958

LATIN AMERICA

Both units were converted from coal to oil, 1923–25, at Balboa, Canal Zone. *Almirante Grau* served as the fleet flagship. Italian Giradelli AA fire directors were added in the 1930s. By the late 1940s, these ships saw very limited service.

All 'R' class submarines received major refits 1935–36 and 1955–56. They acquired their new names in Apr 1957, when those of all submarines were changed to honour famous Peruvian naval battles.

DESTROYERS

Name	Launched	Disp	Fate
GUISE	1917	1350t	Discarded *c* 1947
VILLAR	1917	1200t	Discarded *c* 1954

Guise and *Villar* were rushed to Peruvian Amazon in 1933, when acquired by Peru. They were part of a hastily gathered fleet sent to confront Colombia.

SUBMARINES

Name	Launched	Disp	Fate
ARICA (ex-*R 4*)	10.5.23	576t/755t	Discarded 1960
CASMA (ex-*R 2*)	29.3.26	576t/755t	Discarded 1960
ISLAY (ex-*R 1*)	12.7.26	576t/755t	Discarded 1960
PACOCHA (ex-*R 3*)	21.4.28	676t/755t	Discarded 1960

RIVER GUNBOATS

Name	Launched	Disp	Fate
AMERICA	1904	240t	Inactive
AMAZONAS	1934	250t	Extant 1982
LORETA	1934	250t	Extant 1982

America lies at Iquitos, Peru, in total disrepair. There were also the smaller *Napo* (98t, 1920), *Portillo* (49t, 1902), and the ancient *Iquitos* (50t, 1875, stricken 1967).

In 1947 Peru acquired 2 ex-US YMS type minesweepers *Bondy* (ex-*YMS 25*) and *San Matin* (ex-*YMS 35*), stricken 1974; and 4 ex-US LCT(6) type landing craft, numbered *BT 1–4*; stricken mid-1950s. There were also 6 ex-US Coast Guard cutters (45t type) built in 1943 and transferred 1943–44; stricken 1958–61.

MAJOR SURFACE SHIPS

Originally named *Almirante Grau* by the Peruvians, her name was changed to *Capitan Quinones* in 1973, when Peru acquired the former Dutch cruiser *De Ruyter*. Since the War of the Pacific (1879–83), the name *Almirante Grau* has been reserved for the fleet's flagship. She was transferred on 30.12.59 at Portsmouth, England. She had been reconstructed in 1951–53 at Devonport. Two lattice masts, a new bridge, and improved AA were fitted. Her torpedo tubes were removed at that time. *Capitan Quinones* is fitted with two lattice while *Coronel Bolognesi* is fitted with

Ex-British FIJI class *cruisers*

No	Name	Builder	Acquired	Fate
81	CAPITAN QUINONES (ex-*Almirante Grau*, ex-*Newfoundland*)	Swan Hunter	1959	Discarded 1979
82	CORONEL BOLOGNESI (ex-*Ceylon*)	Stephen	1959	Discarded 1980

one lattice and one tripod mast. *Coronel Bolognesi* was transferred on 9.2.60 at Portsmouth, England. In 1955–56 she had been refitted with a lattice foremast and a covered bridge; her torpedo tubes were removed at

that time. As transferred *Coronel Bolognesi* mounted 9–6in (3×3), 8–4in (4×2), and 18–40mm (5×2, 8×1) – this being 6 more 40mm than her sister, *Capitan Quinones*. The principal electronics were British

radar Types 960, 277; 293 and 274, with US Mk 34 fire control for 2 of the 4in mounts.

For early history see under Netherlands. In 1962–64 the *De Zeven Provincien* was converted to a Terrier missile ship by Rotterdamsche Droogdok Mij, Rotterdam; *De Ruyter* was to have been converted as well, but there was a shortage of funds. After sale to Peru, *Aguirre* had her missile system removed and she was converted to a helicopter carrying ship (the Sea King helicopters carry AM 39 Exocet ASMs) and recommissioned 31.10.77. Electronics now comprise Dutch LW-02, SGR-103, DA 102, ZW-03, 2 new Decca types and M 25 and M 45 fire control. *Almirante Grau* was not modified to any significant degree.

Ex-Dutch DE RUYTER class *cruisers*

Displacement:	9850t standard; 12,250t full load (*Almirante Grau* 9529t standard; 12,165t full load)
Dimensions:	598ft 5in pp, 614ft 7in oa × 56ft 8in × 22ft max *182.4m, 187.3m* × *17.2m* × *6.7m*
Machinery:	2-shaft De Scheide-Parsons geared turbines, 4 Werkspoor-Yarrow boilers, 85,000shp = 32kts
Armour:	Belt 76–102mm, decks 20–25mm
Armament:	4–6in (2×2), 6–57mm (3×2), 4–40mm (2×2), 3 helicopters (*Almirante Grau* 8–6in (4×2), 8–57mm (4×2), 8–40mm (4×2)
Complement:	953

No	Name	Builder	Acquired	Fate
84	AGUIRRE (ex-*De Zeven Provincien*)	Rotterdam, Drydock Co	Aug 76	Extant 1982
81	ALMIRANTE GRAU (ex-*De Ruyter*)	Wilton-Fijenoord, Schiedam	7.3.73	Extant 1982

Initially two more *Fletcher* class units were to have been transferred to Peru, but this was never executed. In 1975 both units had helicopter landing pads constructed over their fantails.

Ex-US FLETCHER class *destroyers*

No	Name	Builder	Acquired	Fate
72	GUISE (ex-*Isherwood*)	Bethlehem, Staten I	15.12.60	Discarded 1981
71	VILLAR (ex-*Benham*)	Bethlehem, Staten I	8.10.61	Discarded 1980

Ferre 1973

Palacios 1975   *Author*

Both units were refitted in 1970–73 by Cammell Laird, Birkenhead. Foremast was enclosed and a Plessey AWS-1 radar installed and 8 Exocet SSMs (4×2) fitted. *Palacios* commissioned Feb 73 and *Ferre* Apr of that year. A helicopter deck was added in 1975 but in 1977–78 a fuller substantial refit replaced the after 4.5in mount with a helicopter hangar, the

Ex-British DARING class *destroyers*

No	Name	Builder	Acquired	Fate
74	FERRE (ex-*Decoy*)	Yarrow	1969	Extant 1982
73	PALACIOS (ex-*Diana*)	Yarrow	1969	Extant 1982

second funnel was raised and streamlined and 2 twin Breda Bardo 40mm mounts replaced the singles in the bridge wings (with Selenia NA-10 director aft); the Squid ASW mortar and sonar were removed.

No modifications carried out before transfer.

Ex-Dutch HOLLAND class *destroyers*

No	Name	Builder	Acquired	Fate
75	GARCIA Y GARCIA (ex-*Holland*)	Rotterdam DD	2.1.78	Extant 1982

No modifications carried out before transfer.

Ex-Dutch FRIESLAND class *destroyers*

No	Name	Builder	Acquired	Fate
71	CASTILLA (ex-*Utrecht*)	Royal Scheldt	6.10.80	Extant 1982
76	CAPITAN QUINONES (ex-*Limburg*)	Royal Scheldt	27.6.80	Extant 1982
77	VILLAR (ex-*Amsterdam*)	Amsterdam	23.5.80	Extant 1982
78	GALVEZ (ex-*Groningen*)	Amsterdam	2.3.81	Extant 1982
79	DIEZ CANSECO (ex-*Rotterdam*)	Rotterdam DD	29.6.81	Extant 1982
	GUISE (ex-*Drenthe*)	Amsterdam	3.6.81	Extant 1982

Meliton Carvajal as completed

Peruvian-built units will differ considerably from the standard *Lupo* design and 2 sisters built in Italy. They will have two masts, a standard hangar, not a telescopic one, will be fitted, and their Albatros reloading system will be hand powered. Armaments will be: (Italian-built units) 8 Otomat SSMs (8×1), 1 Albatros SAM (1×8, with reloads), 1–127mm/54, 4–40mm/70, 2–20 barrelled 105mm rocket launcher, 6 Mk 32 ASW TT (2×3); (Peruvian-built

Italian modified LUPO class *frigates*

No	Name	Builder	Laid down	Launched	Comp	Fate
52	MANUEL VILLAVICENCIO	CNR, Riva Trigoso	6.10.76	7.2.78	25.8.79	Extant 1982
51	MELITON CARVAJAL	CNR, Riva Trigoso	8.8.74	17.11.76	5.2.79	Extant 1982
53	MONTERO	SIMAC, Callao	1978	8.10.82		Fitting out 1982
54		SIMAC, Callao	1979			Building 1982

units) 4 Otomat SSM (4×1), 1 Albatros SAM (1×8, with reloads), 1–127mm/54, 2–40mm/70, 2–105mm RL (2×20), 6–324mm Mk 32 ASW TT (2×3). See under Italy for further details.

Class (former name):
Aguirre (ex-*Waterman*), *Castilla* (ex-*Bangust*), *Rodriguez* (ex-*Weaver*). All three units transferred 26.10.51 under MDAP, arriving in Peru 24.5.52. Prior to transfer, TTs were removed and the ships were recon-

Ex-US BOSTWICK class *destroyer escorts*

ditioned. Pennant nos D 2, D 1 and D 3, changed in 1959 to DE numbers and in 1960 to 62, 61 and 63 respectively. *Aguirre* sank in 1974 in Exocet test. *Castilla* and *Rodriguez* discarded in 1979.

LATIN AMERICA

Class (former name):
Calvez, ex-*Woonsocket* 1944–48)
  Purchased 1948, she was over-
hauled at Norfolk Navy Yard in 1952.
Name often incorrectly cited as

Ex-US TACOMA class *frigates*

Teniente Calvez. Pennant no F 1. Discarded 1961 and broken up.

Class (former name):
Ferre (ex-*Poundmaker*), *Palacios*
(ex-*St Pierre*)
  Both units were purchased in
1947. Modernised with new guns and
fire control at the New York Naval

Ex-Canadian 'RIVER' class *frigates*

Shipyard in 1952. Their names are
often incorrectly cited as *Teniente
Ferre* and *Teniente Palacios*. Pennant
nos F 3 and F 4, became FE numbers in 1959 and in 1960 they were
changed to 66 and 65. Both discarded
in 1966.

Dos de Mayo 1970

SUBMARINES

The *Abtao* class is a modification of
the wartime US *Mackerel* design.
Pennant nos were originally 5–8 and
then SS 1–SS 4. *Abtao* and *Dos de
Mayo* carry a 5in/25 deck gun abaft
the fin. In Apr 1957 names were
changed to those of famous Peruvian
naval battles. *Dos de Mayo* and *Abtao*
were refitted at Groton, Connecticut,
in 1965 and the other pair were refitted in 1968.

ABTAO class *submarines*

Displacement:	825t surfaced; 1400t submerged
Dimensions:	243ft oa × 22ft × 14ft max
	74.1m × 6.7m × 4.3m
Machinery:	2-shaft diesel-electric: 2 General Motors single acting, Type 278A diesels, plus 2 electric motors, 2400hp = 16kts/10kts. Range 500nm at 10kts
Armament:	6–21in TT (4 bow, 2 aft)
Sensors:	Radar SS-2A; sonar BQR-3, BQA-1A
Complement:	40

No	Name	Builder	Laid down	Launched	Comp	Fate
S 42	ABTAO (ex-*Tiburon*)	Electric Boat	12.5.52	27.10.53	20.2.54	Extant 1982
S 43	ANGAMOS (ex-*Atun*)	Electric Boat	27.10.55	5.2.57	1.7.57	Extant 1982
S 41	DOS DE MAYO (ex-*Lobo*)	Electric Boat	12.5.52	6.2.54	14.6.54	Extant 1982
S 44	IQUIQUE (ex-*Merlin*)	Electric Boat	27.10.55	5.2.57	10.10.57	Extant 1982

Name of S 49 changed after a few
weeks, both commissioned 1975 after
refit. Ex-*Tench* also purchased
16.9.76 for spares.

Ex-US GUPPY 1A type *submarines*

No	Name	Builder	Acquired	Fate
S 50	PACOCHA (ex-*Atule*)	Portsmouth N Yd	31.7.74	Extant 1982
S 49	LA PEDRERA (ex-*Pabellon de Pica*, ex-*Sea Poacher*)	Portsmouth N Yd	1.7.74	Extant 1982

First two were ordered in 1969. Units
3 and 4 ordered 12.8.76 and 5 and 6
ordered 21.3.77. Last 4 are slightly
larger at 56.0m and 1000t surfaced.

West German Type 209 *submarines*

| **Particulars:** | As Greek *Glavkos* class |

No	Name	Builder	Laid down	Launched	Comp	Fate
S 32	ANTOFAGASTA	Howaldswerke, Kiel	3.10.77	19.12.79	20.2.81	Extant 1982
S 46	ARICA	Howaldswerke, Kiel	1.11.71	5.4.74	21.1.75	Extant 1982
S 33	BLUME	Howaldswerke, Kiel	1.11.78	1981		Building 1982
S 31	CASMA	Howaldswerke, Kiel	15.7.77	31.8.79	19.12.80	Extant 1982
S 45	ISLAY	Howaldswerke, Kiel	15.5.71	11.10.73	28.8.74	Extant 1982
S 34	CHIPANA (ex-*Pisagua*)	Howaldswereke, Kiel	15.8.78	19.5.81	28.10.82	Extant 1982

AMPHIBIOUS WARFARE VESSELS

Ex-US LSM type *landing ships*

Class (no, former no):
Lomas (36, ex-*LSM 396*), *Atico* (37, ex-*LSM 554*)
  Both units transferred Jul 1959; extant 1982.

Ex-US LST type *tank landing ships*

Class (no, former name):
Paita (141, ex-*Burnett County*), *Chimbote* (142, ex-*LST 283*)
  Acquired 1957 and 1947 respectively. Fitted with landing spaces for helicop-
ters. A third vessel, *Salverry*, was purchased from the merchant navy in 1977.
All extant 1982.

Ex-US AUK class *corvettes*

Class (no, former name):
Galvez (68, ex-*Ruddy*), *Diez Camesco* (69, ex-*Shoveler*)
  War-built US fleet minesweepers transferred under MDAP on 1.11.60. The
minesweeping gear was replaced with sonar and a Hedgehog ASW mortar and
the ships are employed as patrol craft. Transferred to the Coast Guard in 1975,
and stricken 1981.

SMALL SURFACE COMBATANTS

Santillana as completed
NB 1/750 scale

French PR-72P type *missile corvettes*

Displacement:	560t normal; 610t full load
Dimensions:	210ft oa, 193ft 6in pp × 27ft 3in × 8ft 6in
	64.0m, 59.0m × 8.3m × 2.6m
Machinery:	4 shafts, 4 SAGM AGO 240 V16 diesels, 20,000hp = 37kts.
	Range 700nm/2000nm at 30kts/16kts
Armament:	4 MM38 Exocet SSM (2×2), 1–76mm OTO Melara DP,
	2–40mm Breda Bofors (1×2), 2–20mm
Sensors:	Thomson-CSF Triton, Vega fire control
Complement:	45

No	Name	Builder	Launched	Fate
21	VELARDE	Lorient DY	16.9.78	Extant 1982
22	SANTILLANA	SFCN	11.9.78	Extant 1982
23	DE LOS HEROS	Lorient DY	16.9.78	Extant 1982
24	HERRERA	SFCN	16.2.79	Extant 1982
25	LARREA	Lorient DY	20.5.79	Extant 1982
26	SANCHEZ CARRION	SFCN	28.6.79	Extant 1982

All units ordered 1976 and completed in 1980 (first 3) and 1981. Designed by SFCN at Villeneuve-la-Garonne.

Ex-US PGM type *gunboat*

Rio Sama (PC 11, ex-*PGM 78*) was transferred under MDAP in Sept 1966. A second vessel, *Rio Chira* (ex-*PGM 111*) was built at SIMA, Callao with US assistance, and completed in June 1972. Both were transferred to the Coast Guard in 1975 and renumbered 222 and 223. Extant 1982.

VELARDE class *fast patrol craft*

Displacement:	100t normal; 130t full load
Dimensions:	109ft 7in oa, 103ft 4in wl × 21ft × 5ft 7in
	33.4m, 31.5m × 6.4m × 1.7m
Machinery:	2 shafts, 2 Napier-Deltic diesels, 6200bhp = 30kts
Armament:	2–20mm (2×1)
Complement:	25

Class (no, launched):
Velarde (21, 10.7.64), *Santillana* (22, 24.8.64), *De Los Heros* (23, 18.11.64), *Herrera* (24, 26.10.64), *Larrea* (25, 18.2.65), *Sanchez Carrion* (26, 18.2.65)

Designed and built by Vosper, Portsmouth, as multi-purpose patrol, rescue, fishery protection vessels, able to carry guns, torpedoes (side-launching racks), twin RL, mines or DCs (sonar was fitted). Transferred to Coast Guard in 1975 and renamed *Rio Vilor* (229), *Rio Ica* (228), *Rio Chicawa* (224), *Rio Pativilca* (225), *Rio Huaroa* (226), and *Rio Locumba* (227) respectively. All extant 1982.

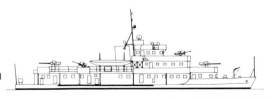

Maranon as completed
NB 1/750 scale

UCAYALI class *river gunboats*

Displacement:	365t full load
Dimensions:	154ft 9in wl × 32ft × 4ft max
	47.1m × 9.7m × 1.2m
Machinery:	2 shafts, 2 British Polar diesels Type M441, 800bhp = 12kts.
	Range 500nm at 10kts
Armament:	2–3in (2×1), 7–20mm (2×2, 1×3)
Complement:	40

No	Name	Builder	Launched	Fate
13	MARANON	Thornycroft	Apr 1951	Extant 1982
14	UCAYALI	Thornycroft	7.3.51	Extant 1982

Santillana as completed   *Vosper Thornycroft*

Stationed at Iquitos on the Amazon River. They have a shallow draft which is necessitated by the river environment. Specially designed for operation in the tropics.

There are also a number of smaller vessels employed on inland waters:
La Pedrera and *Rocafuerte* (Yarrow, 1954) of 150t full load, used as troop transports on the Amazon.
Four Italian-built 37t, 18kt patrol craft for the River Salto built in 1960: *Rio Zarumila*, *Rio Tambes*, *Rio Piwa* and *Rio Salta*; the last was stricken 1966, the rest extant 1982.
Four 14t launches patrol Lake Titicaca, and there are also 4 ex-US Coast Guard 40ft utility boats.

St Kitts

The two islands which make up the State of St Kitts-Nevis form part of the Leeward group of islands in the Eastern Caribbean. St Kitts is the larger of the two (65 square miles) and also contains the capital, Basseterre. The official status of the dependency is a State in Association with Britain which she has been since February 1967. The islands' governor is appointed by the British sovereign and Britain remains responsible for defence. The police force operates one patrol boat.

One 'Spear' class patrol boat, name unknown, entered service 10.9.74, built by Fairey Marine. 4.3t, 29ft 10in in length, 30kts, 2 diesels, 360hp, 2–7.62mm MGs, 2 crew.

'Spear' class patrol boat   *Fairey Marine*

St Lucia

A mountainous and heavily forested island state, St Lucia in the Windward group of islands was a British colony until February 1979; the British sovereign is still the country's head of state. 27 miles long, the island covers 238 square miles and has a population of approximately 120,000. The Customs Service operates a patrol boat from Castries, a port that is highly regarded in the area because of the shelter it affords in heavy weather.

One 40ft Brooke Marine type patrol craft, *Helen*, completed 20.7.70 and built by Brooke Marine, Lowestoft. 14t, 22kts, 2 Cummins diesels, 370hp, 2–7.62mm MGs.

St Vincent

One of the Windward Islands, lying in the Eastern Caribbean, the State of St Vincent incorporates several of the Grenadines and covers an area of just 133 square miles. In 1979 independence was granted and the state is now presided over by a governor general. The Police Force operates a Marine Wing based at Kingstown employing one patrol craft.

One 45ft Brooke Marine type patrol craft; *Chatoyer*, 15t, 21kts, 2 Cummins diesels, 370hp, 3 MG. Lost in a hurricane, 1979.
One 75ft Vosper type patrol craft; *George McIntosh* (SVG 05), entered service Mar 1981, 70t, 24.5kts, 2 Caterpillar diesels, 1–20mm, 11 crew, built by Vosper, Portchester. Replacement for *Chatoyer*.

Surinam

Surinam (formerly Dutch Guiana) lies on South America's northern coast covering an area of 63,250 square miles. Of her three neighbours, Brazil, French Guiana and Guyana, Surinam has had border disagreements with the two latter named. The cause of disagreement in both cases has been over mineral deposits lying within Surinam's territory. Granted independence in 1975, Surinam still relies heavily for defence on the Netherlands. In 1982 there were two attempts, both unsuccessful, to overthrow the country's military government and in both cases rebels were executed. The second attempted *coup* in December was more serious; martial law was introduced and aid of 1.5m dollars held back by the United States. Surinam operates a small navy, employing 160 officers and men and based at Paramaribo. The majority of the navy's craft were acquired from the Netherlands.

Fleet strength in 1982 comprised:
Three 32m, 127t patrol craft built in 1976–77 by De Vries, Aalsmeer: *SO 41–SO 43*, armed with 2–40mm (2×1).
Three 22m, 70t patrol craft built by Schottel in 1976: *C 301–C 303*, armed with 3 MGs

Surinam also operates three 12.6m river patrol craft; *Bahadoer* (RP 201), *Fajablow* (RP 202), *Korangon* (RP 203). Built by Schottel, Netherlands and commissioned Dec 1975 (RP 201, RP 202) and Feb 1976. 15t, 14kts, 1 Dorman 8JT diesel, 280hp, 1–12.7mm, 4 crew.
One 10m river patrol craft, ordered Dec 1974 and entered service Aug 1975. Built by Schottel, Netherlands, 14kts, 1 Dorman 8JT diesel, 280hp.

Trinidad and Tobago

The most southerly of the West Indies, Trinidad and Tobago became independent on 31 August 1962 although a governor general is still appointed by the British sovereign. The regime in the islands is a stable one although internal tensions brought about by economic problems caused rioting to take place in the early 1970s. Although independent, Trinidad and Tobago still rely on Britain in matters of defence. The governor general has direct authority over the Army (approximately 800 men), while the Coast Guard is the responsibility of the home affairs minister. In 1982 the Coast Guard employed approximately 590 officers and men; the main base is at Staubles Bay.

Swedish CG 40 type *large patrol craft*

Displacement:	200t
Dimensions:	133ft 3in × 21ft 11in × 5ft 3in
	40.6m × 6.7m × 1.6m
Machinery:	2 shafts, 2 Paxman-Valenta 16RP200 diesels, 8000hp = 27kts. Range 3000nm at 15kts
Armament:	1–40mm Bofors, 1–20mm
Sensors:	Radar Decca TM 1226
Complement:	22

No	Name	Builder	Comp	Fate
CG 5	BARRACUDA	Karlskrona Varvet	15.6.80	Extant 1982
CG 6	CASCADURA	Karlskrona Varvet	15.6.80	Extant 1982

Ordered Aug 1978. Fitted with optronic fire control for the 40mm. The first export success for this Swedish design. Extant 1982.

Vosper 103ft type *large patrol craft*

Displacement:	96–100t
Dimensions:	(CG 1 and CG 2) 102ft 7in × 19ft 8in × 5ft 6in
	31.4m × 5.9m × 1.7m
	(CG 3 and CG 4) 103ft × 19ft 10in × 5ft 10in
	31.5m × 5.9m × 1.8m
Machinery:	2 shafts, 2 Paxman 12 YJCM Ventura diesels, 2900hp = 24kts. Range 1800nm at 13.5kts. Oil 18t
Armament:	1–40mm (CG 1 and CG 2), 1–20mm (CG 3 and CG 4)
Complement:	17 (19 in CG 3 and CG 4)

No	Name	Builder	Comp	Fate
CG 1	TRINITY	Vosper	20.2.65	Extant 1982
CG 2	COURLAND BAY	Vosper	20.2.65	Extant 1982
CG 3	CHAGUARAMAS	Vosper	18.3.72	Extant 1982
CG 4	BUCCO REEF	Vosper	18.3.72	Extant 1982

All units fitted with roll damping fins, air conditioned. Extant 1982.

SOUTER type *coastal patrol craft*

Class:
CG 26, CG 29
Few details available for these recently built craft (delivery 1982); GRP hulls, 55ft in length, 30kts, 2 GM diesels, 1 MG. Built by Souter (Cowes) Ltd.
Trinidad and Tobago also operate two coastal patrol craft, *Naparima* (CG 01) and *El Tucuche* (CG 25) commissioned 13.8.76 and 1976 respectively. CG 25 slightly larger at 55ft compared to CG 01, 50ft; 2 GM 8V71 diesels (TL 71, CG 25). Built by Tugs and Lighters Ltd, Port-of-Spain.
There is also a 23ft fibreglass coastal patrol craft *Fort Chacon* (CG 9), built in Trinidad, 1 Caterpillar diesel, 27kts; two coastal tugs, *Snapper* and *Bonito*, launched 16.1.80 and 1981 respectively, built by Bodewes, Millengen and a sail training vessel, *Hummingbird II*, a 40ft ketch built in Trinidad 1966.
The first craft operated by the service, the 60ft *Sea Hawk* and the 45ft *Sea Scout* (both built by J Taylor, Shoreham, UK) were stricken in 1975–76.

Trinity as completed   *Vosper Thornycroft*

Uruguay

Economic weakness (and an internal war against Tupamaros guerillas in the 1960s and 1970s) has hampered the growth of the armed forces, and particularly the navy (volunteer personnel 4700 in 1982 including 1000 marines and naval air arm). US aid stopped in 1977 following allegations of human rights violations and Uruguay now renounces all aid, and strongly advocates a policy of non-intervention in other countries. The main naval base is Montevideo.

FLEET STRENGTH 1947

TORPEDO GUNBOAT

Name	Launched	Disp	Fate
URUGUAY	12.4.10	1150t	Discarded 1953

PATROL CRAFT

Name	Launched	Disp	Fate
PAYSANDU	21.7.35	180t	Discarded 1963
RIO NEGRO	22.8.35	180t	Discarded 1969
SALTO	11.8.35	180t	Discarded 1973; survey ship

There was also the ex-US submarine chaser *Maldonado* (ex-*PC 1234*) transferred in 1964 (stricken *c*1969) and the ex-US 63ft ARV *Colonia*, transferred in 1945 and extant 1982.

MAJOR SURFACE SHIPS

Ex-US DEALEY class *frigate*

No	Name	Builder	Acquired	Fate
3	18 DE JULIO (ex-*Dealey*)	Bath Iron Works	28.7.72	Extant 1982

Refit 1979–80, Arsenal de Marinha, Rio de Janeiro; first US-built postwar escort constructed and the least modified of her class.

Ex-US CANNON class *frigates*

No	Name	Builder	Acquired	Fate
1	URUGUAY (ex-*Baron*)	Federal SB	May 1952	Extant 1982
2	ARTIGAS (ex-*Bronstein*)	Federal SB	Mar 1952	Extant 1982

Modernised in late 1960s and now fitted with SPS-5, SPS-6C (not in *Uruguay*) radar and SQS-4 sonar. Armament in 1982 was 3–3in (3×1), 2–40mm (1×2), 4–20mm (4×1)

AMPHIBIOUS WARFARE VESSELS

Ex-US LCM(6) class *landing ships*

Two units *LD 40* and *LD 41* transferred Oct 1972.
Uruguay also operates a 12t, LCU, *LD 42* and two 31t LCUs *LD 43* and *LD 45*.

SMALL SURFACE COMBATANTS

Ex-British 'CASTLE' class *corvette*

Class (former names):
Montevideo (ex-*Arnrior*, ex-*Rising Castle*).
Transferred 1956; used as a training ship; discarded 1975.

Uruguay 1980　　　　　　　　　　　　　　　　　　　　*USN*

Ex-US AUK class *corvette*

Class (former name):
Commandante Pedro Campbell (ex-*Chickadee*)
Transferred 18.8.66. Reclassified as corvettes although still has some minesweeping gear. Carries pennant no 4; extant 1982.

Ex-US AGILE class *corvette*

Class (no, former names):
Maldonado (MS 33, ex-*Bir Hakeim*, ex-*MSO 451*)
A US *Agile* class ocean minesweeper transferred to France in 1964 and then to Uruguay in Sept 1974. All sweeping gear was removed and she operated as an escort; stricken 1979.

Ex-US ADJUTANT class *large patrol craft*

Class (no, former names):
Rio Negro (13, ex-*Marguerite*, ex-*MSC 94*)
Transferred 10.11.69 from France. Minesweeping gear removed.

French VIGILANTE type *large patrol craft*

Displacement:	166t normal; 220t full load
Dimensions:	136ft 2in oa, 124ft 7in pp × 22ft 4in × 6ft 11in *41.5m, 38.0m × 6.8m × 2.1m*
Machinery:	2 shafts, 2 MTU diesels, 5400hp = 25kts. Range 2400nm at 15kts
Armament:	1–40mm (provision for 2–20mm)
Sensors:	Radar Decca TM 1226C, 1229
Complement:	25

No	Name	Builder	Launched	Fate
5	15 DE NOVIEMBRE	CMN, Cherbourg	16.10.80	Extant 1982
6	26 DE AGOSTO	CMN, Cherbourg	11.2.80	Extant 1982
7	COMODORO COE	CMN, Cherbourg	23.1.81	Extant 1982

Ordered in 1978 and all commissioned 25.3.81. Have CSEE Panda fire control.

Uruguay also operates an American-built coastal patrol craft, *Paysandu* (60t, commissioned 1968) and a coastal patrol craft, *Carmelo* (70t, commissioned 1957).

Venezuela

The Venezuelan Navy has dramatically increased in size since World War II. This may be attributed to the development of the nation's vast natural resources, the role played by the Navy in the removal of Marcos Perez Jimenez in 1958, and the growing threat of terrorist forces in the Caribbean area. Venezuela also has a long-standing claim on Guyanan territory, currently in abeyance, but supports Belize against Guatemalan claims. The majority of personnel, 9000 (including 4500 marines and a naval air arm) in 1982, are 18-month conscripts. The main naval bases are Caracas, Puerto Cabella, La Guaira and Puerto de Hierro.

FLEET STRENGTH 1947

GUNBOATS

Name	Launched	Disp	Fate
GENERAL SOUBLETTE	1925	615t	Discarded 1950
GENERAL URDANETA	1925	615t	Discarded 1950

CORVETTES

Name	Acquired	Disp	Fate
CONSTITUCION (ex-*Algoma*)	1946	1060t	Discarded 1962
FEDERACION (ex-*Amherst*)	1946	1060t	Discarded 1956
INDEPENDENCIA (ex-*Dunvegan*)	1946	1060t	Discarded 1953
LIBERTAD (ex-*Battleford*)	1946	1060t	Wrecked 12.4.49
PATRIA (ex-*Oakville*)	1946	1060t	Discarded 1962
VICTORIA (ex-*Westaskawin*)	1946	1060t	Discarded 1962

There were also 4 ex-US Coast Guard 47t cutters, *Antonio Diaz*, *Arimendi*, *Briceno Mendez* and *Brion*, transferred in 1947; *Brion* was renamed *Felipe Santiago Esteves* in 1957.

MAJOR SURFACE SHIPS

Nueva Esparta 1970

Specifically designed for tropic operations, these units are air conditioned throughout and are quite spacious. The single uptake and stack serviced the two independent engine and boiler rooms. The 4.5in guns were British Mk IV.
Nueva Esparta and *Zulia* were refitted at Palmers, Hebburn and Vickers, Barrow in 1959 when 2 Squid ASW mortars were fitted and TT removed. They went on to New York N Yd in 1960 for improvements to their electronics. *Nueva Esparta* was again refitted in 1968–69, at Cammell Laird, when 2 Seacat SAM (2×4) replaced 12–40mm. Electronics by this time comprised SPS-12, SP6-6 (*Zulia*) or AWS-2 and Type 276, with 2 GWS 20 Seacat directors on *Nueva Esparta*.

NUEVA ESPARTA class *destroyers*

Displacement:	2600t standard; 3300t full load
Dimensions:	384ft wl, 402ft oa × 43ft × 12ft 9in max
	117.1m, 122.5m × 13.1m × 3.9m
Machinery:	2-shaft Parsons geared turbines, 2 Yarrow boilers, 50,000shp = 34.5kts. Range 500nm at 11kts
Armament:	6–4.5in (3×2), 16–40mm/60 (8×2), 3–21in TT (1×3), 2 DCT, 2 DC racks
Complement:	254

No	Name	Builder	Laid down	Launched	Comp	Fate
D 31	ARAGUA	Vickers-Armstrong, Barrow	29.6.53	27.1.55	14.2.56	Discarded 1975
D 11	NUEVA ESPARTA	Vickers-Armstrong, Barrow	24.7.51	19.11.52	8.12.53	Discarded 1978
D 21	ZULIA	Vickers-Armstrong, Barrow	24.7.51	29.6.53	15.9.54	Discarded 1978

Nueva Esparta as completed

Navarret Collection

Falcon received a FRAM II modernisation while in US service, and now operates a Bell 475 helicopter from the former DASH platform. A single 40mm aft was added to *Carabobo* in 1978.

Ex-US ALLEN M SUMNER class

No	Name	Builder	Acquired	Fate
D 22	FALCON (ex-*Robert K Huntington*)	Todd-Pacific, Seattle	31.10.73	Stricken 1981
D 21	CARABOBO (ex-*Beatty*)	Bethlehem, Staten I	14.7.74	Stricken 1981

General José Trinidad Moran 1978

This class suffered from many problems, primarily due to their light construction. Ships were air conditioned in living and command spaces. Original 4in main battery was fully automatic and radar controlled. They were rearmed as follows: *Almirante Jose Gacia*, *Almirante Brion* and *General Jose de Austria* at Ansaldo, Leghorn in 1962 received 1 Lanciabas DC launcher; 8–20mm were removed. *Almirante Clemente*, *General Jose Trinidad Moran* at Cammell Laird/Plessey from 1968–75 received 2–76mm OTO Melara Compact, in place of 4–4in, and new electronics. The rest of the armament then comprised 2–40mm (1×2), 6–324mm Mk 32 ASW TT (2×3) with Plessey AWS-2, Decca 1226 and Selenia RTN-10X radar and Plessey MS-26 sonar. Best sea speed for all units in later years was 29kts.

ALMIRANTE CLEMENTE class *frigates*

Displacement:	1300t standard; 1500t full load
Dimensions:	325ft 2in oa × 35ft 5in × 11ft 2in max
	99.1m × 10.8m × 3.4m
Machinery:	2-shaft geared turbines, 2 Foster Wheeler boilers, 2400shp = 34kts. Range 3500nm at 15kts
Armament:	4–4in (2×2), 4–40mm/60 (2×2), 8–20mm/80 (8×1), 2 Hedgehogs, 4 DCT, 2 DC racks, 3–21in TT (1×3)

No	Name	Builder	Laid down	Launched	Comp	Fate
D 23	ALMIRANTE BRION	Ansaldo, Leghorn	12.12.54	4.9.55	1957	Discarded 1978
D 12	ALIMIRANTE CLEMENTE	Ansaldo, Leghorn	5.5.54	12.12.54	1956	Extant 1982
D 33	ALMIRANTE JOSE GARCIA	Ansaldo, Leghorn	12.12.54	12.10.56	1957	Discarded 1977
D 32	GENERAL JOSE DE AUSTRIA	Ansaldo, Leghorn	12.12.54	15.7.56	1957	Discarded 1976
D 22	GENERAL JOSE TRINIDAD MORAN	Ansaldo, Leghorn	5.5.54	12.12.54	1956	Extant 1982
D 23	GENERAL JUAN JOSE FLORES	Ansaldo, Leghorn	5.5.54	7.2.55	1956	Discarded 1978

Almirante Brion 1981

L & L van Ginderen

Almirante Clemente 1979

USN

General Soublette as completed

The Venezuelan units are very similar to the standard *Lupo*s. However, they will have a fixed hangar (for 2 helicopters) and therefore, carry no reloads for the Albatros point defence SAM which will fire Aspide missiles. In 1981 *Mariscal Sucre* successfully fired an Aspide during a UNITAS exercise. See under Italy for full details.

Italian LUPO class *frigates*

No	Name	Builder	Laid down	Launched	Comp	Fate
F 22	ALMIRANTE BRION	CNR, Riva Trigoso	Jun 1977	22.2.79	7.3.81	Extant 1982
F 25	GENERAL SALOM	CNR, Riva Trigoso	7.11.78	13.1.80	Feb 82	Extant 1982
F 24	GENERAL SOUBLETTE	CNR, Riva Trigoso	26.8.78	4.1.80	5.12.81	Extant 1982
F 23	GENERAL URDANETA	CNR, Riva Trigoso	23.1.78	23.3.79	8.8.81	Extant 1982
F 26	JOSE FELIX RIBAS	CNR, Riva Trigoso	21.8.79	4.12.80	Oct 1982	Extant 1982
F 21	MARISCAL SUCRE	CNR, Riva Trigoso	19.11.76	28.9.78	10.5.80	Extant 1982

SUBMARINES

Overhauled at San Francisco Navy Yard 1962; used for training.

Ex-US BALAO class *submarines*

No	Name	Builder	Acquired	Fate
S 11	CARITE (ex-*Tilefish*)	Mare Island N Yd	4.5.60	Discarded 28.1.77

Picuda was overhauled 1979–81 at Puerto Belgrano N Yd in Argentina.

Ex-US GUPPY II type *submarines*

No	Name	Builder	Acquired	Fate
S 21	TIBURON (ex-*Cubera*)	Electric Boat	5.1.72	Stricken 1979
S 22	PICUDA (ex-*Grenadier*)	Boston N Yd	15.5.73	Extant 1982

First two units ordered in 1971 and a second pair on 10.3.77. *S 32* also reported as *Congrio*. They are slightly longer (195ft, *59.5m*) than the standard Type 209, since they incorporate an enlarged bow sonar like the West German Type 206.

West German Type 209 *submarines*

Particulars: As Greek *Glavkos* class

No	Name	Builder	Laid down	Launched	Comp	Fate
S 32	CARIBE	Howaldswerke, Kiel	1.8.73	16.12.75	11.3.77	Extant 1982
S 31	SABALO	Howaldswerke, Kiel	2.5.73	21.8.75	6.8.76	Extant 1982
S 33	–	–	–	–	–	Building 1982
S 34	–	–	–	–	–	Building 1982

AMPHIBIOUS WARFARE VESSELS

Constitucion as completed
NB 1/750 scale

Ex-US TERREBONNE PARISH class *tank landing ship*

Class (no, former name):

Amazonas (T 51, ex-*Vernon County*)

Transferred on loan 29.6.73 and purchased 30.12.77.

Venezuela operates the ex-US repair ship (ex-LST) *Guyana* (T 31, ex-*Quirius*, ex-*LST 1151*); she is used as a transport. There is also the ex-US LSM type landing ship *Los Frailes* (T 33, ex-*LSM 544*), the remainder of a class of 4 transferred in 1959–60, the others being *Los Montjes* (T 21) and *Los Roques* (T 22) stricken in 1979, and *Los Testigos* (T 24) stricken in 1980. Minor landing craft in 1982 amounted to 12 LCUPs built locally to the standard US design, plus a few ex-US LCVPs and LCPLs.

CONSTITUCION class *fast attack craft*

Displacement:	170t full load
Dimensions:	121ft pp × 23ft 4in × 5ft 11in max *36.90m × 7.10m × 1.80m*
Machinery:	2 shafts, 2 MTU diesels, 7200bhp = 31kts. Range 1350nm at 16kts
Armament:	2 Otomat SSM, 1–40mm (*Constitucion, Independencia, Patria*: 1–76mm/62 OTO Melara Compact)
Sensors:	Radar SPQ-2D (plus Orion RTN-10X in gun and vessels)
Complement:	17

No	Name	Builder	Launched	Fate
P 11	CONSTITUCION	Vosper Thornycroft	1.6.73	Extant 1982
P 12	FEDERACION	Vosper Thornycroft	26.2.74	Extant 1982
P 13	INDEPENDENCIA	Vosper Thornycroft	24.7.73	Extant 1982
P 14	LIBERTAD	Vosper Thornycroft	5.3.74	Extant 1982
P 15	PATRIA	Vosper Thornycroft	27.9.73	Extant 1982
P 16	VICTORIA	Vosper Thonycroft	3.9.74	Extant 1982

Vosper Thornycroft designed attack craft in gun and missile armed variants. Laid down Jan 1973–Mar 1974 and completed 16.8.74–22.9.75.

THE NATIONAL GUARD

The National Guard operates a number of small craft, including: 21 *Rio Orinoco* class (65t, 25kts, 1974–78); 12 *Rio Meta* class (45t, 30kts, 1970–71 and 1976–77); 8 *Rio Apure* class (38t, 24kts, 1955), 17 US 'Enforcer' type; 4 new 77ft (*23.5m*) type were ordered in 1980 from R E Direcktor, New York.

Federacion as completed

Vosper Thornycroft

Bahrain

At present the tiny Gulf state of Bahrain has only a coast guard force of 13 patrol craft but the Ministry of Defence ordered two fast attack craft (missile) armed with 4 Exocet and two fast attack craft (gun) from Lürssen in 1979. These are the first stages in the creation of a new naval force. A friendship treaty was signed between Britain and Bahrain after independence in 1971 and Bahrain ordered three patrol craft from Fairey Marine Ltd. As yet, Bahrain has no naval bases as such; there are about 300 volunteer officers and men serving with the naval force. The US Navy's three-ship Middle East Force retained its harbour facilities after British withdrawal until 1977.

Lürssen 'TNC 45' type *fast attack craft (missile)*

Displacement:	228t half load; 258t full load
Dimensions:	147ft 4in × 23ft × 7ft 7in
	44.9m × 7.0m × 2.3m
Machinery:	4 shafts, 4 MTU 16V 538 TB 92 diesels, 14,400bhp = 38kts. Range 500nm/1600nm at 38.5kts/16kts
Armament:	4 MM40 Exocet SSM (4×1), 1–76mm/62 DP OTO Melara (250rds), 2–40mm/70 Breda-Bofors (1800rds) Compatto (1×2), 3–7.62mm MG (6000rds)
Sensors:	Radar WM-28, 4 PEAB 9 LV223; ECM Decca RDL-2 ABC passive warning, Dagaie chaff RL
Complement:	40

Two ordered in 1979. See under UAE and Kuwait.

Al Riffa as completed
NB 1/750 scale

Lürssen 'FPB 38' type *fast attack craft (gun)*

Displacement:	188t half load; 205t full load
Dimensions:	126ft 4in × 23ft × 7ft 3in
	38.6m × 7.0m × 2.2m
Machinery:	2 shafts, 2 MTU 20V 539 TB91 diesels, 9500bhp = 34kts. Range 550nm/1100nm at 31.5kts/16kts
Armament:	2–40mm/70 Breda-Bofors Compatto (1×2), 2–20mm GAM-601 Oerlikon (2×1), mines, Dagaie chaff RL, 2–50mm RFL on 40mm, 2–3 pdr saluting guns
Sensors:	CSEE Lynx, Philips 9LV100G
Complement:	27

No	Name	Builder	Launched	Fate
10	AL RIFFA	Lürssen, Vegesack Apr 1981	Extant 1982
11	HAWAR	Lürssen, Vegesack July 1981	Extant 1982

Two ordered in 1979. Some sources suggest 3 ships were ordered. Originally planned to have 1–40mm/70 Bofors. Commissioned Aug and Nov 1981 respectively.

COASTAL PATROL CRAFT
All these units are part of the Coast Guard and were extant 1982 under Ministry of Interior control.

Three Fairey Marine 'Tracker' class (26t full load, 64ft, 28kts, 1–20mm): *Bahrain* (1) bought 1974, in service since 1975. Two others bought 1980.

Two Fairey Marine 'Spear' class (10t full load, 29ft, 26kts, 2 MG, 3 men): *Saham* (4) and *Khataf* (5) bought 1974, in service since 1975.

Two Vosper type (32t, 56ft, 29kts): *Howar* (3) and *Roubodh*, Singapore-built 1977.

Three small Vosper type (6.3t, 36ft, 27kts): *Al Bayneh*, *Junnan* and *Quaimas*, Singapore-built 1977.

One 50ft Cheverton type (9t, 22kts): *Mashtan* (6) UK-built 1976.

Three 27ft Cheverton type (3.3t, 15kts): *Noon* (15), *Askar* (16), and *Suwad* (17) built 1977.

AMPHIBIOUS WARFARE VESSELS
One 'Loadmaster' class landing craft, *Safra* (7) UK-built 1976 and commissioned Dec 1977.

One utility hovercraft built by Tropimere, UK, 1977.

Cyprus

The Republic of Cyprus, third largest island in the Mediterranean, became independent of British rule in 1960 and has been strife-torn ever since. Civil war between the 80 per cent Greek population and the Turkish minority together with a wider war between Greece and Turkey were only just averted in the period 1963–67. A UN peacekeeping force (UNFICYP) was introduced in March 1964 while Britain continues to hold the two Sovereign Base Areas of Akrotiri and Dhekelia, totalling 99 square miles, in the south of the island.

Both these outside forces were powerless in the face of the Turkish invasion in July 1974, precipitated by the Cypriot National Guard's overthrow of Archbishop Makarios. Makarios returned as president only to find that 38 per cent of the island had become the 'Turkish Federated State of Cyprus' with settlers from the mainland (only 50 miles away) as well as 40,000 troops reinforcing the Turkish minority.

This enforced partition remains the position today and prevents the creation of a significant Cypriot Navy despite the island's large if mainly 'flag of convenience' merchant marine. A force of 330 sailors operates the few warships that have survived the Turkish invasion.

Ex-Soviet 'P 4' class *fast attack craft (torpedo)*

For a considerable period 6 ex-Soviet 'P 4' class MTBs served in Cypriot waters, 4 transferred in Oct 1964 (?1962) and two in Feb 1965 (probably 2 extra engines have been supplied since that time). However the majority were sunk during the Turkish invasion of July 1974; one undamaged craft was beached and captured (now preserved in a marine museum at Istanbul).

French *fast attack craft (missile)*

Two (80t, 4 SS12 SSM, 2–20mm AA) ordered from CN de l'Esterel, Cannes, were not taken up and were transferred to Greece as *Kelefstis Stamou* and *Diopos Antoniou*. Both commissioned 1975. Cypriot names unknown. Wooden hull. For further details see under Greece.

French '32L' type *fast attack craft*

Displacement:	96t
Dimensions:	105ft × 21ft × 2ft 11in
	32.1m × 6.4m × 0.9m
Machinery:	2 diesels, 1900hp = 30kts. Range 1500nm at 15kts
Armament:	1–40mm, 1–20mm
Complement:	?

One unit built by CN de l'Estérel, Cannes. Delivered *c*1982.

Ex-German R41 group *motor minesweepers (patrol craft)*

Three units (launched 1943), Cypriot and ex-German names unknown. Were taken up 1962–63 from mercantile use and rearmed as patrol boats with 1–40mm and/or 2–20mm. One was destroyed by Turkish air attack on 8.8.64 at Xeros (beached near Xeros harbour). One (with radar) had pennant no 15 in early 1970s. Further fates of two ships unknown – probably lost during the Turkish operations of July 1974 (one stricken 1973?).

MISCELLANEOUS
Several of 10 former fishing boats (*c*50t, 1–2 MG or 20mm) were probably lost in July 1974. Some unconfirmed reports give purchase of 3 Type '101' MTBs in early 1970s from Yugoslavia.

Iran

Iran's Navy is the largest in the Persian Gulf area and possesses the greatest missile capability. From the early 1960s the Imperial Iranian Navy was trained in the West mainly by Great Britain and the USA. Iran also had the advantage of having been a member of CENTO and took part in the MIDLINK series of exercises with the US, Pakistan and Royal Navies. Senior Officers therefore have a thorough grounding in sound naval practice and, although a number were lost as a result of the 1979 revolution, a reasonable reservoir of expertise must still remain.

MIDDLE EAST

Before the revolution it was reported that the general standard of ship and equipment maintenance was well below that of Western navies. It is believed that the situation has almost certainly worsened as a result of the departure of Western advisers, disruption of naval administration and difficulty in obtaining spares. It is doubtful if any of the larger ships are fully operational according to Western standards. The most effective units are the most recently acquired 'Combattante II' design (*Kaman* class) fast attack craft with the US-supplied Harpoon missile followed by the *Saam* class frigates fitted with the Italian Sea Killer missile. As regards the three elderly destroyers, an immense effort would be needed to get them to sea.

In 1979 following the cancellation of foreign orders the rapid expansion and technological advances of this navy were halted. The ships in existence suffer from two major problems – lack of maintenance and lack of spares. The British and US maintenance expertise is no longer available and a navy which has never kept very much in the way of spares now has no means of obtaining them; consequently ships have had to be laid up. The task of training conscripts was never an easy one and must be made even more difficult by the departure of foreign assistance. And, with poor morale following the general instability of affairs the Navy cannot be considered as an efficient fighting fleet.

With continued isolation from Western supplies the immediate outlook for the Navy is one of gradual decline although at present morale seems to be high as all are united in the war against Iraq. The future is uncertain and is dependant on the eventual political outcome.

There is no reliable information about losses in the war between Iran and Iraq. Main bases in the Persian Gulf are at Bandar Abbas on the Strait of Hormuz, Bushire, Kharg Island and Khorramshar; in the Indian Ocean at Chah Bahr and in the Caspian Sea at Bandar. There are 20,000 officers and men (two-year conscripts) serving in the Navy.

FLEET STRENGTH 1947

PATROL CRAFT

Name	Launched	Disp	Fate
CHAROGH (ex-*Nilam*)	26.7.31	331t	BU *c*1953
CHANBAAZ (ex-*Hira*)	12.9.31	331t	BU *c*1953
SIMORGH (ex-*Lal*)	3.8.31	331t	BU *c*1953

Charogh and *Simorgh* built by CNR, Palermo. *Chanbaaz* built by OCP, Naples.

MOTOR LAUNCHES

Name	Launched	Disp	Fate
BABOLSAR	1935	*c*30t	Stricken *c*1972
GORGAN	1935	*c*30t	Stricken *c*1972
SEF INDREUDE	1935	*c*30t	Stricken *c*1972

These were stationed in the Caspian Sea armed with 1–47mm Skoda and 1 MG. Built by CNR, Palermo.

MAJOR SURFACE SHIPS

Artemiz 7.5.69   *Vosper Thornycroft*

Artemiz 1975

Ex-British 'BATTLE' class *destroyer*

Armament:	4–114mm/45 QF Mk 4 (2×2), 4–40mm/60 Bofors (4×1), 1 Seacat SAM launcher (1×4; est 16 missiles), 1 Squid ASW mortar (1×3). See notes
Complement:	270
Other particulars:	As British 'Battle' class (1st group)

No	Name	Builder	Acquired	Fate
D 5	ARTEMIZ (ex-*Sluys*)	Cammell Laird	26.1.65	Extant 1982

The former RN destroyer HMS *Sluys* (D 60) was transferred to Iran at Southampton and handed over to the Iranian Navy following a 3-year modernisation by Vosper Thornycroft. Later given pennant no 51. Often referred to as having 8–40mm in early 1970s. 4 Standard SSM launchers (8 missiles) added after refit at Cape Town, South Africa in 1975–76. Now has only 2–40mm (2×1) aft. Plessey AWS-1 air surveillance radar with on-mounted IFF, two Contraves Sea Hunter fire control radars, Plessey MS-26 sonar and Decca RDL-1 ESM.

Ex-US ALLEN M SUMNER class *destroyers*

No	Name	Builder	Acquired	Fate
61	BABR (ex-*Zellars*)	Todd Pacific Shipyards	19.3.71	Extant 1982
62	PALANG (ex-*Stormes*)	Todd Pacific Shipyards	16.2.72	Extant 1982

FRAM II conversions at Norfolk, Virginia in FY 61. *Stormes* replaced the outdated *Gainard* (stricken from USN 1970). However, they are far from being sister ships. For instance, the main deckhouse on *Babr*, ('Tiger') was widened during FRAM refit as far forward as amidships, but only half as far forward on *Palang* ('Leopard'). Both ships underwent a full refit as well as conversion at Philadelphia N Yd before sailing in mid-1974 for Iran. The air-conditioning was improved replacing two 100kW diesel generators by two 500kW units, B gun-mount was removed with its hoists and magazines (which became store rooms since these ships will operate away from suppliers of spare parts), accommodation was altered, a Canadian telescopic hangar similar to the US *Knox* class frigates (AB-204 ASW helicopter), was fitted, the 4 Standard SSM launchers (8 missiles, which can be used as SAM) were sited on a platform between stacks and on the 01 level forward of the bridge, VDS was rigged and 2 Hedgehogs were fitted in B position. *Babr* carried an SQS-43 sonar system that included an SQS-31B hull-mounted sonar and SQA-10 VDS. *Palang*'s VDS was removed to provide spares for *Babr* which has now lost hers. New torpedo stowage was mounted between the funnels (to make room in the hangar) and the landing platform was widened out to the ship's sides while the old hangar was removed and scrapped.

As *Babr* had the small ECM house and mast atop the hangar and *Palang* had the large one, *Palang*'s house was transferred to *Babr* as she was further advanced and due for completion first; a new house and mast was then built for *Palang*. These old ships with their additional SSM/SAM and ASW armament were more effectively armed than many warships currently in the USN. Due to lack of spare parts both in reserve in 1980.

Ex-US DD 713 *Kenneth D Bailey* and DD 881 *Bordelon* (both *Gearing* class) were purchased 13.1.75 and 1.2.77 for spares.

US Modified SPRUANCE class (DD 993 class) *destroyers*

Class:

Kouroush, Daryush, Ardeshir, Nader, Shapour, Anoushirvan

The original order for these superb AA ships placed with the US Navy by the Imperial Iranian Government in 1974 was for 6. They were assigned the US Navy hull numbers DD 993–998 for accounting purposes; Iranian pennant nos 11–16 respectively and named after emperors. Two (DD 995 and DD 997) were cancelled in June 1976 before the order to Ingalls Shipbuilding Corp for the remaining 4 was issued on 23.4.78. On 23.4.78 DD 996 and DD 998 were reclassified DD 995 and DD 996. The Iranian Navy planned to classify them as cruisers. During the Iranian Revolution DD 995 and DD 996 were cancelled on 3.2.79 (French sources give DD 993 and DD 994). On 31.3.79 the two remaining ships DD 993 and DD 994 were cancelled (French sources give DD 995 and DD 996). The 4 were officially acquired by the US Navy on 25.7.79 with the signing of the FY79 supplementary budget request. On 8.8.79 DD 993–996 were reclassified DDG 993–996. These ships are now the USN *Kidd* class. US names: *Kidd* (ex-*Kouroush*), *Callaghan* (ex-*Daryush*), *Scott* (ex-*Nader*) and *Chandler* (ex-*Anoushirvan*). For full details see under United States.

Ex-British LOCH class *frigate*

Babr (ex-*Derby Haven*, ex-*Loch Assynt*) completed as depot ship, acquired in 1949. Served as depot ship for landing craft. No pennant no. Armed with 2–102mm (2×1). Paid off 30.10.69 and officially deleted from the effective list in 1972.

Naghdi as completed

BAYANDOR class (US PF 103 class) *frigates*

Displacement:	900t standard; 1135t full load
Dimensions:	299ft 2in × 32ft 11in × 10ft
	83.8m × 10.0m × 3.0m
Machinery:	2 shafts, 4 Fairbanks-Morse 38D81/8 diesels, 6000hp = 20kts. Oil 110t. Range 3000nm at 15kts
Armament:	2–76mm/50 DP Mk34 (2×1), 2–40mm/60 (1×2), 1 Hedgehog, 4 DCT, 2 DC racks, 60 DCs. See notes
Sensors:	Radar SPS-6, Raytheon, SPG-34; sonar SQS-17
Complement:	133–140

No	Name	Builder	Launched	Fate
F 25	BAYANDOR (ex-*PF 103*)	Levingston SB	7.7.63	Extant 1982
F 26	NAGHDI (ex-*PF 104*)	Levingston SB	10.10.63	Extant 1982
F 27	MILANIAN (ex-*PF 105*)	Levingston SB	4.1.68	Extant 1982
F 28	KAHNAMUIE (ex-*PF 106*)	Levingston SB	4.4.68	Extant 1982

Transferred from the USA to Iran under Mutual Assistance Programme (MAP). Built in two phases, five years apart. Design similar to the Italian-built *Pattimura* class built for Indonesia. Sometimes classified as corvettes. Named after naval officers killed in action with the British in 1941. Pennant nos changed to 81–84 in 1976.

Twin Soviet 23mm AA were bought and have been added forward of the bridge in place of the single Hedgehog ASW mortar. Now reported to have 4–23mm AA (2×2) instead of 2–23mm AA (1×2). Mid-life conversion planned (but now probably cancelled) to include 76mm DP OTO Melara guns. Two reported lost (cause unknown) in the war with Iraq since 1980. Two sister ships; see under Thailand.

Laid down and completion dates: *Bayandor* 20.8.62 and 15.5.64; *Naghdi* 12.9.62 and 22.7.64; *Milanian* 1.5.67 and 13.2.69; *Kahnamuie* 12.6.67 and 13.2.69.

Saam 1972

SAAM class (Vosper Thornycroft Mk 5 class) *frigates*

Displacement:	1110t standard; c1300–1400t full load
Dimensions:	290ft pp, 310ft oa × 34ft 5in × 10ft 6in–11ft 6in
	88.4m, 94.5m × 10.5m × 3.2–3.5m
Machinery:	2 shaft CODOG: 2 Rolls-Royce Olympus TM 3A gas turbines, 46,000shp = 40kts, plus 2 Paxman 16cyl Ventura diesels for cruising, 3800hp = 17.5kts. Oil 150t (overload 250t). Range 5000nm at 15kts
Armament:	1 Sea Killer Mk 2 SSM launcher (1×5), 1 Seacat SAM launcher (1×3; est 9 missiles), 1–114mm/45 DP Mk5 (1–114mm/55 DP Mk8 in *Rostam* and *Faramarz*), 2–35mm/90 Oerlikon-Bührle GDM-A (1×2), 1 Limbo Mk10 ASW mortar (1×3). See notes
Sensors:	Radar Plessey AWS-1, 2 Contraves Sea Hunter 4; sonars Types 170 and 174
Complement:	125–135 (room for 146)

No	Name	Builder	Launched	Fate
DE 12	SAAM	Vosper Thornycroft	25.7.68	Extant 1982
DE 14	ZAAL	Vickers, Barrow	4.3.69	Extant 1982
DE 16	ROSTAM	Vickers, Newcastle	4.3.69	Extant 1982
DE 18	FARAMARZ	Vosper Thornycroft	30.7.69	Extant 1982

Since 1977 new pennant nos 71–74 respectively. It was announced on 25.8.66 that Vosper Ltd, Portsmouth, received an Iranian order for 4 'destroyers'. Three factors made the design possible. The first was the development of the Olympus marine gas turbine with a rating in excess of 22,500hp – a great

Faramarz 1982　　　　　　　　　　　　　　　　*C & S Taylor*

advance on the AEI G6 turbine (7500hp) fitted in the British 'County' and 'Tribal' classes. This made it possible for the gas turbine to become the main source of power instead of merely a boost turbine used in conjunction with conventional steam turbines. Diesel engines for cruising could therefore be added in a CODOG arrangement which considerably simplified gearing. The second factor was the advent of a new generation of smaller and lighter but more powerful weapons systems that did not require such a large ship to carry them. The third factor was the reduced crew needed not only thanks to gas turbines and the higher degree of weapon automation but also to the increased reliability accruing from each of these developments and the consequent reduction in maintenance. Unit replacement methods associated with both gas turbines and modern electronics would ensure faster repairs than would have previously been possible.

As the Mk 5 'destroyer' project which gave birth to the *Saam* class was a private design, the Vosper designers were able to reduce weight and cost – which at £6.5 million was about two-thirds the price of similarly equipped vessels built to the standards demanded by Western navies – by a careful consideration of how far these standards were applicable to the role envisaged for these particular ships. They considered that the standards of shock-resistance laid down by the Admiralty were unnecessarily high, being based on the high probability of near-misses for an older, and less accurate, generation of weapons. Savings were also made by lowering the standards of engine mountings considered essential to reduce underwater noise in a vessel whose primary function was ASW. As a defence against submarine attack the class was to rely on high speed and the manoeuvrability bestowed on them by their KaMeWa CP propellers. *Rostam* completed at Barrow. Ships named after heroes of the Shah Nameh, the national epic. Air-conditioned throughout. Retractable Vosper fin stabilizers. *Saam* and *Zaal* were at HM Dockyard Devonport July/Aug 1975; major refit including replacement of older Mk 5 114mm gun by Mk 8 took place. Completed 1977. Hull-mounted sonar at high speeds retracts into the hull and is covered by doors to protect it against excessive pressures. All weapons and sensors are integrated in a computerised operations room, and all machinery is operated from a similar centralised control room with full instrumentation. Sometimes credited with different range figures 550nm at 36kts (on gas turbines) or 3200nm at 18kts (on diesels); with additional fuel 800 and 4100nm respectively.

Laid down and completion dates: *Saam* 22.5.67 and 20.5.71; *Zaal* 3.3.68 and 1.3.71; *Rostam* 10.12.67 and 26.5.72; *Faramarz* 25.7.68 and 28.2.72.

NATO Standard type *guided missile frigates*

Displacement:	2900–3000 (?3500)t standard; 3750–3800t full load
Dimensions:	419ft 11in × 47ft 3in–47ft 11in × 14ft 5in–15ft 1in (19ft–19ft 8in props)
	128.0–130.2m × 14.4–14.6m × 4.4–4.6m (5.8–6.0)m
Machinery:	2-shaft CODOG (CP): 2 General Electric LM2500 gas turbines, 50,000shp = 30kts, plus 2 MTU 20V956 TB92 diesels = 10,400hp = c18–20kts. Range 4000nm at 18–20kts
Armament:	8 Harpoon SSM (2×4), 1 Mk 13 Mod 4 missile launcher (total c42 Harpoon SSM and Standard SM1–MR) or 1 Sea Sparrow SAM Mk 29 launcher (1×8) instead, 1–127mm/54 DP Mk 45, 2–20mm Vulcan-Phalanx Mk 15 CIWS (2×6), 4–324mm Mk 32 ASW TT (2×2) fixed for Mk 46 torpedoes, 2 helicopters (considered SH-60B LAMPS III or WG13 Sea Lynx or Puma)
Complement:	189

Four units (to be built at West German yards with Bremer-Vulkan as prime contractor), 8 units (to be built at Holland, Rhine-Schelde-Verolme).

These ships were ordered in 1978; after the successful trials of the Dutch *Kortenaer* and the contract for the German Type 122. Although Iran specified that the basic design of the new class should be the same as the NATO Standard Frigate, compatibility was needed with other US systems within the Fleet. This would reduce costs, simplify training and speed up commissioning. Apart from one or two alterations, hull layout was to remain as *Kortenaer* class. The propulsion system was to be the same as in the German Type 122 (*Bremen* class).

The main operational requirement for Iran was to possess vessels with an exceptionally high standard of accommodation for service in the Persian Gulf. With the need to operate over an extended radius of action, far from supporting bases and out of the range of aerial cover, it was essential that the Iranian frigates carried a strong defensive armament backed up by a comprehensive EW system.

The main fire control for the 127mm gun, Harpoon and Standard SM1-MR were to be 2 sets of Lockheed Mk 86 systems (a total of two SPG-60 and one SPQ-9 radars). Long range early warning would be provided by an SPS-48C three-dimensional radar. The other EW system was to consist of an SLQ-32 (V2 or possibly V3). Sonars were to consist of a bow-mounted 80 set with the German VDS set in a well aft. The ships were also to be equipped with NTDS, Tacan, navigational radar, chaff system and Link 11, 14 and 4A.

The contract was cancelled as a result of the Iranian Revolution of 1979.

SUBMARINES

West German Type 209 submarines

Six West German (export) Type 209 submarines (1400t) had been ordered 11.3.78 from Howaldtswerke-Deutsche Werft (HDW), Kiel (builder numbers 140–145). These were cancelled early in 1979, by which time considerable progress had probably been made in the West German yard. First planned to be launched in April 1981, and all planned for delivery at end of 1983.

Ex-US TANG class *submarines*

Agreement on the transfer of 3 ex-*Tang* class submarines (launched 1951) from USN reached in 1975 to provide training for the establishment of a larger submarine force. At the time of the revolution in Iran these 3 ships were earmarked for transfer. *Kusseh* (or *Kousseh*, Iranian pennant no 101 or S 101; ex-US SS 566 *Trout*) had been transferred after extensive renovation on 19.12.78 at New London. Her acquisition was officially cancelled on 3.2.79. She lay at New London until late 1979, with a token crew, when she was towed to Philadelphia and laid up in reserve (handed back to the USN May 1979). The USA has been asked to find a new buyer.

The transfers of the other 2, US SS 563 *Tang* as Iranian *Dolfin* or *Dolphin*, (some sources incorrectly refer to her as SS 567 *Gudgeon*) and SS 565 *Wahoo* as Iranian *Nahang*, were cancelled on 3.2.79 (29.2.80 to Turkey as *Piri Reis*) and 31.3.79 respectively. *Wahoo* was half-way through a two year overhaul when Iran cancelled the project on 31.3.79. Still in a dismantled condition, she was finally decommissioned on 31.3.80 and laid up in reserve.

AMPHIBIOUS WARFARE VESSELS

Hengam as completed

HENGAM class *tank landing ships*

Displacement:	2540t full load
Dimensions:	284ft 9in wl, 305ft 1in oa × 49ft × 7ft 3in *86.8m, 93.0m × 14.9m × 2.2m*
Machinery:	2 shafts (CP propellers), 4 Paxman Ventura Mk2 12 YJCM (*Lavan* and *Tonb* MTU) diesels, 5600hp = 14.5kts (*Lavan* and *Tonb* ?hp = ?kts). Range 3500nm at 12kts
Armament:	4–40mm (4×1)
Sensors:	Radar Decca 1229
Complement:	80 + 227 troops

No	Name	Builder	Launched	Fate
511	HENGAM	Yarrow, Clyde	27.9.73	Extant 1982
512	LARAK	Yarrow, Clyde	7.5.74	Extant 1982
513	LAVAN	Yarrow, Clyde	27.2.79	Extant 1982
514	TONB	Yarrow, Clyde	6.12.79	Extant 1982

Lack the through tank deck of the larger British *Sir Lancelot* class. Flight deck for 1 helicopter aft. Carry up to 9 tanks depending on size (1 Chieftain abreast or 2 T54/55). Cargo capacity of 700t includes 300t of vehicle fuel. Vehicle deck is 140ft × 30ft 9in (*42.7m × 9.4m*) and can accommodate according to some sources 12 Soviet T55 or 6 British Chieftain tanks. Named after Persian Gulf islands. An upper deck 10t crane can handle 2 Uniflote cargo lighters and 12 Z-boat LCPs. In the pure logistics role 10–20t or 30–10t containers would be loaded.

First two ordered 25.7.72 at Yarrow (Shipbuilders) Ltd, Clyde; 4 more ordered 20.7.77. *Hengam* (original no 51) laid down late 1972 and completed 12.8.74. *Larak* laid down 1973 and completed 12.11.74. *Lavan* laid down 6.2.78. Some payments made over, construction continuing slowly but the order had not been cancelled by spring 1980. New customers are being sought for *Lavan* and *Tonb*. Yarrow had already ordered the material for the last two ships by the time of their cancellation in March 1979.

Ex-US LSIL type *landing ships*

Class (former name):

Hengam (ex-French *LSIL 9037*, ex-US *LSIL 768*), *Larak* (ex-US *LSIL 710*)

First transferred from USN to Iran in 1957 under MDAP (between 1953–57 in French Navy). Second was loaned to Iran in Dec 1958. Pennant nos 41 and 42 respectively. Fates uncertain – *Hengam* probably stricken in early 1970s, *Larak* in mid-1970s.

Ex-US LCU type *landing craft*

Queshm (or *Quesham*, some sources give *Gheshme* or *Gheshne*; ex-US *LCU 1431*) was transferred to Iran by USA in Sept 1964 under MAP. Pennant no probably LCU 47, now 501. French references report that she was sunk in 1978 as a Harpoon missile target, but latest British and German reports list as still in service in 1981. For further details see under United States.

British BH 7 'WELLINGTON' class *hovercraft*

Displacement:	33t empty; 50t full load
Dimensions:	75ft 6in–78ft 5in × 44ft 11in × 34ft 1in/42ft height *23.9m × 13.7m × 10.4/12.8m*
Machinery:	1–6.4m diameter prop, 1 Rolls-Royce Proteus Gnome 15M549 (15M541 in Mk 5) gas turbine, 4250hp = 60kts (speed is reduced to 35kts in a 1.4–metre sea). Oil 9–10t. See notes
Armament:	2 Browning MG
Sensors:	Radar Decca 914
Complement:	?

Class (in service):

101 (Nov 1970), *102* (March 1971), *103* (mid-1974), *104* (mid-1974), *105* (late 1974), *106* (early 1975)

Built by British Hovercraft Corporation. First pair are logistics-support Mk 4 version, with a 14t payload, able to carry 60 troops. French reports give speed 65kts and range 400nm at 56kts. The four Mk 5 units have an SSM recess for 2 or 4 Harpoon but missiles are not mounted.

British SR N6 'WINCHESTER' class *hovercraft*

Displacement:	10grt (basic weight 14,200lb, disposable load 8200 lb)
Dimensions:	48ft 7in × 25ft 3in × 12ft 6in/15ft 9in height *14.8m × 7.7m × 3.8/4.8m*
Machinery:	1 Gnome Model 1050 gas turbine, ?hp = 52–58kts. 1 Peters diesel as auxiliary unit. Range 110nm at 30kts
Armament:	1 or 2 MG. See notes
Complement:	?

Class:

01–08

Built by British Hovercraft Corporation. Credited with 1 or 2–12.7mm MG or only 1–7.62mm MG. The Iranian Navy had the world's largest fully operational hovercraft squadron for coastal defence and logistic duties. Building dates uncertain – ordered 1970–72 and, commissioned 1973 (3), 1974 (2) and 1975 (3). Lack of spares must be starting to tell by now and there have been no reports of hovercraft action in the war with Iraq.

Hengam on builders' trials   *Yarrow*

SMALL SURFACE COMBATANTS

KAMAN class ('Combattante II' design) *fast attack craft (missile)*

Displacement:	249t standard; 275t full load
Dimensions:	154ft 2in × 23ft 4in × 6ft 3in *47.0m × 7.1m × 1.9m*
Machinery:	4 shafts, 4 MTU 16V538 TB91 diesels, 14,400hp = 36kts. Oil 41t. Range 2000nm/700nm at 15kts/33–33.7kts
Armament:	4 Harpoon SSM launchers (2×2), 1–76mm/62 DP OTO Melara, 1–40mm/70 Bofors
Sensors:	WM-28
Complement:	30–31

No	Name	Builder	Launched	Fate
P 221	KAMAN	CMN, Cherbourg	8.1.76	
P 222	ZOUBIN	CMN, Cherbourg	14.4.76	
P 223	KHADANG	CMN, Cherbourg	15.7.76	
P 224	PEYKAN	CMN, Cherbourg	12.10.76	?Sunk 1981
P 225	JOSHAN	CMN, Cherbourg	21.2.77	
P 226	FALAKHON	CMN, Cherbourg	2.6.77	
P 227	SHAMSHIR	CMN, Cherbourg	12.9.77	
P 228	GORZ	CMN, Cherbourg	28.12.77	
P 229	GARDOUNEH	CMN, Cherbourg	23.2.78	
P 230	KHANJAR	CMN, Cherbourg	27.4.78	
P 231	NEYZEH	CMN, Cherbourg	5.7.78	
P 232	TABARZIN	CMN, Cherbourg	15.9.78	

Contracted 19.2.74 (first six) and 14.10.74 at CMN, Cherbourg. Meaning of names: bow, javelin, arrowhead, arrow, boiling oil, sling, scimitar, mace, roulette, dagger, spear and battleaxe. The later boats have not yet received their missiles – only 12 Harpoon missiles were delivered but these may have sunk Iraqi 'P 6' FAC and a 'Polnocny' landing ship. Laying down/in service dates: *Kaman* (5.2.75/12.8.77), *Zoubin* (4.4.75/12.9.77), *Khadang* (20.6.75/15.3.78), *Peykan* (15.10.75/31.3.78), *Joshan* (5.1.76/23.3.78), *Falakhon* (15.3.76/31.3.78), *Shamshir* (15.5.76/31.3.78), *Gorz* (5.8.76/22.8.78), *Gardouneh* (18.10.76/11.9.78), *Khanjar* (17.1.77), *Neyzeh* (12.9.77), *Tabarzin* (24.6.77). Last three units, all commissioned 1.8.81, left Cherbourg with approval of French Government (previously embargoed at Cherbourg April 1979 due to non-payment of cash). On way to Iran P 232 seized by a pro-Royalist group on 13.8.81 near Cadiz and briefly returned to Toulon. Three including *Peykan* sunk in 1981 by Iraq: two by SS-N-2 missiles from an 'Osa' class FAC; one by AM39 Exocet missile from a Super-Frélon helicopter.

US Improved PGM 71 *large patrol craft*

Displacement:	105t standard; 146t full load
Dimensions:	100ft 1in × 22ft × 10ft 2in *30.5m × 6.7m × 3.1m*
Machinery:	2 shafts, 8 General Motors 8–71 diesels, 2000hp = 15kts. Range 1500nm at 10kts
Armament:	1–40mm, 2–20mm, 2–12.7mm MG. See notes
Complement:	27

Class (no, former name, launched, in service):
Parwin (PGM 65, ex-*PGM 103*, 1967), *Bahram* (PGM 66, ex-*PGM·112*, c1969), *Nahid* (PGM 67, ex-*PGM 122*, 1970)

All built by Peterson, Bay, Wisc. French sources give 1–40mm, 4–20mm (2×2), 2 Mk22 Mousetrap, 2 DC racks. Names mean Mercury, Mars and Venus. Fitted with navigation radar. All sunk by Iraqi forces 1980–81.

US 'CAPE' class (USCG 95ft class) *large patrol craft*

Displacement:	85t standard; 107t full load
Dimensions:	94ft 10in × 20ft 4in × 5ft 11in–6ft 7in *28.9m × 6.2m × 1.8–2.0m*
Machinery:	2 shafts, 4 Cummins diesels, 2200hp = 20kts. Range 1500nm at 15kts
Armament:	1–40mm, 2 Mk 22 Mousetrap ASW RL, 2 DC racks (8–300lb DC)
Complement:	15

Class (no, former no, in service):
Keyvan (201, PC 61, 14.1.56), *Tiran* (202, PC 63, 1957), *Mehran* (203, PC 62, 1959), *Mahan* (204, PC 64, 1959)

All built by US Coast Guard Yard, Curtis Bay (Maryland). Transferred under MAP–US Contract Nos 95CGMDA1, 95CGMDA3, 95CGMDA8 and 95CGMDA5 respectively. Names derive from islands in the Gulf. *Keyvan* sometimes referred as *Keyvan*, *Kayvan* or *Kaivan*. Fitted with navigation radar. *Mehran* and *Mahan* lost 1980–81 in Iraq war.

COASTAL PATROL BOATS

About 70 US 65ft Mk III class (28.6t std, 3 diesels, 30kts, 3–20mm, 1–12.7mm MG, 5 crew).

Gorz 1978   *C & S Taylor*

20 ordered from Peterson in 1973 and up to 50 more in 1976. Some built under licence in Iran. Totals uncertain some sources report 20 plus 50 (building) employed with the Navy, others give *c*20 plus 50 employed with the Coast Guard.

About 30 US 50ft Mk II class (22t full load, 2 diesels, 26kts, 4–12.7mm MG, 6 crew) built by Peterson for Iranian Coast Guard 1976–77. Numbered *1201–1220*.

Two ex-British Admiralty HDMLs: *SDML 1389* transferred in early 1950s as *FDB 58*. Then renamed *Tahmadou* (pennant no FDB65). British *SML 323* (employed on survey duties; ex-*HDML 1081*) transferred on 21.6.56 as *Asalon*. Both employed as despatch boats. It was officially stated in 1971 that they were taken out of service.

Nine *Azar* class (90ft, 65t std, 2 diesels, 22kts, 2 MG) built by CN Lamar, La Spezia 1954–55: *Azav, Chahab, Darakhsh, Navak, Peykan, Tondar, Tondbad, Toufan, Tousan*. Probably all stricken 1970s though last two may be extant.

Two ex-ASR craft (ex-British MTBs) were handed over to the Custom Guard in 1953. Probably named *Favour* and *Larak* (1942, 25t standard, 40kts).

Three *Gohar* class (70t std, 75ft, 2 diesels, 27–28kts, 1–12.7mm MG, 19 crew): *Gohar, Shahpar, Shahram*. Built by Abeking & Rasmussen, Lemwerder (West Germany) in 1969–71 as fishery protection units for the Iranian Navy, transferred to the Iranian Coast Guard in 1975 and to Sudan the same year as *Sheikan* (?or *Shekan*), *Kadir* (?or *Kader*) and *Karari* respectively. German sources give 95ft 2in × 16ft 5in × 4ft 11in (*29.0m × 5.0m × 1.5m*). Decca 202 navigation radar.

Twelve US 40ft (*Sewart* type) class (10t std, 2 diesels, 30kts, 2–7.62mm MG, *c*7 crew): *Mahmavi-Hamraz, Mahmavi-Taheri, Mahmavi-Vanedi, Mardjan, Mordarid, Sadaf* and 6 others (names unknown – they are possibly *Lovon, Nanang, Schanak, Genbod, Kosay, Dolphin* (Pennant nos 51–56; ex-US Contract Nos *40CGA01, 40CGB01, 40CGC01, 40CGD01, 40CGE01, 40CGF01* – built by USCG Yard Curtis Bay, Maryland).

All served in Iranian Coast Guard. Launches used for port duties, built by Sewart, Morgan City in 1963 and 1970s as Sewart standard 40ft type (according to British reports 6 were transferred June 1953). Now 6 in Iranian Coast Guard (pennant nos 5001 and above, some serve in the Caspian Sea), 4 (built 1970) given to Sudan in 1975 (?1978) and 2 stricken.

MINE WARFARE VESSELS

US MSC class *coastal minesweepers*

No	Name	Builder	Launched	Fate
32	SHAHBAZ (ex-*MSC 275*)	Bellingham Shipyards, Wash	22.11.58	Lost through fire 1975
31	SHAHROKH (ex-*MSC 276*)	Bellingham Shipyards, Wash	c1959	Extant 1982
33	SIMORGH (ex-*MSC 291*)	Tacoma Boat- building, Wash	3.3.61	Sunk 1980–81
34	KARKAS (ex-*MSC 292*)	Peterson Builders, Wisc	1962	Sunk 1980–81

Of wooden construction. Transferred from the USA under MAP in 1959–62. According to British reports *Shahbaz* deleted in 1974 after collision damage. *Shahrokh* is the Iranian Navy's largest unit in the Caspian Sea. Decca 707 navigation radar and UQS 1 sonar. Three later units have pennant nos 301–303 respectively, and probably 2–20mm AA (1×2). Two sunk by Iraqi forces.

US COVE class *inshore minesweepers*

Class (no, former no, transferred):
Kahnamuie (301, ex-*MSI 13*, 3.9.64), *Riazi* (302, ex-*MSI 14*, 15.10.64)

Built by Tacoma Boatbuilding, delivered under MAP – transferred at Seattle, Washington. Sometimes referred to as *Cape* class. In Aug 1967 *Kahnamuie* was renamed *Harischi* as the name was required for one of the new Iranian frigates built in USA (ex-*PF106*). Navigation radar. Given new pennant nos 311 and 312 respectively. Both sunk by Iraqi forces 1980–81.

Ex-British ALGERINE class *minesweeper*

Palang (ex-British *Fly*) acquired in 1949. Served as frigate with 2–102mm (2×1). Without pennant no. Paid off in Dec 1966 and officially deleted from active list in 1972.

Iraq

Although Iraq, an Arab state that maintains close ties with Eastern bloc countries (in 1972 and 1978 the Soviet Union signed treaties of friendship with Iraq), only has a very short coastline – just 58km – she runs an exceptionally powerful naval force. The extensive fleet expansion programme in which Iraq is presently engaged is difficult to understand. With a short coastline and placed at the end of a completely landlocked and rather restricted body of water (the Persian Gulf) with an exit Iraq cannot control, the recent order of February 1981, worth 1.8 million dollars, placed in Italian shipyards for delivery of four *Lupo* class fast frigates, six corvettes and a *Stromboli* class replenishment ship seems nonsense – a deep sea navy without the sea to sail on. This enlarged and modernised navy has probably been developed for a specific reason – to pose a threat and to exert influence throughout the Gulf region. Iraq claims the islands of Bubiyan and Warbah from Kuwait; annexation would improve access to her main naval base, Umm Qasr.

Despite all this, the Navy with its 3000 men is at present the smallest of the three Iraqi armed services. With the Italian-built ships delivered, the Iraqi Navy will present a sizeable force but the problem of training an adequate number of men to man the ships remains to be solved. The training frigate named *Ibn Khaldoum* and built in a Yugoslav yard indicates that this problem is to some extant recognised in Iraq. So far there is little reliable information about naval operations in the war between Iraq and Iran although both sides are reported to have lost 11 minor warships. Iraq's main port, Basra, has been out of action since the beginning.

FLEET STRENGTH 1947

Four 'Thornycroft' type patrol vessels, disp 67t, were launched in 1937 and, now worn out, are used as barracks. Numbered *1–4*, renamed *Abd al Rahman*, *Al Ghazi*, *Dat Al Diyan* and *Janada*.

Ibn Khaldoum design

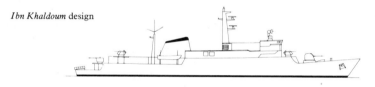

IBN KHALDOUM *training frigate*

Displacement:	1850t full load
Dimensions:	317ft 4in oa, 36ft 8in × 14ft 10in
	96.7m × 11.2m × 3.6/4.5m
Machinery:	2 shaft CODOG (CP propellers): 1 Rolls-Royce Olympus TM-3B gas turbine, 22,000shp = 26kts, plus 2 MTU 16 V 956 TB 91 diesels, 7500bhp = 20kts. Range 4000nm at 20kts
Armament:	1–57mm/70 Bofors, 1–40mm/70, 8–20mm AA (4×2), 2 ASW TT and ASW mortar, DC rack
Sensors:	Radar 2 navigation, 1 search Philips 9LV 200 Mk II; sonar
Complement:	93 + 100 trainees

No	Name	Builder	Launched	Fate
507	IBN KHALDOUM	Titograd, Yugoslavia	1979	Extant 1982

Training ship with frigate characteristics of Yugoslav design. Laid down 1977 and in service 21.3.80. The first of three such ships ordered – one yet unnamed by the Yugoslav Navy and the other named *Hasr Dewantara* by Indonesia, to be completed. Ships differ in machinery and armament (no helicopter pad). These are handsome ships of similar appearance to the Vosper-Thornycroft frigates of the Iranian, Brazilian and Nigerian navies. *Ibn Khaldoum* can carry 4 SSM, used as a transport in the war with Iran.

Italian LUPO type *frigates*

Four modified *Lupo* type frigates were ordered from Italy in Dec 1980. The ships will be similar to the ones built for Peru. Main engines for these ships (FIAT/GE gas turbines LM 2500) were for a time embargoed by the USA on political grounds. 2 were laid down in March and Sept 1982 at CNR Shipyard, Ancona.

Soviet 'POLNOCNY' type *medium landing ships*

Class (delivery):
Atika (1977), *Janada* (1977), *Nouh* (1978), *Ganda* (Sept 1979)
Three ships of 'Polnocny' type built in Poland in 1976–78 by Stocznia Pólnocna, Gdansk. Hull is as originally built; deck structure amidships is new and seems to act as a helicopter platform and a stores lift, closed during helicopter manoeuvres. The same version of the Polnocny design can be found in the Libyan Navy. German reports speak of four ships and it seems that the fourth was named *Ganda*. It is also possible that *Janada* is sometimes mistakenly referred to as *Ganda*. One lost to Iranian Harpoon missiles 1980–81, rest extant 1982.

Italian ESMERALDAS type *corvettes*

Two fast missile armed corvettes of Ecuadorian *Esmeraldas* type are on order in the Italian CNR shipyard at Ancona. These ships fitted with a helicopter landing deck aft are derivatives of Libyan *Wadi M'ragh* type also designed and built in Italy. Laid down on 15.1.82.

Italian improved WADI M'RAGH type *missile corvettes*

Four of an enlarged Libyan *Wadi M'ragh* type are reported on order in Italy. According to some sources these ships were cancelled. Laid down on 22.3.82, 3.6.82 and 2 on 17.9.82.

Ex-Soviet 'OSA I' type *fast attack craft (missile)*

Class:
Hazirani, Kanun Ath-Thani, Nisan, Tamuz, I, II
Six delivered in 1972–74, two since probably deleted. Some names are not reliable.

Ex-Soviet 'OSA II' type *fast attack craft (missile)*

Class:
Sa'd, Khalid Ibn, Al Walid, I—IV
Eight boats of this Soviet type were delivered in pairs in 1974, 1975, 1976 and the last pair since then. Some names may be suspect. Two sunk by Iranian warships and two by Iranian aircraft since Sept 1980

Ex-Soviet 'P 6' type *fast attack craft (torpedo)*

Class:
Al Adrisi, Al Bahi, Al Shaab, Al Tami, Alef, Ibn Said, Lamaki, Ramadan, Shulab, Tamur, Tareq Ben Zaid, I
Twelve units transferred from the USSR, two in 1959, four in Nov 1960 and six in Jan 1961. Probably some since deleted as worn out. Pennant numbers include 217–222. Six sunk by Iranian forces since 1980, some by Harpoon missiles.

Ex-Soviet 'SO 1' type *large patrol craft*

Three ships transferred in 1962. Employed as large patrol craft. Carry pennant numbers 310–312. Extant 1982.

Ex-Soviet 'POLUCHAT I' type *large patrol craft*

Two ships of *Poluchat 1* type were transferred from USSR in late 1960s. Used as patrol craft or for torpedo recovery. Extant 1982.

Ex-Soviet 'ZHUK' type *coastal patrol craft*

Five transferred in 1975. Extant 1982.

Ex-Soviet 'NYRYAT' type II *patrol craft*

Two multi-purpose craft possibly employed as diving craft. There are also two ex-Soviet *PO 2 (Pozarnyj 2)* type fire boats of very similar design. Extant 1982.

Ex-Soviet 'T 43' type *ocean minesweepers*

Class (no):
Al Yarmouk (465), *Al Kadisia* (467)
Built in mid-1950s and transferred to Iraq in early 1970s. Extant 1982.

Ex-Soviet 'YEVGENYA' type *inshore minesweepers*

Three of these GRP-hulled inshore minesweepers were delivered in 1975 ostensibly as 'oceanographic craft'. Armed with 2–25mm.

Yugoslav NESTIN class *river minesweepers*

Three transferred in 1980. Extant 1982.

Israel

The Israeli Navy is a small, but powerful, force centred around three widely separated operational bases at Haifa (the main base where the majority of units and certainly the most modern missile boats are sited), Ashdod (established May 1967) and the Red Sea port of Eilat. Sharm el Sheikh was returned to Egypt in April 1982.

Israel has a really strategical geographical location on the boundary of two important seas: the Mediterranean and the Red Sea. She is surrounded by hostile Arab countries. The peace treaty signed with Egypt at Camp David, USA is of great importance to Israeli industrial and military needs. Among other things it has made it possible for Israeli ships to pass safely through the Suez Canal and so Israeli naval units can be sent from the Mediterranean to the Red Sea in 2–3 weeks instead of sailing round Africa.

THE ARAB-ISRAELI WARS 1948–1982

The Navy has always been the cinderella arm of the Israeli Defence Forces. In the 1948–49 War of Independence it consisted of about 350 sailors with RN and/or 'illegal' immigrant boat experience. Their flagship was the 2150t ex-US Coast Guard cutter *Northland* renamed *Eilath*. They also had a few motor boats and the frogmen amongst them sank the Egyptian sloop *El Amir Farouk* off Gaza. In 1956 the spectacular capture of the Egyptian frigate *Ibrahim el Awal* off Haifa by Israel's two newly acquired destroyers was owed largely to the Air Force and the same Israeli destroyers' shore bombardment of Rafah the next night was no help to the Army.

Before the 1967 Six Day War the Navy had added submarines and home-built landing craft to the inventory of 3 destroyers, 8 MTBs and an ASW ship, but Israel's lightning victory left the Fleet little to do. Three torpedo fast attack craft reached Sharm el Sheikh from Eilat to find the Egyptian naval blockade that had precipitated war no longer existed. Naval frogmen raids on Alexandria and Port Said achieved psychological but no physical damage.

The 1967–70 'War of Attrition' gave more scope to Israel's warships. Their vulnerability to modern missiles was dramatically illustrated by the sinking of her flagship *Eilat*, a lesson that was to be learnt with a vengeance. Meanwhile in the Gulf of Suez tank landing craft carried an armoured battalion into Egypt for a raid in depth (September 1969) that cost the Egyptian naval C-in-C his job.

Israeli Naval Intelligence was less surprised than most by the 1973 Yom Kippur War and events were dramatically to vindicate the Fleet's new emphasis on missile and electronic warfare. Thirteen Israeli missile fast attack craft with 63 Gabriel launchers defeated 27 Arab 'Osa' and 'Komar' boats mounting 84 longer-ranged Styx rockets. Off Latakia (Syria), on the first night of the war and 200 miles from base, five Israeli units fought the first missile versus missile surface action of naval history. They evaded two Styx salvoes of six missiles each, shooting one down with 76mm gun fire, and 18 minutes later, having closed the range, fired a Gabriel salvo that hit all three Syrian ships. Two blew up and the third was finished off with 40mm fire. Two nights later six Israeli craft dodged four Styx volleys (12 missiles) to destroy three out of four Egyptian 'Osa' boats off Damietta, the third vessel again being sunk by gunfire. Another 28 Arab missiles, fired in later actions, all missed. The Gabriel Mk I missile was 85 per cent effective.

The relatively protracted Yom Kippur operations allowed the Navy to come into its own. Constant sorties tied down an armoured brigade on the Syrian Coast. The Egyptians, whose Suez Canal crossing stunned the world, failed entirely off Sinai and in the Gulf of Suez; in one typical action five Israeli patrol boats sank 19 armed fishing boats in the Ras Ghareb anchorage. For a loss of three killed and 24 wounded the Navy sank 19 Arab regular warships.

Israeli naval operations in the 1980s have shown a daring made possible by total air supremacy. In June 1981 fast attack craft hit the PFLP HQ at Tripoli in Lebanon. A year later the Navy made a maximum effort in amphibious and gunfire support of the Army coastal thrust that reached Beirut within four days. The Palestinian military evacuation to Cyprus was effectively regulated by Israel's warships patrolling off the Lebanese capital.

During the Yom Kippur War the Israeli Navy used new coastal warfare tactics; fast attack craft instead of escort ships were employed. The enemy was generally attacked in his own bases, rarely on the open sea. The Israelis deployed their fast attack craft together with helicopters providing mid-flight guidance for missiles and decoys for enemy missiles. Such deployment was a novelty at the time, and gave excellent results ending in grave losses among enemy ships.

Israel, which is in possession of the best trained and equipped fast attack craft group in the Mediterranean, has begun forming the second such unit for deployment on the Red Sea. The rapid build-up of the Libyan Navy induced Israel to order a new type of fast attack corvettes with good seakeeping qualities and designed purely for attack. In her present economic situation Israel cannot afford to build a defensive navy and so the present orders are for attack craft, such as missile armed hydrofoils and small guided-missile patrol boats.

There is a constant danger of infiltration by PLO terrorist groups along the 150-mile coastline. This must be prevented and so there are many coastal radar surveillance stations and 'Dabur' and 'Yatush' class craft are on patrol. These radars and patrols also provide early warning of low-level aerial attacks coming in over the sea.

Israel Aircraft Industries (IAI) is also involved in the development and production of military equipment for the Navy. There are even some small warships built by IAI such as fast attack craft of the 'Dabur' or 'Dvora' (missile) classes.

GABRIEL MISSILES

Surface-to-surface Gabriel type guided missiles designed and produced in Israel are well-known internationally. There are two versions Mk 1 and Mk 2 and the much improved Gabriel Mk 3 is now entering service. Gabriel Mk 1 carried out trials in the late 1950s and during the early 1960s it was decided to adopt the concept of the missile armed fast attack craft as the main unit for future deployment with the Israeli Navy. The Israeli Navy's concept of the missile/gun armed FPB to replace the destroyer and frigate was proved in the 1973 Yom Kippur War with the Gabriel Mk 1 missile which even so suffered from certain disadvantages such as limited range (20km due to the solid fuel rocket motor) and target handling resulting from the semi-active homing system which permits only one target to be selected for engagement. During the early 1970s the Gabriel Mk 2 was developed to carry increased fuel of a more modern type which extended its range to 36km. The range was in fact greater than 36km but the effective range was limited by the extent of coverage of the search and fire control radars then operational. The Mk 2 missile has not been used in action, but the disadvantage of being able to designate only a single target to the semi-active homing missile remained. IAI have therefore developed the Gabriel Mk 3 missile, which is now in production and which uses a fully active homing head enabling the operator to fire the missile and forget it! In fact the Mk 3 missile is unique in the West in that it can operate in three modes: fire and forget (engagement of 4 targets simultaneously possible); fire and update – the missile's computer is updated while in flight to assimilate a target's changing parameters which enables the homing seeker in the head to be activated at the latest possible moment to overcome ECM; fire and control – this incorporates the capability of the Mk 1 and Mk 2 missiles to control the missile throughout the whole of its flight and thus to concentrate on one target alone. Already developments to the Mk 3 are under consideration including an increase in the range (the Mk 3 has a maximum effective range of 40km) and, even more important, an increase in speed to above Mach 1.

The latest concept in missile tactics to gain favour is that of the 'Cocktail' designed to overcome and confuse ECM systems: different types of missiles are fired at the target simultaneously and it is possible that a Mk 2 and Mk 3 Gabriel might be fired simultaneously using different modes of attack. Furthermore it is to be noted that the *Reshef* class are now equipped with the US Harpoon missile so providing even greater possibilities for 'Cocktail' mixes.

GUNS

In addition to developing their missile technology IAI have developed a new twin 30mm gun mount for point defence, the TCM 30, using the Hispano-Suiza 831 30mm. The mount is a low, relatively heavy rigid structure supporting the muzzles and which is designed to help overcome muzzle droop and vibration etc, leading to small dispersion, an essential feature in a gun anti-missile system. The fully automatic system is a completely above deck system with a magazine of 150 rounds per gun fired in bursts of 5, 10, 15 or 20 rounds. Target speeds up to 250–300m/sec can be handled and the barrels have an elevation of −15° to +85°. The mount has undergone satisfactory trials in a *Reshef* class ship and is expected to enter production shortly when it will first equip the *Reshef* class and new vessels under construction and subsequently possibly retrofit the older 'Saar' class boats.

TRAINING AND MANPOWER

The Navy's high-quality personnel are its greatest asset and this quality is assured by its own electronics school training boys for two years from the age of 16 before national service. Most officers and senior petty

MIDDLE EAST

officers are regulars while the 3500 conscripts in the total of 6600 sailors in 1982 also join before their three year period. Naval commando and frogman training is done by 750 men, women take on many shore jobs and there are about 5000 reserves who do up to 60 days annual training. Command is vested in a rear-admiral or commodore.

MAJOR SURFACE SHIPS

PROJECTED *destroyers*

In the mid-1950s construction of two destroyers (1100/1200t, 32kts) was considered.

Ex-British 'Z' class *destroyers*

No	Name	Builder	Acquired	Fate
40	ELATH (ex-*Zealous*)	Cammell Laird	15.7.55	Sunk 21.10.67
42	YAFFA (ex-*Zodiac*)	Thornycroft	15.7.55	Stricken 1972

Transferred at Cardiff Docks. Renamed *Elath* and *Yaffa* (often referred to as *Yaffo*). Refitted before going to Israel in 1956: *Elath* by Harland & Wolff, Langton Dock, Liverpool; *Yaffo* by Crichtons, Trafalgar Dock, Liverpool. Pennant nos 40 and 42 respectively. *Elath*, better known as *Eilat*, sank on 21.10.67 after being hit by 3 Styx SSMs 14½nm off Port Said. The missiles were fired from 'Komar' class Egyptian FAC *inside* the harbour. Casualties aboard the Israeli Navy Flagship were 47 killed or missing and 90 wounded out of 199. This was the first time in history that a warship was sunk by a ship-launched missile. In July 1967 *Elath* and two torpedo FAC had sunk two Egyptian torpedo FAC off Rumani, Sinai.

Ex-British 'RIVER' class *frigates*

No	Name	Builder	Acquired	Fate
?28	MIVTAKH (ex-*Violetta*, ex-*Orkney*)	Canadian Yarrow	1950	To Ceylon 1959
32	MISNAK (ex-*Sharon*, ex-*Halowell*)	Canadian Vickers	1950	To Ceylon 1959
?30	MISGAV (ex-?, ex-*Strathadam*)	Canadian Yarrow	1951	BU 1959–60

Three Canadian-built RN frigates of 1943–44 sold to merchant service 1945 and 1947 from which the Israeli Navy acquired them. Additional 4in gun mounted in *Misgav*, 1956. First two sold in Aug 1959 to Royal Ceylon Navy; third scrapped 1959–60 or stricken only in 1961.

Ex-British 'Modified FLOWER' class *frigates*

Name	Builder	Acquired	Fate
WEDGEWOOD (ex-*Colon*, ex-*Beauharnois*)	Morton	1950	BU 1956
HAGANAH (ex-*Balboa*, ex-*Norsyd*)	Morton	1950	BU 1956

Ex-RCN corvettes sold into merchant service and acquired by the Israeli Navy.

Ex-British HUNT class (Type 1) *frigate*

No	Name	Builder	Acquired	Fate
38	HAIFA (ex-*Ibrahim el Awal*, ex-*Mohamed Ali el Kebir*, ex-*Mendip*, ex-*Lin Fu*)	Swan Hunter	31.10.56	Deleted 1972

Captured off Haifa in the only major naval action of the 1956 Arab-Israeli War. The Egyptian frigate sailed from Port Said and, undetected in the darkness off the Israeli Coast, fired 200rds of 4in from 0330 at Haifa naval installations causing some damage but no casualties. The French destroyer *Kersaint* fired 64rds back but did not pursue as the Israeli destroyers *Yaffa* and *Eilat* were across the Egyptian's line of escape. They fired 436rds from 0527 at ranges under 9000yds but it was two rocket-firing Ouragan jets which at dawn disabled *Ibrahim* and caused her surrender at 0710 with 2 killed and 8 wounded. She failed to scuttle due to rusty valves and *Eilat* towed her into Haifa. Commissioned into Israeli Navy Jan 1957. Served as hulk from *c*1970 until deletion.

SUBMARINES

Ex-British 'S' class *submarines*

No	Name	Builder	Acquired	Fate
71	TANIN (ex-*Springer*)	Cammell Laird	9.10.58	Cannibalised 1968
72	RAHAV (ex-*Sanguine*)	Cammell Laird	Oct 1958	Deleted 1972

RN boats launched 1945, both refitted in Great Britain before delivery to Israel in Dec 1959 (*Tanin*) and May 1960 (*Rahav*). Originally very handy craft, capable of making a 'crash dive' in 30 seconds, and both fitted with 'Snort' mast and sonar domes. *Tanin* put frogmen into Alexandria on 5.6.67. They did not return. *Rahav*, unable to submerge, was discarded after serving as an ASW ship in the Six Day War as worn out in 1968 and was cannibalised to keep *Tanin* in commission, and *Tanin* herself was awaiting disposal in 1972. Used for training.

Ex-British 'T' class (1941 and 1942 Programmes) *submarines*

No	Name	Builder	Acquired	Fate
75	LEVIATHAN (ex-*Turpin*)	Chatham D Yd	19.5.67	Deleted 1975
77	DAKAR (ex-*Totem*)	Devonport D Yd	10.11.67	Lost 25.1.68
77	DOLPHIN (ex-*Truncheon*)	Devonport D Yd	9.1.68	Deleted 1977

Acquisition of these 1943–44 built RN subs by Israel was announced in Nov 1964. Refitted before handover. *Dakar* lost with all hands in the E Mediterranean on passage from Britain. Modernised as British boats: *Turpin* lengthened by 12ft, *Totem* and *Truncheon* by 20ft. All guns and external TT were removed.

German Type 206 *coastal submarines*

Displacement:	420t normal/600t submerged
Dimensions:	157ft 6in (?147ft 8in) × 15ft 5in × 12ft 2in 48.0m (?45.0) × 4.7m × 3.7m
Machinery:	1 shaft, 2 MTU 12V493 TY60 diesels and AEG generators plus 1 electric motor, 1200bhp/500shp = 11kts/17kts. See notes
Armament:	8–533mm TT (bow sub; 2 spare torpedoes). See notes
Complement:	22

Name	Builder	Launched	Fate
GAL	Vickers Ltd, Barrow	2.12.75	Extant 1982
TANIN (ex-*Gur*)	Vickers Ltd, Barrow	25.10.76	Extant 1982
RAHAV	Vickers Ltd, Barrow	1977	Extant 1982

A contract was signed for the building of these boats by Vickers in April 1972. Designed by the well-known German submarine designer Prof Gabler from Lübeck; also known as IKL/Vickers Type 206 or T540. *Gal* (laid down 1973 and commissioned Dec 1976) ran aground on delivery voyage, but has been repaired. *Tanin* (laid down 1974) and *Rahav* (laid down 1976) were commissioned June and 18 Dec 1977 respectively. Some reports give power as 2000bhp/1800shp or 1200bhp/1800shp. Differ from the German Navy's version in having a different conning tower and other changed characteristics. Designed to be equipped with 1 SLAM SAM launcher (1×6, retractable) intended to destroy enemy ASW helicopters. The first type of submarine since 1945 to be designed with armament that cannot be used in standard TT (apart from SLBMs). Electronics: one navigational radar, one TIO fire control radar and one sonar. Tropicalised.

These small submarines, which are extremely cramped by modern standards and really only suitable for short endurance patrols, are excellent ASW units. They are small and quiet and in the variable Mediterranean environment are extremely difficult to detect. They operate as defensive units providing early warning, surveillance and the landing of sabotage teams. It is admitted that 3 submarines are not really sufficient to meet Israeli Navy requirements and they are to some extent limited by short endurance and relatively slow torpedoes. The vessels are armed with a British weapon system incorporating 8 bow TT of the swim out type, the torpedoes being wire guided and controlled by a FCS linked to a one-man operated passive sonar system, with an active system available if required. The tear-drop hull is of single compartment design with a single escape tower in the fin. The forward hatch in the hull is used for battery removal and reloading torpedoes.

AMPHIBIOUS WARFARE VESSELS

Ex-US LSM class *landing ships*

Three purchased in 1972 from civil sources. Armed with 4–20mm. Israeli and all ex-names unknown. Extant 1982.

ETZION GUEBER class *tank landing craft*

Displacement:	182t standard; 230t full load
Dimensions:	See notes
Machinery:	2 shafts, 2 diesels, 1280hp = 10kts
Armament:	2–20mm (2×1)
Complement:	12

Class (no):
Etzion Gueber (or *Ezion Geber*, 51), *Shikmona* (or *Shiqmona*, 53), *Kessaraya* (55)

All built by Israel Shipyards, Haifa. Commissioned 1965. Often credited with other dimensions: 100ft × 19ft 4in × 4ft 3in (*30.5m × 5.9m × 1.3m*) or 120ft × 23ft 4in × 4ft 7in (*36.6m × 7.1m × 1.4m*). All 3 and *Ashdod* (see *Ash* class) transported overland to Eilat in the Six Day War by day and back into the desert by night to tie down Egyptian warships in the Red Sea by simulating a build up for the capture of Sharm el Sheikh. All extant 1982.

Ashdod 1971

ASH class (LCT type) *tank landing craft*

Displacement:	400t standard; 730t full load
Dimensions:	206ft 9in × 32ft 10in × 5ft 11in *62.7m × 10.0m × 1.8m*
Machinery:	3 shafts, 3 MWM diesels, 1900hp = 10.5kts. Oil 37t
Armament:	2–20mm (2×1). See notes
Complement:	20

Class (no, in service):
Ashdod (61, 1966), *Ashkelon* (63, 1967), *Achziv* (65, 1967)

All built by Israel S Yd, Haifa, 1966–67 (one of the latter two units due for completion in Aug was finished in 5 days for the Six Day War) and extant 1982. Helicopter pads fitted aft.

BAT SHEVA

Displacement:	900t standard; 1150t full load
Dimensions:	312ft × 36ft 9in × ?26ft 11in *95.1m × 11.2m × ?8.2m*
Machinery:	2 shafts, 2 diesels, ?hp = 10kts
Armament:	4–20mm, 4–12.7mm MG
Complement:	26

Bat Sheva built in Netherlands (?Germany) 1967 and bought from S Africa in 1968. Sometimes classified as a transport. Extant 1982.

In addition to the above, the Israeli Navy also operates a number of other landing craft. Reported to be a mixed flotilla of ex-US LCTs (including *LCT 640* and ex-*LCT 673*), LCI and LCM types, ex-British vessels of the LCT(6) type and ex-German craft (referred to as *Siebel Ferries* or MFP type). Landing craft of the LCT, LCI and other types, were taken out of commission for disposal before the early 1970s (with the exception of one LCT, which was given to the Israeli National Museum in Haifa). According to the latest German reports 3 LCMs are in service.

SMALL SURFACE COMBATANTS

Saar as completed
NB 1/750 scale

'SAAR 5' class *missile corvettes*

Displacement:	850t full load
Dimensions:	253ft 3in × 30ft 2in (?27ft 8in) × 10ft–10ft 10in *77.2m × 9.2m (?8.4) × 3.0–3.3m*
Machinery:	2-shaft (CP propellers) CODAG: 1 General Electric LM2500 gas turbine plus 2 MTU turbocharged diesels, 20,000–25,000shp plus 8000bhp = 40kts (42kts max; 18–20kts on diesels). Range 4500nm at 20kts on diesels (5500nm with additional fuel), endurance 20 days
Armament:	4 Gabriel SSM (4×1), 2–76mm/62 DP OTO Melara (2×1), 6–30mm/75 AA Hispano-Suiza A32 (3×2), 1–375mm Bofors ASW RL (1×2), 6–324mm AS TT Mk32 (2×3), 1 helicopter (type unknown). See notes
Complement:	45

British source reports 2 building (one laid down early 1981) and probably further 6 planned, but French reports incorrectly: 'this design is a project offered by the shipyard but not yet ordered by the Israeli Navy'. 'QU-09-35' (or 'Q9-O35') known also as 'Corvette 850' is an interim design between 500t missile

boats (high speed, manoeuvrability) and corvettes over 1000t (range, fire power, electronics, CIC). Will probably have a mix of Harpoon and Gabriel SSM launchers. These ships may well be intended for over-the-horizon target data acquisition for Harpoon-fitted *Reshefs* ('Saar 4' and 'Saar 4.5' classes) with command and control facilities, particularly since the trials of a low-mounted helicopter platform in *Tarshish* proved unsatisfactory. Details on armament uncertain – sometimes credited with 8 Harpoon SSM (2×4), 4–30mm/85 Emerlec (2×2), 1 short-range SAM system, 1 single (or twin) 40mm/70 Breda or 1 single 57mm/70 Bofors, without any TT.

Electronic equipment comprises: long range search/surveillance, air search, surface search and navigation radars; gun fire control radar; active/passive sonar; ECM.

'Saar 3' design

'SAAR 1' class *fast attack craft (missile)*

Displacement:	220t standard; 250t full load
Dimensions:	146ft 7in × 5ft 9in mean, 8ft 2in deep *44.9m × 7.0m × 1.7m, 2.5m*
Machinery:	4 shafts, 4 Maybach-Mercedes MD872 (later known as MTU 16V538 TB90) diesels, 13,500hp = 42kts. Oil 30t. Range 2500nm/1600nm/1400nm/1000nm at 15kts/20kts/25kts/30kts
Armament:	'Saar 1' class: 3–40mm/70 Breda Model 58/11 (3×1), 4–32mm Mk32 ASW TT (4×1; Mk46 torpedoes), 2–12.7mm MG. As 'Saar 2' see notes 'Saar 3' class: 6 Gabriel SSM (2×3 trainable mounts amidships), 1–76mm/62 DP OTO Melara, 2–12.7mm MG, 4, 8 or 12 large chaff RL
Sensors:	Radar Thomson-CSF Neptune, Selenia Orion; ECM VHF DIF and intercept gear
Complement:	35–40

Class (no, launched):
Mirtach (311, 11.4.67), *Miznag* (312, 1967), *Mifgav* (313, 1967), *Eilath* (321, 14.6.68), *Haifa* (322, 14.6.68), *Akko* (323, 1968)
Saar (331, 25.11.68), *Soufa* (332, 4.2.69), *Gaash* (333, 24.6.69), *Herev* (341, 20.6.69), *Hanit* (342, 1969), *Hetz* (343, 14.12.69)

All built by CMN, Cherbourg, although designed by F Lürssen Werft of Bremen. First 6 ordered in 1965 had 3–40mm guns (configured like the Italian *Freccia* class patrol boats). Classified as 'Saar 1' class. Next 6 ordered in 1966 with 1–76mm OTO Melara. First 3 units and *Haifa* delivered to Israel unarmed, the former therefore not operational for the June 1967 Six Day War. Last 5 escaped to Israel from Cherbourg on 24.12.69 nominally as Norwegian oilfield supply craft named *Starboat I–V* under Panamanian flag despite the French arms embargo. Arrived in Israel Jan 1970 after world publicity for their endurance and seaworthiness. *Akko* and *Saar* delivered after the embargo was lifted. Only 'Saar 1' class fitted with searchlight sonar ELAC and it became 'Saar 3' after Gabriel SSM fitted. 'Saar 2' 76mm gun and magazine (interim fit before missiles available) left no space for ASW equipment. Armament varies from 1–40mm (fwd) and 8 Gabriel SSM (2×3 trainable launchers amidships and aft, 2×1 fixed mounts fwd or 5 Gabriel SSM (1×3 amidships, 2×1 fwd) and 2–40mm (2×1 fwd and aft) as 'Saar 2' to 3–40mm and 4 ASW TT as all-gun configuration 'Saar 1'. Armaments are now fairly standardised, but triple Gabriel launchers can be interchanged with the after 40mm mounts. 'Saar 3' group can now probably mount 2 Harpoon SSM (2×1) instead of one triple Gabriel. A radar controlled missile system, aided by optical sights, launching a 150lb HE warhead at a low altitude to a range of 12.5nm (22nm in the later versions). Eventually 2–12.7mm MG can be removed. Cost $2 million (late 1960s prices) per unit. *Haifa* was reportedly previously named *Misnak*.

On 'Saar 3' class their superstructure is slightly different forward in order to accommodate the larger gun. This group also has small bridge wings added and relocated inflatable life rafts. 'Saar 2' and 'Saar 3' (and their armament) were not only the most sophisticated vessels in Israel in the early 1970s, but were among the most powerful warships in the Mediterranean. They sank 7 Arab missile FAC without loss in Oct 1973. All extant 1982.

'Dvora' class   *Israel Aircraft Industries*

Yaffo as completed
NB 1/750 scale

'SAAR 4' and 'SAAR 4.5' class (RESHEF type) *fast attack craft (missile)*

Displacement:	415t standard; 450t ('Saar 4.5' class 440t) full load
Dimensions:	190ft 7in ('Saar 4.5' class 202ft 5in) × 24ft 11in × 7ft 10in *58.1m (61.7m) × 7.6m × 2.4m*
Machinery:	4 shafts, 4 Maybach (MTU) diesels, 10,680hp = 32kts ('Saar 4.5' class 34.0kts). Range 4000nm/2900nm/1650nm at 17.5/?/30kts. See notes
Armament:	'Saar 4' class: 6 Gabriel SSM (6×1 all fixed; designed with 7: 1×3, 4×1), 2–76mm/62 DP OTO Melara (2×1), 2–20mm Oerlikon (2×1) or 4–12.7mm MG (2×2) 'Saar 4.5' class: see notes
Sensors:	Radar Thomson-CSF Neptune TH-D1040, Selenia Orion RTN-10X; ECM MN-53 intercept
Complement:	45 ('Saar 4.5' probably 48, although in normal operation no more than 39 are required)

Class (launched, in service):
Reshef (19.2.73, April 1973), *Keshet* (2.8.73, Oct 1973), *Romach* (Jan–March 1974), *Kidon* (July–Sept 1974), *Tarshish* (Jan-March 1975), *Yaffo* (Feb–April 1975)

Nitzhanon (10.7.78, Sept 1978 or March 1979), *Komemiut* (19.7.79, Oct 1979), *Atsmout* (3.12.78, Feb or Nov 1979), *Moledet* (22.3.79, May 1979 or mid-1980).

The development of *Reshefs* began towards the end of 1968. Chaff launchers (4 large single and 6 small 12-barrelled, for long-distance cluttering of radar screens); Israeli-made missiles and electronics and US missiles. An expansion of the building slips at Haifa enabled rapid construction of the next 6 units ordered in Jan 1975. Four Harpoon SSM fitted to 'Saar 4' in early 1978 in addition to the reduced number of Gabriel launchers. Israeli homing systems attached to Harpoons. Gabriel II system, fitted with a TV camera capable of transmitting a picture to the firing ship, was installed after the ships were built.

Present armament: 'Saar 4' class – 4 Harpoon SSM (2×2), 4 Gabriel SSM launchers (4×1), 2–76mm/62 DP OTO Melara (2×1), 2–20mm AA Oerlikon (2×1), 2(?6)–12.7mm MG; 'Saar 4.5' class – 4 Harpoon SSM (1×4), 5 Gabriel SSM (?5×1), 1–76mm/62 DP OTO Melara (aft), 1–40mm/70 Breda (fwd) (*Atsmout* probably has only 2–76mm and no 40mm), 2–20mm AA Oerlikon (2×1), 6 MG.

Tarshish has carried a temporary helicopter deck in place of the after 76mm gun for experimenting with over-the-horizon targeting for Harpoon. The deck has apparently not been successful – hence the order for corvettes. In both classes the 76mm guns have been specially adapted for shore bombardment.

Yaffo deployed in Mediterranean, other 5 of 'Saar 4' class in Red Sea. Quarters are air-conditioned. ELAC Sonar fitted in ships deployed in the Red Sea. VHFD/F and radar warning device.

Excellent sea-keeping qualities and endurance and at cruising speed has a very long range. Four ships made the passage from Israel to the Red Sea round Africa via Gibraltar relying entirely on refuelling at sea. Two sailed to New York in July 1976. The first pair was successfully engaged in the October 1973 Arab-Israeli War. *Reshef* sank a Syrian 'T 43' minesweeper with Gabriel off Latakia.

All details on light AA armament are uncertain. French sources give 4 shafts, 4 MTU MD871 diesels, 14,000hp, range 4000/1500nm at 17/30kts. Three have been built in Haifa for S Africa and 9 more in Durban. Two others bought late 1979 or 1980 by Chile as *Casma* (ex-Israeli *Romach* or a newly built craft) and *Chipana* (ex-Israeli, name unknown or a newly built craft).

Aliya class design

ALIYA class *fast attack craft (missile)*

Displacement:	500t full load
Dimensions:	202ft 5in × 24ft 11in × 8ft 2in *61.7m × 7.6m × 2.5m*
Machinery:	4 shafts, 4 MTU MD 871 diesels, 10,680hp = 34kts. Range 1500nm/4000nm at 30kts/17kts
Armament:	4 Gabriel SSM (4×1), 1–40mm/70 2–20mm (2×1), 4–12.7mm MG Browning (4×1), 1 Bell Kiowa helicopter
Complement:	53

Class (launched, in service):
Aliya (10 or 11.7.80, Aug 1980), *Geoula* (Oct 1980, 31.12.80), *Romat* (1981, Oct 1981)

Hull, bridge and mast similar to *Reshefs*. Have hangars and helicopter deck aft. Planned CIWS – Israeli designed Point Defence System PCM-30 with 30mm Oerlikon gun (twin) fitted in *Geoula*. Between bridge and hangar there is space for 8 Harpoon SSM (2×4). Helicopter hangar removed from *Romat* for more guns. Fourth ship (unnamed) launched in 1981.

'DVORA' class *fast attack craft (missile)*

Displacement:	c38t standard; 47t full load
Dimensions:	70ft 11in × 18ft 4in × 2ft 11in/6ft (props) *21.6m × 5.5m × 0.9/1.8m*
Machinery:	2 shafts, 2 MTU 12V331 TC81 diesels, 2720hp = 36kts. Range 700nm at 27 or 32kts
Armament:	2 Gabriel SSM (2×1), 2–20mm (2×1), 2–12.7mm MG
Sensors:	Radar Decca 926
Complement:	8–10

One or more units (name or names not known)

IAI design, similar to the 'Dabur' class but smallest ever missile craft. Constructed of aluminium alloy. The *Dvora* (meaning 'Seagull') because of her small size, can be transported by land to the required place. Can also be stored on land to ease maintenance. Trials from Dec 1977. It is still uncertain whether this craft's small size will make it acceptable to the Israeli Navy as a missile boat. At the end of 1979 the first units were still undergoing builders' trials. Acquired in 1979 to begin replacing the Coast Guard's 4 patrol boats. Two 'Dvora' class were also ordered by Nicaragua from Israel, but delivery was embargoed in 1979 at US Government request. Price $3–4 million per unit (15 per cent cost of large missile FAC). Extant 1982.

US Super FLAGSTAFF class *missile hydrofoils*

Displacement:	67t light; 101.6t full load
Dimensions:	84ft 5in × 23ft 11in × 5ft *25.6m × 7.3m × 1.5m*
Machinery:	1 shaft (CP propeller) CODOG: 1 Allison 501KE gas turbine plus 2 GM auxiliary propulsion diesels, 5400hp + 260hp = 50–52kts. Oil 22.3t. Range 1700/900nm at ?/48kts. Endurance 3–5 days
Armament:	4 Harpoon SSM (2×2), 2 Gabriel SSM (1×2), 2–30mm CIWS. See notes
Complement:	c15

Class (no, launched):
Shimrit (M 161, 26.5.81), *Livnit* (laid down 1978)

Sometimes known as US 'Flagstaff II' or 'Flagstaff 2' class. The first pair (*Shimrit* means 'guardian') ordered in 1978 from Grumman, USA, with intention to build 10 more in Israel (now authorised). Probably to replace the 'Saar 2' and 'Saar 3' classes. Have a large radome. Many delays in programme. Planned 76mm replaced by second 30mm. *Shimrit* was subcontracted to Lantana BY, Florida, and *Livnit* was laid down by Israel S Yd, Haifa.

Ex-British *motor torpedo-boats*

Class (no):
Lilitt (209), *Shaldagg* (210), *Tinshemett* (212)

At least 3 (possibly 9) British 70ft Vosper MTBs were purchased in late 1940s. Ex-names not known. Reported c1967 to be 'no longer in service'.

Tahmass 1965
NB 1/750 scale

AYAH class *fast attack craft*

Displacement:	62t standard
Dimensions:	85ft 4in × 20ft 8in × 4ft 11in *26.0m × 6.3m × 1.5m*
Machinery:	2 shafts, 4 12cyl Arsenal-Marine-Otto petrol engines, 4600hp = 42kts max. Range 600/300nm at 29/42kts
Armament:	See notes
Complement:	14 (After modernisation 15)

Class:
Ayah, Baz, Daya, Peress, Tahmass, Yasoor

Built by Chantiers de Meulan, France. Ordered in 1949 and delivered 1951–52. Pennant nos T200 series. Wooden hull. Older sources give *Netz* instead of *Yasoor*. Armed as designed: 1–40mm, 4–20mm and 2–457mm TT. Served rather as MGBs without TT. After about 10-years service were modernised. Two new Napier Deltic diesels with total 5000hp replaced the old petrol engines. This also increased significantly safety on board. Superstructure altered and mast with radar added. Armed with 1–40mm, 1 or 2–20mm and 2–457mm TT. Later 1–20mm and TT probably removed. It appears that in early 1970s at least 2 boats mounted 20mm guns forward as well as aft. Probably stricken between 1972 and 1974.

OPHIR class *fast attack craft*

Displacement:	40t standard
Dimensions:	70ft 1in × 17ft 1in × 5ft 1in *21.3m × 5.2m × 1.5m*
Machinery:	2 shafts, 2 Packard-Otto high octane petrol engines, 4000hp = 40kts
Armament:	1–40mm, 2–20mm, 2–457mm TT
Complement:	?

Class (no):
Ophir (T 150), *Shva* (T 151), *Tarshish* (T 152)
Built by Cantieri Baglietto, Varazze, Italy in 1956–57. Wooden hull. Armament variable, torpedoes later probably removed and 1–20mm added. Probably stricken in mid-1970s.

YAR class *large patrol craft*

Displacement:	96t standard; 109t full load
Dimensions:	100ft × 20ft × 5ft 11in–6ft 3in *30.5m × 6.1m × 1.8–1.9m*
Machinery:	2 shafts, 2 MTU diesels, ?hp = 22kts
Armament:	2–20mm (2×1)
Complement:	16

Class (no):
Yarden (42), *Yarkon* (44)
Often incorrectly referred to as *Jarkon Echad* or *Yarkon Echad*. Coast guard cutters, built by Yacht & Bootswerft, Burmester, Bremen-Burg 1956–57. *Yarden* has now become non-naval training craft. *Yarkon* deleted 1976.

KEDMA class *coastal patrol craft*

Displacement:	32t standard
Dimensions:	66ft 11in × 15ft 1in × 4ft 11in *20.4m × 4.6m × 1.5m*
Machinery:	2 shafts, 2 diesels, 1540hp = 25kts
Armament:	2–20mm. See notes
Complement:	10

Class (no):
Kedma (46), *Yama* (48), *Negba* (52), *Tzafona* (50)
Built in Japan during 1968. Handy boats of the small seaward defence type. Steel hull. Used for coast guard and police work in peace time. Later probably all armed only with 2 MG – eg *Negba* has 2–7.62mm MG. Extant 1982.

'Dabur' class   *Israel Aircraft Industries*

'Dabur' class
NB 1/750 scale

'DABUR' class *coastal patrol craft*

Displacement:	25–26t standard; 35t full load
Dimensions:	65ft × 19ft × 2ft 8in *19.8m × 5.8m × 0.8m*
Machinery:	2 shafts, 2 12V-71 diesels, 1920hp = 21.8–25kts (?or 960hp = 25kts). Range 1200nm at 17kts
Armament:	2–20mm (2×1), 2 or 4–12.7mm MG (2×1 or 2×2). See notes
Sensors:	Radar Decca 101 or 926
Complement:	6–9 depending on armament

Class:
*c*25–37 units (names or pennant nos not known)
Twelve built by Sewart Seacraft (USA), others by IAI (RAMTA), 1973–77. Four each exported in 1978 to Argentina and Nicaragua. Five given to Lebanese Christian forces in 1976. Aluminium hull, quarters air-conditioned and spacious. Good rough weather performance. Differences in armament between units.

In some boats 2–?mm TT are fitted forward; reported that some may carry missiles of an unspecified type. Deployed in the Mediterranean and Red Seas; possible as these craft were designed for overland transport. A continuing programme in hand at the IAI (RAMTA). Extant 1982.

'YATUSH' class (ex-US PBR type) *patrol boats*

Ex-USN 6.5t GRP river craft bought since 1974 and up to 28 extant 1982. Two given to Lebanese Christians 1975–76. Armament variously given as 2–3 MG (7.6mm or 12.7mm and/or 1–60mm mortar.

Ex-British FAIRMILE 'B' type *motor launch*

One vessel (ex-*M 17*, ex-*ML ....*) transferred in early 1950s and renamed *Haportzim*. Armed with 3–20mm and 12 DC. Officially deleted from the Navy list in 1961.

Ex-British *harbour defence motor launches*

Class (no):
Dror (21), *Saar* (35), *Tirtsa* (25)
In early 1950s 3 vessels transferred. Original British nos not known. Armed with 1–40(?47)mm, 1–20mm and 8 DC. *Saar* stricken between 1965–68, others armed with 1–47mm, 1–40mm AA and 8 DC or only 2–20mm AA and 8 DC; used for coast guard and police work. *Dror* and *Tirtsa* stricken between 1974–76.

MINE WARFARE VESSELS

WHALECATCHER type *minesweepers*

Displacemnet:	300t
Dimensions:	130ft × 25ft × 13ft *40m × 7.6m × 3.9m*
Machinery:	1 shaft, 1 reciprocating engine, 500ihp = 10kts
Armament:	1–76mm, 1–20mm
Complement:	?

Class:
Drom A I, *Drom A II*
Built in South Africa, probably in 1940s. Broken up in the early 1950s.

MISCELLANEOUS

Ex-US PC class *submarine chaser*

PC 1188 (often incorrectly referred to as *PC 16*) transferred in early 1950s and renamed *Nogah* (since 1960s pennant no 22). Classified as patrol vessel; in mid-1970s served as target for Gabriel missiles. Further fate unknown.

Ex-US NORTHLAND *Coast Guard cutter*

USCG cutter WPG 49 *Northland* (launched 1927) acquired in 1948 (between 1947 and 1948 mercantile *Medina Ivrit*) and renamed *Eilath*. Sloop type, of exceptionally strong construction with icebreaker bows specially built for the Bering Sea. She rammed an RN destroyer during her immigrant running days and had a 60mm mountain gun lashed to the deck during the 1948–49 war. Served in Israeli Navy as TS (mainmast and forward 76mm gun removed) and later as depot ship for MTBs. In late 1950s renamed *Matzpen*. Sold for scrap in 1962.

Ex-US MAYFLOWER *Presidential Yacht/Coast Guard training ship*

Mayflower was one of 3 very large and luxurious steam yachts very similar in size and appearance, all designed by G L Watson. Built by J & G Thompson in 1897, she was bought from the USN in 1898 and armed. In 1902 she was recommissioned as the US Presidential Yacht (in 1905 Roosevelt arranged for the treaty ending the Russo-Japanese War to take place on board). Later became pennant no PY 1. President Hoover withdrew her from service as the Presidential Yacht in 1929. She was laid up in Philadelphia N Yd when she was badly burned in June 1931. The hull was sold to, and refitted by, H L Gielow. The new owner had to sell her, so she went into S American trade as SS *Butte*. The Maritime Commission acquired her in 1942, and after being refitted, armed with 1–127mm and 2–76mm and renamed WPG 183 *Mayflower*, she entered the US Coast Guard where she served as a TS until 1946. Decommissioned and sold, she caught fire and was towed to Baltimore. Purchased and put under the Panamanian flag, she was named *Mala* in 1947 and carried refugees from France to Israel. Purchased by the Israeli Navy *c*1950; served as a patrol craft and TS *Maoz*. Broken up 1955. *Maoz* often incorrectly referred to as ex-USCGC *Tampa* (launched 1921).

Jordan

It was officially stated in 1969 that the Hashemite Kingdom of Jordan had no naval force, but the Jordanian Coast Guard, sometimes called the Jordan Sea Force, takes orders directly from the Army Director of Operations at GHQ. Personnel in 1982: 300 volunteer officers and men, including frogmen. A Dead Sea flotilla no longer exists. Jordan's Sea Force base is at Aqaba.

Four US-built 38ft Bertram 'Enforcer' type coastal patrol craft (8t, 25kts, 3 MG) acquired in Aug 1974: *Faysal, Han, Hasayu* and *Muhammed*.

Two US-built 30ft Bertram type coastal patrol craft (6.5t, 25kts, 3 MG, 8 men): *Ali* and *Abdullah*, GRP hulls. Acquired 1974.

Four unarmed c18ft wooden patrol craft.

Kuwait

Primarily a coast guard force administered by the Ministry of the Interior consisting of lightly armed patrol craft (delivered since 1966) and 4 small landing craft.

The Italian CNR and the Kuwaiti government were negotiating in 1978/79 with a view to signing a sales contract for about eight or ten 550t corvettes, presumably of the type chosen for series construction by Libya and Ecuador. Some sources report that Kuwait is interested in acquiring a frigate. Eight fast attack craft were ordered from Lürssen, W Germany in 1980. In 1977 a Japanese firm was contracted to build a base for the Coast Guard's planned expansion. Volunteer personnel have increased from 120 (1974) to 1100 in 1982.

(For illustration see under UAE)

Lürssen 'TNC 45' type *fast attack craft (missile)*

Displacement:	228t standard; 268t full load
Dimensions:	147ft 4in oa, 139ft 9in pp × 24ft 3in × 7ft 7in *44.9m, 42.3m × 7.4m × 2.3m*
Machinery:	4 shafts, 4 MTU 16V538 TB92 diesels, 14,400hp = 40.5kts. Range 500nm/1600nm at 38kts/16kts
Armament:	4 MM40 Exocet SSM (2×2), 1–76mm/62 DP OTO Melara (250rds), 2–40mm/70 Breda-Bofors Compatto (1×2; 1800rds)
Sensors:	Radar Decca 1226, HSA WM-28; ECM Decca Cutlass RDL-2 Dagaie chaff RL
Complement:	40

Class (no, launched, in service):
Werjia (K 451, March–Aug 1982), K 452 (May 1982), *Mashuwah* (K 453, June 1982, K 454, *Jalboot* (K 455, 1982), K 456 due to be in service Aug 1983.

Lürssen 'FPB 57' type *fast attack craft (missile)*

Displacement:	353t standard; 390t full load
Dimensions:	189ft × 25ft 7in × 9ft 6in *57.6m × 7.8m × 2.9m*
Machinery:	4 shafts, 4 MTU 16V538 TB91 diesels, 16,000hp = 38kts. Range 700nm/1300nm at 35kts/30kts
Armament:	4 MM40 Exocet SSM (2×2), 1–76mm/62 DP OTO Melara (or 2–76mm without missiles), 2–40mm/70 Breda-Bofors Compatto (1×2), 4–30mm/85 Emerlec (2×2)
Sensors:	As Lürssen TNC 45 type
Complement:	40

Two authorised in 1981, similar to W German Type 143 (S 61) class.

Thornycroft 78ft type *coastal patrol boats*

Displacement:	40t standard
Dimensions:	78ft × 15ft 6in × 4ft 6in *25.5m × 4.7m × 1.4m*
Machinery:	2 shafts, 2 8cyl Rolls-Royce V8 marine diesels, 1340hp max, 1116hp = 20kts. Range 700nm at 15kts
Armament:	Reported 1 MG or unarmed
Complement:	12

Class (launched):
Al Salemi (30.6.66), *Al Shurti* (1972), *Al Mubaraki* (16.7.66), *Aman* (March 1968), *Intisar* (1972), *Marzook* (1969), *Mashhoor* (1969), *Maymoon* (April 1968), *Murshed* (1970), *Wathah* (1970)

Two built by Thornycroft before their merger with Vosper and 8 after the merger. *Al Salemi* and *Al Mubaraki* shipped to Kuwait on 8.9.66 and the last pair *Al Shurti* and *Intisar* in 1972.

Welded steel hulls, aluminium alloy superstructures. Twin hydraulically operated rudders, Decca type D202 radar. Modified superstructure and no funnel on later. Designed to have 1–40mm. Extant 1982.

Vosper 56ft *coastal patrol boats*

Displacement:	25t
Dimensions:	56ft 1in × 16ft 1in × 4ft 3in/7ft 7in *17.1m × 4.9m × 1.3m/2.3m*
Machinery:	2 shafts, 2 MTU MB 6V331 diesels, 1350hp = 26kts for first two and 1800hp = 29–30kts for last 3 or 4 boats. Range 320nm at 20kts
Armament:	1–20mm, 2 MG
Complement:	8

Class:
Dastoor, Kasar, Qahir, Sagar, Salam, and probably one with unknown name.

First 2 ordered in Sept 1973 and built by Vosper Thornycroft Ltd, Singapore, laid down 31.10.73 and commissioned June 1974. Steel hulls and aluminium superstructure. 3 more ordered in 1978. Built by Vosper Private Ltd and commissioned 1979. French source gives 2 types – first 2 units built in 1974 armed as above and later 4 with 2–20mm AA (2×1). Second pair ordered 10.3.77, in service Dec 1978 and third pair ordered July 1978, in service 1979. Extant 1982.

Vosper 46ft *coastal patrol craft*

Displacement:	21.5t
Dimensions:	46ft 3in × 14ft 5in × 3ft 11in, 7ft 2in max *14.1m × 4.4m × 1.2m, 2.2m*
Machinery:	Probably 2 shafts, 2 Rolls-Royce C8M-410 diesels, 780hp = 21–21.7kts
Armament:	Can mount 2–20mm AA (2×1), 2–7.62mm MG
Complement:	5

Class: *Mahroos*
Built by Vosper Thornycroft Ltd, Singapore. Ordered in Oct 1974, delivered 1975 and commissioned Jan 1976. Hull is of welded steel construction with aluminium superstructure. Originally not armed. Extant 1982.

Vosper 36ft *coastal patrol craft*

Displacement:	6.8t full load
Dimensions:	36ft 5in × 10ft 10in × 5ft 3in *11.1m × 3.3m × 1.6m*
Machinery:	2 shafts, 2 Sabre 210 turbocharged diesels, 420hp = 27kts
Armament:	4–7.62mm MG (2×2)
Complement:	4

Class:
Antar, Al Salmi II, Al Sebbah, Istiqlal II, Qarah, Warbah plus 8 unnamed.

First ordered from Vosper, Singapore July 1972. Double teak construction with Cascover nylon sheathing. First 4 in service late 1972. Second 4 in April–May 1973, next 3 in 1976 and last 3 on 2.12.77. All extant 1982.

Vosper type *logistic landing craft*

Displacement:	170t/320t
Dimensions:	105ft 11in × 24ft 7in × 8ft 2in *32.3m × 7.5m × 2.5m*
Machinery:	2 shafts, 2 Rolls-Royce C8M-41D diesels, 750bhp = 9.5kts. Range 1500nm at 9kts
Armament:	None
Complement:	?

Class:
Hadiya, Ceriff, Al Jahra
All built by Vosper Private Ltd, Singapore. Ordered July 1978 and commissioned 1979. Unusual design with stern landing ramp.

Vosper type *landing craft*

Displacement:	88t standard; 170t full load
Dimensions:	88ft 7in × 22ft 8in × 4ft 3in *27.0m × 6.9m × 1.3m*
Machinery:	Probably 2 shafts, 2 Rolls-Royce C8M-410 diesels, 752/or 650?/hp = 10kts. Range 1500nm at 9kts
Armament:	None
Complement:	9 (can carry 8 passengers)

Class:
Waheed, Fareed, Regga
Built by Vosper Thornycroft Ltd, Singapore. First 2 ordered in 1970 and third in Oct 1974 by Kuwait Ministry of Interior. Able to carry 6400 gallons oil, 9400 gallons water and 40t deck cargo; a 2.5t derrick employed. Supports landing-parties working on islands off-shore.

Lebanon

Lebanon maintains a small naval force which consists mainly of small patrol boats and craft supported by one old former US utility landing craft. The strength of this navy has remained constant over the years and there are no serious plans for a development programme. A poor country torn by strife and civil war, Lebanon has little money available to buy and equip naval forces. Israel gave seven patrol boats to her Lebanese Christian allies in 1975–76. A strong customs service rather than a navy is required. Some of a 10-year 955 million dollar programme to re-equip the republic's armed forces may find its way to the Navy. The main base is at Beirut-Jounieh; there are a total of 200–400 officers and men serving in the Navy commanded by a colonel.

One large French-built patrol craft (105t standard, 2 diesels, 27kts, 2–40mm, 2–12.7mm MG): *Tarablous* (31, laid down by CNE June 1958, launched June 1959, extant 1982).

Two *Jihad* class large patrol craft ordered in 1975 but sold to Libya Jan 1978 when Lebanon unable to pay.

Two ex-RN Fairmile B motor launches: *Djounieh* (ex-ML ?) and *No 41*. Deleted 1975.

Three *Byblos* class motor launches (28t standard, 66ft, 2 diesels, 18kts, 1–20mm, 2 MG): *Byblos* (11), *Sidon* (12), *Beyrouth* (13) built 1954–55 by CNE of France. Extant 1982.

Two Fairey Marine Tracker Mk2 class patrol boats (31.5t full load, 2 diesels, 29kts, 11 men, armament unknown). In service 21.1.80 and 8.2.80 names unknown).

Six 'Aztec' class 9-metre coastal patrol craft: *CP 1001–1006*, GRP customs boats supplied by Crestitalia, La Spezia, 1980.

One ex-US LCU 1466 utility landing craft: *Sour* (ex-*LCU 1474*) launched 1955 and transferred Nov 1958. Deleted 1980.

Oman

The Sultanate of Oman, a little smaller than Britain in area and with a population of 948,000, is situated at the southern end of the Arabian Peninsula and holds a strategically very important position. From this position she can control the approaches to the Persian Gulf through the Gulf of Oman. And with the small area under her control on the Mussandam Peninsula she virtually controls the narrow Strait of Hormuz which is the only means of entry to the Gulf. The Navy personnel consists of about 1500 volunteer officers and men. It was possible to create a modern navy in the 1970s only with the help of the British and the Navy employs a number of expatriates mainly from the UK. The Commander of the Navy and a few senior officers are on secondment from the Royal Navy. More Omanis are gradually being recruited into the Navy and all officers in the Patrol Boat Squadron apart from the commanding officers are Omanis. In 1982 the first Omani officer to take command of a patrol boat will take up his post. Oman's emerging navy is in grave need of trained officers and men.

Most Omani ships are modern and potent but there is an evident lack of support vessels and auxiliaries. A British firm, Brooke Marine Ltd, is a main supplier of ships as is Vosper Thornycroft to a lesser extent.

The Omani Navy has proved its worth in its involvement in the control of shipping in the Straits of Hormuz Shipping Separation Zones which pass through Omani waters. Requiring two patrol vessels on duty supported by a supply vessel, this is a relatively heavy commitment for such a small force and has been carried out with success since November 1979 and reflects well on the Navy's ability. Patrol boats regularly fired at land targets in an effort to disrupt camel trains during the Dhofar War of 1965–75, although the success of this method was never confirmed. The Navy's role in defeating the Communist led insurgency in the Sultanate's southern province was mainly an unglamorous but essential one of logistic support along the barren coastline.

AL SAID *armed yacht (escort vessel)*

Displacement:	785t standard; 930t full load
Dimensions:	203ft 5in oa, 188ft 4in pp × 35ft 1in × 9ft 10in
	62.2m, 57.4m × 10.7m × 3.0m
Machinery:	2 shafts, 2 Paxman Ventura 12-YJCM diesels, 2470hp = 17kts
Armament:	1–40mm
Sensors:	Radar Decca TM-626
Complement:	32 + 7 staff + 32 troops

Tarablous as completed   *Navarret Collection*

Al Munassir as completed   *Brooke Marine*

Al Said was built by Brooke Marine Ltd, ordered in 1969, launched 7.4.70 and commissioned as the Navy's first ship in 1971. Designed as a yacht for the Sultan of Muscat and Oman, she was converted to a dual purpose ship with a gun on her forecastle and serves as a flagship of the Sultanate Navy. A Fairey Marine Spear patrol boat is carried and she is also fitted with a helicopter deck. Could be used as an escort vessel.

Al Munassir as completed

AL MUNASSIR *logistic support ship*

Displacement:	2000t full load
Dimensions:	276ft oa, 266ft 6in pp × 49ft × 7ft 4in
	84.0m, 81.25m × 15.0m × 2.15m
Machinery:	2 shafts (CP propellers), 2 Mirrlees-Blackstone ESL8MGR diesels, 2400hp = 12kts. Range 2000nm at 12kts
Armament:	1–76mm/62 OTO Melara, 2–20mm (2×1)
Sensors:	Radar Decca TM-1229
Complement:	45 + 188 troops

This unusual ship was built by Brooke Marine Ltd, Lowestoft. Laid down on 4.7.77, launched on 25.7.78, completed on 3.4.79. Equipped with bow doors and ramp for beaching. Bluff-bowed hull shape and slow speed of only 12kts. Can carry 550t of cargo or 8 heavy tanks. Carries a travelling crane of 16-ton capacity which spans helicopter deck; one Westland Sea King or smaller helicopters can be carried. Fitted with Sperry Sea Archer optical fire control. The ship can also be employed as command vessel. She carries hull number *L 1*.

Brooke Marine 93-metre type *logistic landing ship*

Displacement:	2300t full load
Dimensions	305ft × ? × ?
	93.0m × 15.5m × 2.3m
Machinery:	2 shafts, 2 diesels = 16kts. Range 3000nm
Armament	2–40mm/70 Breda-Bofors
Sensors:	Radar Decca, CSEE fire control
Complement:	81 + 240 troops

Ordered in 1982 at Brooke Marine Ltd shipyard in Lowestoft, this ship is a development of the previous *Al Munassir* type but is more suited for landing operations. She has a bow and a stern ramp and so can easily be loaded from both ends. Armament was placed in the bows on the forecastle deck and superstructure is aft over the machinery spaces. Aft of deckhouse is the landing deck which

Artist's impression of new 93m landing ship design

Al Mujahid running trials   *Brooke Marine*

can accommodate one Sea King or smaller helicopters. Unloading is assisted by a travelling hydraulic crane. Probably her hull number will be *L 2*. She is much more traditional in appearance than her predecessor.

The following twin diesel LCUs were extant in 1982 except *Al Doghas* (deleted 1981).

Al Sansoor (C 4), *Al Doghas* (C 5, ex-*Kinzeer al Bahr*), 'Loadmaster' class launched in 1974, in service Jan 1975 by Cheverton Cowes; 60t (130t full load), 6kts, 60ft × 20ft × 3ft 7in, *18.0m × 6.0m × 1.2m*, crew 6.

Sulhafa al Bahr (C 3), 'Loadmaster' class launched in 1975 by Cheverton, Cowes; 30dwt, 45t, 8.5kts, 45ft × 15ft × 3ft, *13.7m × 4.6m × 1.7m*.

Al Dhaibah (C 6), launched in 1975 by Impala Marine, Twickenham; 75dwt, 122grt, 9kts, 75ft × 23ft × 5ft, *22.9m × 7.0m × 1.5m*, crew 8.

Kasab Kumzar, I, II, III, built in 1977 by Impala Marine, Twickenham; 122grt, 9kts, 84ft × 25ft × ?, *25.6m × 7.6m × ?*

Al Neemran (C 7), I, launched in 1979–81 by Lewis Offshore, Stornoway; 85t, 8kts, *25.5m × 7.4m × 1.8m*, crew 8.

Zara (20), built in 1981; 11t standard, 23t full load, 20kts, *18m × 3.8m × 0.5m*, 2–127mm MG (2×1), crew 4.

Saba al Bahr (C 8), launched 30.6.81 by Vosper, Singapore, in service Sept 1981; 230t, 8kts, *30.0m × 8.0m × 1.2m*

SMALL SURFACE COMBATANTS

Dhofar as completed
NB 1/750 scale

DHOFAR class *fast attack craft (missile)*

Displacement:	380t standard; 450t full load
Dimensions:	186ft × 26ft 10in × 8ft 10in
	56.0m × 7.5m × 2.5m
Machinery:	4 shafts, 4 Paxman Valenta diesels, 15,000hp = 40kts
Armament:	6 MM40 Exocet SSM (2×3), 1–76mm/62 OTO Melara, 2–40mm/70 Breda-Bofors (1×2)
Sensors:	Radar Plessey AWS-4
Complement:	40 + 19 passengers

Class (no, laid down, launched, in service):
Dhofar (B 8, 30.9.80, 14.10.81, 7.8.82), *B 9* (9.12.81, May 1982), *B 10* (Dec 1981, July 1982)

Sometimes called 'Province' class. Designed by Vosper Thornycroft (UK) Ltd as a modified version of Egyptian *Ramadan* class FAC. *Dhofar* ordered 1980 and the others boats ordered in 1981 were launched in 1982. All 3 will cost £45 million.

Al Mansur 1978
NB 1/750 scale

AL BUSHRA class *large patrol craft (missile and gun)*

Displacement:	140t standard; 185t full load (B 1–3), 125t standard; 160t full load (*B 4—7*)
Dimensions:	123ft oa × 6ft 11in × 2ft 2in
	37.5m × 6.9m × 1.7m
Machinery:	2 shafts, 2 Paxman Ventura 16 RP-200 diesels, 4800hp = 28kts. Range 3230nm at 13kts (*B 1–3*), 3300nm at 12kts (*B 4—7*)
Armament:	2 MM38 Exocet SSM (2×1), 2–40mm/70 Breda-Bofors (1×2), 2–7.62mm MG (in *B 1–3*); 1–76mm/62 AA OTO Melara (130rds), 1–20mm, 2–7.62mm MG (in *B 4—7*)
Sensors:	Radar Decca TM-916
Complement:	27

Class (no, in service):
Al Bushra (B 1), *Al Mansur* (B 2, 26.3.73), *Al Nejah* (B 3, 13.5.73), *Al Wafi* (B 4, 24.3.77), *Al Fulk* (B 5, 24.3.77), *Al Mujahid* (B 6, 6.10.77), *Al Jabbar* (B 7, 6.10.77)

All 37.5 metre boats built by Brooke Marine Ltd. First 3 ordered on 5.1.71 and commissioned 1973, B 4–7 ordered April 1974 and delivered 1977. B 1–B 3 rearmed with Exocet missiles and Sperry Sea Archer fire control systems by

builders, Nov 1977–Nov 1978. *Al Bushra* lost on 28.11.78 when she was washed off the delivery ship *Trautenfels* by hurricane winds while in the Bay of Biscay. A replacement boat was ordered in 1980 and is a *Dhofar*. B 4–7 fitted with Lawrence-Scott optical director. *B 1–3* originally armed with two single 40mm guns fore and aft.

Ex-Dutch DOKKUM class *coastal minesweepers*

Class:
Al Nasiri (ex-*Axel*), *Al Salihi* (ex-*Aalsmeer*)

Pennant nos 1 and 2. These ex-Dutch minesweepers (launched 1955) were bought by Oman from the Netherlands in 1974. Air-conditioned and fitted as patrol boats by van Giessen de Noord. Similar to British 'Ton' class. Their minesweeping gear was removed and the third 40mm gun placed on the main deck aft. Deleted in 1981.

HARAS 1–5 *patrol boats*

Displacement:	45t full load
Dimensions:	75ft × 20ft × 5ft 10in
	22.9m × 6.0m × 1.5m
Machinery:	2 shafts, 2 Caterpillar D 438 diesels, 1840hp = 24.5kts. Range 600nm at 20kts, 1000nm at 11kts
Armament:	2–20mm
Sensors:	Radar Decca 101
Complement:	11

These boats named *Haras* 1–5 were built in 1975 by Vosper Thornycroft, Singapore. First 4 operational from 22.12.75. Serve on Royal Oman Police duties. GRP hulls. *Haras* 5 delivered in Nov 1978. Extant 1982.

HARAS 7 *patrol boat*

Displacement:	80t full load
Dimensions:	94ft × 17ft × 3ft 3in
	28.7m × 5.2m × 1.1m
Machinery:	2 shafts, 2 MTU 8V331 IC82 diesels, 1866bhp = 25kts
Armament:	2–20mm (2×1)
Sensors:	Radar Decca 1226C
Complement:	13

Small patrol boat built in 1981 by Karlskrona Varvet AB. Swedish type CG 29 (improved CG 27). GRP hull. Sister ship *Haras* 10 also built by Karlskrona, Sweden. Extant 1982.

HARAS 8 *patrol boat*

Displacement:	30t standard; 33t full load
Dimensions:	63ft × 15ft 8in × 4ft
	19.2m × 4.9m × 1.2m
Machinery:	2 MTU 8 V 331 diesels, 1200/1600hp = 30kts. Range 1650nm/2300nm at 17kts/12kts
Armament:	2–12.7mm MG
Complement:	10

Built in 1981 by Le Comte, the Netherlands. Type PT 1903 Mk III. In service Aug 1981. Extant 1982.

SEEB class *patrol craft*

Displacement:	75t
Dimensions:	82ft 10in × 19ft × 5ft 2in
	25m × 5.8m × 1.6m
Machinery:	2 MTU 12V 331TC–92BW255 diesels, 3072bhp = 26kts. Range 2000nm at 8kts
Armament:	1–20mm
Sensors:	Radar Decca
Complement:	13

Class (no):
Seeb (B 20), *Shinas* (B 21), *Sadh* (B 22), *Khasab* (B 23)
Built by Vosper Thornycroft, Singapore; all commissioned Aug 1981. Extant 1982.

Qatar

The naval forces of this tiny but immensely rich Gulf state (4000 sq miles, pop 240,000, GNP 6.58 billion dollars in 1981) have only comparatively recently evolved from a coast guard force. The Navy has expansion plans and to a greater or lesser extent relies on Western assistance to operate their forces. The Navy is incorporated within the Armed Forces which total about 6000 men. The Naval Force consists of 6 Vosper Thornycroft patrol craft acquired in 1975–76 and some 29 coastal patrol craft. Three 'Combattante III M' fast attack craft (fitted with Exocet missiles) were ordered together with some coastal defence equipment from France. Some 400 officers and men serve with the Naval Force, the main base of which is at Doha.

'COMBATTANTE III M' type *fast attack craft (missile)*

Displacement:	345t standard; 395t full load
Dimensions:	183ft 9in oa, 173ft 10in pp × 26ft 9in × 7ft 1in
	56m, 53mm × 8.1m × 2.1m
Machinery:	4 shafts, 4 MTU 20V538 TB93 diesels, 19,300hp = 38.5kts.
	Range 2000nm at 15kts
Armament:	8 MM40 Exocet SSM (2×4), 1–76mm/62 DP OTO Melara,
	2–40mm/70 Breda-Bofors Compatto (1×2), 2–30mm/85
	Emerlec (2×2) Dagaie chaff RL
Sensors:	Radar Decca 1226, Thomson-CSF Pollux, Castor
Complement:	42?

Class (laid down, launched, in service):
Damsah (6.6.81, 17.6.82, Aug 1982), *Al Ghariyah* (26.8.81, 23.4.82, Aug 1982), *R'Biva* (27.10.81, Jan–June 1983)
Ordered from CMN, Cherbourg in Oct 1980. In 1980 Qatar ordered c100 MM40 Exocet missiles for these boats and land batteries. 2 CSEE Panda directors for fire control. Very similar to Nigerian *Siri* class.

Vosper Thornycroft 110ft type *large patrol craft*

Displacement:	120t
Dimensions:	110ft × 21ft × 5ft 6in
	33.5m × 6.3m × 1.6m
Machinery:	2 shafts, 2 Paxman Valenta 16cyl diesels, 6000–6250hp =
	27kts
Armament:	2–20mm (1×2)
Complement:	25

Class (no, in service):
Barzan (Q 11, 13.1.75), *Hwar* (Q 12, 30.4.75), *That Assuari* (Q 13, 3.10.75), *Al Wusaail* (Q 14, 28.10.75), *Fateh al Khair* (Q 15, 22.1.76), *Tariq* (Q 16, 1.3.76)
Ordered in 1972–73. All laid down by Vosper Thornycroft, Portsmouth, between Sept 1973 and Nov 1974. Some sources give displacement 110t standard, 140t full load and power 4000hp. Others refer to these ships as 103ft type with *31.1m pp*, *32.4m oa × 6.3m × 1.6m* and armed with 2–30mm (1×2) and 2–20mm. Q 15 was credited with an incorrect name, *Al Khatab*.

British 75ft *coastal patrol craft*

Two 60t units (names unknown) built by Whittingham & Mitchell, Chertsey, England. In service 1969 with 2–20mm. Extant 1982.

Keith Nelson 45ft type *coastal patrol craft*

Displacement:	13t
Dimensions:	44ft 3in × 12ft 6in × 3ft 7in
	13.5m × 3.8m × 1.1m
Machinery:	2 Caterpillar diesels, 800hp = 26kts
Armament:	1–12.7mm MG, 2–7.62mm MG (2×1)
Complement:	6

Two units (names unknown) built in early 1970s by Keith Nelson, Bembridge, a division of Vosper. A third vessel of this group has been converted into a pilot cutter. Extant 1982.

Fairey Marine 'SPEAR' class *coastal patrol craft*

Displacement:	4.3t/10t
Dimensions:	29ft 10in × 9ft 2in × 2ft 8in
	9.1m × 2.8m × 0.8m
Machinery:	2 shafts, 2 Perkins T 6–354 diesels, 580hp = 26kts
Armament:	3–7.62mm MG
Complement:	4

Class:
No 70–95
All built by Fairey Marine, 1974–77. Seven ordered early 1974. Delivered June 1974–Feb 1975. Contract for further 5 assigned Dec 1975. Three more delivered; 2 on 30.6.75 and 1 on 14.7.75. Order for 10 further craft (4 Mk 1, 6 Mk 2) received Oct 1976 and delivery effected April 1977. Extant 1982.

MISCELLANEOUS
There are 7 British-built Watercraft P 1200 type coastal patrol craft. (12.7t, 2-MGs, 660hp, 2 shafts = 29kts) with a complement of 4 men each. Built 1980.
Also, 2 Fairey Marine 'Interceptor' class fast assault/rescue craft. (1.25t, 270bhp = 35kts with a range of 150nm at 30kts). Delivered 28.11.75.

Barzan as completed   *Vosper Thornycroft*

Saudi Arabia

Of all the Gulf States the Kingdom of Saudi Arabia is certainly the largest and most powerful with a coastline bordering both the Persian Gulf and Red Sea. With the 1355-mile coastline, much of which is unpopulated, divided between two seas, Saudi Arabia has a considerable problem in maintaining adequate surveillance over such an area, as well as presenting a cohesive naval presence to meet a threat in any one particular area. And in addition she formed a Gulf Co-operation Council with the region's smaller states in 1981. The Kingdom's merchant navy expanded stupendously from 43 ships (61,275grt) in 1974 to 286 vessels (3,121,821grt) in 1982 including 64 tankers where there had been four.

Until a few years ago the Royal Saudi Navy (founded with one ship in 1960) was little more than a token force of three MTBs of German origin and small patrol boats. Now as a part of an overall large arms build-up, Saudi Arabia is engaged in a naval programme the relative magnitude of which is unparalleled in naval history. In 1979–80 the Saudi Navy still had less than 2000 men and scarcely more than 1000t of fighting vessels. In May 1981 Saudi Arabia announced a record budget of 298 billion rials (88.1bn dollars), 28 per cent going to defence, a fourfold increase since 1975. With the delivery of the ships presently being built or on order, the Fleet's size will be increased thirteenfold in less than five years!

It is believed that a US expansion programme undertaken by the Saudis was planned as a ten year project (1972–82) and was probably undertaken to match the Iranian Navy. This programme included: 4 MSC 322 type coastal minesweepers, 4 *Badr* class missile corvettes and 9 *Al Siddiq* class missile fast attack craft. In 1980 a new programme was launched, this time involving the French naval industry. With these two programmes completed the Saudis will have a well-balanced, medium-sized fleet. Ships ordered in France under the 'Sawari' programme include four helicopter-carrying frigates of over 2000t each and two large underway fleet replenishment ships similar to the French *Durance* class.

The Saudi Government envisaged problems with the upkeep of equipment from different sources (US and France) and so US ships are provided on the basis of a ten year naval cooperation agreement which includes an extensive training programme and a similar 'total package' agreement has been concluded with France. The main naval bases are at Jiddah and Jubil (Gulf, built by early 1981) with minor ones on the Gulf at Ras Tanura, Damman, Yanbo and Ras al-Mishab. In 1982 the Saudi Navy had 3500 volunteer officers and men; this number is expected to rise rapidly.

MAJOR SURFACE SHIPS

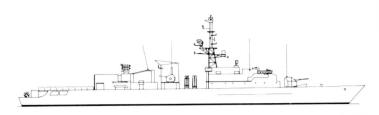

'F 2000' design

These four helicopter-carrying frigates were ordered under the 'Sawari' programme in Oct 1980 from France: the first contract for frigate-type warships won by the French naval industry after the Second World War. Ships will be fitted with the most modern armament and electronics and will be capable of operating independently greatly enhancing the Saudi Navy's capability. They will probably be delivered by the mid-1980s.

It is worth noting the short time from laying down of the first section of the prototype's hull to floating out. Although the frigates are powerfully armed, emphasis so far has been on anti-surface vessel capability which in view of the worthwhile targets which the Saudi Navy presents to those with hostile intentions, should be made good at the earliest opportunity. There have been rumours of a possible order for two 4000t AAW destroyers to give the necessary air protection, but the current large order still being processed together with the

French 'F 2000' type *frigates*

Displacement:	1990t standard; 2610t full load
Dimensions:	377ft 4in oa, 349ft 5in wl × 41ft × 15ft 4in
	115.0m, 106.5m × 12.5m × 3.4/4.7m
Machinery:	2 shafts, 4 SEMT-Pielstick diesels, 16 PA 6 BTC diesels, 32,500hp = 30kts. Range 8000nm at 15kts or 6500nm at 18kts
Armament:	8 Otomat Mk 2 SSM (2×4), 1–100mm/55 Compact, 4–40mm/70 Breda-Bofors (2×2), 1 8-cell Crotale SAM launcher (24 missiles), 4–550mm ASW TT (F17P torpedoes), 1 SA 365F Dauphin helicopter with 2–4 AS-15 missiles
Sensors:	Radar 2 Decca 1226, Thomson-CSF Sea Tiger DRBV-15, DRBC-32E, Castor II FCS, 3 CSEE Naja optronics FCS; Sonar Thomson-CSF Diodon hull mounted sonar, Diodon/Sorel VDS; ECM: Thomson-CSF DR 4000ESM, 2 CSEE Dagaie chaff launchers, SENIT VI CCS
Complement:	189

Name	Builder	Laid down	Launched	Comp	Fate
MEDINA	Lorient Naval Dockyard	15.10.81	15.5.82	1984	Building
	CNIM, La Seyne (Toulon)				On order
	CNIM, La Seyne (Toulon)				On order
	CNIM, La Seyne (Toulon)				On order

considerable expansion in manpower and the intensive training programme entailed, the Saudi Navy may well be advised to wait for a few years before embarking on the acquisition of such a large and sophisticated vessel. If such an order is placed it will almost certainly go to the French shipyards for C 70 AA class destroyers.

These ships ordered on 30.8.77 from Tacoma Boatbuilding, Tacoma, USA belong to the light frigate/corvette type. Named after early Islamic victories. They are powerfully armed for their size, and equipped with modern electronic gear.

BADR class (US PCG type) *missile corvettes*

Displacement:	720t standard; 815t full load
Dimensions:	245ft oa × 31ft 6in × 14ft 7in
	74.7m × 9.6m × 4.5m
Machinery:	2-shaft CODOG: 1 General Electric LM 2500 gas turbine, 16,500hp = 30kts, plus 2 MTU diesels, 3000hp = 20kts
Armament:	8 Harpoon SSM (2×4), 1–76mm/62 OTO Melara, 2–20mm (to get Vulcan-Phalanx CIWS), 1–81mm mortar, 2–40mm army grenade launchers, 6–324mm Mk 32 ASW TT (2×3)
Sensors:	Radars SPS-40A, SPS-60, Mk 92 FCS; sonar SQS-56
Complement:	53

No	Name	Builder	Laid down	Launched	Comp	Fate
612	BADR (ex-*PCG 1*)	Tacoma Boatbuilding	9.4.79	6.10.79	Aug 1980	Extant 1982
614	AL YARMOOK (ex-*PCG 2*)	Tacoma Boatbuilding	20.8.79	13.5.80	1.9.81	Extant 1982
616	HITTEN (ex-*PCG 3*)	Tacoma Boatbuilding	7.1.80	5.9.80	2.9.82	Extant 1982
618	TABUK (ex-*PCG 4*)	Tacoma Boatbuilding	22.9.80	18.6.81	Dec 1982	Extant 1982

Abdul Aziz 21.8.81   *L & L van Ginderen*

AMPHIBIOUS WARFARE VESSELS

AL QIAQ class (US LCU 1646 type) *utility landing craft*

Class:
Al Qiaq (ex-*SA 310*), *As Sulayel* (ex-*SA 311*), *Al Ula* (ex-*SA 312*), *Afif* (ex-*SA 313*) Nos 212, 214, 216, 218

Belong to the US LCU 1646 type. Built by Newport SY, Newport, USA, in 1975.76. Temporary US designations SA 310–313 (SA = Saudi Arabia). Note only even pennant numbers.

HAQIL class (US LCM(6) type) *landing craft*

Class:
Haqil, Al Uquair

These two US LCM(6) type were transferred in the late 1960s.

SMALL SURFACE COMBATANTS

Al Farouq as completed
NB 1/750 scale

AL SIDDIQ class (US PGG type) *fast attack craft (missile)*

Displacement:	320t
Dimensions:	184ft 4in oa, 24ft 11in × 4ft 11in
	56.2m oa × 7.6m × 1.75m
Machinery:	2-shaft CODOG: 1 GM LM 2500 gas turbine, 16,500shp = 38kts, plus 2 MTU diesels, 3000bhp = 18kts
Armament:	4 Harpoon SSM (2×2), 1–76mm/62 OTO Melara, 2–20mm (2×1), 1 Vulcan-Phalanx CIWS (20mm), 1–81mm mortar, 2–40mm Army grenade launchers
Electronics:	Radars SPS-60, Mk 92 FCS
Complement:	35

Class (no, former name, launched):
Al Siddiq (511, ex-*PGG1*, 22.9.79), *Al Farouq* (513, ex-*PGG2*, 17.5.80), *Abdul Aziz* (515, ex-*PGG3*, 23.8.80), *Faisal* (517, ex-*PGG4*, 15.11.80), *Khalid* (519, ex-*PGG5*, 28.3.81), *Amir* (521, ex-*PGG6*), *Tariq* (523, ex-*PGG7*), *Oqbah* (525, ex-*PGG8*, 21.12.81), *Abu Obadiah* (527, ex-*PGG9*)

Ordered on 16.2.77 from Peterson Builders, Sturgeon Bay, Wisconsin, USA. They have the same machinery as the larger *Badr* class corvettes and the same armament (minus 4 Harpoon SSMs and ASW TTs). Very powerful vessels for their size. Named after members of the royal family. Note lower speed on the diesels compared with the larger *Badr* class. To be completed in 1980–82; the first boat was delivered on 8.12.80 last in Nov 1982. All extant 1982.

DAMMAM class (German JAGUAR type) *fast attack craft (torpedo)*

Class:
Dammam, Khabar, Maccah

German *Jaguar* class (Type 141) ordered in 1968 and built by Lürssen, Vegesack in 1968–69. All three were refitted during 1976–77. Extant 1982.

MINE WARFARE VESSELS

ADDRIYAH class (US Bluebird type) *coastal minesweepers*

Class:
Addriyah (ex-*MSC 322*), *Al Quysumah* (ex-*MSC 323*), *Al Wadeeah* (ex-*MSC 324*), *Safwa* (ex-*MSC 325*) Nos 412, 414, 416, 418

Ordered on 30.9.75 from Peterson Builders, Wisconsin. Laid down 1976–77, launched 1976–77 and delivered in 1978. Built in USA under International Logistics Programme. Note only even pennant numbers. Extant 1982.

COASTAL PATROL CRAFT

One ex-USCG 95ft large patrol craft: *Riyadh* (former US contract designation 95CGMDA9) launched in 1959 as one of the US CG Cape type was built and transferred under MDAP from the USA in 1960. Steel hulled. Belongs to the Coast Guard. Built by US Coast Guard Yard, Curtis Bay, Maryland, USA.

Eight SRN-6 type hovercraft. Acquired from the British Hovercraft Corporation Ltd Feb–Dec 1970; 10t, 58kts, 1050hp, 1–7.62mm MG. Extant 1982. Eight more on order.

There are also 68 small patrol boats of under 10m length.

Twelve *Rapier* class (Nos 127–138), launched 1976–77 by Halter Marine, New Orleans; 24t, 28kts, 1300hp, 2–7.62mm MG. Extant 1982.

Twenty-five *Scorpion* class (Nos 140–164), launched 1979–81 by Bayerische Schiffsbaugesellschaft (20) and Arminiuswerft, Bodenwerder (5); 33t, 25kts, 1300hp. Extant 1982.

P 32 type I–VIII, ordered from CMN, Cherbourg in 1976, similar to Moroccan *El Wacil* type; 90t, 29kts, 2700hp, 2–20mm (1×2), wooden GRP sheathed hull. Extant 1982.

Syria

This country has a small naval force equipped mainly with Soviet-supplied ships and equipment; in 1980 the USSR signed a treaty of friendship and cooperation with Syria formalising links going back to 1954. Strong emphasis is still on the Army and Air Force, partly perhaps because of the Navy's poor showing in the October 1973 Arab-Israeli War, and its subsequent inability to interfere with Israeli naval operations against the Lebanese coast. The Soviet Navy's massive and long standing presence at Syrian ports since Egypt's *volte-face* in 1976 must also be a factor. Consequently naval equipment was not included in the recent acquisition of modern defence material, which leaves the Navy with a rather modest base and two 'Petya' class escorts and 12 fast attack craft – missile boats of 'Osa I' and 'Osa II' type and some other minor ships of negligible fighting value. Of the old ships supplied by France in the 1950s, the small submarine chasers of *CH 5* type still survive but are non-operational. Six to ten Ka 25 'Hormone' helicopters form a naval air arm. Bases are at Latakia, Baniyas, Tartus (heavily used by the Soviet Mediterranean Fleet) and Al-Mina-al-Bayda. In 1982 the Syrian Navy had 2500 officers and men (2½ year conscripts) with as many reserves headed by a commodore.

Ex-Soviet 'PETYA I' type *frigates*

Two of these light frigates (nos 12, 14) were transferred in 1975–76. Built 1963. Extant 1982.

SMALL SURFACE COMBATANTS

Ex-Soviet 'KOMAR' type *fast attack craft (missile)*

Nine transferred from the USSR in 1963–66. Pennant nos 41–49. Three sunk during the October 1973 War.

Ex-Soviet 'OSA I' type *fast attack craft (missile)*

Eight transferred in the late 1960s. Two sunk during October 1973 War and later replaced by USSR. Pennant nos 21–26.

Ex-Soviet 'OSA II' type *fast attack craft (missile)*

Six launched in early 1970s, were transferred: 2 in 1978; 2 in Oct 1979 and 2 in Nov 1979. Extant 1982.

Ex-Soviet 'P 4' type *fast attack craft (torpedo)*

USSR transferred 17 during 1957–60: 3 sunk in October 1973 War; 8 still in service; 4 transferred to Egypt in 1970. 2 were decommissioned.

Ex-Soviet 'P 6' type *fast attack craft (torpedo)*

Probably one transferred from USSR. Deleted.

Ex-French CH 5 type *submarine chasers*

Class (former name):
Akba Ben Naseh (ex-*CH 10*), *Al Harissi* (ex-*CH 19*, ex-*RA 1*, ex-*CH 19*), *Tarek Ben* (ex-*CH 13*)

Three built in 1938–41 by AC de France and A C Seine Maritime, were transferred in 1949 (1952?) to form the nucleus of the Syrian Navy. Rebuilt by F C de la Méditerranée in 1955–56 when funnels removed. Non-operational now. *CH 15* was captured by Germans and retroceded incomplete in 1945.

Ex-Soviet 'T 43' type *ocean minesweepers*

Class:
Yarmouk, Hittine
Transferred in 1962. *Hittine* sunk in October 1973 War off Latakia in the first naval action.

Ex-Soviet 'VANYA' type *coastal minesweepers*

Two transferred from USSR in Dec 1972. There is also an ex-Soviet *Nyryat* type ship used as a divers' base ship.

United Arab Emirates

The Armed Forces all came under the control of the Supreme Defence Council when the former Trucial States of seven emirates were merged in 1978. The General Headquarters are at Abu Dhabi. The naval force of Abu Dhabi was formed in March 1968. The present naval forces of United Arab Emirates (UAE) formed on 1 February 1978 consist of 6 Vosper Thornycroft large patrol craft acquired in 1975–76 and over 20 coastal patrol craft. The forces' function is to patrol territorial waters and oil installations in the UAE Marine Areas. Six fast attack craft are on order from Lürssen, to be fitted with Exocet. There are 1200 volunteer officers and men serving with the naval forces (commanded by a brigadier) and main ports are Abu Dhabi, Dubai, Ras al Khaimah, and Sharjah as well as Sharjah on the east coast.

Rodqum as completed
NB 1/750 scale

Lürssen 'TNC 45' type *fast attack craft (missile)*

Particulars:	See under Kuwait

Class (no, launch, in service):
Banyas* (P 4501, Nov 1980), *Marban* (P 4502, Nov 1980), *Rodqum** (P 4503, Dec 1980, July 1981), *Shaheen* (P 4504, Dec 1980, July 1981), *Saqar* (P 4505, 1981, Sept 1981), *Tarif* (P 4506, 1981, Sept 1981)
Belong to Abu Dhabi. First unit laid down by Lürssen 1979. Identical to Kuwait's 6 boats. Carry 350rnds of 76mm ammunition. Two 7.62mm MG (600rds) fitted.
First pair were shipped to UAE in Aug 1980 (without missile launchers), second pair in May 1981. *Sometimes referred to as *Baniyas* and *Rodum*. All extant 1982.

Vosper Thornycroft 110ft type *large patrol craft*

Displacement:	110t standard; 175t full load
Dimensions:	103ft 4in pp, 109ft 11in oa × 21ft × 5ft 3in – 6ft 7in *31.5m, 33.5m × 6.4m × 1.6–2.0m*
Machinery:	2 shafts, 2 Ruston-Paxman Valenta RP200M diesels, 5400hp = 29kts. Range 1800nm at 14kts
Armament:	2–30mm/75 BMARC Oerlikon A32 (1×2), 1–20mm Oerlikon A41A, 2–51mm RFL
Sensors:	Radar Decca RM-916
Complement:	26

Class (no, launched, in service):
Ardhana (P 1101, 7.3–24.6.75), *Zurara* (P 1102, 13.6–14.8.75), *Murban* (P 1103, 16.9.75), *Al Ghulian* (P 1104, 16.9.75), *Radoom* (P 1105, 15.12.75, 1.7.76), *Ghanadhah* (P 1106, 1.3–1.7.76)

Round bilge steel hull construction. All built by Vosper Thornycroft, Portsmouth, for Abu Dhabi. P 1103 and P 1104 sailed out, rest transported by freighter. All extant 1982.

US-built *customs patrol craft*

Displacement:	70t full load
Dimensions:	76ft 9in × 18ft 1in × 4ft 11in *23.4m × 5.5m × 1.5m*
Machinery:	2 shafts, 2 General Motors 12V 71T diesels, 1400hp = 25kts. Range 750nm at 25kts
Armament:	2–20mm (2×1)
Complement:	?

Class:
No 21–No 25
Built by Camcraft, New Orleans. In service since Sept 1975 with the Coast Guard. US P-77A design.

KAWKAB class (Keith Nelson type) *coastal patrol craft*

Displacement:	25t standard; 32t full load
Dimensions:	52ft pp, 57ft 6in oa × 15ft 6in × 4ft 6in *15.8m, 17.5m × 4.7m × 1.3m*
Machinery:	2 shafts, 2 Caterpillar diesels, 750bhp = 19kts. Range 300nm at 10kts. Endurance 7 days
Armament:	2–20mm (2×1)
Sensors:	Radar Decca RM 916
Complement:	11

Class (no, in service):
Kawkab (P 561, 7.3.69), *Thoaban* (P 562, 7.3.79), *Baniyas* (P 563, 27.12.69)
Glass fibre hull construction, designed and built by Keith Nelson, Bembridge, a division of Vosper. Originally operated by Abu Dhabi. Some sources give displacement 32t standard and 38t full load and range 445t at 15kts. Used for coastal patrol, hydrographic survey, and oilfield surveillance. Fresh water evaporators provides 900 litres daily. All extant 1982.

Cheverton type 50ft *customs patrol craft*

Displacement:	20t
Dimensions:	50ft 2in × 14ft 1in × 4ft 7in *15.3m × 4.3m × 1.4m*
Machinery:	2 shafts, 2 GM diesels, 850bhp = 23kts. Range 1000nm at 20kts
Armament:	1–7.62mm MG
Complement:	8

Class:
Al Shaheen, Al Aqab
GRP hull. Built by Cheverton Ltd, Isle of Wight. Commissioned Feb 1975. Originally delivered to the Sharjah Marine Police. Extant 1982.

DHAFEER class *coastal patrol craft*

Displacement:	10t
Dimensions:	40ft 4in × 11ft 3in × 3ft 7in *12.3m × 3.4m × 1.1m*
Machinery:	2 shafts, 2 Cummins diesels, 3700bhp = 19kts. Range 350nm at 15kts
Armament:	2–7.62mm MG or 1–12.7mm MG
Complement:	6

Class (no, launched, in service):
Dhafeer (P 401, Feb–1 July 1968), *Ghadunfar* (P 402, May–1 July 1968), *Hazza* (P 403, May–1 July 1968), *Durgham* (P 404, Sept 1968, 7.6.69), *Timsah* (P 405, Sept 1968–7.6.69), *Murayjib* (P 406, Feb–7 July 1970)
Glass fibre hull construction, built by Keith Nelson, Bembridge. Old sources give range 150nm at 12kts. Transferred to Ministry of Interior (Marine Police), July 1977. All extant 1982.

Fairey Marine 'SPEAR' class *coastal patrol craft*

Particulars:	As Qatar

Six units (names unknown). Glass fibre hull. Belong to police. Order placed in Feb 1974. Built by Fairey Marine, Hamble. Delivered between July 1974 and Jan 1975 – 5 to Abu Dhabi, one to Dubai. Armed with 2 MG. Extant 1982.

NOTE:
UAE also operates a Fairey Marine 'Interceptor' class craft, 10 Watercraft P 1200 class craft and 4 20ft coastal patrol craft. 6 Watercraft 45ft Mk II type craft were on order in 1982 and should be delivered in 1983.

Yemen

Both states of Yemen – the smaller but almost four times richer and populated Yemen Arab Republic (North) and the People's Democratic Republic of Yemen (South, formerly Aden) – have very small naval forces with limited coastal patrol capability and a few hundred men. Frequent attempts to unify the Yemen have failed. The vessels in service are mainly of Soviet origin. They seem not to have featured in the 1971–73 and 1979 border fighting between the two countries.

Since the British left Aden in 1967, the USSR has been using the facilities there, thus establishing a Middle Eastern base. The island of Socotra is also used as a naval base by the USSR. South Yemen signed a friendship treaty with the USSR in 1979 which was ratified in 1980. The naval force of the People's Democratic Republic of Yemen is the slightly larger of the two with four old minesweepers used for patrolling, two 'Osa' missile boats and some MTBs or patrol craft. Yemeni navies are of negligible importance in the Red Sea. The Yemen Arab Republic has her main naval base at Hodeida and personnel amounts to 300 three-year conscript officers and men. The People's Democratic Republic of Yemen uses the base at Aden and one at Mukalla; 950 two-year conscript officers and men make up the Navy.

YEMEN ARAB REPUBLIC (NORTH)

Ex-Soviet 'P 4' type *fast attack craft (torpedo)*

Four built in the mid-1950s and transferred in late 1960s. One has since been discarded.

Ex-Soviet 'POLUCHAT 1' type *large patrol craft*

Four transferred in 1970s to support the 'P 4' type MTBs. Stern ramps for recovering torpedoes. Also used for patrol work.

'BROADSWORD' class *coastal patrol craft*

Displacement:	91t standard; 110t full load
Dimensions:	105ft × 20ft 7in × 6ft 3in
	32.0m × 6.3m × 1.9m
Machinery:	3 shafts, 3 GM 16V71 T1 diesels, 3200hp = 28kts. Oil 16.3t
Armament:	2–23mm (1×2), 2–14.5mm (1×2), 2–12.7mm MG (2×1)
Sensors:	Radar Decca 914
Complement:	14–20

Class (no):
Sana'a ((200), *13th June* (300), *25th September* (400)
Ordered in 1977, built by Halter Marine, New Orleans, USA in 1978. Soviet armament was added after delivery.

Soviet 'ZHUK' type *coastal patrol craft*

Two built in 1978 and transferred in the same year. Unlike other units of this class, the North Yemeni units have their twin AA guns in enclosed gunhouses with hemispherical covers.

Ex-Soviet 'T 4' type *landing craft*

Transferred c1970 and resemble US Navy's LCM(6) type.

PEOPLE'S DEMOCRATIC REPUBLIC OF YEMEN (SOUTH)

Ex-Soviet 'T 58' type *ocean minesweeper (corvette)*

Used as escort vessel with her minesweeping gear removed. Built in late 1950s and transferred in 1978.

Ex-Soviet 'OSA II' type *fast attack craft (missile)*

Six transferred in pairs (2.4.79, Jan 1980, Dec 1980) and a seventh in Jan 1982.

Ex-Soviet 'P 6' type *fast attack craft (torpedo)*

Two, pennant nos 111 and 112, transferred in 1971. Now in poor condition and out of service. Replaced by 'MOL' type.

Ex-Soviet 'MOL' type *fast attack craft (torpedo)*

Two transferred in 1978. Based on 'Osa' type FAC. Sisters are in the Somali and Sri Lankan navies.

Ex-Soviet 'SO 1' type *large patrol craft*

Two transferred in April 1972. Reportedly in bad condition.

Ex-Soviet 'POLUCHAT 1' type *large patrol craft*

One transferred from USSR in early 1970s. May be used as a torpedo retriever or patrol boat.

Ex-Soviet 'ZHUK' type *coastal patrol craft*

Two transferred by the USSR in Feb 1975.

British 'TRACKER-2' class *patrol boats*

Displacement:	31t full load
Dimensions:	19.25m × 4.98m × 0.8m
Machinery:	2 shafts, 2 MTU 8V331 TC diesels, 2200hp = 29kts. Range 650nm at 25kts
Armament:	1–20mm
Complement:	11

Five ordered in Aug 1977 from Fairey Marine, UK for delivery in 1977–78. Used for customs duties. Belong to Ministry of Interior.

Ex-British 'HAM' class *inshore minesweepers*

Class (former names):
Jihla (ex-*Al Saqr*, ex-*Bodenham*), *Socotra* (ex-*Al Dairak*, ex-*Blunham*), *Zinqahar* (ex-*Al Ghazala*, ex-*Elsenham*)
Built in 1956 by British private yards. Transferred on independence in 1967. Renamed after local islands in 1975.

Ex-Soviet 'POLNOCNY B' type *landing ships*

Four medium landing ships of the numerous and successful Polnocny type 'B' version. Built in Poland by Stocznia Pólnocna, Gdańsk. Two delivered in Aug 1973, one in July 1977 and one in 1979.

Ex-Soviet 'ROPUCHA' class *landing ship*

Polish-built after 1975 and transferred 1980.

Ex-Soviet 'T 4' type *landing craft*

Three similar to US LCM(6) type, transferred in Nov 1970.

Bulgaria

During the closing stages of World War II Bulgaria fell into the Soviet sphere of influence and the Bulgarian Army came under Soviet command. The Soviet troops' presence and a strong pro-Russian sentiment in the country were the major factors which enabled the Communists to seize power more easily than in other countries of the recently emerged Soviet bloc. After the peace treaty with the Allies was signed and the new constitution had come into force, the Soviet troops left Bulgaria at the close of 1947 and remodelling of the country on Soviet lines began. Nationalisation of private industry was started immediately, collectivisation of peasant holdings was pursued while industrialisation became one of the principal aims of economic policy regardless of the lack of raw materials and of technically educated manpower for heavy industry.

By 1950 the strict Stalinist course was adopted throughout and in May that year a new Army command was formed with a Soviet officer of Bulgarian origin taking the post of Minister of National Defence and C-in-C of the armed forces. With the help of Soviet advisers the armed forces were equipped and reorganised on the Soviet model. By 1953 they numbered about 220,000 despite the peace treaty limitations. The treaty of 10 February 1947 ordered a considerable reduction of the Bulgarian armed forces as compared with their pre-war status: maximum permitted strength included an Army of 55,000, an Air Force of up to 90 aircraft (with no bombers) while the tonnage limitation for the Navy was set at 7250t with personnel not exceeding 3500. Despite the spectacular build-up of the Army, the naval forces were not so successful as the Soviet Black Sea Fleet had few resources to spare for her ally at that time. However, because of evident neglect of the Bulgarian Navy one 35-year-old *Novik* class destroyer (ordered for the Imperial Russian Navy), 3 war-built *M* class coastal submarines and 4 ex-German *M-boats* of 1935 type were transferred from the Soviet Union to form the nucleus of the 'People's Navy'.

After Stalin's death the country gained a considerable margin of freedom. In 1955 Bulgaria joined the Warsaw Pact and the armed forces were reduced by 45,000 while supplies of modern equipment began to arrive. During the late 1950s one war-built *Ognevoi* class destroyer as well as a number of modern vessels – 2 'Whiskey' class submarines, 2 'Riga' class frigates, 8 'P 4' type MTBs, 2 'Kronstadt' class patrol craft – were purchased in the Soviet Union. In December 1959 command of the armed forces was taken over by a Bulgarian officer and Soviet advisers were withdrawn. However Bulgaria remained one of the Warsaw Pact countries most closely linked with the Soviet Union and unlike Romania – the second Soviet ally on the Black Sea – was entrusted with large modern submarines which could, if necessary, be used against shipping in the Mediterranean. In 1969 four Bulgarian surface warships passed the Turkish Straits for the first time since the war while a decade later combined naval exercises were carried out in the Mediterranean with units of the Soviet Navy.

There were a few additions to the Bulgarian Navy during the 1960s but the period after the Bulgarian Army's participation in the Czechoslovakia intervention was marked by a considerable increase as 2 'Romeo' class submarines, 4 'Osa' class missile craft, 4 'Shershen' class torpedo craft, 4 'Vanya' class minesweepers and 18 'Vydra' class landing craft were transferred from the Soviet Union. Although metallurgy and engineering were well developed as a result of enforced industrialisation the shipbuilding facilities at Varna concentrated on merchant construction only. Therefore the Bulgarian Navy still had to rely only on Soviet supplies and those in the late 1970s comprised 3 'Poti' class corvettes, additional 'Osa' class missile craft, 4 inshore minesweepers as well as 3 patrol craft and a number of LCUs which were reported recently.

Strength of the Bulgarian Navy in 1982: 2 submarines, 2 frigates, 3 corvettes; 4 missile craft; 6 torpedo craft; 6 subchasers; 10 minesweepers; 4 minesweeping boats; 27 landing craft and about 44 auxiliaries. Bulgaria's navy is 10,000 men strong (4000 at sea, 2000 coast defence for 2 regiments with 20 gun batteries and 2 missile battalions, 1000 training, 3000 ashore) and bases are at Varna, Atiya, Burgas and Sozopol. Service is for three years and reserves total 25,000.

FLEET STRENGTH 1947
TORPEDO BOATS

Name	Launched	Disp	Fate
Drski class			
DRSKI	1907	98t	Preserved 1955
KHRABRY	1907	98t	BU 1952–55
STROGI	1907	98t	BU 1952–55

Used for escort service during the war. *Drski* was landed in 1955 and exhibited at Varna.

MTBs

Name	Launched	Disp	Fate
German S 2 class			
F 1–F 4	1939	47.8t	Deleted after 1947
Ex-Dutch T 52 class			
I–III	c1941	30t	Deleted after 1947

German S 2 class
Seized by the Soviets in Sept 1944 and commissioned as *TKA 958–961*. Returned in 1945.

Ex-Dutch T 52 class
Seized by the Soviets in Sept 1944 and commissioned as *TKA 962–964*. Returned in 1945.

PATROL CRAFT

Name	Launched	Disp	Fate
Ex-US SC 1916 type			
BELOMOREC	1917	77t	Deleted late 1950s
CHERNOMOREC	1917	77t	Deleted late 1950s
Ex-Soviet Artillerist class			
I–II	1940s	240t	Deleted c1965

Ex-US SC 1916 type
Seized by the Soviets in Sept 1944 and commissioned as the guard boats *SKA 757–758*. Returned in 1945.

Ex-Soviet Artillerist class
Transferred from the Soviet Union in 1947.

MAJOR SURFACE SHIPS

Ex-Soviet NOVIK class *destroyer*

No	Name	Builder	Launched	Fate
	ZHELEZNYAKOV (ex-*Petrovskij*, ex-*Korfu*)		1925	BU 1956

Transferred in 1949 and commissioned into the Bulgarian Navy under her Soviet name. Exchanged for a *Ognevi* class destroyer.

Ex-Soviet OGNEVOI class *destroyer*

No	Name	Builder	Launched	Fate
	GEORGI DYMITROV (ex-*Ozornoi*)	61 Kommunar Yd	1941	BU 1967 (?)

Transferred 1956 as a replacement for *Zheleznyakov*. She was refitted in 1961 then returned to the Soviet Union in 1967.

Ex-Soviet 'RIGA' class *frigates*

No	Name	Builder	Acquired	Fate
15	DRUSKI	USSR	1957–58	Extant 1982
16	SMELY	USSR	1957–58	Extant 1982

Transferred 1957–58. Refitted 1980–81. Two additional ships *Khrabry* and *Strogi* reported originally but this proved to be incorrect.

SUBMARINES

Ex-Soviet 'M' class *submarines*

Class:
M 1–M 3
   Three units of the Series XII bis transferred in the early 1950s; commissioned as *M 1–3*. Two units exchanged for two 'Whiskey' class boats in 1958; remaining unit deleted in 1967 and probably returned to the USSR.

Ex-Soviet 'WHISKEY' class *submarines*

Class:
Pobeda, Slava
Transferred 1958; given Bulgarian names. Deleted late 1970s.

Ex-Soviet 'ROMEO' class *submarines*

Class (no):
Pobeda (13), *Slava* (14)
   Acquired 1972–73. Took on names of decommissioned 'Whiskey' class. Extant 1982.

AMPHIBIOUS WARFARE VESSELS

D 3 type *landing craft*

Displacement:	420t
Dimensions:	164ft × 20ft 4in × 6ft 6¾in
	50.0m × 6.2m × 2.0m
Speed:	10kts
Armament:	1–37mm

Nine were built during 1954 in Bulgaria to design based on that of German war-built *MFP*s. Some of them were unarmed. Extant 1982.

Ex-Soviet 'VYDRA' class *landing craft*

Class:
421–428 + 10
   A total of 18 craft transferred since 1970. Only eight numbers known. All were in service in 1982. Fitted with Spin Trough radar.

Ex-Soviet LCU type *landing craft*

An unknown number of such craft were transferred from the Soviet Union in 1979.

SMALL SURFACE COMBATANTS

Ex-Soviet 'POTI' class *corvettes*

Class:
33, 34, 35
Transferred Dec 1975 as replacements for 'Kronstadt' patrol craft, numbers of which were given to the first two replacement boats. Extant 1982.

Ex-Soviet 'P 4' type *fast attack craft (torpedo)*

Eight boats of this type were transferred from the Soviet Union in 1956. Four of them were deleted *c*1975 and the remaining boats were all deleted by 1980.

Ex-Soviet 'OSA I & II' class *fast attack craft (missile)*

Class:
20–24
Four acquired 1970–81 (*21–24*). The fifth craft of the 'Osa II' design was transferred *c*1975 and commissioned as *20*. With the exception of *24* which was deleted in 1978, the others remained extant 1982.

Ex-Soviet 'SHERSHEN' class *fast attack craft (torpedo)*

Class:
25–30
First four acquired 1970–71 and followed by two additional craft later. Extant 1982.

Ex-Soviet 'KRONSTADT' class *large patrol craft*

Class:
33, 34
Transferred in 1957 and commissioned as *33* and *34*. Both deleted in 1975 and replaced by 'Poti' class corvettes to which their numbers were assigned.

Ex-Soviet 'SO I' type *submarine chasers*

Class:
41–46
Transferred in 1963–64 and commissioned as *41* to *46*. Extant 1982.

Ex-Soviet 'ZHUK' class *coastal patrol craft*

Five transferred 1980–81.

MINE WARFARE VESSELS

Ex-German M-boat 1935 type *ocean minesweepers*

Four assigned to the Soviet Union after the war, were transferred to Bulgaria in the 1950s, Deleted *c*1962.

Ex-Soviet 'T 43' type *ocean minesweepers*

Class:
47–48
   Transferred from the Soviet Union in 1953. One deleted and cannibalised for parts, the remaining pair with numbers *48* and *49* extant in 1982.

Ex-Soviet 'T 301' class *inshore minesweepers*

Four were purchased in the Soviet Union in 1955. Three were deleted in 1974, one in 1975.

Ex-Soviet 'VANYA' class *inshore minesweepers*

Class:
36–39
Two pairs transferred in 1970 and 1971 respectively and commissioned as *36* to *39*. Extant 1982.

Ex-Soviet 'YEVGENYA' class *inshore minesweepers*

Four were purchased in the Soviet Union in the late 1970s. Extant 1982.

Ex-Soviet 'PO 2' type *minesweeping boats*

Twenty-four boats were transferred from the Soviet Union during 1957–60, although it is possible that they were at least assembled in Bulgaria at that time. Half deleted by 1976, eight further units by 1980. Only four remained in service in 1980 and it is possible they may have been deleted by 1982.

Czechoslovakia

After the war Czechoslovakia, freed from Axis occupation mainly by the Red Army, was rebuilt within the pre-1938 boundaries (with the exception of Transcaucasian Ukraine which was incorporated into the Soviet Union) while her internal affairs were remodelled on the Soviet pattern. Being a landlocked country, Czechoslovakia does not maintain any navy; about 1200 Army personnel operate a small riverine detachment on the Danube. This force was rebuilt after the war and its strength consisted of 20 armed launches in 1982. Since 1955 the country has been a member of the Warsaw Pact. Her small merchant fleet operates from Szczecin (Stettin) in Poland.

East Germany

The German Democratic Republic was proclaimed on 7 October 1949 and the Soviet Military Administration formally transferred power to it, being replaced by the Soviet Control Commission. In February 1950 the military *Seepolizei* (Sea Police) was formed under the Ministry of Interior and in May that year the first flotilla, consisting of the former Danish fishery protection vessel *Hvidbjörnen*, 6 *R*-boats and probably some *Flugsicherungsboote* returned by the Soviets, was commissioned. Construction of 48 *Sperber* class patrol boats was also begun in local yards.

A reduction of reparations by 50 per cent and admission to the COMECON in 1950 benefitted the country economically. An ambitious five-year plan was drawn up in 1951, designed to double industrial production by 1955. In 1952 all military police units were united into the *Kasernierte Volkspolizei* (Quartered People's Police) and the *Seepolizei* became a part of that formation. The *Seepolizei*'s first large ships, namely 6 'Habicht' class minesweepers, were ordered and series construction of over 50 *Delphin/Tümmler* class patrol boats was begun.

After Stalin's death in 1953 the Control Commission was abolished which encouraged the Germans, already under pressure to fulfil the plan, to rise against the authorities in June. Only intervention by Soviet troops restored order; however the government decided to revise economic policy. The Soviets announced an end to the collection of reparations as well as cancellation of debts and reduction of the cost of the Soviet occupied forces. In March 1954 it was announced by the Soviet Union that East Germany was a sovereign state and the following year she was included in the Warsaw Pact. At that time the *Seepolizei* comprised 6 'Habicht' class minesweepers and c100 patrol boats built locally (1950–53) plus ships returned by the Soviets. After completion of this initial programme a further 6 improved 'Habicht' class minesweepers and 50 'Schwalbe' class minesweeping boats were ordered. After the creation of the National Volksarmee (NVA) in January 1956 the *Seepolizei* was transformed into the *Seestreikrafte* (Naval Force). By 1960 this force was increased considerably by the inclusion of 5 'Riga' class frigates (one was burnt out shortly after transfer), 27 'P 6' type MTBs and 16 'SO 1' type subchasers delivered by the Soviet Union as well as 10 'Krake' class minesweepers. From 1957 onwards ships of the *Seestreikrafte* participated in combined naval exercises with units of the Polish Navy and the Soviet Baltic Fleet.

In November 1960 the *Seestreikrafte* was transformed into the *Volksmarine* (People's Navy) and ships were given names instead of the numbers originally carried. The *Volksmarine* was now experiencing shortages of trained sailors. Its role widened in 1961 when, after the erection of the Berlin Wall, the Navy was given full responsibility for direct protection of the sea border and patrol craft of the Frontier Guard were transferred to it. In 1962 an 18-month conscription period had to be introduced. The construction programme could be realised without interruption and by the mid-1960s the Peenewerft Yard at Wolgast had delivered c45 'Robbe' class landing ships and 12 'Labo' landing craft. The enlargement of the *Volksmarine* was completed with transfer of 12 'Osa' class missile craft from the Soviet Union.

The *Volksmarine* began its first modernisation programme in 1969. With the exception of missile craft (another three added in 1976) almost all types were replaced by new ones. New construction included 32 'Libelle' class MTBs, 55 small 'Kondor' class minesweepers, 18 'Bremse' class patrol craft and 14 'Frosch' class landing ships (3 further units were under construction at that time). At least 2 further *Eidechse* class landing ships were under construction in 1980 as well as *Parchim* class corvettes which will replace the 'Hai' class subchasers. Moreover 18 'Shershen' class torpedo craft and recently 2 'Koni' class missile frigates were acquired from the Soviet Union to complete the programme.

The *Volksmarine* which had ranked third among the navies of the Warsaw Pact will find its position considerably improved after completion of the present programme. Its chief wartime missions are control of the western Baltic and seizing of the Danish Straits in close cooperation with the other Warsaw Pact navies operating in that area.

The strength of the *Volksmarine* in 1982 was 2 missile frigates; 6 missile corvettes, 15 missile craft; 18 torpedo craft; 42 light MTBs; 9 subchasers; 18 patrol craft; 55 minesweepers, 14 landing ships, a helicopter squadron and about 83 auxiliaries. They were manned by 16,000 sailors including 3000 in the Frontier Guard sea branch. Reserves numbered 25,000. Nearly all the officers, half the petty officers and 20 per cent of the ratings are members of the Socialist Unity (Communist) Party. Bases are Rostock-Gehlsdorf (Navy HQ), Peenemünde (HQ 1st Flotilla), Warnemünde (HQ 4th Flotilla), Dranske-Bug (HQ 6th Flotilla) plus minor ports at Sassnitz, Wolgast and Tarnewitz. Some 2270 E German servicemen were serving in 6 African and 3 Middle East countries; it is not known how many of these are from the Navy.

MAJOR SURFACE SHIPS

Ex-Danish HVIDBJORNEN *fishery protection vessel*

Armament: 1–85mm, 2–37mm (1×2), 4–25mm (2×2) (after refit)
Complement: 40 + 80 cadets
Other particulars: As Danish *Hvidbjörnen*

No	Name	Builder	Acquired	Fate
	ERNST THAELMANN (ex-*Dorsch*, ex-*Hvidbjörnen*)	Copenhagen N Yd	1950	BU 1968

Built for the Royal Danish Navy as the fishery protection vessel *Hvidbjörnen* (launched 1928). Scuttled 29.8.43 in the Great Belt, raised and pressed into the *Kriegsmarine* then seized by the Soviets in 1945. Transferred to the *Seepolizei* in 1950 and commissioned as the coast defence ship *Dorsch*. Refitted in 1953/4 at the Neptun Yd, Rostock and renamed *Ernst Thälmann* after the German Communist leader murdered by the Nazis. Relegated to training duties only later on and renamed *Albin Köbis* again in 1960 as her former name was transferred to the 'Riga' class frigate. Hulked in 1963 and scrapped in 1968.

Ex-Soviet 'RIGA' class *frigates*

No	Name	Builder	Acquired	Fate
121	ERNST THAELMANN	USSR	Dec 1956	Stricken 1977
122	KARL MARX	USSR	Dec 1956	Stricken 1976
123	FRIEDRICH ENGELS	USSR	1959	Stricken 1968
124	KARL LIBKNECHT	USSR	1959	Stricken 1968

Initially 2 frigates of the 'Riga' class were transferred from the Soviet Union in Dec 1956 and commissioned as coast defence ships *1–61* and *1–62*. Renumbered *KSS 40* and *KSS 41* in 1959 (KSS stands for *Küstenschutzschiffe* = coast defence ship) and 3 additional ships were transferred in that year. Two of them were commissioned as *KSS 42* to *KSS 43* while the fifth ship damaged by explosion burnt out in Rostock soon after transfer. The remaining ships were again renumbered *KSS 401* and *KSS 404* and on 3.11.1960 received the above class names.

Soviet 'KONI' class *frigates*

No	Name	Builder	Acquired	Fate
141	ROSTOCK	Zelenodolsk SY	25.7.78	Extant 1982
142	BERLIN	Zelenodolsk SY	10.5.79	Extant 1982

First export versions of this class, more may follow.

Rostock 1982   *USN*

AMPHIBIOUS WARFARE VESSELS

'Robbe' class early 1970s

'ROBBE' class landing ships

Displacement:	600t standard; 950t full load
Dimensions:	213ft 3in × 37ft 9in × 6ft 6in
	65.0m × 11.5m × 2.0m
Machinery:	2 diesel engines, 4800bhp = 12kts
Armament:	2–57mm (1×2), 4–25mm (2×2), 14 tanks

Class:
Eberswalde, Eisenhüttenstadt, Grimmen, Hoyerswerda, Lübben, Lübbenau, Schwedt, VIII to X

Ten built by Peenewerft Yd, Wolgast in 1962–64. Could carry 500t of stores or vehicles. Seven deleted 1978, 2 in 1979, 1 in 1980.

'Frosch' class as completed

'FROSCH' class landing ships

Displacement:	1950t standard; 4000t full load
Dimensions:	298ft 4in × 36ft 1in × 9ft 2in
	91.0m × 11.0m × 2.8m
Machinery:	2 shafts, 2/40D diesel engines, 9500bhp = 18kts
Armament:	4–57mm/70 (2×2), 4–30mm/65 (2×2), 12 tanks (Type II)
	650t of load, 40 (Type II 36) mines
Sensors:	Type I: Radar Muff Cob, Strut Curve, Don, Square Head, High Pole
	Type II: Radar Don
	Type II: 73
Complement:	

Class (no):
Cottbus (614), *Eberswalde-Finow, Eisenhüttenstadt, Frankfurt/Oder, Hoyerswerda* (634), *Neubrandenburg, Schwerin, Sieger* (631), and 2 others, *Nordperd* (E 35), *Südperd* (E 36)

Built during 1975–79 by the Peenewerft Yd, Wolgast, to a design similar to that of the bigger Soviet 'Ropucha' class. Numbered 611–616, 631–636. The biggest ships of the *Volksmarine*, have no bow doors fitted, only the ramp and the stern doors in addition. First seen in the Baltic in 1976. At least one of the first series has had two 40-barrel MBU 2500 122mm RLs installed in a superfiring position above the forward 57mm turret. The series II ships (last 2) were fitted to act as fast landing transports with the radar outfit reduced and large crane mounted amidships. All extant 1982.

'LABO' class landing craft

Displacement:	150t standard; 285t full load
Dimensions:	131ft 2in × 27ft 9in × 5ft 9in
	40.0m × 8.5m × 1.8m
Machinery:	2 shafts, 4 diesels, 480bhp = 10kts
Armament:	4–25mm (2×2), 3 tanks
Complement:	15

Class:
Gerhard Prenzler, Heinz Wilkowski, Rolf Peters, IV to XII

Built at Peenewerft Yd, Wolgast and launched 1961–63. Ten deleted 1978, last 2 in 1979.

'Labo' class
Twardowski Collection

'Frosch' class
Twardowski Collection

SMALL SURFACE COMBATANTS

Parchim as completed

PARCHIM class corvettes

Displacement:	960t standard; 1300t full load
Dimensions:	252ft 7in × 29ft 6in × 11ft 6in
	77.0m × 9.0m × 3.5m
Machinery:	3-shaft diesels, 20,000bhp = 27kts
Armament:	2 SA-N-5 SAM (2×4), 2–57mm (1×2), 2–30mm (1×2), 2 RBU-6000 ASW RL (2×12), 4–400mm TT (4×1), mines, 2 chaff RL (2×16)
Sensors:	Radar Strut Curve, TSR-333, High Pole, Muff Cob; sonar M/F hull-mounted; ECM Watch Dog
Complement:	60 or 80

Class (no, completed):
Parchim (17, 9.4.81), *Perleberg* (45, 3.9.81), *Lübz, Wismar, V, VI*

Launched 1979–80. Construction of this class which was designated 'Balcom 4' by NATO and 'Koralle' by the Press, begun c1978–79 as a replacement for the 'Hai' class. The design, similar to the Soviet 'Grisha' class, departed from the previous type with greatly increased displacement and diesel propulsion only adopted. Built by Peenewerft Yd in Wolgast. Named after cities. Six extant 1982 with another 6 building.

FORELLE class experimental MTBs

Displacement:	55t
Dimensions:	88ft 7in × 20ft
	27.0m × 6.1m
Machinery:	2 shafts, 2 diesels, 5000bhp = 40kts
Armament:	2–25mm, 2–15mm, 2–533mm TT

Experimental boats, one built by the Schiffswerft, Roslau in 1956 and possibly followed by another two from the Peenewerft Yd, Wolgast. Transferred to Frontier Guard in 1960s, deleted c1970.

Ex-Soviet 'P 6' type fast attack craft (torpedo)

Class:
Adam Kuckhoff, Anton Saefkow, Arthur Becker, Bernhard Bästlein, Bruno Kühn, Erich Kuttner, Fiete Schulz, Fritz Behn, Fritz Heckert, Fritz Riedel, Hanno Günter, Hans Beimler, Hans Coppi, Heinz Kapelle, Herbert Balzer, John Schehr, Josef Römer, Max Roscher, Otto Engert, Rudolf Breitscheid, Willi Bänsch, Willi Sachse, Wolfgang Thiess

The first 9 of these craft were transferred from the Soviet Union in Oct/Nov 1957 and commissioned with numbers *821* to *829* which were changed to *5–61* to *5–69* soon afterwards. A total of 27 boats were transferred by 1959 and numbered in that series. Renumbered in 1959 as *TS 101* to *TS 109*, *TS 201* to *TS 209* and *TS 301* to *TS 309* (TS stands for *Torpedoschnellsboote* = Fast Torpedo Craft). They were given names in 1961, of these the above were reported. Deleted between 1968–78, and scrapped subsequently or converted to patrol boats and target boats.

'P 6' class   *Twardowski Collection*

'Iltis' class ('C' type)   *Author's Collection*

'Libelle' class   *Twardowski Collection*

Ex-Soviet 'OSA I' class *fast attack craft (missile)*

Class (no):
Albert Gast (S 711), *Albin Köbis* (S 713), *Arvid Harnack*, *August Lüttgens* (733), *Friedrich Schulze* (S 712), *Fritz Gast* (754), *Heinrich Dorrenbach*, *Josef Schares*, *Karl Meseberg* (732), *Max Reichpietsch* (S 714), *Otto Tost*, *Paul Eisenschneider* (734), *Paul Wieczorek* (751), *Richard Sorge* (753), *Rudolf Egelhofer* (752), *Walter Kramer*

A dozen units of the 'Osa 1' class were transferred from the Soviet Union between 1964–68, followed by 3 'Osa II' units in 1976. S denotes training boats.

'Iltis' class ('B' type)
NB 1/750 scale

'ILTIS' class *fast attack craft (torpedo)*

Displacement:	25t standard; 30t full load
Dimensions:	47ft 7in × 10ft 4in × 2ft 8in
	14.5m × 3.1m × 0.8m
Machinery:	2 shafts, 2 diesels, 3000bhp = 45kts
Armament:	2–533mm TT (see notes)
Complement:	3

Design based on the German war-built *LS* class light MTBs intended primarily to operate from commerce raiders. Prototypes were ordered in June 1958 in four yards simultaneously; each had to use various hull materials and construction techniques. Peenewerft Yd and Rosslauer Schiffswerft prepared hulls of aluminium alloy, Yachtwerft Berlin built wooden hulls with aluminium alloy frames. The fourth hull designed by the Boots and Reparaturwerft Greifswald was to be made of GRP but did not get further than the planning stage. Trials began in 1961 and series construction was awarded to Pennewerft. At least three design variations were known, the most popular being 'B' type with the flush deck, while 'C' type had the stern cut down at a certain height to compensate weight of the third TT. The stern-firing TTs of all the types were removable, to carry mines instead or accommodate landing parties. A total of *c*45 boats were built (1962–65) and commissioned with numbers in 970 series. Deletion of the first of them began in the mid-1970s, 25 were deleted in 1978, 5 in 1979 and 10 in 1980.

Ex-Soviet 'SHERSHEN' class *fast attack craft (torpedo)*

Class (no):
Max Hoop (811), *Willi Bäntsch* (812), *Arvid Harnack* (813), *Bernhard Bästlein* (814), *Fritz Behn* (815), *Wilhelm Florin* (831), *Erich Kuttner* (832), *Artur Becker* (833), *Fritz Heckert* (834), *Ernst Schneller* (835), *Edgar André* (851), *Joseph Roemer* (852), *Heinz Biemler* (853), *Heinz Kapelle* (854), *Adam Kuckhoff* (855), *Rudolf Breitscheid* (S 814), *Ernst Grube*, *Fiete Schulze* (S 815), *Bruno Kühn* (S 816)

First 4 transferred 1968–69, last 3 in 1976. All 18 extant 1982. S denotes training boat.

'LIBELLE' class *fast attack craft (torpedo)*

Displacement:	30t standard
Dimensions:	64ft 3in × 14ft 9in × 3ft 3in
	19.6m × 4.5m × 1.0m
Machinery:	3 shafts, 3 MSO F4 diesels, 3600bhp = 40kts
Armament:	2–533mm TT (stern), 2–15mm (1×2), mines
Sensors:	Radar TSR-333
Complement:	10

Class:
Karl Baier, Fritz Globig and *c*30 others

An improvement on the 'Iltis' class design built since 1973. The hull was built up higher, so the TTs could be covered which allowed emplacement of double AA MGs. The boats can be used for minelaying and commando/frogmen duties as well. Prototype built during the early 1970s and at least 32 boats were completed by 1980 and commissioned with numbers 911–915, 921–925, 931–935, 941–945, 951–955, 961–965; a further training unit with number unknown. Extant 1982.

'SO 1' prototype
NB 1/750 scale

'SO 1' *experimental submarine chaser*

Displacement:	*c*300t?
Dimensions:	163ft 1in × 19ft 8in × 7ft 3in
	49.7m × 6.0m × 2.2m
Machinery:	3-shaft CODAG: 2 diesels + 1 gas turbines = 25kts. See notes
Armament:	4–25mm (2×2), 4 MBU-1800 ASW RL, 2 DC racks (see notes)

Built 1957–61. Had CODAG experimental power plant which after refinement was to be used in the 'Hai' class for which the 'SO 1' was the prototype. She was completed with two large flat funnels abreast and the turbine exhaust between them. Initially she carried no armament, later being fitted with guns only and finally ASW weapons were introduced. She could also carry a 45mm gun aft. Relegated to training duties after conclusion of trials and experiments.

Ex-Soviet 'SO 1' type *submarine chasers*

Class:
Adler, Bussard, Falke, Habicht, Hai, Kormoran, Kranich, Luchs, Möwe, Panther, Reiher, Schwalbe, Sperber, Tiger, Weihe, Wolf

Transferred from the Soviet Union between 1960–61. Deleted between 1972 and 1978 (4).

'HAI III' class *large patrol craft*

Displacement:	350t standard; 400t full load
Dimensions:	174ft 3in pp, 183ft 9in oa × 20ft 4in × 8ft 9in
	53.1m, 56.0m × 6.2m × 2.5m
Machinery:	3-shaft CODAG: 2 diesels, 4800bhp plus 1 gas turbine, 10,000shp = 25kts max. Range 1000nm at 18kts
Armament:	4–30mm (2×2), 4 RBU-1800 ASW RL (4×5), 2 DC rails (24 DC), mines (see notes)
Sensors:	Radar Pot Head, Drum Tilt, Square Head, High Pole A; sonar Tamir-II
Complement:	45

Class (no):
Bad Doberan (212), Bützow (244), Dirna (215), Gadebusch (211), Grevesmühlen (213), Ludwigslust (243), Lübz (246), Parchim, Perleberg (245), Ribnitz-Damgarter (216), Sternberg (242), Teterow (241), Wismar (214)

Built by the Peenewerft Yd, Wolgast, 1962–69 on the design developed from the 'SO 1' experimental boat. The turbine was used for short bursts of hunting speed; 25 boats had been planned but only 14 were completed finally. Ships of the initial series were armed with 4–25mm (2×2) guns and ASW weapons as above with no Drum Tilt radar fitted. Sometimes called corvettes. All extant except Dirna, Lübz, Perleberg and Wismar deleted c1982; Parchim deleted c1980 and converted to experimental boat V81.

SPERBER class coastal patrol craft

Displacement:	53t standard; 73t full load (Sperber II 56t, 76t)
Dimensions:	85ft 11in (Sperber II 96ft) × 16ft × 5ft
	26.2m (29.3m) × 4.9m × 1.5m
Machinery:	3 shafts, 3 Jumo diesels, 1800bhp = 21kts
Armament:	3–15mm, 10 DCs
Complement:	17

Class:
Sperber I, 3–11 to 3–18, 3–21 to 3–28, G 111, G 112, G 161, G 162, G 171, G 172, G 181, G 182; Sperber II, 3–31 to 3–38, 3–41 to 3–48, G 121, G 122, G 131, G 132, G 141, G 142, G 151, G 152

Sperber I class built at Engelbrecht Yd, Berlin and Sperber II class built at Peenewerft Yd, Wolgast between 1950–54. All deleted c1968.

DELPHIN/TÜMMLER class coastal patrol craft

Displacement:	60t
Dimensions:	95ft 1in × 13ft 8in × 3ft 7in
	29.0m × 4.2m × 1.1m
Machinery:	Delphin class: 3 shafts, 3 Jumo diesels, 1000bhp = 24kts
	Tümmler class: 2 shafts, 2 diesels, 240bhp = 12kts
Armament:	Delphin class: 2–25mm (2×1), 4 DCs
	Tümmler class: 4–15mm (2×2)
Complement:	13 or 14

Class:
Delphin class: 4–411 to 4–16, 4–21 to 4–26, 4–31 to 4–36, 4–41 to 4–46, 4–91 to 4–99

Tümmler class: G 111 to G 334

Both classes built 1953–54 at Engelbrecht Yd, Berlin. All deleted by the early 1970s.

'BREMSE' class coastal patrol craft

Displacement:	25t
Dimensions:	76ft 5in × 16ft 4in × 3ft 7in
	23.3m × 5.0m × 1.1m
Machinery:	2 shafts, 2 diesels, 1000bhp = 14kts
Armament:	2–14.5mm MG (1×2)

Class:
GC 30–39

Ten or perhaps 18 built since 1971 for operations on river and inland waters by the Frontier Guard. Also called KB-123 class.

MINE WARFARE VESSELS

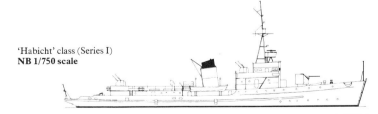

'Habicht' class (Series I)
NB 1/750 scale

'HABICHT' class minesweepers/minelayers

Displacement:	500t ('Habicht II' 550t)
Dimensions:	193ft 7in ('Habicht II' 213ft 3in) × 26ft 7in × 11ft 10in
	59.0m (65.0m) × 8.1m × 3.6m
Machinery:	2 shafts, 2 diesels, 2400bhp ('Habicht II' 2800bhp) = 17kts
Armament:	1–85mm, 8–25mm (4×2), 4 DCT, 18 ('Habicht II' 20) mines
Complement:	70 ('Habicht II' 80)

Class (yard, launched):
Series I: MLR 611 to MLR 613 (Volkswerft Yd, 1952), MLR 614 to MLR 616 (Peenewerft Yd, 1953–54)

'Habicht' class (Series II) after 1960s modernisation   Author's Collection

'Hai III' class   Author's Collection

Series II: MLR 621 to MLR 626 (Peenewerft Yd, 1954–56).

Neptun Yd, Rostock, based this design on the M 40 type but with diesel propulsion instead of the original steam. After the first six ships were completed the design was modernised. Most noticeable features being an extra 20ft section amidships and lattice mast erected to carry a more extensive radar outfit. The numbers previously carried were subject to frequent changes which include MLR 031 to MLR 036, then MLR 331 to MLR 336 and 6–31 to 6–36 for the first series as well as MLR 6–111 to MLR 6–116 and 6–71 to 6–74, 6–91, 6–92 for the second series. MLR stands for Minenleg und Räumboote = minelaying and minesweeping craft. MLR 6–33 sank in April 1958 off Sassnitz during a gale and was raised in 1959 but not returned to active service. In 1959 the numbers were changed again (MLR 181 to MLR 184 were known) and in March 1961 the ships received names Cottbus, Dresden, Greifswald, Neubrandenburg, Sassnitz, Schwerin, Stralsund, Suhl and Wolgast while the pair of the first series were converted into salvage vessels and received numbers R 21 and R 22. During the mid-1960s the second series ships underwent modernisation including additional electronics and replacing the 85mm gun with a twin 37mm.

In 1968 R 21 transferred to the GST for training duties and renamed Ernst Thälmann (deleted 1977) while the remainder of both series were deleted by 1972.

'Krake' class 1971

'KRAKE' class minesweepers/minelayers

Displacement:	650t
Dimensions:	229ft 4in × 26ft 7in × 12ft 2in
	70.0m × 8.1m × 3.7m
Machinery:	2 shafts, 2 diesels, 3400bhp = 18kts
Armament:	1–85mm, 10–25mm (5×2), 4 DCT, 30 mines
Complement:	90

'Krake' class   *Twardowski Collection*

Class:
MLR 6–17, MLR 6–37, MLR 6–41 to *MLR 6–47, MLR 6–91*

Built by Peenewerft Yd, Wolgast, the first four reportedly being designated for Poland, and launched 1957–58. Apparently being developed from the 'Habicht' class. In 1959 their numbers were changed (*MLR 321* to *MLR 324* were known) and in March 1961 they were given names *Berlin, Erfurt, Frankfurt/Oder, Gera, Halle, Karl-Marx-Stadt, Leipzig, Magdeburg, Potsdam* and *Rostock*. *Berlin, Rostock* and *Potsdam* were relegated to training duties while the remaining ships were deleted in the mid-1970s. The last 3 were deleted by 1981.

'Kondor' class (Series II)
NB 1/750 scale

'KONDOR' class *ocean minesweepers*

Displacement:	245t (Series II 310t) standard; 320t (400t) full load
Dimensions:	170ft 7in (II 182ft 1in) × 23ft 4in × 6ft 7in
	52.0m (55.5m) × 7.2m × 2.0m
Machinery:	2 shafts (CP propellers), 2/40D diesels, 4000bhp = 21kts (Series II c20kts)
Armament:	2 (Series II 6)–25mm (1(3)×2)
Sensors:	Radar TSR-333
Complement:	20 (Series II 24)

Class:
Series I: *Ahrenshoop* (G 421), *Anklam* (G 441), *Bergen* (G 412), *Demmin* (G 446), *Graal-Müritz, Griefswald* (G 413), *Kühlungsborn, Neustrelitz* (G 445), *Pasewalk* (G 414), *Prerow G 423, Uckermümde* (G 442), *Vitte* (G 426), *Weisswasser* (G 444), *Wolgast, Zingst* (G 425), *Hettstedt, Meissen* (G 416), *Rerik* (G 443), *Stendal* (G 411), *Zwickau* (G 422), *Prenzlau* (G 415)
Series II: *Altenburg* (311), *Altentreptow, Bansin, Bernau* (343), *Bitterfeld* (314), *Boltenhagen* (342), *Dessau* (316), *Eilenburg* (341), *Eisleben, Freiberg* (336), *Genthin* (312), *Gransee, Greiz* (335), *Grimma, Guben* (346), *Kamenz, Klütz* (325), *Kyritz* (321), *Meiningen* (333), *Neuruppin* (326), *Oranienburg, Poesnnick* (334), *Pritzwalk, Rathenow* (331), *Riesa* (345), *Röbel* (324), *Rosslau* (315), *Schönebeck* (S 321), *Sömmerda, Strasburg* (322), *Stralsund, Tangerhütte* (344), *Tangermünde, Templin, Timendorf* (323), *Torgau* (332), *Warnemünde, Wilhelm Pieckstadt, Wittstock* (S 322), *Zeitz, Zerbst* (313)

A total of 62 ships were built by the Peenewerft Yd, Wolgast as replacements for previous classes. The new design evidently departed from the previous policy being substantially smaller and having no minelaying capacity. Building began in 1968 and the prototype was ready by 1969; series production (5 in service 1970, 15 by end 1971) continued until 1980. Two versions of this class were known – the first one used for Frontier Guard duties with G pennant numbers and training (21 ships completed), the second one being 2m longer and having two additional twin 25mm mountings fitted abaft the funnel (41 ships built) served with minesweeping squadrons. On a base of the first

'Kondor' class (Series I)   *Author's Collection*

'Schwalbe' class   *Twardowski Collection*

series design 2 torpedo recovery vessels and 2 intelligence ships were built while one of the second series design was completed as the state yacht and one as a survey ship. *Pasewalk* was the prototype.

Ahrenshoop and *Anklam* transferred to the GST for training duties in 1977 and renamed *Ernst Thälmann*. All others extant 1982, pennant numbers as of 1982.

R 811–816 *minesweeping boats*

Six war-built *R-boats* of the *R 401* group were returned to the Soviets in 1950 and commissioned with the *Seepolizei*. The numbers were later changed to *7–61* to *7–66*. Two transferred to the GST for training duties, others deleted in the late 1950s.

'SCHWALBE' class *minesweeping boats*

Displacement:	50t
Dimensions:	93ft 10in × 14ft 9in × 4ft 11in
	28.6m × 4.5m × 1.5m
Machinery:	2 shafts, 2 diesels, 1080bhp = 17kts
Armament:	2–25mm (1×2)
Complement:	14

Class:
7–11 to *7–117, 7–21* to *17–27, 7–31* to *17–37, 7–41* to *17–47, 7–51* to *17–57, 7–91*

Built by the Engelbrecht Yd, Berlin during 1954–57; 36 were completed for naval service while an additional 14 unarmed boats went to the hydrographic service, numbered *D 01* to *D 14*. The boats were given names in 1961 and those reported were; *Aue, Born, Brandenburg, Burg, Calbe, Eisleben, Forst, Freiberg, Gotha, Görlitz, Guben, Güstrow, Greiz, Hagenow, Ilemenau, Luckenwalde, Meiningen, Meissen, Nauen, Pössneck, Prenzlau, Senftenberg, Sonnenberg, Stendal, Timmendorf, Torgau, Waren, Weimar, Weisswasser, Wurzen, Zeit* and *Zwickau*. Some of these transferred to coast guard duties and one, numbered *G 422*, sank in a 1962 collision. Two others were sold to Tanzania in 1966 while the remaining boats were deleted by the early 1970s.

Hungary

The armistice signed in January 1945 in Moscow ordered the return of territories seized during 1938–40, 300 million dollars reparations and access to the country's territory by units of the Soviet Army. Hungary was proclaimed a republic in 1946 and in 1947 the Communists seized power in the country following the disbanding of the Allied armistice commissions after signing the peace treaty in the same year. Internal affairs were modelled on the Soviet pattern and in 1955 the country became a member of the Warsaw Pact. In 1956 the Hungarian Revolution forced the government to establish a multiparty system and to announce on 1 November withdrawal from the Warsaw Pact. This resulted in Soviet invasion and a permanent Soviet presence which went unopposed by Western powers at the time. The Hungarian schism had been abolished but thorough economic reform now became possible and the country became the most prosperous of the COMECON states.

Being a landlocked country, Hungary maintained a flotilla on the Danube which at first operated 8 old craft (the 4 *Kecskemet* class 133t ships of 1915–16 were deleted in the 1950s, *Baja* in 1969; the 140t *Sopron* of 1918 also in the 1950s as were the 3 *Honved* class 17t minesweeping boats of 1916) originating from the Austro-Hungarian Danube Flotilla. They were replaced by 10 new 100t diesel-powered patrol craft (1–14.5mm MG) and 10 12t 8mm–armoured, 756bhp minesweeping boats (2 MG, 8 mines) during the 1950s. In 1969 it was officially stated that the flotilla had been disbanded; however, the

12t minesweeping boat   *Twardowski Collection*

country continues to operate about 45 river craft (5 small LCUs, tugs, icebreakers, transport barges and troopships up to 1000t as well as the two 1950s classes) under the Army Maritime Force, employing some 500 officers and men (2 years service).

Poland

The Polish Navy was re-established between 1945 and 1948 with the destroyer *Blyskawica*, 3 submarines, 4 minesweepers, 2 patrol craft and a sail training ship (all of Polish origin), 3 BYMS type minesweepers acquired in Britain and 9 minesweepers, 12 submarine-chasers and 2 MTBs delivered from the Soviet Union as *Kriegsmarine*, allocated as war reparations. The new state had a much longer outlet to the sea. After the possibilities of obtaining ships from external sources had dried up in 1948, a 20-year programme calling for a 44,000t navy was prepared; this was abandoned in 1950 by the Soviet officers in command (they were especially numerous in the Navy as its personnel had been the prewar sailors), in favour of the general rearmament programme authorised at that time. An order for 20 patrol boats was placed in Hungary, and the completion of two patrol craft built on unfinished hulls left by the Germans and the commissioning of 18 landing craft hitherto in civilian service was sanctioned. Furthermore, the old destroyer *Burza* was towed from Britain and refitted in 1952–55 as an AA defence ship. The most significant move, however, was the purchase of 6 'MV' class coastal submarines and 4 'Kronstadt' class patrol craft from the Soviet Union. The licence construction of 'T 43' type minesweepers (12 were built by 1960), 'TR 40' type river minesweepers and 'K 8' type minesweeping boats was also begun between 1954 and 1955.

The enforced rearmament programme resulted in economic breakdown and the serious food shortages experienced in 1952, so the tempo had to be slowed, but only with Stalin's death did both internal and international tensions decrease, the gradual withdrawal of Soviet officers take place and the halting of the programme (in 1955) come about. The Navy reverted to full Polish command after the Poznan riots of June 1956.

Between 1957 and 1970 the Navy was completely modernised and built up, thanks both to Soviet deliveries of warships and to the output of local yards. Personnel in 1958 numbered 10,000 and doubled by 1964. By the early 1960s Soviet transfers had comprised 2 *Skory* class destroyers, 20 'P 6' type MTBs and 4 'Kronstadt' class patrol craft, but from the early 1960s Poland's developing shipbuilding industry was able to supply an increasing number of locally designed and built craft: 12 *Orlik* class minesweepers, 12 'Oksywie'/'Gdansk' class patrol craft, 13 'Obluze' class patrol craft, 11 'Polnocny' class landing ships and 15 'Eichstaden' class landing craft, as well as some auxiliary units. In addition, 4 'Whiskey' class submarines, 12 'Osa' class missile craft and finally a 'Kotlin' class missile destroyer were purchased from the Soviet Union. This programme resulted in a considerable expansion of the Polish Navy, which became the second largest in the Warsaw Pact.

The unrest among the Baltic seaport cities during December 1970, caused by the failure of a closed and centrally controlled economy, recovered the population some of their traditional rights – unprecedented among Communist countries – while the economy was opened to the West and modernised, thanks to the credits obtained. The modernisation of the shipbuilding industry made possible the construction of more advanced warships, although auxiliaries were emphasised at first: 2 *Gryf* class training ships, 2 *Navigator* class intelligence ships, a 'Moma' class survey vessel and 2 *Piast* class salvage vessels, to mention the largest units. Many ships of these or similar types were built for the other Warsaw Pact navies and for Yugoslavia. Warships were also built and deliveries comprised 12 turbine-powered 'Wisla' class torpedo craft, 9 'Pilica' class patrol craft and 12 'Wisloka' class patrol boats, as well as 11 'Polnocny' class landing ships (in mass production for the Soviet Union since 1963) and 4 'Marabut' class landing craft (completed by 1980). According to official statements, conditions for further stages in the modernisation of the Navy, based on local production facilities, were created, as some of the existing craft evidently needed replacement.

After a few years of economic boom, achieved mainly through Western credits, the Polish economy demonstrated signs of crisis caused by poor investment policies. This led to a wave of strikes in August 1980 which resulted in government permission to form a workers' union independent of the party control and the announcing of further reforms. The repeated assurances of its adherence to Warsaw Pact obligations recently made by the Polish government would seem to exclude the eventual possibility of a schism similar to that which took place in Yugoslavia. Mounting demands for democracy and freedom in all spheres forced the Communist government to regain control by means of martial law in December 1981 and to withdraw liberal reforms. The dissatisfaction of the people and the ending of Western assistance have increased the economical breakdown of the country. In July 1983 martial law was lifted only to be replaced by stringent new legislation which leaves the Polish people as badly off as previously.

The strength of the Polish Navy in January 1982 was 1 missile destroyer; 4 submarines; 12 missile craft; 12 torpedo craft, 8 subchasers; 14 patrol craft; 21 patrol boats; 24 minesweepers; 20 minesweeping boats, 22 landing ships; 19 landing craft and about 84 auxiliaries. The Fleet was manned by 7500 sailors with 6000 ashore, 2000 training, 2000 in naval aviation (MiG 17s and helicopters) and 5000 for coast defence (34 ships). Principal bases were Gdynia, Hel and Swinoujscie. Service is for three years and a full admiral commands.

FLEET STRENGTH 1947

DESTROYERS

Name	Launched	Disp	Fate
Wicher class			
BURZA	16.4.29	1540t	BU 1977
Grom class			
BLYSKAWICA	1.10.36	2144t	Preserved 1976

Wicher class
Burza ('squall') served with the Polish Naval Detachment in Britain from 1939 to 1946. She was handed over to the RN in 1946 and not returned to Poland until 1951 because of her poor condition. Rebuilt 1952–55 in the Stocznia Komuny Paryskiej Yard, Gdynia, to serve as an AA defence ship, she was rearmed with 4–100mm (4×1), 8 (later reduced to 6)–37mm (4×2, later 2×2 + 2×1), 4 DCT and 1 double DC rack. The bridge was widened, the two after funnels were trunked into a single uptake, the TTs were removed and a large fire control platform was built up amidships. *Burza* was deleted from the active list on 24.2.60 and converted into a museum ship. In 1976 she was replaced in this role with *Blyskawica* and subsequently scrapped.

Blyskawica after 1961 refit   *Author's Collection*

Sep c 1950   *Twardowski Collection*

Grom class

Blyskawica ('lightning') served during the war with Polish Naval Detachment in Britain and was handed over to the RN in 1946. She was returned to Poland (Gdynia) in 1947, overhauled 1949–50 and had her 4in barrels replaced by 100mm guns to allow Soviet ammunition to be used. In addition she received 10–37mm (4×2, 2×1), 3–21in TT (1×3), 2 DCT (replaced by 4 new-pattern units during a 1957–61 refit) and 2 DC racks. Served as Navy flagship until the early 1960s.

SUBMARINES

Name	Launched	Disp	Fate
Wilk class			
RYS	22.4.29	980t	BU 1954
WILK	12.4.29	980t	BU 1951
ZBIK	14.6.29	980t	BU 1954
Orzel class			
SEP	17.10.38	1100t	Deleted 1970

Wilk class

Minelaying submarines. *Rys* ('lynx') and *Zbik* ('wild cat') were interned by the Swedes in Sept 1939 and returned to Gdynia on 25.10.45. *Wilk* ('Wolf') succeeded in reaching British waters in 1939 and remained there until 1951 when she was towed to Poland and scrapped owing to her poor condition.

Orzel class

Sep ('vulture') returned to Gdynia from Swedish internment on 25.10.45. During a 1946–47 refit the unfinished work was completed and her 105mm gun was replaced with a 100mm weapon to take Russian ammunition. The gun was removed in the late 1950s and *Sep* was subsequently relegated to training duties. She was removed from the active list in 1970 and later scrapped.

MINESWEEPERS

Name	Launched	Disp	Fate
Jaskolka class			
CZAJKA	10.4.35	183t	Deleted 1970
MEWA	10.1.35	183t	Deleted 1970
RYBITWA	26.4.35	183t	Deleted 1970
ZURAW	22.8.38	185t	Hulked 1971
Ex-Soviet T 371 class	1944–45	146t	Deleted c 1959

Jaskolka class

Returned from German service on 12.3.46 with rebuilt sterns and bridges and an armament comprising 4 to 8–20mm guns. The boats returned to their previous names (meaning 'lapwing', 'seagull', 'term', 'crane'), while *Zuraw* was reclassified as a surveying ship in 1948 (renamed *Kompas* in 1951) and rebuilt 1959–63. Her armament was removed and a raised forecastle and tripod mast were fitted. The remaining boats served as patrol craft from July 1949 and were later re-armed with 2–37mm (1×2), 2–0.5in MG (1×2) and 2 DC racks.

Ex-Soviet T 371 class

The Leningrad-built craft *T 23, T 24, T 225, T 228, T 232, T 241, T 243, T 244, T 465*, transferred to Poland on 5.4.46 to represent her quota of German ships seized by the Allies. They were renamed after birds and given two-letter bow identification marks: *Albatros* (AL), *Czapla* (CP), *Jaskolka* (JK), *Jastrzab* (JS), *Kania* (KN), *Kondor* (KD), *Kormoran* (KR), *Krogulec* (KG) and *Orlik* (OK). Service until 1958–59, when *Albatros* and *Kondor* were sold to an inland waterway enterprise while the others were relegated to auxiliary duties.

MOTOR BOATS

Ex-Soviet D 3 type MTBs

TP 1 and *TP 2* formerly *TKA 76* and *TKA 116* (32t) transferred together with the minesweepers. Launched c 1944 and rebuilt in 1954 and used as training boats later on, renumbered *ST* pennant letters were changed to *KT* soon 81 and 82 respectively. Deleted 1958–59.

Ex-Soviet TK type submarine-chasers

Bezwzgledny (BW, 'absolute'), *Bystry* (BS, 'acute'), *Dziarski* (DR, 'brisk'), *Dzielny* (DL, 'brave'), *Karny* (KR, 'disciplined'), *Niedoscigly* (ND, 'inaccessible'), *Nieuchwytry* (NW, 'intractable'), *Odwazny* (OW, 'courageous'), *Smialy*

Rybitwa after postwar refit   *Micinski Collection*

(SM, 'bold'), *Sprawny* (SP, 'efficient'), *Szybki* (SZ, 'rapid'), all with 2-letter bow markings.

Formerly *MO 325* to *MO 329, MO 368* to *MO 372, MO 446* transferred on 5.4.46 with the other boats. Launched 1944, 32t. All deleted 1959.

Ex-Soviet BMO type submarine-chasers

Blyskawiczny transferred from the Soviet Union on 5.4.46, formerly *BMO 552*. Launched 1944 (74t). Deleted early 1960s.

Nieuchwytny class river patrol boat

The river AMGB *Nieuchwytny*, launched 1933, (38.5t), scuttled on 10.9.39, raised by the Germans and commissioned as *Pionier*. Scuttled again in 1944, raised 1947 and recommissioned with the Polish Navy as *Okon* from 1955–57 served with the Frontier Guard. Deleted 1957.

MISCELLANEOUS

Other small units included the frontier patrol boat *Hel* (former customs cutter *Batory*, renamed 7 *Listopada* then *KP 1* later on), 4 ex-German *Pionierlandungsboote* and 10 (later increased to 19) ex-US LCP(L)s used for landing or patrol purposes as well as minor craft including 9 Frontier Guard patrol boats adapted from fishing boats and commissioned during 1947–50. All these smaller craft deleted between 1957–62.

MAJOR SURFACE SHIPS

Ex-Soviet SKORY class *destroyerss*

No	Name	Builder	Acquired	Fate
53	GROM (ex-*Smetlivya*)	Zhdanov S Yd	15.12.57	Deleted 1975
54	WICHER (ex-*Skory*)	Zhdanov S Yd	29.6.58	Deleted 1975

Two units, which included the class prototype, were transferred from the USSR. Names mean 'thunderbolt' and 'hurricane' respectively.

Ex-Soviet 'KOTLIN' class

No	Name	Builder	Acquired	Fate
275	WARSZAWA (ex-*Spravedlivyy*)	USSR	1970	Extant 1982

Transferred from USSR (built 1958) and kept in superb order as Fleet flagship.

SUBMARINES

Ex-Soviet 'M V' class *submarines*

Class:

Kaszub, Kujawiak, Kurp, Krakowiak, Mazur, Slazak

Four, built between 1948–52 in Soviet yards, were delivered to Poland in

Mazur, Kaszub and *Slazak c*1960   *Author's Collection*

1954 and two in 1955: The last one reportedly ran aground in the late 1950s and was badly damaged but repaired later and supposedly recommissioned as *Mazowsze*. The 45mm gun was removed during 1958–59 from all units. All deleted by Feb 1970.

Ex-Soviet 'WHISKEY' class *submarines*

Class (no):
Orzel (292), *Sokol* (293), *Kondor* (294), *Bielik* (295)
     Four bought from the Soviet Union. Transferred on 30.12.62, 24.10.64 and 1969 last two. All extant in 1982.

NOTE:
The ex-German Type XXIII coastal submarine *U 2344* was raised in 1948 and the possibility of recommissioning was considered for some time. This project was abandoned, however, and the boat was scrapped.

AMPHIBIOUS WARFARE VESSELS

Ex-German MFP type *landing ships*

Class:
BDD 1–3, BDD 5–7
     Six were pressed into the Navy in 1950 (2 hitherto in civilian service, 4 incomplete, 1 damaged). The pennant letters were later changed to *ODD* (*ODD* stands for *Okret Desantowy Duzy* = landing ship, large). Deleted 1957–63.

Ex-Italian MZ type *landing ship*

One recommissioned by the Polish Navy in 1950 as *BDD 4*, later changed to *ODD 4*. Deleted *c*1960.

Ex-US LCT 5 type *landing ships*

Class:
BDS 50–60
     Eleven acquired from the civilian service in 1950. The pennant letters were changed later to *ODS* (*ODS* stand for *Okret Desantowy Sredni* = landing ship, medium). *BDD 56* was converted to salvage tender in the early 1950s, the latter were scrapped between 1957–60.

'POLNOCNY' class *landing ships*

Class:
ODS 889–899 (built 1960s), *ODS 801–811* (built 1970s)
     Landing ships designed and built at Gdansk in Poland, three design variations were officially announced in service with the Polish Navy:
I – light tripod mast and one 30mm double mount on the forebridge.
II – bridge lengthened forward, one 30mm double mount there.
III – hull lengthened, bridge lengthened aft as compared with the earlier version to accommodate additional 30mm double mount.
     The first version were modernised later by lengthening of the bridge to allow the second 30mm double mount to be placed aft and heavy solid mast replacing the old one was fitted to accommodate more up-to-date electronics. All were extant in 1982 and the following names were reported at that time: *Brda* (804), *Grunwald*, *Janow* (807), *Lenino* (811), *Narwik*, *Falaise*, *Studzianki* (802) and *Warta*.

Ex-US LCM 3 type *landing craft*

Class:
BDM 100–102
     Three craft of this type were acquired from the civilian service in 1950. The pennant letters were later changed to *ODM* (*ODM* stand for *Okret Desantowy Maly* = landing ship, small). Possibly deleted in the early 1960s.

'EICHSTADEN' class *landing craft*

Fifteen craft of the LCP(L) type were built (1962) in Poland and modernised in 1969 by resiting of the bridge amidships and plating up of the hatch. Can carry 20 troops. All extant in 1982 numbered in *800* series.

'MARABUT' class *landing craft*

Displacement:	60t full load
Length:	70ft × 13ft 9in × 3ft 3in
	21.3m × 4.2m × 1.0m
Speed:	2 shafts, 2 diesels = 10kts
Armament:	2–14.5mm MG (1×2)

Class:
516–519
     Built *c*1975. Can carry a tank or 30 infantry. Plastic hull, one originally numbered 872. Extant 1982.

'Eichstaden' class after modernisation   *Author's Collection*

'Marabut' class   *Twardowski Collection*

'Polncny' class (Series I) as completed   *Author's Collection*

SMALL SURFACE COMBATANTS

Ex-Soviet 'P 6' type *fast attack craft (torpedo)*

Class:
KT 71–80, KT 83–92
 Twenty boats transferred from the Soviet Union Nov 1956–58. (*KT* stands for *Kuter Torpedowy* = MTB). All boats were renumbered *401* to *420* in the early 1960s and 12 were deleted between 1973–75. At least 3 of the remaining boats were converted into a target boats. Only these three were extant in 1982.

Ex-Soviet 'OSA 1' class *fast attack craft (missile)*

Class:
421–433
 Thirteen craft were transferred from the Soviet Union between 1963–65. They carried bridge rather than hull pennant numbers *101* to *112* (plus one other) during the early 1970s and were renumbered *421* to *433* recently. Extant 1982.

WISLA class *fast attack craft (torpedo)*

Displacement:	70t full load
Dimensions:	82ft × 18ft × 6ft
	25.0m × 5.5m × 1.8m
Machinery:	4 shafts, gas turbines + M50-FA diesels, 12,000shp = *c*50kts. Range 100nm/500nm at 50kts/20kts
Armament:	2–30mm (1×2), 4–533mm TT
Sensors:	Radar Pot Drum
Complement:	30

Design work on these units began in the early 1960s and production proper began in the early 1970s. They were built from a light alloy metal and powered by gas turbines. Highly automatised as compared with Eastern standards. 12 boats reported to have been completed by the late 1970s and the programme continues. Pennant numbers in *450, 470* and *490* series.

'Wisla' class   *Author's Collection*

'Gdansk' class as completed   *Author's Collection*

OP 357 ('Obluze' class, ASW version)   *Author's Collection*

Ex-Soviet 'KRONSTADT' class *submarine chasers*

Class (no):
Czujny (361), *Nieugiety* (362), *Zawziety* (363), *Zwrotny* (364), *Zwinny* (365), *Zreczny* (366), *Wytrwaly* (367), *Grozny* (368)
 First four units acquired in 1955; last four on 15.12.57. Deleted 1973–74.

OP 201 *large patrol craft*

Displacement:	140t
Dimensions:	128ft 7in × 18ft 8in × 4ft 11in
	39.2m × 5.7m × 1.5m
Machinery:	2 shafts, 2 diesels = 20kts
Armament:	2–37mm, 2 DC racks
Sensors:	Radar Skin Head

Built on the hull of the ex-German *R-boat* found after the war in Swinoujscie and launched 6.10.56. Probably belonged to the *R 272* series; she retained her armoured bridge. Used by Frontier Guard, deleted *c*1980.

'OKSYWIE' class *large patrol craft*

Displacement:	120t standard; 150t full load
Dimensions:	114ft 10in × 19ft × 5ft
	35.0m × 5.8m × 1.5m
Machinery:	Diesels = 20kts
Armament:	2–37mm (2×1), 4–12.7mm MG (2×2), 2 DC racks
Sensors:	Radar Skin Head; sonar Tamir

Class:
OP 202–OP 204
 Improved version of the *OP 201* type (*OP* stands for *Okret Patrolowy* = patrol craft). Launched 1957 and later reconstructed and fitted with the new mast and RN 231 type radar. Renumbered *302* to *304*; used by Frontier Guard. Deleted 1980–81.

'GDANSK' class *large patrol craft*

Displacement:	170t standard
Dimensions:	134ft 5in × 19ft × 6ft 9in
	41.0m × 6.0m × 2.0m
Machinery:	Diesels = 20kts
Armament:	2–37mm (2×1), 2–12.7mm MG (1×2), DC racks
Sensors:	Radar Skin Head; sonar Tamir

Class:
OP 205–OP 213 (built 1960s)
 Similar but improved design of the 'Oksywie' class. Later reconstructed and fitted with new mast and RN 231 radar. Renumbered *311* to *319*, used by Frontier Guard. Extant 1982.

'OBLUZE' class *large patrol craft/submarine-chasers*

Displacement:	150t standard; 170t full load
Dimensions:	137ft × 18ft 4in × 6ft 7in
	42.0m × 5.8m × 2.0m
Machinery:	2 shafts, 2 diesels = 20kts
Armament:	4–30mm (2×2), 2 internal DC racks, mines
Sensors:	Radar Pot Head (patrol craft only); RN 231, Drum Tilt, Square Head (subchasers only); sonar Tamir

Class:
321–325 (patrol craft), *351–358* (subchasers)
 Built in two series as patrol craft for use by the Frontier Guard or as subchasers, varying in radar outfit. Built by Oksywie between 1965–68 and 1970–72. The subchasers possibly took over names from the 'Kronstadt' class boats as names *Wytrwaly* (352), *Zawziety* (353) and *Zreczny* (356) are reported. Extant 1982.

'Pilica' class
NB 1/750 scale

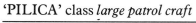

'PILICA' class *large patrol craft*

Displacement:	*c*100t full load
Dimensions:	98ft 5in × 19ft 8in × 4ft 11in
	30.0m × 6.0m × 1.5m
Machinery:	3 shafts, 3 MSO-F 4 diesels, 3600bhp = 24kts
Armament:	2–25mm (1×2), (*166* to *169* 2–533mm TT)
Sensors:	Radar RN 231
Complement:	15

Class:
161–169
Built since 1973. All 8 extant 1982.

BITNY *coastal patrol craft*

Displacement:	c50t
Dimensions:	94ft 2in pp × 15ft 5in × 4ft 3in
	28.7m × 4.7m × 1.3m
Machinery:	2 Hispano-Suiza diesels, 1800bhp
Armament:	2–37(?)mm, 2 DC racks

Built 1951–53 on the hull of the ex-German *Polizeikampfboote* which us found in Torun after the war. Completed in Gdynia, used for experimental purposes, fate unknown.

KP 100 class *coastal patrol craft*

Twenty 60t boats (15kts and 2 MG) were ordered in Hungary for service with the Frontier Guard (built 1953–54). Some of them reportedly existed in the mid-1970s but possible all were deleted by 1982.

KP 141 ('Wisloka' class)   *Author's Collection*

'WISLOKA' class *coastal patrol craft*

A dozen 72ft, c40t, diesel-powered craft were completed by 1980 for service with the Frontier Guard. Armament: 2–12.7mm MG. Numbers in *140* series.

MINE WARFARE VESSELS

Ex-US YMS type *minesweepers*

Class:
Delfin (ex-*BYMS 2211*), *Foka* (ex-*BYMS 2257*), *Mors* (ex-*BYMS 2282*)
Four *BYMS* motor minesweepers were purchased in Britain and 3 of them were commissioned on 19.4.48 with the Polish Navy. Deleted in 1955–57.

Bizon as completed   *Twardowski Collection*

Soviet 'T 43' *ocean minesweepers*

Class (no):
Dzik (604), *Los* (603), *Tur* (602), *Zubr* (601), *Bizon* (605), *Bobr* (606), *Delfin* (608), *Foka* (609), *Mors* (610), *Rosomak* (607), *Rys* (611), *Zbik* (612)
Built by Stocznia of Gdynia under Soviet licence between 1955–60, although the design was lengthened 6ft 6in (*2m*) after completion of the first four to suit Polish requirements and fittings. Completed: 3 (1957), 2 (1958), 2 (1959), 2 (1960), 2 (1961) and 1 (1962). All 12 extant in 1982, *Tur* refitted as radar picket, losing aft 37mm and sweeping gear for a quadripod radar mast.

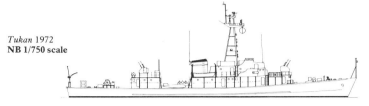

Tukan 1972
NB 1/750 scale

ORLIK class *ocean minesweepers*

Displacement:	500t
Dimensions:	190ft 3in × 24ft 6in × 8ft 2in
	58.0m × 7.5m × 2.5m
Machinery:	2 shafts, 2 Fiat A-230S diesels, 3740bhp = 18kts. Oil 55t. Range 3200nm at 12kts
Armament:	6–25mm (3×2, see notes)
Sensors:	Radar RN-231
Complement:	30

Class (no, completed):
Albatros (618, 1965), *Czajka* (617, 1964), *Czapla* (624, 1967), *Jaskolka* (622, 1966), *Jastrzab* (615, 1964), *Kania* (621, 1966), *Kormoran* (616, 1963), *Krogulec* (614, 1963), *Orlik* (613, 1964), *Pelikan* (619, 1965), *Tukan* (620, 1966), *Zuraw* (623, 1967)
Built by Stocznia Gdynska, Gdynia between 1963 and 1967. Numbers currently in 625 plus series. Built to improved and more compact design as compared with the licenced *Zubr* class. Flush deck hull was provided, close range weapons added. Extant 1982. Some have 4–23mm (2×2) astern instead of 25mm.

Soviet 'TR 40' type *river minesweepers*

Class:
TR 41–47
Seven built between 1954–56 in Poland under Soviet licence (*TR* stands for *Tralowiec Rzeczny* = river minesweeper), later renumbered *811–817*. Deleted 1969–71.

Soviet 'K 8' type *minesweeping boats*

Class:
KTR 951–970
A total of 20 boats were built (1955–60) in Poland under Soviet licence and some of them were commissioned as patrol boats. (*KTR* stands for *Kuter Tralowy* = minesweeping boat). Extant 1982.

New Type *inshore minesweeper*

The GRP-built prototype *Notec* MSB was launched on 18.4.81.

Romania

The peace treaty of 10 February 1947 required a reduction of the Romanian Army to 120,000 men, the Air Force to 150 planes while the Navy was allowed to maintain 15,000t overall tonnage. At the time that tonnage was barely reached as the Romanians operated 2 old destroyers, 1 submarine, 2 escorts converted from the old torpedo-boats, 2 old gunboats and 5 MTBs returned by the Soviets. This force was supplemented by more modern units returned by the Soviet Union by the early 1950s namely 2 destroyers, 2 submarines and a minelayer. At that time the Romanians began the river craft programme which resulted in the completion of 19 such craft for service on the Danube.

WARSAW PACT

Romania's membership of the Warsaw Pact improved her Navy's situation but not to the same extent as with neighbouring Bulgaria. Four 'MV' type coastal submarines, 4 ex-German *M-boats* (1940 type), 3 'Kronstadt' class patrol craft and 21 T 301 class inshore minesweepers were acquired from the Soviet Union during the late 1950s. In addition eight incomplete hulls of the 'TR 40' type river minesweepers were transferred from Poland for completion in Romania and 12 landing craft were laid down in a local yard. In June 1958 Soviet forces left the country.

The early 1960s saw slow, but steady development as 12 'P 4' type MTBs were transferred from the Soviet Union and transfer of the 'Osa' class missile boats was started. Further transfer of Soviet warships was interrupted suddenly in 1964 when Romania refused to follow the Soviet Union's example in relations with Red China or accept COMECON plans for economic development. This rift was widened when Romania took an independent line in her trade relations and refused to participate in the invasion of Czechoslovakia in 1968. Such disobedience resulted in a considerable reduction of Soviet supplies and left the Romanian Navy, except for 3 'Poti' class corvettes, acquired in 1970, with only 5 modern combat naval craft in service ('Osa' class) at the beginning of the 1970s.

Therefore Chinese assistance was willingly invited and licence was bought for construction of torpedo hydrofoils of the 'Huchwan' class and patrol craft of the 'Shanghai' class. Over 25 craft of the former and 30 of the later type were commissioned during the later 1970s. Apart from these boats the Romanians themselves began construction of three types of river craft.

Thanks to these efforts the Romanian Navy operates an effective force of modern vessels. In contrast to the expanding naval forces of Bulgaria, the Romanian Navy is a typical coastal force. The increasing divergence between Romania and the other Warsaw Pact countries, disclosed recently by Romania's refusal to increase defence funds, will compel the Romanians to rely on themselves or Chinese assistance at best when modernising their navy.

The strength of the Romanian Navy in 1982 was 3 corvettes; 5 missile boats; 25 torpedo hydrofoils; 33 patrol craft; 14 minesweepers; 6 minesweeping boats; 12 landing craft; 43 river patrol craft; 8 river minesweepers and about 22 auxiliaries.

In 1982 there were 10,500 officers and men (4500 afloat, 2000 in coast defence with about 110 guns, 1000 training and 3000 for shore support) serving with the Navy; Romania operates a two-year naval period of national service. Mangalia and Constanta are the main Black Sea Fleet bases and the largest existing Danube Flotilla is based between Tulcea, Braila, Galati, Giurgiu and Sulina. Reserves are estimated at 20,000 and a vice-admiral commands.

FLEET STRENGTH 1947

DESTROYERS

Name	Launched	Disp	Fate
Marasti class			
D 11	26.3.17	1391t	Deleted *c* 1963
D 12	30.1.18	1391t	Deleted *c* 1963

Former destroyers *Marasti* and *Marasesti* which were seized by the Soviets in Aug 1944 and commissioned by them as *Lovky* and *Logkij* respectively. Returned in 1946.

SUBMARINE

Name	Launched	Disp	Fate
Delfinul class			
ex-DELFINUL	22.6.30	650t	Deleted 1957

Seized by the Soviets in Aug 1944 and commissioned as *TS 4*. Returned in 1945.

ESCORT VESSELS

Name	Launched	Disp	Fate
Naluca class			
E 1	11.8.14	262t	BU 1960
Sborul class			
E 2	6.8.14	257t	BU *c* 1960

Former torpedo-boats *Smeul* and *Sborul* converted for escort duties during the war, seized by the Soviets in Aug 1944 and commissioned as *Toros* and *Musson* respectively. Returned 22.9.45.

GUNBOATS

Name	Launched	Disp	Fate
Capitan Dumitrescu class			
D 61	1916	355t	Deleted *c* 1960
D 62	1917	355t	Deleted late 1970s ?

Romanian gunboats *Locotenent-Comandor Stihi Eugen* and *Sublocotenent Ghigulescu*, seized by the Soviets in Aug 1944 and commissioned as *Akhutuba* and *Angara* respectively. Both returned in 1945 and served until *c* 1960. *D 62* converted then for surveying service and became *NOD 113*. Possibly stricken during the late 1970s.

MOTOR TORPEDO BOATS

The 72ft Vosper type *Viscolul* returned from the Soviet Black Sea Fleet (*TKA 955*) on 22.9.45 and was BU after 1947.

The 4 70ft *Vantul* class 32t boats (ex-*TKA 951–954*) likewise.

RIVER PATROL BOATS

Three 51t *Captain Nicolae Lascar Bogdan* class 51t units of *c* 1906 returned from Soviet service (*SKA 754–756*) in 1945 and were BU after 1947.

MAJOR SURFACE SHIPS

REGELE FERDINAND class *destroyers*

Name	Builder	Launched	Fate
D 21 (ex-*Letuchy*, ex-*Regina Maria*)	Pattison, Naples	2.3.29	Deleted late 1960s
D 22 (ex-*Likhoi*, ex-*Regele Ferdinand*)	Pattison, Naples	2.12.28	Deleted late 1960s

Distrugatoáre ('destroyers') seized by the Soviets in Aug 1944 and not returned till 1953. Names later changed again to *D 9* and *D 10*.

SUBMARINES

Ex-Soviet 'M V' type *submarines*

Four boats were transferred from the Soviet Union in 1957 and served with the Romanian Navy until deleted in 1967. Names or numbers not known.

NOTE:
The former Romanian submarines *Requinul* and *Marsuinul* the former built in Romania during the war and the latter in the Hague, were seized by the Soviets in 1944 and commissioned as *S 3* and *S 4* respectively. Returned late after the war, scrapped in 1967.

AMPHIBIOUS WARFARE VESSELS

BRAILA class *utility landing craft*

A dozen LCU type landing craft were built in Romania in the late 1950s. Particulars are not known. Extant 1982.

SMALL SURFACE COMBATANTS

Ex-Soviet 'POTI' class *corvettes*

Class:
V 31–33
Three corvettes purchased in the Soviet Union in 1970. Extant 1982. Have 2–533mm TT instead of 400mm and RBU-2500 ASW RL instead of RBU-6000.

Ex-Soviet 'P 4' type *fast attack craft (torpedo)*

Class:
87–92
A dozen such craft were transferred from the Soviet Union probably at the beginning of the 1960s. Only half of them remained in service in the mid-1970s carrying numbers 87 to 92. All deleted by the late 1970s (7 in 1979).

Ex-Soviet 'OSA 1' class *fast attack craft (missile)*

Class:
194–198
Five units purchased in the Soviet Union during 1961–64. Extant 1982.

Chinese 'HUCHWAN' class *torpedo hydrofoils*

Class:
VT 51–69 and others
Three were acquired from China in the early 1970s and licenced production was started in Romania *c*1973 at about 2 a year. Over 25 craft in service in 1982.

'EPITROP' class *fast attack craft (torpedo)*

New class (NATO codename) of FAC reported, building early 1980s in Romania. Displaces 150–200t. Six extant 1982 plus (?) 4 building.

Ex-Soviet 'KRONSTADT' class *large patrol craft*

Class: *VI–V 3*
Three bought in the Soviet Union in 1956. Extant 1982.

Chinese 'SHANGHAI II' class *large patrol craft*

Class:
Patrol version: *VP 21–29*, *VP 31* and others
ASW version: *VS 41–49*, *VS 52* and others
Production of the second type of this class begun under licence at Mangalia in 1973 at about 2 a year. By 1980 at least 30 boats had been commissioned in two versions: patrol, armed with 1–57mm, 2–37mm (1×2) and ASW version armed with 1–37mm, 4 MGs, 2 RBU-1200 ASW RL (2×5), 2 DC racks.

VG class *river patrol craft*

Displacement:	40t full load
Dimensions:	52ft 5in × 14ft 4in × 4ft
	16.0m × 4.4m × 1.2m
Machinery:	2 shafts, 2 3D12 diesels, 600bhp = 18kts
Armament:	1–20mm
Complement:	10

Ten craft built in Galati in 1954 with steel hulls for service with the Danube Flotilla. One numbered *VII*. Extant 1982.

VB 93 1978
NB 1/750 scale

VB class *river patrol craft*

Displacement:	80t
Dimensions:	105ft × 16ft × 3ft
	32.0m × 4.8m × 0.9m
Machinery:	2 shafts, 2 diesels, 2400bhp = 17kts
Armament:	1–85mm, 1–37mm, 4–14.5mm MG (2×2), 2–81mm mortars (2×1)
Complement:	*c*25

Class:
VB 76–94
First units begun in 1973. Built at about 2 a year, 18 extant 1982.

SM class *river patrol boats*

Class:
SM 161–169
Built in Romania 1954–56, 20t units with 2 MG. Extant 1982.

SD class *river patrol boats*

Class:
SD 270, 274, 275, 277, 278
Began building late 1970s in Romania. All 5 extant 1982.

NOTE:
The Romanian river monitors *Ardeal*, *Ion Bratianu*, *Bessarabia*, *Bucovina* and *Alexandru Lahovari* which had been seized by the Soviets in 1944 were returned by them in 1951 and possibly scrapped afterwards.

MINE WARFARE VESSELS

Ex-German 'M 40' type *coastal minesweepers*

Class:
Demokratia (DB 13), *Descatusaria* (DB 14), *Descrobiere* (DB 15), *Dreplatea* (DB 16)
Four ships which had been ceded to the Soviet Union after the war were purchased by Romania in 1956/7. Originally coal burners but converted to oil in 1951 and rearmed with 6–37mm (3×2), 4 MG, DCT. Equipped with navigation radar. Getting new engines and superstructure. Extant 1982.

'COSAR' class *mine countermeasures support ship*

This 1500t, 262ft (*80m*) ship with 4–30mm (2×2) reported as complete 1981. 'Cosar' is the NATO codename.

Ex-Soviet 'T 301' class *inshore minesweepers*

Class:
DR 19, DR 21–29
Twenty-four transferred from the Soviet Union during 1956–60. Individual craft have been deleted since the mid-1970s; only 10 of them remained in service in 1982. Reportedly only half of them are operational.

Soviet 'TR 40' type *river minesweepers*

Class:
VD 421–428
Eight incomplete hulls built 1955–60 were purchased in Poland and transferred to Romania. All of them were completed there by 1960. Extant 1982.

VD 141 class *minesweeping boats*

Class:
VD 141–148
Built since 1975. Later given pennant nos 241–*248*. Extant 1982.

NOTE:
The former Romanian minelayer *Amiral Murgescu* seized by the Soviets in Aug 1944 and commissioned by them as *Don*, was returned late after the war. Deleted *c*1967.

Soviet Union

In 1982 the Soviet Navy is, by various measures, the first or second most powerful in the world. Its present prosperity seems largely due to the exertions of its chief, Admiral of the Fleet of the Soviet Union Sergei G Gorshkov, who has held his post continuously since 1956, and who has supplied the rationale under which the current programme of large surface combatants is being built. Their appearance during the present decade will complete the transformation of the Soviet Fleet from a coastal and near-coastal force dominated by small attack craft, submarines, and missile-equipped bombers into a global sea power capable of challenging the United States Navy throughout the world ocean and based, like the US Navy, on concepts of the command of the seas. This transformation parallels a growth in Soviet ambitions, from interests largely limited to the Eurasian land mass when Admiral Gorshkov took office, to the present world-wide ones. It appears, too, that the Soviet Fleet is on the verge of adding to its current missile arsenal a fully-fledged sea-based air component, perhaps comparable to that operated by the US Navy.

This is not to suggest that the two navies are very similar in structure or in tactics, rather that the Soviets are now at the point where they need not forego any of the tools which have proved so useful to other navies. However, the Soviet Fleet still retains the distinctive tactical style developed over many decades and reflecting the character of the Soviet political system. Operations at all levels are centrally controlled: ideally the commander does not himself participate in the engagement, but rather controls several attackers who fire from maximum range so as to avoid damage to themselves. The Soviet Fleet is still designed to accomplish sea denial rather than sea control, so that its primary tactic is still the massed attack on some particular seaborne target, generally a carrier, an amphibious group or a submarine. Such tactics require a large investment in systems to detect and track the target while the attack is set up, and then to inform the attackers of the precise location of their target. These requirements explain the enormous Soviet expenditure on ocean surveillance: shore-based HF/DF, electronic intelligence satellites, 'Bear' reconnaissance bombers, intelligence ships (AGIs), even specialised 'tattletales' intended to trail potential targets.

Soviet tactics show themselves in Soviet operating procedures and in the designs of many classes of Soviet warships. For example, the concept of co-ordinated group operations externally controlled applies to submarines as well as to surface ships. Since the submarines receive their target data from external sources, they must remain within radio range, which means near the surface, a point brought out by the frequency with which Soviet submarines are photographed at or near the surface, despite their high underwater speeds and impressive depth capabilities. Similarly, the availability of radio target data makes elaborate efforts at silencing unnecessary, as the submarine sonar is not the primary search sensor. On the other hand, in anti-ship operations high mobility is essential: the Soviets tend to be willing to sacrifice silence in the interests of high submerged speeds. Moreover, high submerged speed and good depth performance are the classical means of post-attack escape, and undoubtedly that consideration has been important in Soviet nuclear submarine development. The group attack from long range also explains Soviet interest in stand-off weapons for submarine delivery, such as the SS-N-9 missile fired by 'Charlie' class vessels.

The carrier *Minsk* and a 'Kara' class cruiser refuel from the tanker *Boris Butoma* in the W Pacific June 1979 *USN*

Tactical style is a great constant in Soviet naval development, cutting across a very considerable variation in naval missions and even in favoured war scenarios. The other great constant is the Soviet economic system, geared to a series of five-year plans. Soviet industrial managers are rewarded for their success in fulfilling their 'norms' under the Plan, and such fulfilment is easiest if production rates remain constant throughout the Plan. Thus there is strong resistance to any change in the classes of ships to be produced, and in some cases quite obsolete programmes and concepts have survived well past what should have been a natural demise. Planning also affects the design of new weapons and new platforms, since efforts must always be made to assure the compatibility of all components: changes at any stage are extremely difficult. (This one consideration may well explain much of the Soviet preference for deck-mounted box missile launchers which have minimal impact on the overall ship design, but which are often dismissed in the West as operationally inefficient). Other elements of the Soviet economic system include a relatively backward electronic industry, so that some ships have been commissioned and deployed abroad with important equipment not yet installed, and there have been reports of ships on foreign stations with empty missile tubes.

POSTWAR STRATEGY TO 1953

Within the limits imposed by the Soviet system, the Navy has been the subject of violently shifting political direction. Its modern history can be traced to Stalin's determination to build up a large ocean-going fleet, a decision he announced as part of the 1937–42 Five-Year Plan. Previously a poverty-stricken Soviet Navy had evolved a 'combined-arms' strategy in which shore-based aircraft, coast defence guns, submarines, and torpedo-boats would guarantee the security of the Soviet shoreline against foreign attack. These relatively inexpensive coastal forces responded to the principal requirement of Soviet (and Russian) governments: that the coast be closed to foreigners trying to infiltrate in peacetime or to invade in war, and that it also be sealed against Soviet citizens trying to leave. Thus many naval-type coastal units have always been under the control of the KGB, the border police. The coastal navy has always enjoyed political support, and its existence is the one constant of Soviet naval development. In 1982, it is perhaps best characterised by a variety of missile craft ranging from 'Osas' up through 'Nanuchkas', by very large numbers of submarine-chasers and minesweepers, and by the land-based bombers. All of these forces are controlled from shore, and the efficacy of shore-based target acquisition systems limits their effective offshore range.

In 1937 Stalin resolved to build a second fleet. His motivation is uncertain, since he seems to have had little feeling for the niceties of naval strategy. In retrospect it would almost seem that he felt that for the Soviet Union to take her place as a Great Power she would have to possess a Great Fleet, or, rather, Great Fleets, since the separation of any Russian or Soviet Navy into four fleets is a necessary consequence of geography. One of the earliest indications of Stalin's big-fleet ambitions was his elevation of the Soviet Pacific Squadron to Fleet status.

Stalin's big-fleet programme built the industrial base on which the postwar Soviet Navy rose. Each of the four fleets (Baltic, Northern, Black Sea and Pacific) was to have its own primary yard for new construction. Major shipbuilding centres already existed at Leningrad and at Nikolayev on the Black Sea. Now Molotovsk (renamed Severodvinsk postwar) was built to serve the Northern Fleet; Komsomolsk-on-Amur served the Pacific Fleet. Neither had any considerable industrial hinterland, and each was intended as a satellite of one of the established centres. Thus Molotovsk was to assemble material fabricated at Leningrad, while Komsomolsk worked with Nikolayev. In addition Stalin ordered the construction of a submarine factory at Gorki on the Volga, east of Moscow. Submarines built there could run their trials on the Caspian Sea, and could then travel up the Volga and through the Soviet canal system to the White Sea and the Northern Fleet. However, that canal system in itself imposed limits on the size of submarines built at Gorki and so reduced the value of the Gorki yard postwar as the size of the standard submarine grew.

In 1982 these original yards continue to dominate Soviet warship production, although their functions have changed considerably. Severodvinsk now produces nuclear submarines for the Northern Fleet, as Komsomolsk does for the Pacific Fleet. Designed for year-round operation, it has covered and heated sheds. The Leningrad complex includes the Admiralty yard (nuclear ships and submarines; it built the new *Kirov*), the Sudomekh submarine works, the Zhdanov yard which served as lead yard in postwar destroyer and light cruiser programmes, and the Baltic yard, responsible for *Sverdlov* class cruisers but not for more recent warships. There is also a light warship yard on Petrovski Island. On the Black Sea Nikolayev is a similar concentration. The South Yard builds heavy warships such as the *Kiev* and *Moskva* classes, the North Yard, cruisers such as the 'Karas'. Inland, on the Volga, there is now a light craft yard at Zelenodolsk to supplement the old mass production facility at Gorki. Several of these yards construct merchant as well as naval vessels. There are in addition major fleet bases: Severomorsk for the Northern Fleet, the Leningrad-Kronstadt complex for the Baltic Fleet, Sevastopol for the Black Sea Fleet, and Vladivostok for the Pacific Fleet, with a large base also at Petropavlovsk on the Kamchatka Peninsula.

The Soviet industrial system, including the base for the Navy, was badly damaged by World War II. Leningrad was besieged and its factories and shipyards partly destroyed. Nikolayev was occupied by the Germans. The satellite yards, cut off from their sources of material, were largely idle in wartime, although they were not themselves damaged. In 1945 some of their slips were still occupied by the remains of Stalin's prewar programme, but there was little hope of immediately resuming work on it. All that could be done was the completion of prewar hulls from light cruisers (*Chapayev* class) down.

However, although the Soviet Navy had suffered terribly at the hands of the German invaders, it did derive several important benefits from the Red Army's victory. In East Prussia it seized the Schichau yard at Elbing, a specialist builder of light surface craft; the town of Königsberg, where the yard was located, became the Soviet city of Kaliningrad. The former Walter works fell into Soviet hands, as did several examples of the new and revolutionary Type XXI submarine, and several sets of snorkel gear. In East Germany the Soviets found scientists and engineers who had worked on the German Navy's advanced torpedoes and sonars, as well as on air-launched anti-ship missiles. All of these formed major elements of the postwar Soviet fleet programme. At the same time the Soviet fleet benefitted from Allied Lend-Lease, which provided it with modern radars, sonars and ASW weapons.

In 1945, with the prewar Soviet Fleet and its industrial basis in ruins, Stalin faced enormous costs if he wished to revive his prewar plans. Existing ships were obsolete at best, although the technology for a more modern fleet had fallen into Soviet hands. It could, moreover, be argued that with all the claims on Soviet resources for industrial reconstruction, and indeed with the Army, predominating, funds would best not be spent on naval expansion.

However, as early as July 1945 Stalin proclaimed his intention to build a great sea-going fleet. The shipyards were rehabilitated, prewar designs forming the basis for new cruiser (*Sverdlov*) and destroyer (*Skory*) designs. A new *Stalingrad* class of battlecruisers was laid down, and it appears that classes of heavy cruisers and battleships were planned. Reports differ as to whether Stalin intended to build carriers as well. As they had before 1941, submarines continued to be extremely important in Russian eyes – in 1948 a Soviet admiral referred to a programme to build 1200. It appears in retrospect that they were primarily a means of coast defence: a Soviet Union without important overseas lines of communication did not appreciate fully the significance of classical anti-shipping submarine warfare. Unlike the new surface warships, the submarines did incorporate the new technology developed by the Germans. It appears that the new 'Quebec', 'Whiskey', and 'Zulu' classes began as Soviet design projects in 1943–44, but were extensively modified postwar to reflect German concepts.

Stalin also continued to invest in coastal forces, building large numbers of MTBs and coastal ASW craft. The traditional Soviet coast defence force continued to include large numbers of land-based bombers, and efforts to adapt the wartime German technology of anti-ship, bomber-launched missiles were pressed forward. In addition, large numbers of small warships, which the Soviets designated 'guardships', were built for offshore patrol. The two postwar classes, the 'Kolas' and 'Rigas', apparently originated at Kaliningrad, the 'Kolas' showing a distinct Schichau influence. In 1982 Kaliningrad continues to function as the lead yard for Soviet escorts, having been upgraded to destroyers ('Krivak') or above; it is supplemented by Kerch (Kamysh Borun) in the Crimea, a postwar yard, and by Khabarovsk in the Far East.

KHRUSCHEV'S 'REVOLUTION IN MILITARY AFFAIRS'

Stalin's naval outlook generally reproduced that with which he had entered World War II. In particular, he avoided any admission that the existence of nuclear weapons would lead to radical changes, and indeed he forbade the discussion of the implications of such weapons. His reasoning appears to have been that, were he to admit that nuclear weapons might guarantee victory, he would also have to admit that in a future war errors such as those which had permitted a German surprise attack in 1941 might prove fatal to the Soviet Union. No all-knowing leader could entertain such thoughts.

In effect, then, nuclear weapons were forbidden fruit, suddenly

A 'Zulu IV' and 'Foxtrot' class diesel attack submarines 23.2.68 after the 50th anniversary of the Soviet Armed Forces

accessible within the Soviet military establishment upon Stalin's death. Within two years, the Soviet leadership was to proclaim the 'Revolution In Military Affairs' under which new doctrine they were to be considered decisive in future war. Khrushchev would then announce that he was uninterested in any weapon save 'nuclear-missile' weapons, and a round of inter-service rivalry would begin. The stage for that round was set by general dissatisfaction with the cost of Stalin's fleet. Khrushchev would later characterise the naval shipyards as 'metal-eaters', and the big surface ships as 'coffins'. Cuts began almost as soon as Stalin died, the battlecruisers being the first victims. The heavy cruisers appear not to have been laid down, and several *Sverdlov*s were cut up on the slip; others were launched but never completed. Within a few years the large submarine programme was also to be cut very considerably, as Khrushchev professed no interest in conventional torpedo submarines. It appears that his motive for these economies, as for related cuts in Army and Air Force production and personnel, was to free resources to develop strategic weapons, both missiles and long-range bombers. The one element of Soviet seapower not subject to deep cuts was the coast defence force, including shore-based bombers. By the late 1950s these forces were beginning to receive anti-ship missiles: the shore- and air-based AS-1 'Kennel', and the naval SS-N-1 for destroyers and SS-N-2 ('Styx') for patrol boats derived from torpedo-boats

The Soviet naval leadership of that day sought a new naval mission to justify the existence of a bluewater fleet. In 1955 a Soviet submarine fired the first submarine-launched ballistic missile, and the Navy began to build up a submarine strategic attack force armed with both ballistic (SS-N-4 and then SS-N-5) and cruise (SS-N-3) missiles. This was a large programme, producing at least the various 'Whiskey' and 'Zulu' conversions, as well as new series of nuclear ('Hotel', 'Echo-I') and conventional ('Golf') submarines. If Khrushchev is to be believed, the 'Kynda' class missile cruisers were planned as part of this programme, one per fleet. The Navy was able to avoid inter-service problems because of the failure of the contemporary Soviet bomber and long-range missile programmes: it was the only Soviet service capable of delivering Khrushchev's decisive blow against North America.

Roughly contemporary with the development of this underwater strategic attack force was a revival of Soviet interest in ASW, over a range out to several hundred miles from the Soviet coast. At first this meant the construction of several classes of frigate (eg 'Mirka', 'Petya'). However, the origins of the new 'Alfa' class fast submarine may also be found in this coast defence ASW programme. In each case very fast ASW units were expected to speed out to some previously discovered location before the submarine detected there would have a chance of escaping. In each case, too, the effective range of the ASW system is determined by the time lag between detection and the arrival of the attacker. In effect such a system is the ASW equivalent of the anti-ship system represented by a fast missile boat such as an 'Osa' or 'Komar'.

The precise origin of the late-1950s and early-1960s ASW effort is unclear. The Soviets may well have considered their own strategic system the wave of the future, and may therefore have designed the defensive system required to counter it, on the theory that it would be representative of the threat the West would be able to mount. Alternatively, they may have seen in the US Regulus cruise missile programme precisely such a threat. The distinction is of interest in that it determines to some extent projections of future Soviet naval development, either mirror-imaged or dependent upon Soviet perceptions of the US threat.

By 1960 the greatest threat to the Soviet Navy was a bureaucratic one. The missiles were finally operational, and they now came under the Strategic Rocket Forces (SRF), a new service and Khrushchev's favourite. He was now not merely obssessed with nuclear weapons, but also with missiles as such; no service not heavily endowed with missiles could hope for extensive funding. Admiral Gorshkov and his colleagues needed a new mission, as the SRF would block future construction of naval strategic missiles and their platforms. They found it in the threat presented by NATO carrier forces – a threat which, incidentally, had existed for about a decade. Fortunately the Soviets had available an anti-ship guidance system for the SS-N-3 missile, and were able to convert the existing 'Kynda' design to incorporate it. As for the submarines, the 'Echo-I' gave way to 'Echo-II' which carried the necessary anti-ship guidance equipment in its fin, and a new 'Juliett' class conventional missile-carrier was laid down. At the same time the entire Soviet anti-ship bomber force was transferred to Navy control; in return, the Navy gave up the mission of defending its bases against air attack, transferring its large interceptor force to the Soviet air defence air force, the PVO.

One project of this period is relatively difficult to explain in these terms: the helicopter carrier *Moskva*, which must have been conceived about 1958. Reportedly a companion project for a large surface combatant was cancelled in the early 1960s. *Moskva* herself is often described as a means of attacking Polaris submarines in Soviet coastal waters, but this explanation runs afoul of the disparity between the cost of a single helicopter carrier and the very large ocean area involved. One alternative explanation would be that *Moskva* began as the ASW escort for a large cruiser armed primarily with anti-surface missiles, probably SS-N-3s. Her helicopters would duplicate the tactics of Soviet submarine-chasers, establishing the approximate position of a submarine by combined efforts of many relatively ineffective sonars. In the case of the submarine chasers, such approximate data was normally used to target barrage weapons, or RBUs; in the case of *Moskva*, it would appear that the barrage weapon is the large nuclear ASW missile carried forward, a derivative of the Army's 'Frog'. One would suspect, then, that the big cruiser was cancelled due to Khrushchev's overriding feeling that large surface warships were no more than coffins, but that *Moskva* survived because of her ASW designator, a timely characteristic just when the American Polaris system was taking up Khrushchev's attention.

It does not appear that the anti-carrier orientation remained for long, as the Soviets shifted from the anti-carrier 'Kynda' and 'Kresta I' to the ASW 'Kresta II' and 'Kara' classes after the production of only eight high-seas anti-carrier cruisers. The anti-carrier submarines fared much better, but even they were withdrawn from production during the mid-1960s, in favour of a new generation of ASW types and, probably far more important, a new generation of ballistic missile submarines. These two developments are presumably linked.

THE POST-KHRUSHCHEV ERA

With Khrushchev's fall in 1964, the SRF must have lost its greatest champion, and the Navy have seen the way open for a return to strategic operations, which, in view of the doctrine of the 'revolution in military affairs', carried by far the greatest prestige in the Soviet military establishment. The 'Yankee' programme of ballistic missile submarines apparently dates from this period, and reportedly the details of these submarines attest to an extremely hasty design. Soviet official doctrine also shows a certain hesitancy in returning to strategic affairs. Well into the 1970s Admiral Gorshkov typically argued that his submarines were a reserve force, a modern version of the old fleet-in-being, which would be available for use, or for threatened use, after the primary strategic force, which was still the SRF, had been expended.

It would appear that concurrent with the revival of the strategic submarines was a revival of ASW, except that this time the ASW strike forces were to operate well out from the Soviet littoral. The principal surface ship designs of this period are probably the 'Kresta II' and the 'Kynda', with the 'Krivak' class frigate probably intended to help make up the numbers in Soviet hunter-killer groups. The doctrine of the post-Khrushchev era appears to envisage a non-strategic or even a non-nuclear phase at the outset of a war, during which each side attempts to destroy the nuclear weapons of the other by non-nuclear operations. In this context one might imagine a Soviet naval war plan in which the initial blow would fall on US sea control forces, leaving the way open for the hunter-killers to assault the US deterrent submarine fleet, well before any escalation to the strategic level. This type of strategy was demonstrated in October 1973, when the Soviet Mediterranean Squadron was hurriedly reshuffled in a crisis. The most modern

ships, *ie* the ASW fleet, were moved back into the Black Sea where they came under the protection of land-based aircraft; the older anti-carrier ships moved into the Mediterranean to form classical Soviet anti-carrier groups. Presumably the ASW fleet would have moved back to sweep the Mediterranean free of Polaris submarines, had the carriers been destroyed.

Hand in hand with the construction of ballistic missile submarines, the Soviet Fleet began to receive a new specialised ASW submarine, 'Victor', armed principally with a long-range ASW weapon akin to the US Subroc, as well as a new anti-ship submarine, 'Charlie', armed with a short-range, underwater-launched anti-ship missile, the SS-N-7, comparable in performance to the patrol boat-launched 'Styx', and probably intended as a replacement for conventional torpedoes. The precise relationship between these two classes is not clear. For example, it is sometimes suggested that the main armament of the 'Victor' was derived directly from the US 'Subroc', compromised to the Soviets some time during its test phase. In that case 'Victor' may well be contemporary in concept with the crash-programme 'Yankee'. 'Charlie' is probably an earlier development, and both submarines probably share many important components. 'Victor' is considerably faster than 'Charlie' and thus may not have been designed to combine tactically with it. It is known that about 1960 the Soviets were toying with the concept of an all-submarine task force consisting of specialised types, and one might speculate that both 'Victor' and 'Charlie' were designed to protect groups of 'Yankees' crossing the Atlantic and Pacific towards launch areas off the US coast.

The transit concept was important as a consequence of the Soviet phased war strategy. It meant that most Soviet strategic attack submarines would not be at sea at the outbreak of war, as they would not be needed until well into the conflict. That in turn had important consequences for the standards of reliability and, indeed, of quietness, the Soviets required. To be sure, some 'Yankees' would generally be stationed off the US coast in peacetime, if only as an insurance against surprise attack, but they would represent a far smaller fraction of the 'Yankee' force than would have been the case in the US Navy.

The Soviet building programme of the 1970s would appear to continue the revival of the naval strategic mission. Admiral Gorshkov no longer writes of his submarines as a reserve force, subordinate to his old bureaucratic enemy, the SRF: with the advent of the SS-N-8 ballistic missile, his submarines can fire from Soviet coastal waters against targets in North America. Given the priority of nuclear weapons in Soviet strategy, the primary mission of the Soviet surface fleet became the security of the 'holding areas' in which the new very long-range missile submarines, the 'Deltas', were to operate in wartime. Thus, for example, it would appear that the *Kiev* and her sister ships are intended to seal choke points such as the Greenland–Iceland–United Kingdom (GIUK) Gap against NATO ASW forces which might attempt to move north to hunt 'Deltas' in their holding areas in the Norwegian Sea.

Since the early 1970s, Admiral Gorshkov has been writing about another, very different mission for the Soviet Fleet. According to Soviet ideology, there is a continuous struggle between the forces of 'progress' (pro-Soviet movements) and the 'reactionary' West in the Third World. The primary role of the Soviet armed services is to deter 'reactionary' assault on the centre of 'progressive' movements, *ie* upon the Soviet Union, but this concept is soon extended to shielding pro-Soviet insurrection in the Third World. Perhaps the first explicit example of such an operation was the use of Soviet warships off Angola in 1975–76; Admiral Gorshkov has referred again and again in his writings to the Navy as the principal means of securing State interests overseas in peacetime.

This new concept is extremely important to a Navy which, first, has in the past had a role only in an intense central war and, second, has always suffered from political attack, from the obsolescence of its function rather than of its ships. Given the strategic parity or even superiority which the Soviet Union has gained, it must seem at least possible that deterrence at the strategic level will soon be quite secure, and that in future expenditure should be concentrated on non-strategic or even non-central war forces. Like its foreign counterparts, the Soviet Navy is extremely expensive. In the 1980s it seems likely that the Soviet Union will suffer from declining industrial productivity and a declining manpower pool; at the same time it may well exhaust the easily recoverable resources of European Russia, and considerable capital and manpower may have to be shifted to more expensive resource exploitation in Siberia. In 1982 the Soviet Navy can protect itself from political disaster by pointing to its ability to further Soviet interests short of a central war, and by its unique ability to protect pro-Soviet movements and regimes which can supplement Soviet raw materials. The new building programme now (1982) emerging appears designed for precisely this task: to face down an American carrier battle group, to prevent any future US intervention in a place such as Vietnam. The Soviets will not have any such capability for some years to come, probably not before 1990, but the new ships now under construction appear to fit just this role. They show both a return to the anti-ship weaponry of the early 1960s and a vast increase in unit size and sophistication, enabling them to operate far from the borders of the Soviet Union. The addition of one or more conventional carriers, which is now widely forecast, should increase the independent capability of any such Soviet intervention force.

CRUISERS

Western analysts categorise a wide variety of Soviet ships as cruisers, ranging from the classical cruisers of the *Sverdlov* and earlier types to the 'large ASW ships' of the 'Kresta II' and 'Kara' classes. As in the United States, ship functions and overall tactical concepts changed so radically during the 1950s and 1960s that 'cruiser' persists as little more than an indication of ship size. Moreover, with the general growth of every category of ship in the Soviet Navy, the functional successors of earlier non-cruisers such as the 'Krivaks' may well enter the cruiser size category: for example, *Udaloy* appears to be a 'Krivak' successor in at least some respects. In addition, although the Soviets class the *Moskva* as an ASW cruiser and (at least at first) *Kiev* as a 'heavy ASW cruiser', here both are lumped together as aviation carriers.

The *Sverdlov*s are actually the sole survivors of prewar cruiser concepts; they are improved versions of the *Chapayev*s laid down before World War II. Stalin planned to build larger cruisers, reportedly amounting to 4 battlecruisers with 12in guns and 12 heavy cruisers, but no details have ever become available. With his death the one or two battlecruisers (*Stalingrad* class) under construction were dismantled, and the *Sverdlov* programme curtailed. The 'Kyndas' were the first of a new category of 'rocket cruisers' which reportedly was to have included a large (possibly *Moskva*-sized) cruiser, cancelled early in the 1960s. The cruiser category almost lapsed after the 'Kresta I' class rocket ships, but it was revived in the late 1970s with the construction of the nuclear-powered *Kirov* and with new classes of ASW and surface to surface cruisers (*Udaloy* and *Sovremennyy*). The latter are of particular interest because of the turn to single-ship specialisation, suggesting that the Soviets plan to operate task groups rather than relatively widely dispersing their ships, as previously.

DESTROYERS

The 'Kashins' were the last class of ships the Soviet Navy designated as destroyers, or EM (*Eskadry Mimenosets*, or *Esminets*, meaning fleet torpedo craft). The designation corresponds to a concept of operations long since discarded, that of the traditional balanced fleet with its capital ships, cruisers and torpedo-bearing destroyers. That the 'Kashins' bore this title suggests strongly that, at least in concept, they were little more than conventional destroyers, with their guns replaced by missiles. The 'Kildins' and 'Krupnys' were quite different; they were designated *Raketny Korabl'*, or rocket ships, and were armed primarily with long-range surface-to-surface weapons. It would appear that their construction paralleled the major 'Komar'/'Osa' coastal rocket boat programme, and that they were intended to provide anti-ship fire further from Soviet coasts. Just how they were to survive on the open seas is by no means clear, nor is it clear that they were to have operated much beyond a few hundred miles from the Soviet coast, where they might have enjoyed land-based air cover. They are included under destroyers because of their physical kinship with true destroyers such as the 'Kotlins'.

The *Sovremenny* and *Udaloy* classes, included in this account under the head of cruisers, are currently classified by Western analysts as destroyers, but the distinction between the two has no relation to Soviet practice, just as the distinction between missile cruisers and large missile destroyers in the US Navy appears to be one of convention rather than substance.

FRIGATES

Frigates occupy a very different place in the Soviet Navy from that enjoyed in Western navies; the ships in this section are designated *Storozhevoi Korabl'* or SKR (guard ships). They were intended as coastal pickets rather than as escorts for convoys as a means of keeping Soviet citizens in the Soviet Union and foreigners out of it. This gunboat function explains the heavy gun and torpedo armament of the two postwar classes ('Kola' and 'Riga'); perhaps the early SSM-armed destroyers had a similar operational role. The later SKRs are more heavily oriented towards coastal ASW, operating in groups, often with a 'Kashin' as flagship. In such formations, all sonar outputs are fed to the flagship, which orders a concentration of RBU fire on the presumed submarine as soon as the area of uncertainty of its position shrinks sufficiently to make an attack profitable. Similar tactics obtain with

'Riga' class frigate Phillippine Sea, April 1970 during worldwide Exercise 'Okean'. *USN*

coastal forces such as 'Poti' and 'SO 1' class submarine-chasers, but in that case the role of the flagship is taken by a land control station. It seems noteworthy that the Soviet lightweight torpedo is carried only by SKRs and below; larger ships carry 21in tubes instead. Perhaps that permits them to fire an effective anti-ship weapon as well as an ASW torpedo.

The 'Krivaks' were originally designated 'large ASW ships', or BPK, and when they appeared were generally classed as destroyers in the West. They are certainly out of the category of a 'Mirka' or 'Petya', yet in 1978 they were redesignated SKR. That may reflect their role in helping to seal SSBN sanctuaries against NATO submarine penetration, or it may reflect relatively poor sea-going characteristics, such as short range. Note that the Soviets amended their definition of SKR in the 1970s to include the escort role, which further confuses the issue. However, Soviet naval tactics do not really appear to envisage Western-style screening: Soviet ASW is generally more akin to hunter-killer operations.

SUBMARINES

The Soviet Union operates the largest submarine force in the world; its boats are usually characterised as relatively fast, deep-diving and noisy, compared to those of the United States. These characteristics are in keeping with typical Soviet submarine tactics which, like surface ship tactics, emphasise group attack under the control of detached commanders. Thus Soviet submarines are often seen either on or just under the surface, within communications range of their higher-echelon commanders; their diving capability is probably more for post-attack escape than for pre-attack evasion. As in much of the Soviet Navy, the submarine fleet is designed largely for the massive initial strike, the 'D-Day shoot-out'. Survivability in the face of Western ASW is not too important in that context.

The units which must survive, the missile submarines, do so not entirely by stealth but more by active protection; they operate in sanctuary areas such as the White and Norwegian Seas, at least in wartime. Reportedly only a small fraction remain continuously at sea, as the Soviets do not take day-to-day deterrence nearly as seriously as do their Western counterparts. One might even imagine their strategic submarines as a sea-based equivalent of the once proposed US land-mobile MX ICBM system, secure from attack because of the difficulty of simultaneously locating all of them within a large secure area.

It should also be noted that, large as the submarine fleet is, it is only a shadow of what Stalin apparently had in mind at the end of World War II: in 1948 a Soviet admiral spoke in terms of a fleet of 1200 submarines, and the Gorky plant, which built the 'Whiskeys', was certainly designed with mass production in mind. After all, with a unit life of 20 years, 1200 submarines would imply a steady-state rate of 60 submarines annually, which the Soviets actually exceeded in the early 1950s. As in the case of the surface fleet, the programme was scaled down after the death of Stalin, with major cancellations about 1956–57, as Khrushchev began his 'revolution in military affairs'. At that time he is reported to have said that he cared little for any submarine which did not fire missiles.

It may also be relevant to note that in the late 1950s, a Soviet submarine admiral proposed the creation of balanced submarine fleets, including many specialised units which would operate in concert. Although he did not mention it, such a concept would require highly effective underwater communications, which the Soviets reportedly have; it might explain the decision to build both 'Charlie' and 'Victor' class submarines.

In any case, it is important to distinguish Soviet concepts of submarine operation from Western ones, since Soviet naval objectives differ sharply from those of the more traditional Western navies: for example, Soviet ASW is directed towards the protection of ballistic missile submarines and the destruction of enemy strategic submarines rather than towards the protection of warships and convoys. Moreover, the command an control and sensor system underlying the Soviet ASW differs greatly from that of the West: geography itself prevents the Soviets from building up a SOSUS-like coverage of all the waters in which Western strategic attack submarines can operate. Thus the Soviets may have a much more urgent need (and a much more aggressive research programme) in those physical phenomena which permit submarine detection from space; should their programme succeed, once more Soviet submarine tactics and characteristics would probably differ sharply from those of the West.

It is possible to imagine a rationale for Soviet submarine evolution from the 1950s onwards. In all forms of warfare, the Soviets have generally preferred the longest-range weapons, so that they run the minimum risk of losing their firing platforms. For example, they saw the nuclear torpedo as the solution to the carrier-attack problem, since it could be fired from a considerable distance off the bow of the carrier force. In order to reach that firing position, they needed a fast submarine in contact with external reconnaissance systems: the 'November'. From that point of view a submerged-launch missile such as an SS-N-7 is a 'winged torpedo', and the 'Charlie' is the natural production successor to the 'November', presumably with the next-generation missile. The low rate of 'Charlie' production, and the fact that it is no longer in production in 1983, both attest to the shift away from anti-carrier operations evident in other types of Soviet warship. The emergence of 'Oscar' shows the revival of this type of operation.

Note, too, that the 'Victor' emerged at the same time as the 'Yankee' class strategic submarine and also at about the same time that the Soviets copied the US SUBROC in their SS-N-15. It is difficult to avoid the conclusion that these programmes were related, that as soon as the Navy was permitted to go back into the strategic role, it sought an escort for its valuable SSBNs. At the least, it would be important to help 'Yankees' break through a GIUK Gap barrier to reach firing positions in the Western Atlantic. On this theory the 'Victor' was almost an emergency design, marrying the existing 'Charlie' powerplant to an extemporised weapon system, the stolen SUBROC. 'Victors' remain ASW submarines, and they can now fire the new SS-N-16, which is presumably much more effective than the SS-N-15.

The other major line of development derives from the large strategic submarine programme of the 1950s, a programme cut short when the Strategic Rocket Forces were formed in 1959. At that time Khrushchev much preferred land-based long-range weapons, and the Soviet Navy had to forgo strategic attack missions. It was then building two separate series of missile submarines: the ballistic-weapon 'Golfs' and 'Hotels', and the cruise-missile 'Echos'. In each case the choice seems to have been to claim an anti-carrier role; the SS-N-3 missile was actually modified, as the appearance of the Front Piece/Front Door radar transponder in 'Echo IIs' shows. Note that after the completion of the 'Echo II' and 'Juliett' classes construction concentrated on 'Victors' and 'Charlies' and on ballistic missile submarines. At one time it was assumed that the 'Charlies' were intended as 'tattletales' for wartime trailing of carriers, but they are far too slow, due to their blunt noses and, one suspects, much lower power due to limited internal space

(given the requirements of missile command and control and sonar data processing).

In 1983 it appears that a new attack submarine, presumably a follow-on on the 'Victor', is under construction. Finally there is the exotic 'Alfa', which appears to be unrelated to these classes; it seems to be an extension of the ASW concepts of the 1950s.

POSTWAR COMPLETIONS OF PREWAR-DESIGN SUBMARINES

Beside the tables which follow, reportedly five prewar-type K-class cruiser submarines were completed at Leningrad in 1947; there were also reports that some of these submarines were modernised with snorkels. However, there was no Soviet programme similar to the US or British postwar submarine modernisation.

	Gorki	Sudomekh	Nikolayev
S class			
1945	1		
1946	4		
1947	1		
Shch class			
1945		2	
1946		2	
1947		1	
1948		2	
1949		1	

M-V class (Series XV)
NOTE: Nearly all of these submarines were manufactured in sections in the Leningrad area, assembled at Sudomekh, and then shipped by rail to the Far East and to the Black Sea.

1945			
1946		5	
1947		7	4
1948		9	5
1949		7	8
1950		20	3
1951		10	
1952		4	

AMPHIBIOUS WARFARE VESSELS

Historically Soviet requirements for amphibious warfare have differed sharply from those of the Western powers. Until quite recently (if even now) the primary wartime task of Soviet general purpose forces has been the seizure of Western Europe. Amphibious operations in such a war would be limited to flanking operations against NATO forces in Norway, in the Baltic, and on the Black Sea coast; such operations would not differ in any fundamental way from those which Admiral Gorshkov himself conducted along the Black Sea coastline late in World War II.

However, since the apparent emergence of a Soviet bluewater fleet, the appearance of a Soviet amphibious force comparable to that of the United States has been eagerly awaited; the *Ivan Rogov* and even the *Kiev* were advertised as its harbingers. Politically it seems unlikely that the Soviets will be particularly eager to engage in Western-style power projection. They describe themselves as the protectors of 'progressive' forces in the Third World, which means that they prefer to allow their proxies to fight on the ground, while they shield those proxies from Western intervention. For example, Admiral Gorshkov has claimed that Soviet warships off the Angolan coast deterred the United States from intervening in 1975–76. The troops on the ground were Cubans, not Russians, and no opposed landing seems to have been contemplated. It seems likely that the new generation of Soviet anti-ship warships, such as 'Oscar' and 'Kirov', are designed to further this shielding strategy, and that the non-appearance of large numbers of *Rogov*s may be significant. It may also be important that the *Rogov* herself was transferred in 1979 to the Pacific where the Soviets may need flanking support in a war against China.

Like other elements of the Soviet Fleet, the amphibious forces have suffered from changes in Soviet politics. It is fairly clear that Stalin showed little interest in such issues, merely retaining the German coastal craft seized at the end of World War II. These MFPs were unsuited to rough weather of any sort; they are comparable to the wartime British LCMs. However, soon after Admiral Gorshkov became C-in-C in 1956, a programme of freighter conversions was undertaken. Since the Admiral had already carried out operations with just such craft in wartime, it seems likely that he was personally responsible for the 'MP 2' to 'MP 8' programme. Note that these largely unarmed ships were suitable for administrative, as opposed to combat, landings. In 1956 Soviet doctrine was still quite ambiguous, and weapons and doctrines suited to a jet-age version of World War II remained in production.

However, it is clear in retrospect that Khrushchev had very different

Cruiser *Sovremenny* Jan or Feb 1982 with the new twin 130mm guns and new SS-N-22 quadruple anti-ship missile launcher (Band Stand fire control radome above)　*MoD*

ideas. He abolished the separate Naval Infantry units, and declared that the Army could do well enough without special amphibious units. Only about 1953, as Khrushchev's power began to decline, were the special units revived. At the same time the Soviets apparently began to design landng ships, such as the 'Alligator', which could provide a measure of fire support while the troops landed; note that the earlier 'Polnocny' was initially little more than an updated 'MP 10' lighter.

In this context the *Ivan Rogov* is somewhat difficult to place. She has a significant bombardment capability, but her hovercraft can travel well inland and can cover considerable ocean areas at high speed. In US practice, hovercraft have been associated with keeping the large ships well out to sea, achieving surprise by keeping the enemy from knowing where the attack will fall. In the case of the *Rogov*, it would appear that the hovercraft will be used to drive well inland but that they will be launched close inshore.

One other factor must be kept in mind. The Soviet Union has a large merchant marine subordinated to Navy control at all times. Roll-on roll-off ships can be used as amphibious transports. Heavy booms bought as standard equipment for freighters can lift small landing craft. For many years the Soviets have been exponents of a mobilisation concept of warfare, whereas in the West the civilian economy is generally not included in military calculations – although the Western civil economies are far larger than the Soviet, both in absolute terms and relative to military spending. Reportedly Soviet merchant ships participated in a Soviet amphibious exercise about 1981.

ASW CRAFT/SMALL SURFACE COMBATANTS

The Soviet Navy is the largest operator of coastal craft in the world; in this account, 'ASW craft' correspond to its classification MPK ('small ASW craft'). They are successors to World War II base area defensive craft, their design emphasising high speed with which to reach a reported submarine, rather than the low noise level common in Western concepts. They generally hunt in groups, under the control of a shore station.

From 'SO 1' onwards, there has been a steady progression upwards in unit size, so that the current 'Grisha' is quite comparable with the SKRs of the last design generation. However, a new 'Poti'-sized submarine-chaser, 'Pauk', appeared in 1980. It can be visualised either as successor to 'Osa'-sized harbour defence craft, or as a reversion to a size category left unfilled for some considerable time. 'Pauk' is listed among corvettes because of its similarity to the new 'Tarantul' class.

FAST ATTACK AND PATROL CRAFT

The Soviet Union operated very large numbers of coastal craft, both for military and for political security before World War II, when of the major navies only the Italians did the same. Although all the major navies built up large coastal forces in wartime, only the Soviets kept building MTBs postwar, and in the late 1950s they developed these craft into coastal missile boats, or 'rocket cutters', the famous 'Osas' and 'Komars'. This diversion from standard practice elsewhere in the world deserves some explanation.

First, it can be argued that a coastal MTB or missile boat can be extremely efficient, as she can sink a warship many times her size. In fact, however, because of the short range and very limited sea-keeping ability of the coastal boat, very large numbers are needed to ensure sufficient forces will be available at the point on the coast an enemy may prefer to attack. Alternatively, in an offensive war in relatively restricted waters, as in the Solomons during World War II, large numbers can be concentrated as desired. Only in the Baltic can this argument apply to the Soviets; indeed, their coastal craft were effective there during World War II. Western navies would argue that coast defence *per se* is so small a part of their task that they cannot imagine building up large flotillas simply to secure their coasts against landings, and that failure to intercept and to destroy any invasion fleet relatively far from its objective would in inexcusable. For example, the United States effectively abandoned coastal forces after 1945, returning to them only to fight coastal and riverine wars abroad (*eg* in Vietnam) in the 1960s.

The Soviet point of view is very different. In Soviet eyes *any* foreign incursion is to be resisted. Indeed, it often appears that to Soviet leaders, ordinarily land-orientated, the essential Soviet Fleet consists of coastal craft up to and perhaps including SKRs and coast defence submarines, the craft which keep foreigners out and Soviet citizens in. The very heavy investment in coastal craft follows, despite their large net cost in personnel and in maintenance.

Coastal craft evolution has been largely limited to a series of standardised hull and machinery combinations adapted to the several different tasks: torpedo attack, surface-to-surface missile attack, KGB border patrol, and coastal (almost harbour) ASW (MO series, at first). The earliest postwar type, codenamed 'P 2' in the West, was reportedly a simple derivative of prewar stepped-hull boats descended from the Thornycroft CMB and from some Italian MAS designs. Lend-Lease provided the Soviets with US hard-chine planing craft of Elco design, and many writers consider the 'P 6' descendant of that hull form. The 'Nanuchka' class 'missile corvette' is probably the most impressive departure from such small craft, with its longer-range (but not mid-course guided) weapons and its large sea-going hull. One is tempted to conclude that here was an attempt to reduce the cost of the coastal missile fleet by permitting a smaller number of boats to cover a larger coastal area. In a more general sense, the net size of the coastal fleet appears to be slowly shrinking in the face of higher unit costs and, for that matter, the high cost of building up a large bluewater fleet.

KGB BORDER PATROL CRAFT

The KGB maintains a large force of PSKs, craft intended to deny passage through Soviet sea borders in either direction in peacetime. Both specially built and modified naval types are used; the current specially built types are the 'Pchela' class hydrofoils of 1964–65 and the 'Zhuk' class displacement type patrol boat of more recent construction. There are also very large numbers of modified warships, including 'Grisha II' class frigates; some modified 'T 58' class ex-minesweepers; 'Stenka' class fast patrol boats; and 'Poluchat I', a modified version of the standard Soviet torpedo retriever.

The Soviets also maintain river gunboats, *eg* on the Danube, Amur and Ussuri rivers, most of them consisting of 'Schmel' class boats with tank turrets forward and twin ('P 6' type) 25mm AA guns aft, with a rocket launcher in the waist; they are the successors to the wartime 'armoured cutters' (BK) and are carried in the Soviet Navy as 'artillery cutters' (AK).

MINE WARFARE VESSELS

Since Tsarist times, the Russian Navy has been an enthusiastic proponent of mine warfare. The prewar naval programme included a large number of ocean minesweepers of the *Tral* class, and then, as part of the Stalin programme, fast (24kt) 'Polukhin' class ocean sweepers. Only in wartime did inshore sweeping become important, resulting in the design of the austere 'T 301' class, reportedly suited to construction in a field. Since 1945, the Soviets have continued to maintain massive sweeping forces, numerically well beyond those of the West. However, they do not appear to have adopted the minehunting doctrine of Western navies. That is, many modern mines are so sophisticated that the only real countermeasure is to locate them one by one and then destroy them.

The Soviet mine warfare force is one of the few elements of the Fleet to have had practical overseas experience of its role. In 1972 and 1973 between 4 and 9 minesweepers, with auxiliaries, cleared the Bangladesh port of Chittagong of wrecks and mines – albeit months later than planned. A Western flotilla cleared Chalna which the Soviets had been going to sweep as well. Veterans of the Chittagong operation took part in the 1974 Gulf of Suez clearance by 5 minesweepers from Vladivostok. This was completed 3½ months later than promised and the Soviet Navy found itself left out of the Suez Canal reopening ceremonies in which the US Navy did take part.

SOME GENERAL OBSERVATIONS

This sketch of the evolution of the primary role of the Soviet Fleet emphasises discontinuities in naval doctrine. The effect of industrial inertia is to continue past programmes reflecting earlier emphases, whether or not those emphases continue to be important to the Soviet naval leadership. Existing ships are, moreover, pressed into service to meet the new requirements. For example, the 'Kashin' class missile destroyers, probably the last 'traditional' destroyers ever built by any navy, were initially designated 'fleet torpedo craft' in the Tsarist tradition. With the turn towards ASW/SSBN operations, they were redesignated large ASW ships (BPK) and employed as command ships for group ASW operations by smaller submarine-chasers. It is possible that this involved the installation of specialised computers for sonar data reduction, but the physical changes were small. Similarly, the 'Foxtrot' and 'Tango' class diesel submarines are direct descendants of the 'Zulus' designed for classical submarine warfare in the North Atlantic. However, their relative silence makes them effective ASW platforms, and that appears to be their current mission. Thus, in effect, the Soviet Navy of any one point is an overlay of several quite different navies, and so is the Soviet naval production programme.

It is worth noting that although the Soviet system of industrial planning emphasises long-range programmes and thus imposes considerable rigidity, the Soviets are also very willing to copy their adversaries' equipment, allowing them in selected cases to shift warship missions and characteristics much more quickly than simple, industrial patterns might suggest. Examples of such copies would include the 'Atoll' air-to-air missile, a copy of the US Sidewinder, and quite possibly the SS-N-15 SUBROC equivalent and the SS-N-3 surface-to-surface guidance system. One might contrast the typical Western attitude that if it is 'not invented here' it is not worth having.

It is important, too, to recognise that the warships are only the most visible elements of a much more comprehensive establishment. Reference is frequently made to the large force of land-based strike bombers, at first 'Badgers', but now including many 'Backfire' supersonic bombers, as well as some 'Blinders'. It would appear that the 'May' ASW aircraft was an attempt to apply 'Badger' tactics to the ASW (as opposed to the anti-carrier) problem, the 'May', like a 'Badger', flying out to a pre-determined datum according to the dictates of an external targeting system. Similarly, one might see in the 'Bear-F' ASW reconnaissance aircraft an analogy to the 'Bear-D' which works with anti-carrier strike forces, transmitting target data to them so that they can attack over their horizons. At another remove is the vast Soviet Ocean Surveillance System, for which there is no real Western equivalent, just as there is, in 1982, no Western Navy with quite the same concerns as those which appear to animate Soviet behaviour.

DESIGNATIONS
A word on the designations of Soviet warships is in order here. The Soviets themselves assign a 'Project' number to each new design (or, at least, to each new design selected for production) and typically refer to that type by its Project number throughout its career. This practice is evident in Soviet references to warships of the World War II period and occasionally comes to light in recent contexts. However, the relatively closed character of Soviet society makes unclassified references to Project numbers of postwar classes quite rare, and few have been included in the text which follows. In addition, until very recently, open references to the names of Soviet warships have seldom been encountered, many ships even of destroyer or cruiser size bore no name plates until the mid-1970s, although that practice has now changed sharply. Only a very small fraction of the names of Soviet submarines are known, at least on an unclassified basis. Thus it is standard NATO practice to assign codenames to Soviet warships. Although many of these names appear to be Russian or Slavic in character, in fact they are entirely NATO in origin. The submarine designations are the phonetic equivalents of letters, eg 'Whiskey' for W or 'Alfa' for A. They appear to have been assigned randomly, the first three being W, Q and Z ('Whiskey', 'Quebec' and 'Zulu'). Current practice seems to be to assign the Soviet name of a class where possible, the principal cases being the *Moskva* and *Kiev*, and possibly the new nuclear cruiser *Kirov*.

SOVIET NAVAL WEAPONS AND SENSORS

NUCLEAR WEAPONS
Many Soviet naval weapons have alternative nuclear and conventional versions. Since the late 1950s Soviet military doctrine has consistently emphasised nuclear weapons as the single decisive element in modern warfare, and it is sometimes assumed that such weapons would be used at the outset of a naval war. The detection of nuclear torpedoes aboard the elderly 'Whiskey' class submarine which grounded in Swedish home waters in October 1981 underlined this belief. However, more recently it has been reported that the 'Kynda' class cruiser which sortied into the Mediterranean during the October 1973 crisis was not carrying the standard outfit of nuclear-armed SS-N-3 missiles: one might suspect that, in a period of intense crisis, the Soviet leadership would be chary of unintended nuclear use. One might even go further, and observe that Soviet ideology asserts that the primary war scenario is a *Western* surprise attack on the Soviet Union. Soviet naval forces deploy only in relatively small numbers in peacetime, and one might go so far as to think of the nuclear weapons on board as an emergency 'equaliser' – to be removed in the event of lengthy limited-war warning. The reader is cautioned that such analysis is speculative, but it still seems worth keeping in mind.

GUN SYSTEMS
152mm/57 Triple mount of 1938-pattern in *Sverdlov* and *Chapaev* classes. It elevates to 50 degrees, and is credited with 4–5rpm per gun. Shell weight: 110lb (50kg), effective range reportedly 19,685yds/18,000m = 9.7nm (maximum 27,000m). Muzzle velocity: 3000fps (915 m/sec).
130mm Standard postwar and prewar destroyer calibre. The twin 130/50 semi-automatic 1936–pattern mount in the *Skory* class elevated only to 45 degrees, and was capable of 10rpm per barrel. Shell weight: 60lb (27kg), effective range 15,310–16,400yds/14,000–15,000m (muz-

Quadruple 57mm/70 aboard 'Krupny' class destroyer with triple 533mm TT below and Hawk Screech fire control radar above 1970   *USN*

zle velocity 2870fps or 875 m/sec). The postwar twin tri-axially stabilised 130/58 of 1953 pattern in the 'Kotlins' and their successors appears to have been based on German wartime and prewar practice, the guns elevating through the mount roof to 80 degrees; credited with 10rpm per barrel and with a maximum range of 30,620yds/28,000m (muzzle velocity 2950fps or 900m/sec), and was the last large Soviet naval gun until *Sovremenny*. The latter introduced in 1981 a new twin water-cooled 130/70, credited with 65rpm per barrel, and with a maximum range of 30,620yds/28,000m (15nm), compared with 26,240yds/24,000m (13nm) for *Skory*. This weapon may be designed to use a guided shell; the Soviets are known to have laser-guided bombardment rockets.
100mm Standard frigate and cruiser secondary battery gun. 'Kola' and 'Riga' classes had the 1947-model single 100/56, elevating to 40 degrees and firing 15rpm. Shell weight 30lb/13.6kg, effective range 10,930yds/10,000m (muzzle velocity 2780fps or 850m/sec). The contemporary *Chapaev*/*Sverdlov* mount was a twin German-type, tri-axially stabilised, elevating to 85 degrees. It is often described as a 100mm/50, although that seems inconsistent. It may fire a heavier shell (according to one source, the shell is 15kg, with a muzzle velocity of 2950fps or 900m/sec, and a rate of fire of 15rpm per barrel). This calibre was reintroduced since 1976 in 'Krivak II' and *Kirov* as a single water-cooled weapon firing 80rpm, with an effective range of 8750yds/8000m (4.3nm).
85mm The 1943–pattern twin 85/52 in the *Skory* class elevated to 70 degrees, fired 10rpm per barrel and had an effective range against surface targets of 8750–9840yds/8000–9000m (6560yds/6000m against air targets). Shell weight was 26lb (12kg) and muzzle velocity 2780fps or 950m/sec.
76.2mm Note the calibre, equal to 3in, rather than some round metric number. In its 1961-model twin 76.2/60 form succeeded the twin 57mm, and was credited with 45rpm per barrel. Projectile: 35lb/16kg. Effective range: 6560–7650yds/6000–7000m in AA fire (muzzle velocity 2780fps or 800m/sec). A single fully automatic FAC gun is credited with 120rpm ('Matka' and other classes).
57mm There is an old open 57/70, in single, twin, and quadruple mounts (the latter with the pairs superposed): 150rpm per barrel. Effective vertical range: 4920yds/4500m (6lb/2.8kg shell, muzzle velocity 2950–3280fps/900–1000m/sec). The twin water-cooled 57/70 of 1961 was the first gun of this type without an on-mount crew: 120rpm per gun. Effective vertical range: 5460–6580yds/5000–6000m, which suggests a larger cartridge case and therefore a heavier round, for slower fire.
45mm Quadruple 45/85 mount, early 1950s, 75rpm per barrel. Effective vertical range 4370yds/4000m (4.8lb/2.2kg shell, 2950fps or 900m/sec). Also exists in single form.
37mm Twin mount, early postwar period, 37/63 (model 39AA), 160rpm per gun. Resembles Western 40mm Bofors guns, but with a prominent shield. Reportedly fires a 1.5lb/0.7lb shell at 900m/sec, and is effective against air targets out to 3280yds/3000m (anti-surface to 4000m).
30mm The twin automatic mount, originally in light craft, was introduced in 1959; remote-controlled, 60-calibre, 240rpm. Effective range for AA fire: 2730–3280yds/2500–3000m (1.2lb/0.54kg shell, muzzle velocity 3280fps or 1000m/sec).

In 1970 a 30mm six-barrel Gatling credited with an effective rate of 3000rpm, appeared. Compared with the US Phalanx, it lacks a closed-loop spotting system.
25mm Twin over-and-under 25/60 initially fitted in large numbers in light craft, then in many other types of ship. Maximum rate of fire was 150–200rpm, and the weapon was always optically controlled. Effective range against air targets is reportedly 3000m (¾lb/0.34kg shell, 2950fps or 900m/sec muzzle velocity).

ANTI-AIRCRAFT MISSILES

NOTE: SA-N-1, -2, -3, -4 are all command-guided, their guidance radar systems including both target- and missile-tracking dishes and a command dish. The policy seems to be one guidance radar for each two-arm launcher, so that only one target can be engaged for each pair of missiles fired.

SA-N-1 Naval version of land-based SA-3 'Goa' missile, 1962 prototype in 'Kotlin' class destroyer *Bravyy*. Fire control: Peel Group. Range reportedly 34,450yds/31,500m (17nm) capable of interception between 300 and 50,000ft; 132lb/60kg warhead. The configuration is canard, with relatively large fixed wings, and there is a short booster, the tail fins of which fold out as the missile leaves the launcher. Diameter: 18in/45cm (body), 27in/70cm (booster); length 19ft/5.9m; wingspan 4ft/1.2m. Launch weight is about 1300lb/600kg. Magazine capacity: reportedly 22 (24 in 'Kynda').

SA-N-2 Naval version of land-based SA-2 'Guideline', probably for test use only, in the *Sverdlov* class cruiser *Dzerzhinskiy*. It required a unique height-finding radar (High Lune) as well as the land-type Fan Song fire control set. Range is reportedly 48,100yds/44,000m (23.7nm), 290lb/130kg warhead. Diameter 19ft 6in/50cm (missile), 27in/70cm (booster), length 35ft/10.7m wingspan 5ft 6in/1.7m (missile), 7ft 2in/2.2m (booster), launch weight 4750lb/2150kg. Magazine capacity: reportedly only 10 in *Dzerzhinskiy*.

SA-N-3 The only naval missile without a land-based equivalent. Introduced 1967 and codenamed 'Goblet' by NATO. The only published photograph shows shallow-chord delta wings, and they may indicate a lengthened surface-to-surface range, for something approaching dual-purpose use. Fire control: Head Lights. Range is reportedly 32,800yds/30,000m or 16nm (improved version, in *Kiev*, 60,100yds/55,000m or 29nm), to intercept at 300–80,000ft; 176lb/80kg warhead. Magazine capacity: 22 (*Kiev* 36).

SA-N-4 Point defence missile (NATO codename 'Gecko'), reportedly with a range of about 9840yds/9000m (5nm, based on the land-based SA-8. The twin-arm launcher is housed in a silo, rising when loaded to fire. Presumably this complex loading cycle makes for a low rate of fire. Fire Control Radar: Pop Group. Missile capacity per silo is variously reported as 18 and 20. The vertically-launched point defence missile in *Udaloy* is presumably either a successor or a related development. Range is reportedly 16,180yds/14,800m (8nm); 110lb/50kg (warhead); weight 420lb/190lb, length 10ft/3.2m, diameter 8in/21cm, span 25in/64cm.

SA-N-5 Naval version of the land-based SA-7 'Grail' infra-red guided missile, introduced in the late 1970s and now widespread aboard Soviet patrol and amphibious craft. Fired either from a quadruple launcher, or shoulder-launched; IR-guided, and can home both on a hot tailpipe and, reportedly, on the 'glint' from the forward parts of an aircraft or missile, as can recent versions of the US Sidewinder and Stinger. Approximate range 1100yds/1000m, with 5.5lb/2.5kg warhead; length 30in/76cm, diameter 2.7in/7cm, weight 20lb/9.2kg.

SA-N-6 Naval version (1980) of the new land-based SA-10 area defence missile, employing a phased-array command guidance radar, reportedly with track-via-missile guidance as in the US land-based Patriot system. It appears that each guidance radar can control 6 missiles, based on the ratio of launchers to radars in the nuclear cruiser *Kirov*. Fire control radar: Top Dome. Range is reportedly about 328,000ft/100,000m (54nm), and the vertical launcher holds 8 missiles in a rotating magazine. Length is about 23ft/7m.

SA-N-7 The first Soviet semi-active guided radar, a naval version of the land-based SA-11, itself a development of the land-based SA-6. It first appeared in 1981 aboard *Sovremmenny*. Fire control: Front Dome, a very compact radar similar in appearance to Bass Tilt. Several are provided for each launcher, facing in several directions, so that in theory a ship can engage several targets simultaneously. *Provornyy*, the trials ship for the system, with one single-arm launcher, has 8 of them; *Sovremennyy*, the production version, with two single-arm launchers, has only 6. Reportedly this Mach 3 missile has a range of 30,620yds/28,000m or 15nm (3000m minimum) and can intercept targets from 100–46,000ft altitude.

ANTI-SHIP MISSILES

Most Soviet anti-ship missiles have both conventional (HE) and nuclear warheads. The conventional versions are large shaped charges, the penetrating effect of which is supplemented by liquid fuel remaining in the missile at the end of its flight. This combination is best adapted to attacks against heavily armoured ships, and the sheer bulk of the warhead increases missile size well beyond figures common in the West.

The Soviet missile programme reportedly began with tests of German weapons in 1945, primarily the V-1 and V-2, but including the Wasserfall, Schmetterling, Rheintochter, and Rheinbote AA weapons.

It is often claimed that the first Soviet SAM, the SA-1, was derived directly from the Wasserfall, and that the early SSM weapons were developed V-2s.

Although the SS-N-1 was the first Soviet anti-ship missile to enter operational service, it appears that development work was intensive from about 1945 onwards, and there were probably several experimental weapons still largely unknown in the West. In particular, the air- and land-launched Komet, AS-1/SSC-1, was tested aboard the trials cruiser *Admiral Nakhimov* in 1956–57, according to a Soviet naval officer of that period. Apparently the system was not well liked, and no other installations were made.

Soviet ship-launched missile development shows three very distinct paths: air-breathing cruise missiles, rocket cruise missiles, and ballistic missiles, and it is reasonable to associate them with different design bureaux. In particular the air breathers, from the SS-N-1 onwards, presumably originated with a conventional aircraft designer, the most probable being Semyon A Lavochkin, who dropped out of fighter design about the time SS-N-1 must first have been tested. SS-N-3 was reportedly designed by a bureau headed by V N Chelomei. Note that the experimental Berezhnyak-Isaev rocket fighter of World War II was loosely similar to the later SS-N-2, so that one of the two original designers may have developed that series. It appears that the SS-N-4 and -5 were the products of the Yangel' bureau, which was the second Soviet ballistic missile organisation (after Korolev, who designed the early land-based missiles, including the huge SS-6). However, recent publications suggest that Chelomei took over from the SS-N-6 onwards, and indeed that he also assumed some land-based projects, including the SS-11. Some writers have gone so far as to suggest that the SS-11 was conceived by a naval missile bureau as a land-based anti-ship missile, but that seems unlikely in bureaucratic terms, given the rivalry between the Soviet Navy and the Stategic Rocket Forces.

The list of Western designations cannot be complete. A memoir by a Soviet emigre describes an exhibition, arranged in 1961 by Admiral Gorshkov for Khrushchev; it included what appears to have been SS-N-9, SS-N-8, and possibly an early fore-runner of SS-N-19. However, there was also a project no trace of which has surfaced: a ship-launched satellite intended specifically for target acquisition and guidance to missiles in flight; over-the-horizon data links to aircraft would be developed as an interim solution. The latter may refer to SS-N-3.

SS-N-1 Strela (Soviet name; NATO name Scrubber), the first Soviet shipborne anti-ship missile, a turbojet powered weapon mounted aboard 'Krupny' and 'Kildin' class destroyers. It was housed in armoured 9 or 10 missile hangars, and warmed up before launching. Although Strela range was estimated as up to 150nm on the basis of its size, fire control appears to have been by an extension of standard gun procedures, via modified Wasp Head director with Top Bow radar, which would mean no more than horizon range, perhaps about 30nm. SS-N-1 employed radio command guidance with active radar terminal guidance. Helicopter platforms aboard some of these ships prompted speculation that over the horizon targeting could be assisted by a third-party ship-based helicopter. However, it does not appear that the Soviets had an efficient over-the-horizon targeting system until the appearance of the SS-N-3/Bear D/Hormone A combination in the 1960s. Both conventional and nuclear warheads were reported. SS-N-1 was apparently relatively unsuccessful, the last few ships armed with it completing their time as target-launchers. Diameter 39in/1m, length 25ft/7.6m, span 15ft/4.6m, launch weight 7050lb/3200kg (3.1t).

The Soviet designation of this system was KSSh; it was reportedly tested by Northern Fleet in 1960–61. A Soviet emigre who worked on the project reported that the warhead was designed to detach from the missile as it approached its target, so as to achieve an underwater hit. He also reports that system reliability was not high, and that hit probability was low.

SS-N-2 Styx (as NATO dubbed it in 1959), the first anti-ship missile to sink a ship in anger, when Egyptian 'Komar' class missile boats sank the Israeli destroyer *Eilat* in 1967; it was also used successfully by the Indian Navy in the Indo-Pakistan War of 1971, by the Chinese Navy in combat in the Paracel Islands in 1974 and by the Iraqi Navy in the war with Iran since 1980. However, Styx boats were badly beaten in the October 1973 War, reportedly partly because of the considerable time required to line up gyros before firing. Styx was the first of a series of active radar guided 'fire and forget' liquid-fuel missiles.

The Soviet designation of SS-N-2 is P-15. Development began in 1954, and it entered service in 1958 aboard 'Komar' class attack boats. The Square Tie targeting radar can detect a destroyer under favourable conditions at up to 22nm (maximum theoretical range of the radar is 48nm), and fast patrol boats can be detected at about 10nm. The operator manually sets a range gate around the target, and missile firing data is computed for target ranges of 3 to 15nm. At greater ranges, the impact point has to be calculated manually on a manoeuvring board, which significantly reduces hit probability. The missile platform has to be turned into the direction of the impact point, and in theory the number of missiles launched varies with the target: 7 to 8 for a cruiser, 4 for a destroyer. Hit probability against fast missile boats is lower due to their limited radar cross-section, and the doctrine is to fire 2-4. Styx is launched at 15 degrees to the vertical, then climbs at 45 to an altitude of about 450ft. The seeker, which operates at one of six preset frequencies, is switched on 6 miles from the estimated impact point. It seeks the strongest echo, and (at least in early versions) cannot distinguish fixed from moving targets. The terminal manoeuvre is a dive.

Maximum range was 25nm (50,635yds), but effective range was 16nm. The missile's altitude can be preset at 100, 150, 200, 250 or 300m. The warhead is 880–990lb/400–450kg of HE. Recent SS-N-2s reportedly have an alternative infra-red homer. SS-N-2B was the version with folding wings, in 'Osa II' is a modified version with a range of 45nm and combined radar, infra-red homing. It descends to 2 to 5m (sea-skims) during its final approach. SS-N-2C is carried by modified 'Kashin' and 'Kildin' class destroyers, by 'Tarantul' class missile corvettes, and by 'Nanuchka' II type export missile corvettes. SS-N-7/9 are related developments. Small craft armed with SS-N-2 generally use the Square Tie surface search radar for target designation, but destroyers do not. These weapons are loaded with storable liquid propellants which gradually corrode the missile bodies, and they must therefore be expended after a set period of time, probably about two years. Diameter 30in/75cm, length 21.3ft/6.5m, wing span 9ft/2.75m, launch weight 5070lb/2300lb (SS-N-2A). Cruise speed Mach 0.9 or 666mph. SS-N-2C: 31in/78cm diameter.

Final testing was completed by Northern Fleet (Severodvinsk test site) during 1960–61, although it appears that missile boat production began as early as 1959. Early testing had been done at Feodosia, on the Black Sea. Reportedly no nuclear warhead was designed for it because of its relatively short range, initially about 13nm/25km: Soviet experts believed that at such distances nuclear weapons were dangerous to the launch platform. A rocket rather than an air-breathing engine was chosen to permit very rapid launch, on the theory that an attacking boat would not be able to remain within attack range for very long.

A former Soviet naval missile test officer claims that, at least at first, SS-N-2 had a mid-course command guidance phase, flying at an altitude of 400m/1310ft; it used active guidance only near the target. Its homing radar had alternative wide and narrow gates, permitting it to attack either any ship in a formation or one particular ship. Note that more recent information, presumably based on compromised SS-N-2 missiles, does not mention any command phase; this may reflect the impracticality of that type of operation. Initial Northern Fleet testing was by two 'Osa I' class boats. Soviet estimates of this period were that two hits were needed to sink a destroyer (roughly consistent with the later *Eilat* attack) and that 12 missiles (3 boats) were required to assure this level of damage. Boats were, therefore, organised in units of three, and doctrine was that two units were needed to insure that one would reach the target. Missile installation and arming initially took 15 hours, but was later reduced to 12, and by 1962 an 'Osa' could be outfitted with 4 missiles in 4–6 hours.

SS-N-3 Shaddock in NATO terminology, for many years the primary Soviet long-range anti-ship missile. It is a supersonic turbojet missile, and the first version, fired from 'Echo I' class submarines, was a strategic weapon akin to the US Regulus. About 1960 a new version for anti-ship attack was developed, in line with a revision in Soviet naval doctrine. It transmits its radar picture back to the launching ship for target designation, the ship also benefiting from radar transmission from a 'Bear D' bomber or a 'Homone B' helicopter. In the 'Echo II' and 'Juliett' class submarines, guidance data is transmitted by a Front Door/Front Piece radar. In cruisers that role is filled by Scoop Pair. Most SS-N-3 cruisers also carry the Plinth Net antenna to port and starboard, but its function (apart from SS-N-3 association) is unknown. SS-N-3A is the submarine-launched homing version, SS-N-3B the cruiser version, and SS-N-3C the earlier unguided submarine weapon. Maximum range is 220nm (400km). There are both nuclear (350kt?) and conventional versions. Body diameter is 38.3in/97.5cm, length approximately 33ft/10.2m (reportedly 11.75m in SS-N-3C), and wing span about 6.8ft/2.1m; cruise speed Mach 1.4 (1040mph), and the strategic version has an aerodynamic range of about 450nm. The range of the anti-ship version is determined by guidance considerations rather than by fuel load. The successor system, SS-N-12, is similar but faster; the Trap Door guidance radar on the *Kievs* is apparently related to Front Piece/Front Door.

The Soviet designation of the unguided weapon was P-5, P-5D being an improved type with a doppler altimeter. Chelomei was the designer.

The 'Whiskey' 'Single' and 'Twin Cylinder' submarines were converted for the initial Northern Fleet tests. Reportedly they were disappointing. For example, loading into the cylinders was slow, and onboard tests and prelaunch preparation took more than 40 minutes. A Soviet emigre reports that a submarine at sea with empty containers sank, and that a two-year search failed to find her. The US Navy found somewhat similar potential problems in Regulus missile submarines with large missile hangars communicating directly with the pressure hull.

It appears that P-6 and possibly P-7 were designations for the submarine-launched, nuclear-tipped anti-carrier version of SS-N-3. P-35 was the designation for the surface ship and shore protection version.

SS-N-7 Submarine-launched conventional-warhead liquid-fuel anti-ship missile, active radar homing, fired from 'Charlie' class submarines. Operational since 1969–70. Maximum range is 35nm (64km). Cruise speed is Mach 1.5 (1110mph). Length about 24ft/7m, weight about 7440lb/3375kg.

SS-N-9 Liquid-fuel anti-ship missile, called Siren by NATO, fired from Soviet surface attack craft and probably also from 'Charlie II' class submarines. It considerably outranges SS-N-7, and it is not clear to what extent it benefits from third-party targeting, since ships carrying it ('Nanuchkas') do not display elaborate antennas such as Scoop Pair or Front Door/Front Piece. Moreover, submarines credited with this weapon do not surface to fire. Although this is theoretically a fire-and-forget weapon, it is associated with the Band Stand radar aboard missile craft. Its successor is SS-N-22, reportedly much faster and with a much lower-altitude trajectory. Length 29ft/8.8m, weight 6500lb/2950kg, with a 1100lb/500kg nuclear (200kt) or conventional warhead.

Note that in 1961 Admiral Gorshkov reportedly showed Khrushchev a proposal for a 50–70km patrol boat missile which might well have become SS-N-9.

SS-N-10 Erroneous designation, for a non-existent anti-ship weapon aboard 'Krivak' and 'Kresta II' class ships: these ships are actually ASW craft and carry SS-N-14.

SS-N-11 See SS-N-2C.

SS-N-12 Successor since 1973 to SS-N-3, aboard *Kiev* class carriers and some refitted submarines. Known as Sandbox in the West. Like the earlier weapon, it still requires mid-course guidance (target designation). Range 300nm (555km). Speed Mach 2.5 (1850mph). Warhead about 2200lb/1000kg. The higher speed makes for longer effective range. Length is reportedly 38ft/11.7m.

SS-N-13 Abortive ballistic anti-ship missile, last tested in the early 1970s, and reportedly compatible with a 'Yankee' class launch tube. It had a range of about 400nm (740km), and probably homed on characteristic radar emissions, with a terminal manoeuvring 'footprint' about 30nm in diameter.

SS-N-19 Successor to SS-N-12, suitable for underwater launch, and therefore requiring no mid-course guidance. Presumably that implies very high speed, as the missile cannot compensate for gross target motion during its flight. 'Oscar' and 'Kirov' classes since 1980.

As early as 1961 Admiral Gorshkov appears to have proposed to Khrushchev a cruise missile which could be launched by a submerged submarine against surface ship targets at a range of up to 320nm (600km). A the same time surface combatant missile range was to have been extended to 430nm (800km), and Gorshkov showed proposals for exotic over-the-horizon targeting schemes.

SS-N-22 Successor to SS-N-9, probably in *Sovremmenny* class. Reportedly it is a very fast 28–30ft/8.5m–9m sea-skimmer; with a 1000lb/500kg warhead and a range of 60–90nm/110–180km. Band Stand fire control.

ANTI-SUBMARINE MISSILES

SUW-N-1 Unguided nuclear missile aboard *Moskva* and *Kiev* classes, adapted from the Army Frog-7 with a range of about 16nm (30km), *ie* bottom-bounce sonar range.

SS-N-14 Torpedo-carrying cruise missile (Silex), with a range of about 30nm (minimum range about 4nm), fired by 'Krivak', 'Kresta I', and later classes since 1968. Command guidance by Eye Bowl radars. Guidance is via the Head Lights missile control radar in ships equipped with SA-N-3.

SS-N-15 Soviet equivalent of the US Subroc, a TT-launched nuclear depth charge. Subroc was compromised about 1965, and it is at least arguable that the 1974 'Victor' class was designed around it.

SS-N-16 SS-N-15 equivalent carrying a homing torpedo. Note that the standard Soviet lightweight torpedo is much heavier than the US Mk 44/46 (and is also of larger diameter), so that it is unlikely that SS-N-16 fits a standard 21in torpedo tube. That may account for the change from 'Victor I' to 'Victor II' or III. There may be a nuclear depth bomb variant; for some years there has been intense controversy

SS-N-1 anti-ship launcher aboard a 'Krupny' class destroyer 1970   *USN*

as to whether the Soviets had the means to target their homing torpedoes at the range claimed for both this weapon and for SS-N-14. Nuclear depth bombs of sufficient yield would be a possible solution, although they would pose problems for the launching platform.

STRATEGIC MISSILES

The Soviets fired their first submarine ballistic missile, a modified Army-type Scud, from a 'Zulu' in September 1955. Reportedly this was not the first such attempt. In 1945, in common with the Western powers, the Soviets captured details of a German project for a submarine-towed submersible barge which could carry and then launch up to three V-2 missiles. US trials with a scale model of this device were failures, but reports of Soviet experiments were common in the early postwar years. It appears that intelligence information at this time was far too uncertain for such reports to carry full conviction.

Naval Scud The Soviet designation was R-11FM, and initial installations were aboard 'Zulu' class submarines rebuilt at Severodvinsk (Molotovsk). It was a direct development of an Army weapon, as is suggested by the suffix in the designation. Reportedly the earliest version was non-nuclear, with an 1760lb/800kg warhead; that may reflect delays in Soviet efforts to miniaturise nuclear weapons. A Soviet emigre (who had been a missile test officer) reports that a 'Zulu' could not launch it in sea conditions beyond wind force five. The submarine would surface, open her two launch tubes, lift her platforms (in the tubes), and then turn them to align the missile with the planes of two of the three gyro stabilisers in the direction of fire. This preparation took several minutes, and even then the weapons could be fired only when the submarine was on an even keel. The missile was held by four brackets on the platform while its engine built up thrust. Testing began about 1956, the missile becoming operational in 1959. According to the Soviet naval officer, R-11FM was considered little more than a means of acquiring experience. Even so, when it entered service, a Navy-wide order stated that it gave the submarine fleet a new mission: attacks against large land targets. By this time the next weapon was already under test.

Initial work was done in the early 1950s by a special design office under General Designer Makayev.

SS-N-4 First Soviet submarine-launched ballistic missile, operational 1958 and codenamed Sark by the West; it had to be launched on the surface. Each missile tube was equipped with an elevator, which pushed the missile to the top of the submarine's fin before it could be fired. Liquid fuel, range about 350nm/650km. Diameter 6ft/1.8m, length 46ft/14m, launch weight about 43,650lb/19,800kg. Yield was reportedly 1 megaton, and CEP about 2nm/3.7m.

The Soviet designation of this system was R-13; reportedly designed specifically for the 'Golf' and 'Hotel' class submarines. Early tests were made at Kapustin Yar, and the weapon was ultimately tested by Northern Fleet. The single warhead detached in flight; it weighed about 1.5 metric tons. Missiles were initially carried empty, with fuel in special tanks. Reportedly the Soviets switched to carrying them fuelled after several poisoning incidents due to vibration breaking seals. The launch procedure matched that of the naval Scud, but the missile reached an altitude of 296,000–328,000ft/90–100km, compared with 82,000ft/25km for the earlier type. After reaching apogee, the missile pitched over into a pre-programmed dive, and the warhead separated and flew on. Prelaunch checkout was done submerged, after which the battery in the missile lasted about an hour. Launch itself took about 3 minutes on the surface, and tests were made into a 3 × 3km target area (75 to 80 per cent impacts).

Reportedly submarines carrying three R-13s in 1960–61 had one or two practice weapons with dummy warheads, and only one or two live weapons. No longer in service.

SS-N-5 Successor in 1963 to SS-N-4 (known to NATO as Serb) suitable for underwater launch. Range about 750nm/1390km, later improved to 900nm/1668km. Liquid fuel. Warhead about 800kt, CEP

about 1.5nm/2.7km. Diameter 4ft/120cm, length 42ft/13m, launch weight about 36,700lb/16,650kg.

The Soviet designation was R-21; testing in Northern Fleet began in 1961. At this time the test submarine fired at a depth of 65–100ft/20–30m. The missile was propelled to 100ft/30m above the surface by compressed air. A Soviet emigre claims a range of 1080nm/2000km for this weapon, which is considerably beyond the figure claimed in the West; he claims 650nm/1200km for SS-N-4. Six of the 13 'Golf II' submarines still armed with this weapon in 1982 were in the Baltic Fleet.

SS-N-6 'Yankee' class submerged-launch missile, NATO's Sawfly. Three versions: Mod 1 (1968), 1300nm/2400km; Mod 2 (1973), 1600nm/3000km; Mod 3 (1974), 2 MRVs, also 1600nm range. Liquid fuel. In its single-warhead version the warhead has a yield of about 650 or 700kt; each of the two RVs is 350kt. Accuracy: CEP about 1nm. Reportedly about 1000 were built. Mod 2 is the most numerous Soviet sea-based strategic missile, 400 being deployed in 1982. Diameter 6ft/1.8m, length 33ft/10m, launch weight about 41,600lb/18,900kg.

SS-N-8 'Delta' class submerged-launch missile, using stellar-inertial guidance to obtain useful accuracy even when firing from Soviet home waters. It entered service in 1973. Two versions: Mod 1, 4200nm/7800km range; Mod 2, 4900nm/9100km; one RV (about 800kt) in each case. Accuracy: CEP 0.84nm in Mod 2; reportedly the stellar-inertial system was not always reliable, and initial reports of spectacular accuracy were exaggerated. Such systems, for example, sometimes fix on the wrong star or set of stars. Diameter 64in/165cm, length 42ft/12.9m, launch weight about 45,000lb/20,400kg. Liquid fuel.

The origins of this weapon are unknown. However, in 1961 Admiral Gorshkov ordered a special set of exhibits at the Northern Fleet Test Base for a visit by Khrushchev; they apparently showed new missile systems he wanted developed. Khrushchev did not visit the base as planned, but saw the same material later in the year on the Black Sea. Exhibits included a mock-up of a submarine with vertical launch tubes, in connection with a project for building submarines with 16–24 missiles; an increase of missile range to 3780nm/7000km (as in SS-N-8); solid-fuel propulsion; underwater missile launch; development of improved submarine navigation equipment for ballistic missile launch. All of these projects would seem to prefigure the SS-N-8.

SS-N-17 Limited-production solid-fuel missile to replace SS-N-6 in one 'Yankee' conversion; presumably for system testing, as no more conversions have been reported. Range 2100nm/3890km. First tested 1975, at sea in a 'Yankee' class submarine 1977. It has a MIRV-type post-boost vehicle, but only one RV; this additional guidance may be intended to improve accuracy. Diameter 64in/165cm, length about 36ft/11m.

SS-N-18 First Soviet MIRV missile for submarines. Storable liquid propellant fuel as in SS-N-6/8. Versions: Mod 1, 3 MIRVs, 3500nm/6480km; Mod 2, one RV, 4300nm/7960km; Mod 3, 7 MIRVs 3500nm/6480km. CEP is reportedly 800m. Diameter 6ft/180cm, length 46ft/14.1m, which makes it substantially larger than the SS-N-6/8 series. Mod 1 was introduced in 1977, Mods 2 and 3 in 1979. Yields: Mod 1, 200kt, Mod 2, 450kt. CEPs 0.76nm/1400m in Mods 1 and 2. Deployed aboard 13 'Delta III' class in 1982.

SS-N-20 Typhoon missile, somewhat larger than SS-N-18, first fired 1982. Solid fuel, length 49ft/15m. Six to nine MIRVs, range 4500nm/8330km. A successor is expected to begin tests in 1983.

SS-N-21 Soviet equivalent of the US Tomahawk, a TT launched cruise missile with a range of about 1600nm/2960km. It is not clear whether this weapon can be carried by all Soviet submarines and surface combatants with 21in TT. If in fact SS-N-16 requires a larger tube, one might speculate that this weapon is sized for that larger tube, as part of a family of weapons which could also include a large-diameter torpedo. This will determine whether the Soviets can easily fit strategic weapons in their non-strategic submarine force.

AIR TO SURFACE WEAPONS

Although these are not ship-launched, the Soviet Navy is so dependent on them to counter Western naval formations that they deserve inclusion. In one important case, AS-1, the weapon almost saw shipboard service. Soviet Naval Aviation (SNA) took over all missile-firing 'Badger' bombers (and lost all defensive fighters) in a 1961 reorganisation. However, 'Bears' with AS-3 stand-off strategic weapons were not affected. Reportedly non-Navy units now operate anti-shipping missile-armed bombers, so the SNA order of battle may no longer constitute the full threat to Western surface forces.

AS-1 Soviet designation was Komet, and development reportedly began in 1946; the project was so important that it was headed by the son of Lavrenti P Beria, Stalin's infamous police chief. It was a beam-rider: the bomber had to remain within sight of the target. Propulsion was by turbojet, and range about 50nm/92km; operational from 1958 onwards. Typically a 'Badger' bomber carried two underwing. AS-5 is its successor.

SSC-1 is a ground-launched version for Soviet Coastal Services, a branch of the Navy. Reportedly this latter weapon was designated S-2 in Soviet service, and was developed during 1952–58. It had an airframe derived from that of the MiG-15 jet fighter, and was powered by a used MiG-15 engine (RD-500K) with over 5 hours of running life remaining. A Soviet emigre reported a range of 13.5nm/25km for this version, which was also the one tested aboard the cruiser *Admiral Nakhimov*. The missile was considered good for 5 years of storage, with a check every year; hence the need for a 5-hour engine lifetime, even though running time against a target would be only about 15 minutes. SSC-1 was a beam-rider with active terminal radar homing.

This system was reportedly installed aboard *Admiral Nakhimov* during 1956–57, and several successful launches were made. However, the project was abandoned in view of the size of the launcher and, reportedly, the inefficiency of so large a weapon. In 1958 it was demonstrated for Marshal Tito on the Soviet naval test range at Cape Feolent near Sevastopol; final acceptance (of the land version) occurred in 1958–59. Initially deployed in concrete bunkers apparently only on the Black Sea; in the mid-1960s a mobile system was deployed, and in the early 1970s the S-2 was replaced by a newer missile, the S-35, a land version of the SS-N-3.

AS-2 For many years 'Kipper' was by far the most effective Soviet anti-carrier weapon, a supersonic (1036mph or Mach 1.4) active-radar homing missile with a 2200lb/1000lb warhead and 115nm/200km range. 'Badger' C or G carried one on the centreline, locking it onto the target before dropping it. Weight is about 9260lb/4200kg, length 31ft/9.5m, and span 16ft/4.9m. It became operational in 1960 or 1961.

AS-3 A 33ft/15m unguided strategic stand-off missile, Kangaroo to NATO, apparently a modified SU-7 fighter with a large 500kt H-bomb and guidance system replacing the pilot. Entered service 1961. It is carried only by 'Bear' B and C bombers. Weight 17,600lb/7980kg and speed 1332mph or Mach 1.8.

AS-4 This stand-off anti-ship missile (Kitchen) appears to have been developed specifically for the Tu-22 'Blinder', a supersonic bomber developed in the late 1950s as a 'Badger' replacement. It was first seen in 1961 on a Soviet Air Force 'Blinder' B, and was later adapted for 'Backfire' B and for 'Bear' B and C aircraft of the strategic air arm; it has not been seen on Navy Blinders. It is reportedly a very difficult AA target because it cruises at extreme altitude, then dives steeply as it approaches its target. Guidance is by active radar locked-on before launch, and reportedly there are both conventional and nuclear versions. At least some of the latter may be inertially guided, perhaps as an AS-3 replacement. Speed is estimated at Mach 2.5–3.5 (1850–2590mph), and weight is about 14,330lb/6500kg (length 37ft/11.3m, span 11ft/3.3m). It became operational in 1967. Range 170–300nm (310–555km).

AS-5 This is the active-radar guided HE warhead replacement for AS-1, carried underwing by 'Badger' C and G aircraft. It became operational about 1965–66. Length 28ft/8.5m, 125nm/230km range.

AS-6 This is the replacement (Kingfish) for AS-4, observed so far only since 1977 under 'Badger' bombers, probably with a considerably higher speed but with a similar flight profile. Note that bombers carrying missiles which they must lock-on *before* launch can be forced to close a battle group which is jamming their target acquisition radars. However, for some years the appearance of weapons which can be locked on *after* launch has been predicted. Bombers so armed would be able to launch from below the radar horizon of the target force, beyond the range of the defending fighters.

ASW ROCKET LAUNCHERS

NOTE: The figure in the designation is the nominal range in metres, *eg* RBU-6000 fires to 6000m

MBU-600 The first modern Soviet projector, essentially a copy of the wartime Allied Hedgehog, and widely used in the early 1950s. It was roughly contemporary with RBU-900. Note that the range was far greater than the 300yds of the Allied weapon.

RBU-600 Six barrels, 11.8in/30cm calibre, in two vertical rows; trainable, 198lb/90kg rocket with 121lb/55kg warhead. Only in Modified 'Kotlin' class destroyers. Formerly MBU-4500: Western (not Soviet) assumed designation. All rockets fired simultaneously. Introduced 1962–63.

RBU-900 The Soviet equivalent of the wartime US Mousetrap rocket projector. It consists of two pairs of rocket tracks, one above the other. It does not train. Note the nominal range greatly exceeds that of the original US weapon. This was one of the first postwar Soviet ASW stand-off weapons, and appeared in some early 'Kola' and 'Riga' class ships.

RBU-1000 Same barrels and projectiles as RBU-600 in horseshoe formation, introduced 1962–63. Automatic loading, barrel by barrel, vertically. The barrels fire in sequence. It is trainable. Installed in 'Kara', 'Kresta I', 'Kresta II', *Sovremenny*, 'Kashin' classes and replenishment ship *Berezina*. Formerly referred to as MBU-4500A.

RBU-1200 Two horizontal rows of 9.8in/25cm barrels, three above two. It elevates for range but is fixed in train. The 154lb/70kg rocket has a 75lb/34kg warhead. Mounted in 'T 58' and 'Natya' class minesweepers as well as 'SO 1' ASW craft.

RBU-1800 Five-barrel 9.8in/25cm launcher, three on top, two below, pedestal between the lower pair, introduced 1955–56. It was the first entirely Soviet-designed ASW projector, based on an Army weapon. Manually loaded, aboard early 'Kronstadt', 'SO 1', 'T 58', 'Natya' classes.

RBU-2500 Two horizontal rows of eight 7.8in/20cm barrels each, capable of train and elevation; the standard Soviet ASW weapon of the early 1960s. Manual reloading for 46lb/21kg warheads. Introduced 1957–58.

RBU-6000 Formerly MBU-2500A, 12 barrels arranged in a horseshoe, fired in pairs. Vertical automatic reloading, barrel by barrel. This system is now widely installed. Introduced 1960–61. The radical change in designation suggests the introduction of a new rocket or else an ability to fire at either range (dual-range rocket).

BOMBARDMENT ROCKET LAUNCHERS

The shore bombardment rockets aboard amphibious ships and the 'Shmel' class river gunboats are adapted Army weapons. The 17-barrel 140mm (5.5in) weapon is coded BM-14/17 by NATO, and entered land service in 1954. BM-14/18 is mounted aboard 'Polnocny' class landing ships, and also aboard some 'P 4' torpedo boats; it was designed as a naval weapon from the beginning. Both fire 70lb/32kg rockets to 4.8nm/9km. Some 'Shershens' have a 40-barrel BM-21 (122mm, 101lb/46kg rockets, range 8nm/15km) in place of their TT.

TORPEDOES

Details of Soviet torpedo development are rare, although the presence of TT aboard virtually all Soviet surface combatants suggests that they play an important part in Soviet naval doctrine and tactics. Most are 21in (533mm) steam or electric weapons, and the Soviets have straight runners, pattern runners, and homing weapons. Articles in the unclassified Soviet literature suggest that the standard exploder is a proximity device (active magnetic) adapted to under-the-keel attacks. A nuclear torpedo has been in use since the mid- or late 1950s. It appears to have been adapted initially as an interim strategic weapon for attacks on port facilities, but it also permitted long-range stand-off attacks against carriers, executed from outside their ASW screens.

The presence of nuclear weapons (presumably torpedoes) aboard the Soviet 'Whiskey' class submarine which grounded in Swedish waters in October 1981 suggests how widely such weapons are distributed in the Soviet Fleet, at least in peacetime.

There is also a series of 16in (406mm) electric ASW torpedoes for small combatants and also, apparently, for submarine self-protection. These weapons are also dropped (with parachutes) from ASW helicopters. It is not clear whether the 16in weapon is exclusively for ASW use, nor whether surface ships assigned to ASW carry only ASW torpedoes. However, the absence of some special equipment does show that the older destroyers cannot launch homing torpedoes from their trainable 21in tubes. Note that reportedly Soviet submarines are fitted to fire at least some 16in torpedoes from their 21in tubes, using liners.

Finally, reportedly there is a new large-diameter torpedo; see the entry for SS-N-21 above.

Formerly there were also 18in (457mm) torpedoes for torpedo boats, but they were phased out with the last of the 'P 4s'.

MINES

Again, although unclassified details are extremely difficult to come by, the Soviet Navy is well known as an advocate of mine warfare. Many surface combatants are equipped to lay mines, and minelaying in enemy harbours was one of the major roles of Soviet naval aircraft as early as the 1930s. In fact the current missile attack regiments are direct successors of early Mine-Torpedo Regiments, presumably retaining the mining responsibility. In recent years there has been speculation that Soviet aerial mining would be the best tactic to use against NATO European ports in wartime. As more 'Backfires' enter the SNA inventory, large numbers of obsolescent 'Badger' bombers will be released for just this mission. The reader may recall that the Soviets supplied the North Koreans with the obsolete contact mines which closed Wonsan harbour to UN forces for two weeks in 1950. Current stocks are estimated at 300,000–400,000, several times the US level; some are remaining World War II types.

Western emphasis on minehunting suggests strongly the existence of large numbers of sophisticated Soviet influence mines. Recent interest in deep minehunting, as in the abortive US MCM craft of the late 1970s, suggests a Soviet ability to moor influence mines in deepwater, such as that off ballistic submarine bases. Rising and homing ASW mines have been reported; presumably they are comparable in concept to the US *Captor* (Mk 60) and the abandoned PRAM. Deepwater mines with the NATO codenames Cluster Bay and Cluster Gulf have been reported.

A recent unofficial account lists defensive bottom mines, offensive bottom mines, offensive moored ASW mines, and nuclear mines. The former are moored contact or antenna mines and acoustic mines. The offensive bottom mines are reportedly designated AMD-500 and -1000 (based on weight in kg), with alternative magnetic, acoustic, pressure, or combination triggers. They can be laid by ships or aircraft in 13–230ft/4–70m water, although reportedly the larger mine might be effective against submarines in depths as great as 650ft/200m. There are three basic offensive ASW mines, two rising mines and one (for ship or submarine delivery) triggered by UEP (Underwater Electrical Potential). All three were designed for use as barriers outside NATO submarine bases. Cluster Bay is reportedly intended for use on the continental shelf, Cluster Gulf on the deeper continental ledge. Both are reportedly rising rockets with active/passive acoustic sensors.

There is also reportedly a small stockpile of 5–20kt nuclear bottom mines.

AIR SEARCH RADARS

NOTE: All names are NATO ones usually based on antenna appearance.

Cross Bird Soviet copy of the British wartime Type 291 destroyer air search radar; first Soviet naval air search set. Soviet designation GUIS-2. P-band.
Sea Gull First Soviet-designed naval air search radar (1950), a more directional derivative of Cross Bird, GUIS-2M.
Knife Rest Naval version of the land-based P-8, primarily for the *Sverdlov* class, also on 'T 43' radar pickets (1952). Most vanished by late 1950s, but a successor, Spoon Rest, appeared in 1965. P-band. Large TV-style antenna.
Big Net Large 850mc air search radar in 'Kresta I', and some *Sverdlov* cruisers as well as some 'Kashin' class destroyers; range probably over 100nm/185km. First of a new generation (1955); note also Top Sail in this band.
Top Sail Frequency-scanning 3-D radar, associated with S-AN-3 missile system, c1967. Same frequency band as Big Net; see Top Pair below.
Hair Net First of a new generation of S-band systems, c1957, GP search radar originally fitted to *Kirov* class cruisers and *Tallinn* and 'Kotlin' classes. Succeeded by Slim Net from 1957 on.
Slim Net Destroyer and escort air search radar.
Top Trough S-band system replacing Slim Net and Sea Gull: slotted waveguide feeding a curved reflector.
Head Net Air search radar, S-band. Head Net B is two antennas back-to-back; Head Net C has one of them canted to the horizontal for limited height-finding. Range on a high altitude attack bomber is 60–70nm/111–122km. Head Net series was introduced in the 'Krupny' class, c1958, and Head Net C c1963.
Strut Curve Small ship air search radar, replacing Slim Net: 1962. Last of second generation systems, using somewhat higher frequency than other S-band sets for smaller antenna size.
Boat Sail Long range air search radar on 'Whiskey' class radar picket submarines, introduced 1961–62, with a range of about 100nm/185km at average altitudes.
Spoon Rest P-band system (Soviet P-12) aboard some *Sverdlov*s for very long range air search, from 1965. Too large for a mast, it must be fitted on the superstructure abaft the mainmast.
Strut Pair First Soviet pulse-compression radar, in appearance two Strut Curve antennas mounted back to back.
Top Pair Top Sail and Big Net back to back; *Kiev* class
Top Steer S-band, frequency-scanning 3-D radar, similar in configuration to Top Sail but much smaller. *Kiev* class.

GUN AND TORPEDO FIRE CONTROL RADARS

Ball End/Ball Gun Small combatant target detection and fire control, 1948.
Egg Cup Range-only E-band radar for 152mm, 130mm, and 100mm guns, 1950.
Half Bow Torpedo control, 1952, succeeded by Post Lamp, 1958.
Top Bow 152mm gun fire control, synchronised with optical director but separately mounted. Used in modified form for SS-N-1 missile control.

Sun Visor 100mm and 130mm gun fire control (blind fire), mounted on Round Top or Wasp Head director in frigates and destroyers, 1952.
Hawk Screech 45mm and 76.2mm guns; always used with back-up optical directors. Introduced 1954, replaced by Owl Screech c1960.
Owl Screech Improved Hawk Screech for 76.2mm guns, 1960.
Kite Screech 100mm and new 130mm gun director.
Muff Cob 57mm twin automatic gun fire control; has optical TV camera mounted with it, 1962.
Drum Tilt Fire control for twin 30mm guns, as in small combatants, 1960.
Bass Tilt Fire control for Gatling guns; in 'Matka' and 'Nanuchka III' it also controls a 76.2mm gun.

SONARS

During World War II the Soviets obtained examples of both US and British high-frequency searchlight sonars under Lend-Lease, and these presumably formed the basis for the early postwar sets. There appears to have been little real interest in ASW until the early 1960s, when a range of medium- and low-frequency sets was introduced. Since the capabilities of such equipment depend very much on signal-processing, which is difficult to detect or to estimate, it is not clear to what extent the Soviets were able to exploit such phenomena as bottom-bounce and the convergence zone. Certainly weapons such as the SUW-N-1 and the SS-N-4 suggest such abilities (at least theoretically) in their own range. However, Soviet *tactical* practice is to use the combined outputs of several ship sonars in order to define a region in which the submarine is likely to be located; they then saturate that area with rockets. Thus it is possible that SUW-N-1 fire control in the *Moskva*, for example, was predicated mainly on 'Hormone' (helicopter) dipping sonars.

Early Soviet sonars such as Tamir were apparently copies of the British asdics which the Soviets obtained in wartime: high-frequency searchlights useful for contact-keeping but not for search. Such systems work above about 24khz.

Tamir-5N was introduced in 1947–48, and appeared aboard large surface ships from the 'Kola' class through the *Sverdlov*s. Tamir-5L, for submarines, was introduced in 1947–50. Tamir-10, a related system for small surface ships, was introduced in 1950, followed in 1952 by Tamir-11 and -11M. In 1955 Pegas-2 and -2M appeared aboard large surface ships, from the 'Riga' class up through the *Tallinn*. Like Tamir, it was restricted to high frequency. Feniks (1956) was combined with Tamir-5L aboard submarines.

There were two major lines of improvement beyond the original searchlights: depth-finding through the use of a tilting transducer, and scanning for more efficient search. Since the Soviets adopted long-range ahead-throwing weapons, they would have needed depth capability as the ranges increased; Pegas presumably incorporated that capability. Scanning would have required a major infusion of new technology, and relative Soviet indifference to ASW until the late 1950s argues against that.

However, in 1957 a new high-frequency sonar, Herkules, appeared. It would be reasonable to assume that it introduced the scanning technology already prevalent in the US Navy; it would, then, have been roughly comparable to the US QHB or SQS-10 family, perhaps operating at a slightly lower frequency for longer range. Note, too, that RBU ranges seem to imply slightly better Soviet sonar performance than might be expected of very high frequency sets. Certainly RBU-6000 would seem to demand something like SQS-4 performance.

No Soviet names are known for the succeeding types: a medium frequency bow sonar of about 1966, presumably roughly comparable to SQS-4, and a low-frequency sonar, presumably comparable to SQS-26, introduced in the *Moskva* class. Soviet submarines show large unpainted metal panels which suggest conformal-array passive sonars, both on their bows and on their sails. No names have been announced.

The first Soviet VDS appeared aboard a 'Petya I' trials ship in 1966; it became operational two years later aboard *Moskva*. The 'Victor III' submarine introduced a towed array sonar; no surface ship equivalent has been reported.

FLEET STRENGTH 1947

The data which follows should be taken with considerable caution. It was common in Western accounts of the Soviet Fleet to assume that all Soviet warships were maintained constantly in active status, so that the fleet list equated to the active fleet. That was unrealistic; the Soviets maintained (and maintain) a considerable reserve fleet of uncertain availability, apparently with skeleton crews. Thus it is difficult to determine which of the ships which survived World War II were active postwar or, for that matter, when they were discarded. Soviet ships rarely operated outside home waters through the late 1950s, limiting Western observation of fleet status. The list which follows is not exhaustive, but it includes all ships which reportedly survived the war, plus ships transferred under Lend-Lease and under the Peace Treaties.

Major Lend-Lease units were returned in 1949 in exchange for Italian ships, under the Italian peace treaty. Lend-Lease small craft were scrapped or destroyed in 1955–56 as part of agreements winding up the Soviet Lend-Lease debt; note purchases made at this time.

Note the large-scale scrappings of elderly warships in 1958–60 as part of Khrushchev's programme of reducing the size of the Soviet conventional forces. Presumably many of these ships had not been active for some years.

Note that only a few scrapping dates are available; the data on Soviet ship disposals, at least in the unclassified literature, is extremely sparse. However, the dates which are given below should be considered indicative of the periods during which classes were discarded.

BATTLESHIPS

Name	Launched	Disp (std)	Fate
Gangut class			
OKTYABRSKAYA REVOLUTSIYA	7.10.11	23,000t	BU 1956–57
SEVASTOPOL	29.6.11	23,000t	BU 1956–57
Ex-British Royal Sovereign class			
ARKHANGELSK (ex-*Royal Sovereign*)	29.4.15	29,150t	To RN 4.2.49, BU
Ex-Italian Cavour class			
NOVOROSSIYSK (ex-*Giulio Cesare*)	15.10.11	24,300t	Sunk 29.10.55

Oktyabrskaya Revolutsiya operational 1950, at Kronstadt from at least Nov 1954; superstructure and turrets being removed July 1956. *Sevastopol* BU at her name port. Also reported in existence but inactive 1958. Reportedly the loss of the last ship, a war prize replacing *Royal Sovereign* after being handed over on 15.12.48, on a German ground mine while at anchor in the Black Sea, was the occasion for the removal of Adm Kuznetzov as Soviet Navy C-in-C; he was replaced by Adm Gorshkov.

COAST DEFENCE SHIP

Name	Launched	Disp (std)	Fate
Ex-Finnish Ilmarinen class			
VYBORG (ex-*Väinämöinen*)	28.12.30	3900t	BU by 1965

Flagship of the World War II Finnish Navy ceded as part of the 1947 war reparations. At Kronstadt summer 1956, miscellaneous auxiliary (pennant no 98) 1960.

CRUISERS

Name	Launched	Disp (std)	Fate
Admiralty type			
KRASNY KRIM	21.11.15	6833t	BU 1960
Modified Admiralty type			
KRASNY KAVKAZ	21.6.16	7650t	Target Jun 1960?
Omaha class			
MURMANSK (ex-*Milwaukee*)	24.3.21	7050t	To USN 8.3.49
Kirov class			
KIROV	30.11.36	7880t	Stricken 1975
VOROSHILOV	28.6.35	7970t	BU 1960s
Maxim Gorky class			
MAXIM GORKY	30.4.38	8177t	Hulk 1960
MOLOTOV	23.2.39	8177t	Stricken 1970s
KALININ	Apr 1943	8177t	BU 1960s
KAGANOVITCH	Oct 1943	8177t	BU 1960s
Chapaev class			
KUIBISHEV	31.1.41	11,300t	Stricken 1960s
FRUNZE	31.12.40	11,300t	BU 1960s
CHAPAEV	1940	11,300t	BU 1961
ZHELEZNIAKOV	1940	11,300t	Stricken 1976

Name	Launched	Disp (std)	Fate
CHKALOV	1948	11,300t	Stricken 1980
Ex-German Nürnberg class			
ADMIRAL MAKAROV	6.12.34	6520t	BU 1959
Italian Duca d'Aosta class			
STALINGRAD	22.4.34	8317t	Auxiliary 1960s

Admiralty type
TS from 7.3.45, decommissioned 1958.

Modified Admiralty type
TS from 12.5.47, decommissioned. Expended as SS-N-1 missile trials target.

Kirov class
Name ship overhauled 1950, 1953. Reported at Leningrad 'under overhaul' (ONI) Nov 1954–Feb 1957, then non-operational. Laid up at Krylov Ship-Leningrad 1959–60; hulk by early 1960.

Maxim Gorky class
Name ship BU at Leningrad. *Molotov* renamed *Slava* (1958) and TS from 1960s. *Kagenovitch* renamed *Petropavlovsk* (1957).

Chapaev class
Name ship BU in Arctic. *Chkalov* renamed *Kornsomolets* (1960). Served as TS after transfer to Northern Fleet with *Zhelezniakov* in 1950.

Ex-German Nürnberg class
Handed over to USSR Jan 1946 as war prize. TS 1950, based at Kronstadt to 1956.

Ex-Italian Duca d'Aosta class
Handed over as war reparation 2.3.49. Later renamed *Kerch*. Operational through late 1950s; auxiliary status early 1960s.

DESTROYERS

Name	Fate	Name	Fate
Leningrad class: launched 1933–38, 2150t std			
LENINGRAD	Stricken ?1960s	TBILISI	Stricken ? 1960s
MINSK	Stricken ? 1960s	BAKU	Stricken late 1960s
Novik type: launched 1911–16, 1200–1440t			
KARL LIEBKNECHT	BU 1950s	URITZKY	BU c1953
KUIBISHEV	BU 1950s	NYESAMOZHNIK	
VOIKOV	BU 1950s	ZHELEZNIAKOV	To Bulgaria 1949
STALIN	BU c1953		
Type 7 class: launched 1936–41, 1855t std			
BODRY	Stricken ? 1950s	RESHITELNY	To China 1955
BOIKY	BU 1958	RETIVY	To China 1955
GREMYASHCHIY	Stricken 1958	GROSYASHCHIY	Stricken early 1960s
GROMKY	Stricken ? 1960s	REZKY	To China 1955
GROZNY	Stricken early 1950s	REZVTY	Stricken early 1960s
STEREGUSHCHY	Stricken ? 1950s	REVNOSTNY	Stricken 1950s
RYANY	Auxiliary 1960	RAZARYONNY	A-bomb target 15.11.58
RAZTOROPNY	Target 1959	RAZUMNY	Foundered c1960
RAZYASHCHY	To China 1955	REKORDNY	Stricken ? 1950s
Type 7-U class: launched 1938–41, 2192t std			
STOROZHEVOI	BU 1959	SVIREPY	Stricken ? 1950s
SILNY	Stricken ? 1960s	STROGY	Stricken ? 1950s
VITSE ADMIRAL DROZD	BU 1959	STROINY	BU 1959
STRASHNY	Stricken ? 1950s	SOOBRAZITELNY	Museum ship ship 1966
SLAVNY	Stricken 1960s		
Experimental Type: launched 1935, 1570t			
OPITNY	Decommissioned 1950, BU		

Name	Fate	Name	Fate
Ognevoi class: launched 1940–47, 1800t			
OGNEVOI	Stricken ? 1960s	ODARYNONNY	Stricken ? 1960s
OZARENYY	To Bulgaria 1956	STALIN	Stricken ? 1960s
OTVERZHDY-NONNY	Stricken ? 1960s	VNUSHITYELNY	Target 1959
OSMOTRITELNY	Stricken ? 1960s	VLASTNY	Target 1959
OTLICHNY	Stricken ? 1960s	VYNOSLIVY	Stricken ? 1960s
OBRAZTSOVY	Stricken ? 1960s	OTVAZHNY	Stricken ? 1960s
Ex-British/US 'flush deckers': launched 1917–19, 1090t			
ZHARKY	To RN 28.2.49	DIERZKY	To RN 23.6.49
ZHOSTKY	To RN 8.9.52	DOSTOINY	To RN 28.2.49
ZHIGUCHI	To RN 30.1.50	DRUZHNY	To RN 23.8.52
ZHYIVUCHI	To RN 23.6.49	DOBLESTNY	To RN 4.2.49
Ex-Rumanian Regele Ferdinand class: launched 1928–29, 1400t std			
LYETUCHI	To Rumania 1953	LIKHOI	To Rumania 1953
Ex-German destroyers: launched 1935–41			
PROVORNY (ex-*Z 33*)	BU 1960–62	PYLKIY (ex-*Z 15*)	BU 1960–61
PROCHNY (ex-*Z 20*)	BU 1950s	POSPESHNYI (ex-*Z 14*)	Deleted by 1953
Ex-Japanese destroyers			
TSL-64 (ex-*Harutzuki*)	Target ? c1965	? ex-*Fubuki*	?
Ex-German torpedo-boats			
PRIMERNYY (ex-*T 39*)	BU 1960	PORYVISTYY (ex-*T 17*)	BU 1957
PODVIZHNYY (ex-*T 12*)	BU 1957		
Ex-Italian 'Soldati' class: launched 1937–38, 1690–1820t std			
Z 12 (ex-*Artigliere*)	Stricken 1958	Z 20 (ex-*Fuciliere*)	Stricken 1958
Ex-Italian Ciclone class torpedo-boats: launched 1942, 910t std			
Ex-*Animoso*	Stricken ? late 1950s	Ex-*Ardimentoso*	Stricken late 1950s

Leningrad class
Minsk at Kronstadt 1955–57, auxiliary (pennant TSL-75) 1958–59, used as target-tower from 1959 and transferred from Baltic to Northern Fleet. *Tbilisi* (non-operational at Leningrad Nov 1954, auxiliary April 1956, TS Aug 1957) also used as target-tower from 1959 (TSL-50). *Baku* auxiliary early 1959, still on list 1965.

Type 7 class
Four of these World War II ships went to China in pairs Dec 1954 and July 1955 and are still extant. *Razumny* became an Arctic electronic survey ship from 1958–59 and was beached in a storm off Murmansk.

Type 7-U class
Slavny became a TS c1958, as probably did *Soobrazitelny* until she became a Black Sea museum.

Ex-German destroyers
Provorny served in the Baltic after being handed over by RN in summer 1945. The other 3 were all 1946 war prizes, all considered second line by 1955 and in auxiliary role by 1959. *Pylkiy* was active to 1956 becoming an accommodation ship in 1958.

Ex-Japanese destroyers
TSL-64 (ex-*Harutzuki*) apparently not rearmed; laid up through 1959, then converted as target service ship; active through 1965, probably expended as missile target. In 1959 she had a Knife Rest radar amidships, and a helicopter landing area aft, but no weapons. Former Japanese *Fubuki* class destroyer ? *Ushio* (apparently never rearmed).

Ex-Italian 'Soldati' class
Handed over as war reparation 21.2.49 and 17.1.50 respectively. In 1955 ONI reported that these units were being employed in type training. They had not yet been refitted with Soviet weapons. Both converted to target ships early 1960.

Ex-Italian Ciclone class
War reparations handed over 1949 and considered second line by 1955.

SUBMARINES

Lend-Lease British 'U' class
V 2, V 3, V 4 all returned 10.2.49 and BU 1950.

OPERATIONAL SUBMARINES OF SOVIET PREWAR DESIGN, 1945–64
(Note that this includes postwar construction)

Year	M-V	Schch	L	S	K classes
1947	90	76	28	33	14
1948	97	77	28	34	14
1949	106	79	28	34	14
1950	113	78	22	34	14
1951	133	74	22	34	14
1952	143	70	22	34	14
1953	147	67	22	34	14
1954	134	67	20	34	14
1955	106	65	20	31	14
1956	89	56	19	29	14
1957	83	46	16	29	14
1958	79	32	12	24	14
1959	76	20	10	22	14
1960	75	13	9	20	14
1961	48	8	5	16	12
1962	46	0	2	6	9
1963	41	0	0	0	0
1964	34	0	0	0	0

Note that ONI was still carrying 4 old D (*Dekabrist*) class and two old P class (*B 1* and *B 31*) submarines as second-line units in 1955, even though later lists did not include them.

WAR PRIZES

Ex-German Type IXC
B 25

Ex-German Type VIIC:
S 81–S 84

Ex-German Type XXI:
N 27 (ex-*U 2529*), N 28 (ex-*U 3505*), N 29 (ex-*U 3515*), N 30 (ex-*U 3041*)
    Note that transferred German Type XXI (B 27, 28, 29, 30) and Type XXIII (N 31, the original designation under which it was transferred) submarines were classed as second line by 1955; they may never have been operational.

Ex-Italian Acciaio class:
Z 14 (ex-*Nichelio*)

Ex-Italian Flutto class:
Z 13 (ex-*Marea*)

Ex-Estonian Lembit class:
S 85 (ex-*Lembit*)

FRIGATES

Name	Fate	Name	Fate
Uragan class: launched 1929–35, 450t std			
URAGAN	BU 1958–59	MIETEL	BU 1958–59
TAIFUN		VYUGA	BU 1958–59
SMERCH		TUCHA	
GROZA	BU 1958–59	GROM	
VIKHR		ZARNITSA	
SHTORM		MOLNYA	
SKVAL			
Yastreb class: launched 1940–41, 906t std			
YASTREB	BU 1958–59	SOKOL	stricken early 1960s
ORYOL		KONDOR	
KORSHUN		ALBATROS	
VORON		KIROV	
BERKUT		DZERZHINSKI	

Ex-US Tacoma class
EK 1–28, transferred 1945, all returned 1949 and laid up in Japan; many were transferred to US allies: Japan, S Korea, Thailand, and Colombia. *EK 3* (ex-*Belfast*) foundered off Petropavlovsk 17.11.48.

WAR PRIZES

Six ex-Rumanian torpedo boats, used as minesweepers: 6 units, all returned in 1949; Soviet names are not known.

Ansaldo Type: 810t, 20kts, 3 4in (KGB)
Four ex-Japanese *Matsu* class and modified *Matsu* class: ex-*Hatsuzakura* laid up unarmed, then torpedo retriever; target service vessel TSL-24, 1959. In service through 1965. Ex-*Shii*, ex-*Kaya*, ex-*Kiri* apparently not reactivated.
    Two ex-Japanese *Ukuru* class: acquired 1947 ex-*Ikino* and ex-*Kozu*.
    Eleven ex-Japanese 'Kaibokan' Type C escorts: acquired 1947 ex-Nos *34, 48, 52, 71, 76, 77, 78, 79, 105, 221, 227*
    Most never reactivated, but one Kaibokan No 2 operated as frigate *EK 37* in 1957, and two Kaibokan No 1s were operating as surveying ships, one named *Sorakoram* (G-127); another, at Vladivostok, carried pennant G 111.

COASTAL CRAFT
About 400 MO submarine-chasers of four classes, built in 1935–43, served during World War II.

WARSAW PACT

MO 1 class, 51t, 14kts, 2–12.7mm
MO 2 class, 56t, 24kts, 1–45mm, 2–12.7mm
MO 4 class, 56t, 25kts, 2–45mm, 2–12.7mm
BMO class, 61t, 23kts, 1–37mm, 3–12.7mm

The Soviets claimed a total of 269 MTBs in service in June 1941, and completed another 166 during hostilities; 24 more old boats were reinstated, for a total of 459. However, they lost 122 and had to strike another 52. They also obtained about 12 Rumanian MTBs in 1944. In addition, they received 202 US PT-boats under Lend-Lease. Soviet sources claim a total of 393 operational MTBs as of 2 Sept 1945. Of the Lend-Lease units, 12 were war losses, 66 were broken up, 26 were destroyed before US observers, and the remainder were returned in 1954–58.

'Artillerist' class, 240t, 20kts, 1–3in: 66 ships
Lend-Lease US PTC type, 29t, 28kts, 1–20mm: 26 transferred 1943–44; 5 were war losses, 9 were returned to the USN in 1956, 7 were broken up postwar, and 5 were scuttled in the Barents Sea before US observers in 1958.
Lend-Lease RPC type: 36 transferred 1943–44, 15 were returned in 1955, 1 scuttled in the Barents Sea before US observers in 1956, and the remainder scrapped postwar.
Lend-Lease US SC type: BO 202–246, BO 301–332, transferred 1943–45; 4 lost, 10 returned 1955, 20 scrapped, and 29 scuttled before US observers in 1955–56. The other 5 were purchased by the Soviet Navy.

WAR PRIZES
In 1945–49 the Soviets obtained 23 or more German R-301 class, 26 or more German R-218 class, 14 German R-17 class motor minesweepers ('Raumboote'), and 3 Italian VAS. They also seized 26 or more German S-100 class MTBs, 4 early S-boats, 4 Italian MS-boats, and 2 Italian MAS 501 class MTBs. It is not clear when these boats were discarded.

MINE WARFARE VESSELS

Name	Fate/Comp	Name	Fate/Comp
Ex-Imperial Yacht, minelayer: 6200t			
MARTI (Oka 1957)	BU c1960		
Tral class coastal minesweepers: launched 1935–40, 434t std			
STRELA	To N Korea 1955	GAK	
TROS	To N Korea 1955	RYM	
PROVODNIK	To N Korea 1955	T 215	
PODSEKATYEL	To N Korea 1955	KONTRADMIRAL KHOROSHIN	BU c1947–59
PARAVAN	To N Korea 1955	T 220	
KAPSUL	To N Korea 1955	TRAL	
VEKHA	To N Korea 1955	SCHCHIT	
CHEKA	To N Korea 1955	ISKATEL	
FUGAS		MINA	
GAFEL		ARSENI RASSKIN	
Polukhin class ocean minesweepers: launched 1940–46, 700t std			
VLADIMIR POLUKHIN	1942	TIMOFEI ULYANTSEV	1945
PAVEL KHOKHRYAKOV	1944	MIKHAIL MARTYNOV	1947
ALEKSANDR PETROV	1947	FEDOR MITROFANOV	1944
KARL ZEDIN	1947	LUKA PANKOV	1944

Name	Fate/Comp	Name	Fate/Comp
VASSILI GROMOV	1943	PAVLIK VINOGRADOV	1948
ADRIAN ZOSIMOV	1946	STEPAN GREDYUSHKO	1948
VLADIMIR TREFOLYEV	1946	SEMYON PALEIKOV	1948

Ex-US Admirable class ocean minesweepers: 625t
T 111–T 120, T 272–T 282, T 521–T 526, T 593–T 598. War losses: T 114, T 115, T 117, T 118, T 120, T 278 (possibly postwar loss), T 279, T 522. Destroyed Barents Sea before US observers 1956: T 111–T 113, T 119. Certified unseaworthy and BU in Soviet Union 1954, T 281, T 521, T 523–T 526, T 593–T 598. Purchased by Soviets 1956: T 272–T 277.
Ex-British MMS(1) type: 165t, 11kts, 2–12.7mm MG: T 108–T 110
Ex-British MMS(2) type: 255t, 10kts, 2–20mm: T 121, T 122, T 193–T 202
Ex-US YMS: 203t, 14kts, 1–3in: T 151–T 156, T 181–T 192, T 581–T 592, T 599–T 611.
In 1954 the Soviets stated that T 114, T 116, T 118, T 120, T 152, T 278, T 279, and T 610 had all been lost; that T 181–T 192 in the Black Sea had been declared unseaworthy and BU; that T 151, T 153, T 156, T 271–T 277, T 289, T 282, T 588, T 591, T 602 and T 610 had all been scrapped in the Pacific. In addition, T 522, T 581, T 586, T 587, T 604, T 605, T 606, T 608, T 609 and T 611 in the Pacific were BU c1956. Finally, T 111–T 113, T 115, T 119, T 120, T 154, T 155, T 218, T 521, T 523–T 526, T 583, T 585, T 589, T 590, T 592–T 601 and T 603 were all destroyed before American observers in 1956.

WAR PRIZES: At the end of World War II, the Soviets obtained 14 M-35, 29 M-40, and 17 or more M-43 class German ocean minesweepers. Some writers have suggested that the 'T 43'/'T 58' classes were derived from these ships.

AMPHIBIOUS WARFARE VESSELS

The Soviets appear not to have had any specialised landing ships of their own; they did use a wide variety of merchant ships as extemporised transports during World War II. Under Lend-Lease, the Soviet Pacific Fleet received 30 LCI, 15 LCT, and 54 LCM(3) type landing craft; the Northern Fleet received 2 LCM(3), 2 LCS(S), 2 LCT, and 2 LCVP. At least 5 LCI and 3 LCM were lost in the Pacific.

WAR PRIZES: In 1955 ONI credited the Soviets with 3 Italian MZ class landing craft; 1 German MNL; 8 German SF; 16 German LT class MFP; 29 German F class MFP, and 15 MFP Type D class. The Soviets put these designs into production in the 1950s; see MP-2. The Soviets also obtained 29 German AF type amphibious support ships, built on MFP hulls, and armed with 2–3.5in, 2–37mm and 4 quadruple 20mm, plus 4 RL; 330t (std), 355t (full), 154ft 2in × 21ft 4in × 5ft 3in (max) 47m × 6.5m × 1.6m, and powered by 3 375bhp diesels, with a speed of 10kts. They were coastal craft only.

RIVER CRAFT

The Soviets operated a variety of armoured MGBs before and during World War II and the survivors of that war continued in service through the 1960s until their replacement by the 'Shmel' class described below. A total of 85 modern gunboats armed with two 76mm turrets (Types 1124 and 1125) was in service in June 1941, with 68 more under construction; another 110 were ordered in Aug 1941, and all on order were completed during the war. About 90 were lost out of a total of 270 built. Their Soviet designation was BKA, armoured artillery cutter. There was also an enlarged seagoing version, the MBKA; numbers are unknown.

In addition, the Soviets retained a variety of river monitors for use on the Amur, the Danube, and other Soviet rivers.

MAJOR SURFACE SHIPS

It appears that the Soviets have finally laid down a full-deck aircraft carrier some time in 1983. There has been considerable collateral evidence of Soviet interest, including direct statements by Admiral Gorshkov, and from about 1979 onwards there were reports in the Western press of observations of Soviet experiments, such as catapult tests. Soviet publications have shown paintings of MiG-27 strike aircraft with Navy markings, presumably as a hint of what is coming. Reportedly the carrier is being built at Nikolayev, and there is a general assumption that she will be nuclear powered. However, note that the Soviets have built nuclear surface

NEW aircraft carrier

ships only in Leningrad, and that their primary surface ship reactor, the Artika (ice-breaker) plant, is probably manufactured at or near Leningrad; transportation all they way to Nikolayev might be a problem.

No details of any kind have been released, but the floating drydocks recently delivered to the Northern and Pacific Fleets may represent limits set on the design. The Japanese-built Pacific Fleet dock is 1105ft long and has an 80,000t capacity. Since it would have to accept a battle-damaged carrier, full load displacement of the new Soviet ship is probably closer to 70,000t, and the ship probably approximates to the US Midway class.

This carrier programme can be traced back at least to the 1971–75 Five Year Plan, during which preparations would have been made for the experimental work (eg on catapults) reported during the 1976–80 Plan. If a carrier is actually built, it will represent the third Soviet attempt in that direction. Stalin appears to have ordered the construction of a carrier under the Five Year Plan beginning in 1942, and this project was reportedly revived during the early 1950s, dying with Stalin and his big-ship Navy.

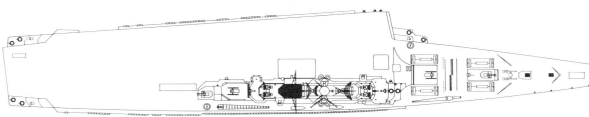

Kiev as completed.
NB 1/1750 scale

For many years Western analysts of the Soviet Fleet looked in vain for a Soviet equivalent of the aircraft carrier, elsewhere universally recognised as the capital ship of the postwar era. Thus when the Soviets produced *Moskva*, and again when *Kiev* emerged, there was, at first, a general perception that the Soviets had finally followed that universal wisdom, or that they were experimenting with a step half-way between cruiser and carrier. In fact there were reports that Stalin had planned a carrier or carriers both before and after the war, and that the postwar plans had been dropped in the general naval disaster following his death. Although both classes of air-capable ships are superficially similar, it seems likely that they represent very different operational concepts.

Moskva was originally conceived as a consort for a large missile cruiser, which was cancelled, probably *c* 1961. Given Soviet concepts of ASW operations by multiple small craft, one might envisage her helicopter complement as a bluewater equivalent, their small dipping sonars locating a submarine well enough for the ship herself to engage it, perhaps with her SUW-N-1 nuclear weapon. Alternatively, the helicopters might form a scouting line or a partial screen for one or two fast warships. Probably *Moskva* and *Leningrad* survived the cancellation of the large missile cruiser because they could be advertised as pure ASW ships. Experience in their operations quite likely contributed to the design of *Kiev*, but it should be kept in mind that the latter, completed as early as 1976 (and therefore built under the 1971–75 Plan), must have been designed, and approved, before their completion in 1967–68. It seems improbable that ships built as part of Khrushchev's Seven Year Plan (1959–65) were designed in 1962 and 1964 but, as the first large Soviet warships in many years, must have been designed as early as 1958.

Chronology suggests strongly that the *Kiev*s were associated with the 'Delta' class strategic submarines, which for the first time could fire from 'holding areas' which the Soviets could hope to control, such as the Norwegian Sea north of the GIUK Gap. It can argued that the massive batteries of these ships were ideally suited to denying passage to NATO ASW forces, be they aircraft (which can be opposed by the Yak-36 fighter), surface ships (against which

KIEV class *air capable ships*

Displacement:	36,000t standard; 42,000t full load
Dimensions:	902ft oa × 108ft wl, 154ft 10in ext × 26ft 11in
	275.0m × 32.7m, 47.2m × 8.2m
Machinery:	4-shaft geared steam turbines, 140,000shp = 32kts. Fuel 7000t. Range 4000nm/30kts, 13,500nm/18kts
Armament:	4 SS-N-12 (4×2, 24 missiles), 2 SA-N-3 (2×2, 72 missiles), 2 SA-N-4 (2×2, 40 missiles),4–76mm (2×2), 8–30mm Gatling (8×1), 10–533mm TT (2×5), 1 SUW-N-1 ASW RL (1×2), 2 RBU-6000 ASW RL (2×12), 31 aircraft. See notes
Sensors:	Radar 2 Palm Frond, Top Sail, Top Steer, 2 Head Lights, 2 Pop Group, 2 Owl Screech, 4 Bass Tilt, Trap Door; sonar L/F hull, VDS; ECM 8 Side Globe, 12 Bell series, 4 Rum Tub, 2 chaff RL (2×2)
Complement:	*c* 1700

Name	Builder	Laid Down	Launched	Comp	Fate
KIEV	Nikolayev	Sept 1970	31.12.72	May 1975	Extant 1982
MINSK	Nikolayev	Dec 1972	May 1975	Feb 1978	Extant 1982
NOVOROSSIYSK	Nikolayev	Oct 1975	Dec 1978	1981	Extant 1982
KHARKOV	Nikolayev	1978	1982		Fitting out 1983

Kiev can release SS-N-12 cruise missiles), and submarines (against which she has a variety of weapons including her helicopters). As in the case of *Moskva*, this is hardly a traditional Western-style carrier function, although one might suspect that operations with the *Kiev*s will teach the Soviets a great deal about the potential of the full-scale carrier. Note, however, that the Yak-36 (12 carried with 18–19 Hormone A and B helicopters) has been observed primarily carrying ground-attack weapons, and appears not to have any air intercept radar. If it is indeed intended to oppose NATO maritime patrol aircraft, especially the P-3, presumably it depends heavily on control by the ship; this would be in accord with standard Soviet fighter-control doctrine. In this context it is suggestive that the 'Forger' has an even design number, since the Soviets reportedly assign old numbers to fighters (eg MiG-21, -23, -25) and *even* ones to attack aircraft (eg Su-22).

In 1983 it appears that the Soviets are very close to building just such ships, again in support of a shift in their naval policy. Since the mid-1970s, Admiral Gorshkov has advertised the Soviet Navy as a 'sure shield' against Western intervention in 'wars of national liberation' in the Third World, ie against US carrier battle groups. Soviet policy appears to be to create forces which can be interposed between local revolutionaries and counter-insurgency (Western) forces. True carriers would make Soviet distant-water operations far more effective. Thus far it appears that the carriers themselves

have not yet been laid down, but catapult experiments have been reported, and Soviet statements about carrier operations have become markedly more respectful in recent years. For that matter, the *Kiev*s, formerly classified as 'large ASW ships' or 'ASW cruisers', are now 'air-capable ships' in *Soviet* terminology.

Certainly among the most spectacular Soviet ships of recent years, these large cruisers or semi-carriers combine the *Moskva* weapon system with the first reloadable SSM system since the *Kynda*s, and with the SA-N-4 point defence missile system. More importantly, to many analysts, they can operate Yak-36 VTOL fighters. It is difficult to divine the relative priorities of these systems: certainly the deep magazine for SS-N-12 missiles takes up a lot of space and even

Novorossiysk 1.6.83

length. Unlike other Soviet ASW ships of their period, they do not have the SS-N-14 torpedo-carrying stand-off missile, although they do have the Hormone/SUW-N-1 nuclear ASW system, and the helicopters can drop torpedoes, and some writers have suggested that the *Kiev*s are intended to support Soviet amphibious operations. That seems unlikely; it is more probable that they are intended to support Soviet ballistic missile submarines by helping to bar NATO access to SSBN 'holding areas' in wartime. In such a role their large hulls improve sea-keeping, and their three-dimensional armament allows them to oppose penetration of their patrol areas by NATO ASW aircraft, surface ship or submarines. However, it should be noted that the second ship to be completed, *Minsk*, went to the

Anpfoto Amsterdam for UPI

Pacific Fleet in mid-1979 instead of supplementing the *Kiev* in Northern Fleet. Moreover, if, as has often been stated, only four ships are being built, that hardly seems sufficient to block the GIUK Gap. *Novorossiysk* first deployed to the N Atlantic mid-1983.

Kiev herself spent considerable time supporting Soviet amphibious exercises since her much publicised maiden voyage through the Mediterranean in July 1976 and many analyses of the Yak-36 suggest that close support or surface support was its design role. Certainly it is only marginally valuable as a fighter, given no airborne intercept radar – which in turn may be explainable in terms of ship-controlled intercept concepts or in terms of the weight an effective radar would consume. The problem is that the Soviets never made the anticipated heavy investment in amphibious assault ships, which might have explained the *Kiev* as a support ship for overseas operations. Nor can the Yak be explained as an anti-ship weapon, since it has no surface search radar (as in the Sea Harrier). To add to the confusion, the Soviets reclassified *Kiev* as a Tactical Aviation Cruiser (TAKR = *Taktycheskiy Avionosnyy Kreyser*) *c* 1982.

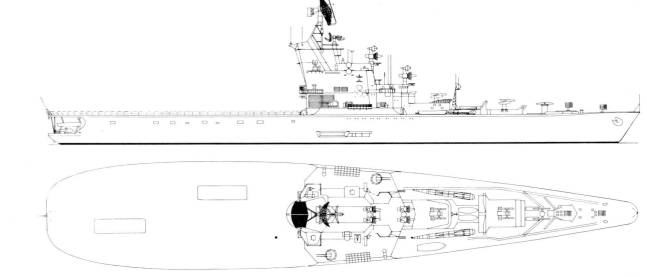

Leningrad 1974

These two ships display several features suggesting either a relatively hurried design or else the incorporation of components under development during the design process. For example, they generally trim by the bow, suggesting that weights forward were improperly calculated at first. The major shipboard ASW weapon, SUW-N-1, is reportedly an adaptation of the standard Army short-range ballistic rocket ('Frog'). It would appear to be associated with sonar-bearing helicopters, as it appears only in these ships and in the *Kiev*s. There may also have been difficulties with the massive hull sonar, by far the largest in Soviet service when they were completed; it is supplemented by a variable-depth sonar, the first in any major Soviet combatant. These ships also introduced the SA-N-3 air defence missile system with its associated Top Sail long-range 3-D air search radar. Given their reported power, one might suspect that they share the pressure-fired steam plant of the 'Kyndas'. The two elevators aft are too small to take the Yak-36 VTOL fighter, but *Moskva* served as test ship for that aircraft.

The construction of only two ships suggests either an unsuccessful or an experimental programme; certainly they cannot be explained as a counter-Polaris measure unless the original programme was far larger. More probably their numbers were curtailed when the original companion SSM cruiser programme was cancelled. Given other Soviet concerns of the late 1950s, when these ships were probably designed, the companion units were most likely intended for strategic attack using SS-N-3 missiles, the *Moskva*s serving ASW and perhaps also as anti-air escorts.

It is also possible that the programme was cancelled in 1964 when Khrushchev was deposed. He had always opposed big-ship programmes, and had accepted these two rather stunted ships only reluctantly.

MOSKVA class *helicopter carriers*

Displacement:	14,400t standard; 19,200t full load
Dimensions:	620ft 1in oa × 85ft 4in wl 111ft 7in ext × 25ft 3in *189.0m × 26.0m, 34.1m × 7.7m*
Machinery:	2-shaft geared steam turbines; 4 boilers, 100,000shp = 30kts. Fuel 2600t. Range 2500nm/30kts, 7000nm/15kts
Armament:	2 SA-N-3 (2×2, 44 missiles), 4–57mm (2×2), 1 SUW-N-1 ASW RL (1×12), 2 RBU-6000 ASW RL (2×12), 10–533mm TT (2×5, removed mid-1970s), 14 helicopters
Sensors:	Radar Top Sail, Head Net C, 2 Head Lights, 2 Muff Cob, 3 Don-2; sonar L/F bow, M/F VDS; ECM 8 Side Globe, 8 Bell Series, 2 chaff RL (2×2)
Complement:	850

Name	Builder	Laid down	Launched	Comp	Fate
MOSKVA	Nikolayev	1962	1964	July 1967	Extant 1982
LENINGRAD	Nikolayev	1964	1966	late 1968	Extant 1982

However, in the post-Khrushchev era Admiral Gorshkov, like his Army and Air Force brethen, was able to ask for far more in the way of non-nuclear forces. Note, too, that it was Khrushchev who steadfastly opposed the production of tactical aircraft (as aboard the *Kiev*s), preferring missiles and nuclear weapons. Under such an interpretation the *Kiev* and Yak-36 projects began *c* 1964.

Another argument in this direction would be the return of the Soviet Navy to the strategic role about 1964, first with the crash 'Yankee' programme and then with the more mature 'Delta'. It seems likely that the 'Delta' and its SS-N-8 missile were conceived (or, more likely, approved) only after the demise of Khrushchev; *Kiev*, the sanctuary guard ship, must have been a central element of the programme.

Moskva 1980

USN

There is no firm data on this class, but large hulls about 700ft long were reported at both Leningrad and at Nikolayev, and the Soviets themselves have referred to these ships as successors of the prewar 'Kronstadt' type. Many sources refer to a 4-ship programme as part of a 10-year building programme begun in 1950, which would have included 40 cruisers: 24 *Sverdlov*s, these 4, and 12 of a new heavy cruiser type, presumably armed either with the existing 7.1in gun or with a new 8in. The data which follows is unofficial and should be treated with caution. They are probably based on the assumption that the 'Stalingrad' design would be a modified version of the prewar 'Konstadt'

STALINGRAD class *battle cruisers*

Displacement:	c40,000t full load
Dimensions:	787ft 5in wl, 836ft 7in oa × 103ft × 29ft 2in 240.0m, 250.5m × 31.4m × 8.9m
Machinery:	210,000shp = 33kts
Armament:	1–2 SSM launchers, 6–12in/50 (2×3), 8–6in/57 (4×2), 12–100mm/70 (6×2), 32–45mm/85 (8×4)

Name	Builder	Laid down	Launched	Comp	Fate
MOSKVA	Baltic	Oct 1952			BU
STALINGRAD	Nikolayev	1951	1965		BU

with better protection and AA armament. In addition it is possible that they would have been armed partly with a naval version of the land- and air-based Kennel anti-ship weapon; contemporary intelligence reports did mention a missile armament. Estimates based on the prewar design gain credence in view of the fact that both the *Sverdlov* and *Skory* designs were direct modifications of prewar types.

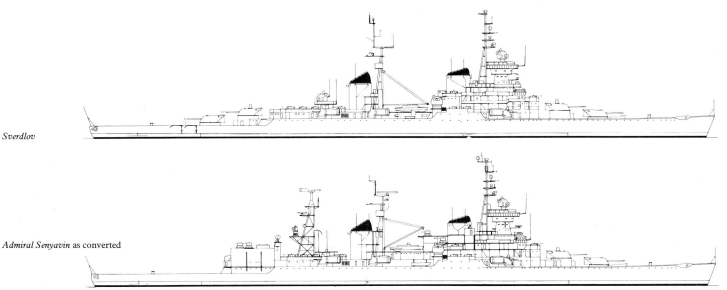

Sverdlov

Admiral Senyavin as converted

Note that some recent writers report that both *Molotovsk* and *Murmansk* were built at Leningrad; the above data come from recently declassified intelligence reports of the mid-1950s. Certainly the name *Molotovsk* would be appropriate to a ship being built in Molotovsk, renamed Severodvinsk later on. TT all removed by the early 1960s. Active units were later fitted with either Top Trough or Big Net for long-range air search. However, some retained their early Sea Gulls. As a missile cruiser, *Dzerzhinski* was fitted (1959–61) with Fan Song (SA-2 guidance) and High Lune (height-finding) radar, the latter removed in 1976.

Out of 24 *Sverdlov*s ordered, 20 were laid down and 17 launched; only 14 were completed, the other three being laid up in the Neva at Leningrad for some years before they were scrapped. Stalin reportedly had a 40-cruiser postwar programme, consiting of 4 battlecruisers (*Stalingrad* class) and 12 large cruisers of a type as yet unknown, plus the *Sverdlov*s, which themselves were improved versions of the prewar-designed (and postwar-completed) *Chapayev*s. The programme appears to have been cancelled; Khrushchev's remark that cruisers were 'floating coffins' cannot but have quickened the disposal of the partly completed hulls.

In the late 1950s *Dzerzhinski* was converted into an experimental SAM cruiser armed with the Army SA-2 test ship, and *Admiral Nakhimov* was converted into a SSM test ship, probably armed with a prototype SS-N-1 missile system. She was scrapped in

SVERDLOV class *cruisers*

Displacement:	16,000t standard; 17,200t full load
Dimensions:	653ft wl, 689ft oa × 72ft 2in × 24ft 7in 199.9m, 210.0m × 22.0m × 7.5m
Machinery:	2-shaft geared turbines, 6 boilers, 110,000shp = 32.5kts. Fuel 3800t. Range 10,180nm/13.5kts, 2470nm/32kts
Armour:	Belt 4⅞in–1⅝in (125–40mm), deck 3in–1in (75–25mm), turrets 4⅞in (125mm), CT 5.9in (150mm)
Armament:	12–152mm/57 (4×3), 12–100mm (6×2), 16–37mm (8×2), 10–533mm TT (2×5). See notes
Sensors:	Radar Sea Gull, Knife Rest A, Slim Net, Top Bow, Egg Cup (for both 152mm and 100mm mounts); sonar H/F hull. See notes
Complement:	1010

Name	Builder	Laid down	Launched	Comp	Fate
SVERDLOV	Baltic	July 1949	13.7.50	Sept 1951	Extant 1982
ZHDANOV	Baltic	Oct 1949	Dec 1950	Jan 1952	Extant 1982
ADMIRAL LAZAREV	Baltic	May 1950	Oct 1951	Nov 1952	Extant 1982
ADMIRAL USHAKOV	Baltic	July 1950	May 1952	Aug 1953	Extant 1982
ADMIRAL SENYAVIN	Baltic	May 1951	Sept 1952	July 1954	Extant 1982
DMITRY POZHARSKI	Baltic	Sept 1951	Apr 1953	Oct 1954	Extant 1982
VARYAG	Baltic	Dec 1952	Oct 1954		
	Baltic	Oct 1953	Apr 1955		
	Baltic	1954	June 1956		
ORDZHONIKIDZE	Admiralty	July 1949	20.9.50	Nov 1951	To Indonesia 1962
ALEKSANDR NEVSKI	Admiralty	Mar 1950	June 1951	Sept 1952	Extant 1982
ALEKSANDR SUVOROV	Admiralty	Oct 1950	June 1952	Aug 1953	Extant 1982
	Admiralty	June 1951	May 1953	Aug 1953	
OKTYABRSKAYA REVOLUTSIYA (ex-*Molotovsk*)	Severodvinsk			1954	Extant 1982
MURMANSK	Severodvinsk	1951		1955	Extant 1982
	Severodvinsk				
DZERZHINSKI	Nikolayev	May 1949	1951	Nov 1952	Extant 1982
ADMIRAL NAKHIMOV	Nikolayev		1949	June 1954	BU 1961
MIKHAIL KUTUZOV	Nikolayev	1950		May 1955	Extant 1982
	Nikolayev	1954	Apr 1956		
	Nikolayev				

Zhdanov as command cruiser 1974   USN

Aleksandr Suvorov April 1970   USN

the early 1960s without ever having departed Soviet home waters. Another ship, *Ordzhonikidze*, was transferred to Indonesia in the autumn of 1962, the Indonesians claiming at the time that they expected to receive another, although none arrived. Two others, *Admiral Senyavin* and *Zhdanov*, were converted to command cruisers, completing in 1972; each had their No 3 triple 152mm turrret replaced by command spaces with a 'pop-up' SA-N-4 missile launcher and 4 twin 30mm guns on top (*Admiral Senyavin* only), with

another set of 30mm guns around the forefunnel; a new tripod mainmast carries the Vee Cone long-range communications antenna. *Admiral Senyavin* lost both of her after 152mm turrets and has a helicopter hangar aft. In 1977 *Oktyabrskaya Revolutsiya* (*Molotovsk* till 1957) completed a refit with an enlarged bridge; *Admiral Ushakov* and *Alexsandr Suvorov* were similarly altered in 1979.

In appearance, they generally resemble the *Chapayev*s but have their hull plating carried much further aft, with an additional pair of

twin 100mm mountings near the bridge, as well as a taller cap to the second funnel.

All three had Egg Cup radars removed from their secondary battery mounts, and exchanged 2 twin 37mm for 4 new twin 30mm controlled by Drum Tilt radars. The two command cruisers were reclassified KU, *Korabl' Upravleniy* (command ship) rather than KR (*Kreyser*, cruiser).

Standard Soviet practice is to pass these ships in and out of reserve, so that a ship can remain out of service for an extended period without going

to the breakers. Even so, there have been breakdowns: *Dzerzhinski* had to be towed home from the Mediterranean in 1979. In 1983 it is not clear whether these ships are being retained for their fire support value or as TS to show the Soviet flag overseas. Certainly without point defence missiles they would not fare well against modern weapons and aircraft; note that they have not received the Gatling close-in (presumably anti-missile) guns.

Grozny in 1974

'KYNDA' class *cruisers*

Displacement:	4400t standard; 5600t full load
Dimensions:	464ft 9in oa × 51ft 10in × 17ft 5in (hull only) *141.7m × 15.8m × 5.3m*
Machinery:	2-shaft geared steam turbines, 4 pressure-fired boilers, 100,000shp = 34kts. Range 2000nm/34kts, 7000nm/14.5kts
Armament:	2 SS-N-3 (2×4, 16 missiles), 1 SA-N-1 (1×12, 24 missiles), 4–76mm (2×2), 2 RBU-6000 ASW RL (2×12), 6–533mm (2×3)
Sensors:	Radar 2 Don-2, 2 Head Net A or C, 2 Scoop Pair, Peel Group, Owl Screech, 2 Plinth Net (2 Bass Tilt in *Fokin*); sonar H/F hull; ECM 3 Bell series, 4 Top Hat
Complement:	375–390

Name	Builder	Laid down	Launched	Comp	Fate
GROZNY	Zhdanov	June 1959	Apr 1962	June 1962	Extant 1982
ADMIRAL FOKIN	Zhdanov	1960	Nov 1961	Aug 1963	Extant 1982
ADMIRAL GOLOVKO	Zhdanov	1961	1963	July 1964	Extant 1982
VARYAG	Zhdanov	1962	1964	Feb 1965	Extant 1982

These four units introduced Soviet bluewater anti-carrier capability, with their pair of quadruple trainable SS-N-3 launchers; there were also 8 reload missiles stowed in the superstructure, although reloading itself was clearly problematical except in very calm water. The use of trainable launchers suggests that they were originally designed to launch the internally-guided strategic version of SS-N-3, since the anti-carrier version can be commanded to turn after launch; on the other hand, the trainable feature allows the forward launcher to clear the AA missile launcher (SA-N-1) in the bows, and the after one can clear the pair of 76mm DP guns aft. The powerplant is often described as a pressure-fired steam turbine, as attested to by the large area taken up by vents in the base of the forefunnel. The helicopter pad at the stern is often associated with the use of a 'Hormone' helicopter for over-the-horizon target verification, in the absence of a Bear D reconnaissance bomber.

The Soviets designate these ships 'rocket cruisers' (RK), and they made

a considerable impression in the West, with their main battery effective at up to 250nm, and their overall level of armament for their size; shorter (albeit beamier) than 'Kashins'. Presumably only their main battery

placed them in the cruiser category. This sort of classification later proved extremely embarrassing to the USN, which had numerous 'frigates' (DLG/DLGN) larger than Soviet cruisers of the 'Kynda' and later clas-

ses, and suffered in comparative tables from its apparent lack of modern cruisers. The problem was solved only with the reclassification of most of the DLG as cruisers in 1975.

Note that the salvo of 8 anti-carrier missiles appears to be a standard unit in Soviet thinking: a 'Charlie' Class submarine has 8 SS-N-7 or -9, *Kiev* carries 8 tubes for SS-N-12, 'Echo II' carries 8 SS-N-3 or -12, and 'Oscar' carries 24, or 3 groups of 8. Note that 2 'Osas' make a like salvo, as do 2 'Kresta II' class cruisers, or 2 anti-ship destroyers. It is not clear, on this reasoning, why *Kirov* carries 20 SS-N-19s. However, these numbers do suggest the sort of attack the Soviets consider the minimum to deal with a carrier.

Admiral Golovko July 1978   USN

Vitse Admiral Drozd after reconstruction

Direct successors of the 'Kyndas', these ships were built in two very distinct series. The 'Kresta I' class of 4 cruisers is armed with 4 (rather than 8) SS-N-3 missiles, carried in fixed-train elevating tubes under the bridge, with an increasing emphasis on self-defence; it is a double-ended SA-N-1 missile ship, with twin 57mm guns as well, and a helicopter in a hangar (indeed, they were the first with this feature). They duplicate the pressure-fired boiler installation of the 'Kyndas', and are designated rocket cruisers.

These ships are reportedly seaworthy, but their armament suit does not fit well with other designs, with too few SS-N-3 to fire an effective salvo, an ineffective SA-1 air defence battery, a poor sonar, poor long-range and 3D radars, and a poor ASW battery; they do not even have the high speed of the gas turbine 'Kashins'. However, they have not been extensively modified. *Vitse Admiral Drozd* was fitted with 4-30mm Gatlings abaft the SS-N-3 launchers and also with a new deckhouse between them; *Sevastopol* received the deckhouse but not the Gatling guns. Some writers have gone so far as to suggest that 'Kresta I' was an attempt to marry an existing SS-N-14-carrying design to existing SS-N-3 missiles so as to complete hulls on time. That seems unlikely; the ships have never been retro-fitted, and they lack the big sonar dome of the later units.

'KRESTA I' class *cruisers*

Displacement:	6000t standard; 7500t full load
Dimensions:	508ft 6in oa × 55ft 9in × 18ft 1in (hull only)
	155.0m × 17.0m × 5.5m
Machinery:	2-shaft steam turbines, 4 pressure-fired boilers, 100,000shp = 34kts. Fuel 1150t. Range 2400nm/32kts, 10,500nm/14kts
Armament:	2 SS-N-3 (2×2, 4 missiles), 2 SA-N-1 (2×2, 44 missiles), 4–57mm (2×2), 2 RBU-6000 ASW RL (2×12), 2 RBU-1000 ASW RL (2×6), 10–533mm TT (2×5), 1 helicopter.
Sensors:	Radar Don Kay, Don-2, Big Net, Head Net C, 2 Plinth Net, Scoop Pair, 2 Peel Group, 2 Muff Cob (2 Bass Tilt in *Drozd*); sonar H/F hull set; ECM 8 Side Globe, 4 Bell series
Complement:	380

Name	Builder	Lai down	Launched	Comp	Fate
VITSE ADMIRAL DROZD	Zhdanov	1965	1965	1967	Extant 1982
SEVASTOPOL	Zhdanov	1966	1965	1967	Extant 1982
ADMIRAL ZOZULYA	Zhdanov	Sept 1964	1966	1968	Extant 1982
VLADIVOSTOK	Zhdanov	1965	1966	1968	Extant 1982

'Kresta I' *Vladivostok* Jan 1969   USN

Admiral Oktyabr'skiy as completed

The 'Kresta II' class can best be described as an ASW derivative, somewhat lengthened 10ft (3m) to accommodate a bow sonar (as evidenced by their more sharply raked bows), and carrying 8 SS-N-14 Asroc-like missiles in place of the SS-N-3 of 'Kresta-I'. The surface-to-air missile is the more capable SA-N-3, requiring a better 3D radar, Top Sail, in place of the Head Net C/Big Net combination of 'Kresta-I'. There is, however, no VDS.

'Kresta II' class ships are officially designated 'large ASW ships' (BPK). The SA-N-3 missile has a substantial SSM capability; it is the only Soviet naval SAM without a land-based equivalent. It is alleged that *Admiral Makarov* bombarded the Angolan ports of Lobito and Benguela on 11–12.2.76 in support of the MPLA during the Angolan Civil War.

'KRESTA II' class *cruisers*

Other particulars:	As 'Kresta I' class
Armament:	As 'Kresta I' except 4 SS-N-14 (4×2, 8 missiles), 2 SA-N-3 (2×2, 44 missiles)
Sensors:	Radar 2 Don-Kay, Don-2, Top Sail, Head Net C, 2 Head Lights, 2 Muff Cob, 2 Bass Tilt; sonar M/F hull; ECM 8 Side Globe, 7 Bell series

Name	Builder	Laid down	Launched	Comp	Fate
KRONSTADT	Zhdanov	1966	1967	1970	Extant 1982
ADMIRAL ISAKOV	Zhdanov	1967	1968	1971	Extant 1982
ADMIRAL NAKHIMOV	Zhdanov	1968	1969	1972	Extant 1982
ADMIRAL MAKAROV	Zhdanov	1969	1970	1973	Extant 1982
MARSHAL VOROSHILOV	Zhdanov	1970	1971	1973	Extant 1982
ADMIRAL OKTYABR'SKIY	Zhdanov	1970	1972	1974	Extant 1982
ADMIRAL ISACHENKOV	Zhdanov	1971	1973	1975	Extant 1982
MARSHAL TIMOSHENKO	Zhdanov	1972	1974	1976	Extant 1982
VASILY CHAPAEV	Zhdanov	1973	1975	1977	Extant 1982
ADMIRAL YUMASHEV	Zhdanov	1974	1976	1978	Extant 1982

Kerch July 1978   *USN*

Admiral Makarov 1974   *USN*

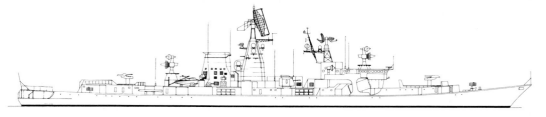

Ochakov as completed

These large ASW ships (BPK in Soviet nomenclature) were built at Nikolayev on the Black Sea. The name ship entered the Mediterranean on 2.3.73. They are, in effect, gas turbine equivalents of the 'Kresta II', with much the same weapon fit, except for the addition of the SA-N-4 point defense missile system and 76mm rather than 57mm guns. In addition, they have a VDS aft and the hull sonar is described unofficially as low rather than medium frequency. One can speculate that the VDS is particularly useful in the Mediterranean, where most of these ships serve. An enlarged superstructure, compared with 'Kresta II', suggests command spaces.

Construction is reportedly complete at 7 ships. One of them, *Azov*, serves as a test ship for the SA-N-6 (naval SA-10) vertical-launch missile system, these weapons replacing her after SA-N-3. Top Dome radar replaces Head Lights in this role. *Petropavlovsk* and *Tashkent* joined the Pacific Fleet in 1979. *Azov* is the only ship not to have deployed outside the Black Sea.

'KARA' class *cruisers*

Displacement:	8200t standard; 10,000t full load
Dimensions:	570ft oa × 60ft × 20ft 4in
	173.8m × 18.3m × 6.2m
Machinery:	2-shaft COGAG, 4 gas turbines, 120,000shp = 34kts. Range 3000nm/32kts, 8800nm/15kts
Armament:	2 SS-N-14 (2×4, 8 missiles), 2 SA-N-3 (2×2, 44 missiles), 2 SA-N-4 (2×2, 40 missiles), 4–76mm (2×2), 4–30mm Gatling (4×1), 10–533mm TT (2×5), 2 RBU-6000 ASW RL (2×12), 2 RBU-1000 ASW RL (2×6, not in *Petropavlovsk*), 1 helicopter. See notes
Sensors:	Radar 2 Don-Kay, Don-2, Top Sail, Head Net C, 2 Head Lights, 2 Pop Group, 2 Owl Screech, 2 Bass Tilt; sonar L/F hull, M/F VDS; ECM 8 Side Globe, 7 Bell series (first 2 ships) or 2 and 4 Rum Tub
Complement:	520

Name	Builder	Laid down	Launched	Comp	Fate
NIKOLAYEV	Nikolayev	1969	1971	1973	Extant 1982
OCHAKOV	Nikolayev	1970	1972	1975	Extant 1982
KERCH	Nikolayev	1971	1973	1976	Extant 1982
AZOV	Nikolayev	1972	1974	1977	Extant 1982
PETROPAVLOVSK	Nikolayev	1973	1975	1978	Extant 1982
TASHKENT	Nikolayev	1975	1976	1979	Extant 1982
TALLIN	Nikolayev	1976	1977	1980	Extant 1982

Kirov as completed
NB 1/1750 scale

This was the first Soviet nuclear-powered surface combatant, referred to by some as a 'battlecruiser' in recognition of her size, but actually more closely equivalent to the defunct US strike cruiser (see Part I), with a combination of high-quality air defence and SSM. She also has a large bow sonar and a new, and also large, VDS aft, with an associated reloadable twin SS-N-14 ASW missile launcher forward. Unlike the strike cruiser, she lacks a large-calibre gun, suggesting that reports of renewed Soviet interest in shore bombardment, at least by such important units, are false. Rather, one suspects that she is intended as an escort for the forthcoming Soviet nuclear carrier, concentrating in one ship the maximum level of area air defence, just as in the case of a US Aegis cruiser. The second *Kirov* reportedly has a greatly improved weapon fit.

KIROV class *cruiser*

Displacement:	28,000t full load
Dimensions:	754ft 7in wl, 813ft 8in oa × 78ft 9in wl, 91ft 10in ext × 24ft 7in hull
	230.0m, 248.0m × 24.0m, 28.0m × 7.5m
Machinery:	2 nuclear reactors plus oil-fired superheaters, 150,000shp = 32–34kts. See notes
Armament:	20 SS-N-19 (20×1), 12 SA-N-6 (12×1, 96 missiles), 2 SA-N-4 (2×2, 40 missiles), 2–100mm (2×1), 8–30mm Gatling (8×1), 1 SS-N-14 (1×2, 14–16 missiles), 8–533mm TT (2×4), 1 RBU-6000 ASW RL (1×12), 2 RBU-1000 ASW RL (2×6), 3 helicopters
Sensors:	Radar 2 Palm Frond, Top Pair, Top Steer, 2 Top Dome, 2 Pop Group, 2 Eye Bowl, Kite Screech, 4 Bass Tilt, Punch Bowl; sonar L/F bow, L/F VDS; probably also M/F for RBU fire control; ECM 8 Side Globe, 10 Bell series, 4 Rum Tub, 2 chaff RL (2×2)
Complement:	800

Name	Builder	Laid down	Launched	Comp	Fate
KIROV	Baltic, Leningrad	1973	Dec 1977	Sept 1980	Extant 1982
	Baltic, Leningrad	Jan 1978	June 1981	1983	Fitting out

The SA-N-6 missile system is reportedly a naval version of the SA-10 strategic SAM currently entering Soviet service; the use of 12 vertical launchers (each almost certainly with a magazine below it for reloads) suggests that the two radar directors can, between them, control 12 missiles simultaneously. Otherwise this inherently fast-firing system would represent an excessive use of valuable deck space, since each missile would have to be controlled from launch to target. The 20 SS-N-19 cruise missiles are more than any earlier cruiser carried; *Kiev* reportedly has a total of 16 reloads plus 8 in her tubes. SS-N-19 is the first very long range Soviet anti-ship missile apparently without a mid-course guidance radar, no such system being identifiable on *Kirov*.

Propulsion, which if of the standard *Artika* class icebreaker reactor type gives 75,000shp, differs from that common in US nuclear cruisers, in that a steam boost system appears to be employed. Apparently it is a fossil-fuel superheater, which in theory can account for up to half the total power of the ship, and which can reduce the total investment in a nuclear plant. Early US nuclear warship designs were difficult because it was not possible to achieve sufficient power in a sufficiently light plant, and combined nuclear and gas turbine and even nuclear and steam turbine plants were proposed. They were all rejected as unnecessarily complex; the superheater system does not appear to have been proposed, although it has been used in land powerplants.

Kirov on trials 1980   *MoD*

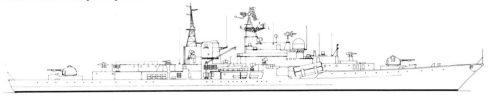

Sovremenny as completed

These SSM cruisers are production successors to the 'Kresta II' class at the Zhdanov yard at Leningrad, although they are now being described as destroyers in the West. They have introduced a new SAM, SA-N-7, a naval SA-11, itself an improved version of the semi-active homing SA-6; the guidance radars are six small illuminators ranged fore and aft along the sides of the ship, suggesting rapid fire from 2 missile launchers and a capability to engage up to 6 targets simultaneously. The associated air search radar is a back-to-back combination of a smaller equivalent of Top Sail, Top Steer, and the Strut Pair two-dimensional air search radar. ASW equipment is extremely austere by Soviet standards, emphasising the specialised nature of the ship: a small bow sonar, no VDS, only 2 RBU-1000 RL and a pair of twin TT – which the Soviets probably think of as the US thinks of its ubiquitous Mk 32 triple 324mm/12.75in tubes.

The powerplant appears to be a pressure-fired steam turbine, as in the 'Krestas' originating in the same yard. One unusual feature of the design is a small telescopic helicopter hangar with a small helipad slightly abaft amidships. This is also the first major Soviet surface combatant with only a single air search radar (apparently both back-to-back units are fed by the same transmitter, since they share a common waveguide feed), suggesting a much increased level of transmitter-/receiver reliability; however, the precise function of the lattice mainmast is not yet clear.

Finally, this class introduces a new surface ship naval gun, a twin 130mm (5.1in) mount. Some analysts had seen in the *Sovremenny* a return to large naval guns, perhaps for shore bombardment.

Moreover, in recent years the calibre of ship-mounted guns has gradually increased, from 57mm to 76mm to 100mm. However, 130mm is not so great a jump as to suggest a major shift in policy. *Sovremenny* entered the Black Sea in Jan 1982 as her first sister started Baltic trials. The former's lengthy trials began in Aug 1980.

SOVREMENNY class *cruisers*

Displacement:	6200t standard; 7800t full load
Dimensions:	511ft 10in oa × 56ft 9in × 21ft 4in
	156.0m × 17.3m × 6.5m
Machinery:	2-shaft geared turbines, 4 pressure-fired boilers, 100,000shp = 35kts. Range 2400nm/32kts, 10,500nm/14kts
Armament:	2 SS-N-22 (2×4, 8 missiles), 2 SA-N-7 (2×1, ?48 missiles), 4–130mm DP (2×2), 4–30mm Gatling (2×2), 4–533mm TT (2×2), 2 RBU-1000 ASW RL (2×6), 1 helicopter
Sensors:	Radar 3 Palm Frond, Top Steer, 6 Front Dome, 2 Bass Tilt, Kite Screech; sonar M/F bow; ECM 8 Bell series, 2 chaff RL
Complement:	350–380

Name	Builder	Laid down	Launched	Comp	Fate
SOVREMNNY	Zhdanov	1976	Nov 1978	1981	Extant 1982
	Zhdanov	1977	Aug 1980	1982	Extant 1982
	Zhdanov	1978	Apr 1981		Building
	Zhdanov	1979			Building

Sovremenny Aug 1982   *USN*

Udaloy 1981   *MoD*

Udaloy as completed

Originally designed Balcom 3 by NATO and resembling nothing so much as a Soviet *Spruance*, this ASW cruiser or large destroyer emerged late in 1980, its main battery consisting of 8 SS-N-14 launch tubes under the bridge, as in a 'Kresta-II' or a 'Kara'. These weapons are loosely equivalent to an American ASROC, but much larger; unlike a *Spruance*, *Udaloy* clearly carries no reloads. She might best be characterised as an enlarged 'Krivak' with two helicopters aft, a new (and unidentified) point defence system, and twice as many SS-N-14 missiles. *Udaloy* is somewhat larger than *Sovremenny*, and her design appears to complement that of the SSM oriented ship.

It may be significant that *Udaloy* the first ship of this type, was built at Kaliningrad, the centre of Soviet frigate (SKR) design and production. In Sept 1981 during the Baltic 'Exercise Zapad 1' *Udaloy* held trials with the new naval helicopter Ka-36,

As this is written, the first unit of a new 'Krasina' (NATO codename) class (8 ships expected), replacing the 'Karas' in production in the Black Sea, is about to run trials. She carries the same advanced AA weapon system (8 vertical-launch SA-N-6), with a total of 64 missiles) as the much larger *Kirov*, and her main battery consists of 16 anti-ship cruise missiles, presumably SS-N-19.

The continuity of ship design in the large surface combatant yards is almost as striking as the radical developments of recent years. Thus from the 'Kynda' onwards, cruisers built in Leningrad have been powered by a standardised pressure-fired steam turbine plant. *Udaloy* follows the Kaliningrad pattern (of the much smaller 'Krivak') in having a gas turbine plant. Nikolayev, which was lead yard for the gas turbine-powered 'Kashin' class destroyers, followed them with gas turbine-powered 'Kara' class cruisers. Some analysts

UDALOY class *cruisers*

Displacement:	6200t standard; 7900t full load
Dimensions:	531ft 6in oa, 485ft 7in pp × 63ft 4in × 20ft 4in *162.0m, 148.0m × 19.3m × 6.2m*
Machinery:	2-shaft COGAG (CP propellers): 4 gas turbines, c120,000shp = 35kts. Range 2400nm/32kts, 10,500nm/14kts
Armament:	2 SS-N-4 (2×4, 8 missiles), 8 vertical launch point defence (?48 missiles), 2–100mm (2×1), 4–30mm Gatling (4×1), 2 RBU-6000 ASW RL (2×12), 8–533mm TT (2×4), 2 helicopters
Sensors:	Radar 2 Strut Pair, 2 Eye Bowl, 3 Palm Frond, Kite Screech, 2 Bass Tilt, 1 for helo control; sonar: 1 oblique bow and L/F VDS; ECM 8 Bell series, 2 chaff RL (2×2)
Complement:	300

Name	Builder	Laid down	Launched	Comp	Fate
UDALOY	Kaliningrad	1978	1980	1981	Extant 1982
VITSE ADMIRAL KULAKOV	Zhdanov	1978	1980	1981	Extant 1982
	Kaliningrad	1979			
	Zhdanov	1979			

Helix, larger than the ubiquitous Hormone; her first sister also began trials then and the third ship followed suit in Jan 1982.

'KRASINA' class *cruisers*

Displacement:	12,500t full load
Dimensions:	613ft 6in × *187.0m ×*
Machinery:	2-shaft, gas turbines, = 34kts
Armament:	16 SS-N-19, 8-launcher SAN-6 system aft (64 missiles), 2–130mm/70 (2×2), 2 multiple TT, 1 or 2 helicopters

Name	Builder	Laid down	Launched	Comp	Fate
	Nikolayev	1976	1979	1983	Extant 1982
	Nikolayev	1978	1980		Building
	Nikolayev	1979	1981		Building

have suggested that there are geographical rationales for these designs, that the 'Kara', for example, is built for the Mediterranean, whereas the 'Krestas' (and, presumably, the *Sovremenny*) are designed for Northern waters. On this argument, the 'Karas' have VDS to operate in the difficult thermal conditions of the Mediter-ranean, whereas the 'Krestas' need no such equipment in colder Northern seas, or at least do not need it as badly.

Tactically, it might be imagined that the role of Soviet surface forces in the Mediterranean would include hunting down enemy ballistic missile submarines in those relatively confined waters, whereas surface forces in the North would be much more concerned with maintaining a positive Soviet SSBN sanctuary. Note that the Mediterranean, unlike the Northern Seas, offers a natural 'choke point' against *Western* penetration in the Sicilian Narrows, which are about 1000nm from the Soviet border. First ship operational March 1983.

Stepenny 1954

Ognenny after modernisation

SKORY class *destroyers*

Displacement:	2240t standard; 3181t full load
Dimensions:	397ft 6in oa, 349ft 5in pp ×39ft 4in × 14ft 9in *121.2m, 116.5m × 12.0m × 4.5m*
Machinery:	2-shaft geared turbines, 4 boilers, 60,000shp = 33.5kts. Fuel 786t. Range 3500nm/14kts, 840nm/30kts
Armament:	4–130mm/50 (2×2), 2–85mm (1×2), 7/8–37mm (4×2 or 7×1), 2 or 6–25mm (3×2), 2 DC mortars, 2 DC racks, 10–21in TT (2×5), 50 mines max. Modernised ships: 4–130mm (2×2), 5–57mm (5×1), 2 RBU-2500 ASW RL, 5–21in TT (5×1), 50 mines
Sensors:	Radar High Sieve, Top Bow or Half Bow or Post Lamp, Cross Bird. Modified ships: Slim Net, Top Bow, 2 Hawk Screech; sonar H/F hull set (Tamir or Pegas); ECM 2 Watch Dog
Complement:	218

Class:
Zhdanov – *Skory* (the prototype, launched 1949), *Smelyy, Serdity, Seriozny, Smotryaschchy, Sokrushitelny, Sovershenny, Stepenny, Stremitelny, Smotryaschchiy, Solidnyy, Sovershennyy, Sposobnyy, Statnyy, Stokyy, Surovyy, Svobodnyy* (17 ships)

Molotovsk – *Ognennyy* (June 1949), *Okhotlivyy* (July 1949), *Ostervenely, Osterozhny, Ostroglazny, Otchayanny, Otretovenny, Ozhivlenny, Otchetlivyy, Otvetstvennyy, Ozhestochennyy, Obrazovanny, Osnovatelny, Osmyslenny, Otchodchivy, Ozoblenny* and 2 others (18 ships)

Nikolayev – *Bditelnyy, Besmennyy, Bezuderzhnyy, Bezukoriznennyy, Buynyy, Bessnervny, Bessmertny, Bezupretchny, Besposhchadny, Bespokoiny, Bestrashny, Beschumny, Bezuderzhny, Bezovertny, Bystry, Buiny, Bezukoriznenny* and 2 others (19 ships)

Komsomolsk – Vazhvy, Vdumchivy, Verduschchy, Verny, Vidny, Vikhrevoy, Vnesapny, Vnimatelny, Volevoy, Vrazumitelny, Vyderzhanny, Vozbushchenny and 6 others (18 ships)

Skory class 28.8.68   *USN*

All 72 completed 1950–53. Transfers: Egypt (2 in 1956, 2 in 1961, 2 in 1968), Indonesia (4 in 1959, 1 in 1962, 2 in 1964, 1 in 1965) and Poland (2 in 1957–58: *Skory*, *Smely*). About 8 were converted to modernised configuration 1958–60 (2 of these being transferred to Egypt 1968: two RBU-2500 ASW RL were mounted on new raised platform forward of the bridge, the forward bank of TT was replaced by a deckhouse, and the former mixed AA battery of two 85mm

and 4 twin 37mm was replaced by 5 single 57mm guns. The former heavy 130mm director atop the bridge was also removed. Some had 7 single 37mm as built; units with 4 twin 37mm have recently received in addition 2 or 3 twin 25mm. Both variants reportedly can lay mines. Modified *Skorys* have raised funnel caps and a heavier mainmast.

Compared to the earlier type, they had a lengthened forecastle with considerable sheer, flare, and rake to the bow. The larger hull, higher freeboard, and longer forecastle presumably made them more seaworthy than earlier Soviet destroyers descended from Italian models, the latter having been designed more with Mediterranean operations in mind. As in contemporary US destroyers of the *Fletcher*, *Sumner* and *Gearing* classes, they had thin armour plating above and abeam their machinery spaces, on their main battery mounts and on their wheelhouse (0.8in STS in the Soviet case). Unlike contemporary Western destroyers, however, they retained the low-pressure, low-temperature steam plants of their predecessors. Machinery arrangement, fore to aft, was two fire rooms, engine room, two fire rooms, engine room, for a total length of about 140ft. Officers were quartered forward on the main deck and in the bridge on the upper deck, with enlisted men forward and aft.

Western observers were struck by the absence of effective AA weapons in a postwar destroyer. Thus the main battery elevated only to 45 degrees, and a 1955 ONI report noted the absence 'of any apparent provision for cross-level stabilisation of the director system, or for elevation discrimination by the associated fire control radar. This would preclude AA blind fire and effective surface blind fire. The whole main battery system is evidently intended primarily for direct surface fire, and has only limited AA capabilities.'

Note, too, that there was no mass modernisation programme comparable to FRAM. As of 1983, 12 were considered active, with about 8 more in reserve.

Neustrashimy 1958   *USN*

NEUSTRASHIMY (TALLINN) class *destroyer*

Displacement:	2700t standard; 3700t full load
Dimensions:	422ft wl, 440ft oa × 44ft × 16ft 1in *128.6m, 134.1m × 13.4m × 4.9m*
Machinery:	2-shaft geared turbines, 4 boilers, 72,000shp = 32kts
Armament:	4–130mm (2×2), 8–45mm (4×2, replaced by 4×4, 1957), 2 MBU-2500 ASW RL, 10–533mm TT (2×5)
Sensors:	Radar Low Sieve, Slim Net, Post Lamp radars; Knife Rest added 1960 in place of 8–25mm (2×4)
Complement:	310

Name	Builder	Laid down	Launched	Comp
NEUTRASHIMY	Zhdanov	1953	1953	1954

Reports suggest that this destroyer was the only one of four laid down to be completed (3 were cancelled and BU on the slip at Zhdanov). Although her funnels resemble those of *Skory* rather than of a 'Kotlin', reportedly she had the high-pressure steam plant of the latter, as well as the latter's more modern battery, with a true HA director and HA 130mm guns. She was often described as a flotilla leader, and some writers suggest that as many as 12 were planned; her high freeboard suggests bluewater operation, but she lacked the high raked bow of the 'Kotlins'. She was unique among modern Soviet steam destroyers in having very widely separated funnels, both sets of torpedo tubes being between them; one writer claims that both engine spaces were between the boiler rooms, rather than the usual alternating arrangement, and that the propulsion system was a prototype partially automated type. Her hull lines were considered (by US observers) consistent with the *Skory* class, with the forecastle extended right aft, rather than with the flush-decked, highly raked form of the 'Kotlins'. When this ship first appeared, many observers commented that she had to be top-heavy, with her director on a pylon; but it appears that the 'Kotlins' carried theirs at about the same height, the difference being that they had taller bridge structures.

Neustrashimy undoubtedly made a much greater impression in the West than in the Soviet Navy, being evaluated at first as a cruiser; for example, she was often credited with a maximum speed of 40kts, which of course she did not reach. Indeed, some observers suspected that the design was abandoned precisely because it was so much slower than the 'Kotlin', with poorer sea-keeping qualities and no more powerful an armament. In effect, *Neustrashimy* was the last of the line of Italian-descended Soviet destroyer designs which began with the *Gordiy* type in the 1930s.

Plamenny as completed

Bravyy after missile conversion 1964

'KOTLIN' class *destroyers*

Displacement:	2850t standard; 3500t full load
Dimensions:	415ft 1in × 42ft 8in × 15ft 1in *126.5m × 13.0m × 4.6m*
Machinery:	2-shaft geared turbines, 4 boilers, 72,000shp = 38kts. Range 3600nm/18kts, 1050nm/34kts
Armament:	4–130mm (2×2), 16–45mm (4×4), 4–25mm (2×2), 6 DCT, 2 DC racks, 10–533mm (2×5) TT, 56 mines max. Missile ships: 2 SA-N-1 (1×2, 22 missiles), 2–130mm (1×2), 4–45mm (4×1, *Bravyy* 3), 2 RBU-6000 ASW RL (RBU-2500 in *Bravyy* and *Skromnyy*), 5–21in TT (5×1)
Sensors:	Radar Neptune or 1/2 Don-2, Slim Net, Sun Visor, 2 Hawk Screech, 2 Egg Cup, Post Lamp or Top Bow; sonar H/F, hull set (Herkules). Missile ships: 1 or 2 Don-2, Head Net C, Peel Group, Sun Visor, Hawk Screech, Egg Cup
Complement:	336

Class:

Besslednyy, Blagorodnyy*, Blestyashchiy*, Byvalyy*, Moskovsky Komsomolets*, Naporistiy*, Plamennyy*, Speshnyy, Spokoynyy, Svedushchiy*, Svetlyy, Vskiy, Vdokhnovennyy*, Vliyatel'nyy, Vozmushchyennyy*, Vyderzhannyy*, Vyzyvayuschchiy*, Dal'Nevostochnyy Komsomolets

Converted to missile destroyers: *Bravyy* (prototype), *Nakhodchivyy, Nastochivyy, Nesokrushimyy, Skromnyy, Skrytnyy, Soznatel'nyy, Spravedlivyy* (to Poland 1970), *Vozbuzhdennyy*.

Builders: Zhdanov, 12 units, of which the first pair were laid down in 1953, launched 1954, completed 1954, the next four laid down 1954, completed 1955, and the last six laid down 1955 and completed 1956); Komsomolsk, 7 units inc *Dal'Nevostochnyy Komsomolets*, completed 1955–57; and Nikolayev, 8 units,

Vdokhonvennyy Oct 1973   USN

completed 1955–57. Total of 27. *Modified 'Kotlin' class. Missile conversions: *Bravyy* 1962, others 1966–72.

Production successors to the *Skory*s, these ships introduced the now characteristic raked bow and flush deck, with a pronounced sheer forward. They also introduced a standard high-pressure high temperature steam plant, reflected in their small funnels. An ONI report dated June 1956 suggests a similarity between their hull lines and those of the 'Kola' class frigate: 'in overall design the 'Kotlin' gives the impression of being an enlarged development of the 'Kola' class . . . [her] hull lines appear to have been derived from destroyer designs evolved by the former Schichau shipyards, once a leading German builder of destroyer type vessels. These hull lines represent a departure from those of the *Tallinn*, whose flush-deck hull appears to be a built-up basic broken deck type.'

From an armament point of view, compared to the *Skory*, they had true dual-purpose capability. They and the similarly-equipped *Neustrashimy* had a full-height radar mast carrying a Hair Net air search set, whereas in the *Skory* the radar mainmast was lighter and carried the simpler Cross Bird antenna (similar to the Type 291 on contemporary British destroyers).

Reportedly a total of 36 was ordered, of which 5 were never laid down and 4 were completed with SSM batteries as the 'Kildin' class; 27 were delivered in their originally planned form, with 10 TT, 4 quadruple 45mm AA, ASW weapons and mines. One ship, *Bravyy*, was modified *c*1960 as the prototype sea-going SA-N-1 platform, the missile system replacing her after 130mm guns. Her TT were removed, and a large pyramidal mainmast carried the 'Peel Group' missile control radar, while her after funnel appears to have been covered in blast-deflection plates. Three of the 4 quadruple 45mm guns were removed. She was later refitted with ASW rockets, TT and 2 more 45mm.

From *c*1966 onwards 8 more units (one of which, *Spravedlivyy*, went to Poland) were converted. In each case one bank of TT was retained, but 3 of the 4–45mm mounts were removed. Two RBU–6000 long-range RL were installed (but *Bravyy* and *Skromny* have RBU-2500s, and both have the three 45mm mounts). *Nesokrushimyy*, *Soznatel'nyy* and *Vozbuzhdennyy* each have 4 twin 30mm. These missile conversions were completed in 1972. In addition, 11 ships were modernised between 1960 and 1962, receiving two RBU-2500s forward and two RBU-600s aft in place of DC equipment; the after bank of TT was removed. *Moskovsky Komsomolets* was unique in having a longer-range automatic-loading RBU-6000 forward, and nothing aft; in 1978 she was fitted with a VDS. Most unmodified ships were later fitted with 4 twin 25mm, a type released by the disposal of lighter units. Three had helicopter decks, 18 extant 1982 with Soviet Navy.

The Chinese 'Luta' class is similar in overall concept, but differs considerably in details; for example, it is larger, with a flat transom stern and a larger superstructure. They also have triple SSM (modified Styx) launchers in place of the two banks of TT of the original Soviet design. This type of modification appears to be unique to Chinese ships.

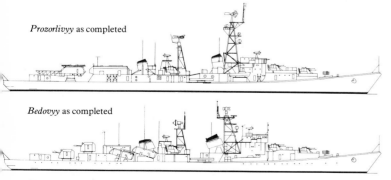

Prozorlivyy as completed

Bedovyy as completed

'KILDIN' class *missile destroyers*

Other particulars: As 'Kotlin' class

Armament:	1 SS-N-1 (9 missiles), 16–57mm (4×4), 2 RBU-2500 ASW RL, 4–533mm TT (2×2). Modified ships: 4 SS-N-2c (4×1), 4–76mm (2×2), 16–57mm (2×2, 45mm in *Bedovyy*), 2 RBU-2500 ASW RL, 4–533mm TT (2×2)
Sensors:	Radar Slim Net, Flat Spin, Top Bow, 2 Hawk Screech; sonar H/F hull set. Modified ships: Head Net C, Owl Screech, 2 Hawk Screech. *Bedovyy*: Strut Pair in place of Head Net C; ECM 2 Watch Dog
Complement:	285 (300 in modified ships)

'Kotlin' class SAM conversion April 1969   MoD

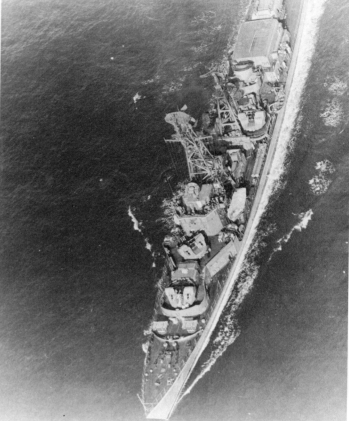

'Kildin' class as converted   USN

'Krupny' class Nov 1970   USN

Class (builder):
Neulovimyy (Zhdanov), *Prozorlivyy* (Nikolayev), *Bedovyy*, *Neuderzhimyy* (Komsomolsk)

The 'Kildin' class represented a shift to anti-ship missile firepower, a single launcher and magazine for SS-N-1 cruise missile being installed in place of the after twin 130mm mount. Laid down in 1957 and 1958 (all launched) at Leningrad and Nikolayev. The first was completed in 1960. They were the first guided missile destroyers in the world; the first ship, *Bedovyy* was almost complete as a 'Kotlin' before conversion, but the others were essentially new construction. The 130mm guns were retained, but all had 4 TT in place of the previous pair of quintuple mounts on the centreline. Estimates of the capacity of the SS-N-1 magazine vary, both 4 and 6 being claimed. The former ('Wasp Head') director was retained, apparently to control the SS-N-1 missile. Three out of four were modified (1973–75) in rough analogy to the modified 'Kashins'; it seems likely that all of these ships are intended primarily as 'tattletales', that is, they are expected to stay with the target formation long enough to provide vital data, then turn astern and retire, adding their missiles to the incoming attack. The modified mounts units retain their quadruple 57mm, adding a pair of twin 76mm DP mounts right aft in place of the earlier SS-N-1 hangar and launcher. *Neuderzhimyy* (unmodified) in Pacific Fleet 1982, other 3 also extant.

Zorkiy after 'Kanin' conversion

Stereguschiy 1973   *USN*

'KRUPNY' and 'KANIN' class *missile destroyers*

Displacement:	4500t full load ('Kanin' 4700t full load)
Dimensions:	429ft 2in wl, 452ft 2in oa ('Kanin' 456ft) × 48ft 11in × 10ft 6in (hull only) ('Kanin' 16ft 5in)
	130.8m, 137.8m, 139.0m × 14.9m × 3.2m, 5.0m
Machinery:	2 shafts, 4 boilers, 80,000shp = 36kts
Armament:	2 SS-N-1 (2×1, 20 missiles), 16–57mm (4×4), 2 MBU-2500 ASW RL, 6–21in TT (2×3); 'Kanin': 1 SA-N-1 (1×2, 22 missiles), 8–57mm (2×4), 8–30mm (4×2), 3 RBU-6000 ASW RL, 10–533mm TT (2×5)
Sensors:	Radar 2 Don-Kay, Head Net A (later replaced by C), modified Top Bow for missile control, 2 Hawk Screech; sonar H/F hull set. 'Kanin': Head Net C, Peel Group, Hawk Screech, 2 Drum Tilt; sonar M/F hull set
Complement:	350 ('Kanin' 300)

Class:
Boiki, Derzkiy, Gnevnyy, Gordyy, Gremyashchiy, Upornyy, Zhguchiy, Zorkiy

Builders: 4 at Zhdanov, 1 at Komsomolsk, 3 at Nikolayev. At least one other was launched but BU before completion, as production shifted to the 'Kynda' class.

These 8 destroyers began as gun-armed successors to the 'Kotlins', but were completed as SSM destroyers, with single launchers for SS-N-1 cruise missiles fore and aft, reportedly with a total of 20 weapons; they also had 4 quadruple 57mm AA, 6–21in TT and 2 RBU-2500 ASW weapons. The first was sighted in June 1961; construction reportedly began in 1958. As in the 'Kildin' class, missile control appears to have required the Wasp Head conventional director; the small helicopter platform aft, the first on a Soviet warship, was probably also associated with the missile system.

Beginning in 1968, these ships were converted to ASW destroyers (BPK rather than RK), their SS-N-1 missiles removed, and a new sharply raked bow added for a bow sonar. An SA-N-1 AA missiles was added aft, an the two waist 57mm guns were removed, the after quadruple mount being moved forward. Other ASW improvements were the provision of quintuple rather than triple TT, and the replacement of the former two hand-loaded RBU-2500s by three RBU-6000s, automatically loaded. Some have received a quartet of small-craft type twin 30mm guns around the second funnel.

These were the most direct descendants of the 'Kotlin' design with the original postwar high-pressure steam plant. Subsequent Soviet surface combatants had either gas turbines or a new pressure-fired steam plant incorporating some gas turbine technology.

Slavny 1980

Krasnyy Krym 1974

'KASHIN' class *missile destroyers*

Displacement:	3750t standard; 4500t full load
Dimensions:	472ft 5in (modified ship 482ft 3in × 51ft 10in × 15ft 5in (modified ships 16ft 5in)
	144.0m, 147.0m × 15.8m × 4.7m, 5.0m
Machinery:	2-shaft COGAG: 4 gas turbines, 96,000shp = 38kts. Range 4000nm/20kts, 1500nm/36kts
Armament:	2 SA-N-1 (2×2, 44 missiles), 4–76mm (2×2), 2 RBU-6000 ASW RL, 2 RBU-1000 ASW RL, 5–21in TT (1×5). Modernised ships: 4 SS-N-2C (4×1), 2 SA-N-1 (2×2), 2 RBU-6000, 4–76mm (2×2), 4–30mm Gatling, 5–533mm TT (1×5)
Sensors:	Radar 2 Don-2 or Don Kay, 2 Head Net A or Head Net C and Big Net; 2 Peel Group; 2 Owl Screech (*Odarennyy*: 2 Head Net C); sonar H/F hull set. Modernised ships: VDS added aft; ECM 2 Watch Dog
Complement:	280 (300 in modified ships)

Class:
Zhdanov (entered service 1963–66): *Obraztsovyy, Odarennyy, Stereguschchiy, Ognevoy*, Provornyy***
Nikolayev (entered service 1963–72): *Komsomolets Ukrainyy, Krasnyy Kavkaz, Krasnyy Krym, Reshitelnyy, Skoryy, Smetlivvyy, Soobrazitelnyy, Sposobnyy, Strogiy, Sderzhannyy*, Smelyy*, Smyshlennyy*, Stroynyy**

Note: *ships converted to modified configuration. ** *Sderzhannyy* was completed to this standard. ** converted as SA-N-7 test ship in Black Sea, mid-1970s. *Otvazhnyy* lost in Black Sea after internal explosion 31.8.74.

These were the first turbine power plants in Soviet surface ships. They were the first large surface combatants to be so powered in the world and are sometimes credited with speeds as high as 39 knots. The 'Kashins' were also the last Soviet general-purpose destroyers; in effect they are missile-armed equivalents of the *Skorys* and 'Kotlins'. Although they were originally classed as EMs, or Fleet Torpedo Craft, they were all reclassified (or completed as) BPKs, large ASW ships.

Gun armament was limited to a pair of twin 76mm guns at the ends, outboard of the twin SA-N-1 launchers, each of which has a large Peel Group director, so that the ship can (in theory) handle two targets at once. The large torpedo battery of earlier Soviet ships was reduced to one quintuple bank; most of the centreline of the ship is taken up by uptakes from the four gas turbines and masts for the air search and missile control radars.

Six ships were modified, conversions being completed from 1973 onwards. They have a towed sonar aft, with a helicopter pad atop it, and four SS-N-2 SSM launchers aft, facing astern, presumably fitting them for the 'tattletale' role. All have 4 16-tube chaff launchers and 4 'Gatling' guns grouped around the after radar mast (carrying a 'Peel Group' S-AN-1 control radar). The original 'Kashins' also have a helicopter pad aft.

In 1979 *Provornyy* appeared with a single-armed SAM launcher and what appeared to be new missile guidance radars; subsequently this was identified with the SA-N-7 semi-active radar guided missiles which is fitted, for example, in the new *Sovremenny* and which probably corresponds to the land-based SA-11 and improved SA-6. She is apparently a trials ship; Head Net C has replaced the Peel Group atop her bridge, and a Top Steer 3d radar is mounted atop a new after mast; the new missile launcher replaces the after SA-N-1. There is no forward launcher.

Three more were built at Nikolayev for the Indian Navy, *Rajput*, the first, entering service in Oct 1980. This was a remarkable case of the revival of a relatively old design, deliveries of the original 'Kashins' having been completed in 1972. Unlike the modified 'Kashins', these ships have their 4 SS-N-2C missiles mounted to fire forward; they are placed abeam the forward SA-N-1 launcher. Tactically, that expresses the difference between the tattle-tale role and a more conventional attacking role as envisaged by the Indian Navy. In these ships, too, the after twin 76mm mount is replaced by a helicopter hangar, exiting to the helicopter pad by an inclined elevator/ramp. They have twin 30mm guns in place of the Gatlings of current Soviet 'Kashins'. Their radar suit differs from Soviet practice in that there is a Big Net air search radar in place of the amidships Head Net C. See under India.

Sovietysky Dagestan as completed

'KOLA' class *frigates*

Displacement:	1900t full load
Dimensions:	314ft 11in × 35ft 5in × 10ft 6in
	96.0m × 10.8m × 3.2m
Machinery:	2 shafts, 2 boilers, 30,000shp = 30kts. Range 3500nm/12kts
Armament:	4–100mm (4×1), 4–37mm (2×2), 3–533mm TT (1×3), 2 MBU-900 (later refitted with MBU-2500), 4 DC rails
Sensors:	Radar Cross Bird and Ball Gun/Ball End; sonar H/F hull
Complement:	190

Class:
Doblestny, Sovietsky Azerbaidjan, Sovietsky Dagestan, Sovietsky Turkmenistan,

WARSAW PACT

Zesky, Zivuchi

Six completed 1950–51 at Kaliningrad. Some early reports claimed a total of 8 units in this class.

The original adjectival names suggest destroyer rather than guardship usage, although the Soviets later classed these units with the 'Rigas' as SKRs. There have even been alternative descriptions of their origins; one school sees them as enlarged flush-decked developments of the prewar *Yastreb* class, another as direct developments of the German light destroyers (T-boats) built by Schichau at Königsberg, later Kaliningrad, the centre of Soviet frigate construction. They differ sharply from the 'Rigas', with alternative engine and boiler rooms in a typical destroyer configuration. ASW armament was limited to a pair of simple Moustrap-type RL (MBU-900).

The prototype was laid down about 1950, and some writers claim that up to 24 were originally planned. The variation in claimed numbers can be traced to their general obscurity. For example, all served in the western fleets (with the last survivors operational in the Caspian), yet as late as 1967 *Jane's* listed several (without names) in the Pacific.

'Kola' class 1955   USN

'Riga' class prototype series rig

'RIGA' class *frigates*

Displacement:	1260t standard; 1510t full load
Dimensions:	295ft 3in × 33ft 6in × 10ft
	91.0m × 10.2m × 3.2m
Machinery:	2-shaft geared turbines, 2 boilers, 20,000shp = 30kts. Range 2000nm/13kts, 550nm/28kts
Armament:	3–100mm (3×1), 4–37mm (2×2), 4–25mm (2×2, added in 1970s), MBU-600 ASW RL (replaced by 2 RBU-2500 in 1960s), 2 DC tracks, 2–3 533mm (1×2 or 3), 28 mines max
Sensors:	Radar Neptune or Don-2, Slim Net, Sun Visor; sonar H/F hull (Herkules or Pegas)
Complement:	175

Class:

Astrakhan'skiy Komsomolets, Arkhangel'skiy Komsomolets, Bars, Barsuk, Bobr, Buyvol, Byk, Gepard, Giena, Kobchik, Komsomolets Gruzhiy, Komsomolets Litviy, Krasnodarskiy Komsomolets, Kunitsa, Leopard, Lev, Lisa, Medved, Pantera, Rys Rosomakha, Shakal, Tigr, Turman, Volk, Voron, Yaguar and 38 others.

Total of 64 units completed 1952–58, plus 4 built in China. Lead yard: Kaliningrad. Also built by Nikolayev and Komsomolsk. Transfers including 8 built for export: Bulgaria (2), East Germany (4), Finland (2), Indonesia (8).

These small coastal craft, always described by the Soviets as guard ships (SKR), were built from 1952 until 1958, the lead yard being Kaliningrad, which as Schichau (Königsberg) had built German T-boats before and during World War II. The flush-decked hull with a sharply raised forecastle would seem to reflect the same design practices which produced the 'Kotlin' class destroyer, although the 'Riga' is of course a much simpler design, with open-mounted 100mm guns and a single triple TT. The original battery included 2 twin 37mm AA guns and MBU-600 ASW launchers; in the 1960s two hand-loaded RBU-2500s were substituted for the former single launcher forward, and two twin 25mm (small craft type) were added in the 1970s in some units. The animal names originally used connect them to prewar SKRs such as the *Albatros* class.

Compared to the 'Kolas', these ships all had the new type of stabilised (Wasp Head) DP director, the prototype of which appeared in the earlier class. One unit, presumably experimental, has (1983) a Hawk Screech director forward and the main director aft.

China built 4, as well as 5 improved versions ('Kiangnan' class). Her former Soviet units were unique in mounting two 'Styx' missiles in place of their TT, although the improved version had no such armament.

'Riga' class April 1969   USN

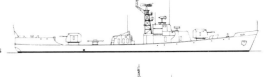

'Petya I' class

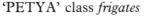

'Petya I' modified class

'Petya II' class

'PETYA' class *frigates*

Displacement:	950t standard; 1150t full load ('Petya II' 1160t)
Dimensions:	268ft 4in × 30ft 2in × 9ft 6in ('Petya II' 9ft 10in)
	81.8m × 9.2m × 2.9m, 3.0m
Machinery:	2-shaft CODAG: 2 15,000shp gas turbines plus 1 6000bhp diesel, 36,000shp = 32kts. Range 4870nm/10kts (diesel), 450nm/29kts
Armament:	4–76mm, 2 RBU-2500 ASW RL, 2 DC racks, 5–406mmTT (1×5), 22 mines max ('Petya II' 2 RBU-6000, 10–406mm TT 2×5)
Sensors:	Radar Don-2, Slim Net ('Petya II' Strut Curve), Hawk Screech; sonar H/F hull (Herkules), helicopter dipping sonar. M/F towed sonar in modified ships; ECM 2 Watch Dog
Complement:	90

All by Kaliningrad and Khabarovsk: 18 'Petya I' completed 1961–64 (10 modified from 1973 on), 27 'Petya II' completed 1964–69 (1 modified 1978). One source claims 46 rather than 45 Soviet units extant in 1982. A modified version with 4 RBU-2500 and 3–21in TT (1×3) has been built for export to India (10), Syria (2), and Vietnam (4); a few also serve with the Pacific Fleet.

These coastal combatants are the production successors of the 'Rigas' designated SKRs. They differ primarily in powerplant configuration. Both are CODAGs, with gas turbines for high speed bursts, but the 'Petyas' have conventional funnel arrangements, whereas the 'Mirkas' have their gas turbines in raised spaces aft, exhausting directly aft, perhaps adding some jet effect for propulsion. Since 'Mirka' production was sandwiched between the 'Petya I' and 'Petya II' series, it is likely that the 'Mirka' represented an interim solution to a problem in conventional CODAG operation, *ie* operation with gas turbines geared to the propeller shafts.

Each class exists in sub-series. 'Petya I', the prototype of which was built in 1960–61 at Kaliningrad, was armed with a pair of twin 76mm DP guns, 4 RBU-2500 ASW RLs, and one quintuple bank of 16in ASW torpedo tubes. Ships of this type were built at Kaliningrad and Khabarovsk. 'Petya I', was well as two banks of ASW TT . A version with 4 RBU-2500s and 3 TT (one triple 21in bank) has been exported to India, Syria and Vietnam; total 'Petya' production was about 65. Nine units were modified with VDS of various configurations aft; the single 'Petya II' modified had one bank of TT removed, and the 'Petya Is' lost 2 of their RBU-2500s. In each case the sonar was housed in a new raised stern deckhouse; however, one trials ship had a large towed 'fish' exposed aft, and another had a deckhouse abaft her uptakes and a towing array, reels and winch on her stern.

'Petya I' class 9.7.79   USN

'Mirka II' class 5.6.67   *USN*

'Krivak I' *Storozhevoy* February 1975   *USN*

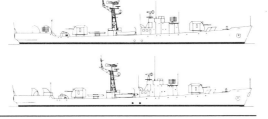

'Mirka I' class

'Mirka II' class

'MIRKA' class *frigates*

Displacement:	950t standard; 1150t full load
Dimensions:	270ft 4in × 30ft 2in × 9ft 6in
	82.4m × 9.2m × 2.9m
Machinery:	2-shaft CODAG: 2 gas gurbines plus 2 diesels, 30,000shp + 12,000bhp = 32kts. Range 4800nm/10kts, 500nm/30kts
Armament:	4–76mm (2×2), 4 RBU-6000 ASW RL, 1 DC rack in some, 5–406mm TT (1×5) ('Mirka II' 2 RBU-6000, 2 sets of TT)
Sensors:	Radar Don-2, Slim Net or Strut Curve, Hawk Screech; sonar H/F hull (Herkules or Pegas); dipping sonar in 'Mirka II'; ECM 2 Watch Dog
Complement:	98

'Mirka I' had 5 banks of TT, and 4 RBU-6000 launchers (two on the forward superstructure and two aft), as in 'Petya I'. 'Mirka II' substituted a second bank of tubes for the after ASW launchers. Production extended between 1964 and 1966, and 'Mirka IIs' have been modernised with a helicopter-type dipping sonar in place of the former internal DC rack. The 'Mirka' machinery arrangement recalls that of the earlier 'Poti' class corvettes. The gas turbine arrangement aft precludes installation of a towed (as opposed to a dipping) sonar aft. Nine of each class, all built at Kaliningrad, extant 1982.

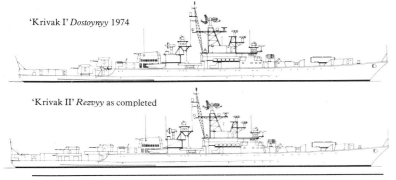

'Krivak I' *Dostoynyy* 1974

'Krivak II' *Rezvyy* as completed

'KRIVAK' class *missile frigates*

Displacement:	3300t standard; 3575t full load
Dimensions:	405ft 3in oa × 46ft 3in × 15ft 1in
	123.5m × 14.1m × 4.6m
Machinery:	2-shaft CODOG: 2 cruise turbines of 12,100shp each, 2 boost turbines of 24,300shp each, 48,600shp = 32kts. Range 4600nm/20kts, 1600nm/31kts
Armament:	1 SS-N-14 (1×4, 4 missiles), 2 SA-N-4 (2×2, 40 missiles), 4–76mm (2×2), 2 RBU-6000 ASW RL, 8–533mm TT (2×4), 20 mines max ('Krivak II' single 100mm in place of twin 76mm)
Sensors:	Radar Don-2, Don-Kay or Palm Frond, Spin Trough, Head Net C, 2 Eye Bowl, Kite Screech, 2 Pop Group; sonar M/F bow set and M/F VDS; ECM 2 Bell Shroud, 2 Bell Squat, 4 chaff RL (4×16)
Complement:	200

'Krivak II' *Rezkiy* 1981   *USN*

'Krivak I' class (21 ships): Kerch – *Bezukoriznennyy, Bezzevetniy, Deyatel'nyy, Boblestnyy, Dostoynyy, Ladnyy*
Zhdanov – *Leningradskiy Komsomolets, Bditel'nyy, Dodryy, Druznyy, Letuchiy*
Kaliningrad – *Pylkiy, Pytlivyy, Razumnyy, Razyashchiy, Retivyy, Siln'nyy, Storozhevoy, Svirepyy, Zadornyy, Zharkyy*
'Krivak II' class (11 ships, in service 1976 on): *Bessmennyy, Gordelivyy, Gromkiy, Grozyashchiy, Neukrotimyy, Pitlivyy, Razitel'nyy, Revnostnyy, Rezkiy, Rezvyy, R'yanyy*

Builders: Kaliningrad (lead), Zhdanov, and Kamysch-Burun SY, Kerch. All 'Krivak II' by Kaliningrad.

Originally rated as BPKs (ASW ships) and in 1978 designated SKRs (guardships, the old rating of the 'Rigas'), these gas turbine small combatants made a great impression with their 4 missile tubes and their pair of SA-N-4 point defence launchers. However, the massive missile tubes turned out to fire ASW weapons (SS-N-4) rather than short-range anti-ship missiles, and speed was ultimately assessed as 31kts rather than the originally estimated 38kts. They have a pair of automatically-loaded RBU-6000 ASW RL and bow and variable-depth sonars. 'Krivak-II' class ships have somewhat larger VDS housing aft, and single 100mm rather than twin 76mm DP guns aft. The VDS fish is not modified, but the housing is shaped to accommodate the larger 100mm gun mount.

The first ship appeared in 1970, as the production successor to the 'Petya', Kaliningrad being the lead yard. It would appear that they were built as part of the same programme which produced the 'Kara' and 'Kresta II' (and *Kiev*) class cruisers, to make up the numbers in ASW hunting groups, much as 'Petyas' or 'Mirkas' combined tactically with 'Kashin' class flagships, operating closer to the Soviet coast. One writer suggests that the switch to SKR designation reflects their limited high-speed endurance, but it may also reflect the strategy of creating ASW (pro-Soviet SSBN) barriers to protect SSBN 'holding areas' in wartime; in that sense such ASW craft act as coast guard ships.

On 9.11.75 part of the crew of *Storozhevoy*, then in the Baltic, mutinied, trying to take their ship to Denmark or Sweden; she was intercepted by naval bombers and warships, and the mutiny quashed. The ship was subsequently transferred to another Fleet and (with a totally fresh crew) made many port visits, presumably to refute Western reports of the mutiny.

'Koni' class 1980

'KONI' class *frigate*

Displacement:	1700t standard; 1900t full load
Dimensions:	311ft 8in oa × 42ft × 13ft 9in
	95.0m × 12.8m × 4.2m
Machinery:	3-shaft CODAG: 1 gas turbine plus 2 diesels, 15,000shp + 15,000bhp = 27kts. Range 1800nm/14kts
Armament:	1 SA-N-4 (1×2, 20 missiles), 4–76mm (2×2), 4–30mm (2×2), 2 RBU-6000 ASW RL, 2 DC racks, 20 mines max
Sensors:	Radar Don-2, Strut Curve, Pop Group, Hawk Screech, Drum Tilt; sonar M/F hull; ECM 2 Watch Dog, 2 chaff RL (2×16)
Complement:	110

Timofey Ul'yantsev completed at Zelenodolsk 1978. Also called *Delfin*. Most built for export, Algeria (2), Cuba (1), E Germany (2), Yugoslavia (1).

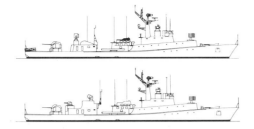

Grisha I

Grisha II

'GRISHA' class *frigates*

Displacement:	950t standard; 1200t full load
Dimensions:	234ft 11in × 32ft 2in × 12ft 2in *71.6m × 9.8m × 3.7m*
Machinery:	3-shaft CODAG: gas turbines plus 4 diesels, 15,000shp + 16,000bhp = 30kts. Range 4500nm/10kts, 950nm/27kts, 2000nm/20kts
Armament:	1 SA-N-4 (1×2, 20 missiles), 2–57mm (1×2), 2 RBU-6000 ASW RL, 2 DC racks (12 DC), 4–533mm TT (2×2), 18 mines max ('Grisha II': second twin 57mm replaces SA-N-4, no Pop Group installed; 'Grisha III': 30mm Gatling aft in addition)
Sensors:	Radar Strut Curve, Pop Group, Muff Cob, ('Grisha III' Bass Tilt); sonar M/F hull and dipping; ECM 2 Watch Dog
Complement:	60

Class:

'Grisha II': *Ametist, Brilliant, Izumrud, Rubin, Saffir, Zhemchug* and one other.

Total of 16 'Grisha I' completed 1968–74, 7 'Grisha II' completed 1974–76, 20 'Grisha III' completed from 1975 onwards. 'Grisha III' production continues. Builders: Khabarovsk, Kamysh-Burn (Kerch), Zelenodolsk.

Production successors to the 'Poti', these 'small ASW ships' or MPKs are comparable in size to the somewhat earlier 'SKRs' of the 'Petya' and 'Mirka' classes, and have somewhat similar characteristics: in effect they have an improved 'Poti' armament on a larger hull, which accommodates an SA-N-4 point defence missile forward, both ASW RLs being moved into the bridgework. As in 'Poti', the machinery is CODAG, but there is no raised compartment aft and it is tempting to draw an analogy with the 'Petya' system. Six 'Grisha II', built for the KGB (border patrol) have a second twin 57mm gun mount forward, replacing the point defence missile; they are designated *Progranichniy Storozhevoy Korabl'* (PSK, recalling some prewar units). Finally, a 'Grisha III' (variant of basic design) adds a 'Gatling' close-in defensive gun; it is the current production variant. All have 2 twin trainable ASW TT, and a dipping sonar as well as a M/F hull unit. In 'Grisha I' and II there is prominent plate, presumably for radiation hazard protection, forward of the 'Muff Cob' radar controlling the 57mm gun aft; in 'Grisha III' this radar is replaced by the 'Gatling' gun. All versions have 2 DC racks and can accommodate mines.

One US analyst called this the best small ASW ship design in the world; the dipping sonar has superior performance for its size, and it carries the large-ship 533mm ASW torpedo rather than the less capable 406mm type carried on other Soviet small ASW ships.

'Grisha I' class 1983   *USN*

SUBMARINES

'Whiskey V' class

'Whiskey Canvas Bag' class

'WHISKEY' class *attack submarines*

Displacement:	1050t surfaced; 1350t submerged
Dimensions:	246ft 1in × 20ft 8in × 15ft 9in *75.0m × 6.3m × 4.8m*
Machinery:	2 Type 37D 2000bhp diesels, 2500shp submerged = 17kts surfaced, 13.5kts submerged. Endurance 40–45 days. Range on snorkel 6000nm at 5kts
Armament:	6–533mm TT (4 bow, 2 aft, 12 torpedoes or 24 mines), 2–57mm (1×2), 2–25mm (1×2, some had 1–100mm and 2 MG)
Sensors:	Radar Snoop Plate; sonar M/F (Tamir) and small passive array; ECM Stop Light
Complement:	50

Class	Gorki	Nikolayev	Komsomolsk	Baltic
1950	1	–	–	–
1951	2	2	–	–
1952	10	6	–	–
1953	15	8	–	–
1954	32	15	1	–
1955	40	14	4	4
1956	35	14	6	8
1957	10	6	–	2

Of a total of 236 units, 12 were converted to cruise missile submarines, 4 to radar pickets (after TT removed, Boat Sail radar on sail). Two became fishery research craft. Transfers (39): 4 to Albania, 2 to Bulgaria, 6 to China, 1 to Cuba, 7 to Egypt, 12 to Indonesia, 2 to North Korea, 5 to Poland. Up to 20 were built in China. In 1982 60 were carried as usable (45 active and 15 in operational reserve), with possibly another 70 in various states of reserve. Of the former radar pickets, one reverted to attack submarine status, and two or three others were broken up.

All guns later removed; many late units were completed without guns. Some may have been modified with 16in torpedoes in the after tubes.

These submarines were the nightmare which afflicted postwar US and British naval planners; a mass-production, Soviet version of the German Type XXI. It took the Soviets somewhat longer than expected to begin series production, the first unit appearing only in 1950, but about 235 had been completed before Krushchev terminated the programme in 1957. Gorki, on the Caspian, was the lead yard, submarines reaching the Northern Fleet via the White Sea Canal and the Volga. Others were built at Nikolayev, Leningrad and Komsomolsk-on-Amur, to supply the four Soviet fleets. There is some controversy as to their precise origins, the Soviets claiming that they are modified versions of the wartime 'S' class incorporating some features of the German Type XXI, and indeed that they are descended from a new medium-range submarine design begun in 1944. There is also some question as to their intended role; it appears in retrospect that the Soviets, at least in Stalin's day, thought of them primarily as a means of protecting the sea approaches to the Soviet Union, rather than as an ocean commerce-raiding force. Only the 'Z' class was considered truly long-range.

'Whiskey V' aground, Karlskrona 4.11.81   *Popperfoto/UPI*

There were several versions, early ones being armed with guns. Some did not even have snorkels, and 'Whiskey I', 'II', and 'IV' all had an enclosed twin (over-and-under) 25mm AA mount forward of the sail; 'Whiskey II' also had a deck gun (57mm or 76mm) abaft the fin, and 'Whiskey III' had the guns removed but retained their platforms. Only with 'Whiskey V' were all guns removed and the fin streamlined; this is the version surviving at present. Since 1958 two 'Whiskeys', *Severyanka* and *Slavyanka*, have been used for oceanographic research. During the 1950s, too, a total of at least 12 were converted to fire SS-N-3 strategic cruise missiles: 5 'Whiskey Twin Cylinder' with 2 missiles abaft the fin, and 'Whiskey Long Bin' with a rebuilt fin and 4 missiles; the single-missile 'Whiskey Single Cylinder' was a prototype reportedly converted in 1957, the 'Twin Cylinders' following in 1959–61 and the 'Long Bins Bag' class) in 1959–62. Finally, 6 were converted into submarine radar-pickets ('Whiskey Canvas Bag' class) *c* 1960–61.

'Whiskey Twin Cylinder' 1973   *USN*

'Romeo' class

'ROMEO' class *attack submarines*

Displacement:	1330t surfaced; 1700t submerged
Dimensions:	252ft 8in × 22ft × 16ft 1in
	77.0m × 6.7m × 4.9m
Machinery:	2 shafts, 2 diesels, 4000bhp submerged = 15.5kts surfaced, 13kts submerged. Endurance 45 days. Range on snorkel 7000nm/5kts and 16,000nm/10kts (surfaced). Diving depth 270–300m
Armament:	8–533mm TT (6 bow, 2 aft, 14 torpedoes or 28 mines)
Sensors:	Radar Snoop plate; sonar M/F (Herkules), passive array (Fenika), ECM Stop Light
Complement:	56

All built 1958–61 at Gorki as successors to the 'Whiskey' class with 2 more TT, greater range and diving depth. 2 in 1958, 3 in 1959, 5 in 1960, 9 in 1961, 1 in 1962. Of this total of 20, 6 were transferred to Egypt, 2 to Bulgaria, and 1 to Algeria; others were built in China and North Korea.

'Zulu I' class

'Zulu II' class

'Zulu III' class

'Zulu IV' class

'Zulu V' class

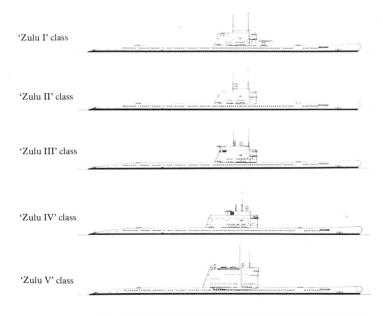

'ZULU' class *attack submarines*

Displacement:	1900t surfaced; 2350t submerged
Dimensions:	295ft 3in × 24ft 7in × 19ft 8in
	90.0m × 7.5m × 6.0m
Machinery:	3 shafts, 2000bhp diesels, 5300shp submerged = 18kts surfaced, 16kts submerged. Endurance 70 days. Range 9500nm/8kts on snorkel, 20,000nm surfaced
Sensors:	Radar Snoop Plate; sonar M/F (Tamir), small passive array
Armament:	10–533mm TT (6 bow, 4 aft, 22 torpedoes or 44 mines), 2–57mm (1×2), 2–25mm (1×2). See notes
Complement:	70

Completions at Severodvinsk 1953 (3), 1954 (2), 1955 (3); Sudomekh 1952 (1), 1953 (5), 1954–55 (6 each)

'Zulu I–III' had deck guns and AA guns on the fin; current 'Zulu IV' has none. Several converted as 'Zulu V' ballistic missile submarines at Leningrad 1956–57, with two tubes in the fin. As of 1982, 11 had been scrapped and 2 had been converted for oceanographic research as *Lira* and *Vega*.

The 26 'Zulus' were longer-range equivalents of the 'Whiskeys'; the shift, in

'Romeo' class 1973   *USN*

the next generation of Soviet submarines, from a concentration on medium-range ('Romeo' class) to one on long-range ('Foxtrot' class) submarines may have been significant as indicating a shift in Soviet concepts of submarine function. As in the 'Whiskeys' early 'Zulus' had deck guns, but all were ultimately converted to a gun-less 'Zulu V' configuration. Six were completed as, or converted to, strategic missile submarines, carrying two missiles in the fin (SS-N-4, surface-launched); they were the world's first ballistic missile submarines, one of them firing a modified Army type weapon as early as Sept 1955.

'Quebec' class

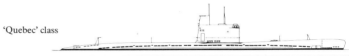

'QUEBEC' class *attack submarines*

Displacement:	400t surfaced; 540t submerged
Dimensions:	183ft 9in × 16ft 5in × 12ft 6in
	56.0m × 5.1m × 3.8m
Machinery:	3 shafts, Kreislauf system; 1000bhp diesels, 2200shp submerged = 18kts surfaced, 16kts submerged. Range 7000nm cruising
Armament:	4–533mm TT (8 torpedoes), 2–25mm (1×2, later removed)
Sensors:	Radar Snoop Plate; sonar M/F (Tamir), passive array (Feniks)
Complement:	30

Completions all at Sudomekh: 3 in 1954, 10 in 1955, 12 in 1956, 5 in 1957, for a total of 30. Four were left in 1982. They were built in alternate groups of 3, 3, and then 4. Launch dates for the first five groups: Sept 1954, then May, July, Oct 1955, and then April 1956. In 1956 US intelligence sources reported first completions in May 1955; the data above may refer to *launch* rather than to completion dates, in which case it would jibe with the more detailed 1956 report.

These small submarines were the functional successors of the prewar and wartime coastal 'M' class, incorporating a closed-cycle (Kreislauf) diesel power system which the Soviets had originally installed in the experimental *M92*. Otherwise they were always regarded as a smaller edition of the 'Whiskey'/'Zulu' group, with only four TT.

The special propulsion system added oxygen to recycled diesel air to keep the engines going, and used special chemicals to scavenge out combustion products. It powered only the centreline shaft. It is not clear whether reports that it was a failure are to be credited. Reports that they had Walter steam turbines were apparently incorrect; it seems that the Soviets briefly tested a Walter plant about 1956, but did not pursue that system, preferring nuclear power. They were specially designed for Baltic and Black Sea operations. Note that the Kreislauf plant would have made possible underwater dashes from, say, Leningrad to the Danish Straits or from Sevastopol to the Bosphorus, both important Soviet naval objectives early in a general war. It would have been far less useful in the role envisaged by the Germans for their Walter boats, escape after an open-ocean convoy battle.

WARSAW PACT

'Foxtrot' class

'FOXTROT' class *attack submarines*

Displacement:	1950t surfaced; 2400t submerged
Dimensions:	300ft 3in × 24ft 7in × 19ft 8in
	91.5m × 7.5m × 6.0m
Machinery:	3 shafts, 2000bhp diesel, 5300shp submerged = 16kts surfaced, 15.5kts submerged. Endurance 70 days. Range 11,000nm/8kts on snorkel, 350nm/2kts on batteries
Armament:	10–533mm TT (6 bow, 4 aft, 22 torpedoes or 44 mines)
Sensors:	Radar Snoop Tray; sonar M/F, passive array
Complement:	78

Class:

Chelyabinsky Komsomolets, Komsomolets Kazakhstana, Kuibishevskiy Komsomolets, Magnitogorskiy Komsomolets, Ul'Yanovskiy Komsomolets, Vladimirskiy Komsomolets, Yaroslavskiy Komsomolets and 69 others

Completions at Sudomekh: 2 in 1958, 5 in 1959, 6 each in 1960 and 1961, 5 each year in 1962–65, 1966 (4), 1967 (2). Severodvinsk completed 3 in 1962. Reportedly 62 units were delivered to the Soviet Navy as 'Zulu' successors: 45 were delivered through 1967, the remainder following from 1971 onwards. Two became the oceanographic craft *Sirius* and *Saturn*. At least 14 more were built specifically for transfer: 2 to Cuba, 8 to India, and 6 to Libya. Heavily deployed in the Mediterranean and Indian Ocean. The class remains in production for export in 1983, with 2 reportedly building for Cuba. Reported names are those of Young Communist city branches.

'Tango' class

'TANGO' class *attack submarines*

Displacement:	3000t surfaced; 3700t submerged
Dimensions:	300ft 3in × 29ft 6in × 23ft
	91.5m × 9.0m × 7.0m
Machinery:	3 shafts, diesels, 6000bhp = 20kts surfaced, 16kts submerged
Armament:	6–533mm TT (bow). Reportedly fitted for SS-N-15 torpedo tube-launched missiles
Sensors:	Radar Snoop Tray; sonar L/F
Complement:	72

All built at Gorki, completed from 1972 onwards; 14 had been completed as of 1982, with production continuing. 'Tango', which first appeared in 1973 at the July Sevastopol Review, is a direct functional successor to 'Foxtrot', with a greater beam and about 50 per cent greater surfaced displacement; it can probably fire the SS-N-15 ASW missile (a Soviet equivalent of SUBROC) as well as conventional torpedoes. Reportedly it has a much higher battery capacity (*ie* underwater endurance) than its predecessors. There is no bow sonar dome visible, and the fin (at least in published photographs) does not show the series of sonar 'windows' apparent in some 'Foxtrots', nor is there a large sonar-transparent 'window' surrounding the bow itself. At least in so far as is visible, the hull is blunter than that of 'Foxtrot'.

'November' class

'NOVEMBER' class *attack submarines*

Displacement:	4500t surfaced; 5300t submerged
Dimensions:	363ft 11in × 29ft 6in × 25ft 3in
	110.0m × 9.0m × 7.7m
Machinery:	2-shaft nuclear, 1 reactor, 30,000shp = 30kts
Armament:	8–533mm TT (bow), 4–406mm TT (aft), 26–32 torpedoes or mines
Complement:	80

Completions all at Severodvinsk: 1 in 1958, 2 in 1959, 1 in 1960, 3 in 1961, 3 in 1962, 3 in 1963, 2 in 1964. Prototype was *Leninsky Komsomol*, commissioned 8.4.58. Made the first Soviet voyage to the North Pole. One was lost off Cape Finisterre April 1970 after an internal fire.

The first Soviet nuclear submarines, these vessels are fast but reportedly unreliable. Soviet sources claim that the decision to produce a nuclear submarine was made in 1953, and reportedly the Soviet Navy was involved in the initial Soviet nuclear powerplant experiments. The first 'November' became operational in 1959, and fourteen were completed through 1965. Components intended for further units were almost certainly diverted to nuclear strategic submarines ('Echos' and 'Hotels').

'Foxtrot' class April 1979 — MoD

'Tango' class April 1979 — MoD

'November' class in distress 10.4.70 — USN

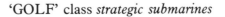
'Golf I' class

'Golf II' class

'GOLF' class *strategic submarines*

Displacement:	2300t surfaced; 2700t submerged
Dimensions:	328ft 1in × 27ft 11in × 21ft 8in
	100.0m × 8.5m × 6.6m
Machinery:	3 shafts, 3 diesels of 2000bhp, 5300shp submerged = 12kts submerged. Endurance 70 days. Range 9000nm/5kts
Armament:	3 SS-N-4, 10–533mm TT (6 fwd, 4 aft)
Sensors:	Radar Snoop Tray; sonar M/F hull
Complement:	80

Completions: Komsomolsk and Severodvinsk 1 each in 1958, 2 and 6 respectively in 1959, 1 and 4 in 1960, 2 and 5 in 1961, Komsomolsk in 1962. Given project number 629. One more was built in China, probably from Soviet components. 'Golf II' was converted to SS-N-5 missiles (13 units, 1965–73), 'Golf III' to SS-N-8 (lengthened to 361ft/*110.0m*, 2900/3300t). One 'Golf I' was converted to 'Golf' IV as a test unit for SS-N-6 missiles about 1970, the hull being lengthened about 60ft; she carries six missiles in a very long fin. One 'Golf II' was converted to a test unit for SS-N-20, with one missile tube in place of her former three. Three converted to command or communications link units 1978, with fin extended aft (SSQ), probably to house a buoy antenna. A fourth was reportedly under conversion in 1983. One boat was lost in C Pacific in April 1968. She was the object of an incredible CIA salvage mission in Aug 1974. The purpose-built *Hughes Glomar Explorer* 'mining ship' reportedly recovered a 38ft nose section of this 'Golf II' from a depth of 17,000ft, over 3 miles down, including 6 of her doomed crew and 2 nuclear torpedo warheads.

These diesel submarines were the first ballistic missile submarines in the world, each carrying three SS-N-4 300nm range missiles in her fin. The missiles had to be launched on the surface; 'Hotel II' and 'Golf II' were modernisations to carry the submerged-launched SS-N-5, whose range is about 750nm. In a product sense, 'Golf' succeeded 'Zulu' and 'Hotel' followed 'November'; presumably there are design similarities. The programme was executed on a crash basis, and ended abruptly as the Navy was forced out of strategic warfare. Indeed, during the 1960s the Soviets sometimes claimed that they intended to use their ballistic missile submarines to attack carrier battle groups on the basis of estimated courses dead-reckoned to the point of impact. In retrospect it would appear that such claims were intended more to serve Soviet internal political interests than as a radical shift in naval policy; the shift in SS-N-3 guidance and role was far more important. In the late 1970s, 'Golfs' were deployed to the Baltic, possibly as an equivalent to US Poseidon submarines assigned to the NATO European theatre.

'Hotel II' class

'HOTEL' class *strategic submarines*

Displacement:	5000t surfaced; 6000t submerged
Dimensions:	377ft 4in × 29ft 6in × 23ft
	115.0m × 9.0m × 7.0m
Machinery:	2-shaft nuclear: 1 reactor, 30,000shp = 20kts/25kts (submerged)
Armament:	3 SS-N-4, 6–533mm TT (bow), 2–406mm TT (stern, total of 20 torpedoes)
Sensors:	Radar Snoop Tray; sonar M/F
Complement:	80

Built only at Severodvinsk: 2 completed in 1959, 1 in 1960, 3 in 1961. One was apparently stricken early in the 1980s. 'Hotel II' had SS-N-4 missiles replaced by SS-N-5 (capable of being launched underwater). 'Hotel III' was trials ships for the SS-N-8 missile, and had to be lengthened to 426ft/130m (5500/6500t) during conversion (1965). Two boats dismantled by March 1983 to conform with SALT provisions; one boat disabled off Newfoundland and towed back to Northern Fleet 1973.

The 'Hotel' nuclear powerplant is reported to be very similar to that of the contemporary 'Echo' and, for that matter, to that of its predecessor, the 'November'; sometimes this system is called 'HEN' after the three classes in which it is found.

'Whiskey Long Bin' class

'WHISKEY LONG BIN' class *cruise missile submarines*

Displacement:	1200t surfaced; 1500t submerged
Dimensions:	272ft 4in × 20ft × 16ft 5in
	83.0m × 6.1m × 5.0m
Machinery:	As 'Whiskey' class
Armament:	4 SS-N-3, 4–533mm TT (fwd)
Sensors:	As 'Whiskey' class
Complement:	60–65

Converted at Leningrad, 1961–63; in 1983 only two are left. Submerged speed reduced to 8kts, surface to 13.5kts.

'Golf II' class 1977 USN

'Echo I' class as converted early 1970s

'ECHO I' class *cruise missile submarines*

Displacement:	4500t surfaced; 5500t submerged
Dimensions:	360ft 11in × 29ft 10in × 24ft 7in
	110.0m × 9.1m × 7.5m
Machinery:	2-shaft nuclear: 1 reactor, 25,000shp = 20kts surfaced, 25kts submerged
Armament:	8 SS-N-3, 6–533mm TT (bow), 4–406mm TT (aft)
Sensors:	Radar Snoop Tray; sonar M/F
Complement:	75

Built at Komsomolsk only: 2 in 1960, 2 in 1961, 1 in 1962. These cruise missile carriers were contemporary with the ballistic 'Golfs' and 'Hotels' in design and in construction; it would appear that the SS-N-3 missile was originally intended as a strategic alternative to SS-N-4. However, when the Soviet Navy was shifted out of the strategic role about 1960 in favour of the new Strategic Rocket Forces, SS-N-3 was amenable to guidance suiting it for the anti-ship role. The original submarines could not accommodate the mid-course command guidance radar required, and they were later converted into pure attack submarines. One boat disabled at sea S of Japan 1980.

'Echo I' class 1975 USN

'Whiskey Long Bin' class 14.5.63 USN

'Hotel II' class 1975 MoD

WARSAW PACT

'Echo II' class

'Juliett' class

'ECHO II' class *cruise missile submarines*

Displacement:	5000t surfaced; 6000t submerged
Dimensions:	377ft 4in × 29ft 6in × 24ft 7in
	115.0m × 9.0m × 7.5m
Machinery:	2-shaft nuclear: 1 reactor, 24,000shp = 20kts surfaced, 23kts submerged
Armament:	8 SS-N-3, 6–533mm TT (bow), 2–406mm TT (aft)
Sensors:	Radar Front Door/Front Piece, Snoop Tray; sonar L/F; ECM Stop Light
Complement:	90

Completions (total 29): Komsomolsk 1, Severodvinsk 2 in 1962, 1 and 3 in 1963, 3 and 4 in 1964, 2 and 5 in 1965, 2 and 4 in 1966, 2 in 1967.

Completed with enlarged fins accommodating 'Front Door'/'Front Piece' antennas for SS-N-3 mid-course guidance. They remain suitable for strategic attack, since their launch tubes can accommodate the inertially-guided version of the missile.

Although 'Echo I' had six launch tubes, 'Echo II' was lengthened by 16ft/5m to house an additional pair. In some units the original SS-N-3 missile was later replaced by the improved SS-N-12, which is also carried by *Kiev*. It was an 'Echo' attack submarine which had an internal accident off Okinawa in Aug 1980, and had to be towed to Vladivostok.

Through 1982 five had been modified to launch SS-N-12 in place of SS-N-3; external differences are bulges to either side of the fin (presumably for a satellite data receiver, Punch Bowl) and a bulge at the forward ends of the missile tubes abreast the fin.

'Echo II' class (SS-N-12 version) 1970   *USN*

'Juliett' class 1973   *USN*

'Yankee' class 1976   *USN*

'Delta I' class 1973   *MoD*

'JULIETT' class *strategic submarines*

Displacement:	3000t surfaced; 3750t submerged
Dimensions:	295ft 3in × 32ft 10in × 23ft
	90.0m × 10.0m × 7.0m
Machinery:	2 shafts, diesel-electric, 5000bhp = 16kts. Range 9000nm/7kts, 15,000nm surface cruising
Armament:	4 SS-N-3, 6–533mm TT (bow, 18 torpedoes), 4–406mm TT (aft)
Sensors:	Radar Front Door/Front Piece, Snoop Slab
Complement:	*c*80

All built at Gorki: 1 in 1961, 2 a year 1962–68, 1 in 1969, for a total of 16. This class was formerly divided between the Northern and Pacific Fleets, but in 1982 at least 4 were assigned to the Baltic.

In effect diesel-electric equivalents of 'Echo II'. They were probably proposed as the SS-N-3 equivalent of the 'Golfs', which suggests that at first a huge cruise missile strategic programme was planned (34 'Echos' and 16 'Julietts'); in contrast to an 'Echo I', a 'Juliett' carries only 4 missiles, and at 90m it is somewhat shorter than a 'Golf' (100m). None was completed before the shift to the anti-ship version of SS-N-3, so there is no strategic version with which the current 'Juliett' can be compared. Even so, it is unlikely that no such submarine was designed and ordered.

'Yankee' class as built

'YANKEE' class *strategic submarines*

Displacement:	8000t surfaced; 9600t submerged
Dimensions:	426ft 6in × 39ft 4in × 29ft 10in
	30.0m × 12.0m × 8.8m
Machinery:	2-shaft nuclear, 1 reactor, 50,000shp = 27kts
Armament:	16 SS-N-6, 6–533mm TT (bow, 18 torpedoes)
Sensors:	Radar Snoop Tray; sonar L/F
Complement:	120

The Komsomolsk and Severodvinsk yards built 34: 2 completed 1967, 4 in 1968, 6 in 1969, 8 in 1970, 6 in 1971, 5 in 1972, 2 in 193, 1 in 1974. As of 1982, 7 had been reduced to attack submarines, with their missile tubes removed. One boat was refitted with 12 SS-N-17 missiles and is now referred to as 'Yankee II.'

It appears that the large 'Yankee' programme was something of a crash effort; reportedly these submarines were not entirely satisfactory, and the short range of their missile must have imposed considerable restrictions. Even so, the Soviets seem to have standardised on the basic design, as the subsequent 'Deltas' are lengthened versions; only with 'Typhoon' did the Soviets produce a genuinely new strategic submarine. The original 'Yankee' was armed with an SS-N-6 missile roughly comparable to early US Polaris missiles, requiring its carrier to operate off the US coast.

At about the same time as 'Delta III' appeared, a single 'Yankee' was refitted to fire the new, and apparently experimental, SS-N-17 missile. Given limits on the total Soviet strategic submarine fleet under SALT-II, the Soviets began withdrawing 'Yankees' from that force about 1980 as they completed 'Deltas'; reportedly they cut the submarine into sections, removing the missile section completely in a process the reverse of that which converted US *Skipjacks* into *George Washington* class ballistic missile submarines. Whether the resulting torpedo-armed submarines are effective attack units is open to some question; they are currently carried on the order-of-battle as 'Yankee' SSNs. The corresponding US practice, in the former US SSBNs, has been to fill the missile tubes with concrete rather than to cut open the submarine hull.

'Delta I' class

'DELTA I' class *strategic submarines*

Displacement:	9000t surfaced; 11,750t submerged
Dimensions:	459ft 4in × 39ft 4in × 28ft 7in
	140.0m × 12.0m × 8.7m
Machinery:	2-shaft nuclear: 1 reactor, 50,000shp = 25kts
Armament:	12 SS-N-8, 6–533mm TT (bow, 18 torpedoes)
Sensors:	Radar Snoop Tray; sonar L/F
Complement:	120

Built at Komsomolsk and Severodvinsk: 1 in 1972, 4 in 1973, 6 in 1974, 2 each in 1975 and 1976, 3 in 1977.

'Delta III' class 1981

Although 34 'Yankees' were built, it appears that their operation was unsatis-factory to the Soviets, who in 1971 introduced 'Delta', on roughly the same hull, carrying 12 400nm SS-N-8 missiles, reportedly with stellar update guidance for a level of accuracy unusual in a submarine-launched weapon. With the appearance of the 'Deltas', Soviet strategic submarine strategy shifted from being a reserve force (with some initial operations against US naval targets) to closer co-ordination with the land-based missile forces; in each case it was assumed that all or most of the Soviet submarines would survive thanks to friendly forces dominating their patrol areas. This is very different from US concepts of SSBN survival.

'Charlie I' class 20.4.74   USN

'Delta II' class

'DELTA II' class *strategic submarines*

Displacement:	10,000t surfaced; 12,750t submerged
Dimensions:	508ft 6in × 39ft 4in × 28ft 10in
	155.0m × 12.0m × 8.8m
Armament:	16 SS-N-8, 6–533mm TT (bow, 18 torpedoes)
Other particulars:	As 'Delta I' class

All built at Severodvinsk: 4 completed 1974–75. 'Delta-II', which first appeared in 1976, was lengthened by about 48ft to accommodate 4 more SS-N-8 missiles in a large hump abaft its fin. Underwater speed fell to 24kts.

'Delta III' class

'DELTA III' class *strategic submarines*

Displacement:	10,500t surfaced; 13,250t submerged
Armament:	16 SS-N-18, 6–533mm TT (bow, 12 torpedoes)
Other particulars:	As 'Delta I' class

All built at Severodvinsk: 2 completed in 1975, 4 in 1976, 2 in 1977, 2 in 1978, and 3 in 1979–81. The 'Delta II' hump was further enlarged to fit the larger SS-N-18 missile with a range of about 500nm and MIRV warhead. A total of 14 launched to early 1983, a few more expected.

'Charlie I' class

'CHARLIE' class *cruise missile submarines*

Displacement:	4000t surfaced; 4900t submerged ('Charlie II' 4300/5100t)
Dimensions:	311ft 8in ('Charlie II', 340ft) × 32ft 10in × 26ft 3in
	95.0m, 103.0m × 10.0m × 8.0m
Machinery:	1-shaft nuclear: 1 reactor, 30,000shp = 27kts ('Charlie II' 26kts
Weapons:	8 SS-N-7 (SS-N-9 in 'Charlie II'), 6–533mm TT (bow, 18 torpedoes)
Sensors:	Radar Snoop Tray, sonar L/F ('Charlie II' Stop Light ECM)
Complement:	80 (85 in 'Charlie II')

All built at Gorki. 'Charlie I' entered service at the rate of 2 per year in 1968–73, for a total of 12; 'Charlie II' one each in 1973, 1974, 1977, 1979, 1980–81 (total 5), programme continuing.

Unlike the 'Echos' and 'Julietts', these submarines can fire their anti-ship missiles submerged; they have relatively short ranges and are, in effect, missile substitutes for torpedoes. The first 'Charlie' became operational in 1968, with 8 SS-N-7 55km missiles in her bulbous bow. An enlarged type, 'Charlie II' fires the longer-range SS-N-9 missile of the 'Nanuchka' class.

The role of this submarine is not entirely clear. They have always been associated publicly with the 'Victor' class SS-N-15-armed ASW submarines, sharing a common level of technology and probably, given Soviet tendencies towards standardisation, a common propulsion plant. However, the large missile tube section forward probably restricts their speeds compared to that of the 'Victor' and therefore limits the extent to which they can combine tactically. Similarly, it may limit their value as a 'tattletales' or even as attack submarines countering fast naval formations such as carrier battle groups.

'Papa' class   USN

'PAPA' class *cruise missile submarine*

Displacement:	6700t surfaced; 7500t submerged
Dimensions:	357ft 7in × 39ft 4in × 27ft 11in
	109.0m × 12.0m × 8.5m
Machinery:	2-shaft nuclear: 2 reactors, 60,000shp = 35–40kts
Armament:	10 SS-N-9, 8–533mm TT
Sensors:	Radar Snoop Tray; sonar MF/LF; ECM Stop Light
Complement:	85

One unit, built at Gorki, completed 1970. Reportedly, although she shares a common turbine with the 'Charlie' class, their reactors differ. 'Papa' class was a pure research and development test bed, for advanced hydrodynamics, a dense powerplant, and possibly new metallurgy. Note her high-powered reactor, reflected in high observed speed.

50 Let SSR

'VICTOR I' class *attack submarines*

Displacement:	4300t surfaced; 5100t submerged
Dimensions:	311ft 8in × 32ft 10in × 23ft
	95.0m × 10.0m × 7.0m
Machinery:	1-shaft nuclear: 1 reactor, 30,000shp = 30kts; 2 small propellers for low speeds
Armament:	8–533mm TT (bow, including SS-N-15 missiles, 18 torpedoes)
Sensors:	Radar Snoop Tray; sonar L/F
Complement:	80

Total of 14 (including *50 Let SSR*) completed at Admiralty, Leningrad, at the rate of 2 a year, 1968–75. These contemporaries of the 'Charlie' class (the first was completed in 1967) were among the fastest in the world until the completion of the 'Alfa'; they appear to have been designed specifically for ASW, with the SS-N-15 missile as well as conventional torpedoes. The former is comparable to the US SUBROC and may have been derived from it. Majority with Northern Fleet though some have gone to Pacific Fleet. Diving depth may be up to 2000ft.

These ships, the 'Charlie' and the 'Yankee' constitute the second generation of Soviet nuclear submarine design, probably with many standardised components.

WARSAW PACT

'Victor II' class

'VICTOR II' class *attack submarines*

Displacement:	4500t surfaced; 5700t submerged
Dimensions:	328ft 1in × 32ft 10in × 23ft
	100.0m × 10.0m × 7.0m
Other particulars:	As 'Victor I' class

Seven completed at Admiralty, Leningrad, 1972–78. For a time the NATO codename 'Uniform' class was allocated to this type. 'Victor II' is slightly larger than the original submarine, about 500t heavier and 5m longer; it is officially credited with SS-N-15, whereas it is not certain whether 'Victor I' carries the weapon. 'Victor II' has Brick Group ESM but is 2kts (28kts) slower than the earlier boats.

'Alfa' class

'VICTOR III' class *attack submarines*

Displacement:	4600t surfaced; 5800t submerged
Dimensions:	347ft 9in × 32ft 10in × 23ft
	106.0m × 10.0m × 7.0m
Other particulars:	As 'Victor I' class

Built at Admiralty, Leningrad, and at Komsomolsk; 8 completed as of 1982, the first having entered service 1978. 'Victor III' is larger still, with new weapons, presumably the large-diameter SS-N-16 missile. The class is a knot faster than 'Victor II'. It also has a prominent teardrop-shaped bulb on its upper vertical stabiliser, which has been described officially as housing a towed acoustic array. Recent reports credit these submarines with two SS-N-16, presumably in two large-diameter tubes, which would leave them with 6–533mm TT. The extra capability is reflected in an increase in length of about 19ft/6m. In April 1983 the US CNO described 'Victor III' as being as quiet as the US *Sturgeon* (SSN 637) class, and about five years behind US practice. A new class of attack submarine is expected in 1983 or 1984.

'Typhoon' class design

'Victor I' class 21.4.74 — USN

'Alfa' class 1982 — USN

'OSCAR' class *cruise missile submarines*

Displacement:	10,000t surfaced; 13,000t submerged
Dimensions:	469ft 2in × 57ft 5in × 36ft 1in
	143.0m × 17.5m × 11.0m
Machinery:	2-shaft nuclear, 1 reactor, approx 30kts submerged
Armament:	24 SS-N-19, 8–533mm (24 torpedoes)
Complement:	?130

First boat built at Severodvinsk, launched April 1980, completed 1982. Second boat launched 1982. The missiles are in two rows of tubes running past the fin, fixed at an elevation angle of about 40 degrees. A US Department of Defence sketch appears to show that the bow planes are retractable.

This giant, *Ohio*-sized submarine is a throwback to the long-range missile tactics of the 'Echos' and 'Juliets'. However, if (as reported) it carries the SS-N-19 missile of *Kirov*, then it needs no mid-course guidance system, and almost certainly it can fire while submerged, on the basis of over-the-horizon intelligence systems: it need not be vulnerable to post-launch attack. A powerful anti-ship submarine is also logical in the context of increasing Soviet interest in out-of-area anti-ship operations against US naval forces. 'Oscar' was built in a large construction hall at Severodvinsk, a building originally advertised as large enough to accommodate a carrier; she was launched in the spring of 1980, and was followed in the autumn by the prototype 'Typhoon'. US official estimate is that a smaller cruise missile submarine will also appear.

'ALFA' class *attack submarines*

Displacement:	2800t submerged; 3680t surfaced
Dimensions:	267ft 1in × 31ft 2in × 23ft
	81.4m × 9.5m × 7.0m
Machinery:	1-shaft nuclear: 1 reactor, 45,000shp = 43–45kts submerged
Armament:	6–533mm TT (18 torpedoes or 36 mines) with SS-N-15 and-/or SS-N-16 missiles
Sensors:	Radar Snoop Tray; sonar L/F bow
Complement:	45

Built at Admiralty/Sudomekh, Leningrad; first one completed 1967 since scrapped. Second entered service 1979, and as of 1982 another 6 had been completed.

These deep-diving titanium-hulled craft had an extremely long period of gestation, having been conceived in the late 1950s, probably as part of the same coastal ASW programme which produced the 'Petyas' and 'Mirkas', as well as WIG semi-seaplanes. Very high speed appears to have been a means of closing a submarine contact fast enough to keep it warm; the Soviets reportedly have referred to the 'Alfa' as a 'submarine interceptor of submarines'. Very deep diving capability, reportedly to as much as 3000ft, would permit the submarine to operate out of reach of her targets, and to evade counter-attack. It might also bring her sonar into particularly good sound conditions for effective target detection, although it is not quite enough to reach the deep channel. The hull is officially described as the most streamlined of any Soviet submarine.

'Alfa' is described as highly automated, with a crew of only 45 men, compared with about 85 in a 'Victor III'. Presumably that means an unmanned engine room, which would contribute to compactness by reducing the need for shielding. Reportedly, too, she has a liquid-metal cooled reactor, which can make for extremely high power density, compared to a conventional pressurised-water type.

Although the existence of an 'Alfa' class submarine was known as early as 1971, it appears to have been a failure, and operational units were not noted until about 1978; reportedly the high power-density reactor used was a failure.

TYPHOON class *strategic submarines*

Displacement:	25,000–30,000t submerged
Dimensions:	551ft 9in × 75ft 6in × ?
	170.0m × 23.0m × ?m
Machinery:	2-shafts nuclear; 1 or 2 reactors; 30kts
Armament:	20 SS-N-20 missiles; 533mm torpedoes

First unit built at Severodvinsk, laid down 1975, launched Aug 1980, began sea trials mid-1981. Second launched 1982, others under construction. Typhoon is a *Soviet* name, and the NATO codename is 'Sierra'.

In Vladivostok in 1974 Chairman Leonid I Brezhnev warned President Gerald R Ford that, were the United States to pursue its Trident submarine programme, the Soviets would pursue a new programme of their own, 'Typhoon'. For some years there was speculation as to whether Typhoon was a new missile or a new submarine; it is both, with the first unit of a huge new class, the world's largest submarine, launched in the autumn of 1980 and undergoing sea trials in mid-1981. It is also the first break with the 'Yankee'/'Delta' design series dating back to the mid-1960s, reportedly half again as large as a Trident submarine, with a broad non-circular hull. In 1981 there were reports that the suspected multiple-hull construction (13–15ft spacing) of Typhoon would defeat existing US ASW weapons, particularly lightweight torpedoes such as Mk 46, and that its advent has led to accelerated development of the new Advanced Light Weight Torpedo.

The design is very unusual in that the fin is abaft the missile tubes. In addition, the two propellers are carried aft on separate bodies of revolution, a configuration known as a double-Hogner stern, and rarely used. It led to speculation that the submarine consisted of two parallel pressure hulls aft. The fin-aft configuration is not entirely novel; it was proposed in the early 1960s for a US non-nuclear ballistic missile submarine, presumably to achieve better fore-and-aft balance. Possibly in the Soviet case it was motivated by the sheer length which had to be devoted to the big SS-N-20 missiles, which would have to be insulated from the reactors in any case. First boat had acceptance trials winter 1982–83, arrived at operational base on Kola Peninsula by March 1983.

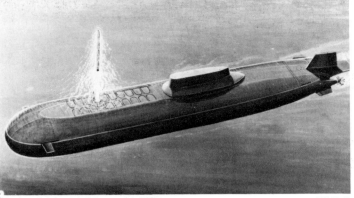

'Typhoon' class, artist's impression 1981　　　　　　　US DoD

'India' class 1980　　　　　　　USN

'Kilo' class

'KILO' class *attack submarines*

Displacement:	2500t surfaced; 3200t submerged
Dimensions:	219ft 10in × 29ft 6in
	67.0m × 9.0m × ?m
Machinery:	Diesel-electric
Armament:	533mm TT

First boat built at Komsomolsk, launched Sept 1980. This new diesel-electric submarine, apparently with a Western-style *Albacore* hull form, is in production at Komsomolsk in the Far East. Its role is uncertain, but it might be a 'Whiskey'/'Romeo' successor, the larger 'Tango' remaining in production as a 'Foxtrot' successor. Note that several Soviet client states now operate ageing 'Whiskeys' or 'Romeos', and that in some cases large submarines would be unsuitable for their waters; they need a successor, and the Soviet Union is the only possible source. Within the Soviet Navy, 'Kilos' are operational only in the Far East in 1983, but they are expected to deploy to the Western Fleets by 1984; perhaps a second yard will enter production as well.

'Bravo' class

AUXILIARY SUBMARINES

The Soviets built a variety of experimental and auxiliary submarines during 1947–82. Details of units built before about 1970 are not available, although reportedly there was a Walter (hydrogen peroxide) test bed, which never became operational. In a sense, 'Papa' was also a test unit, but her armament brings her into the operational category.

At present three classes come into the non-operational list; all may have important military roles in wartime: 'Bravo', 'India', and 'Lima'.

'Bravo' is a training submarine, probably intended as an ASW target. Four were built by Komsomolsk (1 completed 1967, 2 in 1968, 1 in 1970), and distributed among the Baltic, Northern, and Pacific Fleets. 'Bravo' displaces 2900t submerged and is credited with a submerged speed of 16 knots. She has an unusual humped hull form with maximum sectional area abaft the fin. This area presumably surrounds the machinery, and may contain a combination of silencing and simulators of submarine signatures. It is not clear whether TT are fitted.

'India' is a diesel-electric submarine carring two submersibles, usually described as salvage-rescue craft. However, in view of recent Swedish charges, 'India' or related craft may be used to carry special submersibles for covert reconnaissance or sabotage missions. The Royal Swedish Navy has claimed that the Soviets have employed tracked underwater vehicles, which would most naturally be delivered by such a submarine. However, at present 'India' is considered a dedicated rescue/salvage type. Both units were built at Komsomolsk, one completed in 1979 and one in 1980. One is assigned to the Pacific and one to the Northern Fleet, a distribution which would confirm their role in salvage. Fin-mounted planes are an unusual design feature. They displace about 4000t submerged, and are 349ft 9in *(106.0m)* long.

'Lima' is a small experimental submarine, completed by Sudomekh (Leningrad) in 1978, displacing 2400t submerged (278ft 10in × 31ft 2in × 24ft 3in, *85.0m × 9.5m × 7.4m*). Reportedly the sole unit was operating in the Black Sea in 1983.

'Kilo' class July 1982　　　　　　　USN

AMPHIBIOUS WARFARE VESSELS

'MP 2' class *medium landing ships*

Displacement:	600t standard; 750t full load
Dimensions:	182ft 9in × 23ft × 8ft 6in
	55.7m × 7.0m × 2.6m
Machinery:	1-shaft diesel, 1200bhp = 15kts. Range 6000nm/10kts
Armament:	6–25mm (3×2)
Complement:	50 (plus 200 troops)

First specially-built Soviet amphibious ships; 16 built, first laid down 1956, completed 1958. Could carry 4 tanks or 200t. MP was a NATO codename, not a Soviet designation, as in the case of the P-series of MTBs. Now deleted.

'MP 4' class *medium landing ships*

Displacement:	780t full load
Dimensions:	180ft 9in × 29ft 2in × 11ft 2in
	55.1m × 8.9m × 3.4m
Machinery:	1-shaft diesel, 1100bhp = 12kts. Range 5500nm/12kts
Armament:	4–25mm (2×2)
Complement:	50

Converted coastal motor transports: 25 built, laid down from 1956 and first completed 1957–58. One of this type was built in Egypt. Can carry 8 APCs or 550t of cargo. Originally given NATO codename 'Uzka', also referred to as 'Kumos' class; 5 reported in reserve 1982.

'MP 6' class *landing ships*

Displacement:	2000t
Dimensions:	246ft 1in × 36ft 1in × 13ft 1in
	75.0m × 11.0m × 4.0m
Machinery:	Diesels = 10kts. Range 3300nm/9kts
Armament:	4–45mm (1×4), 6–10 tanks
Complement:	?

Converted 'Bira' class freighters: 10 ships rebuilt 1958–61. Classed as VTR (*Voyennyy Transport* or Military Transport). They originally had bow doors, but later these were welded shut, and they served as coastal freighters. Original gun armament optional, now credited with 6–37mm (3×2). There are also several other classes of Soviet freighters classified as VTR; all are unarmed.

'MP 8' class *medium landing ships*

Displacement:	800t standard; 1200t full load
Dimensions:	236ft 3in × 34ft 1in × 8ft 10in
	72.0m × 10.4m × 2.7m
Machinery:	2-shaft diesel, 2500bhp = 14kts. Range 8000nm/10kts
Armament:	4–57mm (2×2)
Complement:	?

Enlarged 'MP 2', 16 built, beginning in 1958; first completed 1961. Could carry 10–12 APCs or 400t of cargo. Now deleted.

'Polnocny A' class after modernisation

'POLNOCNY' class *medium landing ships*

Displacement:	770t full load (800t Type B, 1150t Type C)
Dimensions:	239ft 6in (242ft 9in Type B, 266ft 9in Type C) × 28ft 3in (33ft 1in Type C) × 6ft 7in (6ft 11in Type C) *73.0m, 74.0m, 81.3m × 8.6m, 10.1m × 2.0m, 2.1m*
Machinery:	2 shafts, 2 diesels, 4000bhp = 19kts. Range 1500nm/14kts, 900nm/18kts (5000bhp = 18kts. Range 900nm/17kts Type C)
Armament:	2 SA-N-5 (2×2, 16 missiles) in many; 4 SA-N-5 (4×2, 32 missiles) in one; 2–14.5mm MG (1×2) in some, 4–30mm (2×2) in some; 2–140mm RL (2×18). Some unarmed. Types B and C: 4 SA-N-5 (4×4, 32 missiles) in most, 1 or 2–30mm (2×2), 2–140mm RL (2×18)
Sensors:	Radar Spin Trough or Drum Tilt
Complement:	35 (40 in B and C plus 100 or 180 troops)

All built at Polnocny shipyard, Gdansk, Poland, completed 1961–73. Total of 55 units remains in the Soviet Navy. Beside transfers, 23 were built for the Polish Navy. Transfers (25): Angola (3), Cuba (2), Egypt (3), Ethiopia (1), India (6), Iraq (3), Libya (3), Yemen (4). Soviet designation: SDK, or *Srednyy Desantnyy Korabl'*, Medium Landing Ship. Cargo: 180t in A and B, 250t in C. Early ships carry 6–8 APCs, Type C 8. The decision to provide rockets aboard the landing ship for close-in support would seem to be a major shift in Soviet doctrine. It is possible that the earlier craft were intended for unopposed landings, merely moving tanks more expeditiously than would be possible by land. Note, too, that the 'Polnocny' was the first Soviet amphibious ship apparently designed for troop carrying. Some of the exported ships have helicopter pads immediately forward of the superstructure. SA-N-5s are recent installations.

'Ropucha' class

'ROPUCHA' class *large landing ships*

Displacement:	3200t full load
Dimensions:	370ft 9in × 45ft 11in × 9ft 6in *113.0m × 14.0m × 2.9m*
Machinery:	2 shafts, 2 diesels, 10,000bhp = 18kts. Range 3500nm/16kts
Armament:	4 SA-N-5 (4×4, 32 missiles) on 2 ships, 4–57mm (2×2)
Sensors:	Radar Strut Curve, Muff Cob, Don 2
Complement:	70 (plus 230 troops)

Built by Polnocny Shipyard, Gdansk, Poland at about 2 a year, 12 completed 1975–78 (one to Yemen 1979). Can carry 450t of cargo as well as vehicles and equipment for the 230 troops, 75 per cent of the much larger USN *Newport* class LST capacity. Soviet designation: BDK, *Bolshoi Desantny Korabl'*, large landing ship. Positions for 2 bombardment RLs forward, although no unit has been fitted with them. A combination of bow and stern doors permits roll-on/roll-off operation. Frequently deployed in the Mediterranean, Indian Ocean and off W Africa.

'Polnocny C' class 1981   *USN*

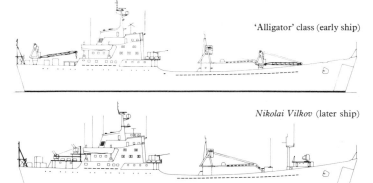

'Ropucha' class 9.7.79   *USN*

'Alligator' class (early ship)

Nikolai Vilkov (later ship)

'ALLIGATOR' class *large landing ships*

Displacement:	3400t standard; 4700t full load
Dimensions:	370ft 1in × 50ft 2in × 14ft 5in *112.8m × 15.3m × 4.4m*
Machinery:	2 diesels, 8000bhp = 18kts. Range 14,000nm/10kts, 9000nm/16kts
Armament:	3 SA-N-5 (3×2, 24 missiles), in some; 2 SA-N-5 (2×2, 16 missiles) in *Petr Il'ichyev*; 2–37mm (1×2, 12 ships), 4–25mm (2×2, last 2 ships), 1–122mm RL (1×40, some ships)
Sensors:	Radar Spin Trough or Don 2, Muff Cob
Complement:	75 (plus 300 troops)

Class:
Aleksandr Tortsev, Donetskiy Shakhter, Krasnaya Presnya, Krymskiy Komsomolets, Nikolay Fil'chenkov, Nikolay Vilkov, Nikolav Obyekov, Petr Il'ichyev, Sergei Lazo, Tomskiy Komsomolets, Voronezhskiy Komsomolets, 50 Let Shefstva VLKSM, plus 2 others.

All 14 built at Kaliningrad 1964–77. Soviet designation, BDK, large landing ship. These ships have bow and stern ramps for unloading vehicles, and are essentially of freighter configuration. Can carry 25–30 APCs or 1500t of cargo. Early units have 3 cranes (15t and 2 5t); later ships have only one crane. Later units have an enclosed bridge and a RL forward (one of these bombarded Eritrean positions around Massawa, Ethiopia, in Jan 1978), and the last two have 25mm guns. Deployment 1982: 2 each Northern and Baltic Fleets, 5 each Black Sea and Pacific Fleets.

Ivan Rogov April 1980   *MoD*

SMALL SURFACE COMBATANTS

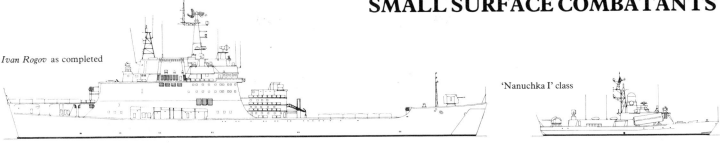

Ivan Rogov as completed

'Nanuchka I' class

IVAN ROGOV class *assault ships*

Displacement:	11,000t standard; 13,000t full load
Dimensions:	518ft 4in × 78ft 9in × 26ft 11in
	158.0m × 24.0m × 8.2m
Machinery:	2-shaft geared gas turbines, 20,000shp = 23kts. Range 12,000nm/14kts, 8000nm/20kts
Armament:	1 SA-N-4 (1×2, 20 missiles), 2–76mm (1×12), 4–30mm Gatling, 2–122mm RL (1×2, 40 tube), 4 helicopters
Sensors:	Radar Head Net C, Owl Screech, Pop Group, 2 Bass Tilt; ECM 4 Bell series
Complement:	200 (plus 550 troops)

Class:
Ivan Rogov and 1 other

When she appeared in 1978, this ship (launched at Kaliningrad 1976 and three times the size of an 'Alligator') appeared to presage a Soviet shift towards amphibious intervention overseas. She can carry a full naval infantry battalion including 10 tanks and 30 APCs and has a unique pair of 'Lebed' class hovercraft to put them ashore as well as 4 Kamov Ka-25 Hormone helicopters. However, construction of the class was relatively slow, the second ship not emerging until 1983, although there were reports of a third unit at that time. She has an integral shore bombardment capability in her 122mm automatic RL. Transferred with *Minsk* from the Black Sea to the Pacific Fleet in the first half of 1979. Sometimes she is compared with the US LPH, although the small hangar in the superstructure is in no way comparable with the standard US hangar deck. Below that deck there is a tank deck forward, and a well deck (with a stern gate) aft. In this sense the concept matches that of the LHA, albeit on a much smaller scale. Unlike the US ship, however, this one beaches to discharge her vehicles through a bow door. Soviet designation: BDK.

'NANUCHKA' class *missile corvettes*

Displacement:	770t full load
Dimensions:	194ft 7in × 41ft 4in × 7ft 11in
	59.3m × 12.6m × 2.4m
Machinery:	3 paired M504 diesels, 30,000bhp = 32kts. Range 2500nm/12kts, 900nm/30.5kts
Armament:	2 SS-N-9 (2×23), 1 SA-N-4 (1×2, 20 missiles), 2–57mm (1×2), 1–76mm and 1–30mm Gatling in 'Nanuchka III')
Sensors:	Radar Band Stand, Peel Pair, Pop Group, Muff Cob (Bass Tilt in 'Nanuchka III'); ECM 2 passive arrays, 2 chaff RL (2×16)
Complement:	60

Class:
Burun, Grad, Maduga, Shkval, Shtorm, Tafun, Tsiklon, Zub' and 8 others.

All 16 'Nanuchka I' built at Petrovskiy, Leningrad, completed 1969–76. Named after weather conditions. Four 'Nanuchka III' completed at Petrovskiy from 1977 onwards. Transfers ('Nanuchka II'): Algeria (3), India (3), Libya (probably 4). Reported to be poor sea-boats. Soviet designations: MRK = *Malyy Raketnyy Korabl'* (Small Rocket Cutter).

The largest craft the Soviets describe as 'rocket cutters' (RK), these vessels are often seen quite far from coastal waters, as in the Mediterranean. They incorporate both a new anti-ship missile, SS-N-9 (which is closely related to the SS-N-7 of 'Charlie' class submarines) and a significant defensive weapon, the SA-N-4 point defence missile set into the deck forward. The twin 57mm defensive gun aft in 'Nanuchka-I' is replaced by a single 76mm dual-purpose gun in 'Nanuchka III'; 'Nanuchka II' was an export version, with 4 late-model SS-N-2s in place of the SS-N-9s of the Soviet ships. They are reportedly poor sea boats, with unreliable engines, M504 diesels paired on each of three shafts. The first appeared in 1969 and production continues in 1982. However, the 'Sarancha' class hydrofoil is a potential successor.

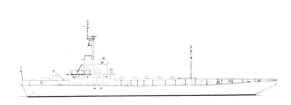

'Vydra' class

MINOR LANDING CRAFT
There are also utility landing craft comparable to the US LCU, developed from the wartime German types. The 'SMB-1' was a commercial modification of the German craft (built 1959–65); some were operated by the Soviet Navy. MP-10 was built for the Soviet Navy 1959–60, a copy of the German MFP-D, differing in having a small cargo hold forward of the bridge, served by a crane; the reduced cargo deck holds only one tank or two trucks. Total production is not known, but in the late 1970s naval SMB-1 and MP-10 totalled about 46.

These were succeeded by the 11kt, 600t full load, Soviet-designed 'Vydra' open-deck 179ft LCU (100 troops or 250t cargo). About 56 were built (1967–69), 15–20 extant with Soviet Navy 1982. Transfers: 10 each to Bulgaria and Egypt; 4 'SMB-1' to Egypt.

From 1954 to 1974 the Soviets built large numbers of T-4, a small 70t, 10kt open landing craft, roughly comparable to the wartime US LCM, but larger (62ft) and more seaworthy; it can be carried as deck cargo by a conventional freighter. From 1978 onwards it has been succeeded by a new 90t 'Ondatra' class of 78ft; *Ivan Rogov* carries one as a tug for 'Lebed' class hovercraft.

Three classes of Soviet hovercraft (built at Leningrad and Gorki) are in the Navy. The 27t 'Gus' (69ft, 60kts, 8t cargo, 24–36 men, crew 4) built since 1968 (1, 2 in 1970, 3 per year 1971–75, 4 per year since 1976). Deployment: 33 or 55 with Black Sea, Pacific and Baltic Fleets 1982.

Twelve 250t 'Aist' (155ft, 80kts, 2 twin 30mm, c 70t cargo or 150 troops) built at Leningrad and Gorki 1970 (1), 1973 (1), one a year to 1979, now 3 a year. Similar to British SR.N4. Bow and stern doors for 4–5 light tanks.

Ten 86t, 'Lebed' class (81ft, 70kts, 1–30mm, 4 crew, 2 PT 76 light tanks or 60–120 troops or 40t cargo) first delivered 1976, 3 a year since 1977. First two classes have Spin Trough radar.

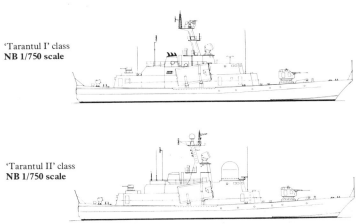

'Tarantul I' class
NB 1/750 scale

'Tarantul II' class
NB 1/750 scale

'TARANTUL' class *missile corvettes*

Displacement:	580t full load
Dimensions:	170ft 7in wl, 183ft 9in oa × 34ft 5in × 8ft 2in
	52.0m, 56.0m × 10.5m × 2.5m
Machinery:	3-shaft CODAG: 2 gas turbines, 30,000shp plus 2000bhp diesel = 36–38kts
Armament:	2 SS-N-2C (2×2), 1 SA-N-5 (1×4, 8 missiles), 1–76mm, 2–30mm Gatling (2×1)
Sensors:	Radar Spin Trough, Bass Tilt, 1 targeting radar; ECM 4 arrays, 2 chaff RL (2×16)
Complement:	50

Begun by Petrovskiy early 1977, 2 completed from 1979 onwards, more (?) building. One writer suggests that this class may have been developed for export. 'Tarantul II' has a 'Nanuchka'-type Band Stand radome in place of the Bass Tilt of 'Tarantul I', and different air intakes and exhaust vents. Both types exhaust through the transom, above water. See also under 'Pauk' class.

'Nanuchka III' 1977   *USN*

'Poti' class 1970   *USN*

'Pauk' class
NB 1/750 scale

'PAUK' class *corvettes*

Displacement:	500t standard; 580t full load
Dimensions:	190ft 3in × 30ft 10in × 8ft 2in
	58.0m × 9.4m × 2.5m
Machinery:	2-shaft diesel, 20,000bhp = 28–34kts
Armament:	1 SA-N-5 (1×4, 8 missiles), 1–76mm, 1–30mm Gatling, 2 RBU-1200 ASW RL (2×25), 2 DC racks (12 DC), 4–406mm TT (4×1)
Sensors:	Radar Spin Trough, Bass Tilt, new air-surface search; sonar M/F hull and dipping; ECM passive arrays, 2 chaff RL (2×16)
Complement:	40

Total of 3 completed so far since 1980. The hull form duplicates that of 'Tarantul', but propulsion is all diesel (probably as in the 'Nanuchkas'). Both carry a 76mm gun forward; 'Pauk' has 4–406mm fixed TT along her superstructure, 'Tarantul' two vertically stacked SS-N-2 'Styx' missiles on each side. Both have an SA-N-5 point defence missile aft, a naval version of the Soviet Army's hand-held SA-7. In addition, 'Pauk' has a 30mm Gatling gun and a dipping sonar aft. Presumably it succeeds the 'Poti' and 'Tarantul' is one of several possible 'Osa' successors. The lead 'Pauk' was seen in the Baltic early in 1979. Soviet designation: MPK (Small ASW craft).

'Poti' class

'POTI' class *corvettes*

Displacement:	500t standard; 580t full load
Dimensions:	194ft 11in × 25ft 11in × 6ft 7in
	59.4m × 7.9m × 2.0m
Machinery:	2-shaft CODAG: 2 gas turbines, 30,000shp plus 2 M503A diesels, 8000bhp = 38kts. Range 4500nm/10kts, 520nm/37kts
Armament:	2–57mm (1×2), 2 RBU-6000 ASW RL, 4–406mm TT (4×1)
Sensors:	Radar Strut Curve, Muff Cob, Spin Trough; sonar H/F Herkules, dipping; ECM 2 Watch Dog
Complement:	80

All built 1961–68. Transfers: Bulgaria (3), Rumania (3). Total: 64 in Soviet service.

Production successors to the 'SO 1' class, these were the first large Soviet gas turbine ships. At 38 knots these were the fastest ASW craft the Soviets ever built; the 'Petyas', 'Grishas', 'Mirkas', and 'Pauks' only managed 32 to 33 knots. The two propellers are mounted in thrust tubes the length of the poop, which contains the two turbines; the jets exhaust through ports above them in the transom, and also power air compressors which exhaust into the propeller tubes, for additional thrust. This is similar to the 'Mirka' plant.

Compared to the 'SO 1', 'Poti' has a single twin 57mm AA mounting amidships and 2 much more powerful ASW RL (RBU-6000) RL, with 2 or 4 single 406mm ASW TT fixed and angled outboard, aft of the gun. The location of one of the two RLs atop the bridge recalls the arrangement of the contemporary 'Petya' and 'Mirka' classes. The first units carried the earlier open 57mm twin mount and smaller RBU-2500 launchers. Three ships transferred to Rumania in 1964–67 had a simplified battery, with 533mm TT, an open, non-automatic 57mm mount and RBU-2500s; three more were transferred to Bulgaria in 1975. Production was completed by about 1967. The Soviets describe them as MPK (small ASW ships).

'P 2' class *fast attack craft (torpedo)*

Displacement:	50t
Dimensions:	80ft 1in × 22ft × 5ft 7in
	24.4m × 6.7m × 1.7m
Machinery:	3 gasoline engines, 5000bhp = 40–50kts. Range 600nm/25kts
Armament:	2–533mm TT, 4–12.7mm or 14.5mm MG (2×2)
Complement:	?

These were apparently the first postwar Soviet MTBs. They introduced ahead-firing torpedo tubes to Soviet practice, perhaps on the basis of experience with Lend-Lease craft in wartime. Large numbers were reportedly exported to China.

Production began 1946, apparently based on prewar D-3 design. Originally designated '603 Class' by US Navy. Estimates of total production vary. However, this class has been sighted so rarely that it seems unlikely that more than a few were completed before production shifted to the 'P 4'. Reportedly all were stricken by 1966.

They appear to have been the last Soviet gasoline-powered MTBs, and their higher power is reflected in the use of 21in (533mm) torpedoes rather than the 18in (457mm) type in the diesel-powered 'P 4'. Externally, the 'P 2' appears to resemble the earlier 'D 3' class MTB, which was descended from Italian MAS designs. Some Soviet accounts imply that these boats were no more than postwar production of a somewhat modified D-3. They were powered by an improved 1250hp gasoline engine.

'P 4' class *fast attack craft (torpedo)*

Displacement:	22t standard; 25t full load
Dimensions:	72ft 2in × 15ft 5in × 4ft 11in
	22.0m × 4.7m × 1.5m
Machinery:	2 M503 diesels, 2400bhp = 42kts. Range 400nm/13kts
Armament:	2–457mm TT, 2–12.7mm or 14.5mm MG (1×2), 4–8 DC
Sensors:	Radar Skin Head
Complement:	12

Laid down from 1950 or 1951, first completed 1952, production ended 1956; about 200 built. Transfers 132: Albania (6), Bulgaria (8), Cuba (12), Cyprus (6), Egypt (4), North Korea (40), N Vietnam (12), Romania (12), Somalia (4), Syria (17), Tanzania (4), N Yemen (3), S Yemen (4). Not certain to what extent the 70 in Chinese service were home-built. At least 15 were built in North Korea ('Iwon' class). Reportedly all stricken by c1975, although carried by Western naval handbooks after that date.

The last Soviet stepped-hull planing craft, these aluminium torpedo boats are direct descendants of prewar Soviet MTBs based on the Thornycroft CMB of World War I. The most striking visual feature is the long foredeck, the cockpit being almost amidships. The 'P 4' design introducing diesel power in the form of the 1200bhp M-50, the first of a series of Soviet small craft diesels. The Soviets have claimed that although small boat diesels of 1000, 1100, 1200, and 1500bhp were developed in wartime, they only entered production postwar. The stepped-hull design made for very high speed but was tactically defective, in that at high speed a boat so designed cannot easily turn, since it has only marginal stability. It cannot turn without slowing down considerably. The Soviet designation was Komsomolets.

'P2' class memorial 16.5.75   *USN*

'P4' class c1968   *USN*

Cuban 'P 6' class 1970   *USN*

'P10' class 1970   *USN*

'Komar' class August 1977   *USN*

'P 6' class *fast attack craft (torpedo)*

Displacement:	64t standard; 73t full load
Dimensions:	85ft 4in × 19ft 8in × 4ft 11in
	26.0m × 6.0m × 1.5m
Machinery:	4-shaft M503 diesels, 5800bhp (5000bhp in newer boats) = 43kts. Range 600nm/16kts
Armament:	2–533mm TT, 4–25mm (2×2), 8 DC
Sensors:	Radar Skin Head (replaced by Pot Head)
Complement:	12

Laid down from 1953, first completed about 1955, over 500 built through the 1960s. About 20 were completed as 'P 8' and 'P 10' classes. Original US designation was '627 Class'. Transfers 199: Algeria (12), Cuba (12), East Germany (27), Egypt (36), Guinea (4), Indonesia (24), Iraq (12), N Korea (45), N Vietnam (3), Poland (20), Somalia (4). About 80 were built in China during 1956–66, and it was produced in North Korea (at least 20 built).

All of these minor combatants were built on a common wooden hull, the first in Soviet practice with a hard chine as in US wartime torpedo-boats; some writers suggest that it was derived from the Elco 80-footers supplied under Lend-Lease. Production began in 1953, with the first delivery in 1955, and it

continued through about 1959. Of over 500 hulls reportedly built, making it the most numerous postwar warship class, many were exported and others converted to targets, yachts, and patrol craft. Beginning in about 1956, about 50 became 'MO VI' class ASW patrol craft, direct descendants of an earlier series of small submarine-chasers. Most had no sonar at all, although in some units one diesel was replaced by a sonar. Their bridges were enlarged, and depth-charge tracks and two projectors added. Three were exported to Nigeria, and the four 'P 6s' (without tubes) exported to Guinea may have been of this type as well.

The 'P 6' was considered more seaworthy than the 'P 4', due to its new hull form; it made a higher speed due to its much more powerful engines. One unusual feature was the asymmetrical position of the forward 25mm gun mount, offset to port. All of these boats are powered by M503 high-speed diesels, 42-cylinder engines consisting, in effect, of seven 6-cylinder radial 'pancaked' together, to achieve 4000bhp at 2.9lb per bhp. It also powers 'Osa I' class missile boats. The larger (56-cylinder) 5000bhp M504 powers 'Osa II' class missile boats. Two M503 driving a common gear box form an M507, the 'Poti', 'Nanuchka', and 'Grisha' diesel; probably there is also a paired M504 engine design. The much higher power of the M503 compared to the M50 is reflected in the much larger size of the 'P 6' hull, and in its 533mm armament.

About 20 units were converted experimentally to a CODAG configuration, gas turbines replacing two of the four diesels, beginning in 1960–61. Hulls were lengthened by about 2m, and a small funnel was added abaft the bridge. The first series of conversions, the 'P 3' class, had a pair of semi-submerged hydrofoils forward, which lifted and stabilised the bow as the boat planed. The 'P 10' class omitted the hydrofoil. Late in 1967 the funnels were removed, presumably indicating a failure of the gas turbine plant, and hydrofoils were removed from the 'P 8s'. The Soviet designation for the 'P 6' class is Type 183. None survive in Soviet service.

'P 8' and 'P 10' *fast attack craft (torpedo)*

Displacement:	90t full load
Dimensions:	91ft 10in × 19ft 8in × 6ft 7in
	28.0m × 6.0m × 2m
Machinery:	3-shaft CODAG: 2 diesels, 2400bhp plus 1 gas turbine, 5100shp = 45kts
Armament:	As 'P 6' class
Sensors:	Radar Skin Head ('P 8') or Pot Head ('P 10')
Complement:	14

'P 8' conversions 1958–59, 'P 10' conversions 1960–61. All reconverted with gas turbine removed, designated 'P 10' class. Another hydrofoil type, tentatively designated 'P 12', was reported in 1961, but has not remained on lists of Soviet warships. All discarded late 1970s.

'Komar' class
NB 1/750 scale

'KOMAR' class *fast attack craft (missile)*

Displacement:	75t standard; 80t full load
Dimensions:	87ft 11in × 21ft × 5ft 11in
	26.8m × 6.4m × 1.8m
Machinery:	4-shaft diesels, 4800bhp = 40kts. Range 400nm/30kts
Armament:	2 SS-N-2 (2×1), 2–25mm (1×2)
Sensors:	Radar Square Tie
Complement:	11

'P 6' conversions, 1958–61; about 100 were built. Transfers 78: Algeria (8), China (8), Cuba (18), Egypt (7), Indonesia (12), Iraq (3), N Korea (10), Syria (9), Vietnam (3). About 40 built in China. None was left on the Soviet list by c1981.

Surely the best known conversion of the basic 'P 6' hull is the 'Komar' class missile boat. Although it was first seen in 1960, after the 'Osa' had been observed, it must have predated the latter; the 'Komar' is the minimum platform which can support a pair of open-ended SS-N-2 missile launchers. It was also the first fast attack boat in the world to engage in combat, as Egyptian 'Komars' sank the Israeli destroyer *Eilat* on 21.10.67.

Egyptian 'Osa I' 28.4.74   *USN*

'Osa II' class
NB 1/750 scale

'Osa I' class
NB 1/750 scale

'OSA' class *fast attack craft (missile)*

Displacement:	175t standard; 215t full load ('Osa II' 240t)
Dimensions:	126ft 8in × 24ft 11in × 5ft 11in (6ft 7in in 'Osa II') *38.6m × 7.6m × 1.8m, 2.0m*
Machinery:	3-shaft M503A diesels, 12,000bhp = 35kts. Range 750nm/25kts, 500nm/34kts ('Osa II' has M504 diesels, 15,000bhp total on 3 shafts)
Armament:	4 SS-N-2B (4×1) or -2C, 4 SA-N-5 (4×1, 8 missiles) in some, 4–30mm (2×2)
Sensors:	Radar Square Tie, Drum Tilt
Complement:	30

Class:

'Osa II': *Amurskiy Komsomolets, Kirovskiy Komsomolets, Tambovskiy Komsomolets, Kronstadtskiy Komsomolets*

Estimated that 175 'Osa I' were built in the Soviet Union (1959–66), and 96 more in China. Similarly, it is estimated that 114 'Osa II' were built in the Soviet Union (1966–70), and that about 60 were transferred making the class easily the world's most numerous and most exported missile FAC. Note 'Osa I' can be distinguished by flat-sided missile hangars *vice* cylindrical tubes. Both types have all-welded steel hulls with aluminium alloy and steel superstructures. They have 'citadel' CBR protective systems. Transfers 175: Algeria (11), Bulgaria (4), Cuba (13), E Germany (15), Egypt (12), Ethiopia (3), Finland (4), India (16), Iraq (12), Libya (12), Morocco (6), N Korea (8), Poland (12), Rumania (5), Somalia (2), Sudan (1), Syria (14), Vietnam (8), Yemen (7), Yugoslavia (10). At least 4 were transferred to China *c*1960; China then built about 96 more. Some 65–70 'Osa Is' and 40–50 'Osa IIs' extant with Soviet Navy 1982. Soviet designation: *Raketnyy Kater*, RK, rocket cutter.

'Osa' appears to have been the first Soviet missile attack craft designed for the purpose, with 4 fully enclosed missile launchers and a steel displacement hull. The first was sighted in 1959; beside their missiles, they introduced the small twin 30mm gun which later appeared as a close-in weapon aboard many Soviet large combatants. It is controlled by a large Drum Tilt radar between the after missile tubes. 'Osa II' is armed with an improved version of the SS-N-2 missile (40nm range rather than 25nm); some were also armed with the lightweight SA-N-5 missile, a naval version of the Army's hand-held SA-7. Production switched from 'Osa I' to 'Osa II' about 1966, and ended about 1970. They are considered much better seaboats than the 'Komars', capable of firing in Sea State 4 (6ft waves). Indian 'Osas' sank the Pakistani destroyer *Khaibar* in 1971 but Arab 'Osas' were outclassed in 1973.

'Shershen' class
NB 1/750 scale

'SHERSHEN' class *fast attack craft (torpedo)*

Displacement:	150t standard; 170t full load
Dimensions:	113ft 10in × 22ft × 4ft 11in *34.7m × 6.7m × 1.5m*
Machinery:	3-shaft M503A diesels, 12,000bhp = 45kts. Oil 30t. Range 850nm/30kts, 460nm/42kts.
Armament:	4–30mm (2×2), 2 DC racks (12 DC), 4–533mm TT (4×1), 6 mines max
Sensors:	Radar Pot Drum, Drum Tilt
Complement:	23

Two 'Turya' class en route to Cuba 1979   *USN*

The Soviets completed about 80 in 1963–70. Transfers 63: Angola (6), Bulgaria (6), Cape Verde Islands (3), Congo (1), E Germany (18), Egypt (6), Guinea (6), Guinea-Bissau (1), N Korea (4), Vietnam (8), Yugoslavia (4). Yugoslavia built 12 under licence. Soviet designation: TK, *Torpednyy Kater*, or torpedo cutter. Yugoslav units carry mines instead of TT, and some Egyptian units have been rearmed with 2 8-tube RL in place of TT. The Soviet Navy had 30 'Shershens' in 1982. Class designation is Type 201.

The 'Shershen' class torpedo boats of 1963–70 were rough contemporaries of the 'Osas', reportedly with the same propulsion plant but with a somewhat smaller hull, at 150t rather than 175t. They have 4 rather than 2 TT (as in 'P 6') and the new-type 30mm gun.

As installed in a 'Shershen', the M503A diesel can operate at 4000bhp (2200rpm) for 10 per cent of engine time between overhaul (TBO); at 3600bhp (1700rpm) for 15 per cent of engine TBO; at a continuous power of 3300bhp (1500rpm) for an unlimited time. TBO is normally 600 hours, but can be extended by an additional 150 if necessary. A former Yugoslav officer described them as having a very favourable power to weight ratio, but noisy and hot. Normally it requires an hour of warm-up before running, and breakdowns (*eg* in the rubber joints of the fuel system) were relatively common above 1500rpm.

'Stenka' class
NB 1/750 scale

'STENKA' class *fast attack craft (torpedo)*

Displacement:	170t standard; 210t full load
Dimensions:	129ft 7in × 24ft 11in × 5ft 11in *39.5m × 7.6m × 1.8m*
Machinery:	As 'Osa I' class except range 820nm/25kts, 550nm/34kts
Armament:	4–406mm TT (4×1), 4–30mm (2×2), 2 DC racks (12 DC)
Sensors:	Radar Pot Drum, Drum Tilt; sonar
Complement:	22

'Osa' hull and engined class of 100 completed since 1967 with enlarged superstructure, 2 twin 30mm and 4 ASW TT and Hormone helicopter dipping sonar. Soviet designation; PSKR, *Pogranichniy Storozhevoy Korabl*', KGB border patrol ship. Some units do not carry the 4 TT, having a motor launch instead.

'MOL' class *fast attack craft (torpedo)*

Displacement:	175t standard; 220t full load
Dimensions:	128ft × 25ft 3in × 5ft 11in *39.0m × 7.7m × 1.8m*
Machinery:	3 M503A diesels, 12,000bhp = 36kts
Armament:	4–533mm TT (4×1), 4–30mm (2×2)
Complement:	30

Transfers (built only for export): Ethiopia (3), Somalia (4), Sri Lanka (1), Yemen (2).

'Turya' class
NB 1/750 scale

'TURYA' class *torpedo hydrofoils*

Displacement:	190t standard; 250t full load
Dimensions:	As 'Osa II' class (41ft × 13ft 1in, *12.5m × 4m* over foils)
Machinery:	As 'Osa II' class = 40kts. Range 650nm/20kts, 400nm/38kts
Armament:	2–57mm (1×2), 2–25mm (1×2), 4–533mm TT (4×1)
Sensors:	Radar Pot Drum, Muff Cob; Hormone helicopter dipping sonar
Complement:	24

Soviet designation: *Torpednyy Kater*, torpedo cutter (TK), 30 completed 1974–79 plus 6 delivered to Cuba since Jan 1979. These craft use a modified 'Osa II' hull and power plant. The forward foils are fixed surface-piercing units, relatively ineffective in rough water. and they bring up the bow when the boat planes on its stern. The stern in turn is trimmed by an adjustable flap mounted on the transom. Later units have semi-retractable foils to simplify docking. Cuban units lack the dipping sonar (mounted aft on starboard quarter for 'spring and drift' operation in Soviet units).

'Matka' class
NB 1/750 scale

'MATKA' class *missile hydrofoils*

Displacement:	250t full load
Dimensions:	129ft 11in × 24ft 11in (41ft over foils) × 6ft 11in (10ft 6in over foils)
	39.6m × 7.6m, 12.5m × 2.1m, 3.2m
Machinery:	As 'Turya' class except 400nm range at 36kts
Armament:	1 SS-N-2C (1×2), 1–30mm Gatling
Sensors:	Radar Cheese Cake, Bass Tilt, new target designation radar; ECM 2 chaff RL (2×16)
Complement:	30

Eight completed by Izhora (Leningrad) from 1978 onwards. Still building. Soviet designation: *Raketnyy Kater*, RK, rocket cutter. This is a missile-armed version of the 'Turya', with a larger superstructure to accommodate the missile combat system, and with different gun arrangement.

'SARANCHA' class *missile hydrofoils*

Displacement:	280t standard; 320t full load
Dimensions:	175ft 11in (166ft 1in foils extended) × 37ft (75.4ft foils extended) × 8ft 6in (23ft 11in foils extended)
	53.6m, 50.6m × 31.3m, 23.5m × 2.6m, 7.3m
Machinery:	2 gas turbines, 4 shafts, 20,000shp = 58kts
Armament:	2 SS-N-9 (2×2), 1 SA-N-4 (1×2, 20 missiles), 1–30mm Gatling
Sensors:	Radar Band Stand, Pop Group, Bass Tilt
Complement:	35

One unit completed by Petrovskiy, Leningrad, 1976; 3 completed by 1980. Sources disagree as to the existence of the latter. Unlike earlier Soviet hydrofils, this one has fully-submerged foils. They require advanced control systems, but should confer very superior rough-water performance. In principle, it would be comparable to the US *Pegasus* (PHM), although actual performance may be very different. Propulsion is by propellers in pods on the after foils. Although displacement is less than half that of a 'Nanuchka', 'Sarancha' has 4 SS-N-9 missiles and an SA-N-4 for self-defence, as well as a 'Gatling' gun aft. She may have been a competitor with 'Babochka'.

'BABOCHKA' class *torpedo hydrofoil*

Displacement:	400t full load
Dimensions:	147ft 8in wl, 164ft 1in oa × 33ft 6in
	45.0m × 50.0m × 10.2m
Machinery:	3-shaft CODOG: 3 NK-12 gas turbines plus 2 cruise diesels, 30,000shp = 45kts
Armament:	8–406mm TT (2×4), 2–30mm Gatling (2×1)
Sensors:	Radar Bass Tilt and new search radar
Complement:	45

One completed 1978. She is the largest Soviet hydrofoil to date (almost the size of 'Pauk' or 'Tarantul' corvettes) and like the 'Sarancha' has submerged foils. The two nests (two above two) of TT are located on the main deck forward of the superstructure, just abaft the bow 30mm Gatling gun; the after 30mm gun is atop the deckhouse, just forward of the gas turbine intakes.

'SLEPEN' class *hydrofoil*

Displacement:	205t standard; 230t full load
Dimensions:	128ft × 25ft 3in × 5ft 11in
	39.0m × 7.7m × 1.8m
Machinery:	3 shafts, 3 M504 diesels, 15,000bhp = 36kts
Armament:	1–76mm, 1–30mm Gatling
Sensors:	Radar Bass Tilt
Complement:	30

Cuban 'SOI' 1970   *USN*

Finally, there is 'Slepen', a trials craft built by Petrovskiy, Leningrad, *c*1969 for small-combatant systems, on a displacement version of the basic 'Osa' hull. Originally armed with a twin 57mm gun forward ('Grisha III' trials), it received the new 76mm there in 1975 to test the weapon for the 'Matka' and 'Nanuchka' classes.

'Kronstadt' class
NB 1/750 scale

'KRONSTADT' class *large patrol craft*

Displacement:	300t normal; 330t full load
Dimensions:	170ft 7in × 21ft 4in × 7ft 3in
	52.1m × 6.5m × 2.2m
Machinery:	3 diesels, 3300bhp = 18kts. Range 3500nm/14kts
Armament:	1–85mm/52, 4–37mm (2×2), 2 MG, 2 RBU-900 ASW RL (RBU-1800 after *c*1960), 2 DC racks
Sensors:	Sonar H/F hull (Tamir)
Complement:	35–40

About 230 completed at Zelenodolsk 1946–56. Transfers 48: Albania (4), Bulgaria (2), China (6, and built 14 more), Cuba (6), Indonesia (18), Poland (9), and Rumania (3). In 1955–56 20 became 'Libau' class AGL (administrative and communications auxiliaries); many served with the KGB.

Postwar successors to the unsuccessful wartime 'Artillerist' class large submarine-chasers, these ships were originally numbered in a BO (*Bolshoi Okhotnik*, or large hunter) series, later designated MPK (*Maly Protivo-Lodochny Korabl*', or small ASW ship). The prototype appeared in 1948, production ending in 1956 at Zelenodolsk, the Soviet lead yard for small combatants; their production (and functional) successor was the 'SO 1'. There were two series, the first with combined DC and mine armament, the second solely with DC. Some had the RBU-900 'Mousetrap' ASW launcher; after 1960 some had 2 RBU-2500s each.

'SO I' class
NB 1/750 scale

'SO I' class *large patrol craft*

Displacement:	170t standard; 215t full load
Dimensions:	137ft 10in × 20ft × 6ft 3in
	42.0m × 6.1m × 1.9m
Machinery:	3-shaft diesels, 7500bhp = 28kts. Range 1920nm/7kts, 1100nm/13kts, 3400nm/28kts
Armament:	4–25mm (2×2), 4 RBU-1200 ASW RL, 2 DC racks, 2–406mm TT (2×1) in some ships replacing twin 25mm mount aft, 10 mines max
Sensors:	Radar Pot Head; sonar H/F hull (Tamir)
Complement:	31

About 150 completed at Zelenodolsk and Khabarovsk 1957–64. There may also have been a prototype, a somewhat earlier design. Transfers 65: Albania (4), Algeria (6), Bulgaria (6), Cuba (3), E Germany (16), Egypt (12), Iraq (3), N Korea (6), N Vietnam (7), S Yemen (2).

This was the production successor to the 'Kronstadt'. They are generally described as poor seaboats, and are rather smaller than their predecessors, at (according to one source) about 170t rather than 310t. Gun armament was sharply reduced to 2 twin 25mm AA, as in contemporary coastal craft, but there were 4 RLS (RBU-1200, former MBU-1800). The first ships, also known as the 'Misha' class, had a 45mm gun and DC aft, but no RL. Compared to the 'Kronstadts', they were considerably faster, with over twice the power, but needed 20 per cent fewer men, in a smaller hull. Late units receiving 2 single 406mm ASW TT in place of the after twin 25mm gun, with shorter DC racks. Being phased out though 35 still extant with KGB in 1982.

'MO V' class *coastal patrol craft*

Displacement:	41t standard
Dimensions:	77ft 1in oa × 13ft 1in × 4ft 3in (max)
	23.5m × 4.0m × 1.3m
Machinery:	2 gasoline engines, 2400bhp = 24kts. Range 365nm/9kts
Armament:	1–37mm, 4–12.7mm MG (2×2), 2 DC racks (12 DC)
Sensors:	Sonar Tamir 10, manually lowered into the water
Complement:	

Produced from 1947 onwards. Successors to a series of *Morskoi Okhotnik* or 'sea hunters' built from 1935 on; earlier types presumably relied on passive sonars. Some, like the later 'MO-VI', were de-rated MTBs. The largest prewar type, 'M0-IV', came to only 56t. A larger BMO, or *Bolshoi* (large) MO, displaced 61t. The number built is unknown.

'MO VI' class 1960   *USN*

'Poluchat I' class 1970   *USN*

'Pchela' class 1970   *USN*

'Schmel' class 1977   *USN*

'MO VI' class *coastal patrol craft*

Other particulars:	As 'P 6' class
Machinery:	4-shaft M503 diesels, 4800bhp = 38.5kts
Sensors:	Radar Skin Head or Pot Head radar; sonar Tamir 4–25mm (2×2), 2 DCT, 2 DC racks

About 50 'P 6' torpedo boats converted 1956–60. Transfers: Bulgaria (10), Guinea (2), Nigeria (3).

'POLUCHAT I' class *coastal patrol craft*

Displacement:	90t full load
Dimensions:	97ft 1in × 19ft × 4ft 11in
	29.6m × 5.8m × 1.5m
Machinery:	2-shaft M50 diesels, 2400bhp = 18kts. Range 450nm/17kts, 900nm/10kts
Armament:	2–14.5mm MG (1×2)
Complement:	20

KGB version of the standard Soviet torpedo recovery boat, 34 completed 1953–56 and extant 1982. Transfers 13: Angola (2), Guinea (3), Iraq (2), Somalia (5), S Yemen (1).

'PCHELA' class *coastal patrol craft (hydrofoils)*

Displacement:	70t standard; 83t full load
Dimensions:	83.0ft × 19.0ft × 4.3ft (without foils)
	25.3m × 5.8m × 1.3m
Machinery:	2-shaft diesels, 6000bhp = 45kts
Armament:	2–14.5mm MG, 4 DC racks
Sensors:	Radar Pot Drum; sonar, Hormone dipping (in some)
Complement:	12

Used for Baltic and Black Sea border patrols, 20 completed 1964–65 and extant 1982. They were the first Soviet seagoing naval hydrofoils, operated by the KGB, to replace an earlier generation of launches similar to MTBs. They employ a half-submerged forward foil and a fully-submerged after set. The electronic outfit is described as elaborate: a dome-enclosed surface-search radar (Pot Drum) and several other antennas under radomes. They are presumably for ESM, to detect intruders. There is also an enclosed fire control position forward of the after 14.5mm gun. A few have Hormone dipping sonars. Soviet designation: PSKR.

'ZHUK' class *coastal patrol craft*

Displacement:	50t full load
Dimensions:	75ft 2in × 16ft 1in × 4ft 11in
	22.9m × 4.9m × 1.5m
Machinery:	2-shaft M50 diesels, 2400bhp = 30kts
Armament:	2–14.5mm MG (2×1, 2×2 in some)
Sensors:	Radar Spin Trough
Complement:	Approx 28

More than 30 completed from 1975 onwards, specially for the KGB. Many (at least 53) have been exported, including 1 each to Algeria and Angola, 4 to Benin, 5 to Bulgaria, 1 to Cape Verdes, 12 to Cuba, 3 to Guinea, 4 to Iraq, 6 each to Mozambique and Vietnam, 6 to Yemens, 1 to Seychelles, 3 to Syria.

'SHMEL' class *river monitors*

Displacement:	60t full load
Dimensions:	92ft 10in × 15ft 1in × 2ft 11in
	28.3m × 4.6m × 0.9m
Machinery:	2 M50 diesels, 2400bhp = 22kts. Range 600nm/10kts, 240nm/20kts
Armament:	1–76mm (tank turret), 2–14.5mm (1×2, early ships) or 25mm (later ones), 5–7.62mm MG, 1–140mm RL (1×17) on later units, 8 mines max. One MG coaxial with tank turret gun; others are portable
Complement:	15

Soviet designation: AK, *Artilleriyeskiy Kater*, or artillery cutter, 85 were completed 1967–74. Earlier types were designated BK, *Bronirovanny Kater*, or Armoured Cutter. These craft replace an earlier generation of river gunboats armed with tank turrets. Three 'Schmels' could embark a platoon of naval infantry, although they would have to be billeted aboard another ship. The turret is the type mounted in the PT-76 tank. The multiple RL was first observed in 1974. Used on the Danube, Amur and Ussuri rivers as well as in the Caspian Flotilla (part of the Black Sea Fleet). A new 'Yas' class has been found in the Pacific Fleet area but no data is yet available.

NOTE: The KGB operates a wide variety of coastal craft for border control. They include converted 'T 43' and 'T 58' class minesweepers, as well *Ivan Susanin* class icebreakers (1974), and two classes of converted tugs (*Okhtenskiy*, which appeared in 1958, and *Sorum*, which appeared in 1974). The 'T 43' entered this service in 1960, and the 'T 58' conversion in 1975.

MINE WARFARE VESSELS

'T43' class

'T 43' class *ocean minesweepers*

Displacement:	500t standard; 569t or 590t full load
Dimensions:	190ft 3in or 196ft 10in × 28ft 3in × 7ft 7in
	58.0m, 60.0m × 8.6m × 2.3m
Machinery:	2 shafts, 2 Type 9D diesels, 3000bhp = 15kts. Oil 70t. Range 3200nm/10kts, 2000nm/14kts
Armament:	4–37mm (2×2), 8–12.7mm (4×2, early ships), 4–25mm (2×2, later ships), 2 DCT, 16 mines max
Sensors:	Radar Don-2 or Spin Trough, Ball End; sonar Tamir II
Complement:	77

Laid down beginning in 1947, first completed 1949, well over 200 built by end of 1950s. Builders: Kamysh Burun (Kerch), Neverskiy and Izhora, Leningrad. Note that 12 were built in Poland 1955–60, and about 20 in China from 1956 onwards. Transfers 28: Algeria (2), Bulgaria (3), Albania (2), China (2), Indonesia (12), Egypt (6), Syria (1). Steel fleet sweepers, replacing the prewar 'Fugas' class and reportedly incorporating some features of standard German minesweepers. A new version, with a smaller bridge, tripod mast, and 2 twin 12.7mm mounts on deck forward of the bridge, and with twin 25mm in place of the 12.7mm on either side of the funnel, appeared in the mid-1950s. Since the late 1960s all but the 37mm guns have been removed.

A radar picket version appeared in 1956, armed with 4–37mm (2×2, and a twin 25mm in most). The initial radar installation was 2 Knife Rest (fore and aft), but later some had the forward Knife Rest replaced by a Big Net, and some at least have only Knife Rest, on a massive lattice mast aft. Twenty units were converted, 6 or 11 extant 1982. Others serve as coastal patrol ships, which the Soviets designate PSKR, *Pogranichniy Storozhevoy Korabl'*, or Border Patrol Ship. They are operated by the KGB. There are also noise-measurement ships, diving tenders, and trials ships. In 1983 these ships are being discarded, but 40–65 are still extant.

'Yurka' class 1981 — USN

'T58' class

'T 58' class *ocean minesweepers*

Displacement:	790t standard; 900t full load
Dimensions:	236ft 3in × 31ft 10in × 8ft 2in
	72.0m × 9.7m × 2.5m
Machinery:	2-shaft diesels, 4000bhp = 18kts
Armament:	4–57mm (2×2), 4–25mmm (2×2, 'T 58 I' only), 2 MBU-1800 ASW RL ('T 58 II' only), 2 mine tracks, about 60 mines
Sensors:	Radar Big Net, Strut Curve
Complement:	82

Class (known names):
Admiral Pershin, Dmitri Lysov, Evgeni Nikonov, Kalingradsky Komsomolets, Komsomolets Bielorossia, Komsomolets Estoni, Komsomolets Kalmycky, Komsomolets Latvia, Primorsky Komsomolets, Sakhalinksy Komsomolets

Two series, begun 1957 and 1959, completed 1960 and 1962. A total of 34 were built, probably no more than 5 in the first series; 14 probably in this series, were converted to 'Valdai' class submarine rescue ships. Transfers: one each to Guinea and Yemen. These were the largest of all Soviet minesweepers at the time of their construction, and appear not to have been entirely successful, since they no longer serve in that capacity, while the 'T 43s' remain. Some, perhaps 2, were converted to radar pickets to replace ageing 'T 43' conversions. They are armed with 2 SA-N-5 (2×24, 16 missiles) and 1 × 2–57mm (1×2), 4–30mm (2×2) and designated KVN, *Korabl' Vozdushnogo Nablyudeniya*, or Radar Surveillance Ships, and first appeared in 1979, converted at Izhora SY, Leningrad.

'T58' class May 1974 — USN

'Yurka' class
NB 1/750 scale

'YURKA' class *ocean minesweepers*

Displacement:	540t full load
Dimensions:	169ft × 28ft 10in × 8ft 6in
	51.5m × 8.8m × 2.6m
Machinery:	2-shaft diesels, 4000bhp = 16kts. Range 3200nm/10kts, 2000nm/14kts
Armament:	4–30mm (2×2), 10 mines max
Sensors:	Radar Don-2, Drum Tilt
Complement:	45

Total of 52 (built from 1963) completed by 1982; transfers: Egypt (4), Vietnam (1). They have an aluminium alloy hull. Soviet designation: MT, *Morskoy Tral'shchik* = Ocean Sweeper.

'Natya' class 16.3.79 — USN

'Natya' class

'NATYA' class *ocean minesweepers*

Displacement:	650t standard; 750t full load
Dimensions:	196ft 10in × 32ft 2in × 9ft 10in
	61.0m × 9.8m × 3.0m
Machinery:	2-shaft diesels, 5000bhp = 18–20kts. Range 5200nm/10kts, 1800nm/16kts
Armament:	4–30mm (2×2), 4–25mm (2×2), 2 RBU-1200 ASW RL (2×25), 10 mines max ('Natya II' 2 SA-N-5 (16 missiles), 4–30mm (2×2), no ASW weapons or 25mm guns)
Sensors:	Radar Don-2, Drum Tilt; sonar H/F
Complement:	70

Class (known names):
Rulevoy, Admiral Pershin, Kontre-Admiral Choroshkin, Miner, Navodvhik, Signalchik

Built by Izhora (32) and Khabarovsk (6), first laid down 1970, completed 1971 (2 ships). Still in production. Transfers: 6 built for India, 2 for Libya. These aluminium alloy minesweepers are also equipped to serve as ASW escorts; they have a H/F hull sonar. They are unusual in having a stern ramp, which suggests some form of towed body beyond the usual cables and paravanes. Designated MT, *Morskoy Tral'shchik*, or Ocean Sweeper.

'T 43' class 24.8.65 — USN

WARSAW PACT

'T 301' class *inshore minesweepers*

Particulars:	See 1922–1946 volume

Production of this wartime class continued at Rybinsk through 1956, very large numbers having been built. In May 1955, for example, the ONI listed a total of 263. These craft were designed specifically for rapid production, without compound curves in their hulls. Production began in 1944, and about 50 had been completed by the end of World War II, the final total being over 200. Reportedly machinery for the early units was provided by the US under Lend-Lease, later units with Soviet diesels being about 3m longer. A total of 80 was reported still in service in 1968. Only about 5 were left by 1977.

Transfers 44: Bulgaria (4), Albania (6), Indonesia (1), Egypt (2), Rumania (22), Poland (9).

'SASHA' class *coastal minesweepers*

Displacement:	250t standard; 280t full load
Dimensions:	147ft 8in × 20ft 4in × 5ft 11in
	45.1m × 6.2m × 1.8m
Machinery:	2 diesels, vertical cycloidal propellers, 2200bhp = 19kts. Range 2100nm/12kts, 1300nm/18.5kts
Armament:	1–45mm or 57mm, 4–25mm (2×2), 12 mines max
Sensors:	Radar Ball End
Complement:	25

These steel sweepers entered service 1954–59. They are designated RT (*Reydovoy Tral'shchik* or Roadstead Sweepers), and some are used as patrol craft. About 50 were built as successors to the wartime 'T 301'. They were the first Soviet flush-deck sweepers. In 1982 only 8 were left, and they were about to be scrapped.

'Vanya' class

'VANYA' class *coastal minesweepers*

Displacement:	200t standard; 250t full load ('Vanya II' 260t)
Dimensions:	131ft 7in × 25ft 11in × 5ft 7in
	40.2m × 7.9m × 1.7m
Machinery:	2-shaft diesels, 2200bhp = 16kts. Range 2400nm/10kts, 1400nm/14kts
Armament:	2–30mm (1×2), 8 mines max ('Vanya II' 12)
Sensors:	Radar Don-2
Complement:	30

About 70 completed 1961–73. Soviet designation: BT (*Basovyy Tral'shchik*, or Base Sweeper). Wooden hulled. At least one was converted to a minehunter, with 2–25mm (1×2), more accurate than 30mm for mine disposal. 'Vanya II' are 1m longer, with larger diesel exhaust amidships. Transfers: Bulgaria (4), Syria (2).

'ZHENYA' class *coastal minesweepers*

Displacement:	220t standard; 290t full load
Dimensions:	139ft 1in × 25ft 11in × 5ft 11in
	42.4m × 7.9m × 1.8m
Machinery:	2-shaft diesels, 2400bhp = 16kts. Range 2400nm/10kts, 1400nm/14.5kts
Armament:	2–30mm (1×2)
Sensors:	Radar Spin Trough
Complement:	40

Three completed 1967–72; plastic-hulled, apparently an alternative to the more successful 'Sonya'. Classed as BT.

Polish 'T301'   USN

'Sasha' class 1977   USN

'Zhenya' class 1975   USN

'Sonya' class
NB 1/750 scale

'SONYA' class *coastal minesweepers*

Displacement:	450t full load
Dimensions:	160ft 1in × 28ft 10in × 6ft 11in
	48.8m × 8.8m × 2.1m
Machinery:	2-shaft diesels, 2400bhp = 15kts. Range 3000nm/10kts, 1600nm/14kts
Armament:	2–30mm (1×2), 2–25mm (1×2)
Sensors:	Radar Spin Trough
Complement:	43

First delivered 1973, 40 built by 1980 (deliveries: 1 in 1973, 3 in 1974, 5 in 1975, 5 in 1976, 6 in 1977, 6 in 1978, 6 in 1979, 8 in 1980). Two transferred to Cuba, 1980. Wooden hull with plastic sheathing, classed BT.

'TR 40' class *inshore minesweepers*

Displacement:	46.3t standard; 49.2t full load
Dimensions:	89ft 11in × 13ft 1in × 1ft 8in
	27.4m × 4.0m × 0.5m
Machinery:	2-shaft diesels, 600bhp = 15kts. Range 500nm/10kts
Armament:	2-25mm (1×2), 2–12.7mm MG (1×2), 20 mines max
Complement:	16

About 55 were built in Poland in the late 1950s for river and coastal operations, as a patrol boat, sweeper, and minelayer; 7 remained in Polish service, and 8 went to Rumania. TR is a Polish designation meaning *Tralowiec Redowy*, or roadstead sweeper, the equivalent of the Soviet term.

'K 8' class *inshore minesweepers*

Displacement:	19.4t standard; 26t full load
Dimensions:	55ft 5in × 10ft 6in × 2ft 8in
	16.9m × 3.2m × 0.8m
Machinery:	2 shafts, 2 3D6 diesels, 3000bhp = 12kts. Range 300nm/9kts
Armament:	2–14.5mm MG (1×2)
Complement:	6

A total of about 130 was built by Polnocny (Gdansk, Poland), 1954–59; 45 left in service 1982 and being replaced by the 'Yevgenya' class. Wooden hulls. The K designation is Polish, standing for Kuter (cutter). With minor modifications these craft became motor gunboats and minesweepers. Poland operated about

30 in her Navy (as sweepers) as well as a like number in her coast guard. Seventy went to the Soviet Union.

NOTE: There was also a small coastal motor boat, 'PO 2', used by the Soviets for sweeping; no details are available. Transfers: 24 to Bulgaria and 2 to Egypt. It dates from the early 1950s.

'YEVGENYA' class *inshore minesweepers*

Displacement:	90t full load
Dimensions:	85ft 11in × 8ft 6in × 4ft 11in
	26.2m × 2.6m × 1.5m
Machinery:	2-shaft diesels, 600bhp = 11kts. Range 300nm/10kts
Armament:	2–14.5mm or 25mm (1×2)
Sensors:	Radar Spin Trough; sonar dipping
Complement:	10

About 40 completed from 1970 onwards; several transferred, including one to Bulgaria, 1977. These minehunters have plastic hulls, and are equipped with a towed television minehunting and marking system effective to 30m depths.

'OLYA' class *inshore minesweepers*

Displacement:	50t full load
Dimensions:	80ft 9in × 13ft 9in × 3ft 3in
	24.6m × 4.2m × 1.0m
Machinery:	2-shaft diesels, 600bhp = 18kts. Range 500nm/10kts
Armament:	2–25mm (1×2)
Sensors:	Radar Spin Trough
Complement:	15

First appeared 1975. Classed as RT, roadstead sweeper. Five, 7 or 10 reported.

'ANDRYUSHA' class *special minesweepers*

Displacement:	320t standard; 360t full load
Dimensions:	134ft 6in wl, 147ft 4in oa × 26ft 7in × 6ft 7in
	41.0m, 44.9m × 8.2m × 2.0m
Machinery:	2 diesels, 2200bhp = 25kts. Range 3000nm/10kts
Armament:	None
Sensors:	Radar Spin Trough
Complement:	40

As of 1982, 3 had been built by Izhora, Leningrad, the first begun 1973–4 and completed 1975; the last completed 1979. They have wooden or plastic hulls, and large cable ducts running down both sides. A prominent stack serves a gas turbine generator, the propulsion diesels exhausting through the hull sides. The cables and generator presumably indicate magnetic sweeping.

'Yevgenya' class 1976 *USN*

'ILYUSHA' class *special minesweepers*

Displacement:	50t standard; 70t full load
Dimensions:	80ft 1in × 16ft 1in × 4ft 7in
	24.4m × 4.9m × 1.4m
Machinery:	1-shaft diesel, 450bhp = 12kts
Armament:	None
Sensors:	Radar Spin Trough
Complement:	10

These 10 drone minesweepers entered service from 1970 onwards. They are radio-controlled while sweeping, but are manned for transit.

'Alesha' class

'ALESHA' class *minelayers*

Displacement:	2900t standard; 3500t full load
Dimensions:	318ft 3in × 45ft 11in × 17ft 9in
	97.0m × 14.0m × 5.4m
Machinery:	4 diesels, 8000bhp = 17kts. Range 4000nm/16kts, 8500nm/8kts
Armament:	4–57mm (1×14), 300 mines max
Sensors:	Radar Don-2, Strut Curve, Muff Cob
Complement:	190

Class:
Pripet and 2 others
Three completed 1967–69, probably on the Black Sea. Soviet designation ZM *Zagraditel' Minnyy*, or minelayer. These ships are used to lay both defensive minefields and ASW harbour defence nets.

Index

Note: Dates and countries given after entries are to distinguish ships of the same name, launch dates where known or else building dates for the class or simply an extant date. *18 De Julio* and similar anniversary names are listed as if the numeral was spelt out. Accents are omitted for simplicity.

C

E

Muavenet (1971) 120
Mubarak 355
Mughetto 65
Muguet 50
Muhafiz 355
Muhammed 442
Muikko 374
Mujahid 355
Mukden 327
Mukhtar 355
Mul (1946) 379
Mul (1952–56) 385
Mulkae 347
Mullany 195
Mullinix 217
Munin (Sweden 1942) 378
Munin (Sweden 1977) 384
Munin (W Germany 1960) 266
Munroe 255
Munsif 355
Murakumo 288
Murane 264
Murasame 286
Murat Reis (Algeria 1979) 299
Murat Reis (Turkey 1940) 119
Murat Reis (Turkey 1970) 122
Murature 394
Murayjib 448
Murban 448
Murchison 273
Murcia 114
Murefte 124
Murmansk (1921) 476
Murmansk (1955) 481
Murotsu 298
Murray (UK 1955) 160
Murray (USA ext 1947) 195
Murshed 442
Murtaja (1898) 374
Murtaja (1958) 376
Musketeer 136
Musko 384
Musson 462
Musvaagen 16
Mutsu 284
Mutsure 298
Muzuki 298
Mvita 308
Myles C Fox 196
Myngs 136
Myo Hyang San 347
Myoko 284
Myong Ryang 347
Myosotis (ext 1947) 24
Myosotis (1954–55) 50
Mysing 384
Mysore 338
Mytho 49

N

N I Goulandris I 60
N I Goulandris II 60
Naaldwijk 90
Naarden 90
Nacken (1942) 378
Nacken (1978) 381
Nadashio 295
Nader 432
Nafratoussa (1953) 58
Nafratoussa (1971) 58
Naga 307
Nagabanda 343
Nagakyay 325
Nagapasa 344
Nagarangsang 343

Nagato 284
Nagatsuki 288
Naghdi 433
Nahang 434
Naharia 303
Nahid 435
Naiad 164
Naifeh 197
Najad (1942) 378
Najad (1979) 381
Najade 264
Najaden 17
Nak Tong 346
Nakha 366
Nakhodchivyy 487
Nala 342
Nalon 118
Nam Du 370
Nam Yang 348
Namdo 385
Namdofjard 379
Namlea 343
Namsen 99
Nan Chang (1946) 328
Nan Chang (1947) 328
Nan Yang (1959) 361
Nan Yang (1974) 361
Nanang 435
Nanawa 421
Nanggala (1959) 343
Nanggala (1980) 343
Naparima 426
Napier 136
Napo 422
Naporistiy 487
Napred 392
Nara 290
Narbada 337
Narcisco 65
Narciso Monturiol (1972) 116
Narciso Monturiol (1974) 116
Narhvalen (1917) 13
Narhvalen (1968) 16
Narushima 298
Narushio 294
Narval (France 1954) 43
Narval (Portugal 1948) 104
Narwal (Spain 1974) 116
Narvik (France 1953–54) 49
Narvik (Norway 1942) 92
Narvik (Norway 1965) 94
Narvik (UK ext 1947) 141
Narwhal (UK 1957) 170
Narwhal (USA 1966) 234
Narwik 459
Nashat 341
Nashville 244
Nasr 303
Nassau 242
Nastochivyy 487
Nasty 97
Natal 319
Natchez 414
Nathan Hale 238
Nathaniel Greene 238
Natsugumo 288
Natsushio 294
Natter 264
Nauen 456
Nautilo (Italy 1942) 64
Nautilo (Portugal 1948) 104
Nautilus (S Africa 1955) 320
Nautilus (Spain 1956) 115
Nautilus (USA 1954) 231
Nautilus (W Germany 1965) 271
Navak 435
Navarinon (1934) 53
Navarinon (1962) 55

Navarra (1920) 108
Navarra (1983) 114
Navia 118
Navmachos 58
Navodvhik 507
Nawarat 325
Nazario Sauro 74
Ndovu 308
Nearchos 55
Neasham 180
Neave 140
Neckar 271
Negba 441
Negros Occidental 356
Negros Oriental 357
Nelson 133
Nemesis 200
Nemuro 295
Nene 139
Nenoshima 298
Nepal 136
Neptun (Denmark 1960–64) 17
Neptun (Sweden 1942) 378
Neptun (Sweden 1978) 381
Neptun (W Germany 1960) 270
Neptuno (Portugal 1948) 104
Neptuno (Spain 1937) 110
Nereide 139
Neretva 389
Nereus 57
Nervion 110
Nerz (1961) 266
Nerz (1982) 267
Nesokrushimyy 487
Ness 139
Nestin 392
Nettleham 180
Netzahualcoyotl 419
Neubrandenburg (1952–56) 455
Neubrandenburg (1975–79) 453
Neuderzhimyy 488
Neukrotimyy 491
Neulovimyy 488
Neuquen 400
Neuruppin 456
Neustadt 272
Neustrashimy 487
Neustrelitz 456
New 196
New Glasgow 6
New Jersey 193
New Liskeard 6
New Orleans 241
New Waterford 6
New York City 235
Newcastle (1936) 134
Newcastle (1975) 156
Newell 197
Newfoundland 135
Newman K Perry 197
Newport (ext 1947) 198
Newport (1968) 246
Newport News 194
Neyzeh 435
Ngahau Koula 368
Ngahau Siliva 368
Ngo Kuyen 369
Ngo Van Quyen 370
Ngoc Hoi 369
N'golo 305
Ngpona 281
N'guene 305
Ngurah Rai (1963) 342
Ngurah Rai (1974) 342
Nguyen An 370

Nguyen Dao 370
Nguyen Duc Bong 369
Nguyen Han 370
Nguyen Kim Hung 370
Nguyen Ngoc Long 369
Nguyen Ngoc Thach 370
Nguyen Van Tru 369
Nhongarhai 365
Nhut Tao 369
Nibbio 76
Nichelio 64
Nicholas (ext 1947) 195
Nicholas (1982) 228
Nicholson 219
Nicola Fabrizi 63
Nicoloso Da Recco 63
Niederosterreich 372
Niedersachsen 261
Niedoscigly 458
Niels Ebbesen 12
Niels Juel 15
Nieuchwytny 458
Nieuchwytry 458
Nieugiety 460
Nieuwpoort 3
Nigeria (Nigeria 1959) 317
Nigeria (Nigeria 1965) 315
Nigeria (UK 1939) 135
Nike 200
Niki 55
Nikola Martinovic 391
Nikolav Fil'chenkov 500
Nikolay Obyekov 500
Nikolay Vilkov 500
Nikolayev 484
Nilgiri 340
Nimble 251
Nimitz 207
Nimr 304
Ninh Giang 369
Ninoshima (1959) 297
Ninoshima (1979) 298
Niobe 270
Niovi 60
Nipat 341
Nipigon (ext 1947) 6
Nipigon (1961) 9
Nirbhik 341
Nire 290
Nirghat 341
Nisan 436
Nisr 304
Nissiros 54
Niteroi 404
Nith 139
Nitzhanon 440
Nixe 271
Niyodo 292
Nizam 136
Njambuur 317
Njord 387
Noa 196
Noakhali 323
Noble 136
Noce 77
Nogah 441
Nogiku 295
Noon 431
Noor El Bahr 302
Noord Brabant 82
Nootka 5
Norain 324
Noranda 6
Norby 17
Nordenskjold 377
Nordkaperen (Denmark 1969) 16
Nordkaperen (Sweden 1961) 381

Nordkaparen (Sweden 1935) 378
Nordkapp (1937) 92
Nordkapp (1957) 100
Nordkapp (1980) 100
Nordkyn 92
Nordperd 453
Norfolk (UK 1928) 134
Norfolk (UK 1967) 154
Norfolk (USA 1951) 222
Norfolk (USA 1981) 235
Norge 100
Norman 136
Le Nomand 40
Nornen 100
Norris 196
Norrkoping (1940) 378
Norrkoping (1972) 383
Norrtalje 383
Norsten 386
Northampton 240
Northland 255
Northumbria 180
Noshiro 292
Notable 251
Noto 295
Nottingham 156
Nouh 436
Novorossiysk (1911) 476
Novorossiysk (1978) 479
Nubian 162
Nueva Ecija 357
Nueva Esparta 428
Nueva Rocafuerte 416
Nueva Viscaya 357
Nueve De Julio 396
9 De Octobre 416
Nuku 342
Numana 77
Nung Ra 347
Nuno Tristao 102
Nuoli 375
Nurton 179
Nusantara 343
Nusret 124
Nuwajima 297
Nyati 308
Nyesamozhnik Zhelezniakov 476
Nymfen 17
Nymphe 271
Nynashamn 383

O

O Tae San 347
Oakham Castle 139
Oakington 179
Oakland 194
Oakley 138
O'Bannon (ext 1947) 195
O'Bannon (1978) 219
Obdurate 136
Obedient 136
Oberon 171
Oberst Brecht 372
Obrazovanny 486
Obraztsovy (ext 1947) 477
Obraztsovy (1963–66) 489
O'Brien (Chile 1972) 410
O'Brien (USA ext 1947) 195
O'Brien (USA 1976) 219
Observation Island 246
Observer 251
Obuma 315
O'Callaghan 226

T

Addenda

PART I: THE WESTERN POWERS

BELGIUM
p4 The first 'Tripartite' minehunter laid down Jan 1982.

CANADA
p5 Six missile frigates ordered from St John Shipbuilding 25.6.83.

DENMARK
p16 May acquire 3 Swedish A 17 type submarines from Kockums instead of German/Norwegian Type 210s.

FRANCE
p28 Further details of the proposed nuclear-powered aircraft carriers have been released: 36,000t full load, 780ft 10in wl × 103ft 4in *(238.0m × 31.5m)* with a flight deck 858ft × 203ft 5in *(261.5m × 62.0m)*; machinery would produce 82,000shp; the projected schedule calls for the first to be laid down in 1988 and completed in 1996.

p37 *Jean de Vienne* began trials 20.11.82.

p41 *Commandant L'Herminier* completed 12.12.82.

p43 *Margouin* paid off 4.10.82; will be cannibalised.

p45 *L'Inflexible* began trials 6.11.82.

p48 Fourth of *Champlain* class, called *Jacques Cartier*, completed 11.4.82.

Twelve LCMs, *CTM 1–12*, being constructed by CMN, Cherbourg and Auroux, Arcachon, 1982–83.

p52 *Cassiopee* commissioned 7.5.83.

GREECE
p56 *Limnos* completed 18.9.82. There has been no progress with Greek plans for more of the class.

ITALY
p66 *Giuseppe Garibaldi* launched 4.6.83.

p72 *Grecale* completed 9.12.82; *Libeccio* completed 12.10.82; *Scirocco* launched 17.4.82 and completed Apr 83; *Euro* launched Apr 83; *Espero* laid down 29.7.82; *Zeffiro* laid down Mar 1983.

p74 *Gugliemo Marconi* completed 16.10.82.

p76 *Astore* completed 6.8.82; *Griffone* completed 16.9.82; *Gheppio* ran trials Feb 1983.

p77 Minehunter *Lerici* launched 3.9.82; *Sapri* laid down Dec 1982; all ordered from Intermarine.

NETHERLANDS
p86 *Abraham Crijnsson* completed 27.1.83; *Jan van Brakel* completed 14.4.83.

p90 *Van Straelen* class minesweepers decommissioned: M 872 10.12.82; M 875 25.12.82; M 876 21.2.83; M 869 4.2.83; M 879 18.2.83; M 882 4.3.83.

p91 *Alkmaar* completed 14.2.83, commissioned 28.5.83; *Delfzijl* launched 29.10.82; *Dordrecht* completed 26.2.83; *Hellevoitsluis* laid down 24.5.82; *Maasluis* laid down 8.11.82; *Makkum* laid down 7.3.83; *Middelburg* and *Scheveningen* ordered 23.7.82.

Dutch minehunter *Alkmaar* 15.8.83 (see p91)
L & L van Ginderen

Spanish *Pizarro* class frigate *Legaspi* 1965 (see p110)
L & L van Ginderen

SPAIN
p114 *Serviola* and *Centinela* sold to Egypt 1.6.83.

p116 *Galerna* began trials Dec 1982; *Siroco* launched 13.11.82.

TURKEY
p121 Gearing FRAM I destroyer *McKean* transferred 1982, *Yucutere* (ex-USS *Orleck*) acquired for purchase 1.10.82. Of 4 MEKO 200 type frigates, 1 ordered from Blohm & Voss, 1 from Howaldtswerke, and 2 for construction in Turkey.

p122 *Yildiray* is being built by Howaldtswerke and was laid down 9.3.81; *Titiray* is first Turkish-built submarine and was laid down in 1982.

p124 A fifth *Dogan* class completed 1982.

UNITED KINGDOM
p156 *Nottingham* completed 21.12.82 and commissioned 8.4.83.

p157 *Edinburgh* launched 13.4.83.

p160 *Hardy* sunk as a target July 1983, after Exocet trials.

RN Fairey 'Tracker' type patrol craft March 1983 (see p178)

Fairey Marine

p167 *Boxer* completed for trials May 1983; *Brave* launched 8.4.82; F96–F99 ordered 14.12.82. Type 23 may be called *Daring* class.

p173 *Trafalgar* class revised details: 4700t/5000t displacement, length 280ft 2in pp (*85.4m*); otherwise as *Swiftsure* class; *Trafalgar* completed 27.5.83; *Talent* ordered 22.3.83.

p174 Mercantile *Grey Master* and *Lakespan Ontario* chartered as RFAs 21.1.83 as temporary replacements for *Sir Galahad* and *Sir Tristram* and renamed *Sir Caradoc* and *Sir Lamorak* respectively. *Sir Tristram* was returned to the UK in the summer of 1983 and is to be refitted. The 27,850t gross *Astronomer*, which had been fitted as an aircraft ferry for the Falklands campaign, was acquired 22.4.83, renamed *Reliant* and is to test the US 'Arapaho' system; she will carry 4 ASW helicopters.

The short-sea ferry *St Edmund* was acquired as a troop transport 15.2.83, was renamed *Keren*, being manned by the Navy for trials.

p176 *Peacock* launched 1.12.82, completed 30.6.83; *Plover* launched 12.4.83; *Starling* laid down 9.9.82.

p178 Five Fairey 'Tracker' type patrol craft ordered 1983 for RNR training (university units); first three *Attacker* (P 281), *Fencer* (P 283) and *Hunter* (P 284) delivered Mar 1983.

p181 *Cottesmore* completed May 83; *Middleton* launched 27.4.83; *Hurworth* laid down Jan 83; M 38 and M 39 ordered 14.11.82.

Details of EDATs minesweepers: displacement 800t, length 277ft 10in oa (*47.6m*), 2 shafts (CP propellers), Ruston diesels, 3040bhp = 13kts; 6 more ordered from Richards and 2 from Clelands (Wallsend) 10.5.83. Reported to be called 'Gem' class, the first being *Amethyst*.

A new single-role minehunter of about 500t is under development.

UNITED STATES

p207 CVN 72 and CVN 73 ordered Dec 1982.

p221 *Yorktown* launched 17.1.83; CG 54–CG 56 ordered from Litton June 1983.

p228 *Vandergrift* launched 15.10.82; *Carr* launched 26.2.83; *Robert E Bradley* laid down 28.12.82; *Reid* completed 19.2.83; *Underwood* completed 29.1.83; FFG 50, 51, 53 and 54 to be called *Jesse J Taylor, Gary, Hawes* and *Ford* respectively.

p235 *Portsmouth* launched 18.9.82; SSN 720 laid down 19.12.82; SSN 724 ordered 11.2.82; SSN 725 ordered 19.4.82; SSN 751 and SSN 752 ordered from Electric Boat 30.11.82; SSN 717 named *Olympia*; SSN 709 named *Hyman G Rickover*.

p238 SSBN 732, named *Connecticut*, laid down 20.6.81; SSBN 734 ordered 7.1.81; SSBN 735 ordered 29.11.82 from Electric Boat; SSBN 733 named *Montana*.

p243 LHD 1 ordered from Litton, Pascagoula; to be laid down mid-1984.

p245 *Whidbey Island* launched 10.6.83; LSD 43 ordered from Lockheed 27.1.83.

p249 *Hercules* completed 17.9.82, commissioned 12.3.83

p251–2 MCM 2 ordered 29.4.83 from Marinette Marine.

WEST GERMANY

p261 *Karlsruhe* (F 223) transferred to Turkey 1983 as *Gazi Osman Pasa*.

p261 *Emden* began trials Feb 1983.

p267 *Frettchen* launched 26.1.83; *Dachs* launched 14.12.82; RAM has now been fitted to early units. *Puma* completed 24.2.83.

p269 The last minesweeping drones, *Seehund 16–18*, were completed 13.5.83.

AUSTRALIA

p275 *Melbourne* is to be put up for disposal; no replacement will be sought.

p278 *Sydney* completed 29.1.83.

p280 *Acute* transferred to Indonesia 6.5.83 and renamed *Kri Silea; Barricade* also transferred in 1982.

Fremantle class: *Launceston* is P 207 (completed March 1982); *Whyalla* is P 208; *Ipswich* (launched 25.9.82, completed Nov 1982) is P 209; *Cessnock* launched 15.1.83 and commissioned 5.3.83; *Bendigo* launched 9.4.83.

An order was placed in 1982 for the first of 6 102ft (*31m*) minehunting catamarans; to be built by Carrington Shipways.

Australian tank landing ship *Tobruk* 13.2.83 (see p279)

NEW ZEALAND

p282 *Dido* was renamed *Southland* not *Salisbury*.

JAPAN

p289 *Sawakaze* completed 30.3.83.

p290 *Shirayuki* completed 8.2.83; *Mineyuki* launched 17.10.82; DDG 129–DDG 131 ordered 30.3.82 from Hitachi, Ishikawajima and Mitsui respectively; DDG 132 ordered 31.3.83 from Sumitomo. DD 171 laid down Jan 1983.

Japanese escort *Isuzu* 1.8.70 (see p291-92)
L & L van Ginderen

Libyan 'Nanuchka II' class missile corvette *Ain Mara* 19.10.81 (see p 310)
L & L van Ginderen

Japanese minehunter/minesweeper *Takami* 17.5.81 (see p298)
L & L van Ginderen

Libyan *Beir Grassa* class missile FAC *Beir Alkur* 6.10.82 (see p311)
L & L van Ginderen

p292 *Yubari* completed 18.3.83; DE 228 named *Yubetsu*, laid down Feb 1982, launched 25.1.83.

p295 *Okishio* completed 1.3.83; *Nadashio* launched 27.1.83; SS 579 ordered 31.3.82 from Mitsubishi.

p298 MSC 658 and MSC 659 ordered 31.3.83 Hitachi and Nippon Kokan respectively. Former launched June 1983, latter 23.6.83.

PART II: THE WARSAW PACT AND NON-ALIGNED NATIONS

AFRICA

ALGERIA

p299 Second *Kebir* class FAC delivered June 1983 and numbered 342.

CAMEROUN

p300 The French-built 18m landing craft *BT 30* delivered on 15.3.83. P 48S type large patrol craft *Bakasi* launched by SFCN 1982 and completed March 1983.

EGYPT

p301 Announced on 1.6.83 that Egypt is to buy the Spanish Navy's *Descubierta* class frigates *Centinela* and *Serviola*.
Six missile FAC ordered from Tacoma Shipbuilding Dec 1982.

LIBYA

p311 FAC *Raad* (ex-*Beir Alkur*) completed 19.5.83. Delivery of last unit, *Laahibe* (ex-*Beir Alkuesat*) due on 27.8.83 but embargoed during Franco-Libyan confrontation in Chad.

NIGERIA

p314 Two landing craft ordered 20.1.81 from Scheepswerf Gravel in the Netherlands.
Two patrol craft ordered March 1983 from De Wiel (Asperen), The Netherlands.

SOUTH AFRICA

p320 Three more 'MOD' class missile FAC building.

TUNISIA

p322 First of 3 'Combattante III' type Exocet missile FAC *La Galite* (501) launched by CMN 16.1.83 for Oct delivery, second in class called *Tunis* (502) to be launched end Sept for Feb 1984 delivery. *Carthage* (503) to be launched end Nov for May 1984 delivery.

ASIA

BANGLADESH

p323 Chinese 'Romeo' class submarine commissioned as *Durjoy* 10.9.82.

MALAYSIA

p350 Type FS 1500 frigates *Kasturi* and *Lekir* launched by Howaldtwerke 3.1.83. Differ from Colombian ships in armament and sensors, and in lacking a helicopter hangar. Armament: 4 MM38 Exocet, 1–100mm, 2–57mm Bofors, 4–30mm Emerlec, 1–375mm ASW RL, WG 13 Lynx helicopter. Sensors: Signaal DA-08, WM-22, 2 chaff Dagaie RL, sonar.

p352 Four missile FAC ordered from Karlskronavarvet Dec 1982.

p353 Two OPVs of 1100–1200t with helicopter ordered from Korea Shipbuilding March 1983.

p353 *Lerici* type minehunter *Mahamiru* launched by Intermarine Dec 1982. Next three are *Ledang*, *Jerai* and *Kinbalu*.

Brunei Exocet missile FAC *Waspada* (see p322)
Vosper, Singapore

Brunei coastal patrol craft *Perwira* (see p324)
Vosper, Singapore

Pakistani ex-British 'County' class missile destroyer *Babur* 28.5.82 (see p354)
L & L van Ginderen

Burmese *Carpentaria* class coastal patrol craft 1980 (see p325)

South Korean ex-US *Gearing* class destroyer *Jeong Buk* with Harpoon SSM midships
28.11.81 (see p346)　　　　　　　　　　　　　*L & L van Ginderen*

PAKISTAN

p354 *Gearing* class US destroyer *Cone* acquired for purchase 1.10.82.

p355 Three coastal patrol craft ordered from Uniflete (Bellingham), USA, June 1982.

PAPUA NEW GUINEA

p355 Landing craft *Bursea* and *Burwave* completed by Sing Koon Seng of Singapore 6.4.82 and 15.5.82.

PHILIPPINES

p356 Two or three missile corvettes on projected order from Bazan (Cartagena) Jan 1983.

SEYCHELLES

p358 Large patrol craft *Andromanche* (605) delivered by Picchiotti summer 1983. Data: 240t, 137ft 2in × 22ft 4in × 5ft 7in, *41.8m × 6.8m × 1.7m*, 2 Paxman Valenta 16 CM diesels, 8000bhp = 27kts. Range 3000nm/16kts. Navigation radar and Foruno radar, 22 men, 1–20mm MG plus SSM fittings.

SRI LANKA

p360 *Pradeepa* class coastal patrol craft: P 447 launched 20.1.82, P 448 launched 27.8.82, P 446 completed 17.9.82, P 449 launched 20.9.82, P 445 completed 30.9.82. Another launched 12.10.82. First of 2 large patrol craft ordered from Colombo D Yd laid down 12.10.82.

THAILAND

p366 Two submarines on projected order from Howaldtswerke or Kockums Jan 1983.

p367 Two Harpoon missile corvettes ordered from Tacoma Boatbuilding 9.5.83.

Austrian river patrol craft *Niederösterreich*
12.4.75 (see p372)
Heinz Stockinger

EUROPE (NEUTRAL)

FINLAND

p375 *Helsinki* class FAC, 3 more ordered (nos 60–63) 26.1.83. Two unnamed 30t, 20kt coastal patrol craft ordered from Rauma-Repola (Savonlinna) Jan 1983.

p376 Six unnamed 18t, 11kt inshore minesweepers ordered from Fiskars-Turun Veneveistamo (Turku) Jan 1983.

SWEDEN

p382 Submarine *Vastergötland* laid down 10.1.83. Amended class data: 2 Hedemora V12A/15 UG diesels, 2160bhp = 12/20kts; 4–21in TT (bow), 17 crew.

p384 *Stockholm* (R 11) FAC laid down 1.8.82, *Malmo* (R 12) 14.3.83. Three unnamed patrol boats ordered from Karlskrona Dec 1982.

p385 Six unnamed 2.25t aluminium minelaying boats ordered 22.11.82 from Marinvarvet (Färösund), 23ft 11in oa, 21ft 4in pp × 7ft 11in × 3ft 11in/1ft 4in, *7.3m, 6.5m × 2.4m × 1.2m/0.4m*, 1 shaft water jet, Volvo Penta TAMD-40, 100bhp = 20kts. Fuel 200 litres for 150nm range.

p386 *Landsort* (M 71) laid down 5.10.81 and launched 20.11.82. *Arholma* (M 72) laid down 13.2.82.

YUGOSLAVIA

p389 Second Soviet 'Koni' class frigate delivered Dec 1982 and named *Koper*.

p390 Third *Sava* class submarine will be completed 1983.

LATIN AMERICA

ARGENTINA

p399 Transport *Bahia Buen Suceso* beached near Goose Green, Falklands, 23.5.82 after British Lynx helicopter attack.

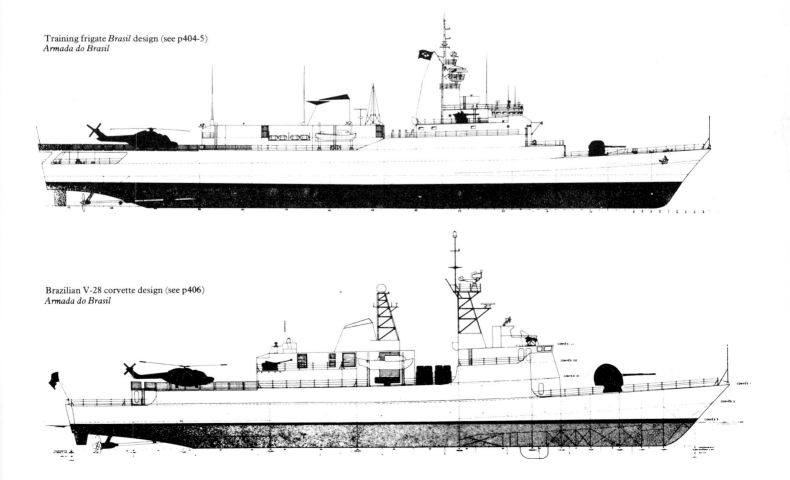

Training frigate *Brasil* design (see p404-5)
Armada do Brasil

Brazilian V-28 corvette design (see p406)
Armada do Brasil

Colombian West German FS 1500 type frigate *Almirante Padilla* 15.5.83 (see p412)
L & L van Ginderen

Argentine MEKO 360 H2 class frigate *Almirante Brown* 15.2.83 (see p397)
Gerhard Koop

BELIZE

p401 Two 36.5t, 20m coastal patrol craft ordered from Souter of Cowes (UK) Jan 1983.

BRAZIL

p401 Fleet ranks 11th in the world with over 100,000t (load), second in the Americas. Arsenal de Marinho (Rio) has 3 dry docks. The Amazonian base of Belem (Val de Caes) was founded in 1949 and has a 225m, 33,000t capacity dry dock. Aratu has a 230m dry dock.

p402 Destroyer escort *Bauru* opened as museum at Rio de Janeiro 22.7.81.

p403 *Minas Gerais* expected to serve until *c*1988.

p404 *Niteroi* class serve as one squadron, the *Força de Fragatas* created in 1978.

p404–405 The training frigate *Brazil* (U 30) has the first 76mm OTO-Melara Compact gun in Brazilian service plus 2–40mm/70 Bofors (2×1). She costs US $124.2 million and 76 per cent of her components will be Brazilian on completion in 1985. Her range will be 7000nm and a crew of 215 will instruct 200 midshipmen.

p405 Submarine force based at Almirante Castro e Silva, Moncangue Grande Island, Rio de Janeiro. Up to 6 new submarines (3 funded so far, 1 ordered 1.12.82) to be built in Rio by the Ferrostaal Consortium, first boat to be laid down by 1984 and not to cost over $100 million. These German Type 209 boats will use British Ferranti KAFS fire control and Mk 24 Tigerfish 21in torpedoes. Data: 1150t/1440t, 200ft 2in × 20ft 6in × 18ft 1in, *61.0m × 6.2m × 5.5m*, 1-shaft, 4 MTU MBV-493 AZ80-GA-3IL diesels/4 Piller generators/Siemens electric motor = 2400bhp/5000shp = 11kts/21½kts. Fuel 118t. Range 8200nm/400nm at 8kts/4kts. Advanced studies on nuclear propulsion were funded in 1981 and a trials/research SSN is planned to be in service by 1995.

p406 Four V-28 corvettes ordered at total cost of $1bn to replace the destroyer force. First ship will have 50 per cent Brazilian materials, rising to 80 per cent before the class is finished. Order reduced to 10 ships. Revised data: 1600t light, 1900t full load, 314ft oa, 295ft 3in pp × 375ft 5in × 10ft 10in, *95.7m, 90.0m × 11.4m × 3.3m*; 2-shaft CODOG, 1 Olympus gas turbine, 2 Ishikawajima-Pielstick diesels. Gun armament to be 1–4.5in/55 Vickers Mk 8 and 2–40mm/70 Bofors (2×1). Radars Plessey AWS-4, Selenia RTN-10X and Orion; sonar. Complement 120. Four missile FAC may be approved. At least 10 LCMs and 4 LCVPs on order, 2 LSD or LPD are planned.

p407 The 6 *Schutze* class form the *Força de Minagem e Verredura* (Minelaying and Sweeping Force) based at Aratu (Salvador, Bahia).

COLOMBIA

p412 Type 1500 frigate amended dimensions: 312ft 8in × 37ft 1in × 10ft 10in, *95.3m × 11.3m × 3.3m*. Sensors: Thomson CSF Sea Tiger, Castor, Canopus. Complement 124.

Peruvian *Abtao* class submarine *Dos de Mayo* June 1966 (see p424)
L & L van Ginderen

ECUADOR

p416 Missile corvette *Manabi*, last of 6, completed 9.4.83.

MEXICO

p420 Spanish B 119 type corvettes/patrol vessels, names, numbers and launch/completion dates: *Cadete Virgilio Uribe*, *Teniente Jose Azueta* (GH 02, 12.12.81, 10.9.82), *Capitan da Fragata Pedro Sainz de Barranda* (GH 03, 29.1–15.10.82), *Contralmirante Castillio Breton* (GH 04, 30.10.82), *Vice-Almirante Orthon P Blanco* (GH 05), *Contralmirante Angel Ortiz Monasterio* (GH 06, 23.4.82, Dec 1982).

VENEZUELA

p430 Landing ships *Capana* and *Esequito* launched 25.3.83 by Korea Tacoma Marine Industries.

Batalla del Lago 38ft class patrol boats and 28ft *General Jose Antonio Piez* class being built by Yamaha Fibra CA.

MIDDLE EAST

BAHRAIN

p431 Two unnamed GRP 34t, 20m coastal patrol craft (24.5kts, 2 MG, 8 men) ordered from Souter of Cowes (UK) Jan 1983. Three 7.2t, 11m coastal patrol craft (24kts) ordered from same yard 20.8.82.

IRAQ

p436 Iraqi warships claimed to have sunk 5 Iranian ships including tankers 50 miles NW of Kharg Island on 2.3.83.

Italian *Lupo* type frigate *Hussa el Hussair* (F 210) launched 16.12.82. Another laid down Sept 1982.

First of 3 LSTs *Al Zahraa* completed by Helsingor Vaerft (Finland) 18.3.83, third of the order launched Nov 1982.

Italian *Esmeraldas* type corvette *Mussa Ibn Hussair* launched by CNR Muggiano (La Spezia) 16.12.82 (first of 6). Second ship laid down 22.3.82 and another on 3.6.82 by Breda (Venice), another at Muggiano 20.5.82. Last 2 ships laid down by Breda 17.9.82.

ISRAEL

p437 As early as 21.2.72 'Saar' class missile FAC landed commandos in Lebanon in successful attacks on Palestinian guerrilla bases. The summer 1982 Lebanon operations saw several amphibious 'hooks' and sustained 76mm gun naval bombardments.

p440 Missile hydrofoil *Livnit* fitting out at Haifa 1982.

KUWAIT

p442 Four unnamed LCMs of 'Loadmaster' type ordered from Cheverton of Cowes (UK) 19.4.83, 67t standard; 76t full load, 68ft 11in oa, 64ft pp × 19ft × 7ft 1in, *21.0m, 19.5m × 5.8m × 2.1m*, 2 shafts, 2 Caterpillar 3412-DITA V12 diesels, 1214bhp = 11kts. Part of £6 million order including 2 harbour tugs and harbour launches.

Kuwaiti Lürssen 'TNC 45' type FAC *Jalboot* 11.10.82 (see p442)

Kuwaiti Vosper type landing craft *Waheed 1974* (see p442)
Vosper, Singapore

Oman ex-Dutch *Dokkum* class coastal minesweeper *Al Nasiri* 1980 (see p444)
L & L van Ginderen

Kuwaiti Vosper type logistic landing craft *Al Jahra 1979* (see p332)
Vosper, Singapore

Saudi Arabian *Addriyah* class coastal
minesweeper *Al Quysumah* 6.8.78 (see p447)
L & L van Ginderen

OMAN

p444 Two LCMs *Al Doghas* (C9) and *Al Temsah* (C 10) sisters to *Saba al Bahr*, ordered from Vosper of Singapore 8.5.82. Both laid down 8.9.82, *Al Doghas* launched 12.11.82 and *Al Temsah* 15.12.82. *Al Doghas* completed 10.1.83 and *Al Temsah* 12.2.83. Second *Dhofar* class called *Al Sharqiyah*, third named *Al Bat'nah*.

QATAR

p445 Four unnamed patrol craft ordered from Fairey Allday (Hamble, UK) Feb 1983.

SAUDI ARABIA

p447 *Al Siddiq* class FAC *Tariq* completed 16.8.82, *Aqbah* 18.10.82, *Abu Obaidah* 3.12.82.

SYRIA

p447 Four 'Nanuchka II' class corvettes to be transferred.

WARSAW PACT
EAST GERMANY

p452 Third 'Koni' class frigate to be transferred.

POLAND

p461 New class of 30m inshore minesweepers building.

SOVIET UNION

p495 'Hotel' class strategic submarines: In the late 1970s US official estimates of the number of 'Hotel' class declined from nine to eight. Given the quality of US intelligence, one would conclude that one was lost at sea; reportedly the Soviet submarine force has sustained numerous unannounced casualties in recent years. Details are difficult to obtain because of the approximate character of published order of battle figures.

p497 'Charlie' class cruise missile submarine sunk in N Pacific off Kamchatka June 1983, later salvaged; crew losses not known. There are reports of additional submarine losses but details not available.